William Caxton,
Paris and Vienne and
Blanchardyn and Eglantine

Middle English Texts Series

General Editor
Russell A. Peck
University of Rochester

Associate Editor
Susanna Fein
Kent State University

Associate Editor
Alan Lupack
University of Rochester

Associate Editor
Anna Siebach-Larsen
University of Rochester

Managing Editor
Pamela M. Yee
University of Rochester

Consulting Editor
Thomas Hahn
University of Rochester

Consulting Editor
Victoria Szabo
Duke University

Advisory Board

Theresa Coletti
University of Maryland

Michael Livingston
The Citadel

Rita Copeland
University of Pennsylvania

David Raybin
Eastern Illinois University

Lisa Fagin Davis
Medieval Academy of America

Eve Salisbury
Western Michigan University

Alexandra Gillespie
University of Toronto

Lynn Staley
Colgate University

Thomas Goodmann
University of Miami

David Wallace
University of Pennsylvania

David A. Lawton
Washington University in St. Louis

Bonnie Wheeler
Southern Methodist University

The Middle English Texts Series produces scholarly texts designed for research and classroom use. Its goal is to make available to teachers, scholars, and students texts that occupy an important place in the literary and cultural canon but have not been readily available in print or online editions. The series does not include authors, such as Chaucer, Langland, or Malory, whose English works are normally in print. The focus is, instead, upon Middle English literature adjacent to those authors that are needed for research or teaching. The editions maintain the linguistic integrity of the original work but within the parameters of modern reading conventions.

William Caxton,
Paris and Vienne and
Blanchardyn and Eglantine

Edited by
Harriet Hudson

A publication of the
Rossell Hope Robbins Library
in collaboration with
the University of Rochester
and the Teaching Association for Medieval Studies

by

Medieval Institute Publications
Kalamazoo, Michigan
2023

Copyright © 2023 by the Board of Trustees of Western Michigan University
Manufactured in the United States of America

The text of this book was set in Arno Pro 11pt, a contemporary typeface inspired by books from the 15th and 16th centuries. It was designed by Robert Slimbach at Adobe.

Library of Congress Cataloging-in-Publication Data

Names: Hudson, Harriet (Harriet E.), editor. | Caxton, William, approximately 1422–1491 or 1492, translator. | Rossell Hope Robbins Research Library, issuing body. | University of Rochester, issuing body. | Teaching Association for Medieval Studies, issuing body. | Pierre, de la Cépède, active 15th century. Paris et Vienne. English

Title: William Caxton, Paris and Vienne and Blanchardyn and Eglantine / edited by Harriet Hudson.

Other titles: Paris and Vienne | Blancandin. English.

Description: Kalamazoo, Michigan : Medieval Institute Publications, 2023. | Series: Middle English texts series | "A publication of the Rossell Hope Robbins Library in collaboration with the University of Rochester and the Teaching Association for Medieval Studies." | Includes bibliographical references. | Summary: ""Blanchardyn and Eglantine" and "Paris and Vienne" were last edited in 1890 and 1957, respectively. This edition incorporates recent scholarship and criticism, including new critical editions of French texts closely related to Caxton's sources for both romances, as well as studies of the two romances and late medieval romance in England and France; gender studies, especially the role of women in these narratives; scholarship relating to the owners and readers of Caxton's romances and associated manuscripts; studies of courtesy literature and its relationship to romance; and scholarship on Caxton, his career, publications, prose style, and language" — Provided by publisher.

Identifiers: LCCN 2023013917 (print) | LCCN 2023013918 (ebook) | ISBN 9781580445566 (hardback) | ISBN 9781580445559 (paperback) | ISBN 9781580445573 (ebook)

Subjects: LCSH: Pierre, de la Cépède, active 15th century. Paris et Vienne. | Blancandin. English. | Caxton, William, approximately 1422–1491 or 1492 — Criticism and interpretation. | Romance fiction, French — 15th century — Translations into English.

Classification: LCC PQ1278 .W55 2023 (print) | LCC PQ1278 (ebook) | DDC 843/.2—dc23/eng/20230510

LC record available at https://lccn.loc.gov/2023013917

LC ebook record available at https://lccn.loc.gov/2023013918

ISBN: 9781580445559 (paperback)
ISBN: 9781580445566 (hardback)
ISBN: 9781580445573 (ebook)

Printed and bound by CPI Group (UK) Ltd, Croydon, CR0 4YY

Table of Contents

Acknowledgments	vii
Abbreviations List	ix
General Introduction	1
Paris and Vienne	
Introduction	17
Text	37
Explanatory Notes	101
Textual Notes	119
Blanchardyn and Eglantine	
Introduction	131
Caxton's Dedication	151
Caxton's Table of Chapters	153
Text	159
Explanatory Notes	285
Textual Notes	301
Appendix: *Paris and Vienne*, Cépède's Prologue	323
Bibliography	325
Glossary	333

List of Figures and Illustrations

    Table 1: Caxton's Translations of Romances and Chivalric Treatises   16

    Figure 1: London, British Library, C.10.b.10, fol. 1. Caxton, *Paris and Vienne*, 1485.   36

    Figure 2: Manchester, Rylands Library, Incunable 15027, fol. 1. Caxton, *Blanchardyn and Eglantine*, 1489.   149

Acknowledgments

Thanks are due to many people whose time, efforts, and expertise have made this edition possible. As the saying goes, "it takes a village . . .". While I produced drafts, these were "raised" by the instruction of scholars and the correction of editors to produce a volume useful to teachers and students of Middle English Literature.

I am grateful for the support of the Editorial Board of the Middle English Texts Series and the diligent work of its Editorial Staff members who did multiple read-throughs of the texts, glosses, and notes at various stages of the editorial process. Pamela Yee, Managing Editor, patiently guided me every step of the way, reading copy, fielding questions, and coordinating the project. I am indebted to the accuracy of Staff Editors Caleb Prus and Steffi Delcourt who read my transcriptions against the British Library and Rylands Library incunables and checked the Textual Notes. I especially want to recognize Steffi's early work on the manuscript read of *Blanchardyn and Eglantine*, and on formatting the text and entering corrections. She and staff members, Eleanor Price and Ashley Conklin, meticulously edited the citations. Readers on the Editorial Board reviewed complete drafts of the edition; Alan Lupack and General Editor Russell Peck read drafts and copy-edited the entire volume, with Alan giving special attention to the glosses and Pamela handling further corrections and emendations. All their work would not have been possible without the continuing support of the National Endowment for the Humanities, which assists with the funding of the Middle English Texts Series.

In addition to the people at METS, other readers reviewed drafts of the whole volume and commented on the content of the Introductions and Editorial Notes. I owe special thanks to the outside reviewers, whose responses were thorough and very helpful, particularly in regard to recent scholarship on critical race theory. Their expertise is deeply appreciated. Thanks are due to my friend and colleague, Kristen Figg, who read drafts of the Introductions, reviewed my translations from French sources, helped to decipher signatures in the manuscripts, and enabled me to obtain copies of essential publications. John Block Friedman was instrumental in identifying an early owner of *Blanchardyn and Eglantine*. I especially want to acknowledge my husband, Richard Knittle, for his many years of support for my academic endeavors and this project.

This edition was made possible by the resources of The Ohio State University Library and by the digital copies of unique surviving texts at the British Library and John Rylands Library.

 ABBREVIATIONS LIST

ACAD	*A Cambridge Alumni Database*, compilers Venn and Emden
BL	*Thystorye of the noble ryght valyaunt and worthy knyght Parys, and of the fayr Vyenne de daulphyns doughter*. Westminster: William Caxton, 1485. USTC: 500113; ISTC: ip00113500. London, British Library, C.10.b.10 [base manuscript for *Paris and Vienne*]
BN	Paris, Bibliothèque Nationale de France, MS fr. 24371 [*Blancandin et L'Orgueilleuse d'Amour*]
BN1	Paris, Bibliothèque Nationale de France, MS fr. 20044 [*Paris et Vienne*]
CT	Chaucer, *Canterbury Tales*, ed. Benson
EETS	Early English Text Society
FRLMA	Brown-Grant, *French Romance of the Later Middle Ages*
Kellner	Caxton's "Blanchardyn and Eglantine," ed. Kellner
KRB	Koninklijke Bibliotheek van België/Bibliothèque royale de Belgique
L	*Paris et Vienne*. Antwerp: Gherard Leeu, 1487. USTC: 70658; ISTC: ip00112800. Paris, Bibliothèque Nationale de France, Département Réserve des livres rares, RES-Y2-159 [*Paris et Vienne*]
Lat	Latin
Leach	Caxton, *Paris and Vienne*, ed. Leach
MWCP	Goodman, *Malory and William Caxton's Prose*
MED	*Middle English Dictionary*, ed. McSparran et al.
METS	Middle English Texts Series
MIFL	Thompson, *Motif Index of Folk Literature*
MWME	Burke-Severs et al., eds., *Manual of the Writings of Middle English*, 11 vols.

OF	Old French
R	Caxton, William. *Blanchardyn and Eglantine*. Westminster: William Caxton, 1489. USTC: 500150; ISTC: ib00690400; ESTC: S108419. Manchester, John Rylands Library, Incunable 15027 [base manuscript for *Blanchardyn and Eglantine*]
Vers. I	Pierre de la Cépède, "Der altfranzosische Roman *Paris et Vienne*." Ed. Robert Kaltenbacher [*Paris et Vienne* (original long version)]
Whiting	Whiting and Whiting, *Proverbs, Sentences, and Proverbial Phrases*

General Introduction

William Caxton's translations of *Paris and Vienne* and *Blanchardyn and Eglantine* are among the first romances to be printed in England. Published in 1485 and 1489, respectively, they continued to be popular for more than a century and have considerable literary significance. They are the earliest English versions of French narratives already well known in medieval Europe. Circulating in verse and prose versions in numerous languages, romances of the faithful lovers were among the most popular narratives of the later Middle Ages and Renaissance. The stories' sustained and widespread appeal had much to do with their lively, sympathetic characters and to their distinctive treatments of familiar plots. The romances both edify and entertain, exemplifying ideals of chivalry and steadfast devotion while incorporating adventure, suspense, deception, and humor. Audiences would also have appreciated their realistic depictions of tournaments and battles.

Paris and Vienne and *Blanchardyn and Eglantine* are important witnesses to the development of English prose style and the genre of romance, being in many ways precursors to the novel. They are unique among the romances that Caxton published, for they are the only independent romances of adventure; all the others are canonical works drawn from the epic cycles of England, France, and Greece and Rome. Despite similarities, the two narratives are a study in contrasts, since they give different but complementary accounts of chivalry and love, and nearly opposite treatments of characters who are Muslim.

The sections that follow review what the romances have in common: their publication by Caxton, ties to the court of Burgundy, English audiences, shared narrative motifs, and fifteenth-century prose style. Commentary on Caxton's translation practice and an explanation of my editorial practice are included. A chronological list of Caxton's romances, manuals of chivalry, and conduct books appears in Table 1.

The remainder of the volume consists of the edited text of each romance preceded by its own introduction addressing matters specific to that narrative, including origin, versions, manuscript history, and distinctive features. Each text is followed by Explanatory Notes and Textual Notes; a Bibliography and a Glossary complete the edition.

William Caxton: Merchant, Diplomat, and Printer

William Caxton was not the author of *Paris and Vienne* or *Blanchardyn and Eglantine*; however, as the person who chose to translate them and print them, he can be said to have authored them into English. His career and publications engaged him directly in the literary, economic, and political life of his times. Caxton was born in Kent around 1420, to parents who sent him to school[1] and arranged his apprenticeship to the

---

[1] In the prologue to *Charles the Great*, Caxton thanked his parents for his schooling, since by it he has been able to support himself, as he says, "to gete my lyvyng."

merchant Robert Large, a member of the Mercers' Company,[2] also Alderman, and later mayor of London. By 1444 Caxton himself was a Mercer engaged in exporting wool and importing fine textiles between London and northern Europe. Trading at Bruges,[3] he rose to become Governor of the English Nation of the Merchant Adventurers[4] there, and in this capacity held what one biographer calls "the most prominent, powerful and lucrative office available to a private Englishman abroad."[5] Bruges was a nexus of trade and cultural diffusion from the continent to England, as well as one of the most important cities in the territories of the dukes of Burgundy. Here staples and luxury goods of all kinds from around the world were bought and sold.[6] Caxton's office in the Merchant Adventurers required him to negotiate both international contracts and local agreements with London, the ports of Flanders, the French staple port at Calais, and the cities of the Hanseatic League.[7] His position of authority, expertise, and knowledge of commerce brought him into contact with important people and cultural trends. Edward IV commissioned him to negotiate shipping treaties and tariffs among the ruling houses of England and Burgundy. In addition to shipping and selling finished cloth and other goods between London and the Continent, Caxton was active in the book trade, supplying volumes in manuscript and print to nobles, gentry, citizens, and courtiers. His clients included aristocratic bibliophiles, literary patrons, and creators of libraries whose desire for books and display of status supported professional translators, scribes, and workshops with ties to the book trade.

At the end of his appointment as Governor in 1468, Caxton ceased his active career with the Merchant Adventurers but remained in Bruges serving as secretary, librarian, and translator in the establishment of Margaret of Burgundy, the sister of Edward IV and wife of Charles the Bold.[8] With access to her library, and time at his disposal, Caxton began to translate a French Troy romance into English and completed the project at Cologne, where he became acquainted with the printing press.[9] In 1473 he printed the romance at Bruges with Colard Mansion, who operated the first press in that city. Having traded in books printed in Germany and at Lyon, Caxton recognized the advantages of the new technology and had experience

---

[2] The Worshipful Company of Mercers was a London livery company, a trade association of merchants who exported wool and imported luxury fabrics.

[3] Bruges, in modern Belgium, is a port city on the North Sea.

[4] The Company of Merchant Adventurers was a trading company and London's foremost guild of merchants selling to overseas ports and markets, especially those that traded in cloth and wool. At major international trading centers like Bruges, merchants and trading associations from foreign regions established bureaucracies and offices for conducting business; these were referred to as "Nations."

[5] Painter, *William Caxton*, p. 44.

[6] Blake, *Caxton and English Literary Culture*, p. 2.

[7] The Hanseatic League was a trading and defensive federation of northern German cities that dominated territories along the North Sea and the Baltic.

[8] Deacon suggests that Caxton played a role in the intelligence network of the Tudors at the court of his patron, Margaret of Burgundy, during the Wars of the Roses (*Biography of William Caxton*, p. 160).

[9] The printing press had been introduced into Europe around 1440 by Johannes Guttenberg of Mainz, who had developed movable metal type. Presses were soon set up in other German cities, notably Strasbourg and Cologne, and German printers and pressmen brought the technology to Italy, France, and eastern Europe. A Benedictine monastery outside Rome set up the first Italian press in 1462. The first printed books in France came from the press established in 1470 at Paris by the Sorbonne. In Cologne, Caxton and Colard Mansion learned the art of printing; the latter set up his press at Bruges in 1472, and Caxton was printing in London four years later. From the 1470s on, presses could be found in cities throughout the Continent.

GENERAL INTRODUCTION 3

supplying the growing demand for books.[10] With these in mind, he returned to London in 1476, after thirty years in northern Europe, to set up England's first printing press in Westminster outside the City of London. Through the instability of the Wars of the Roses[11] he prospered there, translating, editing, publishing, printing, loaning, and selling books until his death in 1491 — a ready conduit to English readers for the fashionable French literature he had encountered on the Continent, as well as a source for material already circulating in English.

CAXTON AS PUBLISHER

During the fifteen years that he operated his press, Caxton catered to the market's demands, printing a variety of materials for a diverse audience. His publications included Latin grammars, standard educational texts, chronicles, indulgences, and such ephemera as handbills. Many of his publications, the books of hours and collections of homilies and prayers, were intended for religious instruction and devotional use. In addition to fostering the spread of literacy generally, Caxton made substantial contributions to English literature. He helped to form its canon, fostered the development of a courtly literary prose style distinct from the older alliterative tradition, and authored prologues and epilogues that are among the earliest examples of literary criticism in English. He edited Thomas Malory's *Morte D'Arthur* before printing it.[12] His many translations from French (also Latin and Dutch) added substantially to those works available to English readers and audiences. Although he created no original work of literature, he was a literary figure in his own right and an author according to literary practice of the period.[13] Major English writers of the fifteenth century, including Malory, Thomas Hoccleve, John Lydgate, and John Skelton, all reproduced pre-existing works by excerpting, paraphrasing, or translating. The years 1400–1530 saw a higher proportion of translated prose, compared to total literary production, "than in any other period of English literary history."[14] Caxton published works by respected authors of earlier generations, commenting on their literary significance and acknowledging his admiration of Chaucer's style. He printed the *Canterbury Tales* (twice) as well as *Troilus and Criseyde*, Gower's *Confessio Amantis*,[15] and Lydgate's *Life of Our Lady*, and his *The Horse, the Sheep and the Goose*.[16] Caxton's edition of Malory's *Morte D'Arthur* was the only known version of the

---

[10] In the fifteenth century, the demand for books increased and there was an "almost insatiable market for liturgical material, particularly books of hours" (Kuskin, *Symbolic Caxton*, p. 109).

[11] The Wars of the Roses (1455–1485) were a series of civil wars in which the noble families of York and Lancaster asserted their claims to the English throne. The male lines of both families were extinguished in a series of battles and political murders, leading to the rise of the Tudors and the establishment of their dynasty.

[12] Caxton created chapters, added a table of contents, and abbreviated Malory's passages of alliterative prose, among other edits.

[13] Blake, *Caxton and English Literary Culture*, p. 4; Kuskin, *Symbolic Caxton*, pp. 18–19.

[14] Despres, "Translation Techniques," pp. 11–12. Henry IV (r. 1399–1413) began the process of shifting to English as the language of the court.

[15] John Gower (1330–1408) is best known for the *Confessio*, a frame narrative of an aging lover's confession to the chaplain of Venus. The poem includes tales illustrating the seven deadly sins and an exposition on the ills of society; it was very popular. Gower also wrote long poems in Latin (*Vox Clamantis*) and French (*Mirour de l'Omme*) for the edification of the court of Edward III.

[16] John Lydgate (1370–1451) was a Benedictine monk and prolific poet, distinguished for his *Troy Book*, *Sege of Thebes*, and *Fall of Princes* (a treatise comprised of stories of historical and legendary figures). His writings include examples of most major genres, among them several saint's lives.

romance until the discovery of the Winchester Manuscript in the 1930s.[17] As notable as the works he did print are those that he did not. Excepting the *Morte* and works by Chaucer, Caxton printed no English romances, and nothing in alliterative verse or prose (and he suppressed Malory's alliteration in his edition). The style of *Piers Plowman*[18] and Richard Rolle[19] doubtless seemed old-fashioned and insular ("rude" and "uplondish"[20]) and their lexicon unfamiliar to one with Caxton's continental tastes. Nevertheless, the earlier verse romances and alliterative works by Langland and Rolle circulated widely in Caxton's England and continued to be popular in the sixteenth century when they were reprinted by his successors.[21]

Caxton and Burgundian Literature

In addition to literature already circulating in English, Caxton printed works new to the language and established a program of chivalric publications that included treatises on conduct and knighthood, chronicles, histories, and romances. With the latter he sought both "to shap[e] and to satisf[y] the taste for romances of chivalry that dominated" the later fifteenth century.[22] Though they were new to readers of English, his romances were in keeping with literary tastes already established in Britain; there, readers of French owned copies of those works, and authors and translators were producing similar prose romances in English. Caxton's publications introduced Burgundian literature with its attendant ideologies and social forms into English culture, contributing to what has been called a Burgundian Renaissance in England.[23] Many of his sources can be identified as works belonging to the collections of Dukes Charles the Bold and Philip the

---

[17] This manuscript shows signs of having been in Caxton's shop (Hellinga, "Malory Manuscript," p. 137). Later treatments of the Arthurian legend, including Tennyson's, were based on Caxton's considerably edited *Morte*.

[18] William Langland (1330–1386) composed several versions of *Piers Plowman*, a dream vision and allegory of moral, spiritual, and ecclesiastical reform in the form of a pilgrimage. This long alliterative poem circulated widely.

[19] Richard Rolle (d. 1349) was a mystic and author of the visionary poem, *The Fire of Love*, among many other works including Latin commentaries on the Bible and a guide for anchoresses.

[20] Ed. Crotch, *Prologues and Epilogues*, p. 109.

[21] Many of the important manuscript collections of Middle English literature, particularly verse romances, were produced in the latter part of the fifteenth century (Cambridge Ff. 2.38, Cotton Caligula A.ii, Rawlinson C86, Ashmole 19.3, and the Thornton manuscripts). Carol M. Meale identifies twenty-one romances (excluding those by court poets) that are extant in manuscripts but also survive in printed editions ("Caxton, de Worde," p. 285). Helen Cooper's appendix catalogues English romances in print after 1500 (*English Romance in Time*, pp. 409–29).

[22] Pearsall, "English Romance," p. 79.

[23] Diane Bornstein uses the term "Burgundian renaissance" to refer to a re-invigoration of English culture and literature, especially at the court of Edward IV ("William Caxton's Chivalric Romances," p. 1). The king had visited Bruges for the marriage of his sister to Charles the Bold, and in exile (1470–1471) had sought refuge in The Hague under the protection of Louis de Gruuthuse (de Bruges). Caxton's translations and publications of works by his continental contemporaries also reveal his connections to literary communities "well beyond the Burgundian world," as Goodman notes ("Caxton's Continent," p. 104).

GENERAL INTRODUCTION 5

Good, among them writings of Christine de Pizan,[24] Raymond Lull,[25] and Geoffrey de la Tour-Landry.[26] The French text closest to Caxton's translation of the latter is known to have been in the ducal library at Bruges.[27] Among Caxton's other publications with sources or analogues in that collection are *The Game and Playe of the Chesse*, *The Consolation of Philosophy*, *Aesop's Fables*, *The Declamation of Noblesse*, *The Golden Legend*, and *The Book of Good Manners*. He translated eight prose romances associated with the court and its sphere of influence, including *The Recuyell and the Historye of Troye* and *Jason*, both authored by Raoul le Fèvre, chaplain and secretary to Philip the Good.[28] The author of *Paris et Vienne*, Pierre de la Cépède, was affiliated with the establishment of Duke Philip in Marseille. Louis de Gruuthuse, Flemish nobleman and bibliophile, owned the manuscript of the *Livre d'Eracles* that Caxton probably used as a source for *Godfrey of Boulogne*.[29] *Fierabras* [*Charles the Great*] was commissioned by Charles Bolomyer, Canon of Lausanne; *Four Sons of Aymon* and *Enydos* have Burgundian connections as well.

Surviving manuscripts of *Paris et Vienne* (in Brussels) and *Blancandin et l'Orgueilleuse d'Amours* (in Vienna) were created in the atelier of the Maître de Wavrin at Lille, a studio of artisans supported by the patronage of Jean de Wavrin, bibliophile and counselor to Philip the Good.[30] Jean de Créquy, another patron of letters and counselor to the duke, commissioned the illustrated Vienna manuscript of *Blancandin* from that atelier.[31] Members of the Croy family, who held titles and offices at the courts of Philip and Charles the Bold, owned the Brussels manuscript of *Paris et Vienne*. Members of the family also commissioned two copies of the romance *Octovyen* from the Wavrin workshop which they dedicated to Créquy.[32] The text of the plainer Paris manuscript of *Blancandin*, which is "undoubtedly" closely related to Caxton's source, is virtually identical to that of the Vienna manuscript and is written in a similar hand. It, too, was likely produced by the same atelier, perhaps for sale.[33] Such workshops in Flanders were the source of many deluxe manuscripts owned by English nobles; Edward IV's fine decorated volumes imported from Bruges became the basis for the British Royal Library.

---

[24] Christine de Pizan (1364–1430) was an intellectual and court writer for Charles VI of France and to the Burgundian court. Her extensive oeuvre includes many treatises of advice to princes and princesses, notably *Book of the City of Ladies* and *Treasury of the City of Ladies*, as well as *Deeds of Arms and Chivalry*.

[25] Raymond Lull (1232–1316) was a Spanish philosopher and missionary. Many of his Latin writings set forth a system of universal logic, but he also authored a treatise, the *Ordre of Chyvalry*, as well as prose narratives in the vernacular.

[26] Geoffrey de la Tour-Landry (1330–1406), a French nobleman, composed books of manners and moral instruction for his sons and daughters. Only the latter survives; it was a popular conduct book in the fifteenth century.

[27] Blake, *Caxton and His World*, p. 68.

[28] Caxton could have encountered the secretary in his diplomatic and mercantile activities. Le Fèvre translated his histories from sources in Latin.

[29] Bornstein, "William Caxton's Chivalric Romances," p. 5. Louis's library commissioned manuscripts from Colard Mansion, the scribe and book-dealer who later brought the printing press to Bruges where Caxton published *The Recuyell* and *The Game and Playe of the Chesse*.

[30] Lille was a major supplier of bespoke manuscripts to noble houses of northern France and Flanders, and of plainer copies to the markets.

[31] Marchal, "L'existence d'un manuscrit," p. 271

[32] Marchal, "L'existence d'un manuscrit," p. 270; *MWCP*, pp. 68–69. Members of the Croy family also patronized Colard Mansion (see note 29, above). Antoine Croy, count of Gueinne (d. 1475) was minister to Philip the Good and Governor General of territories now in Belgium and Luxembourg, as was his son, Philip (d. 1511), who was raised with Charles the Bold.

[33] Marchal, "L'existence d'un manuscrit," p. 266.

Caxton's attempt to introduce French prose romance into England was initially successful, and several of his translations continued in print until the end of the sixteenth century. *The Recuyell of the Historye of Troye* was particularly popular, to judge from the number of editions and copies that survive, and Wynkyn de Worde reprinted that romance as well as *Four Sons of Aymon*, *Morte D'Arthur*, and *Paris and Vienne*.[34] In his own romance publications, de Worde continued to follow Caxton's program of printing "what was currently available, and in demand, on the Continent," that is, new translations of French prose romances.[35] Robert Copland and Richard Pynson, who followed de Worde, kept these four romances in print for more than a hundred years.

Caxton's Audience: Patrons and Readers

Information about Caxton's audiences comes from his prologues and dedications, and from traces left by readers in surviving manuscripts and documents. His dedicatees are both noble and bourgeois, and his writings recommend the romances to the reading of aristocrats as well as to a larger less elite audience. The dedications function as advertisements by calling attention to Caxton's access to the aristocracy and flattering both the patron and aspiring readers of the gentry, merchant, and professional classes. The nature of Caxton's relationship to his patrons and dedicatees varied, and he may not have assumed that they actually read the books dedicated to them. In his prologue to *Jason*, he asks Edward IV, who had commissioned the translation, to allow him to dedicate it to the Prince of Wales, "to the entente he may begynne to lerne rede English," rather than to the king himself, "for as moch as I doubte not his good grace hath it in Frensh, which he wel understandeth."[36] However, Caxton did dedicate *Godfrey of Boulogne* to Edward, whose copy of the book survives.[37] He translated and printed *The Recuyell of Troye* at the request of Margaret of Burgundy; the only surviving copy belonged to her sister-in-law, the queen Elizabeth.[38] *Blanchardyn* was translated for Margaret Beaufort, mother of Henry VII. Caxton had earlier sold her a manuscript of the romance in French that may well have been his source. Caxton was present when Henry VII presented a copy of Christine de Pizan's *Faites d'Armes et de Chevalerie* [Deeds of Arms and Chivalry] to the Earl of Oxford, who in turn conveyed it to the printer for translation. Margaret Beaufort owned a copy of the treatise that he had printed, given to her by her son.[39] These patrons' support for the dissemination of material in print was regarded as a virtuous act of charitable largesse, making books of moral and educational value available to English readers. Such patronage was also a display of status modeled on Italian Renaissance courts where nobles asserted prestige by building libraries and owning luxury copies of important works. Not all

---

[34] Wynkyn de Worde (of Worth, in Lorraine) accompanied Caxton from Bruges to England and continued to work for him, inheriting the business at his death in 1491.

[35] Meale, "Caxton, de Worde," p. 295. De Worde printed a wider range of material already in English than did Caxton, including many popular verse romances (Blake, *Caxton and His World*, p. 214).

[36] In 1477, when *Jason* was printed, the prince was seven years old and would have been learning to read Latin, and French, which was still in use at court. The Tudors decreed English to be the language of government in 1490, though Henry IV (d. 1413) began the shift.

[37] Bornstein, "William Caxton's Chivalric Romances," p. 4.

[38] Goodman, "Caxton's Continent," p. 106.

[39] The copy in the Huntington Library (STC 7269) bears her inscription and her note that the book was given to her by Henry (Nall, "Margaret Beaufort's Books," p. 213).

of Caxton's dedications acknowledge actual patronage; some, like the presentation of *The Ordre of Chyvalry* to Richard III, seem more designed to ingratiate.[40]

While English aristocrats read French, their courtiers and members of their households were more at home with English. In his prologue to the 1483 reprint of *The Game and Playe of the Chesse*, Caxton explains that he translated it for the benefit of those who do not understand French and Latin, and "al them that . . . shal see, here, or rede" the book.[41] In the prologue to *The Nightingale* Lady Anne Beaufort is envisioned reading the poem to her "people" for their moral instruction and entertainment.[42] If the engraving of Margaret of Burgundy in *The Recuyell of Troye* is any indication, the audience would have consisted of ladies in waiting, their maids and pages, and members of the retinue, household, and family.[43] The scene resembles that of other dedicatory miniatures from France and northern Europe where the lady, surrounded by her attendants, receives the book from the kneeling author while others busy themselves on the periphery.[44]

In addition to aristocrats, Caxton dedicated books to several of London's leading citizens. Hugh Bryce, a Mercer, funded the translation and production of the *Mirror of the World*. Caxton dedicated *The Book of Good Manners* to William Pratt and *Charles the Great* to William Daubeney — wealthy tradesmen and city officials. Caxton addressed his publications to "Cristen pryntes, lordes, barons, knyghtes, gentilmen, marchauntes, and all the comyn peple," as well as to clerks, ladies, and gentlewomen.[45] The surviving copies of Caxton's romances belonged to such people: clergy, landed gentry, lawyers, officials, and court servants who would have shared them in their domestic and social circles. Raufe Batson, a member of the Mercers Company at Bruges in 1505, and Roger Thorney (d. 1515), a wealthy London Mercer, owned copies of *Godfrey of Boulogne*.[46] Robert Johnson, a sub-deacon in Ely and rector in Essex, purchased copies of *Godfrey of Boulogne*, *Enydos*, and *Fayttes of Arms and Chivalry* in 1510.[47] John Thynne, who owned *The Recuyell of Troye* and *Enydos*, was steward to the Seymour family and was knighted in 1546. The Troy story seems to have been especially popular, which is to be expected given Britain's myth of Trojan origins. A copy belonged to Thomas Shuckburg, whose family held lands in Warwickshire; he could have obtained the book through an uncle who was listed as a member of the London Drapers Company in 1493.[48] Other copies of *The Recuyell of Troye* were owned by William Saunder, a lawyer in Surrey who held important positions there under Henry VIII; by the Tresham family of Northamptonshire, a member of which was knighted in 1530; and by Margery Wellysborn, of Buckinghamshire, whose husband was MP in 1477.[49]

---

[40] Caxton based his translation of the *Ordre* on a French book belonging to Anthony Woodville, who had been executed by Richard III in the year before Caxton published his book.

[41] Caxton, *Game and Playe*, ed. J. Adams, p. 15.

[42] Krug, "Margaret Beaufort," p. 78.

[43] Kuskin gives a detailed reading of the engraving as it symbolizes the social and literary authority of the printed text (*Symbolic Caxton*, pp. 97–102).

[44] Goodman suggests that the kneeling figure may be a portrait of Caxton himself ("Caxton's Continent," p. 106).

[45] See ed. Blake, *Caxton's Prose*, p. 140; Kuskin, *Symbolic Caxton*, p. 206; and *Blanchardyn and Eglantine*, Dedication.1, for examples of such dedications.

[46] Wang, "Tudor Readers," pp. 180–81. Thorney bound his copy of *The Recuyell of Troye* with Caxton's prints of Chaucer's *Troilus*, the romances of the *Canterbury Tales*, and a manuscript of Lydgate's *Siege of Thebes*. Other owners of copies of Caxton's romances bound them with additional romances and chivalric materials.

[47] Wang, "Tudor Readers," p. 182.

[48] Wang, "Tudor Readers," pp. 182–84.

[49] Wang, "Tudor Readers," pp. 184–88.

Thomas Skeffington, master of military ordinance for the Tudors, owned *Jason* and *The Mirror of the World*.[50] One John Dew of Chesterton, a fellow of Gonville College, inscribed the surviving copy of *Blanchardyn and Eglantine* in 1500.[51] A connection between Caxton and the prominent Paston family can be traced through their scribe, William Ebesham, whose shop was close by Caxton's in Westminster. Ebesham made their "Grete Booke" as well as manuscript copies of Caxton's documents.[52] The Pastons owned a copy of Caxton's *The Game and Playe of the Chesse*.[53]

Caxton's early readers were quite separated by rank, wealth, and locale from his aristocratic patrons and the French nobles who were instrumental in the creation and dissemination of the romances he offered for sale. Their owners belonged to classes that did not fit neatly into the medieval hierarchy of those who work, pray, and fight, and whose growing numbers proved a challenge to the static ideals of feudal society that their reading matter validated. The technology of their books' production was also at odds with these ideals, as mass production and consumption of printed materials had transformative implications for both cultural and economic capital. Caxton could manufacture books in "grete chepe and in grete nombre," a virtue of printing that enabled him to reach a large group of socially diverse customers at once.[54] Though his technology was forward-looking, Caxton's conservative tastes appealed to those of his socially ambitious customers. His prologues and the availability of printed books on chivalric themes suggested that one could rise in social status through appropriate choice of reading matter.[55] That the volumes were valued possessions and symbols of family status is clear from references in wills and other documents. It seems fitting that John Dew, who presumably owned other books he could have written in, chose the one containing *Blanchardyn* to record his family's pedigree and coat of arms.

Chivalry and Courtesy

Caxton's romances are part of his larger program of chivalric publication and commentary on the practice of chivalry in his own times. Significantly, he chose to focus on the cycle of the Nine Worthies.[56] This

---

[50] Wang, "Tudor Readers," p. 185.

[51] I am indebted to John Bloch Friedman for help identifying this individual (E-mail, August 7, 2017).

[52] Kuskin, *Symbolic Caxton*, p. 106. The Pastons' employee, John Pamping, may have purchased an indulgence printed at his press (Painter, *William Caxton*, p. 169).

[53] Ed. Lester, *Sir John Paston's "Grete Boke,"* pp. 54–55. John Paston's inventory of his books lists "A boke in preente off the Pleye of the Chesse." The list was drawn up before 1479, so this must have been Caxton's edition of 1474.

[54] Matheson, "Printer and Scribe," p. 599.

[55] Adams, "Printing and the Transformation," p. 295.

[56] Caxton's program of publications concentrated on this cycle, as he explains in the prologues to *Le Morte d'e Arthur* and *Charles the Great*: "Thenne for as moche I late had fynysshed in enprynte the bok of the noble vyctoryous kyng Arthur fyrst of the thre moost noble and worthy of crysten kynges. and also tofore had reduced in to englisshe the noble hystorye and lyf of Godefroy of boloyn kyng of Jerusalem, last of the said iii worthy, Somme persones of noble estate and degree haye desyred me to reduce thystorye and lyf of the noble and crysten prynce Charles the grete kyng of fraunce and emperour of Rome, the second of the thre worthy" (ed. Crotch, *Prologues and Epilogues*, pp. 96–97). He also mentions his translation and publication of the histories' three pagan worthies: Hector, Aeneas, and Jason. Three Jews (Joshua, David, and Judas Maccabeus) completed the programmatic nine, though Caxton did not publish histories of these Old Testament heroes (also see the prologue to *Godfrey of Boulogne* in ed. Colvin, pp. 1–5). These figures appeared in many narrative cycles, and were a favorite subject for paintings, tapestries, and other artifacts in the later Middle Ages.

group of legendary, biblical, and historical figures had served as a model of chivalric virtue since the early thirteenth century and was a favorite subject of literature and art at the courts of France and England. In these settings, the Worthies played an important role in the performance of chivalry, epitomized by the pageants, celebrations, ceremonies, and tournaments that took place at the founding of the Order of the Golden Fleece by Philip the Good in 1430.[57] Caxton had visited the shrine-chamber at Hesenden that the duke had constructed for the Order and dedicated at its founding. In his prologue to *Jason*, Caxton described its paintings depicting the hero's conquests and the mechanized marvel that produced wind and rain.[58] He could well have attended the celebration of the marriage of Margaret of York and Charles the Bold in 1468, which took place in Bruges amid extravagant pageantry and feats of arms at the Pas de l'Arbre d'Or [Challenge of the Golden Tree]. Here Anthony Woodville, later Caxton's patron, famously jousted with Anton de la Roche, the Bastard of Burgundy.[59] At least four other tournaments were held by members of the Burgundian court while Caxton was in Bruges and Ghent, giving him many opportunities to observe such displays.[60] In London, court and urban cultures blended with the increased frequency of large-scale tournaments. Citizens attended these, and their businesses supported them.[61] Aldermen, officers, and guilds participated in the processions associated with civic and royal ceremonies where chivalric protocol played an important role. In a departure from the practice of earlier sovereigns, Edward IV showed favor to leading London citizens by bestowing knighthoods on aldermen and mayors.[62]

The dedication to *Blanchardyn and Eglantine* recommends romances for their chivalric values:

> [I]t is as requesyte other whyle to rede in auncyent hystoryes of noble fayttes and valyaunt actes of armes and warre which have been achyeued in olde tyme of many noble pryncez, lordes, and knyghtes, as wel for to see and know their walyauntnes for to stande in the specyal grace and love of their ladyes (Dedication.1).

Caxton strikes a note of nostalgia and alarm at his contemporaries' practice of chivalry in his epilogue to Raymond Lull's *Ordre of Chyvalry*:

> [This] booke is not requysyte to euery comyn man to haue, but to noble gentylmen that by their vertu entende to come and entre in to the noble ordre of chyualry the whiche in these late dayes hath been

---

[57] The Order was founded in celebration of Philip's marriage to Isabel of Portugal, to the honor of God and chivalry. Its emblem, a golden sheepskin, commemorated Jason's heroic quest. Its thirty noble members observed quasi-ecclesiastical rituals and passed judgment on cases of unchivalrous conduct, in addition to participating in tournaments and other occasions for displays of arms.

[58] Duke Philip commissioned the composition of the French romance to commemorate the Order. Caxton's translation of *Jason* for Edward IV is related to his induction into the Order at his sister's wedding. The king owned a copy in French.

[59] *MWCP*, p. 10n10.

[60] *MWCP*, pp. 8–10.

[61] The heraldic account of the *Pas de la Perron Féé* [Pass (of arms) of the Magic Pillar] (1462) notes the importance of rich merchants to supply those things necessary to a great feast (*MWCP*, pp. 11–12).

[62] Barron, "Chivalry, Pageantry and Merchant Culture," p. 239. Earlier, in the fourteenth century, leading merchants had the wealth and connections to procure knighthoods, but seldom chose to. While Londoners were aware of the codes and practices of chivalry, they developed their own forms of civic ceremony and pageantry parallel to tournaments.

vsed accordyng to this booke here to fore wreton but forgeten and thexcersytees of chyualry not vsed honoured ne excercysed as hit hath ben in auncyent tyme.[63]

After citing Arthur and the Knights of the Round Table he laments, "O ye knyghtes of Englond where is the custome and vsage of noble chyualry that was vsed in the dayes?"[64] In closing, Caxton appeals to Richard III to make the book required reading for young lords, knights, and gentlemen who aspire to knighthood. Caxton had printed a number of other treatises on chivalry and manners including *The Game and Playe of the Chesse* and *Fayttes of Arms and Chivalry*. Connections can be made between the manuals and the romances published in the same year: the battle plans and siege warfare described in *Blanchardyn and Eglantine* resemble the instructions for mounting defenses and sieges in Christine's *Fayttes of Arms and Chivalry* (1489), while the tournaments and pilgrimage of *Paris and Vienne* are in keeping with the ideals of Lull's *Ordre of Chyvalry* (1485).[65] Caxton's prologues and epilogues are conduct books of a sort, instructing readers in how to approach aristocratic texts.[66]

The romances themselves are courtesy literature, for their characters epitomize proper deportment and chivalric excellence, or the lack thereof.[67] *Blanchardyn and Eglantine* can be read as a mirror for princes and princesses, *Paris and Vienne* as a mirror for adolescents.[68] Blanchardyn is a paragon of courteous behavior: his audiences with Eglantine are models of elegant manners as he approaches the royal personage and "makes the reverence," speaking politely and displaying humility, discretion, and reticence.[69] Such behavior is described in Caxton's *Babee's Boke* and *The Boke of Curtasye*, which include instructions for how properly to greet one's lord or superior, approach them, and engage in conversation.[70] Though Vienne's determination and loyalty to Paris is admirable, her disobedience and refusal of the completely appropriate marriage her father arranges for her are negative illustrations of the ideals of obedience, submission, and respect for parents, especially regarding marriage, that are set forth in *The Book of the Knight of the Tour-Landry*.

---

[63] Ed. Crotch, *Prologues and Epilogues*, p. 82.

[64] Ed. Crotch, *Prologues and Epilogues*, pp. 82–83.

[65] *MWCP*, p. 89.

[66] Adams, "Noble, wyse and grete lordes" p. 56. Conduct literature, designed to inculcate social norms in manners and morals, offered instruction in proper behavior from grooming to deportment and daily devotions. Caxton's *Book of Good Manners* falls into this category; this manual of popular theology for devotional reading includes a treatise on the vices and virtues as practiced by the different orders of society.

[67] Bornstein, "William Caxton's Chivalric Romances," p. 6. Nicholls's *Matter of Courtesy* is a thorough introduction to courtesy books and romance as courtesy literature. See also Bornstein, *Mirrors of Courtesy* and *Lady in the Tower*.

[68] Bartlett, "Translation, Self-Representation," p. 57; Mirrors (*Specula*), treatises ostensibly for the education of rulers, were a form of conduct literature that included instruction in politics, governance, and Christian life illustrated with examples from history and legend. Caxton's *Royal Book* is an example.

[69] The phrase appears at 15.4, 21.2, 23.3, 26.7, and 42.2. The word *curtsy* is derived from *courtesy* (Nicholls, *Matter of Courtesy*, p. 13).

[70] *The Babee's Boke* and *The Boke of Curtasye* are found in ed. Furnivall, *Early English Meals and Manners*. *Generydes*, another fifteenth-century romance, is also concerned with etiquette and courtly manners for "there is much attention to ceremonies of meeting and leave-taking," and observation of proprieties (Pearsall, "English Romance," p. 70). *Jean de Saintré* (1456), which relates the education of a knight, is a fusion of romance and chivalric biography. Geoffrey de la Tour-Landry is thought to be the author of the pedagogic romance *Ponthus et la Belle Sidoine*, an adaptation of *Horn et Rimenild*, "designed to exemplify the rules of behavior proper to a gentleman." An English translation was printed by Wynkyn de Worde in 1505 and in 1510–1511 (Dunn, "Romances Derived," pp. 22, 210).

That treatise, addressed to the knight's daughters, concludes with a debate as to the propriety of "love paramours," or courtly love. He asserts that a knight's love of a lady can inspire him to good conduct and skill at arms while raising the reputation of the lady; his wife argues that men perform feats of chivalry mainly to enhance their own reputations and are more often motivated by lust than by love.[71] *Blanchardyn and Eglantine* and *Paris and Vienne* both mention the lovers' educations and include many dialogues in which the heroes and heroines are advised by their confidantes as to the proper course of conduct, often in terms that resonate with those of didactic writings. Even the format of Caxton's books encouraged instructional reading, and, characteristically for Burgundian works, included prologues and epilogues emphasizing the works' educational and chivalric value. Additionally, tables of chapters and chapter headings called attention to characters' good and bad behaviors and make the text easier for readers to navigate.[72]

Features of Chivalric Romance in *Paris and Vienne* and *Blanchardyn and Eglantine*

Paris and Vienne and *Blanchardyn and Eglantine* share features typical of fifteenth-century chivalric narratives from France. Their authors and redactors composed in prose, a form employed in historical and scientific writings that began to replace verse as the preferred medium for French romances at the time. Descriptions are heightened, as are depictions of emotions, while battles and combats are narrated in formulas that create melodrama and arouse the audience's empathy.[73] Characters are developed through passages of dialogue, monologue, reflection, and self-analysis. Both narratives depict the headstrong lovers humorously on occasion, and have active female characters.

The narratives are composed of elements belonging to the common vocabulary of romance. As MacEdward Leach observes of *Paris and Vienne*, "it is the stock motifs that carry the story."[74] Readers of medieval romance will recognize such familiar memes as the blocking father, the bold Muslim princess, the treacherous steward, three-day tournaments to prove a lady's champion, lovers separated by storms, and recognition by ring. Both romances feature a secondary couple, confidantes of the lovers, who also marry. Both exiled heroes pass as Muslim by appearance and language, ingratiate themselves with Muslim rulers by acts of chivalry, and rescue imprisoned fathers.[75]

Caxton's romances treat generic motifs with literary sophistication and a degree of verisimilitude. Like his sources, Caxton refers to his romances as "hystoryes," making a claim to veracity and fidelity to actual events that the genre of romance does not. The word *history* accords with the fifteenth-century taste for realistic narratives and for true (and therefore instructive) stories. Pierre de la Cépède remarked that he found the material in some romances hard to believe, and so selected the story of Paris and Vienne to

---

[71] The debate concerns whether or not their daughters should be allowed to show "favor" to knights, attend jousts, and give men tokens such as sleeves to wear in a public sign of support. The Knight's is the standard argument for chivalry, but he has earlier expressed disapproval of the conduct of knights at tournaments, based on his own experiences. The wife's negative and conservative position more nearly aligns with her husband's comments elsewhere in the treatise (Caxton, *Knight of the Tour-Landry*, ed. Wright, pp. 171–86).

[72] Bornstein, "William Caxton's Chivalric Romances," pp. 5–9. Caxton points out to the reader the usefulness of these features in his prologue to *Charles the Great* and elsewhere.

[73] Brown-Grant, "Narrative Style," p. 375.

[74] Leach, p. xxi.

[75] The Muslims of *Paris and Vienne* are accepted "at face value" (Cooper, "Going Native," p. 30).

translate because it was reasonable and credible enough [*assez croyable*].[76] The two romances belong to a genre in which chivalric romance can be seen to presage the historical novel. The absence of supernatural elements, the localized settings, and the attention to detail give a realistic cast to the narratives. Unlike many other knights who ride through the forests of romance, Blanchardyn gets hungry and eats the wild fruit and crab apples growing there. Paris's voyage of adventure is not impelled by storms at sea; rather, he arranges passage to and from the Holy Land and pays for his transportation with funds drawn from Missire Bertran's bank. Both romances are set in specific geographic locales. *Blanchardyn and Eglantine* takes place in the Baltic, near Marienbourg where the romance's patron, Jean de Créquy, had rendered military service to the duke of Burgundy. *Paris and Vienne* is set in the city of Vienne and along the Rhone River to the Mediterranean, a region that would have been familiar to its author who lived in Marseille. Characteristically for Burgundian romances, fictional adventures can be traced on historical maps and resonate with actual events.[77]

Despite the romances' commonalities, their differences show them belonging to different sub-genres, and deriving from different literary and regional traditions of chivalric narrative. *Blanchardyn and Eglantine*, the older, is anonymous and originated in northern France, probably Picardy, in the early thirteenth century. What began as a verse romance set in Athens and India made the transition to prose in the mid-fifteenth century in a version set along the North Sea.[78] The story of Paris and Vienne originated in Provence during the late fourteenth century and was composed in French prose by Pierre de la Cépède in 1432. *Blanchardyn and Eglantine* is lengthy and offers an elaborated rendition of Burgundian prose style, while *Paris and Vienne* is a shorter treatment of de la Cépède's embellished romance, with less rhetorical ornamentation and a more linear narrative. *Blanchardyn and Eglantine* is a military adventure of armies, navies, sieges, and gruesome combats in which the knight proves himself by defending his lady and her kingdom from invading armies and treasonous officials. *Paris and Vienne* includes no such episodes, for the lady's person and kingdom are not under attack; instead, Paris demonstrates chivalric prowess in a series of tournaments to become her champion. *Paris and Vienne* is a family romance: the obstacle to the lovers' marriage is parental objection, not the assault of an unwanted suitor, and the matter is complicated by class, for the dauphin of Vienne rejects Paris's suit because of his inferior rank. *Blanchardyn and Eglantine* engages issues of class briefly from a negative perspective in the episode of the treacherous steward and introduces family romance only in the sub-plot of the secondary couple. *Blanchardyn and Eglantine* is interested in governance and *fin amor*, *Paris and Vienne* in adolescent behavior and marriage.

While both heroes disguise themselves as cultural and religious others, the romances offer differing representations of Muslims and use different terms to refer to characters and peoples who are Muslims. *Blanchardyn and Eglantine* is indebted to the *chansons de geste* for its portrayals and employs the words *Saracen* and *pagan* exclusively and almost interchangeably to characterize the enemy king, Alymodes, and his people. The romance portrays these characters in terms of the negative racial stereotypes associated with the label *Saracen*, including dark skin, monstrous bodies, and wrongful aggression against Christians who slay them or force them to convert. While Sadoyne and the Prussians who come to Blanchardyn's aid

---

[76] Painter, *William Caxton*, p. 150; Pearsall makes much the same point ("English Romance," p. 82); Schlauch observes that *Paris and Vienne* and *Blanchardyn and Eglantine*, "belong[ed] distinctly to a medieval tradition, but . . . contribut[ed] to the shaping of later fiction in a realistic vein" (*Antecedents*, p. 65).

[77] *Olyver of Castylle* is set in Iberia, Ireland, and England, regions that French and English readers would have associated with current events (Williams, "England, Ireland, and Iberia" p. 94).

[78] Kellner, pp. cxvii–cvxiii, includes summaries of the verse romance.

are not so vilified, their religious rituals, like those of Alymodes, are said to include the worship of idols and a deity named Mahoun, practices forbidden by Islam but commonly ascribed to Muslims in Christian writings. *Paris and Vienne* uses a term that appears more frequently in the later Middle Ages and refers to Paris and the inhabitants of the Middle East solely as *Moors*. Like Saracens, these Moors differ from Europeans in language, dress, and religion, but they are not racialized or depicted as disfigured, idol-worshiping, enemies.[79]

Blanchardyn and Eglantine is the more conventional romance; the characters of *Paris and Vienne* are the more realistic. Perhaps for this reason, and because of its straightforward narrative and accessible style, it was the more popular and long-lived of the two romances. It was reprinted numerous times while *Blanchardyn and Eglantine* saw no later editions, though both romances were revised and continued in circulation. Their differences extend to their physical formats: *Blanchardyn* is a decorated volume in single columns with dedication, table of chapters, and numbered chapter headings; *Paris* is plainer, in double columns, with less prominent headings and no ancillary matter or table.

Caxton's Translation Practice and Prose Style

Caxton followed the practice of close translation common in fifteenth-century England. As he explains in the prologue to *The Mirror of the World*, "I have to my power folowed my copye. And as nygh as to me is possible I have made it so playn, that every man resonable may understonde it."[80] Thus, he brought into English the prose style of his French sources. In the prologue to *Enydos* he praises this style as "wel ordred" and using "fayr and honest termes."[81] It was also characterized as "compendious."[82] Fifteenth-century writers of French prose narratives cultivated an ornate style notable for *ampificatio* and rhetorical exuberance intended to elevate the subject, and which relied on embellishments like hyperbole and Latinate diction — the gilding of the aureate style. This way of writing was also influenced by curial prose with its learned vocabulary, synonymic doublets, epistolary formulas, and phrases of referential precision ("the which," "that same").[83] Caxton's prose is notable for recapitulation and redundancy, particularly doublets of synonyms in English and French. His syntax follows that of his sources: long chains of clauses and phrases strung together by sequences of subordinate and, more often, coordinate constructions. In neither French nor English is syntax necessarily supported by punctuation and dialogues shift freely from direct to indirect discourse.[84]

Caxton's skill as a translator and prose stylist grew over the course of his publishing career, and both *Paris and Vienne* and *Blanchardyn and Eglantine* are products of his later years. Editors have praised his accomplishments: Leach commends the former for its "clear straightforward style," while Kellner finds the

---

[79] See Rajabzadeh, "Depoliticized Saracen and Muslim Erasure" and Kennedy, "Moors and Moorishness" for discussion of the terms *Saracen* and *Moor*. Kennedy refers specifically to *Paris and Vienne*.
[80] Ed. Crotch, *Prologues and Epilogues*, p. 58.
[81] Ed. Crotch, *Prologues and Epilogues*, p. 107.
[82] Blake, *Caxton and English Literary Culture*, p. 120.
[83] The curial style of writing and of textual presentation, developed by court bureaucrats, supplied necessary clarity to legal and administrative documents. It made use of devices promoting textual cohesion such as titles, headings, and transitions between sections and further adapted to its audience by striving for "congratulatory ceremoniousness" and carefully observing protocol and rank (Burnley, "Curial Prose," p. 596).
[84] Brown-Grant, "Narrative Style," p. 391.

latter "not inferior to Peacock, the greatest prosaist of his time."[85] Caxton aimed for accuracy and intelligibility; though his lexicon imports terms from his source, his vocabulary is midway between the extremes of vernacular, common terms, and ornate, aureate language. As he explains in the prologue to *Enydos*, "Some gentylmen . . . late blamed me, sayeng that in my translacyons I had over curyous termes which coude not be understande of comyn peple and desired me to use olde and homely termes in my translacyons . . . And som honest and grete clerkes have ben wyth me and desired me to wryte the moste curyous termes that I coude fynde . . . Therfor in a meane between both I have reduced and translated this sayd booke."[86] In the dedication of *Blanchardyn and Eglantine*, he asks Margaret to pardon his "rude and comyn Englyshe . . . , for I confesse me not lerned ne knowynge the arte of rethoryk ne of suche gaye termes as now be sayd in these dayes and used" (Dedication.2). Elsewhere he apologizes for his lack of subtle new eloquence while explaining that he avoids the language of "rude uplondish men."[87] Though these are typical instances of the humility topoi in authorial prologues, Caxton's comments recognize the varied and fluid state of the English language, the possibilities of elite and vernacular styles, and the differences between the self-consciously refined literary language of aristocrats and the English widely in use.

EDITORIAL PRACTICE

The texts that follow are based on the single surviving copies of the romances in the Rylands Library and the British Library. Following METS editorial guidelines, I silently regularize *i/j* and *u/v* spellings and use modern capitalization, punctuation, and word division. Thus, dialogue appears in quotation marks, and *hym self* is spelled *himself*. I silently expand the pronoun *thee* to differentiate it from the article *the*, as well as the adverb *off* to distinguish it from the preposition *of*. Standard printers' abbreviations are also silently expanded, as are elided articles where nouns begin in vowels (*the ynstance* not *thynstance*). Transposed and inverted letters are corrected (*for*, Caxton reads *fro*; *Breunes*, Caxton reads *Breuues*). Caxton's punctuation is not regular and consists of marks no longer in use, and his syntax does not conform to modern practice, so I have slightly modernized the punctuation to facilitate reading. I have also edited his paragraphing to follow the narrative more closely. In Caxton's texts, a whole chapter may consist of only one paragraph, or sentences may be punctuated as paragraphs for emphasis. These features are cited in the Textual Notes accompanying each romance.

The following passage from *Paris and Vienne* is found on folio 1v of BL C10.b10:

> . . . And the fayre Vyenne grewe and encreaced ever in soverayn beawte and gentylness so that the renomme of hyr excellent beawte flourysshed not onley thrugh al frau~ce but also thrugh al the royaume of englond & other contrees | It happed after she was xv yere of age that she was desyred to maryage of many knyghtes & grete lordes | & at that tyme was in the daulphyns courte emonge many hys knyghtes | a noble mā of auncyent lygnage & of faye londes | the whiche was wel byloued of the daulphyn & of alle the lordes of the lande and was called Syr James | thys noble man had a moche fayr

---

[85] Leach, p. xxx; Kellner, p. cxi. Leach notes that Caxton's prose style developed over his career as translator but did not rise to the levels of Peacock's or Malory's (p. xxvi). According to Painter, "Caxton was, and knew he was, surpassed by few Englishmen of his time as a master of French and of English prose" (*William Caxton*, p. 39).

[86] Ed. Crotch, *Prologues and Epilogues*, pp. 108–09. This prologue includes lengthy commentary on the state of the English language in the transitional period from medieval to early modern.

[87] Ed. Crotch, *Prologues and Epilogues*, p. 109.

General Introduction

15

sone that had to name Parys | & hys fader made hym to be taught in al good custommes | and whan he was xviii yere of age he was adressed to the dyscyplyne of armes | & demened hym self so nobly & worthely in al maner dedes of chyualrye that wythin a shorte tyme after he was doubed knyght by the hande of the sayd daulphyn | ¶ Noo fayte of knyghthode ne none adventure of chyualrye happed after but that he founde hym self at it in soo moche that the renommee of hym ranne thurgh al the world & men sayde he was one of the best knyghtes þ~ myght be founde in ony contree | & helde hym self ryght clene in armes and lyued chastly & joyefully | & had euer aboute hym fowles hawkes and houndes for his dysporte to all maner of huntyng suffysaunt ynough for a duc or for an erle | and thurgh hys prowesse and hardynes he was acqueynted & knowen of many other grete lordes | and emonge all other he was gretely and louyngly acqueynted with a yonge knyght of the cyte of Vyenne that hyght Edward | and were bothe of one age and moche loued eche other | and as two brethern of armes wente euer to gyder there as they knew ony joustyng or appertyse of armes to be had for to gete honour| ¶ And wete it wel that besyde theyr worthynes in armes they were good musycyens playeng upon alle maner instrumentes of musyke |and coude synge very well | but Parys passed in al ponytes his felowe Edward . . .

Points at which my edited text differs appear in bold type.

. . . And the fayre Vyenne grewe and encreaced ever in soverayn beawté and gentylnesse so that the renomee of hyr excellent beawté flourysshed not onely thurgh al Fraunce but also thurgh al the royame [fol. 1v] of Englond **and** other contrees.

2 **It** happed after she was **fyftene** yere of age that she was desyred to maryage of many knyghtes **and** grete lordes. **A**nd at that tyme was in the daulphyns courte emonge many hys knyghtes **a** noble man of auncyent lygnage **and** of fayr londes, the whiche was wel byloved of the daulphyn **and** of alle the lords of the lande, and was called Syr James. **T**hys noble man had a moche fayr sone that had to name Parys, **and** his fader made hym to be taught in al good custommes. **A**nd whan he was **eightene** yere of age he was adressed to the dyscyplyne of armes, **and** demened hymself so nobly **and** worthely in al maner dedes of ch**y**valrye that wythin a shorte tyme after he was doubed knyght by the hande of the sayd **lord** daulphyn.

3 Noo fayte of knyghthode ne none adventure of chyvalrye happed after but that he founde hymself at it, in soo moche that the renommee of hym ranne thurgh al the world, and men sayd he was one of the best knyghtes **that** myght be founde in ony contree. **And** helde hymself ryght clene in armes and lyved chastly **and** joyefully. **A**nd had ever aboute hym fowles, hawkes, and houndes for hys dysporte to alle maner of huntyng suffysaunt ynough for a duc or for an erle. **A**nd thurgh hys prowesse and hardynes he was acqueynted **and** knowen of many other grete lordes. **A**nd emonge alle other, he was gretely and lo**v**yngly acqueynted with a yonge knyght of the cyt**é** of Vyenne that hyght Edward, and were bothe of one age and moche loved eche other. **A**nd as two brethern of armes wente ever togyder there as they knew ony jousytng or appertyse of armes to be had for to gete honour.

4 And wete it wel that, besyde theyr worthynes in armes, they were good musycyens, playeng upon alle maner instrumentes of musyke and coude synge veray wel, but Parys passed in al ponytes his felowe Edward . . .

Table 1: Caxton's Translations of Romances and Chivalric Treatises

Date refers to the year of the first printing.
Dedicatees are those mentioned in prologues.
Sources are individuals mentioned in prologues and elsewhere who provided the French texts that Caxton translated.

Date	Title	Author	Dedicatee	Source
1473	The Recuyell and Historye of Troy	Raoul le Fèvre	Margaret, duchess of Burgundy	Margaret, duchess of Burgundy
1474	The Game and Playe of the Chesse	Jacobus de Cessolis	George, duke of Clarence and earl of Warwick	
1477	Jason	Raoul le Fèvre	Edward IV; Edward, prince of Wales	
1481	Godfrey of Boulogne [The Siege of Jerusalem]	unknown	Edward IV	
1484	The Book of the Knight of the Tower	Geoffrey de la Tour-Landry	Queen Elizabeth Woodville	
	The Ordre of Chyvalry	Raymond Lull	Richard III	Anthony Woodville, earl Rivers
1485	Paris and Vienne	Pierre de la Cépède		
	Charles the Great	Jean de Bagnyon	William Daubeny	
	King Arthur [Le Morte d'Arthur]	Sir Thomas Malory		At the instigation of Edward IV and request of "noble and diverse gentlemen"
1489	Blanchardyn and Eglantine	unknown	Margaret Beauchamp, duchess of Somerset	Margaret Beauchamp
	Four Sons of Aymon	unknown		John, earl of Oxford
	Deeds of Arms and Chivalry	Christine de Pizan		John, earl of Oxford
1490	Enydos [Aeneas]	Virgil	Arthur, prince of Wales	

Paris and Vienne Introduction

Paris and Vienne is William Caxton's English translation of one of the most popular romances of the later Middle Ages. Originating in the south of France at the end of the fourteenth century, by the end of the fifteenth the story of the faithful lovers circulated in two versions, and the shorter one had been printed and translated into five languages. Caxton's romance, published in 1485, was reprinted many times before being revised in the sixteenth and seventeenth centuries to suit changing literary tastes. The story's combination of chivalric adventure, lively characters, and lovers of unequal status continues to engage readers today. Its didactic appeal and fantasy of upward social mobility would have resonated with Caxton's audience of gentry, merchants, and professionals.

This introduction begins with a review of the versions and genre of the romance and a summary of the plot. Following sections comment on the narrative's distinctive features — its realism, treatment of conventional material, comic elements, and assertive heroine — and explore its instructional agenda and critique of contemporary marriage practices. The concluding sections review scholarship on the romance, assess Caxton's prose style and translation practice, and describe the copytext. A list of witnesses and source texts in French and English follows. Explanatory Notes and Textual Notes following the text provide additional information on topics discussed here.

Origin and Genre

The earliest surviving version of *Paris et Vienne* is a French prose narrative composed in 1432 by one Pierre de la Cépède of Marseille. His was a prominent family there, and a member by the name of Pierre was made Squire of the Stables by Louis II, duke of Anjou, in 1385. Cépède tells us that he translated his romance from a source in Provençal, and his French shows such inflections.[1] Scholars have confirmed that the story of the faithful lovers originated in Provence in the late fourteenth century, probably at the Angevin court, and there is evidence that the pair were familiar to Spanish audiences by 1405.[2] Unlike many French prose romances, *Paris et Vienne* is not a redaction of a verse narrative; while it is possible that it circulated in verse form, no witness survives. The romance is conventional, incorporating motifs and episodes found in other narratives, but it appears not to be indebted to an earlier romance as *Blancandin* is indebted to *The Story of the Grail*, though the author may have been influenced by a contemporary narrative, *Pierre de Provence et la Belle Maguelonne*.[3]

---

[1] In his prologue, Cépède mentions that his source was itself a translation from Catalan.

[2] Francisco Imperial, a well-known poet from Genoa living in Seville, mentioned the lovers in a poem dated 1405 and elsewhere (Leach, p. xxi).

[3] *FRLMA*, p. 80. *Pierre of Provence and the Beautiful Lady of Maugelone* is an anonymous prose romance composed around 1430 in southern France. Like *Paris et Vienne*, it is a tale of youthful disobedience, escaping lovers, disguise, and marriage to a woman of higher status.

Cépède's romance survives in six closely related French manuscripts from the mid-fifteenth century; a shorter version survives in a manuscript from the same period that may have been Caxton's source.[4] The short French romance was printed sixteen times before 1600 and had been translated, and printed in Italian, Catalan, Spanish, Yiddish, German, Flemish, Russian, and Latin.[5] The lovers' story was well-known to sixteenth- and seventeenth-century English readers: John Skelton[6] alludes to the couple in "Philip Sparowe" (1504) as does Gavin Douglas[7] in *Palais of Honour* (ca. 1510, rpt.1553), where they appear in a catalogue of lovers. In 1587, a play of *Paris and Vienne* was performed for the English court by boys of the Westminster School.[8] Caxton's romance continued to be popular and was reprinted five times. In 1618, Matthew Mainwaring published an embellished version revised in the Euphuistic style of the Renaissance which was last reprinted in 1650.[9]

The differences between the long and short versions illustrate different aesthetics. The short version is half the length of the other, greatly expediting the action but lacking or compressing passages of description, dialogue, correspondence, and commentary by the narrator.[10] It also omits Vienne's four prophetic allegorical dreams that appear in Cépède's romance.[11] One manuscript of the long version, Brussels, KBR MS 9632/3, expands the account of Paris's journey in the Holy Land with material incorporated from travelogues and extends the description of the couple's wedding by adding a tournament in which Paris vanquishes all comers. The episode parallels his earlier jousts and gives greater scope to the pageantry and chivalry in favor at northern European courts in the fifteenth century. This elaborated treatment is not unexpected, given that the volume belonged to the library of Duke Philip the Good of Burgundy and was produced at the atelier of the Maître de Wavrin where the romance was adapted to suit the tastes of its

---

[4] See the list of witnesses at the end of this Introduction for a list of extant manuscripts and early prints in French and English. Leach, Brown-Grant, and Crécy posit that the short version is a redaction of the longer, pointing to the facts that the sole surviving manuscript of the short version postdates 1432 and contains inconsistencies that can be explained by material in the longer (Leach, pp. ix–x; Cépède, *Paris et Vienne*, ed. Brown-Grant and Crècy, pp. 7–8). Babbi suggests that the shorter narrative represents a version of the romance circulating in Spain and Italy which was adapted, independently, and it is true that no copy of the short version contains Cépède's prologue or makes reference to Provençal or any source (ed. Babbi, *Romanzo Cavalleresco*, p. 16).

[5] Leach, p. ix. The Italian translation predates Caxton's, surviving in a print from 1482 (ed. Babbi, *Romanzo Cavalleresco*, p. 40).

[6] John Skelton (d. 1529) assumed the title of Poet Laureate under Henry VIII. The poem "Philip Sparrow" is a girl's lengthy lament for her dead bird, with many literary and other allusions. He also wrote *Colin Cloute*, a church satire, and *The Book of Fools*, a court satire, among many other works.

[7] Gavin Douglas (d. 1522) was a Scottish bishop best known for his translation of Virgil's *Aenied* into Scots. His poem, *The Palais of Honor*, is a dream allegory in the courtly tradition of *The Roman de la Rose*, which he dedicated to James IV.

[8] *MWCP*, p. 72.

[9] *MWCP*, pp. 72–73; Cooper, *English Romance in Time*, p. 424.

[10] In the short version, the narrator addresses the audience infrequently, usually in formulas of transition such as "now late us leve to speke of thys mater and retorne we unto Parys," or formulas of abridgement: the names of all attending the tournament "would be overlong to recite . . . [so] we shall reherce of the pryncypallest hereafter the shortest wyse we may."

[11] Vienne dreams of Paris wearing a robe she later recognizes; of being attacked by a lion in her father's garden while Paris is unable to cross a river to rescue her; that Paris is dead; and that she is rescued from prison by an eagle.

patron.[12] The workshop produced long and short versions of texts, so it is possible that the abbreviated romance originated there.[13] All manuscripts of the long version contain Cépède's prologue, which does not appear with any text of the short version; however, it is so relevant to study of Caxton's romance that it is included in an appendix following the edited texts of the romances.

Paris and Vienne is an example of a type of *roman d'aventure* that is widely recognized but variously designated. It is an "idyllic romance," that is, one which concerns itself with the "deeply felt reciprocal love of an adolescent couple and their struggle to marry in the face of parental opposition."[14] These narratives strike a balance between love and chivalry, focusing on tournaments rather than battles as means to win a lady and reversing traditional gender roles when the heroine becomes more active than the hero.[15] Those features are also present in what have been called "society romances," which pay more attention to relationships between characters than to military escapades or supernatural adventures, often have assertive heroines, and employ monologue, dialogue, and other techniques to give vitality and interiority to the characters.[16] *Paris and Vienne* can also be characterized as a "family romance," for its plot centers on families disrupted by generational conflicts and violations of marital taboos, while politics and military campaigns are secondary.[17] The family plot is doubled, since Paris's family as well as Vienne's becomes dysfunctional, and the narrative has other features of family romances, being sentimental, domestic, and giving prominence to female characters.

Plot

The plot is straightforward and without sub-plots, though the narrative shifts its focus between the two lovers. In the initial episodes, Paris wins the love of Vienne; at the midpoint of the narrative, the lovers are separated after a failed attempt to elope; finally, Paris is able to return from exile and they marry. The dauphin of Vienne, Sir Godfrey d'Alaunson, and his wife, Lady Dyane, pray for a child; after seven years a daughter is born to them and named Vienne after the city of her birth. She is sent to nurse with a noblewoman whose daughter, Isabeau, is raised as Vienne's sister. Paris, the son of Sir Jacques (vassal of the dauphin), is knighted by his lord in recognition of his chivalry. He and his brother-in-arms, Edward, win prizes at tournaments and are accomplished musicians. When Paris becomes enamored of Vienne, the two young men disguise themselves and serenade her before the dauphin's castle, arousing much admiration and curiosity. Paris

---

[12] Marchal, "L'existence d'un manuscrit," p. 283. See the General Introduction, p. 5, to this volume for discussion of the Atelier de le Maître de Wavrin. The Burgundian text (KBR 9632/3), suppresses the Provençal dialect forms found in other manuscripts of the long *Paris et Vienne* (Cépède, *Paris et Vienne*, ed. Brown-Grant and Crécy, p. 9). The duke's manuscript was for some time in the possession of members of the Croy family (*MWCP*, pp. 68–69).

[13] Marchal, "L'existence d'un manuscrit," p. 273n47.

[14] *FRLMA*, p. 79.

[15] Cépède, *Paris et Vienne*, ed. Brown-Grant and Crécy, pp. 67–68. Other examples of the *roman idyllique* are *Floris and Blanchefleur* and *Aucussin and Nicolette* from the thirteenth century and *Pierre de Provence et la Belle Maguelone* from the fifteenth.

[16] Schlauch, *Antecedents*, p. 17. *Paris and Vienne*, *Blanchardyn and Eglantine*, and *Arthur of Little Britain* are fifteenth-century examples of society romance. The latter includes supernatural adventures, but presents the progress of the adolescent Arthur's love for Jehanet with a degree of realism.

[17] Ramsey, *Chivalric Romances*, pp. 157–59. Lee Ramsey does not consider Caxton's publications, as his study is limited to narratives in verse, but his chapter on family romances includes discussion of the earlier *Eglamour of Artois* and *Torrent of Portengale*, which have a number of features in common with *Paris and Vienne*.

is determined to remain anonymous, but Vienne and her father are eager to discover the identities of the performers. The dauphin summons all minstrels in the realm to play for him, but Paris and Edward do not attend, and those who do cannot match their music. After another serenade, the dauphin sends guards to apprehend the musicians, but they decline his summons and rout the guards in a scuffle. Paris and Edward then cease their performances. To entertain his daughter, the dauphin arranges a joust at which Paris fights incognito, bearing a white escutcheon and winning the trophies bestowed by Vienne, who suspects that her champion is one of the musicians. The king of France proclaims a tournament to determine which of three noble ladies is the fairest. Paris regards his love for Vienne as hopeless, given the disparity in their social ranks, and begins to take religious instruction from the bishop of St. Lawrence, but he and Edward participate in the king's jousts, again wearing white. Paris is declared the champion, and Vienne is declared the fairest. He returns home, secures his trophies in a private oratory, and then accompanies Edward to visit his lady in Brabant (in modern Belgium) and to enter tourneys there.

Dame Dyane, accompanied by Vienne and Isabeau, visits Paris's father, Sir Jacques, who is ill with worry that his son has lost interest in chivalry. During their tour of Sir Jacques's elegant home, the girls, by a ruse, gain access to the private oratory where Paris's trophies confirm that he is the champion of the jousts. Vienne takes the jeweled collar with her in order to confront him with the evidence of his identity and so meet him. Paris returns home to find Sir Jacques recovered and his prizes missing from his oratory. When he calls on the dauphin to pay his respects, Vienne is present and they are overcome by love for each other. Soon Vienne arranges to meet Paris by asking the bishop of St. Lawrence to hear her confession concerning her theft of the trophies, and to bring Paris with him on the following day so they can be returned. When they are together at last, the couple withdraw from their chaperones and declare their love.

As Vienne is of marriageable age, Sir Godfrey begins to consider possible husbands for her. She assures Paris that she will marry only him and that he should arrange for his father to ask the dauphin for her hand, so that there may be no "deffaulte" (18.5) in their union. Sir Jacques's overture to the dauphin is angrily rebuked and Vienne sends word to Paris that he is in danger and should flee. When he comes to take leave of her, she insists on going with him so they can be married and directs him to arrange for them to elope. Vienne, Isabeau, and Paris depart Aigues Mortes, but a storm causes the river to flood so that it is impossible for them to cross and they are forced to take shelter with a chaplain. The dauphin sends his men to bring home his missing daughter, and the couple, aware of the search party, prepare to part.

Vienne and Isabeau remain in the church while Paris and his servant make their way to Aigues Mortes, then Genoa, to avoid the dauphin's pursuit. Vienne is returned to her father with assurances of her virginity, but when she insists that she will marry only Paris, the dauphin confines her to a chamber on short rations and imprisons Sir Jacques. After a time, the dauphin releases Vienne, and, at her request, restores Paris's father to his former estate; he then proceeds to negotiate his daughter's marriage to the son of the duke of Burgundy. Meanwhile, Paris writes to his father and to Edward, who makes it possible for the lovers to correspond and for Vienne to send letters of credit to her knight. When the son of the duke of Burgundy comes to visit, Vienne declines to meet him, pleading illness. He departs, and the dauphin again imprisons his daughter and Isabeau. When the young duke returns and asks to see Vienne, her father sends clothes and food to the captives, including a quartered hen. As before, she maintains the pretense of her malady and, concealing the fowl in her armpits, lets the odor of its decaying flesh convince her suitor that she is not fit to marry. He withdraws his suit. Her father continues to hold her imprisoned, but Edward secretly gains access to her cell and brings her provisions.

Understanding that his marriage to Vienne cannot advance in these circumstances, Paris undertakes a pilgrimage to Jerusalem and travels to Egypt; here he dresses and speaks as a local, living in poverty. By chance, Paris encounters the sultan of Babylon's hunting party and is able to restore the ruler's sick falcon to health; in gratitude, the sultan installs Paris at his court, never suspecting that he is not an Arab. The dauphin is sent by the king of France to scout a crusade but is betrayed to the sultan. Paris learns of Sir Godfrey's capture and, with the help of two friars, arranges to meet the dauphin, free him from prison, and return him to his realm and his family, all the while maintaining his disguise. In return, the dauphin agrees to reward his benefactor with marriage to his daughter. When presented with the ostensibly Muslim suitor, Vienne again employs the rotten chicken ruse, but Paris, undeterred, reveals himself, and the lovers are married with the dauphin's assent, as are Isabeau and Edward.

While thoroughly formulaic, the romance is distinguished by its realism and active heroine. It handles conventional materials with greater originality than do other similar romances and is subversive, in that the lovers employ deceit and trickery, as much as feats of chivalry, to overcome obstacles to their marriage.

Realism and Convention

Paris and Vienne treats the formulas of medieval romance narrative with unusual circumstantial detail. Fifteenth-century readers showed a preference for verisimilitude in their chivalric narratives, but even among its contemporaries, *Paris and Vienne* is notable for its representation of lived circumstances, being perhaps the most realistic late-medieval prose romance in English.[18] The story has roots in semi-realistic narratives circulating in Provence, and is "more circumstantial, local, and realistic in detail than is at all usual," being an early example of "the absorption of romance into forms of *novella*."[19] Cépède wrote in his prologue that he chose to translate the account of the two lovers because it seemed to him pleasant and "*bien raisonable et assez croyable*" [quite reasonable and credible], more so than the romances he knew of Lancelot, Tristran, and Florimant.[20] The author justifies reading chronicle, romance, and history by quoting Alain de Lille[21] to the effect that one believes those things that appear to be true [*veritables*]. Throughout, Cépède refers to his narrative as an *histoire*. Significantly, it incorporates no supernatural elements. The short version of *Paris et Vienne* dates the events to a specific year, 1275. Vienne exclaims that it is an enchantment when she recognizes her suitor's ring, and he, who has been speaking "Morish," begins to speak French. Paris responds that "hit is none enchaunted work," merely his foreign dress. The unwanted suitor is repelled by the all-too-natural stench of the chicken parts. Paris's travels to exotic India and his years spent in the fabled land of Prester John are passed over in little more than a dozen words. There are no sudden storms at sea to separate the lovers; instead, the point is made that Paris encounters no bad weather during his travels. The river flood is a more plausible functional equivalent. There is no allegory of love: Vienne finds the altar of Paris where he has enshrined the prizes she awarded him in tournaments, but this is the sole suggestion of the religion of love, and Venus is mentioned only once, in a phrase that Caxton added. Vienne feels love's spark ignite in her heart, and Paris laments his separation from her, "O cruel fortune, ful of cruel torment," (18.7) but, in general, the lovers express their emotions directly without recourse to apostrophe or allegory.

---

[18] *MWCP*, p. 64.

[19] Painter, *William Caxton*, p. 150; Pearsall, "English Romance," p. 82. See also Cooper, "Going Native," p. 26.

[20] The story of Paris and Vienne is also more conventionally moral than some: Lancelot and Tristan are adulterous lovers. See the Appendix following the edited texts of the romances for a translation of Cépède's prologue.

[21] Alain de Lille (1128–1203) was the author of *De Planctu Natura* and other influential theological and philosophical works demonstrating that the natural world as well as religious truths could be apprehended by human reason.

Paris and Vienne is noteworthy for its handling of memes fundamental to Europeans' racialized constructions of Muslims, in particular the motif of the Christian knight who passes for Muslim. Paris's years in the Middle East are recounted in only two chapters, and the episodes incorporate few of the negative stereotypes of Muslims typical in romances. The romance does not describe Muslims in racial terms: they do not have dark skin (there is no reference to skin color), and there are no grotesques or giants.[22] The sultan's religious practice is not mentioned, so there are no idols or other distortions of Islam, though the romance does refer, accurately, to its prohibition of alcohol (22.12). Rather, much is made of Paris's conscientious Christian observance throughout the narrative. The Muslims of *Paris and Vienne* are not making war; instead, Christians are the aggressors. The pope preaches a crusade against "fals myscreauntes and hethen men" (20.3), a plan thwarted by Christians who betray his spy for money. The sultan is a chivalrous and generous ruler who offers Paris riches and titles, though he does vow a cruel execution for the captive dauphin. Paris appears sympathetic to his patron, in a kind of double-speak with the friars, when he expresses concern that the sultan's forces will be defeated by the crusaders, since the pope is so powerful. The friars' initial fear of Paris is an instance of negative stereotyping, but the romance's relatively neutral depiction of Muslims may owe something to the fact that authors and audiences in southern France would have encountered them through contacts with Spain and trade throughout the Mediterranean.

Significantly, Cépède and Caxton refer to the inhabitants of Babylon and Alexandria exclusively as *Moors*, not as *Saracens*, another common term for Muslims, Arabs, and North African peoples.[23] The latter is the older term, denoting the racialized, negative portrayal of Muslims common in *chanson de geste* and other European writings from the earlier Middle Ages. By the end of the fifteenth century, *Moor* was becoming the more common word, and Kathleen Kennedy finds that "the late medieval English show few negative connotations in their use of the term."[24] It most often refers to language, textiles, and ceramics, less frequently to religion or physical, racial characteristics such as dark skin.[25] Carpets and cloth were major luxury commodities imported to England from Alexandria and Constantinople, through Venice, Marseilles, and Genoa, cities which figure prominently in the romance. Paris's speech and dress are constantly described as "of a More," "lyke a More," and "Moryske."[26] The friars suppose that Paris is the son of "somme grete Moure" (22.6) because of his rich robes; his beard completes the picture. The romance foregrounds the role of language in Paris's deception when he pretends not to understand French and relies on the friars' translation in the many exchanges with the dauphin and Vienne. His appearance becomes a true disguise only when he uses it to conceal his identity from the dauphin in order to marry Vienne. The motif of the hero who passes as Muslim is fully functional and integrated into the plot of *Paris and Vienne*.

---

[22] Mainwaring's version of the romance includes episodes where Paris wears blackface, fights what are said to be "Saracen" giants and dragons, and evades advances of the sultan's wife, an analogue to the Biblical story of Potiphar's wife (Genesis 39) (Cooper, "Going Native," p. 30).

[23] The term *Moor* is derived from Latin and Old French as a race marker referring to north Africans (Akbari, *Idols in the East*, p. 285). *Moor* and *Moorish* occur more than two dozen times in Caxton's romance; *pagan*, *heathen*, or *Saracen* not at all. Cépède's romance makes a reference to Saracens and Turks.

[24] Akbari, *Idols in the East*, p. 285; quotation from Kennedy, "Moors and Moorishness," p. 228. John Gower, however, makes it a by-word for "ugly": in his "Tale of Florent," the loathly lady is described as grotesque and looking like a "More" (Gower, *Confessio Amantis*, ed. Peck, line 1686).

[25] Kennedy, "Moors and Moorishness," pp. 228–29. *Paris and Vienne* is evidence that "religion did not play a central role in the medieval English concept of Moorishness" (p. 249).

[26] *Moorish* was the name for a pan-Mediterranean *lingua franca*, spoken and written, that arose along trade routes (Kennedy, "Moors and Moorishness," pp. 221–22).

By comparison, Blanchardyn's German speech is mentioned only once, and he does not use a translator; his altered appearance allows him to trick his father and test the loyalty of friends, but it does not directly facilitate his return to his lady and is not referenced in the later parts of the romance.

Paris and Vienne is especially credible [*croyable*] in its treatment of setting and in its attention to planning for travel. Details of everyday life are attended to: Vienne's visit to Sir Jacques's home is a vehicle for descriptions of domestic interiors.[27] Specific features of the city of Vienne are explicit and accurate: in the fourteenth century a church abutted the ducal palace there, so Edward's fictional tunnel from his private chapel to Vienne's prison aligns with architectural fact.[28] Features of local topography and Mediterranean geography are recognizable: the stages along the road from Vienne to Aigues Mortes where Paris engages fresh mounts, the adjacent Rhone River, the proximity of Genoa, the travel to Venice and Alexandria, and the return to Aigues Mortes. Paris's journeys are deliberate: the logistics of his voyages are related with specificity, and he studies the local language in Egypt before undertaking further travel in the region.[29] The narrative refers to obtaining money in foreign cities, engaging passage, and hiring and provisioning boats. Paris draws money from Sir Bertram's bank and later pays a thousand gold bezants for passage for five people from Alexandria to Cyprus.[30] He is practical when he negotiates the dauphin's return to France, stipulating that Sir Godfrey maintain him there in an honorable living since he "can noo mestyer ne crafte" (22.9) and would have no source of economic support. Paris's rescue of the dauphin culminates with the common motif of escape from prison by drugging the guards, but this is the result of much advance planning. Learning of the dauphin's captivity, Paris "thought in hys hert that hys adventure myght yet come to good and effecte" (22.3); he then secures permissions from the sultan to travel to Alexandria to meet the prisoner and arranges access to the prison through friar translators. He regularly visits the dauphin, so the guards are not suspicious when he provides a feast on the eve of his departure from the city. Previously, he has arranged for their their passage to Cyprus.[31] The account of the escape is notable for its details: sending for wine, food, mantles, and towels for the dinner, and the fact (twice mentioned) that the jailers are unaccustomed to wine.

The episodes presented with the most circumstantial detail, even in the abbreviated version of the romance, are the tournaments. A significant portion of the first half of Caxton's text is devoted to them. Their precise dates are announced (May 1, September 8 or 14); the construction of the viewing stands is described, as are the design and décor of the lists, and the feasts before and after the jousts. The scenes are fully realized, including the placement of the spectators and their commentary on the proceedings, the display of prizes, procession of knights, speeches, exchange of challenges, encounters, and awards ceremony. Such attention to specifics suggests that Cépède was familiar with tournament protocol. The catalogue of participants' names and the blow-by-blow accounts of their encounters lend further verisimilitude.[32] At the royal tournament, one challenge narrowly avoids being decided on a technicality when Paris strikes his

---

[27] The long prose version has a more extensive treatment of the visit and décor of Sir Jacques's home.

[28] Leach, p. xix.

[29] Arabic was a "metrolingua franca" of the medieval Mediterranean, fostered by trade and the expansion of Islam (Kennedy, "Moors and Moorishness," p. 222).

[30] The author of the romance seems to have been familiar with routines and arrangements for travel by land and sea, perhaps having traveled himself.

[31] In the long version of the romance, Paris leaves the guards in their drunken state without killing them. The short version explains the violent act as necessary to insure the dauphin's safe escape.

[32] Attempts to identify the names of the participants with those of living persons have been largely unsuccessful.

challenger, Geoffrey of Picardy, causing him to fall to the earth and his horse to slide. Geoffrey's adherents insist that the sliding horse, not the blow, caused the fall. The king knows that the blow caused the fall, but, as judge of the tournament, he asks Paris to consent to a third pass against his opponent to settle the matter. The knight readily agrees, to which the king responds that he showed "grete valoyr and puyssaunce and spake moche swetely and curtoysly" (5.2). Thus Paris answers the challenge to his victory and to the king's expertise as judge, avoiding further confrontations sure to arise from a decision that went against Geoffrey's party. Tournament accounts of the period relate difficult moments of this kind: incidents of "foul play, opponents who refused to surrender, [and] partisan scoring practices."[33] The records compiled by English and Burgundian heralds meld real life with romance, and the same can be said of the letters exchanged by Anthony Woodville (Caxton's patron) and Anton de la Roche, Bastard of Burgundy, regarding their challenge at the celebrated tournament at Smithfield in 1467. This correspondence was much admired at the courts, where copies of the letters circulated.[34] *Paris and Vienne*'s accounts of tournaments are some of the more detailed and accurate in Middle English romance outside of Malory's *Morte d'Arthur*. Cépède's romance and its shorter adaptation are indeed reasonable and believable.

Paris and Vienne (especially Cépède's longer version) comes close to a parody of romance. It subverts generic conventions such as enchantment and exotic locales with its realism. There is a minstrel contest but the hero does not enter it; the attention to money is unusual for a genre in which knights' adventures often have no visible means of economic support. The narrative further contradicts tropes of the genre in its treatment of lovers separated by ocean voyages. One has only to contrast it with *Blanchardyn*'s use of the same motif: there the hero is twice blown off course, his destination unknown and, significantly, determined by "adventure," not by the decision of the character.

Gender, Marriage, Status

Paris and Vienne is notable not only for its realism, but also for its persistent, resourceful heroine whose love for Paris leads her to challenge cultural norms of of gender, marriage, and class. Vienne is striking even among the women of idyllic and family romances, which often present heroines who choose their husbands and determine to marry them despite their fathers' objections as admirable.[35] The romance treats Vienne as a subject in her own right, not simply an extension of the male characters.[36] She advances her agenda as vigorously as Paris pursues feats of arms, becoming "a true heroine, not just the object of a hero's love."[37] She, not he, dictates the action. Though Paris is the first to fall in love, Vienne is immediately attracted to him. She actively seeks to discover his identity, arranges their first meeting, and is the first to declare her love. She proposes that they marry, tells him how his father should approach hers with his proposal, suggests and finances their elopement, and subverts her father's attempts to arrange her marriage to anyone

---

[33] *MWCP*, p. 91.

[34] Bornstein, "Willian Caxton's Chivalric Romances," p. 2. *MWCP*, p. 86. The challenges included another Burgundian bibliophile, Louis de Bretailles, and were based on the earlier much-admired career of Phillipe de Lalaing (Kuskin, *Symbolic Caxton*, p. 164).

[35] Cooper, *English Romance in Time*, p. 226. The romances often go to lengths to reconcile these disruptors of the status quo with social norms. Melusine and Ydoine in *Amadas and Ydoine*, and la Fiere in *Ipomadon* are other examples of such active heroines, as are Cristabelle in *Eglamour of Artois* and Desonell in *Torrent of Portengale*.

[36] Cooper discusses several female characters who share these characteristics, though she does not address Vienne specifically (*English Romance in Time*, p. 231).

[37] Cotton, "Fidelity, Suffering, and Humor," p. 96.

else. Paris, by comparison, is reticent: though he courts his lady with music and feats of arms, he dares not reveal his identity. His reluctance to ask for her hand leads Vienne to chide him: "Sette ye so lytel by me, that ye wyl not enterpryse this? Alas, where is your entendement?" (9.6). The knight's lamentations, though common to courtly lovers, are faintly comic in their melodrama: when faced with separation, he draws his sword to kill himself. Vienne remonstrates, in an explicit role reversal: "O Parys, where is your wysedom and your prowesse? Now whan ye shold have moste strengthe and moost vertuous courage, ye be aferde . . . for now whome that ye ought to comforte, she must now comfort you" (12.4). She is cross-dressed at this point, having worn men's clothing as a disguise to elope, and the fact that she has taken his sword completes the reversal.[38] Only after the lovers' reunion and recognition does Paris assert control: as they go to tell the dauphin that she has agreed to his proposal, he requests that she remain silent until he permits her to speak. When he assents, Vienne addresses her father, revealing Paris's identity and reciting a catalogue of his accomplishments. She takes a more active role than her counterpart in the long version of the romance, where Paris himself orchestrates the revelation.[39] Despite her name, and unlike many heroines of romance, Vienne is not particularly associated with her estates or patrimony, nor is the Dauphiné under attack. Paris does not fight for her or her father against claimants to their territory and initially declines the dauphin's offer of his lands when negotiating his restoration. Vienne needs no champion to defend her from unwanted suitors — she manages that herself.

She does, however, require a champion to represent her in tournaments where his prowess can affirm her beauty and excellence, and his as well. The jousts at Paris are cast as a judicial combat to pacify contesting parties, a simulacrum of warring regional powers, but this ritual combat and the threat of a crusade are the closest the romance comes to warfare. Tournaments, rather than battles, are sites of knightly proving and the construction of chivalric masculinity. Edward makes clear the degree to which that masculinity is defined by the assessment of other men when he tells Paris that by fighting incognito he will win greater praise from the nobles and lords at the tournament (though he also mentions that the mystery will pique Vienne's curiosity).[40]

Paris and Vienne is less interested in defense of patrimony than in issues of parental authority and the liberty to choose a spouse based on mutual affection — the younger generation's alternative to the patriarchal practice of arranging marriages based on status and lineage. The dauphin negotiates the marriage of Vienne and the young duke of Burgundy by seeking the advice of other nobles and employing intermediaries, but Vienne refuses to become an object of exchange between men.[41] Among other reasons she gives the young duke for refusing his proposal is that she is already married, and a case can be made that she and Paris have created a legally binding betrothal in their mutual pledges before God to wed none but each other. According to medieval canon law, a couple's pledges of espousal expressed in the present tense [*verba de presenti*] could constitute a binding betrothal, and a valid marriage required the free and equal consent of the couple. Vienne reminds Paris of this fact — so long as she refuses to agree, her father cannot wed her to another. These empowering statutes notwithstanding, in practice, parents or guardians always arranged

---

[38] Slauch remarks, "One can only hope that in later years he developed a temperament to match hers" (*Antecedents*, p. 69).

[39] The manuscript copy of the short version also has Paris revealing his own identity.

[40] Ruth Karras and Katherine Lewis both note that chivalric conceptions of masculinity are based upon relationships with other men, with relationships with women being secondary (*Boys to Men*, pp. 10–11; *Kingship and Masculinity*, p. 7).

[41] The negotiations are narrated at greater length in the long version of the romance.

aristocratic marriages, and there was very little room for choice on the part of the couple in most gentry marriages of the fifteenth century.[42] An often-cited example is the case of Margery Paston, whose parents sought to nullify her clandestine marriage and disowned her when they were unsuccessful, but continued to employ her husband. Marriage law and church practice became increasingly stringent in the later Middle Ages, only recognizing the validity of witnessed betrothals and unions officiated by a priest. Vienne is careful to follow protocol in having Paris's father ask for her hand, and she insists that their marriage be lawfully solemnized. Edward and Isabel are witnesses to the appropriateness of their conduct.

Part of the Pastons' objection to Margery's marriage was the disparity in the couple's status and wealth, for her husband was employed as her family's bailiff, and they had intended to arrange a socially and financially advantageous marriage for her. Status is also the obstacle to the marriage of Paris and Vienne, though there is little to distinguish Sir Jacques and the dauphin in their behavior and apparent economic status. Paris's father is a noble knight of ancient lineage and fair lands, beloved by the dauphin, and Paris keeps company with great lords and hunts in a manner befitting dukes and earls. The jewels of the tournament prizes and the décor of his home demonstrate his wealth. Vienne's funds enable Paris to live in the style appropriate to a young aristocrat with a display of largesse in Genoa, and, when he is without money, he sorrows at the sight of "other tryumphe and wexe lordes." (20.1) Following the tournament, the dauphin declares Paris to be the most chivalrous knight in all the world, and the French king judges him to be a great lord, but association with the elite, esteem, chivalry, and wealth are not the only factors to be considered.

The facts that Sir Jacques is a vassal of the dauphin and is without a title account for the disparity between the lovers' stations. Sir Jacques is of noble character and respected family, but his lineage is not so great as that of the dauphin, who is related to the French king, or those of the titled dukes and earls who vie for Vienne's favor and unto one of whom her father intends to marry her. Paris's incognito erases his social status while drawing attention to his chivalric accomplishments. Edward reasons that Paris will win more praise from the nobles and great lords if they do not recognize him, for "ye be not of so grete lygnage as they be" (4.7).[43] The youth and his father adhere to convention and are only too aware of their inferior rank and the impediment it poses to marriage with Vienne. Isabeau and Edward also advise the lovers that their union would be inappropriate.[44] While marriage to an heiress was one of the surest ways for English men of the fifteenth century to rise socially and economically, such unions were viewed with suspicion by members of the ruling classes who saw them as a threat to their status.[45] Sir Jacques approaches the dauphin with reverence, humility, and apology; nevertheless, Sir Godfrey is outraged at the knight's affront to his "worship" in speaking of marriage between their children, further denouncing him as "vylayne" (person of low status) and "vassal" (10.1). The marriage's disruption of the lord-vassal relationship has implications for society as a whole, since it destabilizes the ordained hierarchy. The storm and flood that separate the lovers suggest a disturbance of the natural order associated with transgressing taboos and cultural norms. The

---

[42] Studies of late medieval marriage among the English gentry and bourgeoisie show that most unions were arranged by the couple's parents and extended families, especially as primogeniture became a more common practice among these classes (Rawcliffe, "Politics of Marriage," pp. 169–70; Houlbrooke, "Making of Marriage," p. 350). For examples of arranged marriages, see these articles as well as Dockray, "Why did Fifteenth-Century English Gentry Marry," pp. 64–75.

[43] Also, Paris will avoid the possible affront to Vienne should he, a person of lesser status, prove the champion — she will not be "sette by."

[44] Leeu's print of 1487 contains an extended passage of examples of the suffering and punishment endured by lovers (particularly women) who sought to marry someone of lower status.

[45] Cooper, *English Romance in Time*, p. 223.

practice of arranged marriage continues and hierarchies are reaffirmed when the dauphin negotiates noble marriages for his grandchildren and Paris succeeds to his title. As *Paris and Vienne* is a family romance, inheritance is also important for the maintenance of social order. Much is made of the fact that the lovers are sole heirs, and both sets of parents express anxiety about not having children to inherit their title and estates. Paris pledges his inheritance to Edward; later, he instructs his parents to designate Edward their heir, and, when they die, Paris bestows their estate on his adopted brother, elevating his status.

Paris and Vienne manages to reconcile the canonical requirement of individual consent with the practice of arranged marriage, and the lovers' desire for autonomy with their ties to family and society. However, while the romance envisions circumstances in which social advancement and personal autonomy in love are possible, these come about only through such "elaborate narrative strategies" as Paris's disguises and Vienne's distinctive expedient of the rotten chickens.[46]

Comedy, Deception, and Hens

Like other idyllic romances, *Paris and Vienne* employs cleverness and trickery as much as chivalry to bring about the marriage of the faithful lovers and their reintegration into society.[47] This may be a function of the story's origins in southern France. There, a regional genre of short fiction "blended the sophistication and atmosphere of courtly narrative with the down-to-earth comedy reserved for the fabliaux."[48] Vienne is adept at subterfuge: she arranges to identify and meet Paris, elope, and send money. She engages in double-speak with her father and uses his arguments against him. When he praises the young duke of Burgundy, she demurs with a sly reference to Paris saying, "for yf we have not thys man, yf it playse God, we shal have another as good or better" (16.4). Later she appeals to the priority of obedience to God over her duty of filial submission, citing her pledge to remain a virgin until she dies or recuperates from her malady (love-sickness, which would be cured by the return of Paris). Edward's act of devotion, building a chapel, is a cover for his plan to gain access to Vienne's prison. Paris has numerous disguises: as minstrel, as white knight, and a Muslim. Deception creates irony and humor in Paris's linguistic charade with the friars, the dauphin, and Vienne as their French is translated into Moorish, and his replies are rendered back into French. Vienne's secretive inspection of Paris's chamber culminates with a disingenuous reply when she is called to rejoin her mother, and the lovers' efforts to control their expressions when they are introduced is narrated with sly humor. When Vienne presents Paris with the jewels she has taken from his oratory, he replies with profuse thanks for the honor of her visit to his parents and says he would be grateful if she kept the gems. He then apologizes for their unworthiness, a rather awkward display of humility since they both know that she had awarded those trophies. When he further attempts to avoid discovery by explaining that the jewels were given to him by another knight, Vienne cuts him off, interjecting "Ye nede not to say to me from whens these jewels ben comen, for I knowe them as wel as ye" (9.20), and putting a stop to his polite obfuscation and getting right to the point. There is physical comedy in the scene where Vienne convinces the young duke of Burgundy of her mortal illness. Inviting him to approach her, she explains that modesty forbids exposing her diseased body while he quickly withdraws, overwhelmed by the stench of the rotten

---

[46] Brown-Grant, "Adolescence, Anxiety and Amusement," p. 61.
[47] *FRLMA*, p. 101.
[48] Jewers, *Chivalric Fiction*, p. 82. Jewers is referring to *Jaufrey*, a thirteenth-century romance from Occitania, but her statement applies to *Paris et Vienne* as well since it is a later product of the region. Others have commented on the romance's sense of humor (Cotton, "Fidelity, Suffering, and Humor" pp. 96–97; Schlauch, *Antecedents*, p. 67).

chicken. Vienne's outspokenness flares into ironic outrage when she threatens to bash her brains out against a wall rather than marry her Moorish suitor. There is also comedy in Isabeau's expressions of exasperation and amusement at her friend's headstrong behavior, and in her dramatic outburst when she wakes to see Vienne asleep in the chaste embrace of the Moor.

The romance uses humor for didactic ends, nowhere more than in the episodes of the hens' quarters.[49] Vienne's trickery and the reek of the hens' flesh belong to the register of fabliaux.[50] Characters in those narratives often resort to ruses to conduct sexual liasions, but in exempla and saints' lives, the odor of decay preserves chastity. Fifteenth-century audiences could have been familiar with Vienne's ruse from a well-known legend. The story of the Lombard sisters who repelled their Hungarian attackers with the stench of rotten poultry hidden under their arms appears in Paul the Deacon's eighth-century Latin *History of the Lombards*. Their legend became widespread, surviving in Spanish and Mozarabic exempla, and in the thirteenth-century French *Game and Playe of the Chesse*, where it illustrates chastity in a chapter on the virtuous conduct of queens.[51] Christine de Pizan's[52] *Book of the City of Ladies* cites the sisters' example to refute the opinion that women want to be raped.[53] Vienne's circumstances are less dire than the sisters' — her city and person are not under attack — and her appropriation of this defense of virtue in order to evade parental authority is not without irony. Both saint's life and romance valorize those willing to suffer and die for love, and the genres intersect in Vienne's incarceration: her prison is the cell of an anchorite; her illness and the stench of the hens are an impersonation of a virgin martyr.[54] Christine allegorizes the Lombards' odor as sweet, a signifier of moral virtue, and cites the miraculous, pleasant odors said to emanate from the decayed bodies of saints. Vienne explains that she is "half roten," but "the stynche was to Parys a good odour, for he smellyed it not" (22.18), and he vows he will never leave her because of it. Is it a marvel that Paris does not perceive the odor that the friars and the bishop of St. Lawrence cannot withstand? Or is the stench pleasing to him because he recognizes it as sign of his lover's fidelity (Edward having earlier informed him of Vienne's ruse)? Medieval audiences would have appreciated Vienne's clever appropriation of the odor of sanctity, and the rotting barnyard animals' disruption of the decorum of romance's idealization of physical beauty. The hens' quarters are simultaneously fair and foul, spiritual and physical, sacred and profane. Modern readers have sensed a tonal dissonance in these episodes, and, as a recontextualized meme, the chicken ruse is at odds with its generic framework and arouses contradictory expectations.[55] Only by the incongruity of the hens' quarters and deceit does the narrative resolve the conflicting agendas of parent and child, individual and society.

---

[49] Cotton, "Fidelity, Suffering, and Humor" p. 96. Brown-Grant and Crécy discuss *Paris et Vienne*'s use of comedy for didactic purposes in their introduction to the longer version (Cépède, *Paris et Vienne*, pp. 61–62).

[50] Cotton, "Fidelity, Suffering, and Humor" p. 92.

[51] The political treatise was translated by Caxton and printed in 1474 and 1483 (Caxton, *Game and Playe*, ed. Adams, p. 31).

[52] Christine de Pizan (1364–1430) was a prolific writer associated with the court of Charles VI of France. In addition to her *Book of the City of Ladies*, she is known for *The Treasury of the City of Ladies*, *The Book of Deeds of Arms and Chivalry*, *The Epistle of Othea*, and many other works of policy and governance.

[53] Noxious odors have a similar effect in other traditional narratives where bad breath or reeking clothes (*MIFL*, T 320.4.1; T 323.2) prove effective deterrents to unwanted lovers.

[54] Cotton, "Fidelity, Suffering, and Humor," p. 95; *FRLMA*, p. 125.

[55] Cotton, "Fidelity, Suffering, and Humor," pp. 92–93. See also Cartlidge, "Romance Mischief" and Edlich-Muth, "Magic to Miracle" p. 174 for discussion of such dissonance in other romances.

Romance Moralized

Pierre de la Cépède's prologue to *Paris et Vienne* presents the standard moral argument for reading romances: it is good to recall the valiant deeds performed by those who came before, as example and inspiration. The romance features acts of chivalry, steadfast love, and good and bad behavior in a story of adolescents and their maturation: the French texts say the lovers are thirteen and fifteen, though Caxton makes them three years older.[56] *Paris and Vienne*, like other idyllic romances, is sympathetic to young lovers; at the same time, their story is strongly moralized, in keeping with the fifteenth century's taste for didactic literature. The narrative's depiction of adolescents aligns with that found in religious literature, courtesy books, and manuals of chivalry. These works regard adolescence as a stage in the process of maturation during which young people are likely to exhibit rash behavior and to come into conflict with parental authority and social norms, especially those regarding sexuality. That such impulses might be curbed, the writings seek to inculcate youthful chastity, humility, obedience, and willing submission to authority. Young men of the armigerous and aspiring classes are encouraged to channel their aggression into chivalric forms of tournament and crusade, while young women are directed to be silent and modest.

Paris receives the appropriate chivalric education. His father has him trained in good manners, and, when he comes of age, he applies himself to learning feats of arms; his mastery of hunting with hawks and hounds is lauded and later wins him the friendship of the sultan.[57] At the feast preceding the jousts in Vienne, he "ful gracyously and curtoysly" serves and carves before his lady (2.9). In addition to skill in arms, Paris pursues the chivalric ideals of pilgrimage and crusade as set forth in writings by Raymond Lull, among others.[58] Caxton had published *The Ordre of Chyvalry* a year before *Paris and Vienne*, and his earlier prologue to *Godfrey of Boulogne* exhorted knights to embark on crusade. Though fifteenth-century ideals of chivalry favored tournaments as proving grounds for young knights and as occasions of athletic and heraldic display, military service in the defense of Christendom was more highly esteemed and pilgrimage was regarded as a testament to strength of character. Anthony Woodville, second Earl Rivers, who gave Caxton his copy of the *Ordre* to translate, garnered much praise for undertaking a journey to Jerusalem.[59] While the romance passes quickly over Paris's sojourn in the Holy City and his poverty and suffering in Egypt, his pilgrimage and rescue of the dauphin from the sultan's prison complete the knightly ideal.

Vienne is a model of fidelity, but only her outspoken resistance to authority in the name of love maintains this. Didactic texts, like the Knight of the Tour-Landry's[60] book of instruction for his daughters, emphasize the sin of disobedience, especially to parents, and the sin of pride manifest in acts of insubordination to one's elders. Vienne is also not silent or retiring, as the Knight and custom prescribe, though she is obedient and deferential in all matters but those relating to her marriage. Isabeau and Edward offer

---

[56] Brown-Grant discusses adolescence and youthful folly in *Paris et Vienne* and *Pierre de Provence et la Belle Mauglone* (*FRLMA*, pp. 79–103).

[57] No mention is made of the kind of formal schooling in rhetoric, sciences, and literature that Blanchardyn's tutor provides for the young prince.

[58] Raymond Lull (1232–1316) was a Spanish philosopher, missionary, and poet. His *Ordre of Chyvalry* created and codified idealized rules for Christian knights that would support his efforts to peacefully convert Muslims.

[59] *MWCP*, p. 87.

[60] Geoffrey IV of the Tour Landry (1330–1406) was a French nobleman and courtier whose *Livre pour l'Ensignement de ses Filles* (Book for the Instruction of His Daughters) circulated widely. This treatise on proper behavior at court included many stories illustrating moral behavior [*exempla*]. A similar treatise for the instruction of his sons has been lost.

tempering advice to their friends, speaking with the voices of reason and convention.[61] The young duke of Burgundy and Paris both admonish Vienne that "ye ought not to dysobeye the commaundementes of your fader" (22.16). Vienne may be an example of disobedience and rash behavior, but she is scrupulous about marriage and virginity: one of her conditions for eloping with Paris is that "ye touche not my body unto the time that we be lawfully maryed" (10.3), and arrangements are made for her and Isabeau to sleep apart from the men, with a chaperone. Vienne has the men who return her to her father report to him that she is "pure and clene of [my] body" (14.3), and later she, Isabeau, and the chaplain who sheltered them attest to this as well. Earlier romances with similar plots were less insistent on virginity and often punished blocking fathers. In the tail-rhyme romances *Eglamour of Artois* and *Torrent of Portengale*, the lovers are betrothed and secretly consummate their marriages, but when their sons are born, the fathers cast their daughters adrift. After suffering and separation, the couples reunite and put the fathers to death.[62] As sexual morality and civic ordinances became more conservative and restrictive in the later fifteenth century, especially for women, so romances of the period have a stricter, more moral tone.[63]

If Vienne is an example of disobedience, a sin to which children are prone, her father is an example of pride and wrath, particular sins of those in positions of power. His cruelty is highlighted by the fact that, until his daughter elopes, he is an attentive, even indulgent, father: he hosts tournaments for her diversion and to entertain potential suitors, supporting her with rich prizes. Both the members of the search party who return Vienne to the dauphin, and she herself, expect that he will forgive her, and that his wrath will abate. However, his "felonnye and angre" (10.2) are unrelenting once aroused, as shown by his treatment of Sir Jacques following the elopement of their children. Though the dauphin pardons his vassal, he is less forgiving when Vienne foils his arrangements for her marriage — constructing a prison and starving her and Isabeau there. Contemporary examples suggest that such behavior was not exceptional: Elizabeth Paston was confined, silenced, and regularly beaten by her mother for resisting attempts to marry her to an aged, disfigured, but socially prominent widower. Margery Paston suffered similarly before being shunned and disowned by her parents. Though the dauphin is not explicitly punished for his treatment of Vienne, he is imprisoned, the very condition he inflicted upon his daughter, and his life is in jeopardy. His pride is further humbled when, in a reversal of their previous power relation, the dauphin who had demanded respect for his "worship" offers to abdicate in favor of Paris, keeping only a small parcel of land for himself and his wife to live on.

The moral tone of *Paris and Vienne* is heightened by attention to religious observance and churchmen; the friars and the bishop of St. Lawrence have significant roles. While in exile, Paris devotes himself to a life of religion, a choice in keeping with his earlier instruction by the bishop. The romance is careful to note that, though he passes as a Muslim, Paris always keeps his Christian faith. He initiates contact with the friars by professing curiosity about their religion, and their conversations include instruction in the articles of the faith. He further promises the dauphin and Vienne that he will convert, and when he arrives in Cyprus and France, he observes Christian rites and always attends mass. The dauphin insists on swearing his oath to Paris on the mass wafer brought by the friars, putting his soul in jeopardy should Vienne not agree to marry his apparently Muslim rescuer (22.10). Vienne prays for her betrothed throughout her incarceration and, like him, dedicates herself to God should they not be reunited. The romance concludes with the

---

[61] *FRLMA*, pp. 98, 111–12.

[62] Brown-Grant notes that earlier idyllic romances are more accommodating of disobedience and sensuality than later ones (*FRLMA*, p. 127).

[63] McSheffery, *Love*, p. 16.

conventional statement that the couple led most holy lives and adds that, according to the understanding [*entendement*] of some men, they are saints.

The romance features models of courteous behavior and discourse as well as cruxes of moral and spiritual conduct. There are numerous exchanges of formal greetings and leave takings featuring formulas of humility, respect, and gratitude that are markers of proper etiquette as described in treatises on manners. Likewise, polite formulas of salutation and closure appear in the letters the characters exchange. Paris's reply to the dauphin's men-at-arms who have been ordered to apprehend him is particularly polite: "Thurgh your curtosye suffre us to retorne thyder as we came fro, for we be at my lord the dauphyns playsyr . . . but in ony maner, as for thys tyme we may not fulfylle hys commaundement" (2.2).[64] In the extended exchange between Paris and Vienne as they declare their love, she poses a series of *demaundes* in parallel phrases beginning "I wyl that ye say to me yf ye were he that . . ." (9.2), rhetorically heightening the revelation of his identity. Other examples of formal discourse include the dauphin's address to Vienne proposing her betrothal to the duke of Burgundy, which begins "Fayr doughter" and concludes "wherfor we praye you that therto ye wyl gyve your good wylle and playsyr." To which she replies, "Honourable fader and lord, I wote wel that thys that ye entende is for my wele and prouffyt" (16.4), and going on to decline the match with such artful courtesy that he attributes her refusal to modesty.

Paris and Vienne also offers its readers a "sentimental education."[65] The characters experience a range of emotions — love, despair, joy, longing, fear, pity, anger — and the many dialogues, monologues, and letters in which these are expressed promote audience engagement and empathy. Edward's and Isabeau's responses to their friends' plights also direct the audience's sympathies to the couple. The first person direct discourse gives readers unmediated access to the characters' thoughts and emotions, an effect that would have been enhanced when the romance was read aloud to a listening audience.

SCHOLARSHIP

The most recent critical edition of *Paris and Vienne* is that of MacEdward Leach for the Early English Text Society (1957, reprinted 1970), which contains a thorough introduction to the romance and the text, as well as detailed notes documenting Caxton's variations from the French manuscripts. Anna Maria Babbi's introduction to her critical edition of the short French version, BNF fr. 20044, examines the romance's origins, style, and textual relations, and includes a survey of scholarship and surviving manuscripts and prints in French, English, and Italian (1992, in Italian). More recently, Rosalind Brown-Grant and Marie-Claude de Crécy have edited the Burgundian version of the long romance, KBR 9632/3, with a similarly comprehensive and updated introduction that includes descriptions of all the manuscripts of *Paris et Vienne*, a review of scholarship, and discussion of idyllic romance (2015, in French).

One of the earliest literary studies to give attention to Caxton's romance is Margaret Schlauch's *Antecedents of the English Novel, 1400–1600* (1963). Her chapter on society romances and assessment of Vienne's character are still relevant, as is her commentary on other fifteenth-century English romances. "Fidelity, Suffering, and Humor in *Paris and Vienne*," William T. Cotton's article of 1980 focuses on the chicken ruse, its overtones of fabliaux, its origins in exemplum and saint's life, and its reframing of consent to marriage in terms of fifteenth-century life and canon law. Jennifer Goodman's study from 1987, *Malory and William Caxton's Prose Romances of 1485*, considers *Paris and Vienne* in the context of the *Morte*

---

[64] The response of the men-at-arms is less cordial, and the result is a combat in which they are vanquished.
[65] Cooper, "Going Native," p. 26.

d'Arthur, *Charles the Great*, and Caxton's program of chivalric publication, particularly the *Ordre of Chyvalry*. In addition to general background on Caxton's romances, her book covers fifteenth-century tournaments in England and France, the sources and analogues of the chicken ruse, and comparisons to the later versions of Mainwaring and DuPin.[66]

Goodman remarks that *Paris and Vienne* is a narrative of adolescent rebellion, a subject explored at length in Rosalind Brown-Grant's chapter "Youthful Folly in Boys and Girls: Idyllic Romance and the Perils of Adolescence in *Pierre de Provence* and *Paris et Vienne*" (*FRLMA*, 2008) and her article "Adolescence, Anxiety and Amusement in Versions of *Paris et Vienne*" (2010). Both focus on the long French romances, but her analyses are relevant to studies of Caxton's translation. The chapter on youthful folly includes a survey of attitudes toward adolescents in medieval writings and a discussion of *Paris et Vienne*. The article on adolescence contrasts the three versions of *Paris et Vienne* — Cépède's, the longer Burgundian text, and the short version — to find that Cépède used comedy to mock the overwrought couple. By presenting them as tricksters, Cépède created ambivalence about their behavior, while the Burgundian text's additions focus attention away from their deceit. The short version, due in part to its excisions, is more serious in tone and moralistic in depicting the sufferings of the lovers. Articles by the editor of the present volume examine issues of gender and consent to marriage. "Construction of Class, Family, and Gender in Some Middle English Romances" (1994) compares *Paris and Vienne* to *Eglamour of Artois*, *Torrent of Portengale*, and *The Squire of Low Degree*, earlier verse romances involving clandestine marriage and separated lovers. These narratives reflect the late medieval shift from acceptance of pre-marital sex in betrothed couples to an expectation of the woman's virginity and public nuptials. "Rebellious Daughters and Rotten Chickens: Gender and Genre in Caxton's *Paris and Vienne*" (2003) examines the romance's treatment of the hens' quarters as a defense of chastity and re-construction of femininity. A comparison of Paris's and Vienne's chaste embrace with similar episodes in *Generides*, *Degrevant*, and *Partenope of Blois* shows Vienne exercising greater agency than do the heroines of those romances.

Helen Cooper in "Going Native: The Caxton and Mainwaring Version of *Paris and Vienne*" (2011) contrasts these two versions of the romance, casting into relief Caxton's and Cépède's realism, grasp of geography, cosmopolitan outlook, and acceptance of Muslims. Mainwaring treats Muslims negatively as Saracen others, expands the hero's adventures in exotic lands, and expresses a post-Reformation, anti-Catholic bias. Kathleen Kennedy's study, "Moors and Moorishness in Late Medieval England" (2020), traces the origins and racialization of the terms *Saracen*, *Moor*, and *Moorish* over the course of the fifteenth century. The latter two terms refer less often to race markers such as dark skin and more often to sociocultural features, including language and commodities that were imported into England. By Caxton's time, the term *Moor* had few of its earlier negative racial and political/religious associations; thus *Paris and Vienne* is an example of the transition from medieval to early modern constructions of racial and religious difference.

Textual Matters

Caxton's translation aligns closely with the two surviving French texts of the shorter *Paris et Vienne*, manuscript BNF fr. 20044 and Gerard Leeu's print from 1487 — many passages are identical in all three.[67] In places where they differ, Caxton is more likely to agree with Leeu than with the manuscript, though the print is two years later than Caxton's, so it cannot have been his source. In some places Caxton agrees with

---

[66] DuPin published his Latin version in 1516.
[67] Leach, p.xxii.

readings in a French print from 1530 that are not found the manuscript or Leeu, so it is possible that these were present in Caxton's source.[68] The Textual Notes indicate where the manuscript and Leeu agree with each other against Caxton, as these discrepancies could be his own edits. All three texts vary in their placement of chapter breaks and in the wording of headings. Caxton often marks his text with enlarged initials where Leeu and BNF fr. 20044 have chapter headings, and he sometimes modifies or inserts headings in ways that are intentional.[69]

The following passage is a typical example of Caxton's translation practice and additions, indicated by italics (4.5–6).

> But anone the kyng ordeyned a joustes for the love of the sayd thre ladyes and made his maundement that they al shold come wyth theyr armes and hors for to jouste the viii day of Septembre in the cyté of Parys, and they that shold do best in armes at that day, they shold have the *prys* and the worshyp of the feste, and the lady on whos beauté they helde with *shold be reputed and holden for the fayrest damoysel of alle the world.*

> The kyng of Fraunce thenne sente worde to the faders of the forsayd thre ladyes, prayeng them to come atte same feste and that eyther of them shold brynge wyth hym a present of rychesse, the which thre presentes shold be yeven in the worshyp of their thre doughters to the best doer in armes in token of vyctorye. And thus the kyng of Englond fyrst sent for hys syster Constaunce a fayre crowne of gold alle sette wyth perlys and precyous stones of grete value. The duc of Normandye, for love of hys doughter Florye, sente a ryght fayre garlond sette wyth dyvers perlys and precyous stones moche ryche and of grete extymacyon. And the daulphyn, for love of hys doughter Vyenne, sente a moche ryche coler of gold al envyronned wyth precyous stones of dyvers colours, the whiche was worth a ryght grete tresour.* And these thre jewellys were delyvered to the kynge of Fraynce. The forsayd knyghtes thenne made them redy and apparaylled al thynges accordyng to the joustes and in ryche araye came al to the cyté of Parys. And wete ye wel that in Fraunce was not seen afore that day so grete noblesse of barons and knyghtes as were there assembled, for there were the moost hye pryncer and barons of Englond of Fraunce, and of Normandye. And eyther of hem dyd sette al hys *wytte* and entendement to upholde and bere out that they had purposed and sayd. And every baron gaf hys lyverey that they shold be knowen eche fro other. And the bruyt and *renommé* was that my lady Constaunce shold have the honour of that feste for thys that many a fayre and hardy knyght made them redy to mayntene *the quarelle of* hyr beaulté. But nevertheles eyther of these thre partyes hoped to have the worshyp of the feste.

Caxton adds phrases and omits passages from the French. The first italicized example clarifies and reiterates the purpose of the contest, adding the point that the winner will be judged the fairest in the entire world, not just of the three European women. In the second example, indicated by an asterisk (*), Caxton omits a phrase explaining that the jewels were a gift from Vienne's mother [*et lequele luy avoit envoye la contesse de Flandres qui estoit sa dame*]. He adds words creating doublets. *Wytte* is an English equivalent to the French-derived *entendement* [will, intention], while *renomme* [renown, reputation, report] is a synonym for *bruyt* [fame, renown, commotion].

---

[68] Finlayson, "Source of Caxton's *Paris and Vienne*," pp. 134–35.
[69] Leach, p. xxiv. Cépède's long romance is not divided into chapters, though the Burgundian text is (*Paris et Vienne*, ed. Brown-Grant and Crécy, pp. 76–77).

Throughout his translation, Caxton inserts adjectives and adverbs to emphasize value, beauty, virtue, and emotion, and provides occasional transitional formulas ("Now sayth the hystory"). Some of his additions are pointedly chivalric, as in the account of the tournament at Vienne: "[a]nd soo they mostred, rydyng tofore the scaffold of the fayre Vyenne, and were so nobly and rychely armed and arayed, and so godley men they were, that everyone sayd, the floure of knyghthode may now be seen in thys place" (3.1). Caxton also significantly extends the catalogues of musical instruments included in descriptions of various feasts. Other additions, like the French term *quarrelle*, the translation of *lamour* as "fyre of love," or the singular reference to Venus, draw on the rhetoric of courtly love.

Caxton's print is now bound in red leather embossed with the arms of George III in gold. The book measures 8 ½ inches high by 6 ¼ inches wide, and consists of thirty-five folio leaves in five quires printed in double columns of thirty-nine lines; the gothic black letter type is Caxton's font 4*.[70] The text is presented in twenty-one sections set off by an initial paraph symbol and followed by a sentence-length title. This heading is followed by a space and sometimes separated by from the preceding chapter. These rubrics are not numbered; thus all chapter numbers in this edition is editorial. In the print, the initial letters of the first words following the headings are woodblock capitals; these are slightly embellished, three lines high and eight spaces wide. Similar large capitals mark other sections of the narrative and are indicated in this edition. Its unadorned state and double column format would have made it a less costly volume.[71] The book is without a title page, table of chapters, or dedication, which is notable since all Caxton's other romances have a dedication, prologue, or epilogue. Perhaps the political uncertainty of 1485 following the battle of Bosworth Field and the ascension of Henry Tudor led Caxton to avoid arousing disfavor by an ill-timed acknowledgement.[72] Some early readers wrote their names in the book, the most legible inscription being "Cossyn," but the volume reveals little about its owners.

This edition is based on the sole surviving complete copy of *Paris and Vienne*, which is in the collection of the British Library. A digitized version is available at http://access.bl.uk/item/viewer/ark:/81055/vdc_100102251449.0x000001#?c=0&m=0&s=0&cv=76&xywh=-982%2C-345%2C11693%2C6873, and a microfilm of the book is on EEBO. My editorial practice follows METS guidelines as explained in the General Introduction to this volume, pp. 14–15.

---

[70] Leach, p. xi. See Blades, *Biography and Typography*, pp. 306–07.

[71] *Charles the Great* and *Four Sons of Aymon* were also printed in double columns; all Caxton's other romances are single column.

[72] Other romances printed in 1485 are *Charles the Great*, dedicated to the Mercer William Daubeny, and *Le Morte d'Arthur* [*King Arthur*], where the prologue mentions only "noble and dyvers gentylmen."

Witnesses and Source Texts

Long Version

- Brussels, KRB, MS BR 9632/3, fols. 1r–137v. [mid 15c. The longer Burgundian version produced by the atelier Wavrin.]
- Carpentras, Bibliothèque Municipale (Inguimbertine), MS 1792, fols. 285–88. [mid 15c. At the end of Cépède's prologue, Inart Beyssan wrote that he copied (*traylatie*) the book in 1438.]
- Carpentras, Bibliothèque Municipale (Inguimbertine), papiers de Peiresc, n° 23, t. 2, fol. 286.
- Columbia, University of Missouri, Elmer Ellis Library, Special Collections, Fragmenta Manuscripta 157, 1 fol.
- Paris, Bibliothèque de l'Arsenal, MS 3000. [mid 15c.]
- Paris, Bibliothèque Nationale de France, MS fr. 1464. Online at https://gallica.bnf.fr/ark:/12148/btv1b525052213/f9.item. [mid 15c.]
- Paris, Bibliothèque Nationale de France, MS fr. 1479. [The scribe, Guillaume le Moign, dated his copy 1459.]
- Paris, Bibliothèque Nationale de France, MS fr. 1480. [Completed in 1452 according to the colophon.]
- Paris, Bibliothèque Nationale de France, MS nouvelles acquisitions françaises 10169. [15c.]
- Vienna, Österreichische Nationalbibliothek, Cod. 3432. [15c.]

Short Version

French:

- Paris, Bibliothèque Nationale de France, MS fr. 20044. Online at https://gallica.bnf.fr/ark:/12148/btv1b10721305x. [mid 15c.]
- *Paris et Vienne*. Antwerp: Gherard Leeu, 1487. USTC: 70658; ISTC: ip00112800. Paris, Bibliothèque Nationale de France, Département Réserve des livres rares, RES-Y2-159. Online at https://gallica.bnf.fr/ark:/12148/btv1b8600062n. [print, woodcut illustrations]

Italian:

- *Stories dei nobilissimi amanti paris e Viena*. Treviso: Michael Manzolo, 1481. USTC: 999397; ISTC: ip00115500. London, British Library, IA.28369. [print]

English:

- *Thystorye of the noble ryght valyaunt and worthy knyght Parys, and of the fayr Vyenne de daulphyns daughter*. Westminster: Caxton, 1485. USTC: 500113; ISTC: ip00113500. London, British Library, C.10.b.10. Online at http://access.bl.uk/item/viewer/ark:/81055/vdc_100102251449.0x000001#?c=0&m=0&s=0&cv=76&xywh=-982%2C-345%2C11693%2C6873. [Base text. Reprinted by Leeu, Antwerp, 1492; de Worde, London, 1505, 1510; Pynson, London, 1510; Purfoot: London, 1586.]

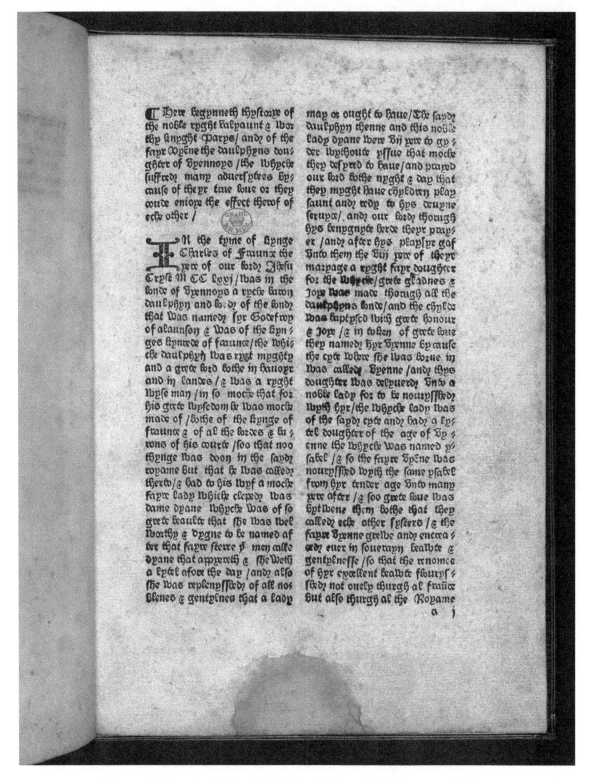

Figure 1: London, British Library, C.10.b.10, fol. 1. Caxton, *Paris and Vienne*, 1485.

Paris and Vienne

[fol. 1r] **Chapter 1: Here begynneth the hystorye of the noble ryght valyaunt and worthy knyght Parys and of the fayr Vyenne the daulphyns doughter of Vyennoys, the whyche suffred many adversytees bycause of theyr true love or[1] they coude enjoye the effect therof of eche other.**

1   In the tyme of kynge Charles of Fraunce the yere of our lord Jhesu Cryst 1271, was in the londe of Vyennoys a ryche baron daulphyn[2] and lord of the lond that was named syr Godefroy of Alaunson and was of the kynges kynrede of Fraunce, the whyche daulphyn was ryght myghty and a grete lord bothe in havoyr[3] and in landes, and was a ryght wyse man, in so moche that for his grete wysedom he was moche made of, bothe of the kynge of Fraunce and of al the lordes and barons of his courte, soo that noo thynge was doon in the sayd royame[4] but that he was called therto. And had to his wyf a moche fayre lady whiche cleped[5] was dame Dyane, whyche was of so grete beaulté that she was wel worthy and dygne[6] to be named after that fayre sterre that men calle Dyane that appyereth and sheweth a lytel afore the day. And also she was replenysshed[7] of all noblenes and gentylnes[8] that a lady may or ought to have. The sayd daulphyn, thenne, and his noble lady Dyane were seven yere togyder wythoute yssue[9] that moche they desyred to have, and prayed our Lord bothe nyght and day that they myght have chyldren playsaunt and redy to Hys devyne[10] servyce. And our Lord, through Hys benygnyté,[11] herde theyr prayer and after[12] Hys playsyr[13] gaf[14] unto them the eight yere of theyr maryage a ryght fayr doughter for the whyche grete gladnes and joye was made thorugh all the daulphyns londe. And the chylde was baptysed with grete honour and joye, and in token of grete love they named hyr Vyenne bycause the cyté where she was borne in was called Vyenne. And thys dough-

---

[1] before
[2] dauphin (feudal title of the lords of Vienne)
[3] property
[4] kingdom (realm)
[5] called (named)
[6] worthy
[7] filled
[8] noble status (refined manners)
[9] children
[10] divine
[11] good will (kindness)
[12] according to
[13] pleasure
[14] gave

ter was delyverd unto a noble lady for to be nourysshed[15] wyth hyr, the whyche lady was of the sayd cyté and had a lytel doughter of the age of Vyenne the whyche was named Ysabel. And so the fayre Vyenne was nourysshed wyth the same Ysabel from hyr tender age unto many yere after. And soo grete love was bytwene them bothe that they called eche other systers. And the fayre Vyenne grewe and encreaced ever in soverayn beawté[16] and gentylnesse so that the renomee[17] of hyr excellent beawté flourysshed not onely thurgh al Fraunce but also thurgh al the royame [fol. 1v] of Englond and other contrees.

2   It happed after she was fyftene yere of age that she was desyred to maryage of many knyghtes and grete lordes. And at that tyme was in the daulphyns courte emonge many hys knyghtes a noble man of auncyent lygnage and of fayr londes, the whiche was wel byloved of the daulphyn and of alle the lords of the lande, and was called Syr James. Thys noble man had a moche fayr sone that had to name Parys, and his fader made hym to be taught in al good custommes.[18] And whan he was eightene yere of age he was adressed[19] to the dyscyplyne of armes, and demened[20] hymself so nobly and worthely in al maner dedes of chyvalrye that wythin a shorte tyme after he was doubed[21] knyght by the hande of the sayd lord daulphyn.

3   Noo fayte[22] of knyghthode ne none adventure[23] of chyvalrye happed after but that he founde hymself at it, in soo moche that the renommee[24] of hym ranne thurgh al the world, and men sayd he was one of the best knyghtes that myght be founde in ony contree. And helde hymself ryght clene[25] in armes and lyved chastly and joyfully, and had ever aboute hym fowles, hawkes, and houndes for hys dysporte[26] to alle maner of huntyng suffysaunt ynough for a duc or for an erle. And thurgh hys prowesse[27] and hardynes[28] he was acqueynted and knowen of many other grete lordes. And emonge alle other, he was gretely and lovyngly acqueynted with a yonge knyght of the cyté of Vyenne that hyght[29] Edward, and were bothe of one age and moche loved eche other. And as two brethern of armes wente ever togyder there as they knew ony jousytng or appertyse[30] of armes to be had, for to gete honour.

---

[15] brought up (nursed)

[16] beauty

[17] renown

[18] customs

[19] applied

[20] conducted (controlled his horse)

[21] dubbed

[22] feat

[23] exploit

[24] fame (renown)

[25] pure (righteous)

[26] entertainment

[27] knightly valor (prowess)

[28] courage

[29] was named

[30] test (expertise)

4   And wete[31] it wel that, besyde theyr worthynes in armes, they were good musycyens, playeng upon alle maner instrumentes of musyke and coude synge veray wel, but Parys passed in al ponytes his felowe Edward. Notwythstondyng, Edward was amerous alredy of a noble lady of the courte of Braban, but Parys as yet knewe nought of amorousté.[32] But not longe after, Venus, the goddes of love, fyred his thought with the hert unto a noble yong lady, that is to wete[33] the fayre Vyenne, the daulphyns[34] doughter of Vyennoys that was his lyege lord.[35] And the more he growed toward his flouryng age, the more he was esprysed[36] and brennyng[37] of her love for the grete beauté that was in hyr. But Parys thought ever in hys herte that this love was not wel lykly ne cordable,[38] for he was not of so hyghe lygnage as the noble mayden [fol. 2r] Vyenne was of. And therfor Parys kept hys love secrete that none shold perceyve it sauf[39] Edward, his trusty felowe, to whom he brake[40] and shewed his counceyl.[41] And the fayre Vyenne perceyved not that Parys was amerous of hyr, nor Parys also durst neyther shewe nor say nothynge to hyr of hyt, but the more that he sawe hyr, the more grewe the fyre of love within hymself.

---

[31] *know*

[32] *being in love*

[33] *that is to wete,* namely, that is to say

[34] *dauphin's (feudal title of the lords of Vienne)*

[35] *liege (lord to whom feudal service is due)*

[36] *inflamed*

[37] *burning*

[38] *agreeable*

[39] *except*

[40] *made known*

[41] *private thoughts*

Chapter 2: How Parys and Edward hys felowe played wyth dyvers instrumentes by nyght tofore the chambre of Vyenne.

1   Parys thenne and Edward wyth one accorde[1] dysposed[2] for to gyve somme melodyous myrthe to the noble mayde Vyenne, and wyth theyr musycal instrumentes as recourders,[3] they yede[4] by nyght tyme togyder toward that parte of the castel where as the fayre Vyenne laye in hyr chambre, and there they sange ful swetely and sowned[5] melodoyously theyr musycal instrumentes and pypes. And certeyn the melodye of their songes and the sowne of heyr instrument was so playsaunt and so swete that it passed al other melodye. And whan the daulphyn[6] and his wyf and the fayre Vyenne, theyr doughter,

---

[1] *agreement*

[2] *resolved*

[3] *recorders (small wind instruments)*

[4] *went*

[5] *made music (sounded)*

[6] *dauphin (feudal title of the lords of Vienne)*

herde this swete and melodyous sowne as wel of mans wyces[7] as of dyvers instrumentes, they had grete joye and took grete playsyr at it, and had grete desyre to knowe what they were that so grete solace and joye made tofore[8] theyr castel. And for to wete and knowe what they were, the daulphyn assygned a day of a feste[9] at the whyche he sente for alle maner mynstrellys in hys londe, chargyng[10] theym upon grete payne that they shold come for to playe before hym and hys barons in hys castel of Vyenne. And whan they were al come, they played and sange in theyr best wyse.[11] But among them were not founde tho mynstrelles that the lord daulphyn sought sore,[12] wherof he was sorouful and desyred more to knowe what they were than he dyd afore. And whan Vyenne herde alle the mynstrellys of the londe that sowned at that feste, she sayd to Ysabel, her damoysel[13] and prevy felowe,[14] "By my fayth, swete syster, these mynstrellys playen nought to the regarde[15] of them that were wonte[16] to come before our chambre. And me dysplayseth moche that I may not knowe them, for certeynly they come not hyther for nought, for they love outher you or me."

2 Whan the daulphin understode hys doughters wordes, he, wyllyng to playse hyr, sayd unto hyr that, yf it were possyble, she shold knowe what they were that soo [fol. 2v] sange every nyght before hyr chambre. Wherfore he ordeyned[17] ten men of armes and commaunded them to hyde themself pryvely[18] there as the sowne was herde, and that they shold brynge to hym, other[19] by force or otherwyse, them that made that swete melodye. Now came the nyght that the two yonge knyghtes, Parys and Edward, that no thynge knewe of the embusshement[20] that was layed for them, came with theyr instrumentes toward the castel, and there they began to synge and sowned theyr instrumentes so melodyously that grete playsyr it was to here.[21] And whan they had songe and wold have retorned thyder as they were come fro, the ten knyghtes lepte and cam forth and salewed[22] them curtoyslle, sayeng that they nedes must come wyth them for to speke with their lord the daulphyn. Thenne sayd Parys to them, "Fayr lordes, abyde[23] a lytel whyle, yf it playse you, and of us ye shal have an ansuer." Thenne wente Parys and Edward aparte and

---

[7] voices
[8] in front of (before)
[9] celebration (feast)
[10] ordering
[11] manner (way)
[12] greatly
[13] lady in waiting
[14] intimate friend (confidante)
[15] esteem (as well as)
[16] accustomed
[17] ordered
[18] secretly
[19] either
[20] ambush
[21] hear
[22] greeted
[23] wait

spake togyder. "Ye see fayr brother," sayd Parys to Edward, "in what party we be now and I wold not that ye shold have by me ony dysplaysyr nor harme, but soo moche I telle you that or[24] I sholde suffre[25] me to be ledde tofore the daulphyn I had lever[26] deye. Therfore, fayr brother, advyse[27] ye what is beste for to do." And Edward, heryng Parys wordes, sayd, "Brother myn, have noo fere of no thynge and lete us doo as ye wyl." Thenne sayd they to the ten men of armes, "Lordes, thurgh your curtosye suffre us to retorne thyder as we came fro, for we be at my lord the daulphyns playsyr and of all the lordes and barons of his courte, but in ony maner, as for thys tyme we may not fulfylle hys commaundement."

3   Whan the sayd ten men of armes saw the two knyghtes dysobeyssaunt, they ansuerd to them, "Ye shal now come to hym other wyth your wylle[28] or by force." And bygan to pulle oute theyr swerdes and came ayenst the two yonge knyghtes that naked[29] were from al armes, sauf[30] theyr swerdes and theyr bowclers[31] wherwyth they coverd them, and so manfully deffended theyr bodyees that they hurte and wounded sore[32] al the ten armed men, insomoche that they maad them alle to voyde[33] and flee fro the place, whether they wold or not.

4   And on the morowe erly, the ten men of armes came tofore the daulphyn alle wounded and sore hurt. And they recounted to hym how two yonge men onely had arayed[34] them so and how they nedes must flee for fere of theyr lyves, [fol. 3r] wherof the daulphyn was ryght angry to see them so sore hurt and took grete dysplaysyr of it and thought wel that the sayd two yonge knyghtes were of grete strengthe and vertue. Wherfore he comanded an hondred men to be redy for to espye[35] and take them the nyght folowyng yf they came ageyn, chargyng that none hurte shold be doon to them but, after theyre songe doon, they shold be brought unto hym. But thys enterpryse[36] came to none effect, for the two yonge knyghtes came not ageyn but kepte alle that they had doon secrete.

5   Whan the fayre Vyenne sawe that she myght not knowe what these mynstrelys were, she thought they were somme grete lordes that were amerous of hyr, and she and hyr damoysel[37] Ysabel spake of none other thynge than of these mynstrelles and had grete playsyr to talke of them. Parys, seyng he durst not say nor shewe the grete love that he had

---

[24] *before*

[25] *permit (allow)*

[26] *rather*

[27] *consider*

[28] wyth your wylle, *willingly*

[29] *unarmed*

[30] *except*

[31] *bucklers (small hand shields)*

[32] *severely*

[33] *leave*

[34] *made a show of armed force [against]*

[35] *spy on (watch for)*

[36] *undertaking*

[37] *lady in waiting*

  to the fayr Vyenne, thought he wold hyde hys courage[38] from hyr, wherfore he took acqueyntaunce wyth the bysshop of Saynt Laurence, the whyche lerned hym holy scrypture.

6   The daulphyn thenne seyng hys doughter ful tryste[39] and pensyful[40] for thys that she myght not knowe the sayd mynstrelles that so melodyously played tofore hyr chambre, he ordeyned[41] a joustyng place wythin his cyté of Vyenne and made lystes[42] and scaffoldes[43] to be sette up and sente his herauldes in Fraunce, in Englond, and in Normandye to anounce and shewe unto al knyghtes and gentylmen that wold doo faytes[44] of armes and of chyvalrye for love of al ladyes and damoyselles, that the joustes shold be holden the fyrst day of May in the cyté of Vyenne. And he that shold doo best in armes,[45] shold have of the Daulphyns doughter a shelde of crystalle of grete valure, and a garlond wyth roses and floures of fyn gold. And wete[46] ye wel that Vyenne, the noble and fayr mayden, was ryght gladde of the joustes that hyr fader ordeyned for hyr sake. For grete talent[47] and desyre she had to knowe hym that was soo amerous of hyr, and she thought he wold be at the sayd fyrst day of May at Vyenne.

7   After the messagers that had pronounced the joustes were comen ageyn to the cyté of Vyenne, the moost parte of the knyghtes and gentylmen of the royame[48] of Fraunce, of Englond, and of Normandye made them redy for to come to the cyté of Vyenne to the sayd joustes. And in especyal many noble barons of the royame of Englond and of France, that amerous [fol.3v] were of the fayre Vyenne for the renommé[49] of her grete beaulté,[50] came to the sayd joustes wyth ryche and noble araye,[51] emonge whome was Johan duc of Bourbon, nevew[52] to the kyng of Fraunce; Edward, the kynges sone of Englond[53]; Anthony, sone to the erle of Provence; Gherard, the marquys sone of Mountferat;[54] and Wyllyam, sone to the duc of Carnes.[55]

8   Parys thenne, knowyng this noble assemblé and the joustes that shold be the fyrst day of May, thought in hymself whether he shold goo thyder or not, but the grete love

---

[38] *feelings (heart)*
[39] *sad [OF triste]*
[40] *pensive (sad)*
[41] *commanded (ordered)*
[42] *lists (barriers surrounding a tournament field)*
[43] *viewing platforms (elevated seats)*
[44] *martial contests (feats)*
[45] *weapons (armed combat)*
[46] *know*
[47] *wish*
[48] *kingdom (realm)*
[49] *reputation (renown)*
[50] *beauty*
[51] *trappings (array)*
[52] *nephew*
[53] Edward, the kynges son of Englond, *the king of England's son, named Edward*
[54] *Montferrat, in southeastern France*
[55] *Tarnès, in southwestern France*

that he had to the fayre Vyenne constrayned[56] hym therto. Nevertheles, he took counceyl of Edward his felowe, the whyche answerd to hym, "Yf ye goo I wyl holde you companye thyder, but we must departe secretly that we be not knowen." And anone they made redy theyr harnoys[57] and pourveyed[58] theym of good horses whiche they harneysed al in whyt, and none other token[59] they had on them wherby they myght be knowen sauf that they were arayed[60] al in whyt and one lyke that other.

9 The day of the joustes thenne approached and al the lordes and barons afore sayd cam two dayes before the feste[61] to the cyté of Vyenne where the daulphyn for love of them dyd doo make[62] a noble scaffold where as the fayre Vyenne was rychely arayed. And al that sawe hyr were amervaylled[63] of hyr grete beauté. To that feste came many noble knyghtes and squyers clothed and arayed rychely after the guyse[64] of theyr contree. And there were many mynstrellys playeng upon al maner instrumentes and many good syngars, whyche the noble mayde Vyenne herkened ful wel, for her hert was onely sette to thynke how she myght knowe hym that was hyr lover. Parys thenne came thyder and was ordeyned[65] for to serve at the daulphyns table where Vyenne satte, and wete ye wel that ful gracyously and curtoysly he served and kerved byfore hyr.

---

[56] *compelled*
[57] *armor (equipment)*
[58] *provided*
[59] *device for a coat of arms*
[60] *dressed*
[61] *festivity (feast)*
[62] dyd doo make, *had made (caused)*
[63] *astonished*
[64] *style (custom)*
[65] *appointed (ordered)*

Chapter 3: How Parys gate the prys of the joustes in the cyté of Vyenne.

1 Whan the day was comen that the lordes knyghtes and gentylmen shold juste for love of the ladyes, Parys and Edward yede[1] to a secrete place where they armed them secretly, and syn[2] came to the lystes[3] with theyr badges and tokens[4] and were horsed and armed ful rychely and wel. Alle other knyghtes there were knowen by theyr armes, but the two whyt knyghtes were unknowen. The daulphyn thenne commaunded that everyone shold mustre[5] [fol. 4r] or[6] the joustyng began along the felde tofore the ladyes and damoyselles. And soo they mostred, rydyng tofore the scaffold of the fayre Vyenne, and were so nobly and rychely armed and arayed, and so godley men they were, that everyone sayd the floure

---

[1] *went*
[2] *then*
[3] *lists (barriers enclosing a tournament ground)*
[4] badges and tokens, *heraldic emblems and ladies' tokens*
[5] *assemble*
[6] *before*

of knyghthode may now be seen in thys place. And emonge al other prynces, Edward of England was moost amerous of al and ryght renommed[7] in armes. The pucelle[8] Vyenne, seyng all these noble knyghtes, sayd to hyr damoysel Ysabel, "Fayr syster, whyche of them al thynke you that moost dooth for the love of me?" And Ysabel ansuerd, "Honourable lady, me semeth he that bereth the lyon of gold in his armes[9] dooth more for your love than the other." "Certes," sayd Vyenne, "yonder two whyt knyghtes that bere none armes in theyr sheldes are more to my fantasye[10] than ony of the other alwaye. We shal see now what they can doo."

2   Thenne were the knyghtes redy to do fayte of armes. And fyrst an hardy[11] and valyaunte knyght that bare in hys armes a crowne of gold bygan the fyrst cours,[12] and ayenst hym ranne the good knyght Edward, Parys felowe, and recountred[13] eche other so vygorously that they brake bothe theyr speres. Many other mette eche other sodaynlye, gyvyng grete strokes. Somme were overthrowen to the erthe, and somme brake theyr speres worthely and kept theyr sterops ryght valyauntly. The other recountred eche other so manfully that bothe hors and man were caste to the grounde, for every man dyd hys best to gete worshyp[14] there. Edward, the kynges sone of Englond, bare hym ful wel and had the better upon many a knyght there. But the strong knyght Parys broched[15] hys hors toward hym and mette hym so vygorously that, atte ende, he overthrewe hym and had the better of hym, wherof he gate grete worshyp and was moche praysed for hys grete prowesse.[16] Thys joustyng lasted tyl souper tyme, and whan the even[17] cam many of them were wery of the jouste and rested them, but Parys dyd thenne more of armes shewyng his mervayllous prowesse than he had doon of al that day, in so moche that none durst approche hym ne withstonde his appertyse[18] in armes. And so moche he dyd that the honour and prys[19] of the joustes rested and abode in hym that day.

---

[7] *renowned*

[8] *maiden [OF pucelle]*

[9] *coat of arms*

[10] *fancy (amorous desire)*

[11] *bold*

[12] *a charge in battle or tournament*

[13] *encountered*

[14] *honor (respect)*

[15] *spurred*

[16] *knightly valor (martial expertise)*

[17] *evening*

[18] *skill (expertise)*

[19] *prize (esteem)*

Paris and Vienne 45

Chapter 4: How the shelde of crystal and the garlond with floures of gold were yeven to Parys as to the best doer in faytes of armes.

1   The feste ended, grete worshyp and loenge[1] abode to the two knyghtes with the whyt [fol. 4v] armes, and Parys was ledde unto the scaffold[2] there as Vyenne was, the whyche delyverd hym the shelde of crystal and the garlond with floures of gold that she helde in hyr honde. And thenne Parys wyth Edward, his felawe, departed then in the secretest wyse[3] that they coude and wente to unarme them to the place where they fyrst armed themself. The barons and knyghtes that were there spake wel of the prowesse and of the chyvalrye of the knyghtes with whyt armes, so that the daulphyn and the other grete lordes had grete desyre to knowe what they were and to have theyr acqueyntaunce. But they departed so secretly fro the felde that no man knewe where they were become[4] nor what waye they toke.

2   After al thys was thus doon, the knyghtes retorned into theyr contrees spekyng ever of the ryal[5] feste and chere that the daulphyn had doon to them and of the prowesse of the whyt knyghtes, and of the ryght soverayn beauté and noblesse of Vyenne. And in the mene whyle, there moeved[6] a stryf betwyxte the barons and knyghtes of Fraunce and of Englond. For somme were there that were amerous of the doughter of the duc of Normandye, and somme were that loved and bare oute the beaulté of the syster of the kyng of Englond, sayeng she was fayrer than Vyenne was, and other were there that helde contrarye oppynyon, sayeng that the daulphyns doughter Vyenne passed in beauté al other wymmen in the world. And for this reason was grete debate and stryf betwyxte the knyghtes of Fraunce and them of Englond for the beauté of these thre damoyselles.[7]

3   Ever multeplyed and grewe more the bruyt[8] and the renommé[9] of the daulphyn by cause of the joustes and tournoyment doon in his cyté of Vyenne, wherof he had grete joye, for they had be moche honourable and playsaunt to al knyghtes. And Vyenne ever thought in hyrself who myght he be that had goten the worshyp and prys of the joustes, and sayd to Ysabel, "Never truste me, dere suster, but the knyght to whom I have yeven[10] the shelde of crystal and my garlond is he that so swetely sang for the love of me tofore our chambre, for myn hert gyveth it me, and by my fayth, syster, he is ful noble and worthy, and in alle hys dedes ryght curtoys and gentyl[11] as we myght have seen whylere.[12] Wherfor I say you, my swete syster, that in hym I have putte the rote[13] of myn entyere herte, my

---

[1] *praise*

[2] *viewing platform (elevated seat)*

[3] *manner (way)*

[4] *gone*

[5] *royal*

[6] *arose (stirred up)*

[7] *young unmarried gentlewoman*

[8] *praise*

[9] *fame (renown)*

[10] *given*

[11] *noble (refined)*

[12] *formerly*

[13] *bottom [of the heart] (root)*

wylle, and al my love. Nor never I shal have playsyr ne joye [fol. 5r] unto the tyme that I knowe what he is, for my love is al hys, and of whatsoever estate[14] he be of, I never shal take myn herte fro hym."

4   Thenne began she to wayle and syghe for the love of hym ful tenderly, for tyl now she had not felte the sparkles of love that spraunge out of hyr hert. But Parys knewe nothyng herof that she desyred to have him and to knowe what he was, but he kepte hys love secrete in hys hert. For he durst not shewe it unto hyr, wherfore he ledde hys lyf in grete trystesse[15] and sorowe. He went ever in the felawshyp of the bysshop of Saynt Laurence and made semblaunte[16] of nothyng. And James, the fader of Parys, that had seen the noble feest and the ryal joustes in the cyté of Vyenne, wenyng[17] to hym that hys sone Parys had not ben there, was ful sory and had grete dysplaysyr of it and sayd, "Fayr sone Parys, I am in a grete malencolye and in a thought for you that ye be not so joyeful ne mery as ye were wonte to be. Here afore tyme, I sawe you ever redy to the joustes and to al maner faytes of chyvalrye for to gete honour, and I now see you al chaunged syn[18] ye took acqueyntaunce wyth thys bysshop, for lothe[19] I were to see you bycome a man of relygyon, as I fere he wyl brynge you to. And ryght wrothe[20] I am that ye were not at that noble and ryal tournoyment that hath be holden in Vyenne, for the sake of alle the ladyes of thys londe. Wherfore, dere sone, I praye you to take hede to yourself that ye lese not your good renommee, your worshyp, ne the praysyng also that ye gate afore tyme, and that ye spende not your yougthe[21] in ydlnesse." And Parys, heryng alle thys, ansuered noo thyng to hys fader but abode stylle pensyfull,[22] thynkyng on the beauté of Vyenne.

5   Now sayeth the hystorye that, as ye have herde above, a grete stryfe befyl emong the knyghtes aforesayd for the love of the thre damoyselles aforesayd. For the erles sone of Flaunders was gretely wrothe for thys cause wyth the duc of Breunes, and had beten and hurte sore[23] each other so that none myght make the pees betwyxte theym, for eyther of hem[24] mayntened[25] and bare oute the beauté of his lady. It happed thenne that fyve knyghtes hardy and valyaunte came forth, the whyche sayd that they were redy to fyght and for to prove by force of armes that Florye, the dukes doughter of Normandye, was the fayrest damoysel of alle the world. And incontynent[26] stert up fyve other knyghtes that said and mayntened [fol. 5v] that Constaunce, the kynges syster of Englond, was the fayrest. And forthwyth other fyve knyghtes rose up that mayntened and uphelde the

---

[14] *social class*

[15] *sadness [OF triste]*

[16] *sign (semblance)*

[17] *thinking*

[18] *since*

[19] *for lothe, sorrowfully (regretfully)*

[20] *angry*

[21] *youth*

[22] *thoughtful (pensive)*

[23] *severely*

[24] *them*

[25] *supported (defended in tournament)*

[26] *immediately (eagerly)*

beauté of Vyenne above alle other wymmen in the world, in so moche that thys debate cam to the knowleche of the kyng of Fraunce, whiche sayd that herof myght growe a grete trouble and dyscorde emong his barons and other lordes. Soo sente he worde to them that they shold come toward hym and that he shold gyve suche a sentence[27] upon theyr stryf that they al shold be therof contente, the whyche message plesed them wel, and came alle toward hym as sone[28] as they myght. And whan they were come tofore the kyng, they spake of theyr stryf. But anone the kyng ordeyned a joustes for the love of the sayd thre ladyes and made his maundement[29] that they al shold come wyth theyr armes and hors for to jouste the eighth day of Septembre in the cyté of Parys. And they that shold do best in armes at that day, they shold have the prys[30] and the worshyp of the feste, and the lady on whos beauté they helde with shold be reputed and holden for the fayrest damoysel of alle the world.

6   The kyng of Fraunce thenne sente worde to the faders of the forsayd thre ladyes, prayeng them to come atte same feste and that eyther of them shold brynge wyth hym a present of rychesse, the which thre presentes shold be yeven in the worshyp of their thre doughters to the best doer in armes in token of vyctorye. And thus the kyng of Englond fyrst sent for hys syster Constaunce a fayre crowne of gold alle sette wyth perlys and precyous stones of grete value. The duc of Normandye, for love of hys doughter Florye, sente a ryght fayre garlond[31] sette wyth dyvers perlys and precyous stones moche ryche and of grete extymacyon.[32] And the daulphyn, for love of hys doughter Vyenne, sente a moche ryche coler[33] of gold al envyronned[34] wyth precyous stones of dyvers colours, the whiche was worth a ryght grete tresour. And these thre jewellys were delyvered to the kynge of Fraunce. The forsayd knyghtes thenne made them redy and apparaylled[35] al thynges accordyng[36] to the joustes and in ryche araye[37] came al to the cyté of Parys. And wete ye wel that in Fraunce was not seen afore that day so grete noblesse of barons and knyghtes as were there assembled, for there were the moost hye[38] pryncyes and barons of Englond, of Fraunce, and of Normandye. And eyther of hem dyd sette al hys wytte[39] and entendement[40] to upholde and bere out that [fol. 6r] they had purposed and sayd. And

---

[27] ruling
[28] soon
[29] written order (command)
[30] prize (esteem)
[31] wreath bestowed on a victor
[32] value
[33] chain or band worn by knights as an identifying ornament
[34] surrounded
[35] prepared (equipped)
[36] proper (pertaining)
[37] trappings (dress)
[38] noble
[39] mental faculties
[40] intention (will)

every baron gaf hys lyverey[41] that they shold be knowen eche fro other. And the bruyt[42] and renommé was that my lady Constaunce shold have the honour of that feste for thys that many a fayre and hardy knyght made them redy to mayntene[43] the quarelle[44] of hyr beaulté. But nevertheles eyther of these thre partyes hoped to have the worshyp of the feste.

7   And Parys, that was in Vyenne the cyté and that wel knewe the grete apparaylle of thys feste, took counceyl of Edward, hys felawe, whether he shold goo to Parys or not. And Edward counceylled hym to goo thyder so that he wente secretly, and sayd, "Yf ye goo thyder secretly, and yf God gyve you grace that ye gete the worshyp of the feste, grete wele[45] and good shal come to you therby. And yf ye goo and be knowen, the daulphyn and the other lordes shal not preyse you soo moche as they shold yf ye were unknowen for cause that ye be not of so grete lygnage[46] as they be. Another is, yf ye goo openly and that my lady Vyenne happeth to have the honour of the feste by your prowesse,[47] she shal nought be sette by,[48] consyderyng the other grete lordes that shal be there procedyng[49] your degree. And yf she gete the worshyp of the feste by a knyght unknowen, the love and honour shal growe the more in hyr courage[50] toward hym that thus hath doon for hyr sake. Wherfore I counceyl you to goo thyder in the moost secretest wyse[51] that ye may, for my truste is that ye shal gete grete worshyp there. And but yf ye goo, trust me I shal make myself redy to goo thyder for you, for I wyl be lothe to see the beaulté of my lady Vyenne to be rebuked."

8   At these wordes graunted Parys to goo to the sayd joustes, and whan he was redy and had al thynges accordyng to a noble knyght, he departed in the secretest manere that he myght toward the cyté of Parys, where as the kyng of Fraunce maad grete provysyon of alle maner metes and of al other thynges necessarye to suche a ryal[52] feste. And in the myddes[53] of the cyté of Parys he ordeyned the place where the knyghtes shold jouste, and dyd doo make[54] many fayre scaffoldes for the ladyes and damoyselles to be sette on for to beholde the joustyng. Also he dyd do make thre baners ful fayre and ryche. The fyrst baner was whyt and there was wryton upon hit in letters of gold, "Vyenne, doughter to my lord Godfroy of Alenson, daulphyn of Vyennoys". The second baner was rede and was wryton theron in letters of gold, "Constaunce, the [fol. 6v] kynges syster of Englond."

---

[41] *identifying device of the wearer's lord (livery)*

[42] *fame*

[43] *support (defend in tournament)*

[44] *dispute*

[45] *well-being (good)*

[46] *lineage*

[47] *knightly valor (martial skill)*

[48] sette by, *affronted*

[49] *surpassing*

[50] *heart (desire)*

[51] *manner (way)*

[52] *royal*

[53] *middle*

[54] dyd soo make, *had made*

The thyrd baner was whyt and in letters of gold was wryton theron, "Florye, doughter to the duc of Normandye." And these thre baners were pyght up[55] at the thre corners of the felde, and wete ye that so grete prees[56] was there that the peple took theyr place upon the scaffoldes two dayes afore the feste for to see the grete peple and the fayr ordynaunce[57] that there was.

9 Whan it was so that the lordes were redy of alle thynges that were necessarye and were departed fro theyr contrees, they assembled al at Parys the fourtene day of Septembre. And never tofore was seen so grete a companye of nobles, for fro alle partyes was comen grete chyvalrye,[58] the somme for to do armes and the other for to see the feste whyche was moche sumptuous and noble. And whan the day assygned came of the joustes, on the mornyng erly he dyd soo sette these thre joyaulx[59] or jewels in the baners, the whyche shone and resplendysshed[60] moche merveillously for the nombre of perles and precyous stones that were in the baners. Now it shold be overlonge to recyte of the barons and of the knyghtes that were in that journeye,[61] for many were comen thyder fro the royame of Spayne, of Aragon, and of many other contrees for to prove their strengthe and persones,[62] and for to mayntene[63] the barons that mayntened the thre ladyes maydens, of whome we shall reherce[64] of the pryncypallest hereafter the shortest wyse we may.

10 And whan it came in the mornyng that every man was armed and apparaylled[65] in the felde, and that the kyng of Fraunce was sette in hys grete scaffolde and began to say al alowde and moche mervayllously that alle the people myght here[66] and understonde, "Knyghtes and barons that been here for to do the fayte of armes, goo ye everyche under that baner that he wyl mayntene for the love of hys lady. And we gyve in comaundement that this felde be of love and of curtosye, as it to you apperteyneth;[67] how be it, we wyl wel that eche of you do valyantly hys armes and hys chyvalryes for that damoysell whyche he wyl mayntene. And he that shal wynne the felde shal have the prys and the honour of the feste, and that lady or damoysel shal be mayntened and allowed[68] for the moost fayre damoysel of the world and shal have the prys and honour of them of Englond, of Fraunce, and of Normandye. And that to thys noo man be so hardy to gaynsay[69] upon the payne to lose his lyf." [fol. 7r] And yet after thys he sayd, "Ye see here a fayre crowne the whyche the

---

[55] pyght up, *pitched (set up)*
[56] *crowd (press of people)*
[57] *display of arms*
[58] *companies of knights*
[59] *gems*
[60] *sparkled*
[61] *a day's combat in a tournament*
[62] *physical power (body)*
[63] *support (defend in tournament)*
[64] *recount (narrate)*
[65] *outfitted*
[66] *hear*
[67] *is appropriate*
[68] *recognized (agreed)*
[69] *contradict*

quene of Fraunce hath ordeyned to the ende that it be delyverd to the fader of the damoysel that shal have the prys and honour of the felde and of the joustes, and the knyght that shal gete the prys and the honour of the joustes shal have all the thre baners and the thre jewels that been in them," and comaunded that the baner[70] of Normandye shold fyrst make hys mustre,[71] and nexte the baner of Constaunce and thenne that of Vyenne.

11   And fyrst under the baner of Normandye were they that folowe, that is to wete: Johan, sone of the erle of Flaunders; Phelyp of Bauyers,[72] newev[73] of the kynge of Fraunce; Edward, sone of the duke of Bourgoyne;[74] Johan, earle of Armynak;[75] Balaxe, brother of the marquys of Saluce;[76] Geffroy, duc of Pycardye,[77] and after them came many other wel armed and habylled.[78] After came the baner of Constaunce the whiche accompanyed Johan, sone of the duc of Bremeos;[79] Gastamons of Gastre, brother of the erle of Foyes;[80] Anthonye Alegre, sone of the duc of Carnes;[81] Larer, newev of the duc of Bourgoyne; the honourable Johan of Braban;[82] Salamon de Launson, brother of the erle of the Marché,[83] and after them came many other barons and knyghtes. And thenne after came the baner of the fayr Vyenne the whyche accompanyed Hughe, sone of the duc of Bourbon; Edward, sone of the kyng of Englond; Wylliam, sone of the duc of Barry; Antonye, sone of the counte of Provynce; Parys, son of Sir Jacques of Vienne; Dormando of Monferrant,[84] sone of the marquys; thre sones of the duc of Carnes; Johan Peryllous, duc of Normandye, and after them came many other barons and knyghtes wel armed and wel horsed. And whan the mustre was made, every baner retorned into hys place, whyche moche noble and mervayllous thynge was it to see and to byholde the noblesse of the barons and knyghtes soo wel horsed and armed as they were. And the daulphyn and Syr Jaques, fader of Parys, were comen for to see the feste and the joustes.

---

[70] *flag for leading troops (a tournament team)*
[71] *assembly for his troops to pass in review*
[72] *Bavaria*
[73] *nephew*
[74] *Burgundy*
[75] *Armagnac*
[76] *Saluzzo*
[77] *Picardy*
[78] *clothed (outfitted)*
[79] *Brennes*
[80] *Foix*
[81] *Tarnès, in southwestern France*
[82] *Brabant*
[83] *la Marché, county in central France*
[84] *Montferrat, in southeastern France*

Chapter 5: How Parys wan the prys at the joustes in the cyté of Parys.

1 Whan thenne it came to the houre of tyerce[1] began the joustes. And cam into the felde moche nobly armed Johan, sone of the erle of Flaundres, and ageyn hym came Johan, sone of the duke of Breunes, and coped[2] togyder so fyersly that they [fol. 7v] brake theyr speres. And Johan, sone of the erle of Flaunders tombled to the erthe under hys hors. And after ayenst Johan de Breunes came Edward, sone of the duke of Bourgoyne. These two knyghtes bete doun puyssauntly[3] Johan de Breunes, unto the tyme that there came ayenst hym Johan Peryllous, duc of Normandye, whyche smote hym wyth so grete force that he overthrewe hym under hys hors and brake hys arme and put hym suche estate[4] that he wyst[5] not whether it was day or nyght. And ayenst Johan Peryllous came Anthonye Alegre, sone of the duc of Carnes, and dyd so moche prowesse wyth his persone[6] that he conquerd Johan Peryllous and fyve other knyghtes myghty men of his partye, whom he smote to the erthe by force of armes. After came ageynst Anthonie Alegre Geffroy of Pycardye and smote Anthonie in suche wyse that he fyl to the erthe and six other stronge knyghtes of hys partye, and after dyd soo mervayllous feates of armes that every man sayd that he had the honour of the felde.

2 And thenne came the free[7] knyght Parys ayenst Geffroy, beryng lowe hys spere, and they gaf so grete strokes that the knyghtes and horses wente al to the erthe. Wherfor the kyng sayd that sythe[8] bothe two were throwen to the erthe, that they shold retorne ageyn to the joustes, and Parys wyth a grete desyre consented, and soo bothe retorned and came rennyng. And Parys gaf to Geffroy so grete a stroke that hys hors slode, and thenne Geffroy overthrewe to the erthe. But bycause that the hors slode, it was sayd that the hors was cause that he overthrewe, for moche they mayntened Geffroy and sayd that he was not vaynquysshed, and that it shold be wel doon that they shold juste ageyn. And by cause that Parys was not knowen, ther was none that mayntened hym ne susteyned. Nevertheles, the kyng of Fraunce knew wel that Geffroy was vaynquysshed loyally[9] and wel, for he had wel seen the adventure[10] and wold do no wronge unto the knyght whyche was of grete strengthe and myght, and anone sente to hym an heraulde whyche sayd to hym in the name of the kynge of Fraunce, that the kyng had wel seen and wel knewe that Parys had vaynquysshed hys knyght. Notwythstondyng, yf he wold yet ones retorne to the juste, by hys noblesse that he shold do hymself grete honour. And thenne Parys maad hys ansuer sayeng that, "The beaulté of my lady Vyenne was so grete that in al the world was none to hyr lyke, that yf it pleased the kyng I am redy for to [fol. 8r] furnysshe[11] the

---

[1] *terce, the third canonical hour around 9 a.m.*
[2] *clashed*
[3] *with military valor*
[4] *state (condition)*
[5] *knew*
[6] *body*
[7] *free knight, one not attached to a lord (noble)*
[8] *since*
[9] *legally (legitimately)*
[10] *danger (risk)*
[11] *prepare for combat (do battle in)*

joustes for hys love ayenst the knyght yet another tyme and to juste tyl that Geffroy shold be vanquysshed, and that was wythoute ony gaynsayeng."[12] And the heraulde retorned and tolde it to the kyng, wherof the kynge was wel contente and sayd that the knyght ought to be somme grete lord, for he was of grete valoyr and puyssaunce and spake moche swetely and curtoysly. And after, Parys chaunged and took another hors, whyche Edward hys felowe had made redy for hym, and retorned to the justes and smote togyder wyth soo grete myght that by veray[13] force Geffrey went to the erthe under hys hors ryght evyl[14] hurte.

3   Thenne, whan it came toward even,[15] the joustes were so grete thycke and stronge that al the thre partyes, as wel of one as of the other, were throwen doun to the erthe, that ther abode no moo[16] of the partye of Vyenne but Parys allone. And of the partye of Normandye thre knyghtes stronge and puyssaunt, and they were Balaxo, brother of the marquys of Saluces; Johan, sone of the erle of Armynack; and Phelyp of Bauyere. And of the partye of Constaunce other thre stronge and myghty, that is to wete Johan of Braband; Larer, nevew of the duc of Bourgeyn; and Salamon da Lanson, brother of the counte de la Marché. And they sayd that the justes shold abyde tyl on the morne, for they were moche wery. And whan Parys saw that they wold have retorned, he fewterd[17] hys spere, and there cam ayenst hym Balaxo, brother of the marquys of Saluces. And Parys at the fyrst stroke strake hym doun to the erthe under hys hors, and in lyke wyse dyd to the other fyve. And moche nobly and valyauntly he wanne the honour of the justes and of the felde.

---

[12]   contradiction
[13]   sheer (strong)
[14]   very badly
[15]   evening
[16]   more
[17]   couched (put into the holder)

Chapter 6: How the kyng commaunded that the thre baners wyth the two jewellys shold be yven to Parys, champyon of Vyenne.

1   The joustes fynysshed, Parys wanne the beauté of hys lady, the fayer Vyenne, and he was ledde to the scaffolde where as the kynge was and the other grete lordes and knyghtes. And there were delyverd to hym the thre baners and the thre jewellys that were in them, and Parys shewed them thurgh all the felde, in sygne that the sayd Vyenne had goten the honour for to be the fayrest damoysell that was in alle the world by the same yonge knyght. And whan Parys had the thre fayr baners and the thre ryche jewellys, he [fol. 8v] and Edward hys felowe departed out of the cyté of Parys and oute of Fraunce the moost secrete wyse that they myght and retorned into Dalphyné.[1] Parys retorned in to the companye of the forsayd bysshop of Saynt Laurence, as[2] he had not been at the feste, and

---

[1]   Dauphiné, county in southeastern France (Viennois)
[2]   as if

alwaye he demaunded³ tydynges of the justes that were made in Fraunce and who had the honour of the joustes.

2 Whan the feste was made, al the barons and knyghtes that were there had grete desyre to knowe who was he that so valyauntly and so nobly had wonne the journeye⁴ and the honour of the justes, for to doo to hym worshyp. But they coude never knowe hym, wherof they had grete dysplaysyr and sayd that the knyght was of grete wysedom bycause he wold not be knowen. And after this, the barons and knyghtes took leve of the kyng and retorned into theyr londes al dyscomforted⁵ bycause they had not goten the honour of the feste. And yet were they more angry bycause they knewe not to whome the honour was gyven of the feste ne of the justes. The kyng of Fraunce, whyche moche loved the dolphyn, made to hym grete feste⁶ and moche grete honour. And the kynge delyverd to hym the crowne that the quene had gyven for to gyve to hyr that shold have the honour of the joustes, to the ende⁷ that he shold gyve it unto hys doughter Vyenne in sygne and token that she was the moost fayr damoysel of the world. And whan al thys was doon, the dolphyn and the fader of Parys retorned into Dolphyné in moche grete honour and grete joye.

3 Whan Vyenne knewe that hyr fader came, she came and mette hym as she was accustomed. Thenne whan the dolphyn sawe hyr, he kyssed hyr and sette on her hede the crowne whyche the kynge had gyven hym and tolde to hyr how she had goton the honour for to be the moost fayrest damoysell of the world. "And loo, here is the fayr crowne that the quene of Fraunce sendeth to you in token that ye have goten the honour, notwythstondyng, fayr doughter, that ye have had many contrarye therto. But ye have had a good deffendour and ryght stronge and hath wel quyted⁸ hym in your nede. For of eche partye were abyden⁹ thre knyghtes moche stronge and puyssaunte, and on your partye was left but one knyght onely whyche vaynquysshed al the other, wythout ony token, and is departed alle secretly that no man knewe hym ne the kyng of Fraunce hath no knowleche of hym. But he hath [fol. 9r] borne awaye wyth hym the thre baners and the two jewellys that were in them and also the prys¹⁰ and the honour of the feste, wherfore, swete and fayr doughter, ye wote never to whom to gyve thankynges of so moche honour as hath be doon for you. But I praye to God of heven and to the glorious Vyrgyn Marye that it playse Hym to gyve to hym good and honour, joye and excellence, and in alle his feates vyctorye. Lyke as¹¹ he is chyef and hede of al honour and of al chyvalrye in thys world, for I never sawe ne herde of knyght that so gracyously and so curtoysly bare hym in his armes and in his chyvalryes."

---

3 *asked* [OF *demander*]
4 *day's combat in tournament* [OF *jour*]
5 *dejected* (downcast)
6 *celebration*
7 *purpose*
8 *acquitted*
9 *remaining (waiting)*
10 *prize*
11 Lyke as, *Likely*

4   And whan Vyenne herde speke of these tydynges and sawe the grete honour and prys[12] that she had goten, and al was comen by this noble knyght, she sayd to Ysabeau hyr damoysel, "My suster, sayd I not to you wel but that late that I was byloved by the moost noble and valyaunt knyght of Fraunce? And by my fayth, my swete suster, this is he that so swetely songe and that wanne the justes in this cyté and bare with hym the shelde of crystal and my garlonde, and went his waye so that noo man myght knowe hym. Advyse[13] you wel, fayr suster, what hanour is comen to me by his prowesse and by his bounté.[14] I may wel be sory and dolant[15] whan I may not knowe who he is, and myn herte is moche hevy and myn entendement[16] that I never can fynde the moyen[17] to see and knowe hym." And yet she sayd, "Certes, my swete suster Ysabeau, I byleve that my dayes be shorte and that I shall deye of somme cruel and fals deth for the grete desplaysyr that I have contynuelly in my herte, for I can none other thynge doo but wepe and waylle and alwaye to contynue in sorouful lyf and hevy." But none apperceyved it but onely hyr damoysel Ysabeau.

5   The fader of Parys, whyche had then ben with the dolphyn in that feste, had not seen there hys sone Parys wherof he had grete sorowe in his herte, for he had seen that he was accustomed to be in al noble justes. But thenne he sawe hym goo with the bysshop of Saynt Laurence and dysposed[18] hym not to doo armes as he was woned,[19] wherfor he sayd to hym on a day, "My sone, I had hoped to have had in thee grete consolacyon, but now thou bryngest me into grete hevynesse and dysplaysyr whan I see that thou wylt not departe from thys bysshop. Wherfor I praye thee that thou leve hym, and doo soo that it may be to me playsaunt and to thee honneste."[20] Parys herde hym wel, but he gaf not a word to ansuer. [fol. 9v]

6   The fader of Parys, seyng thys, went to his secrete felowe Edward and sayd to hym, "I see wel that the grete amytye[21] and love that ye have to my sone, and knowe ye for certayn that I have in my hert grete melancolye[22] whan I remembre that Parys hath had grete honour and fame of chyvalrye, and now I see that he gooth al wyth thys bysshop and leteth[23] hys hawkes, his houndes, and hors to deye for hongre. Wherfore I praye you that ye wyl gyve me somme counceyl, whyche am soo meschaunt[24] that I deye for sorowe." And whan he had sayd these wordes, Edward had pyté[25] of hym and comforted hym the beste wyse he coude, and departed fro hym and wente strayte to hys felowe Parys and sayd to

---

[12] *esteem*
[13] *Consider*
[14] *valor*
[15] *sad*
[16] *understanding (comprehension)*
[17] *means*
[18] *inclined*
[19] *accustomed*
[20] *honorable (appropriate)*
[21] *friendship*
[22] *sadness*
[23] *leaves*
[24] *miserable*
[25] *pity*

hym, "I knowe wel that love constrayneth[26] thee so strongly that thou hast noo power over thyself, wherefore thy lyfe may not longe endure. And also thy fader and thy frendes ben evyl contente ayenst[27] thee, and I say to thee that for to be vertuous and valyaunt it playseth moche to God. And for the love of one woman thou doost moche desplaysyr to thy fader. And also for noo persone, whatsomever he or she be, thou oughtest not to lese the wele[28] and renomee that thou hast of chyvalrye. It appyereth not in thee, that thou hast ony vertu or courage, wherfore I praye thee that thou wylt do somme thyng that it may be playsaunt to thy fader, whych hath desyred and prayed me that I shold soo say to thee." Whan Parys had herde al this, he ansuerd to Edward and sayd to hym, "I knowe wel that these thynges that thou hast sayd to me been vertuous and honnest, but they been to me grevous, for to put me from the thoughtes in whyche I am contynuelly. Nevertheles, I praye thee that thou gyve me counceyl what is beste that I doo." Thenne sayd Edward, "It shold wel playse me, yf it were thy playsyr, that we shold goo into Braband,[29] for it is six monethes passed that I have not seen my lady, and there shall we do armes by which we may gete fame and honour."

7   And Paris agreed therto, sayeng that he was contente yf it playsed hym so to do, and incontynent[30] they made redy theyr harnoys[31] and horses and alle thynges necessarye to them. And or[32] Parys departed, he put in hys chambre[33] al the thynges and pryses that he had wonne by chyvalryes, and closed them fast[34] in his chambre and delyverd the keye to his moder and prayed hir moche derly[35] that she shold not open it, ne suffre[36] that ony persone shold entre therein. And after they wente toward Braband, where as they dyd grete [fol. 10r] feates of chyvalrye and joustes wherof they gate grete honoure and worshyp, and were moche praysed of ladyes and damoysellys. And Parys made countenaunce[37] for to have abyden[38] in Braband for the love of Edward, but hys herte drewe unto the fayre Vyenne whome he so moche loved in hys herte secretly.

---

[26] *compels*

[27] evyl contente ayenst, *ill content (displeased with)*

[28] *good name*

[29] *Brabant, region in modern Brussels*

[30] *immediately*

[31] *armor (equipment)*

[32] *before*

[33] *a private room for personal use*

[34] *securely*

[35] *earnestly*

[36] *permit*

[37] *appearance*

[38] *remained*

Chapter 7: How Dyane and Vyenne hyr doughter wenten to vysyte the fader of Parys the whyche was seek.

1   Now it happened that duryng thys tyme that Parys and Edward duelleden[1] in Braband, the fader of Parys fyl into a sekenesse of fevres or accesse.[2] And the cause came of the thought that he had of hys sone Parys. And he beyng seek, the doulphyn wente on a day to see hym and demaunded[3] the cause of hys maladye and comforted hym the beste wyse that he coude, and after retorned home and sayd to hys wyf that it were wel doon that she shold goo see and vysyte messyre Jaques, whyche was seke. And forthwyth incontynent my lady Dyane, hyr doughter Vyenne, and Ysabeau, hyr damoysel, wyth a grete companye wente to the castel of Syr Jaques and salewed[4] hym moche nobly, as it wel apperteyned[5] and the best wyse that they myght.

2   And whan they were in the chambre where messyre Jaques was and laye, Dame Dyane demaunded hym of his sekenesse. And messire Jaques sayd that al hys dysease came for hys sone Parys bycause he loste so hys tyme, and that he went alway wyth the bysshop of Saynt Laurence. "Wherof I fere me that he shal become a man of relygyon. I have no moo[6] chyldren but hym. I wote not what I shall doo wyth the goodes that God hath gyven to me." And my lady Dyane comforted hym and sayd that hys sone was moche wel byloved of the doulphyn and that he had moche grete amytye[7] of many grete lordes, barons and knyghtes. And also she sayd, that emong al thynges, he shold ordeyne for hys helthe. And after all thys, the moder of Parys prayed hyr that it myght playse hyr to come see the castel, and she ansuered that she moche desyred it. Thenne the moder of Parys shewed hir al the castel, and ledde hir into an halle al ful of armes and abylemens[8] of warre for to fyght in batayll. After, she ladde hyr into another halle where as were many hawkes, faulcens, and many other fowles of chace,[9] and after into many [fol. 10v] other halles and chambres rychely arayed, whyche were over longe to reherce.[10]

3   And after, the moder of Parys shewed unto hyr the chambre of Parys where that he slepte, wherin were many abylments whyche shold wel suffyse the chambre of a grete prynce. And in the sayd chambre were two grete standardes coverd after the guyse[11] of Fraunce. That one was ful of clothe of gold and sylke, and that other of harnoys[12] and of many other thynges. Thenne sayd Vyenne to Ysabeau, "By my fayth, fayr syster, I have noo grete mervaylle of this yonge knyght Parys, though of hym be maad grete mencyon, for

---

[1]   *lived*
[2]   *sudden attack of fever*
[3]   *asked*
[4]   *greeted*
[5]   *was appropriate*
[6]   *more*
[7]   *friendship*
[8]   *equipment*
[9]   *fowles of chace, hunting birds*
[10]   *recount (tell)*
[11]   *style of armor or weapons*
[12]   *arms (equipment)*

the ordynaunce[13] of thyse thynges shewe wel that he is of grete valure." And in byholdyng of these thynges she sawe a coverture[14] of an hors alle whyte. And hyr semed that it was the same that the knyght bare that wanne the prys[15] of the joustes that was made in the cyté of Vyenne, and that had the shelde of crystal and the garlond, whych she tolde to Ysabeau. And Ysabeau ansuerd to hyr, "Never thynke ye soo, for all day been made semblable[16] covertures and tokenes whyte wherof ye may wel be deceyved." Vyenne enforced[17] alleweye hyrself to take better hede, and of the grete joye that she had, she sayd to hyr moder, "Madame I am a lytel crased[18] and sodenly taken, wherfore, yf it playse you, I wold fayne[19] reste a lytel in this chambre. And late me be alle allone wyth my suster Ysabeau, for I wyl have none other." And anone eche body avoyded[20] oute of the chambre, and Ysabeau dyd shytte the dore that none myght come in.

4   Thenne sayd Vyenne, "Now we shal see yf we may fynde ony thynge that we may have better knowleche of, for myn herte sayth yes." After that they had serched and vysyted alle the chambre, they cam on a syde of the chambre where they fonde a lytel dore, of whyche henge[21] a lytel keye by a thwonge,[22] and anone they opened the dore and entred therin. And there was a lytel chambre whyche was twelve foot longe, and was an oratorye where as was the magesté[23] of our Lord Jhesu Cryste upon a lytel aulter and at eche corner was a canstyke[24] of sylver, and thyder cam Parys for to make hys sacrefyse[25] whan he aroos and whan he wente to hys bedde. And there were the thre baners that the noble knyght Parys had wonne in the cyté of Parys, and the thre jewellys of the thre damoyselles aforesayd. And in the same place was also the shelde of crystal [fol. 11r] and the garlond that Vyenne delyverd to hym whan he wanne the prys at the joustes in the cyté of Vyenne. And all these he kepte secrete in that place.

5   And whan Vyenne sawe these thynges, she was sure that Parys was he whome she had so moche desyred to knowe and that soo moche honour had doon to hyr. And for the grete joye that she had, she sette hyr doun on the grounde[26] and there abode a grete whyle and coude not speke a word. And after, she spake to Ysabeau and sayd, "My swete syster, blessyd and preysed be our Lord of thys good journey,[27] for me thynketh I shold never

---

[13] *arrangement (display of arms)*
[14] *covering (trappings for a horse)*
[15] *prize*
[16] *similar*
[17] *encouraged*
[18] *sick*
[19] *gladly (willingly)*
[20] *departed*
[21] *hung*
[22] *thong*
[23] *a representation of Christ in glory*
[24] *candlestick*
[25] *prayer offering*
[26] *floor*
[27] *fortune (undertaking)*

departe oute of thys chambre. Alas, I have so longe abyden[28] to know who he was that so swetely played in his instrumentes so nygh unto me, and now he is so ferre."[29] And thenne Ysabeau began to repreve hyr and sayd to hyr, "Swete lady, I praye you that ye say ne do ony thyng whiche myght torne you to folye, and be ye ruled by wysedom and reason, for notwythstondyng that Parys have so moche good and vertues, yet ye ought to consyder that he is not egal[30] to you in lygnage[31] ne in estate.[32] For I knowe wel that many noble and puyssaunt[33] lordes have demaunded you in maryage and love you and do grete thynges for you, and also the honour of Parys, whyche is your vayssal and subget, is not egall ne worthy unto you."

6   Thenne Vyenne was moche angry on Ysabeau and began to say, "A veray God, I am wel dyscomforted[34] and deceyved by thee, that thus agaynsayest[35] me of hym that I so longe have desyred to knowe. Alas, I had supposed that in noo thyng ye wold have dysplayed me. And in good fayth I say to thee that this man I wyl love and demaunde. And I promyse thee in good fayth that, yf thou ony more gaynsaye me, I shal slee myself and thenne thou shalt be cause of my deth, for I wyl not lese hym that I have so longe loved. But I say to thee for trouthe, that yf thou ever say to me suche wordes of my frende Parys, that thou shalt never after have space to say them ageyn another tyme, for yf thou consyderest wel hys noble condycyons[36] and custommes,[37] thou sholdest preyse hym better than thou doost. And knowest thou not wel that the kyng of Fraunce wold that it had coste hym half hys royame that hys sone Lowys were as valyaunte as Parys is? And also there be many notable lordes that desyre to knowe his name and to have hys amytye.[38] Thenne take hede and byholde, by my fayth, yf ever thou sawe [fol. 11v] man that myght be compared to hym. Certaynly alle vertues been in hym. And sythe[39] that fortune hath brought me to hys love, he is worthy to have my love and yet more than is in me. And have I not reason and cause thenne to love hym, whyche hath doon to me so grete good and honour, and doubtyng[40] noo peryl of hys persone. And is it not wel grete worshyp to my fader to have for vaissal and subget the beste knyght that is in all the world? For in alle the world is noo knyght that I wold forsake Parys fore, ne oone that hath doon so moche for me." And thus to speke of the feates of Parys she coude not stynte.[41]

---

[28] *waited*

[29] *far*

[30] *equal*

[31] *lineage (pedigree)*

[32] *social status*

[33] *powerful*

[34] *injured*

[35] *contradicts*

[36] *circumstances (social status)*

[37] *habits (practices)*

[38] *friendship*

[39] *since (because)*

[40] *fearing*

[41] *stop*

7   Thenne came two damoyselses knockyng at the chambre dore sayeng, "Vyenne, ye must come to my lady." And Ysabeau sprange oute sayeng that she shold come anone. And Vyenne, seyng that she must nedes departe fro thens, sayd to Ysabeau, "My suster, syth we must departe hens, late us take somme of these jewellys. And we shal kepe them secretly tyl that Parys be comen, and we shal see what countenaunce[42] he shal make in hymself." Thenne they took the colyer[43] and the whyte baner of Vyenne and other jewellys and hydde them under theyr clothes and wente into the chambre of messyre Jaques. But Vyenne desyred gretly to speke with Paris and thought longe or[44] he came home. And in the mene whyle, messire Jaques recoverd of his maladye and bycam alle hool wherof Vyenne had grete joye, but she durst not shewe it.

---

[42] *expression*

[43] *collar or band worn by knights as an identifying ornament*

[44] *before*

Chapter 8: How Parys and Edward retorned oute of Braband.

1   After certeyn tyme that Parys had be in Braband wyth hys felowe Edward, he desyred strongely to see the fayr Vyenne, for the love of hyr destrayned[1] hym moche strongly. Nevertheles, he durst not telle it to hys felowe to the ende that he shold take noo dysplaysyr of hys departyng. And sone after the space of fyve dayes, Parys receyved a letter that hys fader was seek and thenne he sayd to Edward, "Ryght dere brother and felowe, pleseth it you to wete that my fader is sore seke, and me semeth it were good that we departed, yf ye consente, but I praye you that ye take noo desplaysyr in thys departyng for, yf it playse God, we shal sone retorne." And Edward, seyng the juste reason of Parys and hys good wylle, sayd to hym that he was wel content and plesyd. Wherfore incontynente they departed oute of Braband [fol. 12r] and came into the cyté of Vyenne, of whose comyng messyr Jaques had soverayn playsyr, specyally bycause he had herde that Parys hys sone had doon valyauntly feates of armes.

2   Now it happed that whan Parys was arryved at home wyth hys fader, lyke as he was accustomed alleweye tofore,[2] or he wente to hys bedde he wente to make hys orysons[3] and prayers. And after he advysed[4] yf he lacked ony thynge, and fonde that tho thynges that he loved beste were taken aweye, wherof he was moche angry, and quasi[5] half in despayr in suche wyse that alle the nyght he coude not slepe. And whan it came in the mornyng, he came to hys moder and sayd, "Moder how is it that ye have not kepte my chambre cloos and shytte? For I lacke certayn thynges whyche I wold not gladly lese, and have for them grete dysplaysir." To whom hys moder ansuerd, "My sone, by my fayth, there never entred therin persone, but on a tyme whan your fader was seek came my lady Dyane and

---

[1] *compelled*

[2] *before*

[3] *acts of devotion*

[4] *considered*

[5] *almost [OF]*

hyr doughter Vyenne, and whan they had vysyted your fader, they wente al aboute for to see thys castel, and thenne they entred into your chambre. But I can not thynke that they took ony thyng for they taryed not longe, sauf onely Vyenne whyche taryed onely allone sauf hyr damoysel, bycause she was eavl at ease[6] in hyr hert. Wherfore, my sone, I praye you to take noo dysplaysyr." And thenne Parys sayd to hymself, "Yf none other theef have taken it sauf she, I shal not be dyscoverd. Nevertheles, I wote[7] never yf Vyenne hath taken it awaye for onythynge."

3   And after he arayed hymself and cladde hym moche nobly, and wente to do the reverence[8] to the daulphyn, and to dame Dyane, and after to Vyenne theyr doughter. And the dolphyn receyved hym moche curtoysly. And the daulphyn demaunded hym tydynges and of many other thynges. And whan the fayre lady Vyenne sawe Parys, of the grete desyre that she had to see hym and of the grete love that she bare to hym, alle hyr chere[9] was coloured lyke a fresshe rose in the monthe of Maye, and coude not be contente ne fylled to beholde hyr fayre love and frende Parys. And the more she byhelde hym, the more grewe and encreaced hyr love toward hym. And Parys, beyng tofore the dolphyn on his knee moche humbly, durst not loke on Vyenne. But in hys herte he had grete payne, and who had wel beholden hym had wel seen in his [fol. 12v] vysage[10] hys thought. And after that the dolphyn had demaunded[11] hym of that it plased hym, Parys took leve of the dolphyn and of my lady Dyane, and of Vyenne, theyr doughter, and retorned home to hys faders hous.

4   After a fewe dayes, Vyenne, in suche wyse as love destrayned[12] hyr, said to her damoysel Ysabeau, "My suster, knowe ye for trouth that me semeth that Parys is moche pensyf, and I byleve that it is for hys thynges whyche he fyndeth not in his oratorye. Me semeth it is beste that we lete hym have knowleche that we have them." Isabeau ansuerd, "It were wel doon soo, but that it be doon honestly[13] and secretely." Thenne sayd Vyenne, "I shal advyse the manere." After certeyn dayes Vyenne sayd to hyr moder, "Madame, I lete you wete that I am a lytel charged[14] in my conscyence, and I wold fayn[15] confesse me to somme good persone. And it is tolde me that the bysshop of Saynt Laurence is a moche honest man and devoute, wherfore, madame, I praye you to sende for hym that I myght speke wyth hym." And my lady Dyane, seyng the good wylle of hyr doughter, sente for to fetche the bysshop. And Vyenne confessyd hyr to hym moche devoutely spekyng alwaye of our Lord and of hys commaundementes, and after that she was confessyd, she prayed the bysshop that he wold come ageyn on the morne, for she fonde grete comforte in his wordes, and that she wold telle hym somme thynges in grete secrete. And on the morne

---

[6] eavl at ease, *ill at ease*

[7] *know*

[8] *ceremonious greeting (act of obeisance)*

[9] *face*

[10] *expression*

[11] *asked*

[12] *compelled*

[13] *honorably*

[14] *heavy (full)*

[15] *eagerly (willingly)*

the bysshop came ageyn to Vyenne, and Vyenne sayd to hym thus, "My ghoostly[16] fader, somme thynges have been taken away in a place, the whiche longen[17] to Parys, sone of messyre Jaques. And the persone that hath them hath therof conscyence.[18] And therfore I praye you as moche as I may that, by your benygnyté,[19] ye say to hym that yf he may, he come tomorne hyther wyth you." And the bysshop, whyche advysed hym noo thyng of the entencyon and thought of Vyenne, said that he shold brynge hym wythoute faute.[20]

---

[16] *spiritual*

[17] *belong*

[18] *scruples*

[19] *goodness (benignity)*

[20] *fail*

Chapter 9: How Vyenne dyscuverd hyr courage to Parys.

1   On the morne, the bysshop came moche dylygently and brought Parys wyth hym. And Vyenne salewed[1] Parys wythoute to make only semblaunte[2] of love, and Parys rendred hys salewes ageyn moche humbly. And thenne Vyenne wythdrewe hyr fro the bysshop and the other, and said to Parys, "It is not longe sythe[3] ye were [fol. 13r] goon into Braband, and that I accompanyed my lady my moder for to goo vysyte your fader whyche thenne was seek. And we sawe and byhelde al the castel untyl we came to your oratorye, and there I sawe certayn jewellys whyche moche wel pleased me, and I took them and have kepte them untyl thys present tyme. And I shal now rendre them to you ageyn. And therfor I praye you that yf I have doon ony dysplaysyr or maad ony defaulte[4] that ye wyl pardonne me, for I promyse to you by my fayth that I have doon it for none evyl." To whome Parys answerd humbly and wyth grete reverence and sayd moche curtoysly, "Madame, by your curtoyse ye came to vysyte my fader, of whyche vysytacyon not onely my fader but alle our frendes have receyved grete and soverayn honour, wherfore myn excellent lady, my fader, my moder, and I been alle youres and alle that we have also. And yf by adventure[5] your ladyshyp had ony playsyr to take of my jewellys, I ensure you by my fayth that myn hert hath therin moche gretter playsyr than hert of man may thynke, yet more shold have yf the sayd jewellys were better the half than they be. Soo thenne I praye you, ryght honourable damoysel, that ye wyl pardonne me for not al onely these jewelles, whyche been of lytel valewe, but my fader, my moder, and I been al youres and al redy to obeye to your servyce. And knowe ye verayly that it is not longe sythen that the sayd jewels were by a Frensshe knyght gyven to me."

2   Thenne sayd Vyenne, "Ye nede not to say to me fro whens these jewels ben comen, for I knowe them as wel as ye." And Vyenne sayd, "I mervaylle me gretely how ye so longe

---

[1] *greeted*

[2] *indication (semblance)*

[3] *since*

[4] *mistake (omission)*

[5] *chance*

have hydde your love fro me. I praye you as moche as I may, and by the fayth that ye have toward me, that ye say to me the trouthe of that whyche I shal demaunde you, for moche I desyre it to knowe." Thenne sayd Parys, "Ryght honourable damoysel, ye ought not to praye me, where ye have power to commaunde me, for alle that your ladyshyp shal plese to demaunde me I shal say to you the trouth wyth good hert and good wylle." Thenne sayd Vyenne, "I wyl fyrst that ye say the trouthe that yf ye were he, that in suche a yere cam every nyght syngyng and sownyng[6] instrumentes so swetely tofore my chambre. After, I wyl that ye telle me yf ye wanne the justes that were made the fyrst day of May in this cyté, and yf ye bare awaye the [fol. 13v] shelde of crystal and the chapelet[7] whyche I have seen in your oratorye. After, I wyl that ye say to me yf ye wanne the justes the eightene day of Septembre whyche were made in the cyté of Parys, where as were so many noble knyghtes and barons, and yf ye had goten there the two baners whyche I have seen in your oratorye. And I praye you that ye telle to me yf ye have doon to me suche servyce, for suche thynges ye ought not to hyde. And yf by adventure ye have doon them for the love of my fader or of hys courte, we be moche holden[8] to you and be bounden to thanke you. And yf by adventure for ony lady or for the love of me ye have doon it, I thanke you as moche as I may, and it is wel reason that ye therfore be rewarded." And yet sayd Vyenne to Parys, "Knowe ye for trouthe that it is long sythe that I have desyred to knowe, and yet desyre strongly to knowe it. Wherfore, yf ye wyl do me ony playsyr, I praye you that ye say to me the trouthe wythout levyng of ony onely[9] thynge or word."

3 Thenne sayd Parys, moche humbly with grete shamefastnes that he had to utter the folye that he had enterprysed,[10] "Ryght honourable and fayr ladye, I am not worthy to be named hym whiche hath doon thys whyche it hath pleased you to demaunde of me. But notwythstondyng that I be a man of lytel estate, I humbly supplye[11] you that in caas ye shal fynde dysplaysyr in my wordes, that it playse you to pardonne me, and that ye take noo dysplaysyr in that I shal say, for your noblesse shal not be the lasse in valure. For my caas[12] enforceth me to say that whyche is to me folye to thynke." Thenne Parys, al shamefast and in grete reverence kneleng upon hys knee, sayd, "Ryght worshypful damoysel, Parys your indigne[13] servaunt is he of whome ye have spoken and demaunded, and shal to you obeye and serve in al thynges that ye have me demaunded. For sythe that I have had ony rememberaunce, my wylle and my thought hath be submysed[14] to your persone and shal be as longe as I shal lyve." Thenne sayd Vyenne, "Parys, my swete frende, it is not now tyme that I make ansuer to your wordes, for it shold be overlonge to recounte. But that not wythstondyng, I wyl wel that ye knowe that your love destrayneth[15] me so stron-

---

[6] *playing (making music)*
[7] *garland*
[8] *obligated, indebted (beholden)*
[9] *single*
[10] *undertaken*
[11] *supplicate*
[12] *circumstances*
[13] *unworthy*
[14] *submitted*
[15] *compels*

gely that there is no thynge in the world that I love soo moche as you. Wherfore abyde in good hope joyously for, yf it playse God, ye shal see that thys whyche I say [fol. 14r] shal be trewe." Thenne sayd Parys, "Madame, who may thynke the joyousté[16] in whyche I am by your ansuer whiche is to me ryght swete, for I never supposed to have had so swete an ansuer of you but for to have endured in payne and in languysshyng. For not onely to me, but unto a kyng shold be overmoche to have your love, and I praye God that I may doo suche thynges as may be to you playsaunt, and that I never lyve to do to you thynge that shold desplayse you ne torne you to melancolye."[17]

4 And thus departed that one fro that other in gretter love than tofore, and took terme[18] to see eche other ageyn as hastely as they myght. And Vyenne retorned more joyously than she shewed and wente into hyr moders chambre. And after, the bysshop departed and Parys accompanyed hym unto his paleys[19] and took leve of hym and retorned home unto hys faders lodgyng, and after tolde to Edward hys felowe alle the parlament[20] that he had had wyth Vyenne. And Edward sayd to hym, "Fayre brother and frende, herein is no jape[21] ne truffes,[22] but I praye you that ye do your thynges secretly, for there ben many false tonges." And Vyenne was moche more joyous than she had ben accustomed, and Parys also. And the sayd Parys and Edward hys felowe made grete chyvalryes and dyd grete armes, whyche were moche playsaunt to the fayre Vyenne.

5 Thenne it happed that after certeyn tyme, seyng the dolphyn that hys doughter was come to fyftene yere of age, treated[23] for to gyve to hyr an husbond. And many tymes he had ben requyred[24] of many noble pryncis, but bycause he had but hyr onely and no moo sones ne doughters, unnethe[25] he wold consente. And in treatyng thus of maryage, Parys herde somme thynges wherof he was sore ennoyed in hymself and thought, "Why thynke not I to have this noble lady whyche is so moch desyred of so many noble prynces and barons?" And sore bewaylled hymself, and dyd soo moche that he spake to Vyenne and sayd, "O swete Vyenne, where is your fayr and agreable promesse that ye made to me whan I departed fro you, and how may it be that your fader speketh for to marye you?"

6 Whan Vyenne herde Parys speke in thys manere, she sayd to hym, "Parys, yf my fader speke to me of maryage, it is noo grete mervaylle, for I may not deffende[26] hym. Nevertheles I have not consented to ony maryage, and ye knowe wel that maryage is [fol. 14v] nothyng worth wythout the consentyng of bothe partyes. Wherfore I praye you to be contente, for I promyse to you that I shal never have man in mariage but you, and I wold that it shold be shortly accomplysshed, yf it pleased God, honestly and justly

---

[16] *joy*

[17] *sadness*

[18] took terme, *appointed a time*

[19] *palace*

[20] *conversation (speech)*

[21] *joke*

[22] *trifles (insignificant things)*

[23] *negotiated*

[24] *requested (asked)*

[25] *hardly*

[26] *forbid*

and not in synne ne in ordure.[27] Therfore I wyl that ye assaye[28] one thynge, which shal be moche dyffycyle to doo and ryght peryllous, but nevertheles it byhoveth[29] that it be doon." Thenne sayd Parys, "Honourable lady, that whyche shal playse you to commaunde me, I shal accomplisshe it with good hert though I shold deye." And thanne sayd Vyenne, "I wyl that incontynent ye say to your fader that he goo to my lord my fader and requyre hym that he gyve me in maryage to you, and that herein ther be no deffaute."[30] And whan Parys herde the wylle and desyre of Vyenne, he was quasi al abasshed[31] and sayd, "Ryght honourable lady, and how wyl ye that I deye thus? I praye you, yf it playse you, that it be not doo." Thenne Veynne sayd, "Sette ye so lytel by me[32] that ye wyl not enterpryse[33] this? Alas where is your entendement?[34] Certes it must nedes be doon." Incontynent Parys ansuerd, "Worshypfull lady, sythe it playseth you, I shal accomplysshe your commandement though I shold deye therefore an hondred thousand tymes."

7   And thus took leve of Vyenne and wente to hys fader incontynent and sayd to hym, "Dere fader, alwaye ye have shewed to me grete love, wherfore I byseche almyghty God that he rewarde you lyke as I desyre. Dere and honourable fader, I wold praye you of one thynge, and bycause it is doubtous,[35] I wyl that ye promyse it to me tofore I say it to you, for ellys I wyl not say it unto you." And hys fader sayd to hym, "My sone, there is nothyng in the world that I may doo for thee, but I shal accomplysshe it by the grace of God; therfor, say to me thy playsyr and wylle." And thenne Parys tolde to hys fader a parte of the pryveté[36] and promesse that he had wyth Vyenne, by cause he shold wyth the better wylle doo that whyche he wold requyre[37] hym. Thenne sayd Parys to his fader, "The prayer that I praye and requyre you is that it playse you to say to the dolphyn that he gyve to me his doughter to wyf and in maryage. And I humbly byseche you that herein ye wyl not faylle me." And messire Jaques, heryng hys sone thys speke, almoost he was fro hymself for the grete folye that he sayd to hym. And he sayd in reprevyng hym that he never shold speke more of that fayte,[38] for he wold not deye for hys doughter, and [fol. 15r] that he shold demaunde of hym somme other thynge, for it were grete folye to speke to hym of suche a thynge. And Parys sayd, "Worshypful fader, as moche peryllous is it to me as to you, therfor I am not abasshed[39] though ye reffused to doo it. But love enforceth and constreyneth[40]

---

[27] *filth*

[28] *attempt*

[29] *is necessary*

[30] *fault (neglect)*

[31] *upset (surprised)*

[32] Sette ye so lytel by me, *Do you esteem me so little*

[33] *undertake*

[34] *will (intention)*

[35] *dangerous (doubtful)*

[36] *private counsel*

[37] *ask*

[38] *deed*

[39] *upset (surprised)*

[40] *compels*

me so strongley that I am half confused, and am as wel contente that he[41] do it not as to doo it, but that ye do your devoyr[42] onely." And so longe Parys prayed hys fader that he promysed hym to doo it.

---

[41] *the dauphin*

[42] *duty (best effort)*

Chapter 10: How messire Jaques demaunded of the doulphyn hys doughter Vyenne in maryage for hys sone Parys.

1 Thenne went messire Jaques to the dolphyn, all chaunged of colour, and sayd to hym, "My ryght redoubted[1] and soverayn lord, a certeyn requeste is made to me whyche I must say unto you, the whiche me semeth is of passyng lytel reason, and therfor it must be at your mercy. And in caas ye fynde therin dysplaysyr, that ye pardonne me and to take noo regarde to[2] my grete folye." The doulphyn, trustyng in the grete wysedom of messire Jaques, graunted hym to say whatsomever he wold. Thenne sayd messire Jaques, "Myn hye and soverayn lord, Parys my sone hath prayed me so moche that I shold requyre of you Vyenne your doughter to be hys wyf, the whiche thynge is not onely to say, but also to thynke, grete presumpsyon and grete folye, but the love of my sone constrayneth[3] me soo strongly that by force[4] I must say it to you." And sodeynly the doulphyn was moeved in grete felonnye[5] and wold not suffre[6] hym to ende hys wordes, but repreved hym moche hardly sayeng, "Vylayne[7] and vassal that thou arte, how kepest thou my worshyp?[8] By God I shal wel chastyse you that ye shal never thynke suche thynges." And comaunded hym that incontynent he shold departe thens and that never he ne hys sone shold come in hys syght. Wherfore messire Jaques departed thens moche rebuked, holdyng doun hys heed, and retorned into hys hous and tolde to hys sone Parys al that had be sayd and doon bytwene hym and the doulphyn, wherof Parys thanked moche hys fader.

2 The doulphyn wente in grete thought thurgh the paleys,[9] havyng grete indygnacyon[10] and alle angry in soo moche that none durst speke to hym ne come in his waye. And he beyng thus in thys manere [fol. 15v], he sente for his doughter Vyenne and made hyr to come to hym, and sayd to hyr, "We have had wordes of grete dysplaysyr. Thys vyllayne, messyre Jaques hath sayd to us that we shold gyve you to wyf and in maryage to hys sone Parys. Advyse you what wysedom it were, by God. Or that I shold do it, I wold rather

---

[1] *revered*

[2] *take noo regarde to, pay no attention to*

[3] *compels*

[4] *necessity*

[5] *ill-will*

[6] *allow*

[7] *Commoner (Tenant)*

[8] *dignity (social standing)*

[9] *palace*

[10] *wrath (displeasure)*

make you a nonne or a menchon.[11] And it shal not be longe to but that ye shal be hyely maryed, so that ye shal holde you contente. And here I swere to you that yf it were not for the grete servyces that he hath doon to me, incontynent I shold do smyte off hys hede." And when Vyenne sawe hyr fader in so grete angre ayenst messyre Jaques and hys sone, she sente for to seche[12] Edward for to come speke to hyr. And whan Edward was come, Vyenne sayd to hym, "Edward, it is soo that my fader is moche angry ayenst messire Jaques and ayenst Parys, wherof I have grete dysplaysyr and have grete doubte[13] that my fader wyl do somme harme to Parys. And therfore I wyl that ye say to hym that he kepe hymself in the moost secretest wyse that he may, and I shal also see the manere yf I may appease his felonnye[14] and angre." Thenne Edward incontynent took leve of Vyenne and went and sayd to Paris all that Vyenne had sayd to hym and sayd, "Fayr brother, me semeth that it were good that ye departed oute of this contrey for to absente[15] you for a space of tyme, for it may be that to the doulphyn shal longe endure hys angre, as I understonde by that whyche Vyenne hath sayd to me." Thenne ansuerd Parys, "Sythe that ye have counceylled me soo, I shal so do, notwythstondyng that it shal be to me a sorouful and an hevy departyng. But er I departe I shal take leve of Vyenne, though I shold deye."

3   Thenne Parys dyd soo moche that he spake unto Vyenne on a derke nyght at a lowe wyndowe where as they myght wel say what they wold. "I am certeyn," sayd Vyenne, "that my fader hath wylle to hurte you, wherof I lyve in grete melancolye, for in al the world is no thynge that I love so moche as you. And yf by adventure ye deye, I wyl not lyve." Thenne sayd Parys, "Honourable lady, it semeth me beste that I departe fro hens a certeyn tyme tyl my lord your fader be more peased[16] and hath passed hys evyll wylle, how be it that it shal be to me a moche sorouful thynge to wythdrawe me fro you, for my lyf shal be moche hevy.[17] Nevertheles, I shal accomplysshe your wylle in alle that ye shall [fol. 16r] commaunde me, whatsomever come therof." And Vyenne, seyng the good wylle of Parys, after many wordes she sayd to hym, "Parys my frende, I knowe well the grete love that ye bere to me, and sythe it so is, I swere to you by my fayth that ye shal never departe fro thys cyté wythoute that I goo wyth you, for it is my wylle. Wherfore, as sone as ye may, make you redy of al thynges necessarye and fynde ye the manere that we may escape oute of the royame of Fraunce, and that we may goo into somme other lordshyppe where as we may lyve joyously and surely.[18] Nevertheles, tofore or we departe from hens, I wyl that ye promyse two thynges. The fyrst is that ye touche not my body unto the tyme that we be lawfully maryed. The second is that Ysabeau parte[19] in al the goodes that we shal have. And other thynge wyl I not as for thys present tyme, but that onely our departyng may be

---

[11] *nun*

[12] *seek*

[13] *fear*

[14] *anger*

[15] *go away*

[16] *appeased*

[17] *sad*

[18] *safely*

[19] *share*

shortely. And I shal pourveye[20] somme jewels and money for our necessyté." And al thys Parys promysed to hyr, and eche departed fro other for to adresse[21] suche thynges as to them shold be necessarye.

4 Whan Parys was departed fro Vyenne, he wente to a man named George and sayd to hym, "George, my frende, alwaye I have trusted in you and have alwaye loved you, wherfore I praye you now that to thys that I shal say you ye faylle me not, for I promyse you ye shal not lese therby." And George promysed to hym to doo al that shal be to hym possyble wyth ryght good hert. And thenne Parys sayd to hym, "Knowe ye for cartayn that I have wrath and rancour to a man of thys toune for certayn desplaysyr that he hath doon to me, wherfore I wyl slee hym. And incontynent as I have slayne hym, I wyl departe out of the royame of Fraunce; wherfore I praye you that ye wyl goo to Aygues Mortes[22] and that ye there make redy a galeye[23] furnysshed[24] of al thynges necessarye tyl that we be arryved there as we wold be. And also I praye you that ye doo ordeyne fro hens to Aygues Mortes fro fyve myle to fyve myle alwaye good horses redy, to the ende that we may surely[25] refresshe us yf it be nede. And also I wyl that ye do thys as secretly as ye may, and loo, here is money ynough for to furnysshe these sayd thynges." George sayd, "I shal doo al thys gladly." And incontynent made hym redy, and whan he came to Aygues Mortes he hyred a galeye and establisshed[26] al the passages and dyd wel al that Parys had charged [fol. 16v] hym, and came ageyn and tolde to Parys how he had pourveyed al that he had charged hym, wherof Parys was moche joyous. And anone Parys wente and told to Vyenne that alle thynges that she had comaunded were doon. And thenne they concluded that the nexte nyght folowyng that at a certeyn houre eche of them shold be redy. Thenne he took leve of hyr and wente home and bad George to take two hors out of hys stable, and that he shold sadle them and abyde hym wythoute[27] the cyté in a certayn place tyl he shold come. And Edward, the felowe of Parys, wyste noo thynge of alle thys, wherof he was moche abasshed[28] and mervayllously[29] angry whan that he knewe it.

---

[20] *provide (arrange)*
[21] *prepare*
[22] *Aigues Mortes, French Mediterranean port*
[23] *seagoing ship with sails and oars*
[24] *equipped (supplied)*
[25] *safely*
[26] *arranged*
[27] *outside*
[28] *downcast*
[29] *wondrously (greatly)*

Chapter 11: How Parys ladde awaye Vyenne and Ysabeau by nyght.

1   Whan Parys was pourveyed of money and of al other thynges beyng to them necessarye, he wente allone the secretest wyse that he myght and came to the place emprysed[1] at the houre taken, and he made a tokene[2] whiche Vyenne knewe. And anone Vyenne and Ysabeau cladde them in mannes araye and lepen oute of the castel by a fauce porte.[3] And so came these two damoyselles to the place where as Parys was allone, whyche awayted upon theyr comyng. And incontynent they departed and went where as theyr horses were, whom they took and rode as faste as they myght. And George rode alwaye tofore bycause to knowe wel the waye. And whyles they thus rode, aroos a storme wyth a grete rayne whyche endured tyl on the morne at nyght. And thenne they arryved nygh unto the lytel towne, but they entred not bycause they wold not be knowen[4] and went and lodged them in a lytel chyrche nygh unto the toun, where they fonde a chapelayn whiche receyved them gladly the best wyse he myght. And thenne whan the nyght came, Parys and the chapelayn slepte in a lytel hous joynyng to[5] the chyrche, George and Parys servaunte slepten in the stable with the bestes, and Vyenne and Ysabeau slepten in the chyrche. And in the mornyng erly they wente lyghtly[6] to horsback and rode tyl they came nyghe unto a ryver whyche was rysen hye bycause of the rayne that had fallen. Thenne Parys was moche angry bycause he sawe wel that it was moche peryllous, and sayd to George that he shold serche and advyse somme good place where they myght passe over. And George wythdrewe hym a lytel from them and chaas[7] a place whiche [fol. 17r] thought hym good, and took the ryver wyth hys hors. And whan he was in the myddes[8] of the streme, hys hors faylled hym that he was drowned and hys hors also.

2   Parys, seyng that George was drowned, was moche sore abasshed and durst make noo semblaunte[9] bycause that fayre Vyenne shold have noo melancolye. And after, Vyenne demaunded of Parys where George was bycomen, and Parys answerd to hyr that he had sent hym for to serche somme good passage, and they wold torne into the chyrche ageyn tyl George were comen. And Vyenne ansuerd to hym that it playsed to her wel soo to doo, for she had grete doubte and fere for to passe the water.

3   And whan they were in in the chyrche, Parys was moche aferde to abyde longe in that place, for he sawe that it was not sure,[10] wherfore he demaunded the chapelayn yf they myght in ony wyse passe that water. And the chapelayn sayd not in thre dayes tyl the water were decreced and avaled.[11] And Parys sayd to hym that he shold goo into the towne to

---

[1] *undertaken*

[2] *signal*

[3] fauce porte, *secret door (postern door)*

[4] *recognized*

[5] joynyng to, *beside*

[6] *quickly*

[7] *chose*

[8] *middle*

[9] *sign*

[10] *safe*

[11] decreced and avaled, *receded and abated*

seche[12] and see yf he myght fynde ony men that wold make a brydge soo that they myght pass, and that he shold spare for no money. "For I shal paye to them as moche as they wyl have." And the chapelayn sayd that he shold doo hys beste. Thus dyd Parys noo thynge but thynke how they myght passe the ryver. Now leve we Parys and torne we to the doulphyn, whych had lost his fayre doughter Vyenne.

---

[12] *search*

Chapter 12: How the doulpyn dyd doo serche and seche Vyenne by hys servauntes.

1   On the morne that Vyenne was loste and departed fro the hous of hyr fader, and that the doulphyn knewe it, he supposed to have goon oute of hys wytte, and al the courte was troubled, and sente hastely men on horsback and afote by dyvers partyes[1] the moost secretely that he myght, and prayed them that they shold brynge home to hym Vyenne, quyck[2] or dede. It happed by adventure that one of his men afote that was sente to seche Vyenne came into the towne where as the chapelayn was comen to seche men to make the brydge. The foteman[3] demaunded every man yf they had had seen two damoyselles whyche were fledde fro the doulphyns courte. Thenne the chapelayn said to hym that it was not longe syth suche tweyne departed wyth other men.

2   And the man supposed that the sayd chapelayn had sayd it [fol. 17v] in jape[4] or in mockyng, and sayd that the doulphyn was moche angry and had sworne that yf ony man or woman knewe where they were and shewed it not, that he shold make them to lose theyr hedes. And whan the chapelayn herde these wordes, he remembred hym of them that were hyd in hys hous and in grete drede sayd to hym[5] that he shold tarye there a lytel, and that for the love of my lord doulphyn he[6] wold gladly seche for them, and as sone as he myght fynde tydynges of them he shold lete hym wyte.[7] And so departed fro thens and retorned home ageyn, and tolde al thys to Parys, and what he had herde in the toune, sayeng also that he doubted[8] that it was for them of hys companye. Wherfore he sayd to hym ferthermore, "Syr, I praye you that ye departe from hens and suffre not that I lese my lyf. But take ye the best counceyl ye can, for there ben fyfty men on horsback that seche you."

3   Whan Parys herde hym say this, it nedeth not to demaunde yf he were hevy and melancolyous, and for the grete sorowe that he had, he chaunged al his colour. And he sayd to the chapelayn, "I praye you that ye tarye a lytel and I shal make you an ansure." And thenne Parys went to Vyenne for to telle to hir al thys feat. And whan Vyenne sawe hym entre and so chaunged in hys colour, sayd to Paris, "What tydynges brynge ye whyche are

---

[1] *directions (groups)*
[2] *alive*
[3] *foot soldier*
[4] *jest*
[5] *the soldier*
[6] *the chaplain*
[7] *know*
[8] *feared*

so pale and your colour chaunged? I praye you as hertely as I can that it playse you to telle me." Thenne Parys sayd to hyr, "The tydynges that I brynge ben evyl for you and for me, for shortly shal be accomplisshed[9] our adventure,[10] and therfore I wyl slee myself." And also he said complaynyng, "O God, how my lyf is sorowful and hevy to have brought thys excellent lady as ye ar in suche daunger. O good God, why gaf thou not to me the deth tofore or that I fette[11] hir out of hyr faders hous? O alas my fader and my moder, what shal befalle of you whan the doulphyn shal knowe that I have stolen from hym hys doughter? O my good felowe Edward, why counceylled not I wyth thee tofore or I had doon thys folye?" And after he retorned to Vyenne sayenge, "And what shal falle of[12] you my lady, whan your fader shal see you? Certes I thynke that how cruel that he be, whan he shal see your noble persone, his hert shal not suffre to do you ony harme. O God almyghty, do to me that grace that I onely may bere the payn of this fayt[13] and none other. O lady, unhappy was that day for you and for me whan [fol. 18r] fyrst ye had acqueyntaunce of me." And whan Parys had fynysshed hys complaynte, he tolde to Vyenne al that the chapelayn had sayd to hym, and forthwyth, as a persone despayred, took hys swerde and wold have ryven[14] it thurgh hys body.

4   And Vyenne, as vertuouse and valyaunte, took to hyr hert[15] and took the swerde fro hym and comforted hym and sayd, "O free[16] knyght, my joye, my lyf, and my solace, what wyl ye doo? Know ye not wel that who that sleeth hymself wytyngly, sleeth the soule and the body? And yf ye deye, I assure you I shal deye also, and so shal ye be cause of my deth as wel as of your owne. O Parys, where is your wysedom and your prowesse? Now whan ye shold have moste strengthe and moost vertuous courage, ye be aferde. O my knyght, thys is noo newe thynge that the persones that lyven in thys world have trybulacyons, of whatsomever lygnage they be. Certes, thys is not the courage of one so valyaunte knyght as ye be, for now whome that ye ought to comforte, she must now comforte you. And therfor, my fayr brother and frende, I praye you as moche as ye may that incontynente ye departe fro hens and that ye goo your waye. And yf ye do not so, I shal slee myself wyth your swerde, for your departyng is as grevous to me as myn shal be to you, but it byhoveth[17] to eschewe[18] of two evyls the werse. And also ye ought to consydere one thyng, that not wythstondyng the grete faulte and trespaas that I have made to my fader, yet therfore he shal not put me to deth, consydered the grete love that he hath alway had toward me. And yf ye were taken,[19] I wote wel that ye and I shold bothe deye. And yet I have good hope that myn entencyon shal come unto a good ende. For be ye sure, though

---

[9]   ended (completed)
[10]   fate (exploit)
[11]   fetched (brought)
[12]   falle of, shall befall (happen to)
[13]   deed (act)
[14]   thrust (stabbed)
[15]   courage
[16]   noble (generous)
[17]   benefits
[18]   avoid
[19]   captured

he never pardonne me, I shal never have other husbond but you, and that I promyse you be my fayth. But alle waye of one thyng I praye you, that for none other lady ye forgete not me, and whan ye shal be in another contreye wryte unto me of your adventure. And to the ende that ye the better remembre me, loo, here is a rynge of gold wyth a dyamonde, the which I praye you that ye wyl kepe for the love of me."

Chapter 13: How Parys departed from Vyenne and lefte hyr in the chyrche.

1   After moche other langage, Paris kyssed Vyenne wyth grete syghes and [fol. 18v] thoughtes, and she comforted hym the best wyse she myght, in prayeng our lord Jhesu Cryste that in short tyme she myght see hym, lyke as hyr herte desyred moost of ony thynge that was in the world. And thenne Parys departed fro Vyenne wyth grete sorowe and hevynesse. And took his waye wyth hys servaunte tyl he came to the ryver wher they coude not tofore have passed, and as despayred doubted noo thynge but entred therin, and the water was soo avaled[1] that they passed wythoute ony peryl. And they rode two dayes wythoute ony mete, for they durst not passe thurgh ony toun. And they passed tyl they came to Aygues Mortes,[2] and there he founde the galeye[3] that George had hyred, whyche anone he took and so longe saylled and rowed tyl that they arryved at Gene.[4] Parys made mervayllous[5] countenaunces[6] in the galeye, that alle they that were therin had supposed he had be a fool, for alleway he was pensyf[7] and ymagynatyf,[8] and unnethe[9] wold speke ne say a word. Thenne whan he was at Gene, he hyred hym a lodgyng and lyved there in grete hevynesse and sorowe. Now leve[10] we to speke of Parys and retorne we to Vyenne whyche abode in the chapelayns hous.

---

[1] receded
[2] Aigues Mortes, a French Mediterranean port
[3] seagoing ship with sails and oars
[4] Genoa
[5] strange
[6] expressions
[7] thoughtful (pre-occupied)
[8] brooding (distracted)
[9] hardly (with difficulty)
[10] cease (leave off)

Chapter 14: How Vyenne was founde in the chyrche by a foteman, and how she was brought ageyn to hyr fader.

1   Whan Parys was departed fro Vyenne, she abode allone wyth Ysabeau makyng the grettest sorowe of the world that it was a grete pyté[1] to byholde, lyke as she had as leef[2] to deye as to lyve. And whan she was wel wery of wepyng, and that it was force[3] that she

---

[1] pity
[2] rather
[3] necessary

must retorne to the mercy of hyr fader the doulphyn, she appeased[4] hyrself. And anone the chapelayn went for to seche the foteman[5] and brought hym into the chyrche. And whan Vyenne sawe hym, she knewe hym wel, for she had oftymes seen hym in hyr faders hows. And thys man sayd to hyr alle hys charge[6] and that many knyghtes were oute for to seche[7] hyr. And Vyenne sayd to hym, "Goo and telle them that thou hast founden me here and brynge them hyther." Thenne the man wente and fonde the knyghtes, that thenne were comen into the towne, and tolde to them how he had founden hyr, and that they shold come with hym and he wold brynge them to the place where she was. Whan the knyghtes herde these tydynges, anon eche made grete haste tyl they cam to hyr. Thenne whan they were [fol. 19r] tofore Vyenne, they salewed hyr and sayd to hyr that the doulphyn had doo seche hyr in dyvers contreyes, and after they comforted hyr and sayd that she shold not be aferde of hyr fader, for he wold doo to hyr noo desplaysyr, "For he shal have so grete joye whan he shall see you, that he shal pardonne you and appease hys yre." And than incontynent they wente to horsbacke and brought forth the chapelayn wyth hyr, to the ende that he shold excuse hyr tofore hyr fader and tolde how she was pure and clene of hyr body.

2   Now sayth the hystory that whan Vyenne was comen tofore hyr fader the doulphyn, he made toward hyr hevy and evyll chere. But notwythstondyng, Vyenne kneled doun on bothe hyr knees to the erthe sayeng and in wepyng, "Redoubted[8] fader, I see wel and knowe in myself that I have mesprysed[9] and faylled toward you, wherof I have grete desplaysyr. Nevertheles, folysshe love hath enforced me to love hym whyche is wel worthy to be beloved of the moost grettest lady of the royame of Fraunce, allewaye seen[10] the noblenes that is in hym. For I wene[11] that in alle the world is none to hym lyke ne pareylle.[12] And also, I thynke that I am not the first that have trespaced by semblable[13] reasons. Wherfore, redoubted fader, I am in your mercy, and take of me vengeaunce suche as shal playse you, and to me chastysement and example to other. Nevertheles, I wyl wel that ye knowe, and that I swere by my soule that I am as pure and clene of my body as I was that day I departed fro hens. And loo, here is the chapelayn whyche can say to you the trouthe." And thenne the chapelayn tolde how she came wyth two men, of whom that one was a moche fayre knyght yonge and curtoys, "the whyche I byleve is drowned in passyng a ryver. And they were in myn hous, and the two damoyselles slept togyder in the chyrch and the knyght slepte wyth me, and the other two slepte in the stable with the horses." Thenne whan the doulphyn herde these tydynges, he had ryght grete playsyr of which he

---

[4] quieted
[5] foot soldier
[6] orders
[7] seek
[8] Revered
[9] committed a fault (mistake) [OF mespris]
[10] seeing
[11] believe
[12] equal
[13] similar

made noo semblaunte, and gaf to the chapelayn moche money and grete yeftes[14] and bad hym retorne.

3   After, the doulphyn took Vyenne by the hande in reprevyng hyr moche gretely, and lad[15] hyr into hyr modres chambre wyth Ysabeau, for hir moder was seke of the grete sorowe that she had for hyr doughter, and there the [fol. 19v] moder blamed them bothe two. And Ysabeau sayd that Vyenne was as pure and clene of hyr body as she was the day that she departed. "Alas," sayd the doulphyn, "thou hast put us in the moost grettest shame of the world. And I promyse that alle they that have consented therto shal be wel punysshed, and especyal that evyl traytre Parys whych is cause of al thys fayte, and yf ever I may have hym, I shal make dogges devoure hym and also bothe ye tweyne shal suffre[16] therfore grete penytence." Thenne sayd Vyenne wepyng, "I see wel and knowe that ye have entencion to do me moche gryef and harm, and I see wel that my lyf shal not longe endure. Therfore I swere to you in good fayth that there is noo man in the world that I so moche love as I doo hym whom ye so menace and thretene; for in hym I have my thought and courage[17] wythoute ever to faylle hym. And yf ye shortly gyve to me my penaunce, so moche shortly shal be my deth. And yf ye suffre me to endure it longe, so moche more shal I bere it, and my soule shal be the more sure tofore almyghty God. And knowe ye for certayn that for hym and hys love I am redy to deye."

4   Thenne the doulphyn yssued[18] out of the chambre in grete indygnacyon and commaunded that the fader of Parys shold be put in an evyl[19] pryson, and that al hys goodes shold be taken fro hym. And also that Vyenne and Ysabeau sholde be enclosed in a chambre and that wel lytell mete shold be gyven to them, and moche he menaced and thretened them. And thus they abode a longe tyme in that chambre, and contynuelly Vyenne dremed of Parys. And whan she myght have ony space to speke to Edward, felowe of Parys, she requyred hym that he shold serche yf he myght have ony tydynges of Parys and that he shold lete hyr knowe therof. In thys maner Vyenne passed hyr tyme in grete sorowe and in grete thought, allewaye desyryng for to here[20] somme tydynges of that noble knyght Parys.

5   Whan Vyenne had ben a grete tyme in thys manere, the doulphyn bythought[21] hym that thenne hys doughter Vyenne had been wel chastysed. And thenne the doulphyn, fader of Vyenne, ordeyned that she came oute of pryson. And thenne he purposed to gyve to hyr an husbond and sette hyr in hyr fyrst estate, wherof alle [fol. 20r] the courte was moche joyous, and in especyal Edward, felowe of Parys.

---

[14] *gifts*
[15] *led*
[16] *endure*
[17] *heart (desire)*
[18] *went (moved)*
[19] *wretched*
[20] *hear*
[21] *considered (reflected)*

6 And after certayn tyme, the doulphyn wrote to the erle of Flaunders that he wold doo marye hys doughter[22] Vyenne, wherupon he requyred hym that he wold gyve to hym counceyll in thys mater, for it was unto hym chargeable.[23] And duryng the tyme that Vyenne was oute of pryson, hyr herte was never in reste, but ever she was hevy and sorouful for hyr swete and faythful frende Parys, whome she myght not see and knewe not whether he were dede or alyve. And whan the doulphyn sawe hyr so hevy, on a day he sayd to hyr, "My swete doughter, wherfore be ye so sorouful? Gyve yourself to playsyr, for as to me, I remembre nomore the thynges passed, and there is noo thynge in the world that ye demaunde me but I shal doo it for you." And thenne Vyenne, whyche had not forgeten Parys, sayd to hym, "Honourable fader, yf I were sure of the thynges passed that they were forgoten by you, I shold be more sure than I am, but I byleve fermely that ye have them yet in your remembraunce, for ye holde alwaye messyre Jaques in pryson, the fader of Parys, whyche is not culpable of ony parte of thys dede ne cause. And yf ye wold do to me soo moche grace that ye wold pardonne hym and rendre to hym al hys goodes and thynges, I shold be moche joyous." And the doulphyn, for the playsyr of hys doughter, sayd to hyr that it wel playsed hym. And incontynent the doulphyn dyd do[24] delyver messyre Jaques out of pryson and dyd do retorne to hym al hys goodes and thynges that had be taken from hym, wherof messyre Jaques had grete playsyr, for yf he had abyden lenger in pryson he had be dede for hungre. There was none that comforted hym but Edward, whiche comforted hym the best wyse he myght and gaf to hym dayly that whyche was necessarye for hys lyf. Whan Vyenne knew that messyre Jaques was oute of pryson, she was moche joyeful and had grete playsyr. Nevertheles, al the consolacyon of Vyenne was whan she myght speke wyth Edward of hyr love Parys. And thus she passed hyr tyme in ryght grete payne and hevynesse the beste wyse she myght.

7 Whan the erle of Flaunders had redde the letters of the doulphyn and understood that he wold marye[25] his doughter Vyenne, whych was [fol. 20v] of the age of fyftene yere, he[26] trayted[27] that she shold have of two barons that one, that is to wete the sone of the kynge of Englond, or the sone of the duke of Bourgoyne, whyche thenne had grete renommee in Fraunce and that was for the grete prowesse that was in hym. And the sayd erle made thys sayd traytye[28] and sente word unto the doulphyn that hym semed best that the sone of the duc of Bourgoyn were beste for hyr, bycause that it shold be grete playsyr to the kynge of Fraunce, and that he was a noble knyght and of grete prowesse. And whan the doulphyn had receyved these lettres fro the erle of Flaunders, he sente to the kyng of Fraunce to wyte of hym whyche shold best playse hym of these two prynces aforesayd that shold have his doughter, for whome that he[29] wold shold have hyr. Wherof the

---

[22] wold do marye his doughter, *would arrange a marriage for his daughter*
[23] *troublesome*
[24] dyd do, *had (caused to be)*
[25] wold marye, *would arrange a marriage for*
[26] *the earl*
[27] *negotiated*
[28] *agreement*
[29] *the king*

kyng had grete plaisyr and reputed it to hym grete honour. And he sente to hym[30] worde that it shold playse hym best that he maryed wyth the sone of the duc of Bourgoyn, hys[31] nevew,[32] and in so doyng he[33] shold doo to hym ryght grete plaisyr and wold do as moche for hym whan tyme and place requyreth. And seyng the doulphyn the wylle of the kyng of Fraunce, sente worde to the erle of Flaunders that he had counseylled wyth hys barons, and also that it was the wylle of the kyng of Fraunce that his doughter shold be maryed to the sone of the duc of Bourgoyne. And thenne the erle laboured so moche in thys mater that he made the sayd sone of the duc to agree as for hys partye.

---

[30] *the dauphin*
[31] *the king's*
[32] *nephew*
[33] *the dauphin*

Chapter 15: How Parys sente a letter to hys felowe Edward.

1   Now late us leve to speke of thys mater and retorne we unto Parys whyche abode in the cyté of Gene[1] moche hevy. And whyles thys maryage was in trayté, Parys dwelled in Gene out of al joyes and playsaunces worldly, and al for the love that he had to the fayr Vyenne whome he had soo moche at his hert. And abode alwaye in hys lodgyng allone and bycame so devoute and soo humble toward God that it was grete mervaylle. And also for the good countenaunces that he made, he was moche wel byloved of al the peple of the cyté, and they helde hym for a noble man and sayd he must nedes be the sone of a grete lord. And Parys, beyng in thys manere, had grete desyre to have tydynges of Vyenne and what was hyr adventure. And anone ordeyned[2] two letters, that one to [fol. 21r] hys fader and that other to hys felawe Edward, of whyche the letter to hys fader sayd in thys manere:

2   "Ryght dere and honourable syr and fader, playse it you to wete that I am moche sorouful and hevy of my cruel adventure, and also I endure grete hevynes, sorowe, and afflyctyon, doubtyng[3] that for me ye have suffred grete payne and trybulacyon. And I late you wete that I am at Genes and dwelle in a lodgyng allone, deposed[4] fro al joyes and consolacyons mondayne,[5] for myn entendement[6] is to serve God and Our Lady fro hens forth, and purpose that ye shal see me no more, for I wyl departe and goo thurgh the world to seche holy pylgrymages. And yf by adventure I shal deye tofore that ye shal see me, I praye you that it may playse you that I deye not in your evyl wylle[7] but humbly byseche you that it playse you to pardonne me and to gyve to me your benedyctyon.[8]

---

[1] *Genoa*
[2] *had made*
[3] *fearing*
[4] *removed*
[5] *worldly*
[6] *intention*
[7] *bad graces (anger)*
[8] *blessing*

Also, dere syr and fader, I praye you and supplye[9] that my dere brother and felowe Edward ye wyl take in my name and place, and that he be recommaunded[10] as your sone instede of me, as wel in your herytage as in other thynges. And the grace of the Holy Ghoost be wyth you. Recomaunde me to my moder and etc." And the letter of Edward sayd thus:

3   "Dere and specyal brother and synguler frende Edward, the peryl of Paris and of hys adventure is poursyewed[11] of alle evyl and cruel fortune. I comaunde[12] me to you as moche as I may say or thynk. Nevertheles, lyke as we have ben accustomed to wryte letters of love and of chyvalrye, now I must wryte letters anguysshous[13] of sorowe and of evyl fortune, for, alas, I am unhappy al allone in a strange[14] contré and exyled fro al joyes and fro alle playsyr, and out of al worldly playsaunce thynkyng nyght and day on the bele[15] Vyenne, the whyche I thynke that for me hath suffred mortal sorowe. And I say to you that, yf I knewe that for me she suffred payne and sorowe, I shold be in despayr, for I am worthy for to be punysshed cruelly for that fayte and none other. Wherfore I praye God and alle Hys sayntes that she may be kepte from al evyl, and gyve hyr grace to prospere in al good and honour lyke as she is worthy and myn herte desyreth. My dere broder and felowe, the moost dere thynges that I love in thys world is fyrst the fayre and swete Vyenne and next you, to whom I praye you yf it may [fol. 21v] be in ony wyse that ye wyl say to hyr in my name how that I am lyvyng in Genes, passyng my lyfe moche hevy and sorouful for the absence of hyr noble persone and for the cruel and evyl fortune that hath poursyewed me. And also say ye to hyr that I crye hyr mercy and that it may playse hyr to pardonne me yf by me she have ony dysplaysyr. And God knoweth myn entencyon and in what trybulacion I lyve. And syth that it hath not playsed to our Lord that we accomplysshe not our desyre and wylle, we ought to bere it pacyently. And also ye shal say to hyr that I praye and supplye her as moche as I may that she yet take no husbond unto the tyme that she shal see the ende of our adventure. And after thys I praye you, dere broder, of the consolacyon of my fader and my moder, and that ye be to them as a sone. For, seyng the love that alwaye we have had togyder, I have wryton to my fader that, in the stede of me, he take you for hys sone and that, after hys lyf, he wyl leve to you hys herytage. For so moche, broder and felowe, I praye and byseche you that ye be to theym humble and obeyssaunt, and the better parte shal be youres. And yf by adventure ye wryte to me ony letter, late the letter be kepte in my faders hous. The Holy Ghoost have you in hys kepyng."

4   And he delylverd thys letter to a courrour,[16] whyche whythin fewe dayes was at Vyenne and secretely delyverd hys letters to Edward, the good knyght. Whan Edward had receyved these letters and knewe that Paris was alyve, he had ryght as grete joye as ony man coude thynke or byleve; nevertheles, he helde the courrour secretely in his hous to

---

[9] supplicate
[10] entrusted (commended)
[11] pursued (harassed)
[12] commend
[13] tormented
[14] foreign
[15] beautiful [OF belle]
[16] courier

the ende that the dolphyn shold not knowe therof. And whan he had herde the letters, he went to the hous of messyre Jaques, the fader of the noble Parys, and sayd to hym, "Messyre Jaques, I brynge to you thys letter." And whan messyre Jaques had redde the letter, he coude not be sacyat[17] of redynge, he took so grete playsyr therin.

5 After that he had redde it at hys playsyr, he prayed Edward to wryte to hym an ansuer wel at large[18] of alle that was byfallen syth hys departyng. And thys doon, Edward departed fro hym and wente unto beale Vyenne, whome he fonde moche hevy and sorouful for hir love and frende Parys. And Edward sayd, "Honourable lady, and how is it that ye be thus hevy?" And Vyenne sayd to hym, "Alas, fayr broder Edward, I have good reason and cause to be hevy, for myn herte abydeth thynkyng day and nyght on my good [fol. 22r] knyght Parys. And I knowe not whether he be alyve or dede, of whyche thynge I moche desyre to knowe, for yf he be deed, I am cause therof, and certes, yf he be dede, I may not lyve after hym. Yf our Lord wold doo soo moche grace that he be alyve, fayn[19] wold I knowe in what londe he is, to the ende that I myght sende to hym a lytel money soo that he have noo necessyte for hys persone." And Edward sayd to hyr, "Madame what wyll ye gyve me yf I telle to you good tydynges and sure[20] of hym?"

6 Thenne sayd Vyenne, "By my fayth there is noo thyng that I have in thys world whyche I may gyve wyth myn honour, but that I shal gyve it to you." Thenne sayd Edward, "Loo, here is a letter whyche he hath sente to me." And whan Vyenne sawe the letter, she opened it and redde it al allonge,[21] and whan she had redde it she had soo grete joye that hyr semed[22] God had appyered to hyr. And the joye that she had in hyr hert shewed wel in hyr vysage,[23] for sythe that she departed fro Parys she had not so good vysage ne chere as she had thenne. And whan the solace had ynough endured, Edward sayd to hyr, "Madame, gyve to me ageyn my letter that I may make to hym an ansuer." And Vyenne sayd, "It pleseth me moche that ye make to Parys my swete frende an ansuer, but surely[24] the letter shal remayne wyth me." Thenne he sayd, "Madame, have ye not promysed to gyve to me that thyng that I shal demaunde you?" "Yes," sayd she. Thenne Edward sayd,[25] "I desyre ne wyll have none other thynge but that ye gyve to me my letter, for as sone shal I gyve to you my lyf, but yf ye wyl demaunde ony other thynge, I wyl wel." Thenne sayd Edward, "I am content that the letter abyde wyth you." And after he ordeyned another letter to Parys whiche sayd in this manere.

---

[17] *satiated (have enough of)*

[18] *at length (copiously)*

[19] *eagerly*

[20] *true*

[21] *entirely (at length)*

[22] hyr semed, *it seemed to her*

[23] *face*

[24] *safely*

[25] See Note

Chapter 16: How Edward sente ansuer of his letter to Parys, whyche abode in the cyté of Genes.

1   "Ryght dere brother frende and felowe Parys, your fader and your moder grete you wel, the whiche have suffred for you moche dysease,[1] payne, and desplaysyr, and in especyal your fader, whiche hath longe been in pryson and alle hys goodes were taken fro hym. And also I certefye you that, by the grace of God and at the request and prayer of Vyenne, the doulphyn hath pardonned hym alle hys evyl wylle and delyverd hym oute of pryson and restored to hym alle hys goodes ageyn. And plese it you to wete, fayre [fol. 22v] brother, that Vyenne hath had so moche joye and so grete playsyr whan she had knowleche that ye were alyve that it is wonder to byleve, for al hyr consolacyon was for to have tydynges of you. And she recommaundeth hyr to you as moche as she may and hath moche grete desyre to see you and also prayeth you not to wythdrawe you fro hyr ne fro that contreye, but that ye wryte ofte to hyr of your estate.[2] And she sendeth to you an eschaunge[3] of thre thousand floryns,[4] of whiche she wyl that ye take your playsyr and joye, for al hyr hope is in you. Also, ye shal understonde that she hath be kepte in pryson a certayn tyme, but, thanked be God, she is now oute. Also, I have shewed to hyr your letter, whyche she reteyneth, and after that she had redde it I myght never have it ageyn, but she sayd that she had lever[5] to lese al that she had than the said letter. And ye shal knowe that the doulphyn treateth a maryage for hyr, the which is the sone of the duc of Bourgoyn, and he hopeth fro day to day that it shal be accomplysshed. Nevertheless, I truste soo moche in Vyenne, seyng that whiche she hath sayd to me, that she wyl never have other husbond but you, wherfore lyve ye forth joyously in hope. Dere brother, I thanke you as I can or may for the presentacyon[6] that ye have doon for me. Your soule be wyth God, to whome I praye that He kepe you in hys holy warde and protectyon and etc." Whan thys letter was wryten, he delyverd it to the courrour,[7] whyche made hasty journeyes so that he arryved at Genes[8] where as the good knyght Parys dwelled and abode.

2   Whan the noble Paris had redde the letter and knewe that Vyenne had been in pryson, almoost for sorowe he was oute of his wytte cursyng his evyl fortune, and after he cursed the day that he was borne and moche dyscomforted hymself, and also he cursed the doulphyn sayeng, "O cruel fader and unconnyng,[9] how may your hert suffre to put in pryson hyr that is soo noble a creature whyche is ful of al vertues, that is the fayre Vyenne, whyche is noo thynge cause[10] of thys fayte? For I myself onely have doon it and ought to bere allone the penaunce. Alas and wherfore dyd not God to me so moche grace that I had be taken in stede of hyr? O fayre Vyenne, what have I doo for you whyche have suffred

---

[1]   *discomfort (tribulation)*

[2]   *circumstances*

[3]   *bill of exchange*

[4]   *florins (coins minted in Florence, Italy)*

[5]   *rather*

[6]   *offering*

[7]   *courier*

[8]   *Genoa*

[9]   *unthinking (ignorant)*

[10]   noo thynge cause, *in no way the cause*

soo moche payne for me?" Thus he made a grete whyle hys sorowe in wepyng strongely. After, Parys sawe that the fayr Vyenne was [fol. 23r] retorned into hyr fyrst estate wherof he was moche joyous. And whan he had receyved the eschaunge[11] that Vyenne had sente hym, he hyred a moche fayr hous and cladde hym honestly[12] and rychely and took acqueyntaunce and amytye wyth the grettest and beste of the cyté, insomoche they dyd hym moche good and honour. And thus duellyd Parys a grete whyle, alway remembryng in hys hert the love of Vyenne, for alleway hys love encreaced. And every moneth they wrote letters eche to other of whyche here is made noo mencyon, for it shold be over longe to reherce. And torne we here into Flaunders for the fayte[13] of the maryage of the excellent Vyenne.

3   Now sayth the hystorye that whan the erle of Flaunders had accorded[14] the maryage with the duc of Bourgoyn, he made redy hys sone and apparaylled[15] hym of companye[16] and of horses, and lete it be knowen to the doulphyn that he shold make redy al thynge necessarye, and that he shold hastely sende to hym his sone. Whan the doulphyn herde these tydynges, that he[17] whome he so moche desyred shold come, he was moche joyous and incontynent dyd doo[18] make redy many grete and mervayllous festes. And duryng the same dyd doo make redy hys sone, the duc of Bourgoyne, horses and peple for to accompanye hym, whiche was a fayre thynge to see. And after sent hym to the erle of Flaunders, whyche receyved hym wyth grete joye and wyth grete honour and fested hym two dayes, and delyverd to hym hys sone in his companye, and sente hym to the doulphyn. And whan the doulphyn knewe theyr comyng, he dyd do make redy to receyve hym. And whan they were by a day journeye[19] nygh unto Vyenne, he rode oute wyth moche grete chyvalrye[20] and receyved them with moche grete joye and playsyr, and eche made grete feste to other whyche were over longe to recounte.

4   Nevertheless, tofore that the doulphyn came to the sone of the duc of Bourgoyn, hee and hys wyf entred into the chambre of Vyenne, to whome the doulphyn sayd, "Fayr doughter, it was the playsyr of God that I and your moder were togyder seven yere wythoute havyng ony chylde, and in the eighth yere our lord comforted us wyth you, in whom we have al our affectyon. For we have neyther sone ne doughter but onely you, ne suppose never to have, so we truste that by you we have one. It is trewe that, so as God wyl and hath ordeyned, we wyl assemble[21] you to a moche honourable maryage the whiche to us [fol. 23v] playseth moche, for I ensure you the doughter of the kynge of Fraunce

---

[11] *letter of credit*

[12] *honorably*

[13] *making (feat)*

[14] *agreed to*

[15] *equipped*

[16] *attendants (entourage)*

[17] *i.e., Paris*

[18] dyd doo, *caused to be, (had)*

[19] a day journeye, *a day's journey*

[20] *knights (display of arms)*

[21] *arrange (join)*

hath moche desyred to have hym[22] that ye shal have, for God hath endowed hym with so moche good and honour as hert of knyght may have. Thus, to the playsyr of God and of the Vyrgyn Marye, we have made the maryage of the sone of the duke of Bourgoyne and of you, wherfor we praye you that therto ye wyl gyve your good wylle and playsyr, and also that ye wyl have the maryage agreable."[23] Thenne Vyenne ansuerd to hyr fader, "Honourable fader and lord, I wote wel that thys that ye entende is for my wele[24] and prouffyt. But notwythstondyng that I be in age for to marye, and that in thys maryage I shold recyve honour more than I am worthy, nevertheles, I shal not yet be maryed, for yf we have not thys man, yf it playse God, we shal have another as good or better. And thynke ye not, myn honourable lord, that I say thys for ony excusacyon,[25] but it is sythen fyftene dayes that I have be evyl dysposed of my persone,[26] and the maladye that I have causeth me to take noo playsyr for to be maryed. For I have avowed unto God never to be maryed to thys man ne to none other as longe as I shal be in thys maladye." Thenne thought the dolphyn that Vyenne sayd it for shamefastness.[27] Nevertheles, he travaylled[28] hyr every day wyth fayre wordes that she shold consente to thys maryage, but it avaylled[29] nothyng all that he dyd, for the wylle of hir was more in[30] Parys than in ony man of the world.

5   Thenne on the morne, the sone of the duc of Bourgoyne and the sone of the erle of Flaunders entred into the cyté of Vyenne, wherof the doulphyn had grete joye and playsyr. And thys feste endured wel fyftene dayes that they dyd no thynge but daunce, synge, and dyd other dyvers playsyrs. And duryng thys feste, the daulphyn sayd to the sone of the duke of Bourgoyn, to the ende that he shold thynke none evyl[31] bycause he abode so longe or that he myght espouse hys doughter. "Fayr sone, I praye you and byseche that ye take you to playsyr and joye. And gryeve you noo thynge of thys longe abydyng here, for certayn my doughter is so seke that unnethe she may speke, whyche doth to hyr grete desplaysyr and shame, for fayn she wold be out of hyr chambre." And thenne the sone of the duc of Bourgoyn, as he that mente but good fayth, byleved it lyghtly.[32]

6   Nevertheles, the doulphyn dyd nothyng nyght [fol. 24r] ne day but admonested[33] hys doughter, one tyme in fayr wordes and another tyme in menaces, but in no wyse he coude make hys doughter to consente, and comaunded that she shold nothyng have but brede and water, and Vyenne abode one day soo in thys manere. And al thys dyd the doulphyn to the ende that she shold consente to the maryage. And alwaye he dyd to hyr more

---

[22] *the son of the duke of Bourgoyne*

[23] *acceptable*

[24] *well-being (good)*

[25] *excuse*

[26] evyl dysposed of my persone, *ill-disposed in my body*

[27] *modesty*

[28] *belabored*

[29] *helped (availed)*

[30] *set on*

[31] none evyl, *nothing bad*

[32] *quickly*

[33] *admonished (counseled)*

harme and payne, and Vyenne was alwaye more harde[34] and ferther fro hys desyre, wherof the doulphyn had moche grete dysplaysyr, and not wythoute cause. And seyng the doulphyn that hys doughter was soo indurate,[35] he thought that by somme good moyen[36] he wold sende home ageyn the sone of the duc of Bourgoyn, for he doubted that yf he abode longe that this feat myght be dyscovered. And he gaf to hym fayr jewellys and after sayd to hym, "Fayre sone, I wyl that ye take noo desplaysyr in that I shal say to you. Me semeth wel that at thys tyme this maryage may not goo forth of you and of my doughter, for after that I see, and as me semethe, the wylle of God is ferther than I wold at thys tyme. For He wyl not that the maryage of you and of my doughter take now effecte, wherfore I have ryght grete desplaysyr in my hert onely for the love of you." Thenne the sone of the duc of Bourgoyne, seyng that at that tyme he myght doo noo thyng, toke leve of the doulphyn and retorned into his countree bycause that Vyenne was not in helthe, and promysed that as sone as he myght knowe that she shold be hool, he wold retorne for to accomplysshe the mariage lyke as the doulphyn had promysed to hym.

[34] *steadfast*

[35] *obdurate*

[36] *means*

Chapter 17: How the doulphyn dyd doo enprysonne Vyenne bycause that she wold not consente to the maryage to the sone of the duke of Bourgoyne.

1   After certayn dayes that the sone of the duke of Bourgoyn was departed fro the cyté of Vyenne, the doulphyn, for grete desplaysyr that he had, dyd do come tofore hym the mayster jayler of hys pryson and dyd doo make wythin[1] hys paleys a lytel pryson derke and obscure. And he dyd do put Vyenne and Ysabeau into that pryson and commaunded that they shold have nothyng to ete but brede and water, and one damoysel in whome the dolphyn trusted shold brynge it to them. And in thys manere Vyenne and Ysabeau passyd theyr tyme in grete sorowe. And thynke not that for thys pryson the hert of [fol. 24v] Vyenne wold in ony wyse consente to the wylle of hyr fader, but alway encreaced wyth hyr the wylle toward hir swete frende Parys. And wyth swete wordes she comforted Ysabeau sayeng, "My dere suster, abasshe[2] you not for thys derkenes, for I have confydence in God that ye shal have yet moche welthe.[3] For, my fayr suster, it is a moche ryghtful thyng that for the good knyght Parys, whyche for me suffreth so moche payne, that I suffre thys for hym, and also I say to you that al the paynes of this world be nothyng grevous to me whan I thynke on hys swete vysage." And in thys manere that one comforted that other in spekyng alle day of the valyaunte knyght Parys.

[1] *inside*

[2] *confound (do not be upset)*

[3] *happiness (well being)*

Chapter 18: How the sone of the duc of bourgoyne departed fro hys contrye for to come see the fayre lady Vyenne.

1   Whan the sone of the duc of Bourgoyne had abyden longe tyme in hys contree, on a day he had grete[1] thought of Vyenne, and that was for the grete beauté of hyr. And it dysplesed hym moche that at hys beyng there he had not seen hyr, and so concluded to goo and see hyr. And it was not longe after that he cam to the dolphyn, and the doulphyn receyved hym moche gladly and with grete honour. Thenne prayed he the dolphyn[2] that it myght plese hym to shewe to hym[3] Vyenne, also seke as she was, for in the world was nothyng that he soo moche desyred to see as hyr. And the doulphyn, seyng the wylle and desyre of hym, wold noo lenger hyde hys[4] courage but sayd to hym, "My fayr sone, by the fayth that I owe to God, I have had grete desyre that thys maryage shold be made, but my doughter for thys present tyme wyl take noo husbond ne be maryed, wherfore I have grete desplaysyr. And that for the love of you, and to the ende that ye knowe that it holdeth[5] not on me, I swere to you that sythe ye departed fro thys toun, I have doon hyr to be kepte in a pryson derke and obscure and hath eten nothyng but brede and water onely, and have sworn that she shal not goo oute of pryson tyl she shal consente to have you in maryage. And thus I praye you that ye take noo desplaysyr yf, at thys tyme, ye see hyr not, for ye may not faylle to have grete maryage in caas that this faylle you." And thenne he[6] ansuerd, "Honourable syr, I praye you moche hertely[7] syth that it is so, that er I retorne I may speke to hyr, and I shal praye hyr as moche as I [fol. 25r] shal mowe,[8] and shal see yf by ony manere I may converte hyr fro hyr wylle." Thenne sayd the doulphyn he was contente.

2   Thenne he sente to his doughter clothyng and vestymentes[9] for to clothe hyr, and also mete for to ete, for in two monethes she had eten but brede and water, wherof she was moche feble, and that shewed wel in her vysage. And thus he dyd bycause she shold consente to the maryage. And thenne it was concluded that the sone of the duc of Bourgoyne shold come see her and speke with hyr. And thenne whan Vyenne sawe thys and had receyved all, and knewe that the sone of the duc of Bourgoyn shuld come and speke wyth hyr, she said to Ysabeau, hir damoysel, "Fayr suster, beholde how my fader and moder wene[10] by these vestymentes and thys henne[11] that I shold ete to deceyve me and put me fro my purpoos, but God forbede that I shold do so." And thenne she took the henne and sayd to hyr that brought it, "Syth it playseth to the sone of the duke to come and speke to me, say ye to hym that he may not come these two dayes, and whan he cometh that he

---

[1] *much*

[2] prayed he the dolphyn, *the son of the duke of Bourgoyne asked the douphin*

[3] *the son of the duke of Bourgoyne*

[4] *the dauphin's*

[5] *depends (is not beholden to)*

[6] *the son of the duke of Bourgoyne*

[7] *sincerely*

[8] *in addition to (more)*

[9] *clothing*

[10] *think*

[11] *hen*

brynge with hym the bysshop of Saynt Laurens." She that had brought to hyr the henne sayd all thys unto the doulphyn and to dame Dyane hir[12] moder. Thenne Vyenne took the two quarters of the henne and put them under hyr arme hooles, and helde ther there so longe that they stonken moche strongley.

3   And whan it came to the thyrd day, the bysshop of Saynt Laurence and the sone of the duke of Bourgoyne camen for to see Vyenne, and or[13] they entred they opened a treylle[14] whyche gaf lyght into the pryson. Thenne whan the sone of the duc sawe Vyenne in the pryson, he sayd to hir by grete pyté that he had, "Noble Vyenne, how wyl ye deye thus for hungre soo folyly[15] by your owne defaulte?[16] And knowe ye not wel that your fader hath gyven you to me to have to my wyf, wherfore I lyve in grete payne and in moche grete sorowe for the duresse[17] of your courage, wherof ye doo ryght grete synne. And doubte ye not that God punyssheth you for thyn obedyence that ye doo to your fader and to your moder. Wherfore I praye you, fayre Vyenne, to telle to me for what cause ye wyl not have me in maryage to your husbond. Doubt ye that whan ye shall be wyth me, that ye may not serve God as wel as ye now do that suffre thys payne? I promyse you by my fayth that ye shal have playsaunces[18] and lybertees[19] in al the maners that ye shal conne[20] demaunde. Thenne I praye you [fol. 25v] that ye wyl not here deye so dolorously, and yf ye wyl not doo it for the love of me, yet at the leste do it for the love of your fader and of your moder whyche lyve for you in grete sorowe and in grete hevynesse, wherfore ye ought to have pyté on them."

4   Whan Vyenne had herde these wordes, she was quasi[21] abasshed and sayd, "Syr, savyng your honour, I am maryed, how be it ye knowe hym not whome I have in my hert. And also I knowe and graunte ryght wel that ye be worthy to have one moche gretter and more hye a lady than I am. And I late you wete that for hym that I desyre I shold suffre more payne than I fele. And therfore I praye you that fro hens forth ye speke to me no more of thys mater. And also I am so evyl dysposed in my persone that yf it endure in me, my lyf shal not be longe, and, yf it were honeste,[22] I shold shewe it you and than shold ye see how it stondeth wyth me. Nevertheles, approche ye ner to me and ye shall the better byleve me." And the sone of the duke of Bourgoyne and the bysshop of Saynt Laurence approuched unto Vyenne, fro whom yssued soo grete a stenche, that unnethe[23] they myght suffre and endure it, whiche savour[24] came fro under hyr arme holes of the two

---

[12]   *Vienne's*

[13]   *before*

[14]   *trellis (window with wooden slats)*

[15]   *foolishly*

[16]   *fault*

[17]   *firmness (hardness)*

[18]   *pleasures*

[19]   *freedoms*

[20]   shal conne, *shall think*

[21]   *somewhat (a little)*

[22]   *appropriate*

[23]   *hardly*

[24]   *scent*

quarters of the henne,[25] whiche were roten. And whan Vyenne sawe that they had felte[26] ynough of the stenche, she sayd to them, "Lordes, ye may now knowe ynough in what adventure I am dysposed."[27] Thenne they took leve havyng grete compassyon on hyr. And they sayd to the dolphyn that Vyenne was thenne half roten and that she stanke, and demed[28] in themself that she myght not lyve longe, and that it shold be grete damage[29] of hyr deth for the soverayn beauté that was in hyr. And incontynent the sone of the duc of Bourgoyn took hys leve of the doulphyn and retorned into hys contrey and recounted to hys fader the lyf of Vyenne, wherof alle they that herde hym had grete pyté in theyr herte.

5   Whan the doulphyn sawe that the maryage was broken by the deffaulte[30] of his doughter, Vyenne, he sware that she shold never departe fro thens but yf she wold consente to hys wylle. And so she abode longe tyme in that pryson where she had grete thought and sorowe for hyr swete and trewe frende Parys. And hyr desyre was on noo thynge but for to here tydynges of Parys hyr love, but in the estate[31] [fol. 26r] that she was in, no man myght brynge hyr tydynges. And Edward, the felowe of Parys, seyng that Vyenne abode in soo grete payne and that none durst speke to hyr, he had in his herte grete sorowe and was moche moeved of grete pyté and also for the grete love that he had to Parys, and concluded to make a chapel in the chyrche that touched on the palays of the dolphyn. And in a corner he dyd do dygge so depe that it was nyghe to the foundement of the pryson wherein Vyenne was, and bycause he wold not have the thyng dysclosed,[32] he wold that they shold dygge no ferther. And whan the chapel was acheyved[33] and fynysshed, Edward alle allone dygged hymself so ferre[34] that he made an hole by whyche he spake to Vyenne whan he wold, whyche cave was made so secretly that no man myght apperceyve it.

6   Soo it happed on a day, Edward byhelde Vyenne thurgh this hole and salewed[35] hyr, and thenne whan Vyenne herd hym and knewe hym, she had so grete joye and consolacyon that she semed that she was rysen fro deth to lyf. And the fyrst tydynges that Vyenne demaunded of hym were yf he knewe ony tydynges of Parys. And Edward tolde to hir that it was not longe syth that he had receyved a letter fro hym wryton at Genes. Thenne said Vyenne al wepyng to hym, "Alas, whan shal the day come that I shal see hym, and that doon I wold be contente that God shold do His wylle of me, for none other thyng I desyre in this world. Alas, fayr brother, what semeth you of my lyf and of this fayr chambre in whyche I dwelle in? Certeynly I byleve veryly that yf Parys knewe it, that for his love I suffre thyus moche sorowe, that the hert of hym shold swelte[36] for sorow." And after she

---

[25] *hen*

[26] *sensed (experienced)*

[27] adventure I am dysposed, *condition I am in*

[28] *thought*

[29] *pity [OF domage]*

[30] *fault (default)*

[31] *situation*

[32] *made known*

[33] *completed*

[34] *far*

[35] *greeted*

[36] *die*

tolde to Edward the parlament[37] that she had with the sone of the duc of Bourgoyne, and also of the henne, and prayed hym that he wold sende worde of al thys to Parys and that she recommaunded[38] hyr to hym, and also that she had none other hope in thys world but in hym. Edward brought to hyr every day fro thenne forthon[39] mete and drynke, and al that was necessary to hyr for hyr lyf and comforted hyr with fayr wordes the best wyse he myght. And Edward wrote al playnly to Parys how for hungre she shold have been dede ne had he ben,[40] whyche dayly pourveyed for hyr al that was to hym[41] necessarye. And he wrote to hym[42] alle the manere that Vyenne had holden[43] wyth the sone of the duke of Bourgoyne. And that thys fayre lady Vyenne desyred noo thynge in this world but for to see hym onely. [fol. 26v] And also that she prayed hym that he shold not departe oute of the countree that he was in.

7   Whan the noble Parys had receyved the letter fro Edward and knewe that Vyenne abode in pryson, it is no nede to demaunde[44] yf he had grete desplaysyr and almoost was in suche caas[45] as to lese his wytte for sorowe. And on that other parte, he had grete drede that she shold be maryed in eschewyng[46] of the grete harme and payne that she suffred, and herein he was pensyf nyght and day, sayeng to hymself, "I see wel that I may not escape but that Vyenne must nedes be maryed, and by that moyen[47] hyr love and myn shal faylle. Alas, now see I wel that now me byhoveth[48] noo hoope ne truste. Alas caytyf[49] and unhappy, what shal byfalle of me? I shal goo so ferre that fro hyr I may never here tydynges ne also she fro me." And after this he bygan ageyn hys complaynte sayeng, "O veray God of heven, wherfore hast thou not doon to me soo moche grace that in the stede of hyr I myght suffre the payne that she suffreth for me? O cruel fortune ful of cruel tormente, and what hath Vyenne doon or made that she must suffre so grevous penaunce? Alas, were it not more reason, justyce, and cause that I whyche have doon alle thys evyl bere the punycyon?[50] Certes yes."

---

[37] *conversation (speech)*
[38] *commended*
[39] *thenceforth*
[40] ne had he ben, *had it not been for him (Edward)*
[41] *them*
[42] *Paris*
[43] *conducted herself*
[44] *ask*
[45] *state (condition)*
[46] *escaping (avoiding)*
[47] *means, course of action*
[48] me byhoveth, *I must have*
[49] *miserable*
[50] *punishment*

Chapter 19: How Parys sente a letter to Edward hys felowe.

1 After that he had made hys complaynte, he wrote a letter unto Edward doyng hym to wyte how he had soverayn sorowe for Vyenne whiche was in pryson, and he thanked hym of the goodnes and dylygence[1] that he had doon toward hyr, in prayeng hym that he never wold faylle hyr but contynuelly ayde and helpe hyr. And after, he wrote to hym how for veray dysplaysyr and melancolye he wold goo into somme straunge[2] contreye, and that fro than forthon[3] he shold sende to hym noo moo letters, and that he never retche[4] for to here moo tydynges fro hym, no more than of a deed[5] persone.

2 Thenne whan Edward had receyved these letters fro Paris and knewe that he wold estraunge[6] hym fro that countree of Genes and wold goo into a strange contreye, he was moche wroth[7] and sore agryeved. And thenne incontynent Edward wente and tolde it to the fader and moder of Parys, [fol. 27r] wherof they toke so grete sorowe that they supposed to have loste theyr wytte. And after Edward wente and tolde it also to Vyenne, wherof it nedeth not to demaunde the grete sorowe that she had, for it was so grete and overmoche that yf Edward had not comforted hyr, she had been dede. And thenne she complayned to Ysabeau sayeng that sythen she never entended to here tydynges of hyr love Parys, she was ryght wel contente to deye, and that she wold never more have playsyr of no thynge that was in thys world, and that thenne she wold that she were dede. And Ysabeau comforted hyr alwaye.

---

[1] effort (persistence)
[2] foreign
[3] thenceforth
[4] expected
[5] dead
[6] estrange (go abroad)
[7] angry

Chapter 20: How Parys wente to shyppe at Venyse, for to goo to the holy sepulcre in Jherusalem.

1 After that Paris had sent the letter to Edward, incontynent he departed fro Genes wyth hys servaunte and wente to Venyse, where he took shyppyng and saylled so ferre that he cam to Alexandrye, where he abode a space of tyme. And after in that contrey he enformed hym and lerned the waye to the mounte of Calvarye and of Jherusalem, and how he myght passe surely.[1] And afterward Parys concluded to goo into that contrey a pylgrymage, but tofore or he took hys waye, he lerned for to speke the langage of Moores.[2] And whan Parys coude wel speke Mouryske, he and his varlet took the waye toward Ynde,[3] and so ferre laboured by theyr journeyes that they arryved in the londe of Prester Johan, in whyche he dwelled a longe tyme. And in that whyle hys berde grewe longe, and

---

[1] safely
[2] Muslims
[3] India

after he took the habyte of a More and also lerned alle the custommes and maners of the contree. And he had alle waye faste[4] byleve in our lord Jhesu Cryste and in the gloryous Vyrgyn Marye hys swete moder. And thus abydyng in thys maner, he had grete wylle to go to Jherusalem to the Holy Sepulture for too see the holy sayntuaryes[5] and for to accomplysshe the holy pylgremage. Thenne whan he was in Jherusalem, he sette al his courage in devocyon and bycam so devoute that it was mervaylle, and prayed contynuelly our Lord that by the meryte of his passyon he wold gyve to hym salvacyon of hys soule and consolacyon for his body, and also for fayr Vyenne. And after, he departed fro thens and wente into Egypte and arryved in the contree of the soudan.[6] And hys money bygan to faylle, and hyred hym a litel hous wherin he dwellyd moche hevy and sorouful [fol. 27v] for hys infortune.[7] And also he had grete desplaysyr whan he sawe other tryumphe[8] and wexe[9] lordes.

2   Now it happed on a day that Parys wente to playe and dysporte[10] hym out of the toun in the feldes and there mette wyth the faulconners of the soudan whyche came fro hawkyng. And emonge them was one fawcon moche seke, and that fawcon the sowdan loved beste of alle the other. Thenne demaunded Parys of the fawconner what sekenesse the fawcon had, and the fawconner sayd to hym that he wyst not. Thenne sayd Paris, "Truly, yf he contynue in the maladye that he hath, he shall not lyve thre dayes, byt yf ye doo that I shal say to you and yf he be not hole therwyth, he shal never be hole." Thenne sayd the fawlconner to hym, "I praye you that ye wyl telle me what I shal do, for I ensure you faythfylly that yf ye may make hym hole, it shal mowe[11] avaylle you and me also, and that I promyse you, for the souldan had lever lose the beste cyté that he hath than this fawcon." Thenne Parys wente and sought certayn herbes and gaf them to the fawlconner and bad hym to bynde them to the feet of the fawcon. And so he dyd, and sone after the fawlcon amended[12] and becam as hole as ever he had be tofore, wherof the souldan was moche joyous. And for the love of thys faulcon, the souldan made the fawlconner a grete lord in hys courte. Thenne the faulconner, seyng that by the moyen of Parys he had goten thys lordshyp, he dyd to hym moche playsyr and shewed to hym as grete amytye and frendshyp as he had ben hys brother, and brought hym in the grace of the souldan and was receyved into hys courte. And the souldan loved hym soo wel that he gaf to hym grete offyce and mayntened hym in grete honour.

3   Ye shal understonde that in thys tyme regned a moche holy pope, the whych was named Innocent, and was a moche holy persone and devoute. And it pleased soo hym

---

[4] firm

[5] sacred places

[6] sultan

[7] misfortune

[8] important (triumphant)

[9] great (powerful)

[10] amuse

[11] more

[12] recovered

that he gaf oute a croysee[13] ayenst the fals myscreauntes[14] and hethen men, to the ende that the name of our lord Jhesu Cryst were more sayntefyed and enhaunced thurghout al Crystyenté. And therfore was maad a grete counceyl emonge the cardynals and prelates, and was concluded by theyr parlament that thys croysee shold be wryton to the kyng of Fraunce and to other kynges Crysten, dukes, erles, and other grete lordes. And so was it doon.

---

[13] crusade

[14] unbelievers

Chapter 21: How the doulphyn came toward the kyng of Fraunce.

1 [fol. 28r] Whan the kyng of France had receyved the letters fro the pope, incontynent he sente for the doulphyn of Vyennoys that he shold come and speke wyth hym, the whiche incontynent came at his commaundement. Thenne the kynge sayd to hym, "Syr Godefroy, we have made you to come hyther, for ye be one of the moost wysest of our courte, and also ye be of our lygnage. And we late you wete that our holy fader the pope hath wryton to us that he hath yeven[1] a croysee ayenst the mescreauntes, wherfore we, for the love and reverence of God, entende for to goo thyder. Nevertheles, we have advysed that ye shold goo fyrst into thoo partyes,[2] and we praye you, for the love and reverence of God, that ye take on you the charge for to espye[3] the contrees and also the passages." Thenne the doulphyn sayd, "I am redy and apparaylled[4] to do your comaundement wyth good wylle. But how shal I mowe do it for to passe surely emonge the hethen peples? For yf they apperceyve in ony wyse that I goo for to espye theyr contre, I shal not conne[5] escape, but that I must deye by cruel deth yf God kepe me not." Thenne sayd the kyng, "Ye may goo and your companye surely clothed in habyte of pylgryms, for ye knowe wel that thys is not the fyrst tyme that many Crysten men have been in the Holy Londe. Wherfore I praye you yet eft ones[6] that in the name of Jhesu Cryst that ye make you redy for to goo thyder, and take wyth you of our knyghtes as meny as it shal playse you."

2 Thenne the doulphyn, seyng the wylle of the kyng and that incontynent he must departe, he sente letters to hys wyf that he wold goo into the Holy Lond to seche the holy sayntuaryes and pylgrymages, and prayed hyr that she moche wysely shold governe hys londe and that Vyenne hys doughter shold not escape oute of pryson tyl he retourned, for in shorte tyme he wold come ageyn.

---

[1] proclaimed (given out)

[2] regions (countries)

[3] reconnoiter (spy out)

[4] prepared (outfitted)

[5] be able to

[6] eft ones, *once again*

Chapter 22: How the doulphyn took hys shyppyng for to goo into Jherusalem.

1 After that the doulphyn had taken hys shyppe and passed into Surrye[1] and Damaske,[2] to Jherusalem and in many other places, and had advysed and espyed moche wysely and wel alle the countree, and enquyred of the Crysten men that dwellyd there many thynges without dyscoveryng his wylle and entente. Nevertheles, somme evyl Crysten men, for to gete money, tolde it unto the souldan of [fol. 28v] Babylone.

2 Thenne whan the souldan knewe it, he maad noo semblaunte, but incontynent he made all the passages[3] to be kept whereas the pylgryms went by in suche manere as the doulphyn was taken and alle hys companye wyth hym in a place called Ramon[4] not ferre fro Jherusalem, whyche was brought tofore the souldan. And he ordeyned that the doulphyn shold be tormented and pyned.[5] The doulphyn, seyng hymself in suche a poynte,[6] sayd that they shold not tormente hym and he wold say to them the trouthe. And thus he recounted to the souldan how the pope had gyven oute a croysee ayenst them, and how he was comen to espye the contreye. Whan the soudan sawe thys, he sayd that he wold advyse hym of what deth he wold do hym to deth in maner that al other shold take ensaumple, and commaunded that anone he shold be ledde into Alysandrye,[7] and there to be put into an harde pryson, and also that none shold gyve to hym but brede and water. Thenne the doulphyn was brought into Alysandrye and was put into an hard and stronge toure, and there he suffred a myserable lyf and had kepars[8] that kept hym nyght and day. Thus was the doulphyn in grete sorowe, thynkyng never to yssue[9] out of that pryson but dede. Nevertheles, the pope and the kyng of Fraunce dyd ofte tymes grete payne to have hym out by fynaunces,[10] but they myght not have hym, for the souldan sayd that he shold do on hym suche punycyon[11] that al other shold take ensaumple. Now late us leve[12] to speke of the doulphyn, and retorne we to Parys that knewe no thynge of these tydynges.

3 Now recounteth the hystorye that Parys was in Babylone, lyke as ye have tofore herde, whyche knewe noo thynge of thys fayte. So it happed that, by adventure, two frers[13] relygyous sought the yndulgences of the Holy Lande and aryveden in Babylone where they wold see the seygnorye[14] and the puyssaunce[15] of the sowdan, for thenne the sowdan helde hym in Babylone wyth moche grete puyssaunce. These two freres were of these par-

---

[1] *Syria*
[2] *Damascus*
[3] *stations on the road (passes)*
[4] *Ramallah*
[5] *tortured*
[6] *predicament*
[7] *Alexandria*
[8] *guards*
[9] *go (leave)*
[10] *ransom (exchange of money)*
[11] *punishment*
[12] *cease (leave off)*
[13] *friars*
[14] *lordship (control)*
[15] *might (strength)*

tyes, whych beyng in tho partyes, it happed as they wente in the towne, Parys fonde them. Thenne Parys salewed them and demaunded of these partyes and sayd to them in thys manere: "After that I have herde say emonge you Crysten men ye have a pope the whyche is moche stronge and puyssaunt. And also ye have many kynges and grete lordes, and so grete townes, cytees, [fol. 29r] and castellys that I have merveyll how he suffre that we that be not of your lawe have the seygnorye of the Holy Lande, whiche ought to apperteyne[16] to you as ye say." And whan the freres had herde Parys thus speke, they were sore aferde, and one of them ansuerd in the langage of the Moure,[17] for they wyst[18] none other but Parys was a Moure, and so dyd al they of the contrey. And he sayd to hym, "Syr, I byleve wel that ye have herd say that in our partyes been assembled grete companyes of peple and men of warre for to come into thyse partyes bycause that our holy fader, the pope, hath graunted oute a croysee.[19] And in the tyme whyles our men of warre assembled, the kynge of Fraunce, whiche is the grettest of Crystyenté, sent a noble baron whyche is named the doulphyn of Vyennoys for to vysyte and espye these partyes. Thenne, he beynge in these partyes, the souldan sette men in suche places where as the pylgryms were accustomed to passe. And sodeynly he dyd do take hym in a cyté named Ramon, and after sente hym into Alysandrye and there sette hym in an evyl pryson wherein I suppose that he be dede, and thus for thys cause, the fayt was dyscoverd." Thenne sayd Parys, "How is that lord named?" Thenne sayd the frere, "He is named Godfroy of Allaunson, doulphyn of Vyennoys." And whan Parys herde thys, he was moche abasshed, but he made noo semblaunter and thought in hys hert that hys adventure myght yet come to good and effecte.[20] Thenne he demaunded them of many thynges, and sayd to them that he wold more speke to them another tyme and demaunded them where they were lodged. And they tolde hym more for drede than for love, for they thought he wold have doon to them somme harme.

4   Whan Parys was departed fro the freres, he was moche pensyf how and in what maner he myght goo into Alexandrye for to see the doulphyn, and how he myght gete hym oute of pryson. And so moche he thought on his fayte that he purposed to goo to the hostry[21] where the freres were lodged and soo wente thyder, and whan the freres sawe hym and were sore aferde. Thenne Parys took them by the handes and ladde them to solace thurgh the cyté spekyng of many thynges alwaye in the langage of Moure, and sayd to them, "I have grete desyre to see that Crysten knyght whiche is in Alexandrye, for I have alwaye had good wylle to the Crysten men. Peradventure I myght yet wel helpe [fol. 29v] hym, and yf ye wyl come with me, I promyse you be my lawe that I shal make you good chere, and doubte ye nothyng."[22] And thenne whan the freres herde hym thus speke they wyst not what to ansuer, they had so grete fere. Nevertheles, they trustyng in the mercy of God,

---

[16] belong
[17] Muslim
[18] knew
[19] crusade
[20] fulfillment
[21] hostel
[22] doubt ye nothyng, *do not worry about anything*

they promysed hym that they shold goo wyth hym though they shold deye, and prayden God in theyr courage that He wold graunte grace that he myght come oute of pryson.

5 Thenne Parys had grete playsyr of the ansuer of the freres and wende[23] never to see the houre that he myght be wyth the doulphyn for to see the ende of his adventure. And so departed fro the freres and wente strayte to the faulconner of the souldan, wyth whom he had grete knowleche, and sayd to hym, "Seynour, I thanke you of the grete honour, curtosye, and gentylnes that ye have do to me, and playse it you to wyte that I wyl departe fro hens into Alysandrye, and I promyse to you that for your love I shall not tarye longe but that I shal retorne hyther ageyn. And bycause I am there unknowen, and that I never was there, I praye you ryght humbly that I myght have maundement[24] of the souldan that he commaunde to the governours that I may goo thorugh alle hys londe surely, for ye knowe wel that one may not kepe hym over wel[25] fro evyl peple. Therfore I praye you and requyre that ye wyl gete me suche a maundement, and also that ye wyl commaunde me humbly to the good grace of my lord the souldan." And forthwyth the faulconner wente to the souldan and made hys requeste for Parys, and incontynent the souldan graunted hym al hys desyre, sayeng that it moche desplaysed hym of the departyng of Parys, and yf he wold abyde and dwelle in hys courte he wold make hym a grete lord. Thenne the faulconner said, "Dere syr, he hath promysed me that in short tyme he shal retorne." Thenne the souldan dyd do make the maundement lyke as he wold devyse, chargyng al his lordes, offycers, and subgettes of townes, cytees, and castellys of his londe that they shold do to hym[26] grete honour, and that they shold gyve and delyver to hym al that shold be necessarye to hym wythout takyng ony money or ony other thynge of hym. And also the souldan gaf to Parys many ryche clothes and vestymentes[27] of cloth of gold and of sylke, and also he gaf to hym grete tresour, prayeng hym that he shold not longe tarye but hastely retorne ageyn, and promysed hym that he shold make hym a grete lord and delyverd hys [fol. 30r] maundement, the whyche was sealed wyth the propre seale of the souldan and sygned wyth hys owne hande.

6 Whan Parys had receyved alle these thynges that the souldan had gyven to hym, he took leve of hym and of hys courte and went with the freres into Alexandrye. Incontynent after he was comen, he shewed the maundement to the admyral,[28] the whyche anon after he had seen it dyd grete honour to Parys and delyverd to hym a fayr lodgyng pourveyed of al thynges necessarye, and delyverd another to the freres. The admyral came every day to see Parys in hys lodgyng for to do hym honour and companye and wente and rode togyder thorugh the cyté, and bycause that Parys was rychely clad, every man made to hym grete honour and sayd that he semed wel to be the sone of somme grete Moure.

7 And on a day as they rode in the cyté they passed forth by the toure where as the dolphyn was in pryson. Thenne Parys demaunded of the admyral what toure it was that

---

[23] *thought*

[24] *command (directive)*

[25] kepe hym over wel, *can not keep himself too carefully*

[26] *Paris*

[27] *robes (clothing)*

[28] *emir (an officer under a sultan)*

was so fayre. Thenne he tolde to hym that it was a moche cruel pryson and terryble, in whyche the souldan helde a prysonner, a grete lord and baron of the weste whyche was comen for to espye these contreyes. Thenne sayd Parys, "I praye you, late us goo see hym," and the admyral sayd he shold gladly. Thenne they alyghted fro their horses and entred into the pryson, and whan Parys sawe the doulphyn, he had in hys hert grete desplaysyr bycause of the myserable and sorouful lyf that he suffred. And Parys demaunded of the kepars what man he was, and they sayd that he was a grete baron of Fraunce. Thenne sayd Parys, "Understondeth he Mourysshe?" And they sayd nay, but that notwythstondyng, yf he wold speke to hym, that they shold fynde tourchemen[29] ynough. Thenne sayd Parys he wold retorne another day for to demaunde of hym of the partyes of the weste, and prayed the admyral to gyve comandement to the kepars that as ofte as he shold come, that they shold shewe hym to hym. And incontynent he comanded lyke as Parys had desyred, and thenne they departed. And a fewe dayes after, Parys returned and came to the pryson and brought one of the freres wyth hym that coude speke Mouryske. And whan they were wythin[30] the pryson, Paris sayd to the frere that he shold salewe hym curtoysly; nevertheles, the frere knew noo thyng that Parys coude speke Frensshe. Thenne the frere sayd to the doulphyn that that lord was come [fol. 30v] for to vysyte hym, and that he loved wel Crysten men, and that he was wel in the grace of the souldan, and that he trusted ys[31] moche in hym as in ony man of hys contrye. And thus the frere demaunded many thynges of the doulphyn in the name of Parys and sayd yf he mygt doo for hym he wold gladly.

8   Whan the doulphyn herde the relygious frere thus speke in the persone of the Moure, he was moche abasshed in hys courage, bysechyng our Lord that he wold put hym in suche courage and good wylle for to brynge hym out of pryson. Parys desyred to here tydynges of the fayr Vyenne sayd to the frere that he shold aske of the doulphyn yf he had ony wyf or chyldren. Thenne the doulphyn began to wepe and said that he had a wyf and a doughter holden for the fayrest of Fraunce, whom he helde in pryson bycause she wold take noo husbond. Thenne Paris began to comforte hym by the mouthe of the frere sayeng that he shold take alle in pacyence and God shold yet ones delyver hym oute of pryson, by whyche wordes the doulphyn was so rejoyced and joyous that hym semed that God had appyered to hym. And the doulphyn sayd to the frere that it was grete pyté that the Moure was not Crysten and prayed our Lord that he wold gyve to hym puyssaunce to kepe hym in that good wylle that he had. And so departed that one fro that other moche comforted. Thenne Parys sayd to the kepars that he had found so grete playsyr in the prysonner that he wold ofte tymes come for to dysporte[32] hym, and they sayd whan it playsed hym he shold retorne and be welcome.

9   And thenne Parys sayd to the freres that were in that place, "Yf I thought to be sure of you, I thynke wel to fynde the moyen[33] to brynge thys prysonner out of pryson." And the

---

[29] interpreters
[30] inside
[31] as
[32] amuse
[33] means

freres were moche admerveylled[34] of thys whiche Parys had sayd to them, and they sayd to hym, "By the fayth that we owe to our God that of us ye nede not to doubte, and in caas that ye be in wylle, late us assaye.[35] But it must be doon secretely, for ye see wel how many kepars been there contynuelly." Thenne sayd Parys, "I shal gyve to you good counceyl and remedye of alle thys, but I wyl have two thynges. The fyrst thynge is I wyl that ye goo wyth me. That other is that he shal gyve to me my lyvyng honourably in hys contré, for I am in grete doubte whan I have delyverd hym and shal be in hys countreye, that he wyl sette nought by me, and I can[36] noo mestyer[37] ne crafte and [fol. 31r] soo I myght be wel deceyved. Therfore, yf he wyl assure me and that he wyl gyve to me a yefte[38] suche as I shal demaunde hym whan I shal be in hys contreye, I shal delyver hym and shal leve my contree for love of hym, and ye may see in what estate I am."

10   On the morne, Parys and the freres came into the pryson and the frere recounted al thys to the doulphyn, and whan the doulphyn understode thys, hym thought that God bare hym awaye, and sayd, "I thanke God and thys Moure of the good wylle that he hath toward me, for I never dyd hym servyce ne playsyr wherfore he ought to do so moche for me; nevertheles, I hope that is the playsyr of God that he shal delyver me oute of pryson. I am redy to swere upon the body of Jhesu Cryst, or I ever departe from hens, that as sone as I shal be in myn owne lande, I shal mayntene hym in more gretter estate[39] than he ne is here. And I wyl that he doo alle hys wylle of al my londe, for it shal suffyce to me onely that I have a lyvyng for me and my wyf, and I shal do al that he wylle. And so say ye to hym of my behalve." And thenne the frere tolde al to Parys that whych the doulphyn had sayd and promysed to do, and to the ende that Parys shold be more sure, he sayd to the frere that he shold bryng tofore hym the body of our lord Jhesu Cryst, and that tofore hym he shold swere to holde alle that he promysed. And the frere tolde it to Parys, and the doulphyn sware it tofore Parys to accomplysshe alle that he had promysed. And whan he had sworne, to the ende that Parys shold be the better contente, the doulphyn receyved the precyous body of our lord Jhesu Cryst, sayeng that it shold be to the dampnacyon of hys soule in caas that he accomplysshed not al that he had promysed whan they shold be in his londe.

11   And whan thys was doo, Parys and the freres departed fro the doulphyn and wente to the porte for to wyte yf there were ony fuste[40] that wold come hytherward. And by adventure they fonde a fuste, and Parys wyth the freres spake to the patrone[41] and promysed hym a thousand besaunts[42] of gold yf they wold lete have passage fyve persones. The patron, seyng the grete tresour, sayd to them that he was contente, but he wold have

---

[34] *astonished*

[35] *attempt*

[36] *know*

[37] *trade (mystery) (occupation)*

[38] *gift*

[39] *status (wealth)*

[40] *small galley with a sail*

[41] *master of a ship*

[42] *bezants (gold coins from Byzantium)*

half at the porte and sayd to them, "Lordes, I praye you make you redy, for in caas that the Moures of thys londe fonde us we shold be al dede." Thenne sayd Parys, "Make yourself al redy for thys nyght at mydnyght I [fol. 31v] shal come." And after thys Parys retorned to hys lodgyng and dyd do make redy moche vytayll[43] and the best wynes that he coude gete, and he with the freres maad provysyon of alle other thynges and mantellys[44] and towellys.[45]

12   Whan al was redy, Parys wente to the kepars of the pryson and sayd, "I thanke you many tymes of the playsyrs thet ye have doon to me. I wyl now departe from hens for to retorne to my lord the souldan. But for your love I wyl soupe wyth you thys nyght and praye yow that we may soupe togyder." And they ansuerd that it wel pleased them for his love. Thenne Parys sente for the vytall and for the wyn, and after it was come they souped togyder. And the kepars, which had not been accustomed to drynke wyn, drank so moche that they alle were dronke, and incontynent layed them doun to slepe and slepte so faste that for noo thyng they coude not awake them. And whan Parys sawe that, he sayd to the freres that they shold unfeter[46] the doulphyn and that they shold opene the yates[47] of the pryson, "and yf ony of the kepars awake, I shal slee hym." Thenne the freres began to unfetere the doulphyn wyth grete drede, prayeng God to be theyr ayde and helpe. And whan the doulphyn was loos, he cladde hym lyke a Moure. After, Parys slewe alle the kepars one after another, bycause yf they awoke they shold not come after them.

13   Thys doon, the doulphyn wyth Parys and his varlet and the two freres camen to the porte and hastely entred into the fuste which was al redy, and wonde up theyr saylle and, by the helpe of God, began so fast to saylle that wythin fewe dayes they arryveden in a place that thenne was Crysten. And there the doulphyn wente alonde bycause he was moche greved and annoyed as wel of the see as for the harme that he had suffred in pryson, and there borowed money. And fro thens came into Cypres where was a kyng whyche had dwellyd in the courte of the kyng of Fraunce, the whiche, as sone as he knewe that the doulphyn of Vyennoys was come, he went to mete hym and prayed hym that he wold come and lodge in hys paleys. And the doulphyn wente thyder, wherof the kyng had grete joye, and there he made hym grete chyere, for many tymes they had seen eche other in the kynges court of Fraunce. And after, the kynge demaunded hym of his adventure, and the doulphyn recounted [fol. 32r] it to hym al alonge. And bycause of the comyng of the doulphyn, he made moche grete feste and receyved hym moche hyely[48] and made hym to sojourne there as longe as it playsed hym. And whan the doulphyn had sojourned there at his playsyr, he look leve of the kyng and of al hys courte, thankyng hym moche of the grete playsyr that he had doon to hym. The kyng, seyng that the doulphyn wold departe, he gaf to hym grete yeftes[49] and dyd do arme two galleyes whyche accompanyed

---

[43] *food*

[44] *cloaks (covers)*

[45] *towels (tablecloths)*

[46] *unchain*

[47] *gates*

[48] *with great honor*

[49] *gifts*

hym and brought hym upon the see, and had soo good wynde that in fewe dayes after they brought hym into Aygues Mortes.

14   Whan the doulphyn was arryved, the knyghtes of the Doulphyné[50] herde it anone and forthwyth maad them redy and went to horsback and mette wyth hym at Aygues Mortes and there receyved hym in grete honour, and so came forth the ryght waye to Vyenne. And for joye of hys comyng, al they of the cyté made a moche noble and mervayllous feste whyche endured wel fyftene dayes, and the playsyr and joye was so grete emonge them bycause they had recouverd theyr lord that noo man shold and coude have thought it. Parys in alle this wyse never chaunged hys vesture[51] ne clothyng but contynuelly wente to masse. And, by the commaundement of the doulphyn, the people dyd hym grete reverence and honour, so moche that Parys was ashamed therof, and spake noo thynge but Mouryske. And he had a grete berde and made to noo persone of the world ony knowleche.[52] And after a whyle of tyme, the doulphyn, for to accomplysshe that he had promysed to Parys, by the frere dyd do say to Parys and do demaunde yf he wold have the seygnourye[53] of hys lond and contree, for he was al redy for to accomplysshe that whyche he had promysed. And Parys made to hym ansuer that he shold kepe stylle hys londe. Thenne the doulphyn dyd do demaunde hym yf he wold have hys doughter, Vyenne, and Parys made the frere to say ye,[54] for that pleased hym wel. And thenne they wente to hyr.

15   Thenne, whan they were tofore Vyenne, the frere spake first. "Madame, ye knowe wel that my lord your fader hath ben a grete whyle in pryson and yet shold have been ne had have been thys Moure whyche hath saved hym, puttyng hys persone in ryght grete peryl and daunger for the love of my lord your fader. And thus ye may wel [fol. 32v] knowe how moche he is holden to hym, and bycause herof your fader is subget to hym ever. Wherfore your fader prayeth you that, upon al the playsyr that ye wyl doo for hym, that ye wyll take hym for your husbond, and he shal pardonne all the desplaysyr that ever ye dyd to hym." When the frere had fynysshed his wordes, Vyenne ansuerd to hym sayeng, "The bysshop of Saynt Laurence knoweth wel, that is here present, that it is longe syth that, yf I wold have be maryed, I myght have ben maryed wyth more honour unto my fader than unto this Moure, for the sone of the duc of Borgoyne had espoused me yf I wold have consented. But God hath put me in suche a maladye that I may not longe lyve in this world, and every day my maladye encreaceth and so enpayreth[55] me that I am half roten. Wherfore I praye you to say to my fader that he holde me excused, for at thys tyme I wyl not be maryed."

16   Thenne they took theyr leve of Vyenne and recounted alle thys to the doulphyn. Thenne the doulphyn sayd to the frere that he shold say it to the Moure, and so the frere tolde it al to Parys. And thenne Parys, which was aferde to lese the love of Vyenne, wente

---

[50] *Dauphiné, county in southeastern France*
[51] *clothing*
[52] *knowledge [of his identity]*
[53] *lordship (rule)*
[54] *yes*
[55] *impairs*

for to see hyr in the pryson with the frere and the bysshop of Saynt Laurence. Thanne whan Parys sawe Vyenne in that dysposycyon,[56] he had moche grete sorowe and grete merveylle,[57] and thenne he made the frere to salewe hyr in hys name, and Vyenne ansuerd unto hys gretyng ryght curtoysly. And the frere sayd in the name of Parys, "Madame, ye knowe wel I have delyverd your fader oute of pryson, wherof ye ought to have synguler playsyr, and yet he shold have been there yf I had not have been and holpen[58] hym oute. And he pardonneth you wyth good hert and good wylle all the desplaysyrs that ever ye dyd ageynst hys playsyr, and prayeth you that ye take me for your husbond and wyll that we have the lordshyp of the Doulphyné; and therfor I praye you that neyther ye nor I lose not thys honour. And yet more though thys were not, ye ought not to dysobeye the commaundementes of your fader."

17   And thenne Vyenne ansuerd to the frere as to the persone of Parys sayeng, "I knowe wel that ye have delyverd my fader oute of pryson, notwythstondyng, my fader shal have suche regarde ageynst you that ye shal lese noo thynge. And I wote wel that ye be a man of grete lyngage and are the worthy to have a gretter lady than I am. But the bysshop of Seynt Laurence, whyche is present, knoweth [fol. 33r] wel that for the maladye that I am in, I may not long lyve." And thenne sayd the frere in his name, "This is bycause I am a Moure that ye refuse me. I promyse you that I shal become Crysten. But I thynke wel that yf ye knewe who that I am and what I have lefte for to brynge your fader oute of pryson, that ye wold preyse me more than ye doo. Knowe ye for certeyn that your fader shal be parjured,[59] for he hath promysed that ye shal be my wyf, wherof ye shal have blame. Therfore, yf it playse you, graunte ye hym hys wylle." Thenne sayd Vyenne, "Lord, I have herd say moche good of you, and that ye be he that have doon so moche for my fader, but nevertheles, in the maladye in the whyche I am, none ought to counceyl me to take an husbond, for my lyf may not longe endure. And bycause that ye may knowe that I say trouth, approche ye ner to me and ye shal fele and smelle in what dysposycyon I am of my persone."

18   And thenne they approuched ner to hyr. And Vyenne had put two quarters of an henne under hyr two arme hooles, and there yssued so grete stenche that the bysshop ne the frere myght not suffre it. Nevertheles, the stynche was to Parys a good odour, for he smellyd it not and sayd, "I wote not what ye smelle, for I fele none evyl savour."[60] And they mervaylled strongely bycause he felte not the odour. And the frere sayd in Parys name, "For this odour shal I never leve you, and I assure you I shal never departe fro hens untyl ye have consented to that your fader wyl." And Vyenne answerd moche angrely and sayd, "By the fayth that I owe to God, I shal rather renne[61] wyth my hede ayenst the walle that I shal make my brayn oute of my mouth, and so shal ye be the occasyon of my dethe." Thenne sayd the frere, "Ye shal not so doo, madame, for I promyse you fro hens forth that I shal never speke more to you, sythe that it is not your wylle ne plesyr. But atte leste

---

[56] *condition*

[57] *astonishment*

[58] *helped*

[59] *perjured*

[60] *scent*

[61] *run*

of one thyng I praye you, that this nyght ye advyse you, and I shal retorne to morn for to have of you an ansuer. And ye shal take counceyll of your felowe, and I praye to God that ye may be wel counceylled." And alle these thynges sayd the frere in the name of Parys to Vyenne. And after, they took theyr leve of Vyenne and sayd alle to the doulphyn, wherof he was thenne moche dyspleased, and had the frere to telle it alle unto Parys for to excuse hym and that he shold not lye the blame on hym.

19   And whan they were departed fro Vyenne, she sayd to Ysabeau, "My [fol. 33v] fayr suster, what semeth you of the wysedom of my fader that thynketh that I shold take thys Moure to my husbond and have refused the sone of the duke of Bourgoyne? But God forbede that ever in my lyf I have other lord than Parys to myn husbond, whome I hope yet to have." And Ysabeau sayd, "Certes madame, I wote not what to say of your fader whyche wold gyve you to a Moure in maryage. I have therof grete thought, for he hath sayd that he shal retorne to morn to see you and hath sayd that ye shold remembre and advyse you."

Chapter 23: How Parys came to see Vyenne in the pryson, and how she knew hym.

1   And on the morn betymes,[1] Parys cladde hym moche more rychely than he had be accustomed and gyrde wyth a moche ryche swerde and came to the pryson with the frere. And the frere sayd to hyr, "Madame, we been retorned for to knowe your good answer and your entencyon." And Vyenne ansuerd, "Lordes, myn entencyon is that I shal never breke my promesse that I have made. For I have avowed that I shal never take husbond, ne goo oute of this pryson but dede,[2] sauf[3] hym to whome I have promysed, and therfor retorne ye in good tyme."

2   Thenne sayd the frere, "By my fayth, I wote not what to say, for it is grete dommage[4] that ye suffre so moche sorowe and payne. And syth it is thus your wylle and that ye wyl none otherwyse do, nevertheles, the Moure prayeth you that it may playse you to do to hym so moche grace that, syth ye wyl not take hym in maryage, that ye wyl were thys rynge for the love of hym." Now thys rynge was the same rynge that Vyenne gaf to Parys whan he departed fro hyr in the hows of the chappelayn, and Vyenne, bycause they shold nomore come ageyn, took the rynge. And whan she had receyved the rynge, Parys sayd to the frere, "I praye you that ye tarye a lytel wythoute,[5] for I wyl see what countenaunce[6] she wyl make of the rynge." And the frere sayd, "Gladly," nevertheles, he mervaylled moche. And incontynent the frere wente oute. And Vyenne began to beholde the rynge, and whan Parys sawe that Vyenne byhelde the rynge so strongely, he began to speke in hys playne tongue[7] and sayd, "O moche noble lady, why be ye so moche admervayled[8] of that

---

[1] *early*

[2] *dead*

[3] *except (saving)*

[4] *pity [OF domage]*

[5] *outside*

[6] *expression*

[7] *French, not Moorish*

[8] *astonished*

rynge?" Thenne sayd Vyenne, "Certes, to my semyng[9] I sawe never a fayrer." Thenne sayd Parys, "Therfore I praye [fol. 34r] you that ye take therin playsyr, for the more that ye byholde it, the more ye shal prayse it."

3   Whan Vyenne herde the Moure thus speke, thenne she was more admervaylled than tofore and was as a persone al abasshed and sayd, "Alas, am I enchaunted, and what is thys that I see and here speke?" And in sayeng these wordes she wold have fledde for fere oute of the pryson, bycause she herde the Moure so speke. Thenne sayd Parys, "O moche noble lady Vyenne, mervaylle ye noo thynge ne have ye noo doubte. Lo, here is Parys your true servaunte." And Vyenne was thenne abasshed more than tofore. "Certes," sayd she, "this may not be but by werke enchaunted." And Parys sayd, "Noble lady, hit is none enchaunted werke, for I am your servaunt Parys whyche lefte you with Ysabeau in suche a chyrche, and there ye gaf to me the dyamond whiche now I have delyverd to you, and there ye promysed to me that ye wold never take husbond but me. And be ye noo thynge admervaylled of the berde ne of the vesture that I were, for they take aweye the knowleche of me." And many other wordes sayd Parys to Vyenne, by whyche she knewe clerely that he was Parys. And for the soverayn love that she bare to hym, and for the grete joye that she had, she began to wepe in hys armes and to embrace and kysse hym moche swetely. And there they comforted eche other wyth swete wordes, and so abode longe tyme. Vyenne coude not ynough kysse hym and enbrace hym, and also Parys demaunded of hyr of hyr adventure, and she tolde hym alle.

4   And of alle thys Ysabeau had nothyng herde of, for she was faste aslepe bycause she had watched[10] alle the nyght byfore. And for the grete joye and swetenes that Parys and Vyenne demeaned[11] bytwene them, she awoke. And whan she sawe Vyenne beyng enbraced with the Moure, she sayd, "Madame, what is thys that ye do? Have ye loste your wytte that so enbrace this Moure? Hath he enchaunted you that ye suffre hym soo famylyer wyth you, and is this the fayth that ye kepe to Parys, for whom ye have suffred so moche payne and sorowe?" And Vyenne sayd, "Swete suster, say ye noo suche wordes, but come and take your parte of the solace that I have, for also wel have ye founden good adventure as I have. See ye not here my swete Parys whome so moche we have desyred?" Thenne Ysabeau approched ner to hym and byhelde hym wel and sawe that it was Parys, and she wente and kyssed hym and demened so moche [fol. 34v] grete joye bytwene them thre that there is noo persone in the world that myght say ne thynke it, but so abode a grete whyle in thys soulas and joye, tyl atte laste Parys spack. "Swete Vyenne, it byhoveth that we goo hens tofore my lord the dolphyn, your fader, for now fro hens forth it is necessarye that he knowe alle our fayte; nevertheles, I praye you to say nothyng tyl I desyre you."

5   And al thre came oute of the pryson and fonde the frere, whyche mervaylled gretely, and alle they togydre wente to the doulphyn, whyche had soverayn playsyr whan he sawe them, and nevertheles, he was moche abasshed how his doughter was so come. And thenne Parys sayd to the frere, "Say ye to the doulphyn that I have converted hys doughter

---

[9] to my semyng, *in my opinion*
[10] *kept watch*
[11] *expressed*

to hys wylle and to myn, and that it playse hym that she be my wyf." And the frere sayd soo. Thenne the doulphyn sayd to hys doughter, "Wyl ye take thys man for your husbond, whyche hath delyverd me oute of pryson in grete peryl of hys persone?" Thenne demaunded Vyenne of Parys yf he wold that she shold speke, and Parys sayd, "ye." And thenne Vyenne sayd to the doulphyn, "My fader, I am redy to do your commaundement and hys, and praye you to pardonne me and to gyve to me your benedyctyon." And whan she sayd thys, hyr fader pardonned hyr and gaf to hyr hys blessyng and kyssed hyr. Thenne sayd Vyenne, "Loo, here is my good frende Parys whome I have so moche desyred and for whome I have suffred so moche payne and sorowe. And, fader, thys is he that so swetely songe and floyted[12] and that wanne the joustes in thys cyté and bare with hym the shelde of crystal and my garlonde, and also thys is he that wanne the joustes in the cyté of Paris and wan there the thre baners wyth the two jewellys and went awaye with them wythoute knowyng of ony man. And also, he hath delyverd you out of pryson, puttyng hys lyf in jeopardye for you." And whan the doulphyn understood al thys, he was mervayllously glad and joyous.

6   After al thys, Parys went to his fader, and whan he sawe hym and knewe that he was hys sone Parys whome he had so longe desyred to see, he enbraced hym and kyssed hym, and for the joye that he had he coude not speke a word, and after alle the other lordes and knyghtes ranne for to embrace and kysse hym. And after this joye, Parys fader sayd to the doulphyn, "My lorde, playse it you that I may borowe[13] my sone home to my hous for to see his moder and hys felowe Edward?" [fol. 35r] Thenne sayd the doulphyn, "It playseth me ryght wel onely for thys day, for tomorn I wyl that the maryage of hym and my doughter be made and solempnysed[14] here." And thenne messyre Jaques wente with hys sone unto hys hous, and whan he was there, verayly his fader, his moder, and hys felowe Edward wyst not where they were for joye and playsyr that they had. And that was noo wonder, for they had no moo chyldren but hym, and he shold wedde the doughter of their lord, and also Parys was in that tyme become a valyaunte knyght and ful of al beaulté.[15] And for many reasons, it was no mervayll though they had in hym grete joye and playsyr. And Edward demaunded of hym of hys adventure and many other thynges, and he recounted and tolde hym alle.

---

[12] *played the flute*

[13] *be surety for*

[14] *performed (solemnized)*

[15] *courtesy*

Chapter 24: How Parys espoused and wedded Vyenne, and of the feste that was there made.

1   Thenne on the morne, the dolphyn gaf his doughter in maryage to Parys and the feste was moche noble and sumptuous for moche peple were comen thyder for to see the feste, and it endured fyftene dayes. And the playsyr and solace whyche was doon for the love of Parys and of Vyenne was soo grete that unnethe it may be byleved, whyche Parys and Vyenne lyved togyder a grete whyle in ryght grete consolacyon and playsyr. But after the accomplysshement of the maryage, the fader and moder of Parys lyveden not longe after in thys world. And Parys had by Vyenne, hys wyf, thre chyldren; that is to wete two sones and one doughter. And the doulphyn ordeyned for them moche noble matrymonye. And Parys, after the deth of hys fader and his moder, wold that Edward, hys dere felowe, shold be herytyer[1] of al the goodes that hys fader lefte, and gaf to hym Ysabeau to hys wyf, whyche lyved togyder longe tyme in grete love and concorde. And sone after, the doulphyn and hys wyf deyeden. And thenne was Parys doulphyn and had the possessyon of al the seygnourye, the whyche lyved wyth Vyenne in thys world fourty yere and ledde a good and holy lyf, insomoche that after the entendement[2] of somme men they be sayntes in heven, and they deyed bothe in one yere. And semblably[3] Edward and Ysabeau deyed bothe tweyne in one yere. Therfore, late us praye unto our Lord that we may doo suche werkes in this world that in suche wyse we [fol. 35v] may accompanye them in the perdurable[4] glorye of heven. Amen.

2   Thus endeth the hystorye of the noble and valyaunt knyght Parys and the fayr Vyenne, doughter of the doulphyn of Vyennoys, translated out of Frensshe into Englysshe by Wylliam Caxton at Westmestre,[5] fynysshed the last day of August the yere of our lord M CCCC lxxxv,[6] and enprynted the ninetene day of Decembre the same yere, and the fyrst yere of the regne of kyng Harry the seventh.

    Explicit[7] par Caxton

---

[1] *heir*
[2] *belief*
[3] *similarly*
[4] *everlasting*
[5] *Westminster*
[6] *1485*
[7] *it ends [Lat.]*

Explanatory Notes to *Paris and Vienne*

MacEdward Leach's edition of *Paris and Vienne* includes explanatory notes and detailed annotations and comparisons of the manuscript, Leeu's print, and Caxton's translation, including passages from the French texts. The following notes incorporate information from his citations, adapted and expanded in keeping with METS editorial policies. Leach's transcriptions of passages in French have been summarized and translated.

Chapter 1, Paragraph 1

kynge Charles. No king Charles ruled France in 1271, and Vers. I gives no date; however, a series of kings from the Valois family had that name (ruled 1364–1461). Cépède composed his romance during the reign of Charles VII.

Vyennoys. Vienne, south of Lyons, is the principal city of the region of Vienne, whose lords took the title *dauphin* [Fr. dolphin] from the emblem and sobriquet of a family founder. Young Charles V inherited the province from his grandfather in 1349 and used the title until his coronation; following this precedent the title and territories passed exclusively to the successor to the French throne. The region itself was referred to as Dauphiné.

Godefroy of Alaunson. No such person has been identified.

that men calle Dyane. This phrase does not appear in BN1. The reference is confusing, for in Roman mythology, Diana is the goddess of the moon, while Venus is associated with both the morning and the evening star.

redy to Hys devyne servyce. See MED *redi* (adj. 3, senses 1(a), 5 (a)). This makes the gloss, "Children pleasing and eager to serve God."

prayer. The infertile couple whose prayer for a child is answered (*MIFL* D1925.3, T548.1) is a staple of romance plotting. Often, as here and in *Blanchardyn and Eglantine*, it is the initial episode leading to the birth of the protagonist. The meme also appears in the Middle English verse romances *Sir Tryamour*, *Northern Octavian*, and *Sir Gowther*.

nouryshed. It was a common practice among the nobility and gentry to place their infants with wet nurses, often members of their households or affinity. The romance's attention to the pedigree of the protagonist's breast milk is similar to that in *Blanchardyn and Eglantine* (1.2).

beawté and gentylnesse. Vers. I includes several more sentences detailing Vienne's accomplishments: reading books of romances and histories, mastery of dancing, singing, and many musical instruments, and being in all things gracious and pleasant. Her musicianship complements that of Paris.

Chapter 1, Paragraph 2

fyftene. L says she is twelve; BN1 gives no age. Caxton makes Vienne older, perhaps a reflection of the English practice of later marriage. In Vers. I the couple are younger — he is sixteen and she is eleven, which more nearly accords with marriage practices in southern Europe.

knyghtes. L and BN1 mention royalty among her suitors, including kings, princes, and dukes.

Syr James. BN1 and L give the name Jacques, which Caxton uses in the rest of the romance.

by the hande of the sayd lord daulphyn. Caxton added the detail of the dauphin knighting Paris. L reads *et dedans peu de tamps fut fait chevalier* [and in a short while was made knight]. BN1 lacks this concluding phrase.

Chapter 1, Paragraph 3

huntyng. Hunting was the purview of the aristocracy and part of the performance of chivalry. Many romances include episodes of hunting and members of the nobilty and gentry owned manuals of hunting. See, for example, *The Master of Game* by Edward of Norwich, second duke of York; the *Book of St. Albans*, by Juliana Berners; *The Art of Hunting*, by William Twiti.

honour. BN1 and L vary from BL and each other. BN1 says the knights went to tournaments throughout the land [*monde*], while L says they especially attended those in the kingdom of France. Both BN1 and L conclude by remarking on the couples' exemplary youth and beauty.

Chapter 1, Paragraph 4

musycyens. Musicianship was associated with chivalry, especially the ability to perform courtly melodies and lyrics. Sir Tristrem was a noted harper; his lessons with Isolde kindled their love affair. Chaucer says of his Squire that "syngynge he was, or floytynge [piping], al the day; . . . He koude songes make and wel endite" (*CT* I [A] 91, 95).

Venus, the goddes of love. The phrase was added by Caxton; it is the only reference to the gods and religion of courtly love in the short version. BN1 and L say only that before a year had passed Paris began to fall in love with Vienne.

hyghe lygnage. Paris's father is a vassal of the dauphin and without a title.

Explanatory Notes to *Paris and Vienne* 103

Chapter 2, Rubric

by nyght tofore the chambre of Vyenne. BN1 and L read *aubades*, a word from Old Provençal referring to love songs, literally dawn songs. According to convention, they would be performed beneath a lady's opened window.

Chapter 2, Paragraph 1

theyr musycal instrumentes. Caxton has introduced details into this account of Paris's and Edward's performance, namely recorders, pipes, other instruments, and men's voices.

mynstrellys. Vers.1 devotes more attention to the episode of the minstrel contest, a convention of romance in which the hero in disguise is judged the winner, often in competition for the favor of a lady. In *Paris and Vienne*, the hero declines to participate and is still judged the champion.

Chapter 2, Paragraph 2

came. BN1 and L include a detail missing from Caxton, a boy [*enfant*] who carries the instruments. Paris and Edward are concerned for the child should they be discovered; L explains that they send him back to the hostel.

Chapter 2, Paragraph 4

they recounted. In BN1 and L the men relate that three of them were wounded — in the head, the arm, and the leg.

Chapter 2, Paragraph 5

Saynt Laurence. In Vers. I the name is Saint Vincent. No such place has been identified in the city of Vienne.

Chapter 2, Paragraph 6

lystes and scaffoldes to be sette up. Caxton has added details to this passage to heighten the splendor of the event, specifically the construction of the stands and the presence of heralds and knights from Normandy, the fine gold of the jewels, and the nobility and beauty of Vienne.

fyrst day of May. May Day was traditionally a time to celebrate the coming of spring (and love) and a day of festivals. In the later Middle Ages, many tournaments were held around May Day and Whitsuntide; Froissart notes that English knights assembled for the jousts of St. Engelvert (1390) at the beginning of May (*Chronicles*, ed. Brereton, pp. 373–81).

Chapter 2, Paragraph 7

Johan duc of Bourbon . . . duc of Carnes. The names of the knights in this and other lists of tournament participants do not always agree with those in BN1 and L, which vary from each other; Caxton adds references to English knights. Attempts to associate the names with historical personages have met with limited success.

Chapter 2, Paragraph 9

wete ye wel . . . byfore hyr. Gracious table service and skill at carving were regarded as necessary accomplishments for young gentlemen and knights. See, for example, Chaucer's Squire who "carf biforn his fader at the table" (*CT* I [A]100). Caxton printed *The Babee's Boke* and *The Boke of Curtasye* which include instructions on table manners (ed. Furnivall, *Early English Meals and Manners*, pp. 250–58; pp. 175–205). *The Boke of Kervynge*, printed by Wynkyn de Worde, gives detailed instructions for carving and serving (ed. Furnivall, *Early English Meals and Manners*, pp. 147–74). BN1 and L conclude the scene differently. While serving, Paris observes Vienne's beauty and feels the love in his heart grow; however, he takes great care that no one should notice it.

Chapter 3, Paragraph 1

juste. The tournament episode incorporates several familiar motifs: the knight who participates incognito in a three day tournament for the hand of a lady, in which he proves his valor and defeats other suitors (*MIFL* R222, also H331.2).

rydyng tofore . . . Edward of England. Not in BN1 or L. Caxton adds details of the muster as the knights, in full regalia, parade by Vienne's scaffold.

floure of knyghthode. A conventional expression and metaphor: the flowering, the perfect development of chivalry; a gathering of those knights held to be the most accomplished in feats of arms (see Whiting F311).

Chapter 3, Paragraph 2

worshyp. Worship was synoymous with respect, honor, esteem, and high social status. In the context of chivalry, it refers to praise and renown for deeds of arms (*MED worship(e* (n.) senses 1a; 3a).

Edward. The king of England's son is not mentioned in Vers. I, which contains an extended technical account of Paris's combat with a nameless knight. All texts of the short version agree in identifying him as Edward.

Explanatory Notes to Paris and Vienne 105

Chapter 4, Paragraph 1

themself. Vers. I includes extended conversations between Paris and Edward and between Vienne and Ysabel.

Chapter 4, Paragraph 3

estate. The term refers to social status or rank and to the three estates constituting medieval society: clergy, nobility, and commons. It also has the meanings of wealth and possessions (*MED estat* (n.), senses 10a; 14a)

hym. In Vers. I Vienne expounds upon her lovesickness at length, as does Paris in the passage that follows there.

Chapter 4, Paragraph 4

sparkles of love. This is a conventional image of the heart aflame with love common in the literature of courtly (and spiritual) love.

sayd. Vers. I gives an extended version of messire Jacques's advice to his son, followed by a lengthy reply from Paris expressing filial devotion and remorse for displeasing his parents.

thys bysshop. Here, and later (6.5; 7.2), Caxton suppresses an anti-clerical comment. In both BN1 and L messire Jaques calls the churchman a *dyable devecque* [devil of a bishop].

Chapter 4, Paragraph 5

Breunes. A region in Champagne. BL and L agree, but BN1, the 1482 Italian print, and Vers. I all read *Bohemia*. Vers. I gives an extended account of the combat.

Constaunce. A Constance (d. 1461) was sister to Edward Langly, Duke of York.

joustes. Vers. I includes a more detailed description of the field and scaffold, and their decorations.

eighth day. In 4.9, the tourney is said to take place of the fourteenth of September.

Chapter 4, Paragraph 7

secretly. Vers. I does not include the justifications for secrecy found in BL, L, and BN1: that the nobles will praise Paris's exploits less if they are aware of his lower status, and that status might also be an affront to Vienne, should he become known as her champion.

Chapter 4, Paragraph 9

for fro all partyes. BN1 says that never before was seen such nobility in France, England, or Flanders. Caxton changes the order of ideas in this passage and introduces new details which emphasize the chivalry and splendor of the occasion. L lacks a detail found in BL and BN1: the three jewels in the banners. Caxton embellishes with a phrase about the sparkle of their gems and pearls.

shortest wyse. The composer of the short romance expedites the narrative, giving an abridged account of the combats described in Vers. I. That romance gives much more detail throughout the tournament episode. Nevertheless, Caxton's romance touches on all the main elements of the tournament: the sending out of heralds to announce it, the establishment of prizes, the construction of lists and scaffolds, the gathering of the participants, the opening address of the sponsor, the parade of knights and catalogue of names and arms, the series of encounters, the awarding of prizes to the victor. As jousts became more and more ceremonial in the fifteenth century, books of instructions and regulations for tournaments began to appear. Sir John Tiptoft, earl of Worcester and constable under Edward IV, wrote *Ordinances for Justes and Triumphes,* a manual including rules for scoring; the Paston's *Great Book* included similar items.

Chapter 4, Paragraph 10

felde be of love. The king declares that these will be combats *à plaisance,* for sport, not *à la outrance,* that is to the utmost, i.e. death. Knights were considered defeated when their lances were broken and they were unhorsed.

Chapter 4, Paragraph 11

Bourgoyne. Burgundy was a region in west central France, seat of powerful dukes who, in the fifteenth century, also ruled much of northern France, modern Belgium, and the Netherlands.

Bremeos. Later, Caxton refers to this character as Johan of Breunes (5.1).

Carnes. Perhaps Tarnès, in southwestern France.

horsed. Vers. I treats the rivalry of the three knights at greater length.

Chapter 5, Paragraph 1

overthrewe hym. The brief accounts of these combats, in which no one is killed, can be contrasted with the extended, graphic combats of *Blanchardyn and Eglantine.*

Chapter 5, Paragraph 2

gaf so grete strokes. Vers. I treats the tournament at greater length and includes different details, making it a more equal contest.

sayeng. Paris's speech is much longer in Vers. I, though its content is the same.

Chapter 6, Paragraph 1

knyght. Vers. I gives an extended account of the awarding of prizes and the declaration recognizing Vienne as the fairest of the ladies.

Fraunce. The region around Paris in what is now central France.

Chapter 6, Paragraph 3

Whan. In Vers. I, the homecoming celebration in Dauphiné is described in detail and the dauphin makes a speech recounting the events of the tournament.

Chapter 6, Paragraph 5

thou. Messire Jacques here uses the familiar singular pronoun, signalling reproach as well as his son's subordinate status. In the following paragraph, Edward uses this form of address to remonstrate with his friend about his conduct.

Chapter 6, Paragraph 6

sayd. In Vers. I messire Jacques's speech is much longer.

melancolye. Melancholy, besides being a state of sadness, is one of the four humors (fluids) of which the human body was composed. According to the medieval system of physiology, each humor corresponded to one of the four elements comprising all of creation. Melancholy, or black bile, was associated with earth and depression; choler, or yellow bile, was associated with fire and anger; blood was associated with air and a sanguine (active and cheerful) temperament; phlegm was associated with water and a placid or sluggish temperament. The medieval theory of disease associated each humor with a particular organ: blood with the liver, yellow and black bile with the gall bladder and spleen, respectively, and phlegm with the lungs and brain. Good health required that the humors be kept in balance, so when messier Jaques is saddened and upset by Paris's behavior, he suffers from a preponderance of black bile and develops a "sekenesse of fevres" (7.1). Disease, whether actual or feigned, is a recurring feature of the romance.

thou. Paris's response to Edward's remonstrations uses the same familiar pronouns as his friend, though here they may signal intimacy as well as objection to the offered advice.

Chapter 7, Paragraph 2

over longe to reherce. The composer of the short version abbreviates the passage. Vers. I describes more chambers in the *hostel* of messire Jacques, giving further details of luxurious apartments and a description of Paris's robe, which Vienne recognizes from an earlier dream.

Chapter 7, Paragraph 4

oratorye. This is a small room for private prayer, often adjacent to a bed chamber. The homes of aristocrats and gentry often featured oratories, which were expressions of both affluence and piety. Paris's, at twelve feet long, is large.

Chapter 7, Paragraph 5

speke. In Vers. I, Vienne calls out Paris's name three times and addresses him in a lengthy passage of apostrophe and exclamation while shedding many tears.

Chapter 7, Paragraph 6

thee. Vienne here uses the familiar singular pronoun to express her anger and scorn for Ysabeau's advice.

stynte. The concluding phrase, which restates Vienne's infatuation with Paris, does not appear in BN1 and L. In L, the exchange between Vienne and Ysabeau concludes with Vienne citing the example of other noble women who loved knights of lower rank, specifically the example of Susana, daughter of the king of Armenia, who became enamored of her chamberlain who had put himself in peril on sea and land for the love of her and her father. Knowing that such prowess must arise from noble extraction, she makes discreet inquiries and discovers that he is Bauduyn, son of the Count D'Austin. This story features lovers who are only apparently of unequal status, and so confirms that chivalry and noble lineage go hand in hand. Vienne laments as she thinks of other lovers, men and women of unequal rank who could not marry and died of despair, and predicts her own similar demise.

Chapter 7, Paragraph 7

hymself. In Vers. I, the conversation is is extended.

home. In Vers. I, Vienne dreams that night of Paris clothed in a rich robe.

Chapter 8, Paragraph 1

After certeyn tyme . . . feates of armes. This paragraph has no counterpart in Vers. I, which says only that Paris and Edward came back from Brabant before narrating the call on the dauphin.

Explanatory Notes to Paris and Vienne

Chapter 8, Paragraph 3

reverence. An act of respect, especially a bow (*MED reverence* (n.), sense 2). Attendance on the lord or lady was a matter of protocol in a noble household as described in Caxton's publication, *The Babees Boke* (ed. Furnivall, *Early English Meals and Manners*, pp. 250–58).

sawe Parys. In Vers. I, Paris wears a robe from Brabant identical to the one in Vienne's dream.

hous. Vers. I tells how Paris goes to the dauphin's castle, where Vienne sees him from a window and converses with Isabel.

Chapter 8, Paragraph 4

sayd to hyr moder. In Vers. I the exchange between Vienne and her mother is longer.

Chapter 9, Paragraph 1

On the morne. The episode that follows is a synopsis of that in Vers. I.

Chapter 9, Paragraph 2

praye me, where ye have power to commaunde me. Paris's reply is couched in the terms of courtly love service where the lady is dominant and the lover her servant. It is also a recognition of her superior social status.

Chapter 9, Paragraph 4

Edward sayd to hym. This scene does not appear in Vers. I; instead, there is a similar exchange between Vienne and Ysabel.

Chapter 9, Paragraph 5

fyftene yere. Vers. I says fourteen.

Chapter 9, Paragraph 6

consentyng of bothe partyes. According to canon law, a valid marriage required the consent of both parties.

Chapter 10, Paragraph 1

thou. The dauphin uses the familiar singular pronoun to emphasize his anger and scorn for messire Jaques and his inferior status as a *vassal* and *vylayne*.

fader. In Vers. I this scene is followed by Vienne's dream of being attacked by a lion in her father's garden and of Paris being unable to rescue her because he cannot cross a river.

Chapter 10, Paragraph 2

We, us. The dauphin here uses formal plural pronouns to refer to himself — the "royal we" — emphasizing his superior status and power.

nonne. In BN1 the dauphin says he will have Vienne dead or keep her in prison; in the Burgundian adaptation of Vers. I, the dauphin threatens to cut her into little pieces and eat her (*FRLMA*, p. 102).

And when Vyenne. In Vers. I Vienne and Ysabeau have a long conversation about her father's response, followed by a similar one between Edward and Paris.

Chapter 10, Paragraph 3

touche not my body unto the tyme. Not in Vers. I.

Chapter 10, Paragraph 4

I have wrath. In Vers. I Paris explains that he is making the arrangements for a friend who has angered the dauphin.

Aygues Mortes. Aigues Mortes, on the Rhone River delta, was an important Mediterranean port. It was a point of preparation and departure for the seventh and eighth crusades in the thirteenth century. Its name, from the Occitan, translates as "dead waters," a reference to the marshes and swamps in the region. As these silted up, the city's importance waned.

fyve myle to fyve myle. George is to arrange for fresh mounts every five miles at regular stages on their journey.

galeye. Vers. I gives a fuller account of George's activities.

passages. BN1 and L include the word *chevaux* [horses]. George arranges the party's itinerary and permits for travel.

two hors. BN1 provides more details of Paris's instructions to George: that he go to his father's house and with the stable hand take two horses, making sure that his father does not know.

Chapter 11, Paragraph 2

Parys, seyng that George . . . passe the water. Not in Vers. I. The composer of the short version has Paris lie to protect Vienne from disturbing news.

Chapter 12, Paragraph 4

who that sleeth hymself wytyngly. Vienne here invokes the Catholic teaching that suicide is a sin and will send one's soul to Hell, though she herself threatens suicide later (22.18). Paris's eagerness to commit suicide is a convention derived from the tradition of troubadour lyrics where lovers profess to die when separated from their ladies. He is perhaps over-reacting, especially in comparison to Vienne's sober assessment of their situation.

whome that ye ought to comforte. Vienne's comment is both a rebuke to Paris's masculinity and an assertion of her own agency, not often seen in romance heroines.

never have other husbond. Vienne's promise, on her faith, to marry only Paris, and his later plea that she take no husband but him (15.3) could be considered a binding betrothal according to medieval canon law. See note 18.4 below.

Chapter 13, Paragraph 1

hevynesse. Vers. I tells of Paris riding alone so overcome with grief that he falls from his horse and is rescued by merchants.

fool. One who is mentally impaired, a person without reason (*MED fol* (n.), sense 1a). The word also has the sense of "fool of kynde," that is one born with mental or physical challenges, since Paris appears to be mute. Other knights of romance driven mad by love are Tristrem and Lancelot, though their cases are extreme: both at times live as wild men in the woods.

Chapter 14, Paragraph 2

The whyche I byleve is drowned. This is an odd statement, though perhaps the chaplain is referring to George, who did drown, or is covering for Paris.

Chapter 14, Paragraph 3

penytence. Repentance is the penance imposed by a priest after hearing a confession. After confessing her love for Paris, Vienne asks to receive penance, saying her suffering will strengthen her soul. Paris, too, seeks penance for causing Vienne's suffering (16.2, 18.7).

deye. Vers. I extends this scene.

Chapter 14, Paragraph 6

he wold doo marye. The dauphin is asking the earl of Flanders to advise him about suitable husbands for Vienne. In keeping with medieval practices of arranged aristocratic marriages, the negotiations continue with the king of France who must approve the proposed union.

myght. Vers. I contains a detailed account of Paris's life in Genoa.

Chapter 15, Paragraph 1

letter. Paris's letter in Vers. I begs his father's pardon for causing him suffering and asks for news of him, but says nothing of his intention to serve God and go on pilgrimage, or about treating Edward as a son and heir. In the short version Paris's journey is expiatory, an attempt to atone for his transgressions of disobedience to his parents and causing the suffering of Vienne (*FRLMA*, p. 124n120).

Chapter 15, Paragraph 2

letter of Edward sayd thus. In Vers. I, messire Jacques shares the letter with Edward who recounts the news to Vienne. She has Edward write to Paris, instructing him to go to the bank of Bertran de Picartville should he need funds.

Chapter 15, Paragraph 3

faders. In BN1 and Vers. I, he is to send the letter to a Jacques de Plaisance in Genoa.

Chapter 15, Paragraph 4

herde. Perhaps Edward is listening to someone reading the letters aloud.

Chapter 15, Paragraph 6

Edward sayd. This is a mistake; Vienne is still speaking. BN1 and L read "'Il est verite,' dist Vienne, 'mais ne me parler plus de la lettre'" ["It is true," said Vienne, "but do not speak to me more of the letter."]

Chapter 16, Paragraph 1

eschaunge. A letter of credit or exchange, arranging a transfer funds. Letters of exchange became common in the later Middle Ages as international trade flourished and a banking system developed.

letter, whyche she reteyneth ... said letter. This detail, Vienne's refusal to return the letter, is not related in BN1 and Vers. I.

Chapter 16, Paragraph 4

we. Vienne uses the formal plural.

maladye. The word has a double meaning, referring to her physical illness but also to her lovesickness for Paris. As long as she suffers this malady she will marry no one, and only Paris can cure her.

EXPLANATORY NOTES TO *Paris and Vienne*

CHAPTER 16, PARAGRAPH 6

doulphyn. The dauphin's harsh treatment of Vienne here and in following episodes is extreme, but historical examples show that parents did use such measures to compel their daughters to accept arranged marriages. See the Introduction to this romance, p. 30.

CHAPTER 17, PARAGRAPH 1

After. Vers. I has a different order of episodes. There, Paris hears rumors of Vienne's marriage to the son of the duke of Burgundy and writes to Edward explaining his plans to travel to Venice and points east. This letter is similar to the letter appearing in a later chapter (19.1). In Vers. I Edward's receipt of the letter is followed by his discovery of Vienne's prison and the building of a chapel to gain access to it. BL, BN1, and L abbreviate this episode, which appears following Vienne's second imprisonment (18.5–6).

CHAPTER 18, PARAGRAPH 2

quarters of the henne. Breast or leg quarters of a chicken, presumably cooked since they are intended for Vienne to eat (*MED quartere* (n.), sense 1b).

CHAPTER 18, PARAGRAPH 4

I am maryed. Vienne's pledge to Paris (12.4) and his to her could be considered a binding betrothal. See Introduction to this romance, pp. 25–26, for discussion of medieval marriage laws.

stenche. Similar ruses appear in folklore, where women use foul odors to defend their chastity and repel unwanted suitors (*MIFL* T320.4.1, bad breath; T323.2, smelly cloak). A story of Lombard sisters who repelled their attackers by concealing rotten chicken flesh in their clothes circulated widely in the Middle Ages.

CHAPTER 18, PARAGRAPH 5

chapel. A church was adjacent to the castle of the dauphins of Vienne in the fourteenth century.

CHAPTER 18, PARAGRAPH 6

Alas, fayr brother ... best wyse he myght. This passage appears only in the short version. Vienne's sarcastic comment about her "fayr chambre" is in keeping with her character.

CHAPTER 18, PARAGRAPH 7

complaynte. Paris's speech takes the conventional form of the lover's lament: despair and dread that that he will lose Vienne to another suitor; hopelessness that impels him to exile; apostrophe to God and to cruel fortune, beseeching that he might suffer the "grevous penaunce" that Vienne endures in prison, for his sake.

Chapter 20, Paragraph 1

Venyse. Vers. I gives a longer account of Paris's departure from Venice, then back to Genoa, and then with Bertran de Picartville to Romanie [Romania], then back to Venice before departing for Jerusalem. The Burgundian treatment of Vers. I expands further by incorporating material from contemporary travelogues.

mounte of Calvarye. This is the site outside of Jerusalem where Jesus was crucified. A visit to this shrine was a major objective of pilgrimage (See Matthew 27:33, Mark 15:22).

Moores. The term refers to North Africans (Akbari, *Idols in the East*, p. 285) and in the fourteenth century began to displace *Saracen* as term refering to Muslims.

Mouryske. This refers to a language that was also spoken and written by those who do not otherwise live as Muslims.

Prester Johan. Prester John was the purported ruler of a legendary Christian kingdom in Asia, noted for its marvels and great riches. Well-known travel books by Marco Polo and John Mandeville describe journeys to his fabled realm, as well as to India, China, and pilgrimage sites in Palestine (Ed. Kohanski and Benson, *Mandeville*, lines 1716–22, 2392–2753).

berde. Christians associated long beards with Muslims. Fifteenth-century European fashions favored a clean shaven face.

Holy Sepulture. This is a Church in Jerusalem containing the sepulchre from which Christians believe Christ arose from the dead. (See John 20:2.) It is a major site of pilgrimage.

Chapter 20, Paragraph 2

out of the toun in the feldes. In romances, dejected, impoverished knights often go to disport themselves in the countryside where they encounter a helper. See *Sir Launfal* (ed. Laskaya and Salisbury), where the helper is a fairy.

fawcon. Arabs were conventionally noted for their skill in falconry.

bynde. BN1 says that he should feed the herbs to the bird, which seems more logical.

mayntened. To affirm the dignity of one's rank by expenditures; spend money on a household, a court (*MED maintenen* (v.), sense 3a).

Explanatory Notes to *Paris and Vienne* 115

Chapter 20, Paragraph 3

Innocent. In 1202 pope Innocent III preached a crusade (the fourth) to conquer the Egyptian sultanate and then Jerusalem; neither of these goals were achieved, though the armies sacked Constantinople. Vers. I has an extended account of the proclamation and gathering of troops for the crusade, and places it immediately after Paris's arrival in Egypt. Crusades would have been on the minds of Caxton's audience. In 1480 Pope Sixtus IV had preached a crusade against the Ottoman Turks who had captured Otranto. Caxton printed indulgences for this, and his crusading romance *Godfrey of Bolougne* appeared in the following year with a prologue that promoted campaigns against Muslims.

Chapter 21, Paragraph 2

sholde governe hys londe. Medieval wives were expected to play a role in the administration of their husbands' property in their absences. Knights and nobles traveled frequently for military service or other duties for their overlords.

Chapter 22, Paragraph 1

evyl Crysten men. The men resemble Judas, who betrayed Jesus for money.

Babylone. BN1 also reads *Babilone*, or Babylonia (*MED Babiloine* (n.), sense 1), though Cooper notes the word was also a European name for Cairo ("Going Native," p. 31).

Chapter 22, Paragraph 2

the pope and the kyng of Fraunce. The offer of ransom does not occur in BN1 or Vers. I.

Chapter 22, Paragraph 3

yndulgences. The friars sought the remission of sins granted by indulgences that the pope issued to those who visited holy sites. They would also have sold indulgences to pilgrims at the sites.

partyes, whych beyng in tho partyes. BL omits a phrase that BN1 renders as *partie de elevante* [of the levant/east] and that L renders as *parties devers le vent* [regions in the direction of the wind]. Caxton's source text may have been unclear; BN1 and L vary in other details here.

we that be not of your lawe. Here Paris speaks in character as a Muslim. See also 22.5.

Chapter 22, Paragraph 5

hande. Vers. I turns to Vienne in prison, where she dreams that she is freed by an eagle.

Chapter 22, Paragraph 7

tourchemen. The *OED truchman* (n.) lists *Paris and Vienne* as the earliest recorded instance of this word in English. Caxton found it in his source.

Chapter 22, Paragraph 10

swere. In Vers. I the dauphin also swears to give Paris his daughter in marriage, as he had previously offered.

body of Jhesu Cryst. This refers to the Communion wafer symbolizing Jesus's body sacrificed to redeem human sin. According to Catholic theology, when blessed by a priest, the bread is transformed into the actual body of Jesus. This miracle is the essential ritual of mass.

receyved. The dauphin participates in the ritual of Holy Communion, receiving the consecrated wafer and consuming it.

Chapter 22, Paragraph 12

not been accustomed to drynke wyn. Pierre de la Cépède here refers accurately to the Muslim practice of avoiding alcohol (*MIFL* K625.2, escape by making watchman drunk.)

Chapter 22, Paragraph 14

fyftene dayes. Conventional length of time for celebrations in romance. See also 24.1.

dyd do say. BN1 includes an passage not present in BL or L in which Paris negotiates with the dauphin through the friars, reminding him of his promise to give his rescuer whatever he asked, as well as his lands. Paris concludes by asking to marry Vienne, and promises to become Christian. The dauphin is pleased to grant his request, but says he doubts his daughter will comply, since she is always unwilling to marry; he then calls for the bishop of St. Lawrence and the friar to accompany them to visit Vienne the next day. Vers. I treats this episode at greater length.

Chapter 22, Paragraph 16

doulphyn. In Vers. I, Vienne dreams that Paris is dead.

Chapter 22, Paragraph 18

good odour. MIFL V222.4.1, aromatic smell of saint's body.

Explanatory Notes to *Paris and Vienne*　　　　　　　　　　　　　　　　　117

Chapter 23, Paragraph 1

swerde. Fine swords were associated with Muslims (especially steel from Damascus). See note 23.5 below.

Chapter 23, Paragraph 2

rynge. MIFL H94, identification by ring.

Chapter 23, Paragraph 4

enbraced. Other romances feature lovers who chastely embrace; such episodes appear in *Generides*, *Sir Degrevant*, and *Partenope of Blois* where they are tests of chastity and the couples are less passionate than Paris and Vienne.

Chapter 23, Paragraph 5

kyssed hyr. BN1 includes a passage not in BL and L in which Paris, holding the point of his sword, kneels and surrenders it to the dauphin, asking pardon for failing in his duty to his lord, and explaining that he is not the first to do so and that wise men have as well. He then reveals that he is Paris, a vassal the son of messire Jaques, and asks for mercy but offers his sword for the dauphin to take vengeance "on my body" if he is displeased. The dauphin and his men are amazed to hear the Moor speak French and identify himself, the dauphin especially since he had seen Paris so often and had not recognized him. In this text Paris reveals his identity, not Vienne, though her declaration to her father follows as in BL and L.

Chapter 23, Paragraph 6

borowe. To take with a promise to return, often securing the promise with a pledge or bond; to stand as surety for (*MED borwen* (v.), senses 1a; 2). Messire Jacques is here speaking as vassal to his lord, who is also lord of Paris.

Chapter 24, Paragraph 1

dayes. The Burgundian treatment of Vers. I contains an extended description of the wedding, which includes a series of tournaments paralleling those at the beginning of the romance and reaffirming Paris's superior chivalry and noble status.

Ysabeau to hys wyf. Edward, and the author, seem to have forgotten his lady in Brabant (1.3), though years have passed since his visit there. By romance convention, confidantes of the protagonists marry each other.

sayntes in heven. It is conventional for romances to end with a reference to the sainthood of the protagonists, though the author introduces a disclaimer.

Textual Notes to *Paris and Vienne*

Leach's notes to his edition of *Paris and Vienne* include variant readings from the French manuscript, Leeu's print, and Caxton's translation from which the following notes are adapted. I cite instances where Caxton's translation departs from both BN1 and L, and instances where BN1 or L include headings that do not appear in his print.

Chapter 1, Rubric

Chapter 1. So BL. The rubrics in BL are not numbered.

Here. So BL. A leaf has been inserted preceding Caxton's text — a title page on which is printed his colophon. The type belongs to the eighteenth century, when the book was rebound.

Chapter 1, Paragraph 1

In. So BL. First letter is an enlarged capital.

1271. So BL: *MCClxxi*.

that men calle Dyane. This phrase does not appear in BN1. See Explanatory Note.

gladnes and joye. So BL. BN1, L: *feste*.

bothe. So BL. BN1, L: *que lune ne povoit estre sans laultre* [that the one could not be without the other].

contrees. BN1 and L include a phrase to the effect that Vienne was also renowned for the great dignity of her father and mother.

Chapter 1, Paragraph 2

lygnage. So BL. BN1, L: *moult puissant de terres de chateaulx et de richesses* [very powerful in lands in castles and in wealth].

Syr James. So BL. BN1 and L: *Jacques*.

eightene. So BL: *xviii*. BN1, L: *xv*.

by the hande of the sayd lord daulphyn. L: *et dedans peu de tamps fut fait chevalier* [and in a short while was made knight]. BN1 lacks this concluding phrase. See Explanatory Note.

119

Chapter 1, Paragraph 4

But not long after ... noble yong lady. So BL. Not in BN1, L.

Venus, the goddes of love. So BL. Not in BN1 and L.

fyre of love within hymself. So BL. Not in BN1, L.

Chapter 2, Rubric

played wyth dyvers instrumentes by nyght. So BL. BN1, L: *faire les aubades* [perform songs]. See Explanatory Note.

Chapter 2, Paragraph 1

melodyous myrthe. So BL. BN1, L: *aubades.*

recourders. So BL. Not in BN1, L.

pypes. So BL. Not in BN1, L.

as wel of mans wyces as of dyvers instrumentes. So BL. Not in BN1, L.

Chapter 2, Paragraph 2

Whan. So BL. First letter is an enlarged capital. L heading: *Comment le daulphin ordonna dix hommes bien armez pour faire amener devant luy les dits menestriers* [How the dauphin ordered ten well-armed men to bring before him the said minstrels].

Chapter 2, Paragraph 3

Whan. So BL. First letter is an enlarged capital L heading: *Comment Paris et Edouard son compaignon se deffendirent contre dix hommes darmes* [How Paris and Edward his companion defended themselves against ten men of arms].

not. So BL. BN1, L: *mais bien fut grief a iceuls espies de laisser la place et plus que deux mesmes mais pour doubte de mort sen fuirent et par ainsi sans nul dommaige ils eschapperent* [but indeed it was painful to those scouts to yield the place, and more that for two only, but for fear of death they fled from there and in this manner escaped without any injury].

Chapter 2, Paragraph 4

And. So BL. BN1 heading: *Comment Paris se miste avec levesque de saint Laurens* [How Paris went with the bishop of Saint Lawrence].

chargyng that none hurte shold be doon to them. So BL. Not in BN1, L.

Chapter 2, Paragraph 6

made lystes and scaffoldes to be sette up. So BL. Not in BN1, L.

herauldes. So BL. Not in BN1, L.

Normandye. So BL. Not in BN1, L.

of fyn gold. So BL. Not in BN1, L.

noble and fayr mayden. So BL. Not in BN1, L.

and she thought . . . at Vyenne. So BL. Not in BN1, L.

Chapter 2, Paragraph 7

Normandye. So BL. Not in BN1, L.

erle. So BL. BN1, L: *conte* [count]. Caxton always uses the English term; the rank is equivalent.

Chapter 2, Paragraph 9

two. So BL. BN1: *v.* L: *ung* [one].

Chapter 3, Paragraph 1

tofore the ladyes and damoyselles. So BL. Not in BN1, L.

Chapter 3, Paragraph 2

kept theyr sterops. So BL. Not in BN1, L.

Chapter 4, Rubric

in faytes of armes. So BL. Not in BN1, L.

Chapter 4, Paragraph 4

sparkles of love that sprange out of hyr hert. So BL. Not in BN1, L.

bysshop. So BL. BN1, L: *dyable devecque* [devil of a bishop].

that hath be holden in Vyenne. So BL. Not in BN1, L.

Chapter 4, Paragraph 5

Now. So BL. First letter is an enlarged capital. BN1 heading: *Comment le roy de France va ordonner unes joustes in la cité de Paris* [How the king of France proclaimed jousts in the city of Paris].

Breunes. BL: *Brennes;* twice later spelled *Breunes.* See note 4.11, below.

mayntened. So BL. Not in BN1, L.

reputed and holden . . . alle the world. So BL. Not in BN1, L.

Chapter 4, Paragraph 6

tresour. So BL. BN1, L: *et lequele luy avoit envoye la contesse de Flandres qui estoit sa dame* [and which her mother, the countess of Flanders, had given to her].

wytte. So BL. Not in BN1, L.

renommé. So BL. Not in BN1, L.

quarelle. So BL. Not in BN1, L.

Chapter 4, Paragraph 9

Whan. So BL. First letter is an enlarged capital. BN1 heading: *Comment le roy de france va ordonner unes joustes en la cite de Paris* [How the king of France proclaimed a joust in the city of Paris].

fourtene. So BL: *xiiii.* BN1: *viii.*

somme for to do armes and the other. So BL. Not in BN1, L.

moche sumptuous and noble. So BL. BN1, L: *merveilleuse* [marvelous].

these thre joyaulx. So BL. Not in L.

whyche shone and resplendysshed . . . in the baners. So BL. Not in BN1, L.

Chapter 4, Paragraph 11

Bremeos. So BL. So L: *fiz du duc du Breuues* [son of the duke of Breunes; *u/n* printer's error]. BN1 and Vers. I read *Bohemia.*

Chapter 5, Paragraph 3

Thenne. So BL. First letter is an enlarged capital.

Chapter 6, Paragraph 2

Whan. So BL. First letter is an enlarged capital.

Chapter 6, Paragraph 5

The. So BL. First letter is an enlarged capital.

bysshop. So BL. BN1: *dyable deveque* [devil of a bishop].

Chapter 6, Paragraph 7

worshyp. So BL. Not in BN1, L.

Chapter 7, Paragraph 1

accesse. So BL. Not in BN1, L.

Chapter 7, Paragraph 2

bysshop. So BL. BN1: *dyable devesque* [devil of a bishop].

Chapter 7, Paragraph 3

lytel crased and sodenly taken, wherfore. So BL. BN1 and L read *grant mal mest venu* [great sickness is come to me]; BN1: *sur le cuer* [in the heart].

that none myght come in. So BL. Not in BN1, L.

Chapter 7, Paragraph 4

whyche was twelve foot longe. So BL. Not in BN1, L.

Chapter 7, Paragraph 5

wysedom and reason. So BL. BN1, L: *bon sens* [good sense].

Chapter 7, Paragraph 6

veray. So BL. Not in BN1, L.

And thus ... she coude not stynte. So BL. Not in BN1, L.

Chapter 7, Paragraph 7

other jewellys. So BL. Not in BN1, L.

Chapter 8, Paragraph 2

and prayers. So BL. Not in BN1, L.

shytte. So BL. Not in BN1, L.

Chapter 8, Paragraph 3

contente. So BL. Not in BN1, L.

Chapter 8, Paragraph 4

After. So BL. First letter is an enlarged capital.

Chapter 9, Paragraph 2

Thenne. So BL. First letter is an enlarged capital.

eightene. So BL: *xviii*. BN1, L: *viii*.

Chapter 9, Paragraph 3

Thenne. So BL. First letter is an enlarged capital.

Chapter 9, Paragraph 6

Whan. So BL. First letter is an enlarged capital.

Chapter 9, Paragraph 7

doughter. So BL. BN1, L: *folie* [folly], which Caxton mistook for *fille* [daughter].

Chapter 10, Paragraph 2

menchon. So BL. Not in BN1, L.

Chapter 10, Paragraph 3

Thenne. So BL. First letter is an enlarged capital. L heading: *Comment Paris parla a Vienne par la fenestre* [How Paris spoke to Vienne at a window].

Chapter 10, Paragraph 4

Whan. So BL. First letter is an enlarged capital.

passages. So BL. BN1 and L include the word *chevaux* [horses].

Chapter 11, Paragraph 1

secretest wyse. So BL. Not in BN1, L.

taken. So BL. BN1, L: *premier somme* [first sleep, early in the night].

endured tyl on the morne at nyght. So BL. BN1, L: *dura jusques a lendemain a vespres* [lasted until the next day at vespers/evening].

Chapter 11, Paragraph 2

and fere. So BL. Not in BN1, L.

Chapter 14, Rubric

How. So BL. BN1: *Comment Vienne se retourna a la merci de son per* [How Vienne returned to the mercy of her father]. L: *Comment Vienne fut ramenee a lotel de son pere* [How Vienne was led to the dwelling of her father].

Chapter 14, Paragraph 2

Now. So BL. First letter is an enlarged capital. BN1 heading: *Comment Vienne demanda pardon a son pere* [How Vienne asked pardon of her father]. L: *Comment Vienne fut ramenee a lotel de son pere* [How Vienne was led to the dwelling of her father].

soule. So BL. BN1, L: *en dieu* [God].

Chapter 14, Paragraph 5

Whan. So BL. First letter is an enlarged capital. BN1 heading: *Comment le dauphin fist mestre sa fille hors de prison* [How the dauphin had his daughter brought out of prison].

Chapter 14, Paragraph 7

Whan. So BL. First letter is an enlarged capital. BN1 heading: *Comment le conte de Flandres manda au daulphyn une lettre* [How the count of Flanders sent a letter to the dauphin].

Chapter 15, Paragraph 1

allone. So BL. BN1, L: *avec son vartlet* [with his servant].

Chapter 15, Paragraph 2

Ryght. So BL. First letter is an enlarged capital.

Chapter 15, Paragraph 3

Dere. So BL. First letter is an enlarged capital.

Chapter 15, Paragraph 6

Edward sayd. So BL. BN1 and L read "*Il est verite,*" dist Vienne, "*mais ne me parler plus de la lettre*" ["It is true," said Vienne, "but do not speak to me more of the letter."] See Explanatory Note.

Chapter 16, Paragraph 1

letter, whyche she reteyneth . . . said letter. So BL. Not in BN1 and Vers. I.

Chapter 16, Paragraph 2

Whan. So BL. First letter is an enlarged capital. BN1 heading: *Comment Paris receust le change de iii mille florins* [How Paris received the change of three thousand florins].

Chapter 16, Paragraph 3

Now. So BL. BN1 heading: *Comment le fils du duc de Burgoine alla la cite de Vienne* [How the son of the duke of Burgundy went to the city of Vienne]. L heading: *Comment le filz du duc de Bourgoigne avec belle compaigne vint au Daulphine pour veoir Vienne son espeuse, et pour lemmener avec luy, and comment il fut receu en grand joye du daulphin, pere de la dicte Vienne.* [How the son of the duke of Burgundy with good company went to Dauphiné to see Vienne his betrothed, and to bring her away with him, and how he was received in great joy by the dauphin, father of the said Vienne].

Chapter 16, Paragraph 4

honourable. BL: *honouble.* Omitted letters added.

Chapter 16, Paragraph 5

Thenne. So BL. First letter is an enlarged capital.

Chapter 18, Paragraph 4

Whan. So BL. First letter is an enlarged capital.

Chapter 18, Paragraph 5

Whan. So BL. First letter is an enlarged capital.

Chapter 18, Paragraph 7

Whan. So BL. First letter is an enlarged capital.

Chapter 19, Rubric

hys felowe. So BL. Not in BN1, L.

Chapter 19, Paragraph 2

Edward. BL: *Parys*; this is an error; Leach emends to *Edward*, which I follow.

Chapter 20, Paragraph 1

Egypte. So BL. L: *aultre pt.* [other part]; BN1: *Babilone.* Leach suggests *Egypte* is a misreading.

Chapter 20, Paragraph 2

bynde. So BL. BN1: *quil luy en donnast a menger* [which they gave to him to eat].

Chapter 22, Rubric

How the doulphyn . . . goo into Jherusalem. So BL. Not in BN1, L.

Chapter 22, Paragraph 3

Now. So BL. First letter is an enlarged capital.

partyes, whych beyng in tho partyes. BN1: *partie de elevante* [region of the levant/east]; L: *parties devers le vent* [regions in the direction of the wind].

Chapter 22, Paragraph 4

Whan. So BL. First letter is an enlarged capital.

Chapter 22, Paragraph 6

Whan. So BL. First letter is an enlarged capital. BN1 heading: *Comment Paris alla en Alixandre pour veoir le dauphin* [How Paris went to Alexandria to see the dauphin]. L heading: *Comment Paris avec deux freres sen alla en Alexandrie et la fut receut de lamiral moult honnorablement* [How Paris with two friars went to Alexandria and there was received by the emir with much honor].

Chapter 22, Paragraph 7

weste. BL: *theste*. I follow Leach who emends to *west*, which is accurate in context, and BL elides "w" elsewhere: *thorthy*, [the worthy], so readers could have read the word as "the west." However readings in the French texts point to eastern lands. L: *du vent* [of the Levant], BN1: *levant* [Levant].

Chapter 22, Paragraph 8

Whan. So BL. First letter is an enlarged capital.

and be welcome. So BL. Not in BN1, L.

Chapter 22, Paragraph 10

On. So BL. First letter is an enlarged capital.

God and. So BL. Not in BN1, L.

Chapter 22, Paragraph 12

Whan. So BL. First letter is an enlarged capital. L heading: *Comment Paris delivra le daulphin de prison en Alexandrie* [How Paris delivered the dauphin from prison in Alexandria].

Chapter 22, Paragraph 13

Thys. So BL. First letter is an enlarged capital. L heading: *Comment le daulphin et Paris sen retournerent par mer* [How the dauphin and Paris returned by sea].

Chapter 22, Paragraph 14

Whan. So BL. First letter is an enlarged capital. L heading: *Comment le dauphin et Paris furent receus de peuple de France en grand joye and en grand honneur* [How the dauphin and Paris were received by the people of France with great joy and with great honor]. BN1 heading: *Comment chevaliers du dauphine vindrent au devant du dauphin* [How knights of Dauphiné came before the dauphin].

Chapter 22, Paragraph 16

And yet more . . . your fader. So BL. This sentence is punctuated with paragraph marks (¶) for emphasis.

Chapter 22, Paragraph 18

two quarters of an henne. So BL. BN1: *Vienne avoit fait la mediecine quelle avoit fait au duc de bourgoigne des quartiers* [Vienne had made the remedy which she had made to the duke of Burgundy of the quarters].

Chapter 23, Paragraph 3

Whan. So BL. First letter is an enlarged capital.

Chapter 24, Paragraph 1

world. So BL. BN1 and L add *et croy que leur adventure fut mieulx de dieu que de nulle aultre personne* [and think that no one else had a life as godly as theirs].

Chapter 24, Paragraph 2

Thus. So BL. Beside the colophon, in very faded grey ink, is written *This was my boke* followed by another word, perhaps *omnis*, and below that the word *annus* and the Roman numeral *vxx*. *Cossyn* is written near the bottom of the colophon, and again below. There is faint lettering also at the top of the page. The hand appears to be Elizabethan secretary.

translated. So BL. L: *Emprientee en Anvers par moy Gherard Leeu, lan Mil CCCClxxxvii, le xv jour du mois de May* [Printed in Antwerp by me Gherard Leeu in the year 1487, the fifteenth day of the month of May].

🌿 BLANCHARDYN AND EGLANTINE INTRODUCTION

When William Caxton printed *Blanchardyn and Eglantine* in 1489, the lovers' story had been circulating in French verse for over two hundred years. The original romance had been composed in the early thirteenth century in northern France; in the later fifteenth century this narrative was adapted in prose for the court of Burgundy.[1] It was this version that Caxton translated into English. The story of Blanchardyn and Eglantine maintained its appeal for many years. English versions circulated as late as the seventeenth century. Audiences would have appreciated its tale of faithful lovers and chivalric combat, as well as its literary sophistication and realistic treatment of conventional material.

This introduction to *Blanchardyn and Eglantine* begins with an overview of the romance's origin and genre and a summary of its plot, followed by sections devoted to its patrons and setting, instructional agenda, treatment of race and religion, construction of gender, attention to emotion, and review of scholarship. The concluding sections address technical matters, including Caxton's translation practice, a description of his copytext, and evidence of early owners. A list of witnesses and source texts in French and English follows. Explanatory Notes and Textual Notes accompanying the text provide additional information on topics discussed here.

ORIGIN AND GENRE

The lovers' story originated early in the thirteenth century in the northern French region of Picardy, where an anonymous author composed a verse romance known as *Blancandin et l'Orgeuilleuse d'Amours* [*Blancandin and the Proud Lady of Love*].[2] This person drew on other romances and *chansons de geste* for themes and incidents, and incorporated entire lines from the *Roman d'Eneas* [*Romance of Aeneas*].[3] Several episodes resemble those in the romance *Richard le Beau* [*Richard the Good*].[4] The first part of *Blancandin* shows the influence of Chrétien de Troyes's *The Story of the Grail*, whose protagonist, like Blanchardyn, is forbidden the knowledge of chivalry, learns the art of combat, and claims a kiss from an unwilling lady. The heroine shares her name with several proud ladies in this and others of Chrétien's romances: *l'Orgueilleuse de Logres* [the Proud Lady of Logres], *l'Orgueilleuse de la Roche* [the Proud Lady of the Rock], and *l'Orgueilleuse de la Lande* [the Proud Lady of the Wilderness]. Other names suggest the author's familiarity with

---

[1] Burgundy is a region in northeastern France. The territories of its dukes included much of northern France, the Low Countries, and parts of modern Germany.

[2] Sweetser, *Blancandin*, p. 7.

[3] Sweetser, *Blancandin*, pp. 36–37. The *Roman* was composed in 1160.

[4] Sweetser, *Blancandin*, p. 33. In *Richard* (thirteenth century, Picardy), a knight accepts a challenge from a host for lodging. *L'Histoire des Seigneurs de Gavre* [*History of the Lords of Gavre*] contains passages identical to those in the long prose *Blancandin*; its composer may have been associated with the atelier Wavrin (ed. Greco, *Blancandin et L'Orgueilleuse*, p. 67n86; Stuip, "Blanchandin, Jean de Créquy," p. 356). See the General Introduction to this volume for discussion of the atelier Wavrin (p. 5).

chansons de geste: Blancandin [from Fr. *blanc*, white] has analogues in the *Song of Roland* and elsewhere, while the names Daryus, Rubyon, and Sadoine are found in *Ogier le Danois* [*Ogier the Dane*], *Godefroi de Bouillon* [*Godfrey of Boulogne*], *Tristan de Nantueil* [*Tristan of Nantueil*], and elsewhere.[5]

The narrative's blend of chivalric love and warfare proved popular. The earliest version survives in four verse texts from the thirteenth and early fourteenth centuries and the story's continuing appeal in the fifteenth century is attested by its adaptation into two prose versions at the court of Burgundy during the reign of Duke Philip the Good (1396–1467).[6] A copy of the longer prose version was Caxton's source for his translation, and a fifteenth-century German verse translation also survives. With Caxton, *Blanchardyn and Eglantine* made the transition from manuscript to print and wider circulation, and the romance continued to be read in the seventeenth century, for 1595 saw the printing of a version refashioned for Tudor audiences.[7] The story owed its appeal to a plot based firmly in formulas of romance and feats of chivalry, and to its morally and socially uplifting messages. These would have appealed to Caxton's audience — a mix of gentry, courtiers, merchants, and professionals who read English more readily than French, and who wanted access to the chivalric literature fashionable at the courts of England and northern France.

Blanchardyn and Eglantine has been variously characterized as a composite romance, as a non-cyclic *roman d'aventure*, and as a romance of chivalry and *fin amor*.[8] It is a sentimental romance, devoting much attention to the characters' emotions and to engaging those of the audience.[9] It can also be described as a pedagogical romance, for it incorporates the story of both the hero's and the heroine's educations and provides models of chivalric behavior and governance. Caxton, like his source, refers to the narrative as a history, a term of prestige that makes claims of veracity and fidelity to actual occurrences that the term romance does not.

Plot

Caxton's romance is long and its narrative complicated, though the plot consists of three main episodes: the proving of a knight; his adventures in foreign lands with his brother-in-arms; and his return to rescue his lady. Romance plots are notable for their repetition, and *Blanchardyn and Eglantine* does not disappoint. There are two storms at sea separating the lovers, two exchanges of messages, two raids to capture supplies, two marriages, two pleadings for imprisoned heroes, three episodes of capture and imprisonment, and four full-scale battles. Not only is the plot repetitive, the narration is redundant. The same details and events are

---

[5] Stelboum, "William Caxton's Romance," pp. 101–02; Sweetser, *Blancandin*, p. 38; ed. Greco, *Blancandin et l'Orgueilleuse*, p. 11. In *Tristan de Nantueil*, the name Blanchandine is that of a female character who becomes a transgender man.

[6] Stelboum, "William Caxton's Romance," pp. 69–71; ed. Greco, *Blancandin et l'Orgueilleuse*, p. 44.

[7] The author claims to translate a Latin source, but no evidence of such has been found and the narrative is indebted to Caxton's text. A claim to Latin authority would have recommended the book to Renaissance readers. In the 1595 print, the dedication concludes with the initials P. T. G.; a second print from 1597 substitutes a name, Thomas Pope Goodwine. Such a person has never been identified, though scholars have assumed it is that of the reviser. Rebecca Olson argues that the name is a pseudonym for a female reviser who had earlier hid her gender in initials ("Continuing Adventures," pp. 308–09).

[8] Refined or "courtly" love. Composite romances are late romances incorporating elements derived from earlier courtly narratives (Hornstein, "Miscellaneous Romances," p. 147).

[9] Schlauch used the term "society romance" to describe English verse romances in which the characters' "sentimental relations are the ones most frequently presented" (*Antecedents*, p. 17).

related multiple times; the audience is advised of what is going to happen, told about the event as it occurs, then again when it is reported by a character, and reminded once more in the narrator's transitions at the beginnings and ends of chapters.[10] The chapter headings themselves refer to the events yet another time.

As the story begins, the king of Frisia has no heir; the queen prays for a child and gives birth to a son who is named Blanchardyn. He is well educated, though forbidden to learn the art of war; nevertheless, inspired by the legends of Troy, he secretly departs his peaceful kingdom to prove himself a knight. He rescues a maiden, slays her oppressor and returns her to her dying lover, whereupon she too expires — greatly impressing upon Blanchardyn the value of such true love. He encounters a knight who helps him to cross a river, and directs him to the city of Tourmaday where the queen, Eglantine, is besieged by the Muslim king Alymodes. Blanchardyn can vanquish these attackers if she will accept him as her champion, but that requires that she fall in love with him, which can only be accomplished by a kiss. This is no easy task, for the queen is known as l'Orgueilleuse d'Amours because she refuses all suitors.[11] Blanchardyn is able to accomplish this feat, much to the lady's displeasure, and arrives in Tourmaday where he jousts, then lodges with the provost. News of the knight's victory reaches Eglantine, who, on the advice of her governess, relents and puts him in charge of her armies. The provost and his daughters supply Blanchardyn with arms, and he joins the battle against Alymodes. Eglantine observes the knight's prowess and begins to fall in love with him; she has him brought to her and they declare their love, which is confirmed by a flame descending from heaven. Blanchardyn accepts the challenge of Alymodes's giant, Rubyon, and kills him, wounds Alymodes's son, Daryus, and siezes his sister, Beatrix, but is captured by enemy forces.

Alymodes sends his prisoner to Rubyon's brother, but the ship is wrecked in Prussia, where Blanchardyn disguises himself to pass among the local inhabitants, who are Muslims. He offers his services to the king and leads his troops to victory over the invading Poles, befriending the Prussian prince, Sadoyne. Meanwhile, Daryus sails to renew the siege of Tourmaday, is driven off course to Frisia where he plunders the countryside, seizes Blanchardyn's father, and sends him prisoner to Alymodes. When Daryus arrives at Tourmaday, the provost captures the stolen provisions and repels his assault. Back in Prussia, Blanchardyn tells Sadoyne of his love for Eglantine, and they set sail to come to her aid. En route, they meet the provost, so Blanchardyn, still in disguise, sends a letter to Eglantine telling of his imminent arrival. Before he can land, a storm drives his ships away, but when Sadoyne throws his idols overboard, the sea becomes calm and the fleet makes land at Cassydoyne, Alymodes's capital. Blanchardyn defeats the Cassydonians, kills Daryus, and betroths Beatrix and Sadoyne, who are baptized, married, and take possession of the city. Blanchardyn then releases his father from prison and, with Sadoyne, sets sail again for Tourmaday. They encounter the provost, who returns to Eglantine with the news of Blanchardyn's arrival. In the battle that follows, he and his father rout Tourmaday's attackers, and Sadoyne kills Alymodes's brother but is captured and imprisoned at Cassydoyne.

Eglantine and Blanchardyn are betrothed; he then leaves to rescue Sadoyne, appointing the steward, Subyon, as guardian. When Subyon claims Eglantine for himself, she escapes with the help of the provost and the knight of the ferry. Meanwhile, Blanchardyn and his father arrive in Cassydonye in time to save his friend from the gallows. Together the three men conclusively defeat the forces of Alymodes and take

---

[10] This redundancy is even more pronounced in *Valentine and Orson*, another Burgundian romance (Schlauch, *Antecedents*, p. 56). The repetition would have refreshed the memories of readers and listeners as they returned to the story, insuring textual cohesion and clarity.

[11] This name appears throughout Caxton's text, sometimes translated as "the proude mayden in amours/love;" only twice is the character referred to as Eglantine.

him prisoner. Beatrix and Sadoyne are crowned. The provost reaches Cassydoyne with news of Subyon's treachery, so Blanchardyn and his compatriots sail a third time for Tourmaday, kill Subyon and a band of outlaws, and rescue Eglantine. Finally, the lovers are married and Blanchardyn is crowned king of Frisia and Tourmaday.

Patrons, Politics, and Setting

We owe *Blanchardyn and Eglantine* to the request of Margaret Beaufort, duchess of Somerset and mother of Henry VII. In his dedication, Caxton says she asked him to translate the romance into English.[12] He had earlier sold her a manuscript of the text written in French, and it seems likely the story had particular significance for her since she wanted to make it available to English readers. This possibility is further supported by the fact that it is the only secular work commissioned by this important patron of books and early printers. Caxton justifies the reading of "noble historyes" for, there, gentlemen can learn of chivalry and "stande in the specyal grace and love of their ladyes." The ladies, in turn, can learn "to be stedfaste" to those they "have promysed and agreed to," and who "have putte their lyves ofte in jeopardye for to playse theym to stande in grace" (Dedication.1). These phrases may have resonated with Margaret since she, with Queen Elizabeth Woodville, had earlier negotiated the marriage of their children, Henry Tudor and Elizabeth of York. Perhaps the duchess saw in the separations of Blanchardyn and Eglantine similarities to the protracted courtship of the royal couple, for though they were betrothed in 1483, they did not marry until 1486.[13] Elizabeth may be the lady steadfast in her promise to Henry who has put his life in jeopardy for her (and his) kingdom. The heroine's name, which first appears in the long prose version, may have suggested to Margaret an association with the future English queen, since *eglantine* is a name for the sweetbriar, or briar rose, which is also known as the English rose.[14] Caxton emphasized the name by referencing it four times, while his source mentions it only once; he was also the first to include it in his title, for all the French texts refer to the romance as *Blancandin et l'Orgueilleuse d'Amours*.

If Margaret saw in the French romance parallels to her own political and personal circumstances, the narrative may have appealed to Duke Philip the Good for similar reasons. Blanchardyn became king of Frisia,[15] and so did the duke, who assumed that title in 1447.[16] Philip may have regarded *Blancandin* as an

---

[12] Caxton's edition of *The Fifteen Os*, a popular prayer, was also undertaken for Margaret and Elizabeth Woodville. A pious woman, Margaret fostered the distribution of books of devotion and commissioned Wynkyn de Worde to print *The Scale of Perfection*, as well as engaging Richard Pynson to print works of religious usage for the Abbey of Syon. She translated the *Mirror of Gold for the Sinful Soul* and the fourth book of the *Imitatio Cristi* from French to be printed by Pynson(Krug, "Margaret Beaufort," pp. 107, 106). Margaret also owned a copy of Caxton's *Faytes of Arms and Chivalry* (Nall, "Margaret Beaufort's Books," p. 213).

[13] Painter, *William Caxton*, p. 166; Cooper, *English Romance in Time*, pp. 348–49; Krug, "Margaret Beaufort," pp. 88–90.

[14] Cooper, *English Romance in Time*, p. 349. Two references are especially prominent, appearing in the Dedication and at the beginning of the Table of Chapters.

[15] Frisia was a region along the northeastern coasts of present day Netherlands and Germany.

[16] He never underwent a formal coronation (ed. Greco, *Blancandin et l'Orgueilleuse*, p. 45n60, p. 49). Duke Philip owned several tapestries depicting Frisian heroes and a manuscript of the romance *Rambaux de Frise* has been associated with his court (Farber, "Tapestry Collection of Philip the Bold"; Sargent, *Roy Rambaux*, p. 30). This legendary king is said to be the son of Blanchardyn and Eglantine at the conclusion of their story (Stuip, "*Blanchandin*, Jean de Créquy*," p. 354). Jan Veenstra discusses Rambaut and Philip's claims to Frisia ("Le Prince," pp. 209–18).

ancestral romance; the fact that his library included two versions suggests he attached some importance to it.[17] The longer prose version, composed 1454–1474, was commissioned by Jean de Créquy, Philip's chamberlain and counselor.[18] The illuminated copy now in Vienna (Österreichische Nationalbibliothek 3438) would have been intended for a high-ranking member of the court, if not the duke himself, perhaps to commemorate his ascension to the Frisian throne.[19] Créquy was probably responsible for a significant modification to the story — a change of setting.[20] The verse narratives of *Blancandin et l'Orgeuilleuse d'Amours* refer to Blancandin's home as Phrygia (once); they and the short prose version are set in the eastern Mediterranean on the model of *chanson de geste* and Oriental romances such as *Floris and Blaunchefleur* and *Partonope of Blois*.[21] Blancandin is shipwrecked in Greece, befriends the king of Athens, and defends Constantinople. Other characters come from Alexandria, Babylon, Jerusalem, Persia, and India. The long prose romance, however, unfolds in northern Europe and along the Baltic: in Frisia, Prussia (northern Germany), Poland, and Norway, all regions parts of which were claimed by Burgundy at one time or another.[22] The romance's locale as well as the protagonist's title would have resonated with the duke, and readers seem to have accepted the conflation of Prussians who practiced a Germanic religion with Mediterranean Muslims.

Blanchardyn's sojourn in Marienburg fighting the Poles may have recalled contemporary events to audiences in Burgundian regions. The castle there on the river Nekar (in modern Poland) was a key defensive and administrative position of the Order of Teutonic Knights, as well as a major trading center for the Hanseatic League.[23] The territories surrounding the fortress there were the site of frequent military campaigns in the fifteenth century as Poles, Prussians, and the Order struggled for military, religious, and commercial hegemony there.[24] In 1410, the Order was defeated at the Battle of Wittelsbach by Wladyslaw Jagiello, king of Poland and duke of Lithuania, who had accepted Roman Catholicism in 1385. The Poles were driven out of Marienburg by the Prussians in 1454. Accounts of these battles and other campaigns in the region may have influenced the long prose *Blancandin*'s depiction of the victory of the Prussians over the Poles, which is greatly expanded from the account in other versions of the romance.[25] Créquy himself was

---

[17] These versions are Brussels MS 3577 and Vienna MS 3438 (Stelboum, "William Caxton's Romance," pp. 79, 92, 94).

[18] Marchal, "L'existence d'un manuscrit," p. 271.

[19] This manuscript was produced in the Wavrin atelier at Lille, as was the Paris MS of *Blancandin* which was quite possibly Caxton's source (Marchal, "L'existence d'un manuscrit," p. 266).

[20] Ed. Greco, *Blancandin et l'Orgueilleuse*, pp. 52–54. Stuip, "*Blanchandin*, Jean de Créquy," p. 354.

[21] It has been suggested that the authors of the prose *Blancandin* misread "Phrygia", or intentionally read the word as a garbled rendering of Frisia (Kellner, p. cxvii; Stuip, "*Blanchandin*, Jean de Créquy," p. 355).

[22] The change of locale is also in keeping with literary trends of the fifteenth century. *Melusine* (*Romance of Partenay*), the Middle English *Sir Tryamour*, and *The Squire of Low Degree* are set in northern Europe; also, Chaucer's Knight had fought non-Christians in Lithuania and Prussia. Romances with crusading themes remained popular in the later Middle Ages, but the locus of historical campaigns of Christians against Muslims had shifted from the Middle East to the Balkans and eastern Europe following the Turks' conquest of Constantinople in 1453.

[23] A largely reconstructed castle remains at modern Malbork.

[24] Ed. Greco, *Blancandin et l'Orgueilleuse*, p. 49. Burgundy laid claim to territories in present Belgium, Holland, and northwest Germany, as well as France.

[25] Schlauch, *Antecedents*, p. 66n32; Stuip, "*Blanchandin*, Jean de Créquy," p. 353. In the long version, the battle occupies thirteen pages, in the short version, two.

in the service of the duke of Burgundy and participated in battles in the region around Marienburg.[26] The setting would not have seemed remote to English audiences, for England had long had political and commercial interests there: Caxton was in London when the king of Poland visited to intercede with Edward IV on behalf of the Hanseatic merchants in his city.[27] A century earlier, Chaucer's Shipman knew all the creeks and havens from Gotland to Finistere, and readers of Caxton's romance, especially merchants, would have been aware of events taking place in the Baltic, Germany, and Scandinavia.

INSTRUCTIONAL ROMANCE

Caxton's dedication to *Blanchardyn and Eglantine* stresses the moral and pedagogic value of reading histories, and chivalric education was an important axiom of his publishing agenda, as discussed in the General Introduction to this volume, pp. 8–11. He recommends the story as being "honeste and joyefull to all vertuouse yong noble gentylmen and wymmen" (Dedication.1) to read for their pastime, as an alternative to studying overmuch in books of contemplation. Accounts of chivalry have moral value of their own, and Caxton's Dedication stresses specific values of valor in combat and steadfastness in love, going beyond the brief, conventional defense of reading histories found in Pierre de la Cépède's prologue to *Paris et Vienne*. The romance itself is about an education: the first episodes of *Blanchardyn and Eglantine* are devoted to the instruction of the hero, for while his superior character is innate, his chivalry is learned. He is educated as a young royal of the fifteenth century: under the tutelage of a clerk who teaches literature, manners, grammar, logic, and philosophy; later Blanchardyn writes his own letters. He also excels at table games, chess, polite conversation, hawking, and hunting, pastimes appropriate to one of his status. The youth's natural inclination for chivalry is evident in his curiosity about the scenes from the Trojan War depicted in the palace's tapestries, and his tutor's explanation is a lesson in deeds of arms. Inspired by their example, Blanchardyn sets out prove himself in knightly combat. His first encounter is a lesson in love, as he vanquishes the felon knight. Thereafter he proves himself in a graduated series of challenges against the provost, the giant Rubyon, and Alymodes, to become the commander of armies and navies. Earlier episodes emphasize his novice status by referring to him as *chylde* or *jovencel*, terms that designate a young man of noble birth or an aspirant to knighthood. Blanchardyn later becomes a mentor to Sadoyne, whose father sends him into battle for the first time under the instruction of the proven warrior.

Eglantine, too, is educated by her governess and by the god of love, one giving political, the other emotional instruction. In a series of lengthy dialogues followed by passages of reflection, her mistress counsels Eglantine to restrain her anger at Blanchardyn and to consider her duty to secure peace for her kingdom. Eglantine is further educated by Reason, who restrains her with "premysses" and "conclusyons" (23.4) to temper her pride and emotion in the debate with Love. The lady herself is a source of instruction as she admonishes the provost about his daughters' "wanton" looks and the impropriety of their considering marriage to someone so far above them in rank as Blanchardyn. Eglantine's advice is motivated more by jealousy than concern for her official's family; nevertheless, her comments are instructive. The same precepts are conveyed by *The Book of the Knight of the Tour-Landry*, which also cautions young women to control their gaze and not to seek husbands above or below their station.

---

[26] A seigneur de Créquy and others are mentioned in *Jean de Saintré* (1456) as having fought against "Saracens" in Prussia and joined other Christian forces at a battle at Torun, a castle of the Teutonic Order in Poland (Stuip, "Blanchandin, Jean de Créquy," p. 355).

[27] Ed. Crotch, *Prologues and Epilogues*, p. lxviii.

The characters are models of courtly manners. Blanchardyn is a paragon — even Alymodes's men admire him for his "grete beaulté and worthynes" (25.1). He is always and often described in superlatives. Those he meets recognize his noble lineage in his courtesy, impeccable bearing, extraordinary horsemanship, and skill at arms. His audiences with Eglantine are the epitome of protocol and humility. He demurs when she takes him by the hand, making "hymself to be prayed and drawen sore or ever he wolde vaunce hymself for to sytte hym doune by her, but force was to hym to obeye her commaundement" (23.3). Though his reticence is not without irony, such behavior is described in Caxton's *The Babee's Boke* and *The Boke of Curtasye*, which includes instructions for how to properly greet one's lords and superiors, approach them, and engage in conversation.[28] Eglantine's resistance to the game of love, and to kissing, is exactly what the lady of la Tour-Landry recommends to her daughters, as is her concern for reputation and avoiding rumor and gossip.[29] Both hero and heroine exemplify self-control and governance of strong emotion.

The romance also provides models for the governance of states. Frisia, under the rule of Blanchardyn's father, enjoys the "wele of peas" (1.1), while Alymodes is a "grete tyraunt" who has "ravysshed . . . by stronge hande upon his neyghbours . . . all that he fonde of grete value" (38.6), as we see in the ravaging of Frisia. Portraits of good governance are found throughout the romance. When Blanchardyn approaches Tourmaday, he beholds a "most fayre and most riche cyté" (13.1) with walls of stone surrounded by fields, orchards, and rivers — the picture of prosperity befitting the seat of a great lord. Illuminations in the duke of Berry's *Tres Riches Heures* [*Very Rich Hours*] and *The Hours of Mary of Burgundy* depict similar scenes of peaceful castles, towns, and their fruitful surroundings. The citizens of Tourmaday are not absent; they cooperate under the leadership of the provost to defend the town, secure provisions, provide weapons, and process with their lady to their church for prayer. All rally before the final battle with Alymodes, donning their best clothes, festooning the streets, and parading through them by rank to musical accompaniment. These scenes present an ideal of a well-ordered, prosperous society, the civic equivalent of the flourishing landscape. When Sadoyne becomes king of Cassydonye, he eliminates bad customs and enacts new laws. In highlighting such regnal contrasts, *Blanchardyn and Eglantine* reveals affinities with another pedagogical genre, the mirror for princes, and even offers "a covert political manual for its politically-engaged aristocratic, noble and gentry women readers."[30] Eglantine acts to insure the security of her kingdom and the welfare of its people. She convenes councils, consults advisors, provisions armies, plans battles, negotiates ransoms, and decrees sentences. Christine de Pizan, in *Treasure of the City of Ladies*, advises noble women about the importance of preparing themselves for such responsibilities. Her *Faytes of Arms and Chivalry* includes instructions for mounting a siege, plans for attack, defense, and types and placements of weapons, just as the romance depicts such preparations and provisioning. Loyalty is especially emphasized: the long prose *Blancandin* makes a point of denouncing Subyon and his corrupt barons, both for their treason and for his social climbing. Caxton adds several proverbs to those in his source, reinforcing the message that people of the lower classes and those who seek to rise in status are not to be trusted: "[T]herfore I saye

---

[28] *The Babee's Boke* and *The Boke of Curtasye* are found in ed. Furnivall, *Early English Meals and Manners*. *Generydes* is another romance much concerned with etiquette and courtly manners, including ceremonies of greeting and leave-taking and observation of proprieties (Pearsall, "English Romance," p. 70).

[29] Caxton, *Knight of the Tour-Landry*, ed. Wright, pp. 185–86.

[30] Bartlett, "Translation, Self-Representation," p. 58. See also Bornstein "William Caxton's Chivalric Romances," p. 10.

that of churles, both man and wyff can departe noo goode fruyte" (44.4).[31] The episode is an argument for the established social hierarchy and noble privilege, and a warning to those in positions of authority to choose their officials carefully. Usurpation and troth-breach could well have been on the minds of Caxton's audience during the Wars of the Roses, and of the Burgundians and the French during the final phases of the Hundred Years War.[32]

Marvels and Others

Blanchardyn and Eglantine is composed of elements tracing their origins to Chrétien de Troyes and the *chansons de geste*, but the author of *Blancandin* did not adopt the marvelous elements of its sources, and its conventional construction of Muslim difference is complicated by the fact that the followers of Islam have been transplanted to the Baltic.[33] An overt instance of the suppression of the marvelous is the provost's observation that Blanchardyn's prowess in battle is such that he seems to be more "a man of the feyré than . . . humayn" (21.3). The comment simultaneously invokes and dismisses the topos of the hero's supernatural taint, and perfectly illustrates "the transfer of wonder from the marvelous to the human" that is a generic marker of romance.[34] The lovers' first kiss is a realistic cousin to the disenchanting kisses of Sleeping Beauty and the *fier baiser* of *Lybeaus Desconus*.[35] In the verse romance of *Blancandin*, the test requires the traditional number of three kisses. While it may recall episodes of enchantment, the kiss is described with specificity. The author of the prose version takes pains to explain how such a manouver could be executed on horseback. Eglantine turns to determine the source of a noise behind her; at that moment Blanchardyn rides past, leaning so that their lips meet — an impressive display of horsemanship. The flame of love that descends to sanctify their pledges to one another belongs to the conventions of courtly love, and the calming of the sea is a Christian miracle, not uncanny.

Blanchardyn and Eglantine incorporates the negative stereotypes of Muslims as aggressors and religious and racial others that originated in the Crusades. The romance refers to the Prussians and Norwegians as *pagans* and as *Saracens* interchangeably and exclusively. Both words denote non-Christians, but the latter is also Islamophobic and racialized.[36] The terms appear most frequently in reference to Alymodes and his troops, usually coupled with the adjectives *false*, *infidel*, and *untrue*. These expressions are repeated throughout the narrative, and Caxton himself added such doublets, reiterating the romance's Islamophobia. Almost

---

[31] The romance is notable for its proverbial expressions, frequently introduced by the formula "But men saye in comyn langage . . ."). According to Brown-Grant, the long prose *Blancandin* contains a higher percentage of proverbial expressions than similar romances ("Narrative Style," p. 405). Here, elites appropriate common language — both in the sense of widespread and in the sense associated with ordinary people — to express aristocratic social attitudes.

[32] Megan Leitch points out that others of Caxton's romances from the 1480s, including the *Morte d'Arthur*, *Godfrey of Bologne*, *Charles the Grete*, and *The Foure Sonnes of Aymon*, are concerned with treason, loyalty, and maintaining bonds of chivalry and trust, which were also matters of concern to the readers of these texts ("Thinking Twice," p. 41).

[33] Sweetser, *Blancandin*, p. 41.

[34] Cooper, "Going Native," p. 27.

[35] The knight's fearless kiss restores a serpent-woman to her human form.

[36] While *Saracen* may refer specifically to Muslims, medieval writers also used it generally to refer to those of religions other than Christianity (as in Jean de Saintré's reference to Frenchmen fighting "Saracens" who are Poles and Prussians, and known by the French not to be followers of Islam; see Stuip, "*Blanchandin*, Jean de Créquy," p. 355).

half of the narrative is devoted to battles in which Blanchardyn decimates armies of religious others. He and his allies slaughter Alymodes's male relatives in a series of battles where their deaths are described in grisly detail, though Alymodes himself is spared and taken prisoner. The romance is Islamophobic, but Alymodes is not fighting a war of religious aggression; his motives are territorial and matrimonial.

Common racial stereotypes of Muslims are present in the romance: they are dark-skinned, grotesque, even demonic. This physiognomy was attributed to the climate of Africa, said to be their homeland by the atlases, encyclopedias, and travel writings of the time. Christian allegory accounted for these characteristics as physical manifestations of Islam's perceived spiritual distortion and false belief.[37] Though *Blanchardyn and Eglantine* acknowledges these conventions, it rarely exaggerates racial difference and takes no notice of the fact that a marriage of Eglantine and Alymodes would be interracial. There is a single instance of the monstrous: Rubyon, the giant who challenges Blanchardyn, is described as foul and hideous in the sole reference to his size and appearance. Alymodes has other stereotypically "Saracen" attributes: irascibility, cruelty, hatred of Christians, and ugliness.[38] With the distortion typical of medieval Christian misrepresentations of Islam, the romance's Prussians pray to Muhammed as a deity and worship idols, both practices that are counter to actual Muslim doctrine and practice, but which mirror Christian belief in the divinity of Jesus and the cult of saints. Beatrix denounces her father's religion as false, deceiving, and without efficacy, while lecturing him on the articles of Christian faith.

Though the Prussians are racialized by their dark skin, this feature is mentioned only in reference to Blanchardyn, who blackens his skin with herbs to blend in at the Prussian court. In a nod to realism, the author of the prose romance explains that this was the "coloure suche that the folke of that contrey had hers [theirs] atte that tyme" (26.6), in recognition of the fact that fifteenth-century Prussians did not have dark skin. This awkward detail had made sense in the verse *Blancandin*, which was set in the Middle East.[39] The romance mentions Blanchardyn's complexion twice more when the provost fails to recognize him and attributes his skin color to the heat of the southern sun. This pigmentation does not occlude the knight's whiteness (purity) and racial identitification stated in his name.[40] Alymodes's skin color is not mentioned; Beatrix is said to be "fayer," which means beautiful, but in context suggests fair-skinned as well; princesses in romance and *chanson* named as "Saracen" are often white.[41] The illustrations in the Vienna manuscript do not depict these characters with darkened coloration, suggesting that the audience may not have expected it.[42]

Blanchardyn is one of many Christian knights in romance who travel in Muslim lands and adopt the local language, style of dress, and physical appearance. He speaks German (appropriate to the setting), as well as speaking in character as a Muslim when he interjects "thanked be Mahon" (26.8) when introducing

---

[37] Cohen, "Saracen Enjoyment," p. 119. See also Rajabzadeh, "Depoliticized Saracen and Muslim Erasure" and Heng, "Jews, Saracens" for discussion of the construction of racial difference in medieval English literature, including the fourteenth-century romances *Isumbras*, *The King of Tars*, and *Fierabras* (or *The Sultan of Babylon*).

[38] A hot, wrathful temperament was associated with an imbalance of humors (blood), astrological influence, and the hot sun of Africa.

[39] Though dark-skinned Muslims would have been rare in Prussia, Kennedy and others point out that dark-skinned people were present in Europe to a degree often overlooked by historians ("Moors and Moorishness," p. 227).

[40] See Heng, "Jews, Saracens," pp. 260–62; *Invention of Race*, Chapter 4, especially pp. 183–85, on the importance of skin pigmentation to racist cultural representations of cultural others.

[41] de Weever, *Sheba's Daughters*, p. xviii.

[42] Alymodes and Beatrix are distinguished by headdress: she wears a turban, he a peaked cap and crown. The giant Rubyon is depicted as a large, armed figure with an angry expression.

himself to the Prussian king; several times he identifies himself to Christians as a "paynem" and a "Sarasyn" (35.1), all without reflection on his part or comment by the narrator.[43] Blanchardyn's passing for a Muslim Prussian becomes a disguise that enables him to play the trickster and test the loyalty of those who know him. He tells the unsuspecting provost that he has heard of Blanchardyn's marriage, to which the provost responds that this cannot be true, for the love of Blanchardyn and his lady is indissoluble. In another instance of deception, he frees his father from prison only to pretend to be a companion of Blanchardyn's and to have had news of his friend's death. Aside from these episodes in the first part of the romance, there is no mention of the knight's disguise.

Eglantine rejects marriage to Alymodes because he is an "infidel" and worships "false ydols," but these grounds are not sufficient to deter the friendship of Blanchardyn and Sadoyne. The pair have analogues in other Christian knights who become brothers-in-arms to Muslims who convert (Roland and Otuel, Tristan and Palomides).[44] Often in romances, political allegiances of Christians and Muslims follow on conversion of the latter, but the alliance of Blanchardyn and Sadoyne is established long before. Though Blanchardyn passes as a Muslim, the permeability of boundaries between Muslim and Christian is shown to operate principally in the other direction, namely in Muslim assimilation, though conversion is voluntary, not compelled by the sword as in the *chansons*. Sadoyne readily jettisons his idols (though not before Blanchardyn tells him to save their gold and jewels). The baptism of Beatrix, Sadoyne, and their people takes place in the Christian ghetto of Cassydonye which produces the priest, tubs, and holy water necessary for the public ritual.

Sadoyne and Alymodes are contrasting constructions of cultural others, one featuring assimilation, the other, extermination. Sadoyne and the Prussians are Blanchardyn's allies, not enemies; their troops join Blanchardyn to defeat other Muslims. While the romance is conventionally anti-Islamic, it is less negative and extreme in its treatment of Muslims than the giants and monstrosities, the idol-bashing, and crusading genocide of earlier romances such as *Isumbras*, *Fierabras* (or *The Sultan of Babylon*), and *The King of Tars*, or Caxton's *Godfrey of Bolougne*. In *Blanchardyn and Eglantine*, shared chivalric values of loyalty, feudal service, and military valor supersede the religious differences — the Christian Subyon's betrayal of these values makes him a villain. Military and political alliances outweigh racial and religious differences.

Gender and Character

Like other romances, *Blanchardyn and Eglantine* constructs gender according to chivalry's code of aristocratic masculinity. This code included a model of female command and male service, but was based on a patriarchal system in which men controlled the marriages of women to secure alliances with other men.[45] Women are thus mediators, supporting "men's agency, as well as the harmony of masculine communities."[46] Blanchardyn succeeds in his quest to marry his lady (and become king) because he has the support of

---

[43] His counterpart in the verse romance gives a more factual account, including the shipwreck.

[44] Unlike Blanchardyn, Roland and Tristan are not in Muslim disguise.

[45] Karras characterizes masculinity as a culturally constructed system through which men "exert dominance over men of [their] own social stratum as well as over women and other social inferiors" (*Boys to Men*, p. 21). This dominance was established in competition with other men and also through bonds with other men established in that competition, and through the exchange of women. See Karras's chapter, "Mail Bonding: Knights, Ladies, and the Proving of Manhood," pp. 20–66, for a useful discussion of chivalric masculinity.

[46] Summit, "William Caxton, Margaret Beaufort," p. 164. Her analysis of the economic relationship of patroness and printer applies to the relationship of romance heroine and hero as well: Caxton "redirects the object of masculine

other men who are loyal to her, and together they vanquish her challengers. As in many other romances, the absence of women is noticeable in the treatment of family. Fathers play a role throughout the narrative: Alymodes is a constant presence, and Blanchardyn's father is active in the second part of the story, insuring the succession to the throne of Frisia.[47] In contrast, Blanchardyn's mother is there to nurse him, lament his departure, die of sorrow (off stage), and be mourned by her son. Eglantine is without a family: her parents are dead, her absent uncle dies, and her governess and surrogate mother is rarely present after the couple declare their love. The long prose version of the romance makes a gesture to compensate for the lack of a maternal presence by adding the initial episode of the childless queen's answered prayers, and references to mothers breast-feeding the hero and heroine.

The courtly model of male service and female command suggests the possibility of marriage based on love rather than solely on practical or dynastic considerations, but Eglantine, as an orphaned heiress, is very much identified with her kingdom. The knight of the ferry, the provost, and her mistress refer to their lady's marriage pragmatically, the latter goes so far as to advise her to wed Alymodes in order to secure peace. Though Eglantine insists on her own choice of a husband, she, too, is pragmatic in choosing husbands for the provost's daughters. The exchange of women here is a function of the queen's jealousy and status, as she exercises a ruler's prerogative to arrange marriages and alliances. Social and emotional harmony are restored: all parties are agreeable as the unions are socially correct and advantageous. Blanchardyn arranges the marriage of Beatrix to Sadoyne, treating her as a spoil of war, a gift promised to his fellow in recognition of their friendship and loyalty. When her city falls, Beatrix courteously yields to the victorious Sadoyne and willingly accepts Blanchardyn's proposal to wed her to that prince. The union has been foreshadowed, since the lady had previously admired Sadoyne from afar and had been attracted to Blanchardyn by his excellence, at one point even wishing she were his "lady paramours."[48]

Beatrix resembles other strong-willed Muslim princesses of romance who are attracted to Christian knights, convert, and marry them, though she marries a converted Muslim.[49] She happily leaves her father's camp with Blanchardyn to avoid an arranged marriage to the giant Rubyon. Later, she challenges Alymodes when he berates her for disobedience, and asserts her right to marry without his knowledge or consent; she then mounts a rebellion, commanding her father's troops and defending his city against him. Muslim heroines are often depicted as "gruff, forthright, and even brutal in their speech and manners," and Beatrix is no exception.[50] In a memorable scene she approaches her father with humility and polite appeals, "swetly"

---

economic ambition away from competition with one another toward an idealised economy of 'virtue' and reward ... effected ... through the mediatory figure of the female patron" (p. 160).

[47] The reviser of the 1595 *Blanchardyn and Eglantine* seems to have found Blanchardyn's treatment of his parents callous and lacking in filial piety. That version makes more of it and of the guilt he feels for their grief, expanding the final scene to incorporate the son's penance for his departure and lamentation for the death of his mother.

[48] The verse romances detail the growing love of Beatrix and Sadoyne in passages of courtly rhetoric that have no counterparts in the prose adaptations; the latter move quickly to the couple's conversion and marriage (*FRLMA*, p. 43).

[49] Josian in *Bevis of Hampton*, Marsabele in *Octavian*, and Floripas in *Fierabras* (or *The Sultan of Babylon*) are examples of the type. Like Beatrix, Floripas betrays her father and attacks him with his own forces which follow her to France with her Christian love, Guy of Burgundy. Her behavior is extreme; in some versions of the romance she pushes her governess out a window to her death and punches her father's counselor on the nose. See de Weever, *Sheba's Daughters*, for an in-depth study of Muslim women in French epics. Many of her obervations pertain to English romances as well.

[50] Schlauch, *Antecedents*, p. 12.

urging him to convert and make peace with Blanchardyn and Sadoyne. When he refuses, calling her a "false and renyed [renegade] strompet," she lashes out: "Olde unfamouse myschaunt [wicked one], how arte thou soo follyshe and so overwenynge as for to wene to have her [Eglantine]? Thou haste that berde of thyne over-whyte therto, thy face is too mykel wonne [pale], and that olde skynne of thyn ys over mykel shronken togyder." He is too old to marry, she says, and should take himself to some "fayr hermytage" (48.6–8). Despite the humor of Beatrix's rebuttal, a reader looking for models of filial behavior might be taken aback by her mocking repudiation of her parent, and by the inversion of the accepted father-daughter power dynamic.

Unlike the absent ladies of some romances, Eglantine and Beatrix are very much present in the narrative, whether in the scene or in the thoughts and conversations of others. However, the two never meet, so there is no sisterly bond to parallel the brotherhood of Blanchardyn and Sadoyne. Many episodes are narrated from their point of view and there are frequent instances of the female gaze as Eglantine and Beatrix, from their castle windows, *chuse* their men in the commotion of battle. The word is apt, meaning both "to choose" as well as "to see," in the sense of discerning, or recognizing.[51] The intensity of the women's gaze suggests their agency in constructing chivalric masculinity. It is also possible that these are episodes of male narcissism — "the author's appropriating the woman's gaze merely for the purposes of male self-admiration."[52]

The limits of chivalry's gender-role-subverting conventions are apparent when Eglantine's resistance to masculine control is overcome by the kiss. The episode may have been suggested by the stolen kiss in Chrétien's *The Story of the Grail*; though subdued by comparison, Blanchardyn's kiss still "resonates with sexual violence."[53] The test of manhood and horsemanship is a transgression: Eglantine falls to the ground in a faint and insists that her person has been violated, the outrage being compounded by the fact that the perpetrator is a complete stranger. Her mistress minimizes the significance of the kiss and discourages Eglantine from seeking public retribution, pointing out that, since there were no other witnesses to the kiss, the lady's reputation will not be sullied by gossip. The romance thus presents two responses to the act: the mistress is more pragmatic and conventional while Eglantine is principled and absolute in her rejection of love and male dominance.

Although the plot turns on the love of Blanchardyn and Eglantine, the narrative devotes equal attention to bonds between men, that is Blanchardyn's network of loyal supporters which includes his father, Sadoyne, the king of Prussia, the earl of Castleford, the knight of the ferry and the provost, both mentors. The story of Beatrix and Sadoyne takes on a life of its own in the latter part of the romance when his capture by Alymodes and rescue by Blanchardyn postpone the wedding and prolong the "bromance," a term that captures the nature of the bond of male friendship depicted in romances.[54] The narrative speaks frequently of the love the two men have for one another, and it is telling that, on the point of dying, Sadoyne laments

---

[51] *MED chesen* (v.), senses 1, 9.

[52] Cooper, *English Romance in Time*, p. 236.

[53] Summit, "William Caxton, Margaret Beaufort," p. 162. See also Alberghini, "'A kysse onely,'" on Eglantine's refusal of consent. That scene is depicted in the Vienna manuscript: at the center the couple kiss on horseback, while, on the left the mistress looks on from behind a hedge. On the right, the hindquarters of the horses of the entourage are shown at the edge of the illustration, making it clear that the moment is observed by no one but the chaperone.

[54] One text of the verse romances (BNF fr. 375) omits the capture and rescue of Sadoyne and the treason of Subyon to conclude with the marriage of Blanchardyn and Eglantine following the defeat of Alymodes at Tourmaday; it thereby creates a more streamlined plot with fewer battles and greater focus on the heterosexual relationship.

that Blanchardyn is not present to avenge his death (and honor their oath) as much as he laments that death will separate him from Beatrix.

Blanchardyn and Eglantine's conception of chivalric masculinity is grounded in warfare. The long prose romance pays more attention to military matters than does the earlier verse romance, abridging passages of courtly sentiments while adding and enhancing episodes of combat. There are four full-scale battles and four individual challenges; the battle between the Prussians and the Poles and the capture of the king of Frisia are greatly expanded and are not mediated by female witnesses.[55] These engagements are described in detail, including the arming of leading warriors, individual combats, and deployments of troops under various leaders, their advances, retreats, casualties, and captures. The culminating combat of Blanchardyn and Alymodes is described as though it were a tournament, including single combats separate from the meleé, observed by a lady who sends a sleeve to her knight. Roughly fourteen chapters, comprising half the lines of the text, are devoted entirely to fighting.

Courtly Love and Affective Romance

Blanchardyn and Eglantine is attentive to the characters' emotions and to the literary conventions of courtly love, as is suggested by the heroine's soubriquet, The Lady Proud in Love.[56] While in the verse romances the lady refuses suitors because she has not yet found a knight who meets her standards, in the prose versions, her absolute refusal to love is an example of youthful pride and dangerous disregard for her kingdom.[57] Her obstinacy is treated with a degree of irony and humor. In her fury after the kiss, Eglantine debates what manner of execution would cause Blanchardyn the most suffering: "late hym be hanged, brente, or drowned, his hed to be smytten off from his shulders, or to make hym to be drawen and quartred" (16.2). Soon, under threat of Alymodes's attack, she decides to pardon Blanchardyn and appoints him commander of her troops. She ends her deliberations with the declaration that "never daye of my lyffe hym nor other I wyll not love . . . for all syche thynges I repute and take for foly . . . and shal be alleways my soverayne desyre and fynall conclusion" (17.1). The folly of her overstatement is emphasized in a later episode when the narrator comments, "at the same owre was taken the fynal and faste conclusion and altogydre was of her determyned to make of Blanchardyn her lover and her specyall, that a lytyl before that for one kysse onely was so ferre from her gode grace and in daunger of his lyf" (20.10).

Eglantine displays all the symptoms of courtly love. She becomes jealous of the provost's daughters. She is love-sick: wounded by love's arrow, her heart is enflamed and her body's humors thrown out of balance so that she is unable to eat, drink, or sleep. The rhetoric of courtly love is much in evidence in oxymorons, as when Eglantine shakes with cold caused by the arrow's heat, and when Blanchardyn declares that to be her servant would be great freedom. There is the allegory, personification, and metaphor of love, as when Love serves Eglantine a sour meal of jealousy and sends her servant, Care, to wait upon the lady and make her anxious. Love is likened to a religion with deities, conversions, temples, chapterhouses, and rituals. There are passages of debate between Reason and the lady's Pride. There is also a lover's soliloquy

---

[55] *FRLMA*, pp. 39–40.
[56] French and English use the terms *fin amor* [refined, idealized love], or *par amours*. While scholars have debated the nature of the phenomenon and its origins, by the fourteenth century its literary conventions were well-established in love lyric and romance and had been codified in the *Roman de la Rose*, including a physiology and a religion of love.
[57] *FRLMA*, pp. 41–42.

in a walled pleasure ground among "fayere flouris wherof nature had fayre appareylled the gardyne" (33.1). In a scene familiar from the *Roman de la Rose*, Blanchardyn sees a rose whose perfection reminds him of Eglantine, prompting him to lament their separation bitterly and at length.

The conventions of courtly love and debate enabled medieval authors to depict characters' emotions, and passages of dialogue and monologue make the reader privy to their thoughts and feelings. The plot often advances in series of conversations: those between Eglantine and her mistress concerning the kiss and Alymodes's proposal, followed by that between Eglantine and the Provost regarding his daughters and Blanchardyn, which is followed by the provost's communication with the knight, and finally the exchange between Blanchardyn and Eglantine in which he becomes her commander in chief and they declare their love. These passages shift fluidly between direct and indirect discourse, a feature of fifteenth-century prose that brings immediacy to the exchanges.[58] Formal speeches of lamentation, declaration, and supplication heighten emotion, promoting audience engagement.[59]

Blanchardyn and Eglantine portrays its characters' emotional states and appeals to those of the audience. Among romances of sentiment, it is distinguished for its exploitation of "empathy-creating devices ... to promote maximum identification with the characters," and for breaking "the temporal and spatial barriers between the narrator, audience and text."[60] There are many scenes of melodrama and pathos. Twice Eglantine joyously anticipates Blanchardyn's arrival only to despair as his return is thwarted by capture or storm. Sadoyne, on his way to the gallows, faints and is beaten with staves. He laments, "Alas, yf nedes I shal dey . . ." (48.10) and expounds at length upon his sorrow in response to a series of rhetorical questions, each also prefaced by "Alas." The lamentations of the king and queen of Frisia on the loss of their son are reiterated in several passages. The later sufferings of the captured king are narrated with specificity and repeated. He is "sore beten wyth the flayel of fortune" in a "tenebrouse and derke" dungeon (32.5) where he languishes dirty, starving, and nearly blind. The pathos of the father-son reunion is heightened by Blanchardyn, who does not reveal himself and instead inflicts more suffering on the poor man.

Techniques of narration also bring the reader into the action and minimize distance from the characters. We experience battles from the perspective of Eglantine and Beatrix. The narrator addresses the audience, creating "eavesdropping" effects that position the reader as a witness to the action.[61] The narrator refers to the audience directly as "we" and "you," as listeners and as readers, and interjects familiar *occupatio* such as, "Yf . . . I wold reherce and telle, I sholde over longe tary myself" (51.4). The voice contributes humor in comments and ironic asides, as when Eglantine arranges marriages for the provost's daughters: "I saye not that jalousy was cause of this thynge, but I leve it in the jugement that in suche a caas can good skyle" (24.1). Appeals to the audience in transitions between episodes are frequently empathetic, reminding the audience of the characters' emotions: "So shal we leve hym thus makyng his sorowfull complayntes tyl that tyme befor to speke of hym, and shal retourne to speke of his sone the goode yonge knyght Blanchardyn, whiche we have left wythin the paleys of Maryenborugh wyth Sadoyne" (32.5). The narrator even invites the audience to participate in the action by consoling the characters: "[let us] retourne to helpe the sorowful kynge and quene for to complayne and wepe for the absence of theyre dere sone Blanchardyn"

---

[58] The "rapid and almost invisible shifting from *discours indirect* [indirect discourse] to *discours direct* [direct discourse] . . . [creates] a dramatic and free-flowing quality which mimics 'real life' conversation" (Brown Grant, "Narrative Style," p. 391).

[59] Schlauch, *Antecedents*, p. 56.

[60] Brown-Grant, "Narrative Style," pp. 399, 378.

[61] Brown-Grant, "Narrative Style," p. 399.

(3.2). As it is a constant presence in the romance, the narrator's self-conscious persona becomes a kind of character, speaking to the audience in a tone that is familiar, even colloquial in its use of proverbs. Since the romance was read aloud, the voice would have spoken directly to the listeners, making the reader's performance more engaging.

Descriptions further appeal to the audience through synesthesia by invoking multiple senses. Episodes of feasting, private entertainment, and public celebration are often embellished with catalogues of musicians' instruments that invite the audience to form aural as well as visual images of these scenes, as though they are onlookers. Battles are rendered in grisly, if formulaic, realism that puts one on the battlefield amidst the blinding dust, the blast of trumpets, and the explosions of siege guns so loud the four elements seem to be colliding. Wounded knights are trampled under the hoofs of their mounts while injured horses run trailing their bowels; bodies are pierced by spears that are jerked out, and swords stab "lunge and lyvre" (20.4). Caxton sometimes adds such details where they do not appear in his source, compounding the depiction of carnage. The Vienna manuscript of *Blancandin* gives visual emphasis to the violence with its numerous illustrations of massed armies and battlefields heaped with dismembered dead and bloody wounded.

SCHOLARSHIP

Sources of information on the development of the romance, the French manuscripts, and Caxton's text can be found in Leon Kellner's brief Appendix to the Introduction of his 1890 edition of *Blanchardyn and Eglantine*; it provides a concise but outdated survey of the surviving verse and prose manuscripts.[62] Rosa Anna Greco's 2002 edition of the French prose *Blancandin* romances, short and long, includes stemma for both verse and prose texts and a thorough introduction (in Italian). Judith P. Stelboum's 1968 dissertation, "William Caxton's Romance of *Blanchardyn and Eglantine*," is designed as a companion to Kellner's edition with discussion of the romance's sources and the relationships of its surviving versions and texts, as well as Caxton's style and translation practice. "Translation Techniques in the Romances of William Caxton," Joanne M. Despres's dissertation of 1991, compares three of Caxton's romances to show his development as a translator and includes a semantic and syntactic analysis of *Blanchardyn and Eglantine* with attention to additions and omissions from his source. Both dissertations note that the romance had received little critical attention.

For the most part, scholars have approached the romance through its Burgundian connections and in the context of Caxton's other romances and chivalric publications. One of the first to do so was to was Margaret Schlauch, whose *Antecedents of the English Novel* (1963) examines late medieval prose narratives, termed society romances, that are more interested in human relationships than in military exploits. Diane Bornstein's article, "William Caxton's Chivalric Romances and the Burgundian Renaissance in England" (1976), examines the cultural diffusion of Burgundian chivalric practice and its literature into England, particularly through the court of Edward IV. This movement's lingering influence was due largely to Caxton's translations and other works from his press. Because Caxton's translation of *Blanchardyn and Eglantine* is faithful to his source, recent studies of the French prose romances are also useful: Rosalind Brown-Grant's "Narrative Style in Burgundian Prose Romances of the Later Middle Ages" (2012) compares narration in chronicle and romance, and notes ways romances decrease the distance between audience and character. Her analysis of the long prose *Blancandin* shows it to be particularly concerned with promoting empathy and engagement. Matthieu Marchal, in "De l'existence d'un manuscrit de la prose de *Blancandin et*

---

[62] Kellner, pp. cx–cxxvi.

l'Orgueilleuse d'Amours produit dans l'atelier du Maître de Wavrin" (2018), identifies the Vienna manuscript of the romance as a product of the Wavrin workshop and includes information about its production and connections to the Crèquy and Croy families.

Other studies of *Blanchardyn and Eglantine* examine it through a central figure in the Burgundian connection, Margaret Beaufort, and her program of patronage. All these studies address gender and the role of women as literary patrons, readers, and owners of books: see Patricia Pender's "'A Veray Patronesse': Margaret Beaufort and the Early English Printers" (2017), Rebecca Krug's "Margaret Beaufort's Literate Practice: Service and Self-Inscription" (2002), and Jennifer Summit's "William Caxton, Margaret Beaufort and the Romance of Female Patronage" (1995). The latter demonstrates how Caxton's dedication of *Blanchardyn and Eglantine* uses the language of courtly love and chivalry to represent the relationship of printer and patron according to the model of gendered behavior present in the romance itself. Anne Clark Bartlett reads the romance as a mirror for princesses in "Translation, Self-Representation, and Statecraft: Lady Margaret Beaufort and Caxton's *Blanchardyn and Eglantyne*" (2005) and finds the romance to be "a highly idealized, and deeply didactic account of its patron's own exercise of governance."[63] Other scholars discuss *Blanchardyn and Eglantine* in terms of Margaret's political activities and negotiation of the betrothal of Henry VII, in particular George Painter's biography of Caxton (1976) and Helen Cooper's *The English Romance in Time* (2004).

Studies have also focused on the romance's female characters and how contemporary audiences would have read *Blanchardyn and Eglantine*. Rosalind Brown-Grant's chapter "Chivalric Prowess and the Threat of Female Autonomy in Versions of *Blancandin*" (in *FRLMA*, 2008), compares French verse and prose versions, noting that the latter's treatment of chivalric masculinity gives less importance to love for women, and more importance to their land. Amy Vines's Introduction to *Women's Power in Late Medieval Romance* (2011) notes that Caxton's dedication of *Blanchardyn and Eglantine* suggests "new opportunities for female readers to consolidate and enact social and cultural power."[64] Though she does not discuss the romance itself, her observations about the female characters of similar romances are relevant. In "'A kysse onely': The Problem of Female Socialization in William Caxton's *Blanchardyn and Eglantine*," Jennifer Alberghini examines Eglantine's and her mistress's responses to Blanchardyn's kiss, and his removal of Beatrix from Alymodes's camp, in light of modern concerns for issues of female consent.

Textual Matters

Caxton is a faithful, accomplished translator, leaving nothing out and endeavoring to render the style of his French prose source into English.[65] However, his romance is wordier than his source and longer, though he adds no episodes.[66] Besides creating many doublets, often to emphasize misfortune, violent action, and emotion, he adds expressions of pious or chivalric sentiment such as "[H]e whom God wolde preserve can not peryshe" (25.3) and "as longeth [is appropriate] tyl a knyght to doo" (23.4). In addition he adds Islamophobic intensifiers such as "false Sarasyns" (21.2) and embellishes the episode of Subyon

---

[63] Bartlett, "Translation, Self-Representation," p. 58.
[64] Vines, *Women's Power*, p. 4.
[65] Stelboum, "William Caxton's Romance," p. 31; See the General Introduction, pp. 13–14, for discussion of fifteenth-century prose style.
[66] Despres estimates Caxton's text to be as much as twenty percent longer than his source ("Translation Techniques," pp. 185, 190, 197).

with additional proverbs. Caxton's deviations from the French texts are indicated in the Textual Notes and Explanatory Notes. The following passage, the end of the chapter in which the King of Frisia is taken prisoner, is a typical example of Caxton's additions which are indicated by italics (32.5).

> Whan Kyng Alymodes knew the same he wexed sore angry and wroth, but no remedy he myght not put therto, *for or ever he was advertysed therof, the provost and his felauship were almost oute of syght.* Well he had wold that they myght be met wythall by Daryus his sone, but he oughte not to care for it, for Daryus and hys navey helde their waye toward Cassydonye wher they arryved in fewe dayes wythout eny fortune. *And the provost saylled and rowed toward the costes of Nourthweghe.* Whan Daryus was come to lande into the haven of Cassydonye, *where he arryved wythin short tyme wythout ony fortune, as it is sayd*, he made the kyng of Fryse and other his prysoners to be had out from the shippes into a grete and strong toure whereas was a tenebrouse and derke dongeon, wherin the poure sorowfull kynge, replenysshed and sore beten wyth the flayel of fortune, was cast in pryson there to consume his olde dayes ful myserably, unto that tyme that by his right wel beloved sone Blanchardyn he be had out from this grete poverté and myserye. So shal we leve hym thus makyng his sorowfull complayntes tyl that tyme befor to speke of hym, and shal retourne to speke of his sone *the goode yonge knyght* Blanchardyn, whiche we have left wythin the paleys of Maryenborugh *wyth Sadoyne*.

As these examples show, Caxton's additions, besides supplying rhetorical flourishes, add continuity to the narrative by knitting up the threads of the preceding episodes and carefully locating all the characters.

Caxton's publication survives in a single copy, now in the John Rylands Library at the University of Manchester. This volume consists of ninety-six folios in fourteen quires of four leaves. Its present dimensions are 230 mm high (8 ¾ inches) by 178 mm wide (6 ¾ inches). The pages are printed in single columns, usually thirty-one lines per page. All the type is Caxton's gothic black letter font number six.[67] The text is ornamented with large woodcut capital letters at the beginnings of chapters, and usually chapter headings are set off by spaces between the preceding and following text. There are fifty-four chapters, ranging in length from one to twenty-one pages. Several leaves are missing from the Rylands volume: folio five containing the last leaf of the Table, the leaf following gathering Bii in chapter nine, and the conclusion to the romance after leaf Miiii. In this edition, the missing narrative is supplied by my translation of BNF fr. 24371. The book is now bound in red leather stamped with the arms of John, duke of Roxburghe, an eighteenth-century bibliophile and antiquarian. The volume has been restored, perhaps when he had it bound. Leaves have been inserted at the beginning including an engraved portrait of Caxton, a decorated title page, and a leaf, written in professional Gothic hand, which replaces one missing from the Table of Chapters. Headings in decorative script and annotations have been added to the pages of the Table and the Dedication. Before the restoration, a single writer had added folio numbers and was responsible for a program of textual annotation and correction.[68] There are further annotations in several seventeenth-century hands, well as traces of other readers, and several sets of marginal brackets that mark passages of particular significance. These features are referenced in the Textual Notes.

Earlier owners and readers have left their marks in the volume. John Dewe of Chesterton wrote that the book belonged to him in 1500, and described his family's coat of arms granted by Richard II. A John Dew (d. 1517) received his B.A. 1484–1485 at Cambridge and was a fellow of Gonville Hall there in the years

---

[67] Kellner, p. cxxiii. See Blades, *Biography and Typography*, pp. 338–39.
[68] The leaf added to the table interrupts the foliation sequence, so those notations predate the current binding.

1488–1500.[69] Chesterton is part of modern Cambridge, so it is possible that this person was the book's owner, perhaps its first. Others have left their names on its pages, the most legible being a Mary, a Richard, and John New. In 1776, John Ratliff, a London tradesman and bibliophile, sold the book to John Mason, who in turn sold it at auction to the duke of Roxburghe. When his library was auctioned in 1812, the book was purchased by the earl Spencer from whose collection it passed to the Rylands Library in 1894.[70]

This edition follows the METS guidelines explained in the General Introduction to this volume, where they are accompanied by comments on my editorial practices, with examples. The text is based on the only surviving print of *Blanchardyn and Eglantine*, that in the Rylands Library; it is available online at https://luna.manchester.ac.uk/luna/servlet/detail/Manchester~20~20~17~190274:Bookreader-15027.

Witnesses and Source Texts

French:

Verse

- Paris, Bibliothèque Nationale de France, MS fr. 375, fols. 254v–267r. [End 13c.; omits captivity of Sadoyne and treason of Subyon.]
- Paris, Bibliothèque Nationale de France, MS fr. 19152, fols. 174–192v. Online at https://gallica.bnf.fr/ark:/12148/btv1b52513419n?rk=42918;4. [Beginning 14c.]
- Philadelphia, University of Pennsylvania, Kislak Center for Special Collections, Rare Books and Manuscripts, Lawrence J. Schoenberg Collection, MS Codex 862 (formerly MS French 22). [Beginning 14 c. (incomplete); likely source of prose version.]
- Turin, Biblioteca nazionale universitaria, MS L V 44, fols. 136r–188r. [13 c.; destroyed by fire 1904.]

Prose: all mid-fifteenth-century

- Brussels, KRB, MS 3576/7. [Short prose version.]
- Paris, Bibliothèque Nationale de France, MS fr. 24371. Online at https://gallica.bnf.fr/ark:/12148/btv1b90580821/. [Caxton's source.]
- Vienna, Österreichische Nationalbibliothek, Cod. 3438.

English:

- Caxton, William. *Blanchardyn and Eglantine*. Westminster: Caxton, 1489. USTC: 500150; ISTC: ib00690400; ESTC: S108419. Manchester, John Rylands Library, Incunable 15027. Online at https://luna.manchester.ac.uk/luna/servlet/detail/Manchester~20~20~17~190274:Bookreader-15027?qvq=q:Bookreader%2B15027&mi=0&trs=1.USTC 500150. [Base text].

---

[69] *ACAD*, "Dew, John."

[70] Spencer wrote on the volume's flyleaf that he had planned to purchase it from Mason when it went to Roxburghe in uncertain circumstances and notes with satisfaction that it has come into his hands at last.

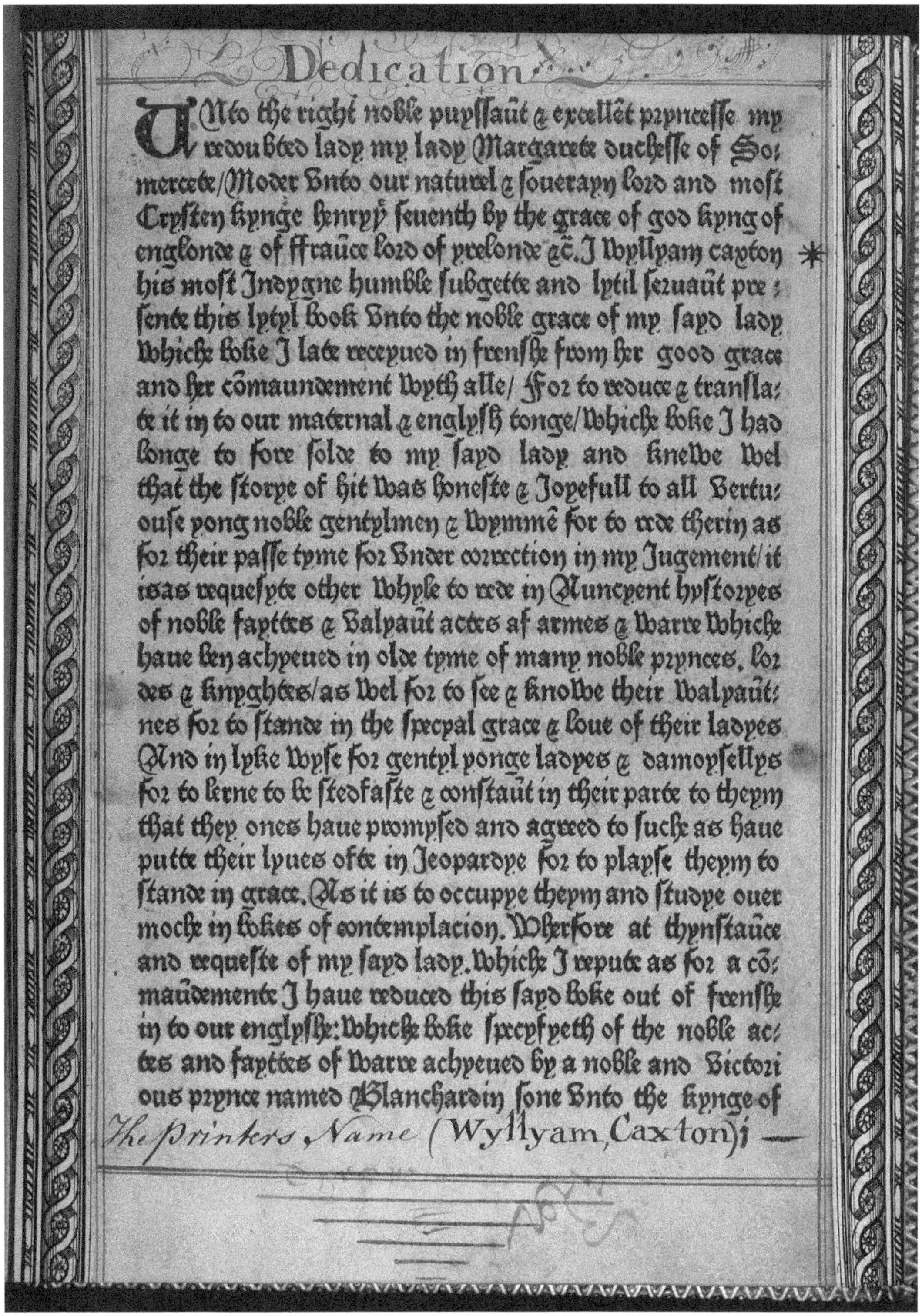

Dedication

Unto the right noble puyssaut & excellêt pryncesse my redoubted lady my lady Margarete duchesse of Somercete/Moder vnto our naturel & souerayn lord and most Crysten kynge henryj seuenth by the grace of god kyng of englonde & of ffraûce lord of yrelonde &c. J wyllyam caxton his most Jndygne humble subgette and lytil seruaût presente this lytyl book vnto the noble grace of my sayd lady whiche boke J late receyued in frensshe from her good grace and her cômaundement wyth alle/ ffor to reduce & translate it in to our maternal & englysh tonge/whiche boke J had longe to fore solde to my sayd lady and knewe wel that the storye of hit was honeste & Joyefull to all vertuouse yong noble gentylmen & wymmê for to rede therin as for their passe tyme for vnder correction in my Jugement/ it was requesyte other whyle to rede in Auncyent hystoryes of noble faytées & valyaût actes af armes & warre whiche haue ben achyeued in olde tyme of many noble pryncés. lordes & knyghtes/as wel for to see & knowe their valyaûtnes for to stande in the specyal grace & loue of their ladyes And in lyke wyse for gentyl yonge ladyes & damoysellys for to lerne to be stedfaste & constaût in their parte to theym that they ones haue promysed and agreed to suche as haue putte their lyues ofte in Jeopardye for to playse theym to stande in grace. As it is to occuppe theym and studye ouer moche in bokes of contemplacion. Wherfore at thynstaûce and requeste of my sayd lady. Whiche J repute as for a cômaûdemente J haue reduced this sayd boke out of frensshe in to our englysshe: Whiche boke specyfyeth of the noble actes and faytées of warre achyeued by a noble and victorious prynce named Blanchardin sone vnto the kynge of

The Printers Name (Wyllyam Caxton)j

Figure 2: Manchester, Rylands Library, Incunable 15027, fol 1. Caxton, *Blanchardyn and Eglantine*, 1489.

Caxton's Dedication

1 [fol. 1v] Unto the right noble puyssaunt[1] and excellent pryncesse my redoubted[2] lady, my lady Margarete duchesse of Somercete,[3] moder unto our naturel and soverayn lord and most Crysten kynge Henry the seventh, by the grace of God, kyng of Englonde and of Fraunce, lord of Yrelonde, et cetera., I Wyllyam Caxton, his most indygne[4] humble subgette and lytil servaunt, presente this lytyl book unto the noble grace of my sayd lady. Whiche boke I late receyved in Frenshe from her good grace and her commaundement wythalle for to reduce[5] and translate it into our maternal and Englysh tonge. Whiche boke I had longe tofore solde to my sayd lady, and knewe wel that the storye of hit was honeste and joyefull to all vertuouse yong noble gentylmen and wymmen forto rede therein as for their passetyme. For under correction in my judgement, it is as requesyte[6] other whyle to rede in auncyent hystoryes of noble fayttes[7] and valyaunt[8] actes of armes and warre which have ben achyeved in olde tyme of many noble prynces, lordes, and knyghtes, as wel for to see and know their walyauntnes[9] for to stande in the specyal grace and love of their ladyes. And in like wise for gentyl yonge ladyes and damoysellys for to lerne to be stedfaste and constaunt in their parte to theym that they ones have promysed and agreed to, suche as have putte their lyves ofte in jeopardye for to playse theym to stande in grace, as it is to occupye theym and studye overmoche in bokes of contemplacion. Wherfore at the ynstaunce[10] and requeste of my sayd lady, whiche I repute[11] as for a commaundemente, I have reduced this sayd boke out of Frenshe into our Englysh. Whiche boke specyfyeth of the noble actes and fayttes of warre achyeved by a noble and victorious prynce named Blanchardin, sone unto the kynge of [fol. 1v] Fryse,[12] for the love of a noble pryncesse callyd Eglantyne otherwyse named in Frenshe lorguylleuse damours, whiche is as moche to saye in Englyshe as the proude lady of love, quene of Tormaday; and of the grete adventures, labours, anguysshes and many other grete dyseases of theym

---

[1] *powerful*
[2] *honored*
[3] *Somerset, county in southwestern England*
[4] *unworthy*
[5] *translate*
[6] *necessary*
[7] *deeds (feats)*
[8] *brave (valiant)*
[9] *valiantness*
[10] *urging*
[11] *consider (regard)*
[12] *Frisia, coastal area in Holland and Germany*

bothe tofore they myghte atteyne[13] for to come to the fynall conclusion of their desired love, as alonge by the grace of God it shall be shewed in the historye of thys present book.

2   Bysechynge my sayd ladyes bountyuous grace to receyve this lityll boke in gree[14] of me, her humble servaunt, and to pardoune me of the rude and comyn Englyshe whereas shall be found faulte, for I confesse me not lerned ne knowynge the arte of rethoryk ne of suche gaye termes as now be sayd in these dayes and used. But I hope that it shall be understonden of the redars and herers. And that shall suffyse.

3   Besechynge allmyghty God to graunte to her moste noble goode grace longe lyffe and the accomplysshement of hir hihe,[15] noble, and joyes desires in thys present lyff. And after this short and transytorye lyff, everlastynge lyff in heven. Amen.

---

[13] *achieve (attain, reach a certain state)*

[14] in gree, *favorably*

[15] *high*

Caxton's Table of Chapters

1   [fol. 2r] Here begynneth the table of the victoryous prynce Blanchardyn, sone of the noble kyng of Fryse, and of Eglantyne quene of Tormaday otherwyse callyd lorgoylleuse damours, whiche is to saye the proude lady in love.

2   The first chapitre[1] conteyneth how Blanchardyn departed from his fader and moder wythout lycence. *Capitulo primo.*[2]

3   How tofore[3] his departyng he devysed[4] wyth his mayster,[5] enquyring hym of the batayles of Troye the grete cyté, whiche he sawe in tapysserye[6] the fygures of the knyghtes, and other affyares. *Capitulo ii.*

4   How Blanchardyn departed wythout knowleche of the kynge his fader and the quene his moder, and ledde wyth hym the beste hors and courser[7] that the kynge his fader hadde, and his goode swerde. *Capitulo iii.*

5   How the kyng of Fryse sent out men for to folowe and to seche Blanchardyn his sone, and of the grete angre and displayser that the kynge and the quene hadde. *Capitulo iiii.*

6   How Blanchardyn fonde in his waye a knyght wounded to the deth by another knyght whiche had taken his lady from hym, and how by the sayd Blanchardyn was promysed to rescowe hir agayn, and how he receyved the order of chivalrye of[8] the wounded knight. *Capitulo v.*

7   How Blanchardyn wente after the knyght soo ferre that he fonde hym, and wolde have enforced[9] the lady of the hurte knight. *Capitulo vi.*

8   Of the bataylle that betwene Blanchardyn and the knyght whiche soo longe fought togyder that Blanchardyn slewe hym and rescowed the mayden, whom he brought agayn to her love and frende whome she fonde ded, wherfor the mayde deyde for sorowe. *Capitulo vii.*

9   How Blanchardyn fonde a knyght whiche sente to hym a [fol. 2v] bote to passe over a ryver, and of the dyvyses that they had togyder and of the good chier that the goode knyght dyde to Blanchardyn. *Capitulo viii.*

---

[1] *chapter*

[2] *Capitulo primo, first chapter* (Lat.)

[3] *before*

[4] *conversed*

[5] *tutor*

[6] *tapestry*

[7] *war horse*

[8] *from*

[9] *raped*

10	Of the devyses and fayr exhortacions[10] that the knyght of the fery[11] gaaf to Blanchardyn, and how he conveyed hym on the waye toward Tormaday curtoysly. *Capytulo ix.*
11	The tenth chapter conteyneth how Blanchardyn departed fro the knyght of the ferye and went all alone after the orguylleuse damours. *Capitulo x.*
12	How Blanchardyn rode so ferre that he overtoke the orguyllouse damours and kyssed her, for to accomplysshe his enterpryse,[12] wherof she was in grete sorow. *Capitulo xi.*
13	Of the grete anger and sorowe the orguylleuse damours had of the kysse that Blanchardyn had receyved of her and of the complayntes that she made to hir maystresse,[13] which dyde grete payne to appease her. *Capitulo xii.*
14	How after that Blanchardyn had kyssed the orguylleuse damours departed fro hir and rode thynkyng all on her tyl that he cam to Tourmaday and arryved at the ostell[14] of the provost[15] for to lodge there, where as he dyd mervayllus armes.[16] *Capitulo xiii.*
15	How Blanchardyn justed wyth the provost and overthrewe hym, and by two damyselles doughters of the saide provost was ladde into their hous for to be lodged honorably. *Capitulo xiiii.*
16	How Blanchardyn was richely lodged and receyved into the hous of the provoste by his two doughters, and of the complayntes that the orguylleuse damours made to her maystresse of Blanchardyn. *Capitulo xv.*
17	Of the complayntes and grete thretenynges and menaces that the orguylleuse damours made to her sayd maystress of Blanchardyn. *Capitulo xvi.*
18	How the orguylleuse damours after many remonstraunces[17] [fol. 3r] whiche by her maystresse were made to hir, bygan to modere[18] her anger and hate whiche she hadde toward Blanchardyn for the kysse. *Capitulo xvii.*
19	How the orguylleuse damours made the ordynaunce[19] for the defence of the cyté, and how the Kyng Alymodes arryved and toke the porte nyghe unto Tormaday where he sette his siege. *Capitulo xviii.*
20	How a doughter of the provoste brought to Blanchardyn a whyte coverture[20] for his hors and gaaf to hym one of hir sleves praying hym to bere it on his helme, which he dyde gladly. *Capitulo xix.*
21	Of the grete bataylle whiche was tofore Tormaday ayenst the people of Kynge Alymodes, and of the grete prouesses[21] that Blanchardyn dyde that daye, and how the

---

[10] *urgings*

[11] *ferry*

[12] *undertaking (feat of arms)*

[13] *governess*

[14] *residence (lodging)*

[15] *chief magistrate of the city (military officer)*

[16] *feats of arms*

[17] *appeals*

[18] *moderate*

[19] *orders (military equipment)*

[20] *trapping for a horse (cover)*

[21] *acts of knightly prowess (martial expertise)*

Caxton's Table of Chapters

155

orguylleuse damours becam amorouse of hym, and of the devyses whiche made to her maystress of Blanchardyn and other thynges. *Capitulo xx*.

22　　How the orguylleuse damours by the grete love that she had sette upon Blanchardyn bycam moche jalouse and sore doubted leste[22] he shold sette his love in one of the doughters of the provost, for whom she sente moche hastely and speke to hym secretely. *Capitulo xxi*.

23　　Of the devyses that were bytwene the provost and the orguylleuse damours and of the grete love that she had sette in Blanchardyn. *Capitulo xxii*.

24　　How the provost retourned home and recounted to Blanchardyn all that the orguylleuse damours had sayd to hym, and how she sent for Blanchardyn to com to her, the whiche cam and of the devyses and how their loves were confermed. *Capitulo xxiii*.

25　　How Blanchardyn retourned home wyth the provoste and the fayr stede or courser all white and of the sleve of cloth of golde which his lady the orguylleuse damours sente to [fol. 3v] him, and of the grete bataylle bytwene Blanchardyn and a geaunt whiche was slayn, and of the merveluose prouese doon by Blanchardyn, and also how he was taken. *Capitulo xxiiii*.

26　　How Kyng Alymodes wold have put to deth Blanchardyn, but at the request of his doughter fayr and good respyted[23] him of hys deth, and how the orguylleuse damours sent the provost to Alymodes to offre hym raenson[24] for his delyveraunce whiche wold not accepte it. *Capitulo xxv*.

27　　How Daryus by the commaundement of the kyng his fader ledde Blanchardyn toward the Kyng of Salamandre,[25] but the ship was perished[26] and all drowned except Blanchardyn, whiche arryved on londe and cam to the kyng of Maryenborugh[27] whiche reteyned[28] him and made him conestable[29] of his oost.[30] *Capitulo xxvi*.

28　　How a knight wounded cam and reported tydynges to the kynge of Maryenborugh that the kyng of Polonie[31] his enmye was entred into hys royalme wyth a grete armye. *Capitulo xxvii*.

29　　How the kyng of Maryenborugh delyvered his sone Sadoyn wyth fourty thousand men to Blanchardin for to fyghte wyth his enmyes and chased them oute of his royalme.[32] *Capitulo xxviii*.

---

[22] sore doubted leste, *was anxious lest (greatly feared that)*

[23] *spared*

[24] *ransom*

[25] *Alexandria*

[26] *wrecked*

[27] *Marienburg, now Malbork, in Poland*

[28] *employed*

[29] *commander (chief military officer)*

[30] *army*

[31] *Poland*

[32] *kingdom (realm)*

30	How Blanchardyn and Sadoyn wyth ther armye dysconfyted[33] their enmyes and Blanchardyn toke the kyng of Polonye prysoner whom he delyverd to the kyng of Maryenborugh. *Capitulo xxix.*
31	How Daryus sone of Kyng Alymodes by fortune of the see arryved in Fryse, where he tok the kyng fader of Blanchardyn and dyde there grete dommage[34] and ledde hym prysoner into Cassydonye.[35] *Capitulo xxx.*
32	How Darius arrived in the ost[36] of the kyng his fader where he was receyved with grete joye bycause he brought grete foyson[37] of bestaylle[38] and all manere of vitayll[39] to the oost. *Capitulo xxxi.*
33	How the goode provoste wente oute of Tormaday and toke all the bestayll that Daryus hadde broughte in to the [fol. 4r] ooste and ladde it into the cyté, wherof they hadde grete nede. *Capitulo xxxii.*
34	Of the complayntes that Blanchardyn made, and of the grete comforte that Sadoyne made to hym promysyng that to his power he wolde ayde hym. *Capytulo xxxiii.*
35	How Sadoyne toke leve of his fader and also Blanchardyn and wente to the see wyth a grete navye full of men of armes for to socoure[40] the orguylleuse damours, and of the goode provoste whiche they mette in the see of whome Blanchardyn was joyous. *Capitulo xxxiiii.*
36	Of the grete devyses of Blanchardyn and of the goode provoste, and of the lettres that he sente to the orguylleuse damours, and of the joye that she had. *Capitulo xxxv.*
37	Yet of the joye that the orguylleuse damours had for the comynge of her frende and love and of the grete sorow that sone after she demened[41] whan she sawe the tempest and fortune that so soone put hym soo ferre fro the porte. *Capitulo xxxvi.*
38	How Blanchardyn and Sadoyne arryveden tofore Cassydonye where they fonde Daryus whiche cam and spake to theym. *Capitulo xxxvii.*
39	How Blanchardyn sleue Daryus and of the grete batayll where Cassydonyens were slayen and dyscomfyte[42] and the cyté taken, and how Sadoyne and the fayr Beatryce dyd do baptyse theym and their people. *Capitulo xxxviii.*
40	How Blanchardyn fonde ther his fader kyng of Fryse whiche ther was prysoner, and of their pituose[43] devyces that thei had togyder. *Capitulo xxxix.*
41	How Blanchardyn, Sadoyne, and the kyng of Fryse wente to the see wyth a gret puyssance[44] for to com to socoure the fayr orguillouse damours, where they arryved in the

---

[33] *defeated (overcame)*

[34] *harm*

[35] *possibly Chalcedon in Asia Minor*

[36] *army*

[37] *abundance*

[38] *livestock*

[39] *food*

[40] *aid (succor)*

[41] *expressed (exhibited)*

[42] *defeated (overcome)*

[43] *pitiful (sad)*

[44] *military strength (power)*

42   ende wyth right grete joye by the prouesse[45] and valyaunce[46] of armes that they dyde. *Capitulo xl.*

42   [fol. 4v] How Blanchardyn recounted to the kynge his fader and to Sadoyne the beaulté and bounté of his lady and of the provoste whiche cam for to mete theym. *Capitulo xli.*

43   Of the grete joye that the orguylleuse damours had whan she herd saye of the provoste the joyous tydynges of the comyng of Blanchardyn her frende and love. *Capitulo xlii.*

44   Of the grete bataylle tofore Tourmaday ayenst the kyng Alymodes whiche was descomfyted, and of the takynge of Sadoyne and of the sorowe that Blanchardyne made. *Capitulo xliii.*

45   How Blanchardyn made hym redy and toke his men in his shippe for to goo socoure his felawe Sadoyne whom Kyng Alymodes ledde wyth hym prysoner in grete distresse. *Capitulo xliiii.*

46   How Blanchardyn put hymself to the see for to socoure his sayd felawe Sadoyne. *Capitulo xlv.*

47   How Subyon, to whom Blanchardyn tofore his departing had lefte the governaunce of his love the orguylleuse damours, had made conspyracion[47] ayenst her for to take hir to his wyff and make hymself kyng, and of his grete alyaunces.[48] *Capitulo xlvi.*

48   How the erle of Castelforde, the provoste, and the knyght of the ferye toke and ledde the lady by force to Castelforde maulgré[49] Subyon and alle his puyssaunce. *Capitulo xlvii.*

49   How the kyng Alymodes arryved tofore Cassydonye and how he spack to his doughter the fayr Beatryce, and for to doo her despyte[50] he ded reyse a payr galowes supposyng to have hanged theron Sadoyne her husbonde. *Capitulo xlviii.*

50   How the fayr Beatryce sente socours to her husbond Sadoyne and was rescowed fro deth and brought wythin Cassydonye maulgré the kynge Alymodes. *Capitulo xlix.*

51   [fol. 5r] How Blanchardyn arryved in the haven of Cassydoyne, before whiche towne he founde Alymodos the kynge. Chapter 50, folio 90.

52   How grete the batayll was bytwyx Blanchardyn and Kyng Alymodos before Cassydonye and how Alymodes was overcome, take, and broughte prysoner into the cyté, and of the coronacyon of Sadoyn and of his wyff Beatryx. Chapter 51, folio 90.

53   How the proude mayden in love sent the provost toward Blanchardin whiche after thees tydynges exployted[51] so sore that he arryved wyth alle his exeercyte[52] nyghe to the oost of Subyon. Chapter 52, folio 92.

---

[45] *prowess*

[46] *bravery*

[47] *conspiracy*

[48] *alliances, especially through noble marriage*

[49] *in spite of [OF maugré]*

[50] doo her despyte, *to spite her*

[51] *hurried*

[52] *army (host)*

54   How Blanchardyn and Sadoyne dyscomfyted Subyon and of the grete bataylle and manere how he was taken and what followed after. Chapter 53, folio 94.

55   How Blanchardin wedded his love the proude pucell[53] in amours, and of the grete joye that was made there, and of the kynge of Fryses deth. Chapter 54, folio 96.

---

[53] *maiden [OF pucelle]*

[fol. 6r] **The first chapitre of this present boke conteyneth how Blanchardyn departed out of the court of his fader kynge of Fryse. Capitulo primo.**

1 That tyme when the right happy wele[1] of peas[2] flowrid for the most parte in all Christen realmes, and that moche peple dyde moche peyne[3] to gadre and multyplye[4] vertues, regned in Fryse a kynge of right benewred[5] and happy fame, loved, doubted,[6] and well obeyed of his subgettis. Ryght habundaunt of the goodes of fortune; but privated[7] and voyde[8] he was of the right desyred felicité[9] in mariage, that is to wyte[10] of lignage or yssue[11] of his bodye, wherof he and the quene his wyffe were sore[12] displesed. I leveto telle[13] the bewayllyngis and lamentaciouns that the goode lady the quene made full often by herself al alone in solytary places of her paleys[14] for this infortune.[15]

2 But she, knowyng the vertuouse effecte of devote and holy oryson,[16] excercysed with al her strengthe her right sorowful grevous herte to this gloriouse occupacion. And after this fayre passetyme, by veraye[17] permyssion devyne,[18] conceyved a right faire sone whiche was named Blanchardyn. Now it is soo that atte his byrthe and comyng into this world, sourded[19] and rose up one not acustomed joye and gladnesse of the kynge and of the quene, of the prynces and lordes, and of all the comyn[20] people of the lande that judged hemself right happy of a successoure legytyme. Yf unto you I wold recounte and

---

[1] *common good (well-being, prosperity)*

[2] *peace*

[3] *care (diligence)*

[4] gadre and multyplye, *gather and enhance*

[5] *happy [OF ben eurez]*

[6] *honored*

[7] *deprived*

[8] *devoid (lacking)*

[9] *happiness*

[10] that is to wyte. *that is to say (know)*

[11] *progeny (child)*

[12] *greatly (very much)*

[13] leveto telle, *leave off telling (cease)*

[14] *palace*

[15] *misfortune*

[16] *prayer (the recitation of a set of liturgical prayers)*

[17] *true (authentic)*

[18] *divine*

[19] *soared*

[20] *common (those without rank or title)*

telle the joye and the myrthe that atte that daye was made, I myght overmoche lengthe oure matere. Blanchardyn the chylde was taken into the handes of a right noble lady of the lande for to norysshe[21] and bryngen up. [fol. 6v] But well ye knowe that he was not hadde sore ferre[22] from the kynge his fadre nor fro the quene his modre. For never daye nor owre[23] the childe Blanchardyn toke noo fode of none others brestis, but all onely of the quene his modres owne brestis. The childe grew and amended sore[24] of the grete beaulté[25] wherof he was garnysshed.[26] None can telle it you bycause that it was so grete, that God and nature had nothyng forgoten there.

3   Blanchardyn grewe in beawté, wytte,[27] and goode maners beyonde mesure and passed all other of his age. Thenne whan he came atte the yssue[28] of his childhode he was take for to be endoctryned[29] in lytterature and in goode maners to a clerck the whiche wythin short tyme made hym expert and able in many and dyvers sciences, that is to wyte in gramayre, logyke, and philosophie.

4   Blanchardyn, emonge other passetymes, delyted hymself in hawkynge and hunting, whereas right moderatly and manerly mayntened[30] hymself. Of the tables[31] and ches playinge, and of gracyous and honeste talkynge, he passed them that were his elder in age. And for to speke the trouthe, he was naturelly inclyned and used alle that whiche the herte of a noble man appeteth[32] and desyreth, reserved that[33] he nevere had borne noon armes nor herde speke therof, nor also had not seen the manere and the usuage of joustynge and tournoyinge. And that was for bycause of the right expresse commandementes of the kynge his fadre, doon to theym that hadde the chylde in governaunce. Notwythstandyng, he lefte[34] not to knowe theym, for it is sayde in comyn langage[35] that the goode byrde affeyteth[36] hirself, and so dyde Blanchardyn, as ye shall mowe[37] here heraftre.

---

[21] *nurse*

[22] he was not hadde sore ferre, *he was not placed (had) very far*

[23] *hour*

[24] amended sore, *improved greatly*

[25] *beauty*

[26] *adorned*

[27] *intellect (mental ability)*

[28] *conclusion*

[29] *instructed*

[30] *conducted*

[31] *gaming tables (gambling)*

[32] *aspires to (seeks after)*

[33] *with the exception that*

[34] *omitted (neglected)*

[35] in comyn langage, *idiomatically (commonly)*

[36] *teaches*

[37] *more*

[fol. 7r] **The seconde chapytre conteyneth how Blanchardyn byfore his departyng talked and devysed wyth his mayster, demaundynge of the bataylles of Troye, whiche he sawe fygured in tapysseryes, and the signyfycacion of the names of the knyghtes, of theyre armures and of theyre fayttes.**

1   It happed that on a daye emonge othre, Blanchardyn fonde hymself in advyses[1] wyth his mayster[2] walkynge wythin[3] the paleys. And by adventure[4] entred into a chambre hanged wyth right fayre and riche tapysserye of the destruttion of Troye, well and alonge[5] fygured.[6] Blanchardyn, that nevere had taken theratte noo hede, ryght instantly dyde advyse[7] and sette his syghte toward the sayde tappysserye, and coude not merveylle[8] hymself too moche in beholdynge upon the same of the dyverse and strange werkes that he perceyved.

2   Thenne dylygently he demanded his mayster of the subtylnes[9] of the werke[10] of the historye, and of the personnages. And first recounted unto hym his mayster the puyssaunce,[11] the right grete cyrcuyte,[12] and the noblesse of the cyté of Troyes. And syn[13] the horryble and merveyllous bataylles of the Grekes ayenst[14] the Trojans, the right grete valyaunce[15] of Hector, of Troylus, Parys, and Deyphebus brederen,[16] and of Achilles and of many othre, of whom he sawe the representacyon in the sayde tappysserye that sore movyd and styryd his noble and hyghe[17] corage,[18] and gaffe hym a wylle for to be lyke unto those noble and worthy knyghtes wherof he sawe the remembraunces.[19]

3   After he demaunded of his mayster the names and blasure[20] of the armes that the sayde knyghtes bare, that well and alonge dide advertyse[21] [fol. 7v] the chylde. And for to abredge[22] longe taryeng,[23] tofore they departed fro the chambre, by the ynstruction of

---

[1] *discussions*

[2] *tutor*

[3] *inside*

[4] *chance*

[5] *fully (at length)*

[6] *depicted (portrayed in figures)*

[7] *notice (examine)*

[8] *wonder (marvel)*

[9] *details (subtleties)*

[10] *the tapestry (fortification)*

[11] *military might (power)*

[12] *encircling defensive walls*

[13] *afterwards*

[14] *against*

[15] *bravery*

[16] *brothers*

[17] *exalted (elevated)*

[18] *courage (spirit)*

[19] *memorials (commemorations)*

[20] *blazon (heraldic design, coat of arms)*

[21] *that well and alonge dide advertyse,* that one [his master] did at length inform

[22] *shorten*

[23] *delay (pause)*

his mayster, he was sage[24] endoctryned[25] of the names and usages for the moost parte of the habylymentes[26] necessary and servynge to the werre. From that oure[27] forth on, the right noble jovencel[28] Blanchardyn concluded in his corage that he shold fynde hymself, yf God graunted hym helthe, in som place where by experyence he shuld lerne to bere armes and shuld excercyce[29] and take payne and dylygence upon hymself to knowe the wayes of the same for the grete plesure that he toke in herynge therof speke, thynkyng in hymself that the use therof shulde be to hym ryght moche agreable and plaisaunt. And so thenne departed from his mayster more pensefull[30] than he had be byfore tyme.

[24] *wisely*
[25] *instructed*
[26] *equipment (apparatus)*
[27] *hour*
[28] *youth (young man) [OF jovencel]*
[29] *practice (exercise)*
[30] *thoughtful (brooding)*

The thirde chapitre conteyneth how Blanchardyn departed wythout the knowlege of his fadre, the kynge of Fryse, and bare awaye wyth hym his goode swerde, and toke his goode courser. And of the sorowe that the kynge and the quene made for his departynge.

1   Blanchardyn, after the departynge that he made from his mayster, cam into his chambre al alone. And there al his thoughtes he concluded in one, for to fynde the manere and facyon[1] for to departe out of his faders hous the kynge. And it is not to be doubted but or evere[2] he myght come to the chyeff[3] of his enterpryse[4] for to make his departynge, that his mynde was full sore troubled wythal bycause of the dyverse and many conclusyons that his fantasyouse[5] wylle dyde present byfore hym. Neverthelesse [fol. 8r] all rewthis,[6] layde a departe[7] as well for his fader as for his modre, kynrede[8], and fryndes, as other infynyte thynges that are wont to tarye[9] the corages[10] of some enterpryses, concluded[11] by hymself his departynge wythout shewyng[12] tyl[13] onybody. And dyde so moche by his

[1] *mode*
[2] *before*
[3] *main point*
[4] *undertaking*
[5] *full of fantasies*
[6] *regrets*
[7] layde a departe, *laid plans for a departure*
[8] *family (kindred)*
[9] *impede (slow)*
[10] *courage (spirits)*
[11] *carried out (completed)*
[12] *revealing*
[13] *to*

subtyll[14] engyne[15] that he gate a ryght goode and riche swerde that longed[16] unto the kynge his fadre, whiche afterward was to hym wel syttynge.[17] Whan he sawe hymself thus garnyssed[18] therwyth he was ful glad. Thenne went he all fayre and softe[19] donne fro the paleys evyn about the oure[20] of mydnight; the mone shone bright and faire. Blanchardyn toward the stables tourned his waye where he fonde, standing aparte, the best courser[21] of the kinge his fader, whiche was the fairest and the best that coude have ben founde in ony countrey at that tyme, so that for the fyersnes[22] of the sayd courser he was kept in a litil stable by himself nere ynoughe the grete stables. The jovencel[23] Blanchardyn, joyful and gladde, cam and entred into the stable and sette the sadell and the brydell to the riche and myghty courser, upon whiche right quykly he mounted and, smyting wyth the sporys,[24] went his waye anone,[25] to the ende[26] that he shulde not be herde nor aspyed[27] of noo man. So rode he all that nyght, that was to hym of avauntage[28] for cause of the mone that spredde her bemes abrode, wythout that onybody coude telle ony tydynges where he was becomen.[29]

2   Thus as ye here, the jovencel Blanchardyn, all alone wythout companye, departed from the kynge his fader, the whiche God wyl kepe and guide. So shal we leve him drawing[30] on his waye and shal retourne to helpe the sorowful kynge and quene for to complayne and wepe for the absence of theyre dere sone Blanchardyn.

---

[14] *clever (subtle)*
[15] *scheme (wit)*
[16] *belonged*
[17] *suited*
[18] *adorned*
[19] *quietly (gently)*
[20] *hour*
[21] *war horse*
[22] *fierceness*
[23] *youth (young man)* [OF *jovencel*]
[24] *spurs*
[25] *immediately*
[26] *to the ende, in order that (in such a way that)*
[27] *seen (discovered)*
[28] *advantageous*
[29] *where he was becomen, where he had gone*
[30] *traveling*

The fourth chapitre conteyneth how the kynge of Fryse made to pursyew his sone Blanchardyn and of the grete sorowe that he and the quene his wyf made for hym.

1   [fol. 8v] After the partynge that Blanchardyn made, that alone and wythout companye rode lighteli[1] to the end he shold not be folowed of noo man, the nyght passed and the fayre daye came and the sonne rose up spredyng his bemes upon the erthe. The

---

[1] *quickly*

owre[2] cam that every man was rysen up wythin[3] the paleys. Right thus as many knyghtes and esquyers[4] went there walkyng and spekynge one wyth other, cam the yomen[5] and grommes[6] of the stable makynge grete noyse and crye for that grete courser[7] of the kynge whiche that night was stolen fro theim. So moche that the bruyt[8] and the tydinge therof ranne thrughe all the pallays.[9] The kynge and the quene his wyf atte that owre were rysen up, herynge the bruyt that there wythinne was made for that myschyef[10] that so was fallen, and had grete merveylle.[11] Dyverse[12] there were that unto them brought the tydynge of the same, but not longe hit taryed[13] whan tolde and recounted was to theim the harde[14] departynge of theire right wel beloved sone Blanchardyn, that al alone was gon no man knewe where.

2   Whan the good kyng and the quene understode the voyce of theym that the pyteouse tydynges brought unto theim, there nys[15] no tonge humayn that coude to yow recounte ne saye the grete sorow and lamentacion that they bothe togidre made, and so dyde al they that were wythinne, for the grete love that they al had unto that jovencel. But the lamentable sorowynge that the king and the quene made passed all other for they were bothe fal in swone so that no lyf coude be perceved in theire bodyes. But trowed[16] all they that were present that they had be bothe deed, wherof the pyteouse cryes, wepyng, and lamentacions bygan to be more grete, so that thurgh the cyté were herde the voyces wherby they were soone advertysed,[17] wherfore suche a sorowe was made wythin the palays.[18] In the cyté and thurgh al the [fol. 9r] royalme[19] wept ladyes, maydens, men, and wymen. Within a short while the palays and the cyté were tourned from joye unto tristresse[20] and replenysshed[21] wyth sorowe ful byttir. The kynge and the quene, after that they had layen in a swoune a goode while, came ayen[22] to theyme self. And the kynge

---

2   hour
3   inside
4   squires
5   household attendants (yeoman)
6   grooms
7   war horse (swift horse)
8   report (clamor)
9   palace
10 misfortune
11 astonishment (surprise)
12 Several
13 remained, i.e., news of the missing horse was quickly eclipsed by that of Blanchardyn's absence
14 bitter (harsh)
15 is no
16 believed
17 informed
18 palace
19 kingdom (realm)
20 sadness [OF triste]
21 filled
22 again

ascryed[23] hymself a-hyghe[24] saynge, "O my right beloved sonn, the gladnes and joye of myn herte, who moved you to leve me and to parte soo? Certeynly I perceyve in me the shortynge[25] of my dolaunt[26] and sorowfull lyff."

3   After the rewthes[27] and lamentacions of the kynge commauded expressely to al his barons and knyghtes in the cyté and thurghe alle the realme that, upon the love[28] that they ought[29] to hym and upon as moche as they entended to do hym plasire, that they alle sholde mounte on horsbacke for to enquyre and seke after hys most dere and wel beloved sone, and to brynge hym ayen unto him. Thenne were anone[30] steryng out of alle partyes knyghtes, noblemen, and burgeys,[31] and they parted fro the cyté toke dyverse wayes, enquyrynge in every place where they passed by for to here and understande some goode and true tydynges of the jovencel Blanchardyn. But so moche they coude not seke nor enquyre that ever they coude lerne nor here ony tydynges of hym, wherof alle dolant and confuse tourned ayen to the kynge of Fryse that of this adventure[32] was full sory and dolaunt, and so was his wyf the quene. I shal leve[33] to telle yow of the kynge and the quene, suffryng[34] theym to demayne[35] their rewthis and complayntes unto that tyme and oure[36] shal be for to retourne to the same.

---

[23] exclaimed (called out)
[24] on high (loudly)
[25] shortening
[26] sad [OF dol]
[27] sorrows
[28] feudal loyalty (love)
[29] owed
[30] immediately
[31] burgesses (town officials)
[32] event (fortune)
[33] cease (leave off)
[34] allowing
[35] express (exhibit)
[36] hour

The fythe chapitre speketh how Blanchardyn founde a knyght on his waye wounded to deth by another knyght that from hym had taken his lady awaye. And how by the [fol. 9v] same, Blanchardyn was made knyght that promysed to rescue his lady unto hym.

1   As byfore ye have herde of, Blanchardyn, that alone was departed wythout leve[1] of the kynge his fader, holdynge the covert[2] wayes bycause that of his faders folke he shold not be folowed or overtaken. So moche and so longe a space he rode wythout fyndyng of ony adventure that ought to be recounted or tolde, that passyng forth on his waye thurghe the londe, founde hymself in a hyghewaye brode ynoughe that ladde hym unto the

---

[1] permission
[2] hidden (secret)

ende of a grete forest, in whiche he entred and rode styl[3] tyl the morowe none[4] wythout ony adventure wherof men ought to make mencion. And so rode all nyght unto the next morowe tenn of the clocke, and gooynge doune from a hylle into a valeye founde a knyght that lay there on the grounde armed of al pieces,[5] the whiche full pyteouly complayned and made grete mone. Thenne Blanchardyn, seeyng the knyght there alone, taryed hymself, mervellyng why nor what cause moevyd hym thus to sorowe and complayne. He stode styl makyng humble salutacion unto hym and syth[6] demaunded hym of the causes of his sayde sorowe and grevaunce. The knyght, right humbly, and wyth a right lowe voyce as he that hurt was to deth, rendryd[7] hym ayen his salewyng and well alonge advertysed[8] the jovencel Blanchardyn of his mysadventure, shewyng to hym the place and wounde that drue hym toward to dethe by the hande of a knyght that had taken his lady from hym, the whiche thynge was but late doon unto hym.

2   Thenne Blanchardyn, moved of pyté,[9] alyght[10] from his courser and sette fote on erthe and disarmed the knyght from his armures, and syth wrapped his wounde wherof he so sore sorowed, [fol. 10r] and dyde covere hym wyth his mantell, axyng yf he that injurye had doon to hym myght be but lytyll ferre[11] goon. The knyght answerd and sayde that he myght wel have goon a myle and nomore. After this, he toke hymself to syghe full sore saying, "Alas my right dere lady that so moche I loved, this day shal the separacion be made of the two hertes that so stedfastly loved eche other. I fele deth atte the entrance of my soroweful herte, prest[12] and redy to make me pryvatod[13] of the swete remembraunce of our entyre[14] and feythfull love. But moche more werse and grevouse is to me that, by vyolent opressyon, that traytour that hath wounded me to deth shall enjoye[15] youre[16] youghthe[17] unpolusshed."[18] To thees wordes sayde Blanchardyn to the knyght and prayed hym that he vousshesauff[19] to helpe hym that he were doubed[20] knyght wyth his armes. And that in favoure and compassion of his infortune,[21] he sholde avenge hym of his enmye

---

[3] *continually (noiselessly)*

[4] *noon*

[5] of al pieces, *completely*

[6] *afterward*

[7] *gave (returned)*

[8] *informed*

[9] *pity*

[10] *dismounted*

[11] *far*

[12] *prepared*

[13] *deprived*

[14] *complete (undivided)*

[15] *take advantage of*

[16] *i.e,. his lady's*

[17] *youth*

[18] *morally pure (unblemished)*

[19] *swear (consent) [OF voucher sauf, warrant safe]*

[20] *dubbed*

[21] *misfortune*

and that he shulde yelde ayen his lady unto hym. Thenne the knyght sore hurt to dethe, wyth grete peyne rose up on feet and armed Blanchardyn with his armes and gaaff[22] hym the necstroke[23] of knighthode, and dowbed knight for to strengthe the more the good wylle that he had toward hym.

3   That tyme that Blanchardyn sawe hymself armed of all his armures, he was right gladde and joyous and sore desyrynge for to avenge the dsyhonnoure and shame that to the knyght had be late don. He cam toward his goode courser on whiche he lyght[24] ful quykly, the shylde alonge the brest and the helmet wel clos laced, the spere on the rest and his goode swerde y-girded. Whan Blanchardyn sawe hymself on horsbacke and thus wel armed, made a tourne upon the playne therefor grete joye, and to the knyght began thus to say, "Vassell, enforce[25] yourself and take [fol. 10v] ayen your corage, for, to the playsyre[26] of our Lorde, your love and lady I shal yelde unto you this day, and also youre enmye taken or ded." Thenne brocheth[27] Blanchardyn forth wyth the sporys[28] his ryche courser, takyng his leve[29] of the knyght sore wounded and kept the way that the knyght dyde shewe.[30] Ful wel and right fayre dyde Blanchardyn conteyne[31] hymself in his harneys,[32] seen[33] that never had borne non armes afore,[34] and right wel halpe hymself wyth his spere and handled and tourned hit at his playsyre.

[22] *gave*
[23] *neck stroke [OF coleé, col, neck]; (see note)*
[24] *mounted (alighted)*
[25] *exert (strengthen)*
[26] *pleasure, i.e., if it please God*
[27] *charged (dashed)*
[28] *spurs*
[29] *departure*
[30] *show*
[31] *control (bear)*
[32] *armor (equipment)*
[33] *since*
[34] *before*

The sixth chapytre conteyneth how Blanchardyn went after the knyght so longe that he founde him where he wold have enforced the lady of the wounded knyghte.

1   Blanchardyn, that wyth all his herte desyred to fynde him that he went sekynge, rode forth wythin the forest so moche that he founde the foot[1] of the hors of hym for whom he wente in enqueste,[2] wiche he folowed ryght quyckly insomoche that fro ferre he entré[3] herde the cryes ful piteouse of a mayden, wherby he thought and knewe for trouthe that it was she that he went sekynge. So tourned he that parte[4] and soone chose,[5] in the

[1] *hoof prints*
[2] *search*
[3] *within (ahead)*
[4] *direction (region)*
[5] *saw (discerned)*

shadowe under a busshe, the knyght that he soughte and the gentyl mayde or damoysell[6] dolaunt and ful sprenct[7] wyth grete teerys, ryght fowly handled and sore beten by the sayde knyght for the reffuse that she made to his shameles concupyscence.[8] Blanchardyn, herynge the cryes and seeynge the wepynges, the grete sorewe and doleaunce of the vertuose and noble mayden, broched wyth the spowrys and swyftli waloppyd[9] that parte, tyl that he cam to the place whereas the sayde pucelle[10] cryed so pyteously, whereas atte the approaches that he made said ful instantli to the knyght, "Vassal, kepe[11] that ye nomore attouch[12] that pucel and defende yourseelf from me. For hir sake I wyl fight with you in favoure of the good knight, her true lover, that whiche falsly as an untrewe knyght ye have betrayd and wounded vylaynously, wythout a cause goode or raysonable. So yelde ye her ayen lightli[13] to me by love, and I shal lede [fol. 11r] her ageyn surely and saufly[14] toward her right dere love."

2   The knyght thenne beholdynge the jovencell Blanchardyn that right yong was, and sawe hym alone, rose anone[15] upon his feet all chaffed[16] and full of yre, as half madde for the contraryté[17] of his wylle that he founde in the same mayde. Moche fyersly behelde Blanchardyn and sayde unto him that in vayne he traveylled[18] for to require[19] her from him for another, in sainge to him that of suche purpose he wolde ceasse. And that he shulde noo more speke therof, or ellys he shulde shewe hym by his swerde that the pursyewte[20] that he had made, and wolde yet make for her, shulde be to his shame, and that he shulde therfore dye shamefully in that place.

---

[6] damsel (a young woman of rank)
[7] besprinkled (spattered)
[8] lust
[9] galloped
[10] maiden (young woman) [OF pucelle]
[11] take heed (restrain from)
[12] touch
[13] quickly
[14] safely
[15] immediately
[16] enraged
[17] opposition (contradiction)
[18] labored
[19] claim
[20] attack

The seventh chapytre conteyneth and speketh of the bataylle that was made betwyx the sayde knyght and Blanchardyn. And so longe they fought that Blanchardyn slew hym sterke ded and rescued the pucelle, the whiche deyde for sorowe bycause that she founde her true lover ded.

1   Whan Blanchardyn understode the knyght thus went thretnyng hym, and that so moche inhumaynly entreated the gentyll pucelle,[1] sayde unto hym, "Vassell goo thou

---

[1] maiden [OF pucelle]

and lyght upon thy destrer,[2] for syth[3] that by fayre meanes thou wylt not yelde ayen the pucelle, thou most nedes deffende thee nowe ayenst[4] me the right that thou pretendest upon her. And yf thou avaunce[5] or haste not thyself, I shal doo[6] passe this same spere thrughe the myddes[7] of thy body, for thy lyffe is to me so gretly displeasaunte.[8] But that it were for shame that I see thee afote, I sholde have separed[9] alredy the sowle of thee from the body." The [fol. 11v] knyght heryng the grete wordes of the jovencell Blanchardyn, answerd hym and sayde, "O thou proude berdles boye and full of arrogaunce, over grete haste thou makest to the purchas of thy deth, whiche is right sore[10] nyghe,[11] and the which I shal presente anone unto thee wyth the yron of my spere whiche is full sore trenchaunt."[12]

2 Thenne, wythout moo[13] wordes, the knyght mounted hastely on horsbake and toke his spere, whiche he cowched[14] and cam gyvyng the spores ayenst Blanchardyn, that had his spere all redy prest[15] in hande. Soo ranne the vasselles togyder and roughte[16] eche other by suche a force upon the sheldes that they were brusen[17] and broken all to peces; theire sperys, that sore bygge and stronge were, broke also all to pyces, and thenne toke theire swerdes wherof they gaaffe[18] many a grete stroke tyl eche other.

3 Blanchardyn, sore angry and evyl apayde[19] of that he sawe the untrewe knyght to endure so longe, approched hymself ayenst hym and heved[20] up his good swerde wyth bothe his handes, wherof he gaffe to the knyght suche an horryble and dysmesurable[21] a strok, in whiche he had employed alle his strengthe and vertue, that he detrenched[22] and cut his helmet and the coyffe[23] of stele, in suche manere a wyse that the goode swerde entred into the brayne, porfended[24] and clove[25] his hed unto the chynne, and

---

[2] *steed (charger)*
[3] *since*
[4] *against*
[5] *advance*
[6] *make (cause)*
[7] *middle*
[8] *displeasing*
[9] *separated*
[10] *very*
[11] *near*
[12] *sharp (piercing)*
[13] *more*
[14] *couched (lowered for attack)*
[15] *prepared*
[16] *attacked*
[17] *smashed*
[18] *gave*
[19] evyl apayde, *displeased*
[20] *raised*
[21] *excessive*
[22] *sliced to pieces*
[23] *coif (hood of chain mail)*
[24] *split through*
[25] *cleaved*

syn[26] wringed[27] his strock[28] atte the pullyng out ayen that he made of his swerde. So fell the knyght doune from his hors that nevere moeved fote nor legge. The pucelle, thenne seeynge that she was delyvered by the dethe of the knyght, wyst[29] not what a manere she shulde kepe nor how to thanke humbli ynoughe Blanchardyn, whiche made the pucelle to lyght[30] upon the hors of the knyght so slayne and deed, fro the [fol. 12r] whiche incontynent[31] he dyde cut of the hed and henged[32] hit atte foreende[33] of his sadel for to shewe hit to the knyght wounded, that he shulde take the more comfort wyth the ryght wysshed desyre of the syght of hys present maystresse.[34]

4   The noble pucelle, ryght desyrouse to here tydynges of her right true lover, demaunded of Blanchardyn whether he wyst not that her lover was alyve. "Bewtefull suster," sayde Blanchardyn, "that owre that I parted from hym, I lefte hym strongly greved[35] and sore hurt, but I hope that yet, to the plesure of our Lorde, we shal fynde hym alyve. So late us ryde a goode paas[36] to the end we may gyve hym comfort." "Alas syre," sayde the mayden, "I make grete dowte, seen[37] his grete sore, that never I shal see hym alyve. And yf thus it happed, that God forbede, I shuld quyte[38] and gyve up the remenant of my lyffe. Syth that we two helde but one party, for our herte thenne shulde be departed, yf deth parted us asondre in takynge fro me my lover, and my parte shulde be wythout powere and as imperfyht, drawyng[39] to the perfection of his partye." In suche devyses[40] as ye here, Blanchardin and the maiden rode forth tyl that they cam to the place where the knyght her lover laye, whiche they founde ded and the sowle departed fro the body. Whan the pucelle sawe her feythfull love dede, of the grete sorowe that she toke therof, she fell donne dyverse tymes in a swoune upon the corps or[41] ever the usaunce[42] of speche was in her restored, for to complayne the intollerable evyll that for this infortune envyroned[43] her herte out of all sydes.

---

[26] *afterwards*

[27] *twisted*

[28] *stroke*

[29] *knew*

[30] *mount (alight)*

[31] *immediately*

[32] *hung*

[33] *front*

[34] *lady*

[35] *injured*

[36] *pace, i.e., ride quickly*

[37] *seeing*

[38] *quit*

[39] *attracted (drawn)*

[40] *manner*

[41] *before*

[42] *use*

[43] *surrounded*

5   And for to abredge,⁴⁴ after the rewthes, syghes, and wepynges that so moche incessauntly or wythout ceasse made, the noble pucelle fell donne sterk ded upon the stomak of her moost dere lovere. This seeyng, [fol. 12v] Blanchardyn right moche abasshed⁴⁵ hymself, and sayde in hymself that thees two persones loved eche other full truly. Wherof moche grete pyté⁴⁶ toke hym in tendryng⁴⁷ theym, so muche that the teerys ranne donne from his eyen, and right muche dyspleased hym that he muste leve them there. Ryght gladly, yf he had myght, wold have brought them bothe wythin some place for to gyve the corsses a sepultre, to the ende⁴⁸ they shulde not abyde⁴⁹ there to be fode for birdes and bestes. But so ferre he was from all townes that a grete day journay nyhe were there noo dwellers, wherfor it behoved⁵⁰ hym for to leve hem there seeyng that noon otherwyse he myght doo. But disarmed hymself of the armures of the sayd knyght, toke ayen his mantell, and syn departed sore troubled atte herte for the pyteouse dethe of the two true lovers. And also had wel in remembraunce the knyght that he had slayne. Blanchardyn, all mournyng and pensefull,⁵¹ departed and went his waye. And from that tyme forthon⁵² began to fele a lytel of the state of love, and praysed and comended⁵³ hit in his herte and was remembred of it allewayes.

---

⁴⁴ *shorten (abridge)*
⁴⁵ *was surprised (taken aback)*
⁴⁶ *pity*
⁴⁷ *considering with compassion*
⁴⁸ *result (purpose)*
⁴⁹ *remain*
⁵⁰ *was necessary*
⁵¹ *melancholy*
⁵² *forth*
⁵³ *entrusted*

The eighth chapitre conteyneth how Blanchardyn fonde the knyght that made hym to passe over the ryvere wythin a bote that he sent hym. And of the devyses that they had togydre and of the goode chere that the knyght made to hym.

1   After that Blanchardyn was goon fro the place where he lefte the two lovers wythout lyffe, he began to ryde faste by the forest, in whiche he was bothe the daye and the nyght unto the morowe aboute the owre of pryme¹ wythout adventure² to fynde that doeth to be recounted. Ryght wery and sore travaylled³ he was for hunger and for thurste that he felte, for syn that he was departed from his fadres house, the kynge of Fryse, had nothre eten nor [fol. 13r] dronken but onely that whyche he fonde upon the trees growynge in the grete forest, as crabbes⁴ and other wylde frutes that are wonte⁵ to growe in wodes. So

---

¹ *around 6 A.M., hour of the first liturgical service of the day*
² *chivalric encounter (happening)*
³ *troubled (beset)*
⁴ *wild (crab) apples*
⁵ *accustomed*

longe rode Blanchardyn by the forest that, in comynge doun from an hylle he sawe there under in a playn a moche ample and a grete medowe, thorough whiche passed a grete ryver wyth a streme sore bigge and right grete. Blanchardyn, seeyng this rivere of so bigge a streme, so depe and so sore grete, was moche abasshed[6] how nor by what manere he sholde mowe[7] passe hit over.

2   So descended and cam doune the hylle and rode thurgh the medowe tyl he cam to the banke of the ryvere whiche he fonde grete and large, wherof he was sore displesed, for impossyble was to hym for to passe over. Tyl that, by adventure, atte the other syde of the ryvere he sawe a knyght armed of al peces that went hastly rydynge along the ryvage, the whiche, whan he sawe Blanchardyn, anone escryed[8] hymself hyghe[9] sayeng, "Vassall, beware that ye putte not your self wythin this ryvere by noo manere for to passe hit over, for nother ye nor your hors sholde never departe out wythout[10] ye sholde be bothe perysshed.[11] Suffre[12] a lytel whyle, for soone I shal sende you a vessell for to passe for you and your hors over." Thenne Blanchardyn, herynge the knyght that to hym wolde do this curtosye to make hym pass over, alyghted[13] from hys courser and sette fote on grounde. Not long he had ben there whan toward hym arryved a marener[14] that brought hym a boote goode and sure that from the knyght of the fery was sent unto hym. He entred the vessell ledynge his hors by the brydell, thenne began they to rowe so that wythin a short whyle they were over. Whan they were passed over, they founde the [fol. 13v] knyght that awayted after theym that well and curtoysly saluted Blanchardyn, whiche thanked hym moche of his curtoysy that he had shewed unto hym of his goode advertysynge, and of the vessell that he had sent hym for to pass over the ryver.

3   The knyght wyth grete merveyll bygan to byholde Blanchardyn, and the more he loked upon hym, the more lyked[15] hym to be a childe[16] comen of a hyghe extraction,[17] saynge in hymself that never noo day of his lyffe a fayrer jovencell had he not seen, and that the disposicion of his membres[18] judged hym to be a man of grete myght. After he mynded and dyde byholde his joyouse esperyte[19] and his assured contenaunce and goodely manere that right moche pleased hym. So aproched himself nygh Blanchardyn and began to demaunde hym, axyng of whens he was and whyther he wold drawe[20] to.

---

[6] confounded
[7] be able to
[8] shouted
[9] loudly
[10] unless
[11] killed
[12] Wait (Endure)
[13] dismounted
[14] boatman
[15] compared (likened)
[16] youth of noble birth (an aspirant to knighthood)
[17] lineage
[18] disposicion of his membres, *arrangement of his limbs, i.e., physique*
[19] spirit (nature)
[20] travel

Blanchardyn full curtoysly answerd hym sayeng that he was of the roalme of Fryse, and bycause, thanked be God, that the marches[21] there werre in peas, he had sette hymself to journaye for to fynde som contreye where were[22] was for to prove his barnag,[23] excercisyng hymself in the noble crafte of armes for to aquire lawde[24] and pryce,[25] as tyl a knyght apparteyneth.[26] Thenne the knyght, heryng the haulte[27] corage and goode wylle that the yonge knyght Blanchardyn had, was ryght well apayed of that answere and praysed and comended hym ryght moche in his herte.

---

[21] territories

[22] war

[23] bravery (prowess) [OF barnage]

[24] praise

[25] glory (reputation)

[26] is appropriate (pertains)

[27] high

The ninth chapitre conteyneth and speketh of the devyses and fayre exortynges that the knyght of the feery made unto Blanchardyn and how he conveyed hym unto the the waye of Tormaday.

1   After many dyvyses made betwene the knyght and Blanchardyn by the shorys of the ryvere, the knight . . .[1] led him into his castle, where he was received with great reverence by the wife of the knight. If they thought well of him and his destrier,[2] there is no need to ask. For of all the good things with which one could ease the body of a man, Blanchardyn was well served with as much as he needed. Blanchardyn, after he had eaten at his leisure and when they rose from the table, asked and enquired of the knight the name of the region and country where he had arrived. The knight, hearing the youth, answered him and said that he was in the service of the maid of Tormady, who was successor to the crown of the kingdom of Darye, of which Tormaday was the capital and leading city of the said kingdom, of which a near neighbor was a very old pagan king named Alimodes of Cassidonie, who by his force and presumption would have to wife the said damsel, l'orgueilleuse d'amours[3], whom many great Christian princes wanted very much to have on account of her goodness and the nobleness of her kingdom, which is very rich.

2   "But because of the refusals that the maiden has made to King Alimodes, he is prepared and arrayed to make a great war against the said young lady, because she was so much admired and prized for her very excellent beauty, and also for the great virtues with which she is adorned. She among the other young ladies of the world is reputed to be the best. If I wanted to tell the whole story of her beauty, humility, and virtues, it would keep you here too long. Nevertheless, though she be such as you hear me report, even as all the common report says, one could not too much praise and esteem her. The reason is because she never wanted or would open her ears to the offers, pleas, or requests that

---

[1] See T-Note

[2] steed (charger)

[3] l'orgueilleuse d'amours [OF orgueilleuse (n. fem.), proud one]

anyone had made in love, no matter how grand or well disposed. For this, she is called by all princes near and far 'l'orguilleuse d'amours;' even though she has the name Eglantine."

3   The knight marveled greatly hearing Blanchardyn speak. So graciously did he converse that the knight was amazed that the young knight could already have so many virtues, such as excellent beauty, graciousness, prudence, so that at this occasion he could not refrain from telling Blanchardyn, "Would that it pleased God, sir, that my mistress, l'orgeuilleuse d'amours, would make you her friend, for thus it would be your desire and obligation to defend her against King Alimodes." Blanchardyn then responded to the knight and said to him, "Sir, I thank you for the goodness and the honor that you do me, but I know well enough that such a great bounty is not due to me. And it would be presumptuous for me to think of it, seeing that, as you say, so many good men have wished to ask for her and no matter what they did, she would not hear pleas [fol. 15r] nor requeste of noon of theym, be he never of so grete perfection." "Certes," sayde thenne the knyght, "me semeth not that this manere at long rennynge[4] may endure. The arowes of love ne hir dartes right sharp, som daye, yf God be plesed, shall not be ydle about her. But peradventure she so quykly hitte atte her herte ther wythall,[5] that daunger[6] nor refuse shal have no more lawe for to rule nor governe hir prowde corage as touching love. God gyve grace that this may be soone, and that he to whom ye wolde wysshe moste good in this worlde because of the reformacion of suche an obstynate wylle." Moche humbly remercyed[7] Blanchardyn the knyght, excusynge hymself in dyvers facions[8] by gracyouse langage of this thynge. How be it that[9] within hymself alredy, by the admonestynge[10] of the good knyght, byganne for to desyre the goode grace of the same proude pucelle in amours, wythout makynge of eny semblaunt[11] not to dyscovere it to the knyght.

4   After many wordes servyng to the purpos aforsayd and utteryd betwyxt them bothe, the knyght sayd unto Blanchardyn, "Syre, ye be a right fayre jovencell and of noble representacion,[12] well syttyng on horsbacke and tyl[13] a wysshe wel shapen of alle membres,[14] and to my semynge ryght wel worthy to have the grace and favore of the right gentyll damoyselle the proude mayden in amours. Doo thenne after my counseyll; my advyse is that the effecte that shal procede therof shal be to you moche prouffytable.[15] I have tolde

---

[4]   *continuance (running)*
[5]   *by this means, i.e., love's arrows*
[6]   *disdain*
[7]   *thanked [OF merci]*
[8]   *ways (manners)*
[9]   How be it that, *Although*
[10] *counselling*
[11] *sign (semblance)*
[12] *expression*
[13] *to*
[14] *limbs*
[15] *beneficial*

you her[16] byfore that the paynem[17] Kynge Alymodes apparreylleth[18] hymself to make werre[19] to my lady, my maystresse the proude pucelle in amours, and commeth for to besyege the cyté of Tormaday. And for this cause departeth now my sayd lady from a castell of hers not ferre hens and draweth[20] toward Tormaday, [fol. 15v] for to gyve a corage to the knyghtes and other men of werre that ben in the towne for the deffense of the same ayenst the Kynge Alymodes. Right well it were your fayt[21] and welthe[22] for to goo rendre[23] your persoune unto her for to serve her as a soudyoure,[24] for to acquyre praysynge of worthynesse and goode renomme[25] that thurghe this cause shall mowe growe to you ward[26], so moche that the bruyt[27] wherof haply[28] shal come to her knowlege, unto the prejudyce[29] of her pryde dampnable and to the felycyté of your benewred[30] persoune, deservynge therby her goode grace. I doubte not but that ye shall fynde her by the waye, ryght nobly accompanyed of knyghtes and noble men, of servauntes, of ladyes and damoyselles. And bycause of her delyciouse[31] custume[32] and tendernes,[33] of herself she rydeth the lytyl paas[34] upon her swete and softe[35] palfraye.[36] And of her custome whan she rydeth by the feldes awaye, she commeth alleways behynde ferre ynough from all her folke, havynge onely besyde her a goode auncyent damoysell[37] whiche dyde norysshe her of her brestys in her moost tender and yonge age, and is called her nouryce[38] and maystresse. Wherfore I counseylle you to fynde the waye and the manere for to have a kysse or cusse of her mouth, howsoever that it be. Yf ye doo so, I ensure yow ye shal be the happyest of alle other, for my herte judgeth yf ye may have that onely cusse. And ye wyll, but yf it be long on yow,[39] hit shal be occasyon of a love inseparable betwyx her and you in tyme to

---

[16] here
[17] pagan
[18] equips
[19] war
[20] travels
[21] destiny
[22] good fortune
[23] submit
[24] soldier
[25] reputation
[26] to you ward, *toward you*
[27] report (renown)
[28] by chance
[29] detriment
[30] fortunate (happy) [OF ben eurez, indeed happy]
[31] charming (elegant)
[32] custom
[33] delicacy
[34] path (way)
[35] gentle
[36] riding (leisure) horse
[37] lady in waiting (lady of rank)
[38] nurse, governess
[39] yf it be long on yow, *if it is attributable to you*

come. How be it[40] I knowe right well and make noo doubte at all but that first of all, hit shall tourne for pryde of her tyl a grete displeasire unto her and shal be therof wors apayed,[41] more then reason requyreth. But care you not, for that ye be well horsed, [fol. 16r] passe forthe wyth the spore, wythout eny spekynge as for that tyme, and ryde fast awaye wythout taryeng tyl ye come to Tourmaday. And whan ye come there, thynke to do that wherby ye may be comended."

5   Whan Blanchardyn herd the knyght thus speke, he was ryght glad and promysed hym to do soo yf possyble were to hym, whatsomevere shold falle therof. And after the curteys thanke that wel coude make,[42] Blanchardyn toke his leve[43] of the knyght and of the lady his wyf, thankyng the knyght of the goode counseyll and advertysinge that he had gyven unto hym. Thenne departed forth the chylde[44] Blanchardyn. But the knyght, that was right curteys, guyded hym and conduyted a whyle and shewed hym the waye that he muste holde for to furnysshe[45] his enterpryse,[46] prayeng our lord God that a gode adoventure he myght fynde as the herte of hym dyde desyre, and syn[47] toke leve of Blanchardyn and tourned homward ageyne.

---

[40] How be it, *However*

[41] *repaid*

[42] curteys thanke that wel coude make, *courteous thank-yous that he knew well how to make*

[43] *departure*

[44] *youth of noble birth (an aspirant to knighthood)*

[45] *carry out*

[46] *undertaking*

[47] *soon*

The tenth chapitre conteyneth how Blanchardyn parted fro the knyght of the fery and rode on his waye al alone after the proude damoyselle in amours for to acomplysshe his desyrable entrepryse, as foloweth.

1   After that the knyght was retourned home, Blanchardyn bygan to ryde on a good paas,[1] desiring with all his herte to overtake the proude pucell in amours for to fulfylle his desyre and the promesse that he made to the knyght. So thought he moche in hymself by what manere he myght execute and brynge at an ende the werke that he hath undertaken, that is to wyte,[2] to kysse the proude mayden in amours, wherof in this manere of [fol. 16v] thoughte was his noble herte all affrayed[3] and replenysshed[4] wyth grete fere lest he shold faylle of his entrepryse. For wel it was the advis of Blanchardyn that the thyng ought well to be putte in a proffe,[5] syth his promesse was thus made to the knyght. And for this cause entred wythin his thoughte a drede as for to be so hardy that he sholde vaunce[6] hymself

---

[1] good paas, *quick pace*

[2] *say (know)*

[3] *troubled (afraid)*

[4] *filled*

[5] be putte in a proffe, *put to the test (proven)*

[6] *advance (be so forward)*

for to kysse suche a pryncesse that never he had seen byfore, and wherof the acquentaunce was so daungerouse. But love, that wyth her dart had made in his herte a grete wounde, admonested[7] hym for to procede constantly to his hyghe entrepryse, and after all varyablenes and debates y-brought at an ende wythin the mynde of this newe lover, his resolucion fynall was that he sholde putte peyne[8] for to have a cusse of the proude pucelle in amours, althoughe deth sholde be unto him adjudged onely for this cause. And herupon went Blanchardyn sayenge, "O veraye[9] God, how well happy shold myn herte be, that presently is overmoche pressed bycause of myn enterpryse yf I myght obteyne that one cussynge.[10] And if myn infortune or feblenes of corage sholde lette[11] me fro this adventure that so sore I desyre, deth make an ende of me."

[7] *exhorted*
[8] putte payne, *exert himself (strive)*
[9] *true*
[10] *kissing*
[11] *deter*

The eleventh chapitre speketh how Blanchardyn overtoke the proude mayden in amours and kyssed her, wherof she toke a grete anger.

1   Thus as ye here, the jovencell Blanchardyn went stryvyng in herte for fere that he had lest he myght not brynge his enterpryse at an ende, and rode thus thynkinge a goode while, tyl that soone after he herde the bruyt[1] and the voyces of the proude pucelle in amours folke, and in tornynge of a narowe waye, by the knowlege that the knyght of the fery had yeven[2] to hym of her araye,[3] knewe [fol. 17r] that it was she that he went sekynge, and thought it was tyme to endevoyre[4] hymself. He gaf the spore to the hors and forced hym as moche as he coude for to overtake the fayre pucelle, soo that by his dylygence taken wyth an ardaunt desyre, fonde hymself nyghe her and of her maystres wythin a short space of tyme.

2   Blanchardyn, seeyng the oure and the poynt[5] that he sholde furnysshe[6] hys enterpryse that ful sore he desyred to fynysshe, smote hys courser wyth the spore for to kysse her as he furth by her went. Wherof happed, by the bruyt that his hors made, that she loked bakward for to se what he was that so hastely rode after her. And so well it fortuned Blanchardyn that bothe theyre mouthes recountred[7] and kyst eche other fast.[8]

[1] *commotion (noise)*
[2] *given*
[3] *the order of her retinue and its attire*
[4] *exert*
[5] *moment*
[6] *carry out*
[7] *collided (came together) [OF recontrent]*
[8] *firmly*

3 Yf Blanchardyn was right glad of this adventure it is not to be axed,[9] and of that other party, the proude mayden in amours coude not kepe her behavoure[10] in this byhalve[11] for the grete dyspleasyre that she toke therfore. But Blanchardyn, wyth a glad chere, waloped[12] his courser as bruyauntly[13] as he coude thurghe the thykkest of all the folke, lepyng alwaye here and there as hors and man had fowgthen[14] in the ayer, and dyde so moche in a short while that he had passed ladyes and damoselles,[15] knyghtes and squyers, and all the grete companye of this proude pucelle in amours, gyvyng a gracyouse and honourable salutacion to them all where he went forth by. It is not to be axed yf he was well loked upon of all them of the rowte.[16] And in especall of the ladyes and gentyl women that, all in one, sayde he was a knyght right goode and fayre, and that it semed wel by countenauce[17] to be a man comen of hyghe extraction,[18] merveyllyng hemself[19] what he myght be and fro whens he came there, thus alone wythout eny companye.

---

[9] asked
[10] demeanor
[11] in this matter, i.e., the kiss
[12] galloped
[13] noisily
[14] fought
[15] maids in waiting (young women of gentle birth)
[16] crowd
[17] bearing (courtly manners)
[18] lineage
[19] themselves

The twelfth chapitre conteyneth and speketh of the grete [fol. 17v] **wrathe and anger that the proude mayden in amours had for the kysse that Blanchardyn had taken of her. And of the complayntes that she made therfore unto her maystres that peyned herself full sore for to pease her, as herafter foloweth.**

1 Whan Blanchardyn sawe that he had brought at an ende his enterpryse, and that he had passed alle the rowtes and compaynes[1] of the proude pucelle in amours, he was ryght glad of this fayre adventure. Soo toke his waye, as right as he coude as was tolde hym by the knyght, and rode toward Tourmaday. A lytyl shal here ceasse oure matere to speke of hym, unto tyme and oure[2] shal be for to retourne to the same. And shal shewe the sorowes and the complayntes of the proude pucelle in amours and the manyere that she kept after the kysse that Blanchardyn toke of her.

2 Incontynente[3] that she felte herself to be thus sodaynly kyst of a man straunger, out of her knowlege[4] she fell doune from here amblere[5] as a woman from herself and in a swone. And whan she myght, speke unto her maystres that he that this injurye had doon to her

---

[1] entourages
[2] hour
[3] Immediately
[4] out of her knowlege, *unconscious*
[5] horse for easy riding

whatsoever he be, yf he may come in her handes or in her power, noon shal mowe save hym but he shal lese his hed for the same. Of the teerys that from her eyen fyll doune, her gowne that she had on was therof charged,[6] as grete shoure of rayne had come doune from the hevens.

3   Thenne her maystres, that sage[7] and dyscrete was, comforted her, blamyng gretly the grete sorowe that she made for a cusse. But the proude pucelle in amours kept so hard that same kisse in her corage, whiche she reputed for an injurye doon to her that fayre speche nor non excusacion[8] that her goode mastres coude make nor [fol. 18r] shewe to her for to pease[9] her of her anger. Myght not in nothynge confort her, but semed that she sholde slee herself to be more hastely venged. Her maystres saide unto her, "Alas, my goode damoyselle, I have right grete merveylle how a prynces of so grete renomme[10] as ye be of may make so grete a sorowe of a thynge of nought. Yf a gentylman hath kyst you, take we hit for a folye or dishonoure, whiche is not so; noon but I have seen it, and make no doubt that evere hit sholde be discovered nor knowen by me. Soo pray I you that ye wyl cesse your grete sorowe." Thenne ansuered the pucell to her maystres, "How may ye requyre me to leve myn anger, but that I sholde complayne me? No lenger may suffre[11] me God to lyve in suche a sorowe, yf that shame done to me be not right sone[12] avenged. Now knowe I not yf he be a gentylman or not. Alas, that my knyghtes knowe not and my folke that marchen byfore me; this adventure soone ynoughe they wolde avenge me. Certaynly, I shal doo folow hym, and byleve for certayn that his laste daye is comen and shal deye." "O madame," said the maystresse unto the yonge damysell, "ye shal do more wyseli,[13] for yf thys thynge shuld come oute and be knowen, your sorow ought to double sore therfor. Yf men sayden that of everi man ye had taken a kysse, yet ought ye to maynten and holde the apposite saynge strongly ayenst hit, and ye wyll scandalyze and uttre your mysfal[14] that is now happed to you of one man. Lepe upon your palfraye,[15] your folke ben ferre afore[16] you, and put out of your ymaginacyon[17] suche casuall fryvolles[18] and that over moche do greve yourself, for it is for youre best and worship[19] grete yf ye wol understande hit well."

---

[6] filled
[7] wise
[8] justification (defense)
[9] appease (placate)
[10] reputation (renown)
[11] allow
[12] soon
[13] wisely
[14] misfortune
[15] riding horse
[16] before
[17] thoughts (fantasy)
[18] trifles (things of little importance)
[19] honor (renown)

The thirteenth chapitre conteyneth how Blanchardyn, after he had [fol. 18v] **kyst the proude mayden in love, went forth on his waye havyng styl his thought fast upon here beaulté, tyll that he cam to the cyté of Tourmaday where he alyghted at the provostis house for to be lodged there, as herafter foloweth.**

1 After many shewynges[1] that the olde damoyselle had don unto her lady, the proude pucelle in amours, wyth what peyne and grief that it was, atte the ynstance[2] and requeste of her sayde maystresse she mounted anon upon her whyte palfray amblyng, and sayde she sholde fynde at Tourmaday hym that had doon her this vyolence, and that by the morowe next she sholde make him to be hanged. Sore troubled of wyttis and gretly vexed wythin her mynde, as ye here, rode forthe the gentel pucelle after her folke towardes her cyté of Tourmaday. But we shal leve her sorowyng wyth her maystresse that conforteth her, and shal speke of Blanchardyn that alredy was nyghe comen unto the cyté of Tourmaday whiche he dyde beholde well, havynge merveylle of the comodyouse[3] and riche contrey where the towne was sette. And hym semed the most fayre and most riche cyté that ever he sawe. The see was nyghe betyng on the walles atte one syde of the towne; at the other syde were the grete medowes, the fayre vynes, and the londe arable, the wodes, swete ryveres, and dyverse fountaynes.[4] And sayde in hymself that he that had suche a noble cyté of his owne were a grete lorde. Blanchardyn exploytted[5] so that he soone entred the cyté and rode a goode waye wythynne, beholding on eche syde the fayre houses and ryche palayces and the grete edyfyces[6] as monasterys, chirches, and chapelles. And also he sawe the grete multytude of peple, the fayre stretes ample and large, tyl that he cam to the chyeff market place, where he dyde calle a man to hym for to brynge hym to a [fol. 19r] good lodygys[7] for hymself and his hors. The man ansuered hym that wyth grete payne he sholde be lodged, and that the men of armes of the proude pucelle in amours were comyng in so grete nombre for to awayte on the siege that the kynge Alymodes wolde leye aboute the cyté there, that the towne was not suffysaunt for to lodge hem[8] alle. But wel he tolde hym that he sholde be well lodged in the provostys[9] house of the towne, yf he wolde receyve hym for his hoste.

2 Blanchardyn thanked hym humbly and prayed hym that he wold shewe hym the provostys hous, and he wyth goode wylle dyde soo. Blanchardyn drue thytherward and fonde the provost syttyng at his gate. He salued[10] hym, prayng that for to paye[11] well and largely content him, he wold vouchsauf[12] to take hym for his hoste and lodge hym in his place.

---

[1] *examples*

[2] *insistence (urging)*

[3] *productive (profitable)*

[4] *springs*

[5] *hurried*

[6] *buildings*

[7] *lodging*

[8] *them*

[9] *chief magistrate (provost, military officer)*

[10] *greeted (saluted)*

[11] *please*

[12] *consent [OF voucher sauf, warrant safe]*

The provost stode up anon and dede beholde Blanchardyn, whiche he praysed moche in his herte and sayde unto hym thus, "Syre, the manere of this lodgyse is suche that noon may lodge hymself here but yf he doth that whiche is wryton in that marbel stone above the yate."[13] Than casted Blanchardyn his sight upward and sawe writon graved[14] wythin a marbel stone the verses that herafter folowen, wherof he was glad, for non other sporte nor non other thing he desired.

3   Here foloweth the ballade that was wryton upon the gate of the provostis place of Tourmaday.

> Who that wol lodge hymself herynne
> Most furst befyght the host of herynne
> Wyth spere, swerde, and eke[15] of axe.
> Here nedeth non other craftes to gete ynne,
> For who that wol be receyved wyth chere fyn
> May thynke that nedes he muste therto.
> But God graunte hym grace herto
> To overcome his host, thylke hardy[16] foo,
> He shal mowe lawfulle entre this inne.

---

[13] gate (entry)
[14] carved (engraved)
[15] also
[16] bold (courageous)

[fol. 19v] **The fourteenth chapitre conteyneth how the jovencell Blanchardyn josted and fought ayenst the prevost and overthrewe hym, and how two yonge damoselles doughters to the provost cam and toke Blanchardyn for to have hym to be lodged wythin her faders place.**

1   Whan Blanchardyn had wel loked and rede the verses that graven were in the marbell upon the gate and well understode theire sentence a lytyl, he bygan to smyle as he that lytyl dyde sette therby.[1] And the provost axed[2] hym yf he was counseylled[3] for to fulfylle the construction[4] of that texte. Blanchardyn ansuered that he was therof right wel content, so that he myght have harneys[5] to arme hymself wythall. The provost sayd it sholde not lacke on that, and that gladly he sholde furnysshe[6] hym of goode and mete[7] harnoys to arme his body wythall.[8] And he dyde soo, for he made to be brought unto hym

---

[1] lytyl dyde sette therby, *thought little of it*
[2] asked
[3] was counseylled, *had concluded*
[4] meaning (terms)
[5] equipment (armor)
[6] supply
[7] suitable
[8] fully (completely)

by his folke al suche armures and harneys as to hym behoved[9] to have and that to suche a caas[10] apperteyneth. Blanchardyn sette fote a-gronde and made hym to be armed and well appoyntted by the provostis men, whiche was all prest and redy poyntted[11] to the jouste.

2 Whan Blanchardyn sawe hymself well armed of alle peces, right quykly he lept upon his courser, the helme on his hede, the shelde atte his necke, and the spere in his fyste, wythout takyng ony avauntage.[12] Wherof all the assystents,[13] that were comen there for to see hym joust with the provost of the toune, sayde that they nevere sawe no fayrer man of armes nor better pyght[14] nor better syttyng on horsbak. Grete multytude of peple was there assembled for to see the joustynge of the two vasselles. The provost, seyng Blanchardin redy, monted upon his hors, the spere in his fyste, and lepte out of his place. He semed wel by his behavoure and mayntenaunce[15] [fol. 20r] to be a man of right grete fayte,[16] for to saye trouthe, he was a myghty man of body wel renommed of prowesse.[17] And the valyant Blanchardyn, the spere couched on his thye, awayted for hym in the strete all redy for to assaylle hym. The provost sayde to Blanchardyn, from as ferre as he coude chuse[18] hym, "Syre thynke to deffende yourself well, for, yf ye overcome me, I shal lodge you in my house where ye shal be right richely served wythout your cost. But yf I may, it shal not come therto, for I shal brynge you to dethe or to me ye shal yelde yourself."

3 Blanchardyn herkned to the provost, to whom boldly he answered that he shold doo the best and the worst that he coude, and that he shulde take noo thoughte but onely for hymself, and that he sholde putte peyne[19] that his honoure sholde be kepte and his body ayenst hym. Thenne toke the provost his spere and so dyde Blanchardyn the his, whiche was strong and bygge that it was mervayll, and as moche as the horses myght renne,[20] came eche ayenst other. The provost brak his spere upon Blanchardyn but he hurted hym not, for his goode shelde kept hym, and his stronge bones suffred hym not to bowe bakward by the right grete vertue wherof he was garnysshed. Blanchardyn hytt the provost in the myddys of his shelde so myghtly that it was perced all thourgh that the yron was seen at the other syde of the shelde. And yet the provostis harneis was hole and nought dommaged[21] of nothyng. But notwythstandyng, the strok was so myghty grete and so sore peysaunt[22] that hit lyfted the provost out of the sadel to the grounde more thenne tenn fot ferre bakward. And with that renne, Blanchardyn his courser ran over the provost

---

[9] *was necessary*

[10] *circumstance (case)*

[11] *appointed (outfitted)*

[12] *unfair advantage*

[13] *squires (assistants to the knights)*

[14] *equipped*

[15] *conduct*

[16] *ability*

[17] *valor (martial strength)*

[18] *see*

[19] putte peyne, *take pains*

[20] *charge (run)*

[21] *damaged*

[22] *forceful (heavy)*

that he tradd[23] upon one of his armes so that it was hurt full sore. [fol. 20v] But he was so gretly astonyd[24] of the myghty stroke wherby he was fallen doun that he wyst not where he was. Blanchardyn right quykly alyghted[25] from his hors, his swerd in his hande for to cutte the laas[26] fro the helmet of the prevost and so to smyte off his hede, yf he wolde not yelde hymself to Blanchardyn and gyve hym fre entré wythin his hous.

4   But whan the two doughters of the provost, that right praty[27] and full fayre were, dyde see this harde bataylle and theire fadre in parell[28] of deth, lepte hastely out of their house and cam to the place, where as bothe of hem puttyng themself upon theyre knees byfore Blanchardyn, sayde unto hym, "O thou free[29] knyght, replenysshed[30] wyth prowesse and of grete wordynesse,[31] have mercy upon our fadre." And Blanchardyn, full of curtoysye, to them answered that, for the love of them, he sholde be sauf from all evyll. And evyn at these wordes cam the provost tyl his owne knowlege ageyne,[32] and understandyng that he had lost the felde for cause of the stourdy stroke that he had receyved of the spere of Blanchardyn. And sayde in this maner, "A,[33] right gentyl knyght, to whom none oughte to compare hymself, for[34] that right grete vertue that in you is entred and sette, I yelde myself unto you and present my hous to your plesure and behouffe,[35] prayeng right affectually[36] that in pacyence ye wyl taken hit wyth suche as ye shall fynde in hit." And thenne, wythout taryeng, drewe his swerde and toke it unto Blanchardyn, that wyth goode wyll gaff it hym ageyn and wythall[37] pardoned hym alle that he myght have had mysprysed[38] ayenst hym, in that that he wold fyght wyth Blanchardyn, wherof the provost thanked hym gretly.

---

[23] *trod (stepped)*
[24] *stunned*
[25] *dismounted*
[26] *lace*
[27] *pretty*
[28] *peril*
[29] *gracious (generous)*
[30] *filled*
[31] *worthiness*
[32] *cam . . . tyl his owne knowlege again,* regained consciousness
[33] *Ah*
[34] *because of*
[35] *disposal (advantage)*
[36] *ardently*
[37] *completely*
[38] *offended*

[fol. 21r] **The fifteenth chapytre conteyneth how Blanchardyn was moche richely lodged and receyved in the provostis hous of the two doughters of the provoste. And of the complayntes that the proude mayden in amours made unto her maystres of Blanchardyn.**

1. After this that Blanchardyn atte requeste of the two yong damoyselles had pardoned theyre fader the provost his evyll wylle, dyverse folke of the towne that had seen the valeauntnes[1] and prowes,[2] the grete humylyté and curtoysyes that were in Blanchardyn, praysed and commended hym right moche, sayeng comonly that a fayrer knyght they had not seen nor herd speke of in their tyme, and that by his behavoure and contenaunce men myght well knowe that he was departed and come of noble extraction[3] and hyghe parentage.

2. Soone after, Blanchardyn, havyng the two yong damoyselles by the handes, was lad[4] by the provoste into his house where he was receyved and festyd,[5] God knoweth how. So was he by the two doughters brought into a chambre full richely dressed and hanged wyth riche tapysserye, where he was desarmed by the two damoyselles that helped him, whiche toke him a longe gowne furred wyth fyn martrons[6] that was her faders for to clothe hym wyth. And syth dyde sende for the wyn[7] and made hym the best chere for the first acqueyntaunce that ever coude be made to a knyght.

3. It is not to be tolde but that Blanchardyn mayntened hymself talkyng emonge hem more gracyously than evere dyde man, and shewed hymself of so goodly and honneste behavoure that right sone[8] he conquered the hertes and goode wylle of the two forsayde praty[9] maydens. That was not a lytell thyng, for moche fayre and gentyl they were, whiche, on that other part, sawe in [fol. 21v] Blanchardyn so grete a beaulté[10] that nevere was seen by them noon suche in noo man, wherfore it was noo mervaylle yf they gladly behelde hym.

4. We shal leve to speke of this matere and shal retourne to speke of the proude mayden in amours whiche alredy had exployted[11] so moche that she entred wythin her towne of Tormaday, and, in a dyspleasans right bytter of her accustumed corage, descended into her paleys wyth her stoute[12] rowte[13] of folke of armes, and syth moche tryste[14] and

---

[1] *bravery*

[2] *valor (martial strength)*

[3] *lineage*

[4] *led*

[5] *hospitably entertained (fêted)*

[6] *fur of martens, a sign of luxury and status*

[7] *wine*

[8] *soon*

[9] *pretty*

[10] *beauty*

[11] *hurried*

[12] *large*

[13] *crowd*

[14] *sad [OF triste]*

pensefull[15] entred her chambre, callyng wyth her her mastres that fulle soone cam there. Wherfore that night, noon of them alle, were he never so moche her famyllyer, cam to see her, but onely the captayne of Tormaday that cam for to make unto hir the reverence.[16] And, emonge other devyses[17] that ynough brief were, recounted unto her how a knyght straunger was come to the cyté which was the fayrest gentylman that myght be seen, and had befought the provoste and overcomen hym.

5   Thenne the proude pucelle in love, after a lytyl musyng, understode well by the wordes of the captayne and by the cognyssaunce[18] that he tolde her of his horse, that he was that self[19] knyght that the kisse had taken of her. But she therof made noo semblaunt.[20] The captayne gaff the goode nyght to the damoyselle, toke his leve of her and went. The proude mayden in amours, seeyng the captayne goon from her presence, sayde anon unto her maystres, "I shal suffre, for this nyght, hym that so grete a dysplaysure hath don to me this day by the waye to be festyd in the provostis hous. But ther nys[21] man alyve that so gretly be my frende that myght kepe me, but that I shal tomorowe make hym for to deye of an right evyll deth, yf I am woman alyve. And wyth this yf the provost wolde not delyver hym unto me, I shal destroye hym[22] [fol. 22r] and shal make hym pryvated[23] from all his tenementes[24] that he holdeth of me." Thus, as ye here, the proude pucelle in amours in her harde herted wyll abode all that nyght for to make Blanchardyn to deye. Wherof for this cause for grete anger that was in her, she had nother lust[25] nor myght for to ete nor drynk, nor also to take the reste of slepe.

---

[15] *melancholy (thoughtful)*
[16] *greeting of respect (bow)*
[17] *reports (consultations)*
[18] *identifying emblems on the horse's accoutrements (information)*
[19] *same*
[20] *indication (sign)*
[21] *is not*
[22] *i.e., the provost*
[23] *dispossessed*
[24] *lands (property)*
[25] *desire*

The sixteenth chapitre conteyneth yet of the complayntes and grete thretenynges that the proude pucelle in amours made unto her maystres of the knyght Blanchardyn.

1   In suche a state and of the wrathe wherin she was, talked and devysed[1] herself sore harde and angerly wyth her maystres, whiche dysconseylled[2] her by al manere wayes of the deth of Blanchardyn. But what argument nor remonstrans[3] that she coude make to

---

[1] *schemed (considered)*
[2] *counseled against*
[3] *appeals*

the proude damoyselle in amours, coude not nor myght not moeve her for to have awaye her corage from the obstynacioun[4] that she had toward Blanchardyn.

2   Thenne sayde the fayre damoyselle that so fyers was ayenst the god of love, "Of what dethe myght I do make hym to deye for to tormente hym moost therby, other late hym be hanged, brente,[5] or drowned, his hed to be smytten off from his shulders, or to make hym to be drawen and quartred, for to gyve unto hym his payment of the grete oultrage by hym commytted in my persone." Her maystres, heryng her wylle, conclusion, and haulte[6] corage insaucyble,[7] that right sore touched the honesteté and honoure of alle pryncesses, was therof right impacient and bygan to saye suche or semblable[8] wordes, "Alas madamoselle, he that ye so sore do hate hath not desserved dethe, thoughe he hath taken a kysse of you. To my semyng, ye sholde forclose[9] and take awaye out of your herte all inutyle[10] sorowfulnesse, wherof ye overmoche doo hurt hit, and garnysshef hit [fol. 22v] of a newe joye. The rayson[11] wherby I so saye, I shal shewe hit unto you yf ye pleased to understande it. Al ynough ye may thynke and knowe that whatsomever he be, he hath a gentyll[12] herte and is a man of hyghe facion[13]. And where allredy ye have mowe knowen by the relacion of youre captayne of Tourmaday, ye may understande of his worthynesse. Ye may well knowe that yf he had not chosen[14] you full praty and ryght fayre, and more than eny other accomplysshed in all manere of beauté and faycture,[15] byleve certaynly that he nevere wolde have vaunced hymself to take a kysse of you, nor had not put hymself in daunger of youre indyngnacion[16] that gretly ought to be drad.[17] Wherfore, atte my requeste and for the love that evere ye had to me, by all the servyces and pleasures that I have mowe doon unto you and that herafter I myght doo, beseche you that this evyll wylle and grete indygnacion that ye have to that yong knyght ye putte and chasse out from you, and that ye wyll ceasse youre sorowe and take ayen unto you the state of joyfull lyvyng, for upon my sowle, it is the beste that ye can doo in this world."

---

[4] *stubbornness (hardness of heart)*
[5] *burned*
[6] *high (strong)*
[7] *immoderate (insatiable)*
[8] *similar*
[9] *shut out completely (exclude)*
[10] *useless*
[11] *reason*
[12] *noble (refined)*
[13] *stature*
[14] *discerned (seen)*
[15] *stature (bodily form)*
[16] *anger*
[17] *feared (dreaded)*

The seventeenth chapytre conteyneth how the proude pucelle in amours after dyvers and many remonstracions made by her maystres unto her bygan to wexe moderate puttyng awaye from her the hate that she had upon Blanchardyn.

1   After that the proude mayden in love had largely herde of her maystres, that all ynough semed her raysonnable, wyst nomore what to replyque¹ nor gaynsaye,² and bygan to lene³ her eerys⁴ thurghe a subtyl and soubdayne⁵ hete of love that perced the veray hert rote of her, for the delyverance of the yong knyght Blanchardyn. She helde herself [fol.23r] styl a longe whyle wythout speche and becam penseful with a contenaunce full sadde,⁶ more than ever she was byfore. But, at the ende of a whyle began for to saye wythin herself, "O veraye God, what bruyt of cruelnes and of tyrannye sholde be spred over all the worlde of me that am a woman, yf I, for by cause of a kysse onely sholde make to deye soo gentyll a knyght? I nedes muste saye that he loveth me truly, and overmoche straunge sholde be the reward of his love unto hym, yf deth sholde folowe therby by the sentence of me that may conforte hym. But alas, I make a grete doubte that overmoche sholde greve me, yf by adventure it happed that he fonde hymself somwhere, as he presently doth wyth the doughters of the provost, sholde boste hymself to have kyssed me. This remors prycketh⁷ me to the herte; how be it, I holde hym so curtoys and dyscret or wyse that noo bostyng shold not mowe come out of his mouthe, and in especyall of her unto whom he hath shewed so grete a token of love. It is force,⁸ and herto I am constrayned, that I confesse that he hath the corage areysed⁹ unto parfytte¹⁰ noblenesse, and that yf he were otherwyse, he sholde nevere have made force¹¹ to kysse me. Men see atte ey¹² his beaulté wherof he is endowed hyghly, his valyauntnes is alredy well preved, and therfore I chuse¹³ hym and make hym myn senescall¹⁴ and cheff of my werre, for he is a man worthy to be taken soo. And by al thus, but yf it holdeth on hym,¹⁵ yf eny malyvolence or evyll wylle I have had byfore this unto hym, I altogydre pardone hym. But alwayes, yf he hath eny love to me, it is for nought, for never daye of my lyffe hym nor other I wyll not love. So wot¹⁶ I never what love ment nor what it is of love, nor I loke not after to knowe it, for all syche

---

¹ *reply*
² *speak (argue) against*
³ *lend (lean)*
⁴ *ears*
⁵ *sudden*
⁶ *serious (sad)*
⁷ *pierces (pricks)*
⁸ *necessary*
⁹ *raised*
¹⁰ *perfect*
¹¹ *aggression (bold)*
¹² *eye*
¹³ *choose*
¹⁴ *seneschal (chief officer of a noble's household and overseer of its estates)*
¹⁵ but yf it holdeth on hym, *unless it is his fault*
¹⁶ *knew*

thynges I repute and take for foly, as [fol. 23v] certaynly they be. And wol that every man knowe that it is and shal be allewayes my soverayne desyre and fynall conclusion."

The eighteenth chapitre conteyneth how the proude pucelle in amours made her ordonaunces for the kepynge of her cyté, and how Kynge Alymodes arryved and toke lande nyghe the cyté of Tourmaday whiche he beseged wyth a myghty power of folke.

1   In this dyversyté[1] of purpos the proude pucelle in amours, to what a peyne that it was, passed the tyme of the nyght. And on the morowe she made the castell and her sayde cyté of Tourmaday to be garnysshed[2] right wel of vytaylles,[3] of men of warre and of al manere of artyllary, bycause that she had had tydynges that same daye that for certayn she sholde be beseged there. After whiche ordynaunces[4] so made by her knyghtes and captaynes, she wythdrewe herself into her castell of Tourmaday. She entred in her chambre and cam toward a wyndowe out of whiche men sawe right ferre into the see, and there she had not be no longe whyle whan she had perceyved the playn[5] choys[6] and syght of a right grete and myghty navye, and of many a hyghe mast that bare grete saylles, and many penoncelles,[7] baners, and standardes that the wynde shok here and there, wherof the golde and the azure[8] was glysteryng tyl unto her eyen bycause of the bryght bemes of the sonne that spred were upon them. All the see was covered wyth shippes and galeyes[9] that wyth a full sayll cam to take porte and to caste theire ankers byfore the cyté of Tourmaday.

2   The damoselle, seeng that grete armee commyng, knewe all ynoughe that it was the excercyte[10] of the sayd Kynge Alymodes, by the banners and cognyssaunce[11] that she sawe appyere upon [fol. 24r] the see. She called to her them that were in her chambre to whiche incontynent[12] she commaunded that they sholde goo arme themself for to resiste ayenst her enmyes at their commyng on lande, whiche she sawe approched alredy right nyghe. After this commaundement made, they all went to arme and arraye hemself,[13] and thourgh all the cyté every man toke his harneys on hym and made grete haste toward the haven.[14] Trompettes, claryons,[15] and other instrumentes bygan to blowe thurgh every

---

[1] *diversity*
[2] *supplied*
[3] *food*
[4] *commands*
[5] *clear (plain)*
[6] *choice (view)*
[7] *pennants*
[8] *bright blue (a heraldic tincture)*
[9] *sea-going ships with sails and oars*
[10] *company of men at arms*
[11] *heraldic designs used to identify knights*
[12] *immediately*
[13] *themselves*
[14] *harbor (port)*
[15] *slender, shrill sounding trumpets*

part of the towne, and were all in affraye¹⁶ for to lepe out, to the ende they myght be at the descendyng of theyr enemyes to lande.

3   Never so soone they coude comen but that the kynge Alymodes had alredy taken lande, and his sone Daryus wyth hym, and one of his doughters that he had whiche was moche fayre and a praty mayden that it was mervaylle. So had he one kynge in his companye that hyght¹⁷ Rubyon, and wyth theym was come another kynge right myghty and grete beyonde mesure, whiche of heyght was fifteen fote long and wythall right foul and hydouse¹⁸ for to see. So moche they dede that they cam all out of their vesselles and had out all theyr horses, tentes and pavyllyons, artylleryes, and harneys, and sprade themselves thurgh the medowes that be there full ample and large. They of the cyté coude never lette¹⁹ hem²⁰ nor defende, but that atte their pleasure they descended from their shippes and toke lande, for so grete a nombre they were that men called them about four score²¹ thousand men of werre²² or more, besyde thos that kept their shippes. Ryght grete bruyt and grete noyse they made at their comyng a-lande of hornes²³, bussynes,²⁴ and of tambours,²⁵ so that an horryble thyng it was to here. The kynge Alymodes and his son Daryus, acompanyed wyth the two other kynges, mounted upon theire coursers²⁶ and palfreys and [fol. 24v] twenty thousand men wyth them and came tofore the cyté. The kyng Alymodes, so ferre²⁷ that he was nyghe by the gate, hevyng upward his hand sayeng to them that kept theire warde²⁸ that they sholde yelde up the cyté unto hym or ever²⁹ that the lande aboute were wasted, sweryng upon all the goddes that he worshiped that he ne sholde departe from byfore the cyté unto the tyme that he had the proude pucelle in amours tyl his spouse and wyff. They of wythynne, thenne heryng Alymodes the kynge speke, that wel they knewe, ansuered unto hym that they had noo fere of hym and that theyre damoyselle and maystres doubted³⁰ nor feered hym nought in noo thynge.

4   This ansuere y-herde Alymodes the kynge, replenysshed wyth wrath and ire more than ever he was tofore, made his oost³¹ to approche as nyghe the cyté as he coude. He made there his tentes and his pavyllyons to be pyght³² and his folke to be lodged aboute

---

[16] in affraye, *ready to attack (disturbed)*
[17] *was named*
[18] *hideous (monstrous)*
[19] *stop*
[20] *them*
[21] four score, *eighty*
[22] *war*
[23] *bugles*
[24] *straight trumpets [OF busine]*
[25] *large drums used in battle*
[26] *swift war horses*
[27] *far*
[28] *guard*
[29] *always*
[30] *feared (worried)*
[31] *army (host)*
[32] *pitched (set up)*

hym, and made his chieff standard to be sette al on hyghe upon his riche pavyllyon, ayenst whiche they of the cyté casted full fast and often serpentynes[33] and gunnes,[34] wherof they dyde grete dommage unto their enemyes. But whatsomever thinge that men evere dyde unto them nor that of theire folke, was made grete occysion[35] and slawghter. Nevertheles, they lefte not[36] to lodge hemself there, what for daunger[37] nor moleste[38] that men coude do to them, and all as nyghe the cyté as myght be, makyng redy their canons and their bombardes for to bruse[39] and bete doune the walles of the sayd towne.

---

[33] *small canons*

[34] *siege engines for firing missiles*

[35] *killing (carnage)*

[36] lefte not, *did not neglect*

[37] *resistance*

[38] *harm*

[39] *break*

The nineteenth chapytre conteyneth how the doughter of the provost brought to Blanchardyn a fayre coveryng all of whyte sylke to covere his hors wythall and one of her sleves prayng hym that he wold bere hit upon his helme. And he dyde so.

1   [fol. 25r] When they of the cyté had seen the manere and the rewle of their enemyes, and that all wyth leyser[1] they had seen their puyssaunce[2] and their manere of doynge, the captayne and the provost of the towne dyde ordeyne a stronge and a bygge warde[3] that they sette by a goode ordenaunce along the walles and into the yates[4] for the defence of the towne. And this doon, toke wyth them two thousand men well chosen, and all in a goode array lept out of the cyté and sodaynly, wyth a grete cry that they made, charged upon theyre enmyes, wherof at their commyng on they dyde putte to deth grete foison[5] of Kynge Alymodes folke, whiche was right sory for it. But soone ynough, by the provysion that he putte therto, reculed[6] his enemyes abacke tyll wythin the barreys[7] of the towne. Another posterne[8] of the cyté was open, wherof the enemyes toke noo kepe,[9] out of whiche yssued[10] out a thousand men, goode and hardy fyghters, well shapen and strongly herted for to hurt their felon[11] enmyes. So smot they hemself wythin, callyng up a hyghe[12]

---

[1] *opportunity (leisure)*

[2] *military might (power)*

[3] *guard (sentries on the city walls)*

[4] *gates (portcullises)*

[5] *many (abundance)*

[6] *pushed back (retreated)*

[7] *outworks (barriers at the approach to the gate of a fortification)*

[8] *back gate (secret passageway)*

[9] *notice*

[10] *rushed out (exited)*

[11] *wicked (fierce)*

[12] *loud*

crye into the thikkest of their enmyes where they slew and detrenched[13] many one, and dyverse tentes and pavyllyons they pulled doune and brought to dethe theym that were wythynne. Soo that the cry and the callyng camen unto the kynge Alymodes pavyllyon, that hastely came there acompanyed wyth ten thousand of his men. The noyse and the cry bygan thenne to be efte[14] as grete than it was tofore, so that the folke of the proude pucelle in amours were constrayned to wythdrawe themself ayen into that cyté, after that they had brought and slayne wel xiiiic[15] of their enmyes wythout eny losyng of theire owne folke. Wherof Alymodes the kynge was right sory and dolaunt, and sore troubled and hevy[16] wythdrewe hymself into his pavyllyon, commaundyng his folke that [fol. 25v] every man shold loke to lodge hymself, trowyng[17] to be in a sewreté[18] that his enmyes, as for that same day, sholde not comen nomore out of their cyté.

2   Blanchardyn, that at the same owere was in the provostis hous, heryng the bruyt and the noyse that wythout[19] the towne was made by Kynge Alymodes folke, the whiche he had seen and advysed[20] from over the walles where he went up, and seen the battaylles and scarmysshynge[21] that by them of the towne and their enmyes were made. So began he to be ful of thoughte and all annoyed of hymself bycause he was not armed tyl his plesure, and that he myght not yssue out upon the proude pucelle in amours enmyes wyth her folke. The provost, that ryght wyse was and subtyll, asked Blanchardin what moevyd hym to be so sore sad and pensefull and yf he was not well lodged at his ease and to his playsure, and yf he wanted eny thynge that myght be recoverd for gold or sylver, that he sholde telle it hym and that he shold late hym have hit incontynent, al sholde he putte in jeopardye bothe lyf and goode for to fulfille his wylle. "Alas," said Blanchardyn, "sire, of your lodgis and goode chere I am right wel content and thanke you moche therfore, but one thynge wol I telle you syth that it playseth you to knowe the cause of my grete dysplaysaunce. Ye shall understande that I have habandonned[22] and forsaken bothe fadre and modre, kynnesmen and frendes, and eke[23] lyflode[24] and lande where I toke my byrth and noureture, for to excercyse and able myself in the noble crafte of faytes[25] of armes and to take and lerne the dyscipline of knyghthode. And I se nowe that for defaulte[26] of armures I may not sette a-werke nor employe my good wylle, whiche full sore greveth me, and moche more than I telle."

---

[13] *sliced to pieces*
[14] *afterward (again)*
[15] *1400*
[16] *depressed*
[17] *thinking (believing)*
[18] *guarantee (surity)*
[19] *outside*
[20] *scrutinized (examined)*
[21] *skirmishes*
[22] *abandoned (left behind)*
[23] *also*
[24] *livelihood (inheritance)*
[25] *deeds (feats)*
[26] *lack*

3   The provoste, hering the goode wylle and grete affection that this yonge knyght had, was therof right glad and sayde unto hym, "Vassell, come wyth me [fol. 26r] and I shall delyvere you hors and eke harneys right goode so that ye shall have noo cause for fawte[27] of armures, but that ye shal mowe prove your prowes[28] whiche I holde right grete." "Syre," sayde Blanchardyn, "of the curtosye that ye have doon and proffre[29] unto me, I thanke you moche." Thenne the provost toke Blanchardyn by the hand smylyng and to hym sayde, "Come you wyth me and I shal gyve you the choys of suche armures as ye shal lyke." They two went togidre and entred into a chambre that well garnysshed[30] was of all manere of armes suche as atte that tyme were used.

4   The provost dilygently armed Blanchardyn of suche armures as he wold chose, and syth made eche hemself to be armed hastely. Whan dressid and redy they were, they made theire coursers to be had forth out of the stable, whiche were brought anone to the mountyng place byfore the halle. Thenne one of the doughters of the provost, knowyng that Blanchardyn was armed and redy to goo out wyth her fader, she cam and brought wyth her a fayre whyte coveryng of damaske clothe wherof she made the hors of Blanchardyn to be covered wyth, and unto hym she gaffe one of her gowne sleves that was of damask blake, prayng hym that for her sake and love he wolde vochesauf to were and bere it upon his helmet. Blanchardyn toke the sleve of the damoysell sayng that he sholde fulfylle her request, and she, thankyng hym therof, sayde she sholde, because as her semed that God sholde gyve hym some goode fortune that day.

---

[27] lack (want)
[28] valor (martial skill)
[29] offer
[30] supplied

The twentieth chapitre speketh of the grete bataylle that was byfore the cyté of Tourmaday ayenst kyng Alymodes folke and of the grete prowes that Blanchardyn made there that day and how the proude mayden in amours becam sore enamoured over him and of the devyses or communyng that she made wyth her maystres.

1   [fol. 26v] After that the provoste and Blanchardyn were armed of all peces[1] and set upon the myghty coursers, the shelde at the necke, theire helmes bokled, and eythre of them the spere in the hande, toke leve of hem that were there and departed out of the place and cam to the towne gate where they fonde thre thousaund men alredy for to yssue out, the whiche, by the motion and warnyng of the provoste, had appareylled[2] themself for to kepe hym felawship[3] and folowe hym.

2   When the provoste was come to the yate, hit was soone open, thurghe whiche they alle yssued out in goode and fayre ordynaunce.[4] Blanchardin, whiche was sore desyryng

---

[1] of all peces, *completely*
[2] equipped (made ready)
[3] comradeship (company of soldiers)
[4] battle array (military equipment)

for to prove hymself and shewe his strengthe and vertue, to have bruyt and comendacion[5] and that he mygbt be knowen, dyde putte hymself in the forefront, havyng a ryght bygge spere in his hande.

3   They bygan alle to vaunce[6] and marche forth out of the barres[7] of the towne, and syth all at ones gaaf a grete crye, wherof theire enmyes, that all redy awayted there for them, were alle affrayed. They byganne thenne to renne[8] one upon other by so grete strengthe, that for the noyse and sowne[9] that the erthe gaffe bycause of the horses that ranne harde upon it, semed to them of wythin and wythout[10] that the foure elementes had fought theire togydre. The duste rose up fro the grounde that derked[11] the lyght of the sonne wyth the shot that drawe was[12] of bothe sides, one parte ayenst that other.

4   Blanchardyn, that in the forefronte was the first man of all, had his spere in the rest and ranne upon Corbadas, that nevewe[13] was to Kynge Alymodes. And so grete a stroke and so hevy he gaffe hym that the sperehed appiered[14] at the backe thurgh the body of the sayd Corbadas, and, pulling ageyn his spere, he overthrew him doune sterke ded [fol. 27r] to the erthe. And syth anone he rought[15] another of Kynge Alymodes knyghtes in suche a wyse that he made his spere to entre his body thurghe lunge and lyvre and so kyld hym. And so moche he made atte the first empraynte[16] that, ar[17] evere his swerde was broken, he threwe doune ded syx of his enemyes from their sadelles, the whiche emonge the horses fete fynisshed myserably theyre dayes. And syn[18] aftre he lyghtly dyde sette hande on the swerde, of the whiche he smote here and there wyth bothe his handes by suche a strengthe that him that he rought wyth full stroke was all to-brused[19] and cloven in two peces. He detrenched[20] and kutte bothe horses and knyghtes, he clove and rent[21] helmes and sheldes, and brake the grete routes[22] and made his enemyes to sprede abrode. Moche better he semed to be a man of the fayré[23] than a creature of the worlde. All fled byfore hym and made hym waye to passe. There was noo man, how hardy that he was, that

---

[5] *praise*

[6] *advance*

[7] *outworks (barriers at the gate of a fortification)*

[8] *charge (run)*

[9] *sound (noise)*

[10] wythin and wythout, *indoors and outdoors*

[11] *darkened*

[12] shot that drawe was, *arrows that were drawn*

[13] *nephew*

[14] *appeared*

[15] *attacked with a blade*

[16] *assault*

[17] *before*

[18] *soon*

[19] *crushed*

[20] *dismembered*

[21] *tore*

[22] *squadrons (companies of soldiers)*

[23] *fairy*

durste[24] mete hym, so sore fered and doubted[25] hym his enmyes. Wythin a lytyl whyle, he made so moche of proesse that his enemyes were therof ryght sore abasshed and that his swerde was well beknowen emonge hem. Ryght grete and horryble was the battaylle, and so moche that they of Tourmaday and his enemyes merveylled gretly of the grete strengthe and hyghe proes[26] that they sawe in Blanchardyn, the whiche his enmyes fledde as the larke doth the sperhawke.[27]

5   The howlyng and the noyse bygan to ryse up a-hyghe and so moche that the fayre proude mayden in amours, that lened atte a wyndowe seeyng the grete proesses and merveyllouse faytes[28] of armes that by Blanchardin were there made, asked of her maystres that was nyghe her yf she [fol. 27v] knowe not the knyght that had his hors coverid with whit rayment,[29] and syth she also perceyved the black sleve that upon his helmet was sette fast.[30] Her maystres thenne wyst not what to thynke nor also what he myght be, but well ynough sayde that he was the most valyaunt and that dyde best that day of al bothe partyes. And she sayde, "A, madame, loke nowe ye may see that they all fle aweye byfore hym, and ye may well perceyve that no man dare abyde hym. Moche grete desyre I have to wyte[31] and knowe what he may be."

6   Even atte this oure that the proude mayden in amours and her maystres were in suche talkyng, came unto them a squyer that cryed on hyghe and sayde, "O my right redoubted[32] lady, yonder wythout[33] may you chuse[34] and see the floure of knyghthode, the subduer and sleer of your enemyes, not yet satysfyed nor fylled of the deth of many of hem but styl destroyeth them. He heweth and felleth doune right al byfore hym; his armes were not longe syth all clere[35] and whyt, but now they be dyed in red wyth the blode of your enemyes that he hath slayne and brought to deth. Madame, knowe for a trouthe that it is the fayre knyght whiche is lodged at the provostis house."

7   Whan the proude lady in amours understode the squyer speke thus, the bloode ranne up at her face and wexed[36] red as a rose. Well perceyved hit her sayde maystres and that the love of hym smote her, but no semblaunt[37] she made therof to her. Right gladde and joyeful was the pucelle whan she knewe that it was Blanchardyn and bygan to thynke in herself that he was wel worthy to be beloved. Thenne she sayde to her maystres, "Certes that knyght that I see yonder dooth merveylles of armes. I see the provost that of nyghe

---

[24] *dared*

[25] *respected*

[26] *prowess*

[27] *sparrow hawk*

[28] *deeds (feats)*

[29] *cloth*

[30] *firmly*

[31] *understand*

[32] *honored (respected)*

[33] *outside*

[34] *discern by sight*

[35] *pure (bright)*

[36] *became (waxed)*

[37] *sign (indication)*

foloweth him. It is to be thought that he shal wyl give him one of his doughters in mariage with [fol. 28r] a grete parte of his grete havoyre,[38] but on my fayth it were dommage,[39] for he is a man of noble corage and right valyaunt, and nought it is to be doubted but that he is come of som noble hous." The maystres, that right sage was, dyd perceyve incontynent by her wordes that her indygnacion[40] and evyll wylle that she byfore that had conceyved ayenst Blanchardyn was moderat[41] in her herte, and wyst not what she therof shold thynke but that love had overcome her evyll erroure, wherof she shold have ben right glad. And lyke as her thought was to be, so it was indede happed. Among other comynyng[42] and devyses, that she myght more playnly[43] knowe how it was therof, right subtyly bygan to saye thus to the proude pucelle in amours, "Madame, as for this, I knowe and can perceyve youre pryde shal be cause, but yf[44] ye take hede, of the totall distruction of your royalme.[45] Concedere you not that ye be occasion and the cause movyng of the assemblé of the ostis[46] that are for[47] your towne, and of the shedyng of bloode that procedeth therof? Yf ye wolde wedde the kynge Alymodes, all your lande shal be in sureté,[48] quyete, and peas." Than the proude mayden in amours, after this exhortyng herde of her maystres, sayde that she sholde noo more speke therof unto her and that never the dayes of her lyff she sholde wedde paynem[49] nor noo man infydele.[50]

8 And for this cause cessed a while their talkyng and loked bothe toward the felde where they saw the knygtes ful sore fyghtyng of bothe partyes. But Blanchardyn hath the praysyng over hem alle, for ther was no man of nother syde that of prowes and worthynes coude go beyonde hym, wherof Kynge Alymodes knyghtes had grete envye[51] over hym, and grete cure[52] and laboure toke upon them for to slee hym, but non of them, how hardy that he was, durste not proche[53] nor nyghe[54] [fol. 28v] hym, for as many as he myght reche unto, he feld hem doune or slew hem and wounded them grevously.

9 The proude pucelle in amours folke bare themself right wel that day. This bataylle lasted tyl the nyght came, wherfore Kynge Alymodes, seeyng that he myght not by noo manere putte nor close them fro the cyté, bycause of the wyse wyt and worthynes of the

---

[38] estate (wealth)
[39] unfortunate (misfortune) [OF domage]
[40] anger
[41] moderated
[42] conversation (communication)
[43] clearly
[44] but yf, unless
[45] kingdom (realm)
[46] armies (hosts)
[47] before
[48] safety (security)
[49] pagan
[50] non-beliver, i.e., non-Christian
[51] envy (hostility)
[52] difficulty (care)
[53] approach
[54] come near

goode knyght Blanchardyn that conduyted them, made to sowne[55] and call the retreyte[56] or wythdrawe his men to his losse and grete confusion, and wythdrewe hymself into his tente right wrothe[57] and sorowfull for the losse of dyvers his knyghtes, and all thurgh the vertue and strengthe of one knyght onely. Blanchardyn and the provost wyth theire folke wyth grete glorye and tryumphe entred ayen into the cyté and brought wyth them many a riche prysonner. And to the provostis house toke Blanchardyn his waye, wherunto he was conveyed[58] of the most parte of the noblemen, makyng to hym the gretest honoure that men can or may doo to a knyght, as to hym that best had doon that day. And to saye the trouthe, many of the gretest of hem had ben slayn or taken yf by the vertue and strengthe of Blanchardyn they had not be socoured[59] and holpen[60] that day. Some he helped ayen upon theire horses whan they were feld doune, some he rescued from the hande of theire enmyes that had hem as prysoners. So bare himself that wyth grete tryumphe and grete glorye he retourned fro the bataylle wyth them unto the sayde provostes place, to the grete benyvolence and gladnesse of the peple of the cyté. And there alyghted from his hors and the provost wyth hym, whos two doughters that were right fayre and praty came there ayenst them, for bothe of hem loved sore Blanchardyn and right enamored they were over hym. There [fol. 29r] abode twenty knyghtes at souper wyth Blanchardyn, for to chere and feste[61] hym and to be acoynted[62] of hym. Harpe, lute, sawtrye,[63] and dyverse other instruments of melodyouse musyke were sent for, for to rejoysshe the noble felawship[64] that was full fayre, for there were comen diverse ladyes, many a gentyl woman, maydens, and noble bourgeyses[65] at the requeste and prayers of the provoste and of his two doughters, that were right besy for to chere and serve Blanchardyn wyth all dyligence.

10   Atte the same owre that this joye and feste was in makyng in the provostis house, the proude pucelle in amours was in her castel lenyng upon one of her chambre wyndowes that had syght wythin the towne, and herde the noyse and the feste that was adoyng[66] in the provostis house for love of Blanchardyn and for to doo hym worshipe[67] and honoure, wherof she was advertysed[68] alredy. And how be it[69] that, as ye have herde anone, she had gyven herself in hir herte to the sayd Blanchardyn, allewayes at the same owre was

---

[55] blow (sound)
[56] retreat
[57] angry (wrathful)
[58] accompanied (guided)
[59] aided (succored)
[60] helped
[61] celebrate (feast)
[62] acquainted
[63] small harp with a shallow soundbox
[64] company (group of people)
[65] burgesses (officials of the town)
[66] taking place
[67] respect (honor)
[68] informed
[69] how be it, however it is

taken the fynall and faste[70] conclusion and altogydre was of her determyned to make of Blanchardyn her lover and her specyall,[71] that a lytyl before that for one kysse onely was so ferre from her gode grace and in daunger of his lyf, yf the goddesse of love that is so myghty of her grace had not purveyed[72] better for hym. At the begynnyng of this new alyaunce,[73] amoures, or love, served her wyth a messe[74] sharp and sowre[75] ynoughe tyl her tast. That is to wyte of a lovely care that is as moche worthe as a suspecyouse jalousye of the doughters of the provoste and her specyall[76] Blanchardyn. But she thought in herself that she sholde purvey therto of a remedye mete[77] and goode to the cause, whiche thynge she dyde as ye shal here herafter. Love, that departeth wyth her goodes[78] whereas it semeth her [fol. 29v] best employed, forgate not her newe servaunt, but atte her first comyng made her to be vysited and wayted upon by a servaunt of hers named Care, that well sore movyd and troubled her spyrites. And she that was not lernyd to receyve suche geestes, sore harde was his queyntaunce[79] to her. And yet, wythin a whyle after, Love smote her ayen with a darte to the quycke[80] tyll the herte of her, so that the fayer pucell wyst not her behavyng nor how to mayntene herself, and also had no power to drynke, nor ete, nor coude not slepe ne take no maner of reste. But held her hert so esprised[81] and so over-pressid wyth love that she had to Blanchardyn, that she myght noo lenger hyde her falle.

11   Thenne cam to her maystres and said to her in thys maner, "Alas, who shall mowe recover helth to this pacient[82] sore syke, that suffreth wyth goode wyll of herte both grete thurste, honger, and shaketh for colde caused thrughe a hete intollerabyll?" The maystres perceyved anoone by her wordes and maner that she had ben in the chapiter[83] of the god of love, and by his grace men shuld have gode accompte[84] of the pryde that over longe a tyme had ruled her dismesurable[85] herte. She thought that she had ben taken wyth Kyng Alymodes love and syth said unto her, "Madame, ye oughte to yelde grete graces and thankes to the myghty god of love, seyng the unknoulege that ye have had always here byfore of his vertues, that hath daynd to vysite you and to altre and change your corage.

---

[70] *firm*

[71] *beloved (sweetheart)*

[72] *provided*

[73] *alliance, one established by noble marriages*

[74] *meal (portion of food)*

[75] *sour*

[76] *beloved (sweetheart)*

[77] *suitable*

[78] departeth wyth her goodes, *distributes her gifts*

[79] *acquaintance*

[80] *living, sensitive flesh*

[81] *inflamed (overtaken) [OF esprise]*

[82] *patient*

[83] *chapter house (ecclesiastical assembly building)*

[84] *account (reckoning)*

[85] *excessive (exceeding due measure)*

I byleve now, that for cause of thys soudayn mutacion, ye be seke and sore passioned[86] of one accident[87] that nameth hymself the sore of love." "Alas," said the pucell, "the sore of love is ryght anguyssous and hevy forto bere, as me semeth." "Madame," sayd her maystres, "men must suffre for better to have. This evyll shalle be cause of your perfection, and knouleche[88] that love is that thynge that [fol. 30r] moost embellisheth and decoreth[89] the nobyl corages. And I can not thynke that ever man and woman havyng bruyt or name of some goode vertues passyng other, have come nor raughte[90] therunto wythoute[91] that they were or had ben in the service of love." The proude mayden in amours herkened her maystres, but the fevere that love had takn her for to plucke oute the roote of pryde from her herte lettid[92] here sore, and atte the ende of a whyle biganne to say, "Alas, amours I have longe defendyd mysylf ayenst the harde assautes[93] and impetuous excitacions that often tymes thy messangers made unto me. Now have I nother power nor wyl to defende me eny more, unto thee I yelde me."

---

[86] *tormented (impassioned)*
[87] *fortuitous happening*
[88] *know*
[89] *adorns*
[90] *reached (achieved)*
[91] *unless*
[92] *troubled*
[93] *assaults*

The twenty first chapter conteyneth how the proude pucell in love, by the grete love that she had sette upon Blanchardyn, bycam jalouse and douted leest he shuld sette his love on one of the doughters of the provoste, whom she hasteli sente for and spake to hym as it foloweth.

1   The maystres, herynge the complayntes of the proude pucelle in amoures, had no lityl joye to here suche tydynges, and tyll her feete fell herself and sayd, "Thanked be God, madame, the werre wiche is cause of so many evilles shal ceasse in your realme, yf it please God, for from that owr that ye shal wold gyve your love unto Kynge Alymodes, the right happy wele[1] of peas shal be publysshed[2] thurgh alle the countrey. But and yf ye suffre the siege to abyde any lenger byfore youre cyté, ye ought to wyte that the countrey about shal utterly be dystroyed of Kyng Alymodes folke. Wherfore at my request, use youreself after the dyseyplyne of amours, to whome ye have made obeyssance[3], and take to youre lord and husbande the kynge Alymodes. How well [fol. 30v] he ys overraged,[4] take no hede and care not therfore; he hath yet strenghe ynough ye see what it ys of warre." And thenn the proude mayden in love answerd and sayde to her maystres, "I have absoluteli sayde to you ones for alle that, while I lyve, Kyng Alymodes shall never wedde me. I merveylle

---

[1] *common good (well-being)*
[2] *proclaimed*
[3] *homage (submission)*
[4] How well he ys overraged, *Though he is quite old*

me gretli of you that ar ferre in age and ought wele to knowe so ferre, that a lesse evyll it were for to suffre all my lande to be wasted, than to wed and take to my lorde a kynge full of idolatrye acursed and apostata[5] of oure holy Crysten feyth. Thynke not that I sorough[6] for hym, but byleve that there is grete choys[7] of Alymodes, and hym for whom love hath taken my fayth that never I shall change hym." The maystres wyste not goodely what she shulde thynke, but ynoughe she doubted that Blanchardyn had that grace from whiche he was a lytyl afore sore[8] ferre cast.

2 Sone after, wythoute lityll taryeng, the proude pucelle in amoures sent for the provoste sayeng that she had nede of his counceyl. "He is sage, dyscrete, and experte in many thynges," sayd she, "I am sure that he hath in his house a rote[9] that, as to my semyng, shal gyf me help and shal lyght my herte of the soris[10] wherof I am full sore passyonned." Her maystres, wythout more enquyre to be made, sent one for the provost that cam sone toward the proude mayden in amours and made to her the reverence.[11] She toke hym by the hande and made hym to syt doune by her for to breke[12] her matere and to come to a conclusyon. She made her premysses[13] for to speke of her werre,[14] but she forgate not to telle hym how the knyght his hoste,[15] that is to wyte, Blanchardyn, and he hymself, had borne hemself that day right valyauntly, wherof she was right well content, and that, yf it pleased God, she sholde have knowlege som day of thoos that helpeth her to mayntene [fol. 31r] her were ayenst the false Sarasyn[16] Alymodes.

3 She that ardauntly sought occasion to fynde matyere for to spek of Blanchardyn sayde unto the provost in this manyere, "Provost, I have founde you always goode and trewe servaunt unto me, wherof I fele me moche beholden[17] to yow, and wyl advertyse you of one thyng that dyspleseth me sore whiche is sayd of youre doughters, that is that they wyll enamoure hemself of that knyght youre ghest whiche is now lodged wyth yow. Whiche is a thynge of grete oultrage and grete dyshonoure unto them, knowyng that he is a man come of a grete house and extracted[18] of hyghe parentage and a grete lorde in his contrey. I make no doubte, but holde myself wel certayn that he the lesse therfore setteth by them. And also, it is no merveylle theyre grete foly displayseth me moche, for it is to be presumed that this myght be cause to mynusshe[19] your worship and their goode

---

[5] *apostate (opposed)*
[6] *sorrow*
[7] *choice (contrast)*
[8] *very*
[9] *root (medicine)*
[10] *sorrows*
[11] *bow (gesture of respect)*
[12] *disclose (reveal)*
[13] *preliminary plans (preparations)*
[14] *war*
[15] *guest*
[16] *Muslim*
[17] *indebted*
[18] *descended*
[19] *diminish*

renomme." "Madame," sayd the provost, "I have not perceyved me of this that ye telle me, but yf it were soo that the knyght wherof ye speke were wyllyng to take one of hem, I sholde holde her to be employed to the most valiaunt knyght that men evere speke of, to the moost free[20], sage, and curteys that I trowed[21] evere to be acqueynted of. Now wolde God that his wylle were suche, and that he had a grete desyre to take her as I sholde be wyllyng for to gyve her to hym, oure bargayne shold be all thus lyghtly doon. That sore lytyll that God hath lent me of goodes sholde not be straunged[22] unto hym by me, for he is worthy to have mykel more. Hath he not taken this daye tenn knyghtes prysonners, besydes threty coursers that he hath conquered upon youre enemyes? And so many of them he hath cloven and slayne that grete merveylle it were to reherse the same. And, to my demyng,[23] I trowe better that he is a man of the feyré[24] than [fol. 31v] otherwyse, for his prowes and worthynes that ben hyghe are not to be tolde ne compared to the humayn or wordely werkes."

---

[20] generous (of noble character)

[21] thought (believed)

[22] estranged (removed)

[23] judgment (opinion)

[24] fairy

The twenty second chapitre conteyneth and speketh of the devyses that were betwene the provost and the proude pucelle in amours, and of the grete love that she had sette to Blanchardyn the yonge knyght, as it folowed here.

1 The proude pucel in love, heryng the provost, was right glad for she herkened not to the rewthes but onely to that loenge[1] and praysynge of her lover and frende specyall. But well she bethought herself that the doughters of the provost sholde not longe trouble her heedes, for she sholde purveye[2] therto of a remedy convenable.[3] And whan she spake ageyne, her wordes were suche: "Provost, as byfore I have sayde unto you, the knyght of whom I speke paraventure[4] is of byrth right hyghe, and suche and so vertuouse in armes as ye knowe. It nedeth not to be doubted that he is comme to his extremyté of prowes and valyantnes, wythout that amours hathe be the cause in the persone of some hyghe a pryncesse. And for to telle you I knowe well soo moche that he is this day in the goode favoure and grace of a kynges doughter, right ryche, myghty and well in lynage,[5] and endowed, as men sayen, of all that that can be desyred in the body of a woman. And therfore grete foly it is to youre doughters to have suche an overwenyng[6] wylle, wherof men gyven them a dysmesured[7] proclame.[8] Nevertheles, as dere as ye have my playsure to

---

[1] esteem (praise)

[2] provide

[3] suitable (reasonable)

[4] perhaps

[5] lineage

[6] conceited (exaggerated)

[7] exaggerated

[8] reputation (fame)

fulfylle, and above all to renne into[9] myn indygnacion, holde the hande to[10] this: that they forbere hemself to the smylynges and fayre shewes[11] of their eyen whiche wauntonly thay caste full often upon that yonge knyght. And to the ende that ye may have them to[12] [fol. 32r] soner awaye from the love of the sayd knyght, gyve me hem bothe and make them to be brought here wythin, and wythout enythyng to youre charge nor cost I shal mary hem right wel."

2   The provoste, heryng his lady soverayne, right humbly thanked her of the grete offre and curtosye that she wolde do to his doughters and was ryght glad. He toke his leve of her in his most goodly manere, as to suche a caas[13] apparteyneth.[14] After the fayre offres had don unto hym and at his partyng from her, she sayde unto hym that she wold wel see the knyght of whom they had spoken, and that he sholde brynge hym to her the next day for to make aqueyntance betwyx hem bothe. And sayde that she was wel holden to doo so, knowyng that he was in hir servyse, and that he exposed his body for the deffence of her countrey. "I wol," saide she, "knowe yf he shal be wyllyng to dwelle wythin this my towne, takyng suche wages as ben acoustumed, or ellis, yf not soo, I shal doo so well reward hym that he shal by reason be well content of me, and be sure yf he serve me as he hath bygonne, yf God be pleased, I shal rewarde hym right well. And I hope that thurgh his ayde my werre shall take a good conclusion. And that doon, yf it pleaseth hym, he shal mowe take to his spouse hyr that so moche is his and that so truly hath gyven herself to hym. And yf it cometh to purpos, forgete not to say that it were yl don of hym for to forgete her. But on my fayth, this that I speke the cause is moved bycause that the forsayde, his specyall maystres and true lover, is my cosyn germayn.[15] And also that she bereth in hir herte care ynough and dyspleysure for the love of hym and may nother slepe nor take no manere of naturall rest, so moche she is enamored on hym. I doubte not that yf by adventure she were out of his remembraunce and by hym putte [fol. 32v] in oblyvyon, that God forbede, but that sholde dey sodaynly after that suche pitteuouse tydynges were brought tyll her. Gryevous sore and payne tendreth to pité the very herte of myn owne body, and nedes muste I putte peyne[16] to the relevyng of her grete sorowe. For wythout fawte, it were domage yf suche a lady that is so well condycioned and in all manere norreture[17] right parfyt, sholde perysshe thorugh the coulpe[18] of a knyght."

---

[9]   renne into, *incur*

[10] holde the hand to, *stop (refrain)*

[11] *expressions*

[12] *two*

[13] *circumstance*

[14] *pertains (is appropriate)*

[15] cosyn germayn, *close kin*

[16] putte peyne, *take pains (exert oneself)*

[17] *breeding*

[18] *fault*

The twenty third chapter conteyneth how the provost retourned tyll his house and recounted unto Blanchardyn that the proude pucelle in amours had tolde hym, and how she sent for hym that she sholde come toward her, and how Blanchardyn went thither, and how they talked togydre at leyser to the grete pleasure of bothe partyes, and how theyr love was knytted and confermed.

1   After the humble leve that the provost toke of the lady, he went homward agayn tyl his place all penseful of the wordes that he had herde of the pucelle. It was tyme to go to bed, so cam he toward Blanchardyn that was alredy goo into his chambre, and gaff hym the goode nyght. And on the morowe after the masse, the provost sayde unto Blanchardyn that he wold talke wyth him atte leyser, and Blanchardyn ansuered, "Fayre hoost, in good oure be it." Thenne they two sette hemself upon a benche. The provost bygan hym to recounte and telle hou the proude mayden in amoures, the even last past, had spoken wyth hym of many thynges and emonge other tolde hym that she was right well content of his servyce and wolde reteyne[1] hym in wages and gyve hym of her goodes, for he was worthy therof. "Morovere," sayde the provost, "sire, she hath tolde [fol. 33r] me that ye be enamored of a hyghe and a riche pryncesse, wherof I merveyll me not for, on my feyth, ye be well the man that ought to chuse your specyall love in a hyghe place. But alleways it is force that I bere you in hande[2] that it is her owne silf, for it semeth me not wel possyble that yf it were in som other place, hit sholde not have comen to her knowlege. How wel that here is one doubte that retardeth[3] myne ymagynacyon[4]: she sette nevere nought by amours and love, but japeth[5] and playeth[6] herself of theym that ben amerouse. I wote[7] not alleways yf the god of love myght have shewed his vertues in her. Alas, we sholde wel desyre that it were so, to the ende she myght take a goode lord for to deffende us and her lande."

2   After that the provost had sayde to Blanchardyn all that semed him good to be tolde, Blanchardyn, curtoysly wyth a smylyng contenaunce, ansuered hym that God hath well kept hym from so moche an hap[8] and so hyghe,[9] as for to have the grace of so noble and so grete prynces as was the proude pucelle in amours. "And also I byleve," sayde Blanchardyn, "that ye make yourself these tydynges. But I can not bythynke[10] to what purpos ye have seen eny token ne apparence for to coloure your gracyouse suspecion. I never spake wyth her, nor never in my dayes I dyde see her. Wherof sholde to me come suche a wylle?" "I wot[11] not," sayde the provost, "I telle you that that I have herde of my lady. Yf ought[12] be

---

[1]   *engage in service (employ)*
[2]   bere you in hande that, *assert that*
[3]   *pauses (delays)*
[4]   *thought*
[5]   *mocks (japes)*
[6]   *amuses*
[7]   *know*
[8]   *chance (unforseen occurrence)*
[9]   *exalted (lofty)*
[10] *understand (think)*
[11] *know*
[12] *anything*

ther to your avauntage, soo take hit. Now pleased God that she were that woman that suffred so moche of sorowe and angwysshe[13] at her herte for the love of you." "I thanke you," sayde Blanchardyn, "I wolde not that noobody sholde suffre for love of me anythyng to his dyspleasure whereas I myght [fol. 33v] by ony manere of waye putte a remedy. But alwayes," sayde Blanchardyn, "I can merveyll me not too moche wherof suche langage commeth, and can not thinke that it shold come of the doughter of a kyng. For thus to say, she in a manere mocketh me; suffyse her yf I am come to serve her in kepyng my worship. And as to me, suche an use[14] I seke not, but I wyl onely prove and adventure honorably my body as a gentyl man ought for to doo. Joustyng, tournoynge, and behourdyng[15] are my passetyme, and no wyffe I thynke not to take." "Aa, sire," sayde the provost, "I wold well kepe[16] me and be loth for to denounce[17] thynge unto you that sholde tourne you to a displeasure, and praye you that ye wyll not take the thynge otherwyse than I have told hyt to you and thynke nomore upon it. But let us go see my lady, for in goode ernest she doth sende for you by me." Blanchardyn graciously ansuered to his hoste that he was content, excusyng hymsilf alwayes of that love that he had spoken to hym of, howbeit he felt the contrary at his herte.

3 They cam to the ladyes palays and went though the grete halle into a fayre chambre, and after that announced was there comyng, men made them to entre into the chambre of parement[18] wheras the right gracyouse and fayre the proude pucelle in amours was wyth many of her ladyes and other her gentyll women, and spake at that same owre wyth certayne of her counseyll[19] upon the faytte of her werre. Blanchardyn and the provost entred into the chambre, and thenne, as Blanchardyn sawe and perceyved the noble pucelle, he dyde vaunce himself toward her and make unto her the reverence so gracyously and so boldly in all worship that non coude amende[20] it, and consequently to all the lordes, ladyes, and gentyl women so goodely and wel that everyone saide good of hym. The noble [fol. 34r] mayden behelde hym moche humbly, whiche toke a right grete pleasure to see his gracyouse and assured behavyng that tysed[21] and doubted in her herte the fyre of love, wherof she was sore esprysed.[22] And thenne after the fayre and swete welcomynges, the lady wythdrewe her toward a couche that was in the sayd chambre and toke Blanchardyn by the hande and made hym to sytte besyde her. He made hymself to be prayed and drawen[23] sore[24] or ever he wolde vaunce hymself for to sytte hym doune by her, but force[25]

---

[13] *suffering (anguish)*
[14] *way of life*
[15] *participating in informal jousts*
[16] *restrain (refrain)*
[17] *declare (communicate)*
[18] *richly decorated room hung with tapestries*
[19] *advisors (council of officers)*
[20] *improve*
[21] *stirred up (teased)*
[22] *inflamed (kindled)*
[23] *persuaded*
[24] *very much*
[25] *necessary*

was to hym to obeye her commaundement. Wherof al they that thenne were wythin the chambre coude not tourne their eyen from Blanchardyn, for his right grete beaulté, fayre behavoure, and good manyere.

4   And she to whome the dede most touched had grete joye at her herte to fynde herself in the presence of hym, and for to saye the trouth, she was so enbrased[26] and taken wyth the brennyng fyre of love that she not coude kepe her contenaunce. And yf rayson had not restrayned her, wythout other premysses[27] nor conclusyons she sholde have gladly of pryme face[28] tolde unto Blanchardyn how love constrayned her for to love of hym. And at ende of a while, the best wyse that she coude, wyth a lowe voyce she sayde unto Blanchardyn, "Syre, ye knowe the werre that the untrewe kynge Alymodes hath alredy don to me dyverse tymes, wherfore I mystered[29] gretly of the ayde and socours[30] of you and of other. So praye I you that ye wyl helpe and conforte me in my said werre, and I shal rewarde you so that ye shal be content." "Madame," sayde Blanchardyn, "I ensure you on my feyth that in all that I shal mowe,[31] I shal employe me in your servyce. I wyll not spare myself. I am come out of myn owne contrey for to fynde me in a place whereas I myght excercise the fayttes of armes as longeth[32] tyl a knyght to doo, and thanked be [fol. 34v] God I am here right well arryved. I aske nothynge of you, but I praye you, syn[33] that it pleaseth you to gyve me wages that ye wyl doo them to be delyvered unto myn hooste youre provost, for moche beholden I am to hym. And I shal gladly dwelle wyth you in the companye of your other knyghtes, and shal serve you truly." "Syre," sayde the pucell, "I promette[34] you that youre hoste shal be altogydre contented of you and alle of myn owne." And after thees wordes she dyde cast a profound syghe that proceded from the depnes of her herte that sore was pressed. She was so over perced[35] and enflammed of love that she had so moche on it as the herte of eny lady myght bere or comprehende, unto the grete extremyté. And the reyson is goode, for the strenthes and vertues of the gode of love, that departeth wyth whereas hym semeth goode, are suche that the more that the persone is more harde to be convertysed[36] and tourned to his lawe, the more ought she afterward, whan she is overcome, to be more constant and stedfast to kepe hit. This experyence was playnly shewed in this lady.

5   Blanchardyn trowed[37] to perceyve a lytyl her manere and remembred hymself of the wordes that his hooste had tolde hym the same daye, and syth sayde to the lady, "Madame, myn hoste hath tolde me this daye that ye knowe well my lady paramours and that she is

---

[26] *seized (embraced)*

[27] *premises of an argument, introductory statements*

[28] of pryme face, *at first sight* [Lat. prime face]

[29] *needed (lacked)*

[30] *assistance (succor)*

[31] *do (be able)*

[32] *is appropriate (belongs to)*

[33] *since*

[34] *promise*

[35] over perced, *completely pierced*

[36] *converted*

[37] *thought*

of your lynage. By my feyth, this thynge semeth me right straunge." Thenne the proude pucelle in amours byganne to ansuere and sayde, "The lady of whom I touched the provoste, your hoste, is well trusted wyth me, and I wolde doo for her as moche honoure as I wolde for myself." "A, madame," saide Blanchardyn, "pardoune me yf I desyre by manere of replycacyon[38] to knowe the name of her of whom ye have made nowe mencyon, for I ensure you, madame, that whan [fol. 35r] I dyde that grete oultrage wherto I was constrayned by force, to nyghe and touche youre swete mouthe, I had not seen no lady nor non other gentylwoman of whom I desyred to be reteyned[39] her servaunte. But syth I have ben fayne[40] of the servyce of one whiche I repute to me a grete fredom,[41] in suche a wyse, that yf I sholde deye for deffawte[42] of her socours, yet coude I not nor wolde not departe nor be from her for no thyng of the worlde. And therfore, my ryght redouted[43] lady, I beseche you in all humylyté that it please you of your grace to pardoune me my vayne[44] wylle, for in you lyeth my bytter deth or my prosperouse lyf. I am and shal be, yf it pleayse you, youre feythful and true servaunt for to employe myself in youre servyse in al that shal please you to commaunde me, as longe as lyf shal be in me, whatsomever happeth to me for."

6   Whan the pucelle herde this swete and graciouse langage, of the heryng of whiche she toke no displeasure, wold no lenger suffre hym to be in peyne upon whom she had sette her herte, and in whom she hoped of goode servise for to brynge her werres tyl and ende, but saide unto him, "Aa, gentyl knyght, forced I am atte this houre present, syth it is your wylle, that I declare and saye that whiche my herte thynketh and suffreth for your sake. Be ye sure that all that I sayde unto the provost toucheth noobody but only to myself, for so helpe me God, as I love you wyth all my veraye herte, and am so esprysed[45] wyth your love that reherce it to you I can not. I have debated the quarelle ayenst the god of love, but, at the last, I have ben subdued and uttirly overcome though the graciouse maneres, honeste behaving, hardy and noble corage that I have perceyved in your persone, whiche I love moche better than alle the remenant of the world. And from hens forth I reteyne you myn onely true lover and goode frende, never to chaunge [fol. 35v] unto the oure of deth." Wherof men may thynke al ynough that in spekyng and uttraunce of suche wordes they were not wythout mutacion of coloure, chaungyng of contenaunce, and suche other thynges in this caas acostumed. And whereupon is to byleve that Blanchardyn ws nevere in hys lyff half so glad, and not wythout a cause, as whan he understode this joyouse tydynge, and as that thinge whiche most he desyred in this world dyde accepte this gracyouse and desyrable ansuere. And how he thanked that noble mayden, it is not to be demaunded, for he forgate noo worde that therto served to be sayde.

---

[38] *reply (answer)*
[39] *engaged in (love) service*
[40] *glad (eager)*
[41] *liberty*
[42] *lack*
[43] *respected (honored)*
[44] *futile (foolish)*
[45] *inflamed*

7   And thenne, thourghe a soubdayne[46] fyre that descended from the hevens above, was theire love confermed togydre, and fro that oure abode bothe their hertes in one hole wylle. The provost at the same tyme perceyved well that Blanchardyns besynes was in non evyll waye, howbeit he coude knowe noo thynge therof but by suspecyon. Betwix the lady and Blanchardin were noo wordes more for that tyme, but that the yonge knyght toke a gracyouse leve of the fayre pucelle that myght not tourne her eyen from Blanchardyn.

---

[46] *sudden*

The twenty fourth chapitre conteyneth how Blanchardyn toke leve and went ayen to the provostis house, and of the fayre whyt courser and of the sleve of cloth of gold that his lady dyde sende to him, and of the grete battayll that was byfore Tourmaday betwix Blanchardyn and a gyant whiche was dyscomfyte,[1] and of the grete mervaylles of armes that Blanchardyn made there and of his takynge.

1   After their devyses, the provost vaunced hymself for to take Blanchardyn by the arme and have hym to his house. But or[2] they went, the proude pucelle in amours [fol. 36r] sayde to the provost that he sholde not leve[3] to bringe her two doughters the next morowe, and that she holde marye hem right well, as she dyde unto two of her knyghtes right noble and gentyl wythin fewe dayes after. I saye not that jalousy was cause of this thynge, but I leve it in the jugement that in suche a caas can good skyle.[4]

2   After the gracyouse leve of the lady, Blanchardyn and the provoste came ayen in the sayd place and was dynertyme. The provost, that wyth all his herte loved Blanchardyn, conjured[5] hym sayng it semed hym that he sholde be yet kynge and lorde of the londe of Tormaday, and that their lady had hym well in her grace. Thenne Blanchardyn, that well beholden was to the provost and that knewe hym for a trusty man and secret,[6] mystrusted not hym but recounted and tolde hym al alonge the fayttes of his werkes in amours, wherof the provost was not lesse rejoysshed than Blanchardyn was. The dyner was redy and made an ende of theyr proces[7] tyll another tyme. They sette hemself at the table, and had not be longe at their meet when the lady sent to Blanchardyn a fayre whyte courser, and wyth it her right sleve whiche was of riche clothe of golde crymosyn, to the ende he sholde bere hit upon his helme when he shold go upon her enmyes bycause she myght the better knowe hym emonge other.

3   This present was not to be reffused, and the messanger sayde to Blanchardyn that well he ought to areyse[8] his corage when so gentyl a lady wolde sende him suche a present. Blanchardyn thanked the messager and prayed hym curtoysly that he wold have hym

---

[1] *defeated*

[2] *before*

[3] *neglect (forget)*

[4] can good skyle, *have sound judgment*

[5] *urged (beseeched)*

[6] *discreet*

[7] *conversation*

[8] *rouse*

for humbly recomended⁹ to the goode grace of the noble pucelle that so fayre a present had sent to hym. Blanchardyn dyde putte his hand in to his aulmonere¹⁰ and drewe out of it [fol. 36v] a riche ouche¹¹ of golde, upon whiche was sette a right riche ruby auyrouned¹² wyth fyve grete perles, and gaffe hit to the messager, whiche thanked moche humbly Blanchardyn, of whom he toke his leve and departed. And taryed noowhere unto the tyme that he had tolde and reherced to the lady the joye that Blanchardyn had made at the recepcion of the present that she had sent unto hym. And syth recounted her of the riche gyfte that Blanchardyn had don to hym, wherof the proude mayden in amours was wel payd,¹³ sayng in herself that suche largesse¹⁴ proceded to¹⁵ hym of veraye noblenes.

4 Here we shal leve to speke of her and shal retourne to speke of Blanchardyn, that in the provostis house was sette atte dyner. Right soone aftre the last messe¹⁶ was served, a lytyll affray¹⁷ and alarme roos wythin the towne for bycause of the kynge of geauntes, called Rubyon, that was in the playne wythout¹⁸ the cyté byfore the walles of the towne. And demaunded after the joustes for his ladyes sake that doughter was unto Kynge Alymodes, the whiche had taken hym a sleve that was of satyn vyolet and had sette hit upon his helme for the love of her. But bycause he was of so hyghe and bygge corpulence, and so stronge of body and renomme of grete proes,¹⁹ the proes²⁰ was not grete of the knyghtes nor of other folke of Tourmaday for to furnysshe his apetyte²¹ nor fulfylle his requeste.

5 The bruyt of this werke²² cam to the knowlege and understandyng of Blanchardyn, the whiche for this tydyng was gladde by over mesure, and sayde of a goode herte and a free wylle that he shal furnysshe Rubyon of his requeste and that he was comme in tyme. Redyly and soone he made hit to be knowen to Rubyon lest he sholde departe thens, whiche was right joyous of the tydynges, for right moche he desyred to shewe hymself [fol. 37r] for his ladys love, doughter to Kyng Alimodes, of whiche he was amorouse. And of that other partye, Blanchardyn made hymsylf to be armed quyckeli and syn mounted upon that myghty courser that the fayer the proude pucell in amours had sente to hym. He forgate not the sleve of cloth of gold that unto hym had be presented from her bihalf, the whiche he couched along his sholder in stede of gardebras.²³ And for that daye he

---

⁹ commended (entrusted)

¹⁰ purse

¹¹ brooch (pin)

¹² encircled (surrounded)

¹³ pleased

¹⁴ generosity

¹⁵ proceded to, resulted from (originated in)

¹⁶ course (meal)

¹⁷ commotion (disturbance)

¹⁸ outside

¹⁹ prowess

²⁰ courage

²¹ desire

²² action

²³ armor protecting the arms and shoulders

wold have therto noon other armour, wherof the provost was not wele content. Whan he was redy appareilled, mounted, and armured of all his armures except the haulte[24] pece where the pucelles sleve kept stede,[25] he made the signe of the crosse over hym and so departed oute of the provostes place and cam ridyng thorugh the toun, accompaned wyth the provoste and of many other knyghtes. He was sore loked upon and praysed of the ladyes and gentyll women as he passed by, for al prayd to our Lord that wyth honoure and joye he wolde brynge hym ayen.

6   So long rydde[26] Blanchardyn that he cam to the toun yates oute of whiche he yssued and parted, the spere in the hande, the shelde sette afore hym, the helmet lacid[27] and clos, redy forto renne[28] upon his ennemye that he sawe byfore hym that walked before the barres[29] of the toun, awaityng after hym that shuld furnyshe hym of batayll, thynkynge that none shuld dare come bicause he had taryed there longe, whereof he bare hymself wel proude. Whan he see Blanchardyn, that all prest[30] was to furnyshe[31] hys enterprise,[32] gaffe to hymself grete mervaylle and praised hym but litell. He asked hym of whens he was. Blanchardyn answerd that for no drede nor fere that he had of hym he shuld not kepe his name from hym, and tolde hym that he was of the realme of Fryse and his name was Blanchardin that unto him was sent by the fayer the proude [fol. 37v] pucell, his maystres in amours, for to juste and to aprove hymsylf upon hym. Thenne answerd Rubyon to Blanchardyn that the doughter of the myghty Kynge Alymodes the even byfore had gyven unto hym her sleve, the whiche in presence of her fader she had taken it from her ryght arme, to the ende that for the love of her he shuld doo some thynge wherby she myghte the better have hym in her grace. "Vassayll," sayd Blanchardyn "thynke to do your werke. Ye see me here redy to furnysshe your requeste." Thenne bothe of them went abacke for to take their cours[33] and tourned ayen, brochynge[34] their horses wyth their spores, that one ayenste the other, the speres in the rest, wherof they roughte eche other upon the sheldes by so grete a strengthe that nother of their sheldes abode there hole but were all quartred in peces. And in suche a wyse they recountred[35] eche other that their speres brake unto their handes that the shyvers[36] flowe upward, and syn passed beyonde for to parfurnyshe[37] their enterprise. And in tornynge hemself ayen layde hande on their swerdes, wherwyth

---

[24] *top (high)*
[25] *place*
[26] *rode*
[27] *laced*
[28] *charge (run)*
[29] *outworks (barriers)*
[30] *ready (prepared)*
[31] *carry out*
[32] *undertaking*
[33] *charge*
[34] *spurring on*
[35] *met (collided)*
[36] *slivers (splinters)*
[37] *complete (carry out)*

they began to smyte one upon that other by so grete and horrybyll strokes that the fire cam oute of their helmes.

7   Evyn atte the same oure that the two vasselles befoughte eche other, the proude mayden in amours was lenyng at a wyndow thorugh whyche she sawe pleynli the bataylle of her speciall[38] and of Rubyon. Wherfore all ynoughe ye maye byleve that she had grete fere that Blanchardyn shulde not retourne atte his honoure. How well she helde hym so valiaunt as he was, that her advyse was for ryghte grete and goode desire that she had that her beste biloved was alleredy com to his above[39] overe Rubyon. The doughter of Alymodes the kynge was atte this owre setytnge byfore her pavillyon for to beholde the batayll of the two champions. [fol. 38r] She dyd prayse and commende so moche Blanchardyn, and prevely[40] atte her herte whished hersilf hys lady peramours for the grete worthynes and proesse that she perceyvid in hym there, for he smote so grete strokes wyth his swerde and so ofte that he had all astonyed[41] alredi his enmye Rubyon.

8   Blanchardyn, seeng Rubyon in that plyght, lefte[42] uppe his swerde, of the whiche he raughte[43] Rubyon wyth a revers[44] myght by the eere[45] wyth suche a mervelous stroke that he overthrewe hym doun from his hors. The batayll had ben sone finysshed bytwyx them both and Rubyon ded, ne had ben[46] Kynge Alymodes folke that cam for to socoure Rubyon, to whom[47] Blanchardyn had smytten the hed off, yf they had not come right soone. But the proude pucell in amours, for the grete care that she had to sende socoure and helpe unto her lover, that she sawe in danger and enclosed with three score men that aboute hym were for to slee hym and brynge hym to deth, sent hastely her men for to socoure hym, for he was assaylled of eche side of good men of werre. But not wythstondyng thys, right vygoriously defendid hymsylf ayenst them all and yelded them ynoughe to do wythoute that they ever coude hurte nor wounde hym unto the tyme that socours cam to hym. For he detrenched and kyt[48] them both legges and armes, and clove their heedes unto the brayne, and so fiersly mayntenid himself ther that none durst no more vaunce to approche nyghe hym. Whan they of Kyng Alymodes oost[49] sawe them of the cité that were comen oute, they mounted on horsebacke and came towarde them as faste as they might come. And atte the reconntre[50] that both partyes made one ayenst that other were many a spere broken, and many a knyghte broughte to grounde that were troden wyth the feete of the horses so that fewe of hem rose [fol. 38v] up alyve. And in

---

[38] *lover*

[39] *victory*

[40] *secretly (privately)*

[41] *stunned*

[42] *lifted*

[43] *pierced*

[44] *back-handed stroke*

[45] *ear*

[46] ne had ben, *had it not been for*

[47] *of whom*

[48] *cut*

[49] *army (host)*

[50] *collision (coming together)*

conclusyon, all they of Alymodes partie had ben there slayne or taken, yf his son Daryus had not come the same tyme, that brought with him a grete companie of folke and assembled and called ayen togydre theym that fled fro the battaylle.

9 And thenne entred hymself into the battaylle where he bygganne to do merveylles of armes, for a ryght gode knyght he was yf he had ben a Crysten man. Grete slawghtyr he made of them of the cyté. But Blanchardyn, that sone was aware of his commyng, cam ayenst hym the swerde in hande by right on hyghe, whiche he lete fall upon Daryus wyth suche a stourdy[51] strok and so grete that he amasyd hym wythall and overthrewe hym doune from his hors. And right sone wolde have taken the hede wyth the goode helmet from the body of hym, yf he lyghtly had not be socoured of his men that wyth right grete peyne, strong wounded and sore hurt, remounted hym on his hors and had hym to his pavyllyon wher he kept his bed the space of thre dayes. Rubyon, the kynge of gyauntes, that of Blanchardyn had ben overthrawen as it is sayde afore, faught full sore ayenst theym of Tourmaday beryng to them grete domage. But Blanchardyn, that alle his mynde and thoughte had sette to fynde hym to the ende he myght be avenged over hym, loked aboute at the right syde of hym whereas he chose Rubyon that made merveylles of armes and had overthrawen doune the goode provoste, whos hed he sholde have stryken off right soone yf Blanchardyn had not be, that hastely brake the presse[52] and camen there and socoured hym,[53] creynge upon Rubyon in this manere of wyse, "Ha, a thou false paynem[54] and cursed man, this shall be thy laste daye, for by false and grete traysen, and by a watche[55] thought[56] before, wolde have madest me to be [fol. 39r] murdered. And by suche meanes thou escaped ones fro my handes, but to me nor to noon other thou shalt nevere werke trayson." And thenne Blanchardyn, that had a stronge axe in his handes, smote atte Rubyon wyth al his strenthe and gaff hym suche a stroke that his goode armures coude not waraunt[57] his lyff, but was feld doune sterk ded, wherof the cry and the noyse rose up ryght grete. Whan the Sarrasyns saw the kynge of the gyauntes dede, they were sore frayed and gretly abasshed, for in hym was alle their hope. They fled toward their tentes as faste as they myght.

10 Blanchardyn and they of Tourmaday pursued them, smytyng and overthrawyng hem ded unto their tentes. And so moche that Blanchardyn cam to the kyng Alymodes tente, before the whiche he fonde his doughter syttyng that behelde the battaylle that was afore the sayde towne. Whan Blanchardyn sawe the yong damoysell that was there syttyng, he bowed hymself douneward upon his hors necke and toke the mayden by the myddes of her body and sette her up byfore hym wythout any resystence made by the pucelle whiche made therof noo refuse. And syth retourned ayen as fast as he myght toward the cyté of

---

[51] *powerful (fierce)*

[52] *crowd, i.e., the thick of the fight*

[53] *the provost*

[54] *pagan*

[55] *ambush*

[56] *plotted*

[57] *protect (defend)*

Tourmaday. But Alymodes, seyng this harde adventure so befalle, as a man madde[58] and alltogyder from his wyttes, cam rennyng after Blanchardyn wyth more than foure thousand Sarrasyns wyth hym that folowed faste at the backe of hym for to socoure their lady. And Blanchardyn, that bare the pucelle byfore hym, sawe a Sarasyn[59] that moche nyghe folowed hym. He tourned his horse hed toward hym, lyfte upward his swerde, and gaff suche a merveyllouse stroke to the Sarrasyn that he clove his hede [fol. 39v] to the harde tethe.

11   Alas, why dyde he tary hymself for to slee that Sarrasyn? For so sore nyghe he was pursiewed by Kynge Alymodes and his folke that they closed hym anone rounde aboute. The provost and the other of the towne entred ayen into the cyté, wenyng to them that Blanchardyn had be wyth them. But he was not, but was enclosed from al sydes and in suche wyse opressed that they had all redy slayne his horse under hym and was afote amonge the Sarrasyns, where he fought wyth the swerde in the hande, wherof he made grete slawghter of them. But what occysion[60] or defence that he made myght not warauntyse hym, for aboute him were more than foure thousand Sarrasins that desyred all for to purchasse hym his deth.

12   The kynge Alymodes, seeyng the grete prowes that was in Blanchardyn and that non so hardy durste approche hym, he bygan to crye alowde on hyghe, "Fy on you all untrewe paynemys, cursed be the owre of youre natyvyté, whan for the body of one knyght alone, I see you, more than foure thousand men, to tourne and recule[61] abacke. Full yl have I employed the godes[62] that I have doon unto you. A full sory norysshyng I have doon over you." Thenne the Sarasyns that herde their lorde soo speke to them, whiche they dyde ferre ryght sore, all att ones ranne upon Blanchardyn, that sore wery and traveylled was of the grete strokes that he had gyven and receyved soo that the blode ranne out of dyvers places of his body. Wel he saw that it was impossyble to hym to laste eny lenger but that he muste be other slayne or taken. Notwythstandyng this, Blanchardyn, lyke as other a tygre or a lyon that is broken loos from his boundes, heved upward his swerde wyth bothe the handes and smote a knyght therwyth, that nevewe[63] was unto Kyng Alymodes, wyth suche [fol. 40r] a strengthe that he cleved hym unto the chynne[64] bone. But as he wythdrewe his swerde toward hym from that grete and merveyllous stroke, his fotyng faylled hym for cause that the grasse wherupon he trad[65] was sore weet and slyther[66], and so nedes he muste falle. Thenne cam upon hym sodaynly out of all sydes grete foyson[67] of paynemys and toke and bonde hym full fast. Whan the Sarasyns dyde see hym thus fallen

---

[58] crazed
[59] Muslim
[60] killing (carnage)
[61] retreat (move back)
[62] goods (gifts)
[63] nephew
[64] chin
[65] trod (stepped)
[66] slippery
[67] abundance (plenty)

13 At the same owre, the proude pucell in amours that yet was styll at her wyndowe and had seen her folke turne agayn into the towne wyth grete haste, and syth herde the crye and the grete noyse that was made wythout the cyté, and of another part she sawe a grete nommbre of folke that retourned to the tentes, thoughte wel, and also her herte judged and gaf it to her, that that was the worthy Blanchardyn, her lover, that Sarasins ledde wyth them prysonner. Seyng this confusion thus to be happed, she wyst not how to conteyne herself[68] and byganne full sore to wepe wyth grete teerys that fell doune alonge her swete vysage,[69] and sayde, "Alas, my right dere and feythfyl lover, yf God thurgh his grace putteth noo provysion her unto, this day shal be broken and undoo oure sore desyred acqueyntaunce."

14 Thenne the provoste, right sorowfull and gretly dysplaysed, wyth a sad chere entred into the chambre where the right desolate the proude pucelle in amours made grete mone, whiche he fonde fallen in a swoune in the lap of one of her gentyl wymen. And syth whan she was come ayen to herself that she had the myght to speke, she sayde to the provost that soone and incontynent he shold go toward the kyng Alymodes for to wyte yf for golde or sylver he [fol. 40v] wolde take to raenson[70] the knyght that was a straunger, whiche was but as her sowldyour in this her werre, and, yf his playsure was, to sende hym ayen to her, "I shal gyve him for his raenson seven dromadaryes[71] al laden with fyn gold, so that he wyll sende hym to me sounde and hole." Whan the provost sawe the grete amarytude,[72] or, by termes,[73] grete sorowe, whereas his lady, the proude pucelle in amours, was inne, and the promesse that she made for the delyveraunce of Blanchardyn, he, moeved wyth pyté, ansuered and sayde to the pucelle that wyth all possyble dilygence he sholde do so moche that, or[74] ever the nyght sholde come, he sholde knowe the certeynté of that that Kynge Alymodes wolde doo in this behalve. He toke his leve of the proude pucelle, whiche he lefte sorowynge wythin her chambre wyth her maydens, and went anone hastly upon a hyghe toure that had syght toward Kyng Alymodes oost. And there he called out of the batelmentes as hyghe as he myght upon a knyght Sarrasyn that went forth by the same toure, to whom he prayed sore moche that he wold doo hym as moche curteysy toward the kynge Alymodes, that he myght undre gode surtye[75] and saufcondyt[76] goo to speke wyth hym for to shewe and annonce to hym certayn message from his lady, the proude pucelle in amours. The paynem knyght, that was full curteys, made a token

---

[68] conteyne herself, *control her behavior*
[69] *face*
[70] *ransom*
[71] *camels*
[72] *bitterness (sorrow)*
[73] *words (manner of expression)*
[74] *before*
[75] *security*
[76] *safe-conduct (escort)*

to hym that his request he dyde graunte. Soo went he hastely and dyde so moche that he brought to hym a goode saufcondyt, where the provoste right moche thanked hym.

15 The provost anone after made hymself redy toward his waye and cam nygh ynoughe to the tente of Kynge Alymodes, and as he passed by he saw Blanchardyn that was kept in holde of six squyers syttyng byfore a [fol. 41r] pavyllyon. That tyme that Blanchardyn perceyved the provost that passed forth by hym, he demaunded of hym what thyng he went there sekynge. The provost tolde hym that he went toward Alymodes the kyng for his delyveraunce, saynge to hym that he sholde not be abasshed of no thynge and that he sholde not care, but sholde make good chere, and that he sholde not abyde behynde so that for eny golde or sylver he coude be had. "Frende, of that ye telle me," sayde Blanchardyn, "I am right glad and joye wel to thanke God therof. I praye you that ye wyl doo the beste that ye shal may toward the kynge Alymodes, for my confyance[77] and trust is in you." The provost toke leve of hym and dyde so moche that he cam and alyghted byfore Kynge Alymodes tente, and syth entred inne where he fonde Kynge Alymodes and his barons aboute hym. He right reverently salued[78] hym, sayeng unto hym that he was come there for to beye[79] ayen the straunge knyght that he helde prysonner, "whiche is a souldyour[80] and reteyned into wages wyth the proude pucelle in amours. And the cause that moeveth her herto it is bycause that he is a straunger and that he is comen from ferre lande to take wages, thus right gladly she wolde have hym ayen yf your plesure were for to putte hym to raenson.[81] And my lady the proude pucelle offreth you for hym seven dromadaryes al charged of[82] fyn golde and a thousand coursers and as many amblynge horses and armures goode and fyn, ynoughe for to arme a thousaund knyghtes."

16 Whan the kynge herde the provoste that soo grete offre made for to have ageyne Blanchardyn, he gaf hymself grete merveylle and bethoughte in hymsilf a lytyl whyle. And syth dyde sende [fol. 41v] for Blanchardyn whiche he behylde so moche whan he was come afore hym, and sayde wythin hymself that never in his lyff he had not seen noo fayrer knyght, nor more better made and myghty of body. He dyde coveyte moche sore the grete havoyre[83] that was proffred[84] hym for his raencon, but a soubdayne[85] sparkle of jalousye cam to hym byfore, that was lest this yonge and fayre knyght Blanchardyn were reteyned of the proude pucelle in amours as her owne specyall lover, the whiche thynge kept hym so sore at the hert of hym that he, movyd wyth grete wrath and yre, wold have ronne upon Blanchardyn for to have slayn hym, sayeng for to cover his right false jalousy that it was for the grete damage and grete slawghtir that he had don of his folke, and that,

---

[77] confidence
[78] saluted
[79] buy, i.e., ransom
[80] soldier
[81] ransom
[82] al charged of, loaded with (full of)
[83] estate (wealth)
[84] offered
[85] sudden

by the feyth that he owed to his goddes, he sholde not abyde longe alyve, for he sholde nother ete nor drynke tyll that he sholde see hym deed.

The twenty fifth chapiter conteyneth how Kynge Alymodes wolde make to be put to deth Blanchardyn, but at the request of the fayre Beatryx his doughter he respyted hym, and how the proude pucelle in amours had sent the provost toward the kynge Alymodes offryng to hym a grete raenson for the delyveraunce of Blanchardyn whiche he refused.

1   Thus after as ye have herde, Kynge Alymodes made his avowe[1] and sware his goddes that he sholde neyther ete not drynke tyl that Blanchardyn had lost his lyff. Wherof Daryus, the sone of the same Kynge Aymodes and many other barons that were there present had grete pyté, for the right grete beaulté and worthynes that they sawe and knewe in Blanchardyn. But the best of them all was not so hardy that he durste speke one worde nor praye for hym, bycause they [fol. 42r] drad and fered ever sore Kynge Alymodes.

2   And thenne his doughter Beatryx that was there, whiche had taken goode hede and well over loked the grete beaulté of Blanchardyn, and well had also consydered the grete and merveyllous faytes of armes that she had seen hym do that day, prosterned[2] or casted herself doune byfore her faders feet on her knees, humbly requyryng, wyth bothe handes heved up faste togydre, that pyté and compassyon he wolde have of the yonge knyght and that his lyff myght be saved. Kynge Alymodes, heryng the request and humble prayer of his doughter, whiche he loved tenderly, ansuered to her and sayde, "My ryght dere and right well beloved doughter, I wold for mekell goode that ye had not requyred me herof and that ye had not ben here at this tyme, for the presence and syght of hym for whom ye have caused your humble supplycacion reneweth alle my sorowes. But for to obtempre[3] youre requeste, for this tyme I graunte hym his lyff. But ye shall wyte that I shall sende hym into the royalme of Salmandry[4] unto the kynge of the geauntis brother, that is to wyte Rubyon, whiche he hath slayne and the whiche I loved as myn owne persone, for yf he had ben yet man alyve, I wolde have gyven you tyl his wyff. So may ye knowe that he shal doo goode justyce of hym and shal take cruelle vengeaunce, and noon other wyse wyll I doo." And syth dyde caste his eyen upon the provoste full proudely as by grete despyte[5] and tolde hym that he myght well go home ayen, and that he sholde not leve but that he sholde departe his presence incontynent, or ellys he sholde make hym soone deye an evyll deth. And that nother for noo golde nor for no yefte[6] that myght be don to hym, nor for noo manere of raenson he shold not respyte[7] nor yelde ayen Blanchardin, but he sholde sende hym into a suche place from [fol. 42v] whiche he sholde never retourne ayen.

---

[1] *vow (pledge)*

[2] *prostrated*

[3] *comply with (grant)*

[4] *Alexandria*

[5] *contempt*

[6] *gift*

[7] *spare (reprieve)*

3   And thenne the provoste departed anone, and, full sory of the aunsuere that Kyng Alymodes had gyven to hym, ful sore wepyng went toward Blanchardyn and recounted hym the harde tydynges that had be made of hym. And evyn thus as they sholde never have seen eche other, they toke leve one of other. And after their leve taken, Blanchardyn, lokyng right pyteously upon the provost, prayed hym that he wold have hym for recomended[8] unto the fayre the proude pucelle in amours, besechyng her on his byhalve[9] that she wolde not putte in oblyvyon nor forgete hym that is in her servyse, for he whom God wolde preserve can not peryshe. The provost, heryng Blanchardyn speke that charged hym his eraunde to be do unto the proude pucelle in amours, departed sonn wythout eny morre that he coude say to Blanchardyn. For he had no power to speke no more for the grete pyté that he had over hym, but retourned to the cyté so ful of hertely sorowe that no man can expresse it to you. And rested hym not tyl he come to the paleys where he alighted doune and went forth into the halle and syth entred into the chambre wher the noble pucelle was, unto whom he recounted and tolde the harde and pytoyable[10] tydynges and the proude ansueres that Kynge Alymodes had gyven unto him, wherof the right noble mayden made suche a sorowe and grete hevynesse that never was sen like. We shal leve her makynge her pytoyable complayntes and shal retourne to speke of Kynge Alymodes, the right and evyl tyraunt that all taken was wyth anger and wrathe.

---

[8] have hym for recomended, *convey his regards (recommend him)*
[9] *sake (account)*
[10] *pitiful*

The twenty sixth chapitre foloweth whiche conteyneth how Darius had a commaundement don unto hym in his faders byhalve that he shold have Blanchardyn forth into Salamaundrye. And how the ship in whiche Blanchardyn was inne was perysshed by fortune and tempeste [fol. 43r] **of the see and were all drowned except Blanchardyn. And how he cam toward the kynge of Maryenbourgh that reteyned hym in servyse and of hym he made his constable.**

1   After the departynge of the provost, Alymodes the kynge gaaff commaundement unto his sonn Daryus that he sholde tourne ayen into Cassydonye, whiche is in the lande of Nourweye of whens he was kynge. And that he sholde take wyth him his suster and kepe wel his lande and countreye duryng the tyme that he sholde kepe his siege before Tourmaday. And that he sholde have wyth hym Blanchardyn, whome he sholde sende forth hastely, as sone as he were comen to Cassydonye, to be pressented on his byhalve to the kynge of Salamandrye whos brother Blanchardyn had brought to dethe, for to have wrake[1] upon hym. Daryus, heryng his fadres commaundement, made to be redy a shippe right bygge and grete wherinne he and his suster entred, wel garnysshed wyth folke and vytaylle.[2] And in another small shippe that was there redy he made Blanchardyn to be brought ynne wyth thre score men that had the kepyng of hym. Whan they were redy,

---

[1] *revenge*
[2] *food (provisions)*

thy wonde[3] theyr saylles up and departed. Grete pyté it was to see and here the pyteouse rewthe and complayntes that Blanchardyn made, for well he wend[4] that he sholde nevyr have seen ayen her for whom he was brought in suche angwysshe and sorowe.

2   We shal at this tyme leve to speke of hym and shal retourne to speke of the proude pucelle in amours, and of the grete tyraunte Alymodes, that wasted al the countrey aboute the cyté of Tourmaday and greved sore the towne and them of wythynne wyth his engynes[5] as moche as he coude, howbeit that the cytezeynes[6] yssued oute often and slew fuson[7] of their enmyes. And the [fol. 43v] fayre the proude pucelle in amours, that evermore had her sight that parte that she wyst her best beloved goon, whiche she wysshed sore agayne, lamentyng for hym for she sawe playn ynough whan he departed from the porte, toke in her herte her leve of hym full sore wepynge. She brought thenne in remembraunce how swetly he had kyssed her, wherof she had take so grete a dyspleasure. "But alas," sayde she, "this displeasure passed over many folde that other and more than I can telle. Ha, a, fortune, shal I nevere have noon other but alwayes dysplaysure?" And after thes wordes she fel in a swone as half ded, and the ladyes and other gentyl women, full pyteously wepyng, toke her up anone and had her to bedde where fro she parted not six dayes after.

3   Of that other part, Daryus and his folke, his suster wyth hym, and Blanchardyn in the lytyl shippe, saylled soo longe that they arryved in the lande of Northweye evyn at the havene[8] of the cyté of Cassydonye where they ancred. But or that Daryus went out of his shippe, he commaunded and ordeyned to them that had kepynge of Blanchardyn that they shold have hym streyght forthe to the kynge of Salmaundrye, and that they sholde delyvere hym[9] in his[10] hande and telle hym that it was he[11] that had slayne Rubyon, his[12] brother, byfore Tourmaday where his[13] fader, Kynge Alymodes, was yet kepyng the syege, whiche made hym a present of hym that had kylled his brother for to take vengeaunce therof atte his wylle. They that had the charge to doo this ansuered that they sholde doo hys commaundement. They departed from Cassydonye, but ye may be wel in certayne that this departynge dysplaysed moche unto Beatrix, Daryus suster, and ful fayne[14] wolde have putte therunto a remedy yf [fol. 44r] by ony meanes she had coude, but atte that oure she had noo power to do soo. Blanchardyn, that in the lytyl ship was, was sore dolaunt whan he sawe hymself to be had forthe from the other, and thoughte well that a present

---

[3]   *wound*

[4]   *believed (imagined)*

[5]   *siege machines or structures for assaulting walls*

[6]   *citizens*

[7]   *great numbers (abundance)*

[8]   *harbor*

[9]   *Blanchardyn*

[10] *the king of Salamandry's*

[11] *Blanchardyn*

[12] *the king of Salamandry's*

[13] *Daryus's*

[14] *eagerly (desiring)*

sholde be made of hym in some straunge lande. He dyde reclame[15] and calle upon oure Lord God, right devoutly besechyng that, of His grace, He wold have pyté and mercy upon hym that he myght yet ones come to his sore desyred wylle, that is to wytte,[16] to see his fayre lady, the proude mayden in love, and that He wold kepe her sauff[17] from Kynge Alymodes handes. Ye may byleve well that Blanchardyn made grete sorowe and lamentacyon, wyshyng full often that he may yet see ones his lady that he loved truly above all other.

4   And whan they were comen two dayes saylyng nyghe the coste of Salamandré, a grete tempeste roose in the see and so horryble that the saylle of their shippe was all to-rent[18] in peces that all the maryners coude putte therto noo remedye. Suche and so grete was the tempeste that they muste gyve nedes to the wyndes and wawes[19] of the see the kepynge and the gydynge bothe of their shippe and of them alle that were therinne, whiche soone were brought besyde a grete roche[20] wherupon their ship smote by suche a force that she cloved anone in two peces. Wherby alle the mareners[21] and the sayde thre score men were peryssshed and drowned in the see and nevere non of them saved, but onely Blanchardyn, that couched[22] hymself alonge upon the mast of the shippe whiche enbraced and colled[23] sore fast wyth bothe his armes. They were nyghe the lande, as it is sayde, where as the sayd mast and Blanchardyn upon it was cast off the wawes unto the shores. Whan Blanchardyn felt hymself so nyghe agrounde and fast by the lande, he forsoke his maste and lept from hit [fol. 44v] to the lande. And whan he was come there he kneled doune right sone upon bothe his knees and havyng his handes heved up toward the hevens, rendred and gaff lovynge and thankes unto oure Lord that thus had delyvered hym from that grete parell[24] where he was inne.

5   After that he had made his oryson[25] to our Lord, he toke on his waye all afote for to drawe hymself to that adventure that God wolde sende hym. And walked so longe tyl that he fonde not fer wythin the contrey a right fayre towne whiche is now called Maryenbourgh, and is in the lande of Pruce,[26] wythin the whiche at the same tyme was a right myghty kynge that kept ther a grete feste wher atte he had called alle his barons and lordes and alle the gentylmen of thereaboute, whiche alle arryved there upon the daye that to them was prefyxed[27] or poynted[28] for to come.

---

[15] *cry out (clamor)*

[16] *that is to wytte, that is to say [lit. know] (namely)*

[17] *safe*

[18] *torn (broken)*

[19] *waves*

[20] *rock*

[21] *sailors*

[22] *laid down*

[23] *hugged [OF col, neck]*

[24] *peril*

[25] *prayer (a set of liturgical prayers)*

[26] *Prussia*

[27] *agreed upon*

[28] *appointed*

6 Blanchardyn thoughte wythin hymself that he wolde make black his vysage[29] or of coloure suche that the folke of that contrey had hers[30] atte that tyme. He toke and gadred som herbes that served hym therto and rubbed therwyth his vysage all aboute, and in lyke wyse his handes, bycause that of noobody he sholde not be knowen. He coude well speke dyverse langages, and in especyall the hyghe Duche tonge. He purveyed and dyde ordeyne hymself so that yf he had ben met of them that had seen hym afore, they myght not thenne have knowen hym.

7 Whan he had apareylled hymself well, he toke his way forth on, and folke he met ynough by the waye of whom he asked the name of the towne that he sawe afore hym, and they tolde hym that it was the cyté of Maryenbourgh. He went so longe that he cam into the towne and asked whiche was the waye to the paleys, for right well he coude speke the langage of the contrey, as it is sayde. Men shewed [fol. 45r] hym the paleys, and he went in where he fonde the kynge amonge his barons, to whom he made the reverence righte humbly and honorable as ful wele coude he doo it. The kynge thenne demaunded of hym yf he was a yoman[31] or els a squier. And Blanchardyn tolde hym that he was a knyght and that from his contree, that sore ferre was thens, he was departed for to come and serve hym for by cause of the grete renommee that he had herde speke of him. And how, thorugh fortune and tempeste of the see, his ship was perished[32] and he only had saved hymsilf. The kynge ful besily[33] behelde Blanchardyn that semed to hym a full faer yonge man and wele shapen of all membres. And wyth thys he praysed hym ryght gretly that he was a knyght, and so thought in hymself that he was come of som highe and nobyl extraccion, for his fayr behavore and assured contenaunce that the kynge sawe to be in hym gaffe demonstracion of the trouthe of what byrthe he was come of. Wherfore the kynge was right wele content, and reseyved hym of his hous and commaunded to his stewarde that he sholde be brought to a chamber that all suche thynges that necessarye were to hym shulde be delyverd wythoute onye gaynsaynge[34] unto hym, the whiche thynge after the commaundement yoven[35] was doon. He was ledde into a chambre fayre and clere[36] where was raymentes[37] and full riche clothynge were to hym delyverd, wherwyth he dyde araye hymsilf. Whan he was thus clothed and richely arayed,[38] he semed wele to be a man comen of some nobyl hous. He cam ayen anon toward the kyng that ful gladli sawe hym and moche plesed him, and so dyd he to all the knyghtes and other of the kynges courte.

8 The kynge, that gretli desired to knowe of his estate, asked of hym what he was, of what lande, and of what lynage. Blanchardyn aunsuerd that [fol. 45v] he was of the lande of Grece and sone to a kynge. "But sire, for cause of the right grete renomme and goode

---

[29] *face*
[30] *theirs*
[31] *free man (household attendant)*
[32] *wrecked*
[33] *carefully (attentively)*
[34] *denying (gainsaying)*
[35] *given*
[36] *shining*
[37] *clothes*
[38] *dressed*

fame that renneth of you over all the world, is a wylle entred wythin me to departe secretly out of my countreye wyth a fewe men of myne, wythout license of the kynge my fader, and brought wyth me but thre score men. We toke the see and cam nyghe by the castell of Mocastre, byfore the whiche a right grete and impetuouse tempeste rose that lasted us thre dayes and thre nyghtes wythout ceasse, insomoche that fortune thrugh stormes of wyndes made our vessel to smite ayenst a grete roche[39] and brake so that all my men were drowned and noon escaped sauf[40] onely myself that ye see here. And wyth grete peyne and traveyl all afote I am come toward you hether. Yf I sholde all suche adventures as I have fonde by the waye reherce unto you, over moche myght let you the heryng of hem, but thanked be Mahon[41] that this grace hath doon unto me. I am comen to do you servyse after my powere." "Vassell," sayde the kynge, "of your commynge unto me I am right glad, and wel pleaseth me your servyse and wyl not reffuse it. And for the grete losse and grete trouble and peyne that ye have had for to seke me, rayson requyreth that ye shold have a goode reward of me. Well ye are come to passe for to serve me in a were, whiche to us is happed of newe ayenst a kynge whos countrey is not fer hens. And for thys werke to conducte and brynge to an ende, I graunte you even now and chese you for to be in oure byhalve conestable[42] and hed captayne of oure present armye, for the grete trust and hope that we have in your worthynes and personne."

---

[39] *rock (cliff)*

[40] *except (saving)*

[41] *Mohammed*

[42] *commander (chief military officer)*

The twenty seventh chapitre conteyneth how a knyght all sore wounded cam and brought tydynges to the kynge of [fol. 46r] **Maryenborugh that his enmye the kynge of Poleyne was entred wythin his royalme.**

1   Whan the kynge had precented this grete worship to Blanchardyn, it nedeth not to be asked yf he was therof gladde, or yf he forgate to thanke the kynge for the same, yet he dyde thrin[1] his devoyer[2] so well that none coude have doon it better, sayeng to hym in this manere, "Syr, sith[3] that this grete honoure ye have proffred me, evyn now forth wythall I do accepte it, promyttynge[4] you that all my strenghe, myght, and understondynge that the goddes have gyven to me I wyll putte and applie in your servyse." The kynge thenne wyth a right glad chere receyvyd Blanchardyn and toke hym by the hande and sayd unto hym, "Vassel, yf ye serve me well a grete rewarde shal be redy yeven[5] to you therfore of me."

---

[1] *therein*

[2] *duty (task)*

[3] *since*

[4] *promising*

[5] *given*

2   Ryght thus as the kynge was talkynge so wyth Blanchardyn, cam there a knyghte armed of all peces that was sore hurt in dyverse places of his body, his shelde crasyd[6] and broken, and his helmet all to-kutte. He cam byfore the kynges presence sayeng to hym all an hyghe, "Alas, noble kynge, where is now becomen the grete prowesses and hardynesse that were wont to be in thee, that soo well hast ruled and kept us of soo long tyme paste, whan thou suffrest now thyn enmyes to sette thy land al on a fyre and wymmen and children to be slayn of them are comen ferre wythin they royalme? And but yf thou putte a provysyon therto shortly, thou shalt are[7] thre dayes be passed see thyself beseged wythin the cyté of Maryenbourgh. And knowe for certeyn that the kynge of Polonye, thy mortall adversarye, is there in his persone whiche hath avaunced hymself for to brenne and waste all the lande, the whiche thynge he shal mowe well doo yf remedy be not [fol. 46v] sone putte by thee therunto. And alredy thou mayste see by me that they be not fer from hens, for as I was commynge towarde thee I dyde fynde thyn enmyes byfore me whiche have broughte me to the plyght that thou seest me nowe ynne. And yf wele y-horsed I had not ben, I shulde never have escaped but other I muste deye or be taken of hem." Whan the kyng herde the knyght speke, he understode wele by his wordes that the thynge wente evyll[8] for hym. He asked hym in what countree of his realme he had lefte his enmyes. "Syr," aunswerd the knyght, "hyt is wele thirty myle from hens to the place where I lefte them. But to myn advyse,[9] or ever thre dayes be past, but yf ye se a remedy, ye shal se them lodged here byfore the toun in their tentys and pavyllyons." The kynge thenne, after the knyght had thus spoken to hym, he gaff commaundement to his styward that he sholde be seen wele to, that he were helyd of his woundes that were grete by his owne leches,[10] cyrurgyens,[11] the whiche thynge was doon as he had commaunded. The kynge wyth grete haste assembled them of his counseyll for to see how a remedye shulde be had to the grete daunger that lykely was to comme, wythoute a goode provysion were had.

---

[6] *shattered*
[7] *before*
[8] *badly*
[9] *opinion*
[10] *physicians*
[11] *surgeons*

Chapter 28 How the kyng of Maryenborugh toke Sadoyne, his sone, to Blanchardyn and thre score thowsand men wyth for to goo ayenste his enmyes to fyghte wyth hem, and to caste hem oute of his realme.

1   After that the kynge had herde the knyght that had rehersed to hym the commynge of his enmyes, he sent for his lordes and barouns whiche cam to hym in his paleys, and to them he shewed all that he had understonde of the sayd knyghte, prayenge them that they wolde gyve hym counseyll therupon, to the ende he myght resyste and goo ayenste the dampnable[1] [fol. 47r] enterpryse of his enmyes. The barouns and counsellers answerde to the kynge that they shold speke togyder, for to advyse the manere and how

---

[1] *damnable*

this thynge myght be conducted. They wythdrewe themself asyde and assembled them in grete nombre to have consideracion upon this matere, the whiche they sore debatyd emonge themself by many and dyverse oppynyons. But, at the last, they dyde conclude togyder all of one accorde that the kyng shold sende his new conestable ayenst his adversaryes, acompanyed wyth thre score thousaund of the most valyaunt and best chosen men of his royalme, and that he sholde have wyth hym the kynges sone that called was Sadoyne, bycause that the barons and knyghtes of the sayd royalme sholde go wyth better wylle wyth hym. They went ayen to the kynge and proferred and tolde hym their advyse.

2 Whan the kynge had herde speke his barons, the thynge was to hym right agreable. He called Blanchardyn, his new conestable, and tolde hym how by hym and his barons was ordeyned to hym the charge and conduyte of his werre, and that wyth thre score thousaund men he sholde go ayenst his enmyes for to fyght wyth hem and dryve hem oute of his royalme. Whan Blanchardyn understode the kynge, he was therof right glad and thanked hym of the grete honoure that he dyde unto hym. Thenne sent the kynge his letres myssyfe[2] into al the partyes of his royalme, to be directed in all haste to his barons and knyghtes that they sholde wythout delaynge come hastely toward hym. The messagers were sone redy that bare the letters to them unto whom they were dyrected, and so grete a dilygence they made that wythin short terme dyde arryve in the cyté of Maryenbourgh. Fro the first to the last, wel thre score thousaund men of werre alredy prest and well apparelled[3] for to deffende their royalme and to go ayenst their [fol. 47v] enmyes. And whan the kyng sawe his men that were comme, he was of them right glad and so was Blanchardyn that had the rule over hem all, to whome he gaff in commaundement that they sholde be redy on the morowe bytymes[4] for to departe in the felaweship of Sadoyne, the kynges sone, and of hym.

3 Whan the morne cam, trompettes and claryons[5] bygan to blowe thourgh the towne and in the subarbes[6] of the same. They alle departed from their lodgis and cam wel apparelled in gode araye[7] to the felde, where they awayted after the conestable that shold be their ruler and their guyde, the whiche camm toward the kynge, and Sadoyne wyth hym, and to take their leve of hym. The kyng, seyeng his sonis[8] departyng, saide to Blanchardyne, "Vassall, vassal, to whom I have taken in hande that thynge most dere to me in this world, that is my sone, my royalme, my knyghtes and my barons. I beseke and praye thee, in the worship of the goddes, that at tyme of nede for the defense of my royalme thou wylt uttir and shewe that whiche I see appiere wythin thee that callest thyself the sone of a kynge, in whom ought to be graffed[9] and sette the floure of knyghthode with proesse and hardynesse wherwith thou art armed, as I holde." "Syre," sayde

---

[2] *conveying a command (missive)*
[3] *equipped*
[4] *promptly*
[5] *slender shrill sounding trumpets*
[6] *areas outside the town walls*
[7] *order*
[8] *son's*
[9] *grafted (implanted)*

Blanchardyn, "as for me though the helpe of the goddes, I shal so moche do that wythin fewe dayes your enmyes shal have no cause to be glad therof. And in their folysshe pryde I shal succombe[10] and brynge a-lowe their corage." And thenne wythout mo[11] wordes, Sadoyne and Blanchardyn toke leve of the kynge.

---

[10] *subdue (overwhelm)*

[11] *more*

The twenty ninth chapitre conteyneth how Blanchardyn and Sadoyne and their folke discomfyted their enmyes, and how Blanchardyn toke prysoner the kynge of Polonye, the whiche he putte in the handes of the kynge of Maryenbourgh. And of the worship that they made to Blanchardyn.

1   [fol. 48r] After their leve taken of the kynge, the two barons mounted on horsbacke and camen to the felde where they fonden their folke renged[1] nyghe togydre, to whome they commaunded to departe holdyng their waye toward their enmyes, whiche they fonde two dayes after all redy aparailled for to fyght, for they were advertysed afore of the commyng of Blanchardyn. Whan they two oostes sawe eche other, the noyse and the cry began to be grete on bothe sydes. Soo beganne they to marche forth toward eche other in right fayr ordonnaunce made by Blanchardyn that conduyted the first bataylle,[2] and had lefte Sadoyne in the seconde baytayllen the kepynge of two noble pryncess that were there comen with hym. The shot beganne to fle of bothe partyes so fast and soo thycke that the lyght of the sonne was kept wythal from the fyghters. And syth cam to joyne hemself togyder wyth sperys, and wyth dartes, and wyth swerdes and axes, wherof they hewe eche other insomoche that the felde was sone coverd wyth the bodyes ded that were slayne there. The horses went travayllyng[3] after theym their owne bowellys, rennyng over hylles and dales here and there. And Blanchardyn thenne, that in proesse and hardynes was entred, toke his spere doune and ranne ayenst the brother of the kynge of Polonye[4] that grete damage had done to the Prusyens.[5] He rought hym so sore and wyth so grete a strenghthe that he shoved and passed his spere alle thourgh and thourgh his body that he fel doune sterk ded, wherof the noyse and the cry rose up grete though the batallof the Polonyens. Ful sone cam the tydynges therof to the kynge, that grete sorowe made for his brothers dethe. He sware and made his avowe[6] that he shold never have joye at his herte unto the tyme his brothers deth were avenged; sore an angred and ful of wrath smote hymself into the thyckest of [fol. 48v] the bataylle,[7] where he dyde upon the Prussyens grete merveylles of armes, so that there as he arryved no man durste not abyde nor come nyghe hym.

---

[1] *drawn up in battle order*

[2] *batallion*

[3] *dragging (laboring)*

[4] *Poland*

[5] *Prussians*

[6] *vow (oath)*

[7] *battle*

2   Of that other parte was Blanchardyn that so many fayttes of armes had doon that, or ever his spere was broken, he had slayne and brought to deth and borne to the grounde more than twenty four of his enmyes, and syth toke in hande his swerde wher wythall he brake the grete presses.[8] He kutte and clove the Polonyens by so grete fyersnes that his swerde and bothe his armes were dyed wyth red blode. He semed not to them that sawe hym to be a man mortall, but semed better to be a fende or a spiryte of the fayrye. He brake the arayes[9] of them that were renged,[10] and the grete presses he departed and made waye byfore hym. Alle fled and non durste abyde hym for the grete and merveyllouse faytes of armes that he made there, wherof they of Prusse that wyth hym were gaff hemself grete merveylle. They folowed after at the backe of hym as the yonge lambe do the sheep. Sadoyne and his bataylle dyde approche their enmyes. They smote hemself wythin them callyng a grete crye, wherfor they of Polonye lepte and reculed six passes or moo. But the kynge of Polonye, seeyng his folke go backe, was ful sory. He ascryed[11] and dyde calle upon his mayster conestable that he sholde ryde forth upon his enmyes, the whiche thynge he dyde. Wherof the batayll began to be reforced[12] ayen so that the Prussyens, wolde they or not, muste lose grounde and goo abak, and sholde have be full sore dealed wythall yf they had not be soone socoured of Blanchardyn, the whiche, seeyng his folke recuyelle abacke, gaffe the spore to his hors and cam ayenst hym that bare the cheff standarde of Polonye, to whom he gaaff soo merveylouse a stroke wyth his goode swerde that he clove hym unto the brest and fell [fol. 49r] doune emonge the hors feet.

3   Thenne byganne the noyse and the crye to ryse up grete of the Polonyens that trowed to have taken up ayen their standarde. But Blanchardyn, whiche at that owre slept not, smot hymself emonge them. He kutte and clove them that nother helmet nor shelde coude helpe there, soo that none was so hardy to approche hym. His folke dyde folowe hym and putte hemself upon their enmyes, so that it was force the Polonyens to recule abak the space of an acre of lande or more. The kynge of Polonye, that sawe his folke recule and fle and his standarde y-brought to the grounde thourgh the valyauntnes and strengthe of one knyght alone, sware his goode goddes that he sholde nevere have joye at herte tyll that the deth of his brother and the domage that he had receyved were by hym avenged. He smote hymself into the bataylle and relyed[13] his folke togyder as well as he coude. Soo chose he Blanchardyn, that grete slawghter dyde make over his men. He toke a bygge spere in his hande and drewe that part where he sawe hym that so moche of evyll and damage had borne to hym. Blanchardyn sawe hym right well commynge toward hym; he toke also a grete spere from the hande of a knyght of his that was nyghe hym and cam ayenst the kynge of Polonye that soone perceyved hym. They brought alowe their sperys and ranne sore one upon the other and gaff eche other soo unmesurable strokes that the kynge of Polonye spere brake al to peces, but that other spere that Blanchardyn had, that

---

[8] *crowds*

[9] *battle formations (arrays)*

[10] *drawn up in battle order*

[11] *exclaimed (called out)*

[12] *reinforced (renewed)*

[13] *rallied (regrouped)*

was of wode right stronge and harde, brake not but roughte the kynge of Polonye wythall by suche a strengthe and vertue that he bare hym from his horse doune to the grounde.

4   Blanchardyn anon cast from [fol. 49v] hym his goode spere and syth toke his goode swerde in hande and cam to the kynge for to have smytten off his hed, but the kynge, seyenge that noon of his folke came for to socoure hym, dyde take[14] his swerde to Blanchardyn, yeldynge hym up unto hym, and prayed hym to save hym his lyff. Thenne was the kynge redely taken to mercy of Blanchardyn, that toke hym by the hande and gaf hym to tenn knyghtes for to kepe hym, that had hym out of the presse bycause that they sholde be more sure of hym. Whan they of Polonye sawe and knewe their kynge to be take, they wyst wel ynough that he was not to be recovered of hem, wherfor gaffe up the place and fled awaye. And so fynably[15] were all the Polonyens discomfyted,[16] taken, or brought to dethe that fewe of them escaped. But grete gayne[17] made there they of Prusse, whiche was departed by Blanchardyn to them that had hit deserved.

5   After this bataylle doon and that they had chassed their enmyes oute of their royalme, Blanchardyn wyth grete glorye and grete tryumphe, and Sadoyne his trusty felawe wyth hym, retourned toward Maryenborugh and their folke wyth them, where they were receyved of the kynge wyth grete joye and praysynge. Thenne cam Blanchardyn to the kynge and to hym sayde, "Syre, I do yelde and delyvere into your handes the kynge of Polonye your enemye, whiche I have taken wyth the helpe of your sone and of your noble and worthy chevalrye.[18] And ye may now doo wyth hym what youre goode plesure is or shal be." The kynge, that herof was well advertysed by his sone and by his other barons, that the bataylle had ben overcome and the kynge of Polonye taken though the right excellent and hyghe proesse of Blanchardyn, toke hym in his armes and syth sayde unto hym, "Ha, my right trusty frende and right noble knight, fulfylled with al gode maners [fol. 50r] and vertues, that hath be the pyler[19] susteynynge under thy swerde bothe myself and all my royalme, I am not a power[20] to reward thee after the meryte that ye have deserved to have of me. Well ye have shewed and doon perfytly to be understande the excellent vertu of humylité that is in you, and the right hyghe and noble lynage that ye be descended of. But fro this owre now I betake myself, my sone, and my royalme in your protection, and wol that all your commaundementes be obeyed and put to execucyon in all manere poyntes."[21] The noble Blanchardyn, thenne heryng the kynge that suche honoure made unto hym, sayd, "Sire, suche a worship apparteyneth not[22] to be doon to me, for I am not to the value therof. And it suffyseth me right well to be symply taken and kept as one of youre knyghtes wyth you and youre soone." The kynge wyst not to thanke hym ynough,

---

[14] *surrender*

[15] *finally*

[16] *defeated (overthrown)*

[17] *gain (profit)*

[18] *knights (mounted warriors)*

[19] *pillar*

[20] I am not a power, *I do not have the resources*

[21] *particulars*

[22] apparteyneth not, *is not appropriate*

that soo had delyvered hym from his enmyes and had put in his handes that kynge that moost he hated in this world. Wherfore he sayde unto Blanchardyn that he had a cosyn[23] that was of a right excellent beaulté whiche he wolde gyve hym right gladly to be his wyff. But Blanchardyn dyde excuse himself, saynge that in his countrey he was trouthplyght[24] tyl another. The kynge, herynge Blanchardyn, helde hym therof for excused. Right grete honoure was don unto hym of the kynge and of all his barons, but above al other he was most beloved and dere y-holde of Sadoyne, the kynges sone, that was a fayr knyght and yonge, right hardy and valyaunt. And also Blanchardyn loved hym moche, and yet more he wolde have do yf he had be a Crysten man, but nought he durste to hym speke therof.

6   Here we shall leve to speke of Blanchardyn and shal leve hym wyth the kynge of Maryenbourgh in Prusse and wyth his sone Sodoyne, that soo dere loved hym [fol. 50v] that wythout[25] he was always wyth hym he myght not endure. But whatsoever goode sporte and pleysure that Blanchardyn sawe ther make for his sake, nothyng coude playse nor brynge hym tyll his hertys ease. But evermore reforced[26] and redoubled his sorowe at alle tymes that he remembred wythin hymself his right swete lady and goode maystres, the whiche he had lefte beseged wythin her cyté of Tourmaday by the untrewe and crymynel tyraunt Alymodes, kynge of Cassydonye, that had made his othe nevere to departe thens into the tyme that he had tyl his wyf the right fayre and proude pucelle in amours.

---

[23] cousin, i.e., close kin
[24] betrothed
[25] unless
[26] reinforced

The thirtieth chapitre conteyneth how Daryus the sone of Alimodes by fortune of the see arryved in the lande of Fryse where he dyde grete hurt damage and toke the kynge of Fryse the fader of Blanchardyn and had hym wyth hym prysoner unto Cassydonye.

1   Well ye have herde byfore how Blanchardyn was taken and had prysoner by Kynge Alymodes folke, the whiche betoke hym to his soone Daryus for to brynge hym to Cassydonye, and the manere how he escaped the fortune of the see and cam and arryved in the lande of Prusse. Duryng the whiche tyme, Daryus the sone of Alymodes the kynge, beyng in his cyté of Cassydonye awaytyng after tydynges of them that had forth Blanchardyn toward the kynge of Salamandrye. But his awaytyng that he made was in vayne, for they were all peryshed and drowned in the see as ye have herde here above.

2   Whan Daryus sawe noo tydynges he coude not understande of them, he made redy a grete navye laden wyth men of werre, and wyth artylary and vytaylles for to goo agayn to the syege of Tourmaday toward his fader. [fol. 51r] Whan all these thynges were redy, he toke his leve of his suster Beatryx, to whom he betoke his citye to kepe. He syn entred his shyp, made to drawe up ancres[1] and began anoon for to sayle so that wythin a lytil whyle they were oute of syghte and fer from the haven. And so longe they saylled wyth goode wynde that they were anoon nyghe the realme of Tourmadaye. But as they shulde have

---

[1] anchors

taken lande, a storme began to come, grete and horribyll wynde to blowe that rose oute of the landes, soo that, wether they wolde or not, they must habandounne[2] their barkes[3] and galleys[4] to the wyndes and wawes[5] of the see, wherfor they were ful sore afrayed. The wynde and the see were so horryble to here and see that they wende[6] all to peryshe anoon.

3   They were full sone y-caste from the realme of Tourmaday, and the wynde brought them into a lytyl isle longyng[7] to the realme of Fryse, the whiche was fruytfull and right fayr and replenyshed wyth all maner of goodes. So that bycause of the grete commodytees[8] of that isle, Blanchardyns fader, kynge of Fryse, went for to sporte hym there thre or four tymes in the yere, that he shulde forgete therby the grete sorowe that was atte his herte for love of his sone Blanchardyn, of whom no tydynges he had syth his departynge from hym. And also for of the grete dysplesure that he had of the quene his wyffe, that suche a sorowe made for her entyerli beloved sone Blanchardin whiche she wyste not where he was becom, that nobody lyvyng myghte gyve her consolacion, nor brynge her herte oute of trystesse[9] and sorowe. And therfor the noble kynge, wyth a fewe of his folke, was come to the sayde isle for to dysporte[10] hym there and to dryve his fantassye[11] away, in the whiche isle he had do make a fayre paleyce ryghte delectable.[12]

4   Duryng [fol. 51v] the tyme that he was thus there, the sayd adventure happed that Daryus, the sone of Kynge Alymodes, wyth his grete navé, by fortune of the see arryved there, as it is sayde, even at that same haven that was most nyghe to the sayde paleys where the kynge of Fryse lay. Daryus, that of his beynge ther was soone advertysed, came anone wyth his puissaunce[13] of men to the paleys where they founde but litil resistaunce. Whan they were come there, they fonde there of the kynge of Fryses servauntes, to whom they asked to whom belongeth that paleys and how the lande was called. The sayd thre men ansuered them wyth grete fere that the paleyce and the ysle was bylongyng unto the kynge of Fryse that was come there thre dayes afore that. "Frendes," sayde Daryus, "what lawe[14] is there kept amonge you in this lande?" "Syre," sayde one of hem, "we holden on the Crysten feyth and are bylevyng in Jhesu Cryste." Thenne Daryus, knowyng that he was fortunatly arryved upon the Crysten peple enmye of his lawe, commaunded that they sholde be all slayne and brought to deth, the whiche thynge was putte to execucyon after his commaundement, except upon one of hem that escaped, that dyde soo moche that

---

[2] *abandon (surrender control)*
[3] *boats*
[4] *seagoing vessels with sails and oars*
[5] *waves*
[6] *thought*
[7] *belonging*
[8] *resources*
[9] *sadness*
[10] *entertain*
[11] *brooding (musing)*
[12] *delightful (pleasing to the senses)*
[13] *military might (strength)*
[14] *faith*

he went and entred into the paleys thurghe the wykettes[15] of the gate that of a custume were alleways lefte open. And whan he was come wythynne, he made a scrye[16] and called alowde after the watche, so that every man cam forth for to doo his devoyre,[17] eche of hem in his rowme[18] in defending the place after their powere. And whan he was come as ferre as the halle wythin the paleys, he byganne to reforce his callynge, cryinge wyth a hyghe voyce sainge that they were al lost and that the Sarrasyns were descended from their shippes byfore the paleyce in grete nombre. Thenne rose and cam they of wythin out of all partyes of the place armed and arrayed [fol. 52r] as haste requyred and no bettre.

5   Soone was the tydynges herof brought to the kynge, that at that owre was at his rest and slept fast as a man that doubted hymself of noo suche adventure to befalle. He awoke out of his slepe thurghe the pyteouse crye that of his men was made; notwythstandyng, he made hymself redy and made a goode ordynaunce as a prynce of hyghe corage and grete vertue, for in all poyntes he was a right valyaunt and a hardy prynce, but over sodanly he was taken. Neverthelesse, full nobly lyke a man of grete corage, he admonested[19] his folke and trowed to have goon to the yate of his palayce, the whiche was allredy wonne and taken and Daryus and his folke were entred inne. The kynge of Fryse, seynge his paleys wonne, a grete sorowe toke hym at his herte of that he was so taken unbeware,[20] and anone hastely he and his folke went and sought wythin the place where they myght save hymself best. But over sore oppressed they were, and of so nyghe chassed that never one of them escaped but he was taken or ded. The kynge was taken and seasid,[21] the handes y-bounde, and the eyen y-blynded,[22] and sent into the shippes by Daryus, and lykewyse was doon of all his barons that were there. After that this grete myshap was thus falle to the kynge of Fryse, Daryus and his folke serched the paleys. They robbed alle the richesses and goodes that were therinne, and were al brought into Daryus shippes.

6   Thees pytoyable[23] thynges thus y-happed, they made their horses to be had out of their shippes and anone over-ranne all the ysle and wasted and dystroyed all the countrey and slewe men, wymen, and children bothe yonge and olde. They toke and ravyshed alle the bestyall[24] as oxen, kene,[25] and shepe, wherof was wythout nombre, and had them into their shippes, whyche they [fol. 52v] charged wyth the praye[26] and gayne that they made there in the sayd isle. And syn they dyde putte the palayce all in afire and toke wyth them grete nombre of prysoners and entred ayen into their shyppes wyth grete joye and gladnes for the goode adventure that they had fonde. All thus in grete dyspleasure and

---

[15] *small door or gate in a fence*

[16] *shout*

[17] *duty (best effort)*

[18] *appointed area (particular place)*

[19] *exhorted*

[20] *unaware*

[21] *seized*

[22] *blindfolded*

[23] *pitiful*

[24] *livestock (beasts)*

[25] *cattle*

[26] *plunder (spoils)*

hevynes was taken that kyng of Frise and was broughte as a prisoner sore wepyng and sorowynge his byttirnesses. The poure, sorwfull kyng had his herte all replenished wyth sorowe and hevynes, of the whiche the nobel quene his wyff shall have parte whan thees pituable tydynges shall come to her eeris. For she toke in herself suche a sorow and so grete a displesure therfor, with that she sorowed before for the departynge of her dere sone Blanchardyn, that she was constrayned thorugh grete passion and bytternes of hert to falle in a swoune, for her legges nor feete myghte not bere her, and not wythoute a cause. And bycamme so sore febil and so full of sorowe that, atte the laste, what for her sone Blanchardyn as for the love of her goode husbonde and her lorde, she toke suche a sekenes that her soule departed from the body of her. And thus the noble ladye and goode quene of Fryse ended her dayes in hevynes and sorowe for the love of her lorde that she so myserably has loste.

The thirty first chapiture conteyneth howe Daryus arryved into the ooste of kynge Alymodes his fader, wher he was receyvyd wyth grete joye for love of the vitaylles that he broughte unto them there.

1   Whan Daryus entred ayen in his ship, he thanked moche his goddes of adventure and goode fortune the was happed to hym. He made the ancres to be drawen up and the sayles to be haled[1] alofte. The wynde and the see were apeased and a softe wynde goode for them bygonne to ryse oute of [fol. 53r] the west that droef forth their shypes there as they wolde, and wythoute lettyng arryved on the therde daye byfore the cytye of Tourmaday whereas the oost of Kyng Alymodes was lodged. They cast their ancres and ful sone they were knowen of Kynge Alymodes, that hastly cam wyth hys barons toward the haven for to welcom Daryus, his sone, whiche was com a-lande and fonde his fader that wyth grete joye and gladnes receyved, askyng of hym how he had doon syn his partyng from hym. Daryus al alonge recounted to hym how by fortune of the see they arryved and entred into an isle of the see whiche was Crysten, where they dyde fynde a kyng ryght puyssaunt, whiche he had broughte wyth hym prysoner. And also tolde hym how he had dystroyed the sayd isle and brente the paleys that was there, and had brought wyth them a grete praye and vytayll ynough, as wyne[2] and corne,[3] sheepe and oxen for to susteyn his ooste the space of thre monthes and more. Wherof Kyng Alymodes and they of his oost were oute of mesure glad. But and yf God wol kepe the goode provost of Tourmaday, he shall have, or thys two days be paste, his parte of the sayd praye, wherof the joye shal be renewed emonge the knyghtes and pepyll of Tourmaday, that grete scarcenes had of fleshe and of other vytaylle.

2   After that Daryus had thus recounted to his fader his adventure that to hym was of late happed, they two both togyder cam toward theire tentes talkyng of many thynges. Daryus demaunded of his fader how they of the cytye dyd and yf hit was longe agoo that they made eny yssue[4] oute of their toun. Alimodes aunsuerd to hym and sayd that

---

[1] *hauled*

[2] *wine*

[3] *grain*

[4] *sortie (assault)*

it was more than a monthe ago that they never made noo yssue wherof men sholde take eny hede, and that he thought wele that grete defaulte of vytaylles they had wythin. "And that they were [fol. 53v] made full symple⁵ syth that the yonge knyght was taken, whiche I betok you for to be brought unto the kynge of Salamandrye." "Syre," sayde Daryus, "I have doon of hym as ye commaunded me, but never syth that they parted from me I have herde noo tydynges of hem nor of hym nor of thre score men of myne owne that I dyde sende for to make present of the knyght Crysten, wherof I have gyven me full ofte grete merveylle." They thenne seased their wordes. He was al nyght wyth his fader Alymodes, unto the morowe that Daryus made hymself redy by the ordonnaunce of his fader for to retourne in his cyté of Cassydonye. Ryght grete joye and gladnes made they of the oost, for they made no doubte at all of their enmyes. Daryus, after the feste and joyouse talkyng that he had wyth his fader and wyth his barons, he toke his leve for to retourne and take his shippynge. The kynge and the barons dyde conveye hym unto the ship where he entred ynne, comaundyng hym in the kepyng and protection of all their godes.⁶ The maronners bygan to saylle and seaced never tyl that he camen into the havone of Cassydonye where he was receyved wyth grete joye.

---

⁵ destitute (feeble)
⁶ gods

The thirty second chapitre conteyneth how the goode provost yssued out of Tourmadaye and cam to fet¹ bestyall that Daryus had brought in the oost whiche was brought into the cyté wyth grete joye.

1   Evyn at the same owre that Daryus toke shippyng upon the see, and that his fader the kynge Alymodes and a grete parte of his barons were goon to conveye hym, and were there tyll he was departed from the haven and ferre fro the cleves,² the provost of Tourmadaye and many other barons of the cyté were upon the walles beholdynge the manere and the governauns of them of the oost. [fol. 54r] And were alredy advertysed of a spye howe that, the daye byfore, Darius, the sone of Kyng Alymodes, was arryved in the oost and had broughte wyth hym grete plenté of vytayles, and that he retorned into his countree and toke the see that same daye. And wyth this they sawe the grete nombre of bestes that toke their pasture in a grete medowe not ferre thens, and that noo body kept hem, for they went³ to have be sure though all the ooste, bycause that they of the cyté had not made longe tyme afore that no manere of entrepryse nor dyde not come out of their towne. And also that the custume of them of wythin was that they never made non yssue⁴ but it were in the mornyng or at evyn. And for this cause, the provost, that thought upon the same, delybered⁵ in hymself consideryng that whiche he sawe at eye: how all the oost was styll and that Kyng Alymodes, nor his barons, nor his princypal capitaynes were not

---

¹ fetch (bring)
² cliffs
³ thought
⁴ exit (go out)
⁵ reflected

comen yet from the seesyde, where they were all gon for to conveye and see Daryus take his shippynge.

2   Of that other part, he sawe also afore hym nyghe by the walles of the towne the grete multytude of bestes that were wythout kepynge, whiche was the thynge wherof they had most nede wythin the cyté. He, seeng and consyderyng this that he sawe at his eye, descended hastely from the walles and dyde calle to hym al the capitaynes, barons, knyghtes, and noblemen, whiche he made to come byfore theyr lady the proude pucell in amours. And byfore her he declared unto them all his purpos and what he entended for to doo. Whan the lady wyth her barons had well understande the provost, they all in generall accorded wyth him for to putte to execucion the wordes afore spoken. And for to do the same they went prevely[6] and armed themself. And whan they were redy, they fonde six thousand of [fol. 54v] hem all a-horsebak the whiche were conducte by the provost, and another of the capitayns had the charge of the foure thousand archers fotemen,[7] whiche yssued oute at a posterne[8] that was nyghe the see and lepte anon into the medowe where the sayd bestes were fedyng.

3   And of that other partye, the provost and his felauship wente oute of the gate whereas they were wonte to goo oute whan they made their issues. Whan the capitayne of fotemen was wele advertysed and that he wyste the provost to be come oute of the toun, he made his folke to vaunce hemself forth softly[9] and by order alonge by the toune dyches[10] whiche were drye at that syde of the toun, and so made them to walke al under coverte[11] unto the seesyde all along the dyches, tyl that they cam and saw the bestes that wythoute eny kepyng were enclosed wythin a maner[12] of a parke. And after they had putte hemself betwyx the bestes and the oost, they taryed and herkened there after there men on horsbacke, the whiche they herde full sone makyng their cryes in their enmyes tentes whereas they foughte wyth hem. The fotemen thenne entred wythin the close[13] medowe where the bestes were pasturyng, whiche they brought all togydre on a flok and byganne to chasse them afore hem to the towneward, where they brought inne bothe oxen, kyen,[14] and sheep wyth all other manere of bestyall that was there. Wherof the peple of the cyté was gretly rejoiced and syth cam and put hymself[15] byfore the yate of the towne in fayre ordennaunce, awaytyng that the provost and his folke sholde tourne ayen whiche were wythin their enmyes tentes and pavyllions, whiche they powlyd[16] and brought doune, and slewe many of their enmyes or ever that Kynge Alymodes nor his folke coude be garnysshed of their armures. And whan the provost sawe that it was tyme for to departe, and

---

[6] secretly (privately)

[7] infantry (foot soldiers)

[8] back door (secret passageway)

[9] quietly

[10] ditches (moat)

[11] cover

[12] kind (type)

[13] enclosed

[14] cattle

[15] themselves

[16] pulled

that the [fol. 55r] bestes myght well be brought into the cyté by that tyme, he made his trompette to be sowned that every man shold withdraw hymself. And so cam ayen wythin the cyté wythout eny losse of his men, to their grete glorye and praysynge, and grete confusion to theyr enmyes to whom they had born so grete domage that never byfore that they had receyved suche. Wherby the kynge Alymodes and alle his oost was right sore affrayed and in grete hevynes of the grete losse that they had susteyned by the sayd provost and his folke. And also of that other part, whan they knewe how alle their bestes were had aweye fro the medowe and brought into the towne, their sorowe redoubled them full sore.

4 The provost, that lytyl dyde care[17] therfore, hymself and all his folke bothe a-fote and a horsback, in gyvyng thankes and graces unto our Lord entred agayne into the cyté wyth grete gladnes and joye, where they were ful curtoysly receyved of their lady that graciously thanked theym. The cyté of Tourmaday was purveyed of vytaylles of the same for a hole yere, and their enmyes oost sore dysgarnyshed therby, wherfor they made emonge hemself grete sorowe. But whatsoever joye and gladnes that they made wythin the towne, the fayr pucelle and proude in amours myght not seasse[18] nor leve her sorowe therfore that she contynually made for her right dere frende Blanchardyn, that for the love of her she trowed that he had other be lost or ded and wyst not what she sholde thynke therof. But sawe wel that, yf by proces of tyme[19] she had som socours, that force sholde be to her to yelde up and deliver her cyté unto Kynge Alymodes, but rather she wolde deye than she sholde see suche a sorowe to befalle to her. And for to see a remedy to the same, she dyde sende for the provost to whome she sayde thus, "Provoste, oure cyté is nowe garnyshed, thanked be [fol. 55v] oure Lorde, both of vytaylles and of artyllerye for a grete space of tyme, and wyth this for the defence of the same, hit ys wele and suffysaunly furnyshed of goode knyghtes and of goode souldyors[20] grete foyson. Wherfore ryght instantly I praye you that ye doo make redy a galleye, and I shal furnysshe her welle wyth vytaylles and wyth goode artylerye for the defence of yourself and of them that shall be wyth you, and ye shal goo as myn ambassatour toward myn uncle, the kyng of Grete Norweyghe, to whom ye shall declare and shewe in my behalf the estate[21] where presently I am inne, prayeng hym in my behalf that now, atte my grete nede, he wolde sende me folke for to helpe and socoure me, or els that mysylf and my royalme are in wey of perdycion."[22] "Madame," sayde the provost, "wyte ye for certeyn that, to the pleasure of our Lorde, I shall doo therin my best wyth all deligence unto me possyble. And I hope I shall brynge you good tydynges and suche a socours that shal not be pleysaunt unto Alymodes the false kyng." The provost, after many other devyses, toke his leve of the pucel and cam to hys hous. He made a galee to be dressyd wyth all her apereylle,[23] and whan all his thynges

---

[17] lytyl dyde care therfore, *cared little for (the sorrow of Alymodes)*

[18] *cease*

[19] proces of tyme, *passage of time*

[20] *soldiers*

[21] *circumstances (status)*

[22] *great harm (destruction)*

[23] *equipment*

was redy and preste, he went oute of a posterne pryvely wyth suche as he wolde take in his companye toward the seesyde, and entred his ship so prevely in the mornyng that none of his enmyes coude see hym tyl that they were gon awaye from the lande and wythoute fere of them.

5   Whan Kyng Alymodes knew the same, he wexed[24] sore angry and wroth,[25] but no remedy he myght not put therto, for or ever he was advertysed therof, the provost and his felauship were almost oute of syght. Well he had wold that they myght be met wythall by Daryus his sone, but he[26] oughte not to care for it,[27] for Daryus and hys navey helde their waye toward Cassydonye wher they arryved in fewe dayes [fol. 56r] wythout eny fortune. And the provost saylled and rowed toward the costes of Nourthweghe. Whan Daryus was come to lande into the haven of Cassydonye, where he arryved wythin short tyme wythout ony fortune, as it is sayd, he made the kynge of Fryse and other his prysoners to be had out from the shippes into a grete and strong toure whereas was a tenebrouse[28] and derke dongeon, wherin the poure sorowfull kynge, replenysshed and sore beten wyth the flayel[29] of fortune, was cast in pryson there to consume his olde dayes ful myserably, unto the tyme that by his right wel beloved sone Blanchardyn he be had out from this grete poverté and myserye. So shal we leve hym thus makyng his sorowfull complayntes tyl that tyme befor to speke of hym, and shal retourne to speke of his sone the goode yonge knyght Blanchardyn, whiche we have left wythin the paleys of Maryenborugh wyth Sadoyne.

---

[24] *grew*
[25] *wrathful*
[26] *the provost*
[27] oughte not to care for it, *need not have worried about it*
[28] *gloomy (dark)*
[29] *whip (flail)*

The thirty third chapyter conteyneth how Blanchardyn made pyteouse complayntes for his lady wythin a gardyne, and of the grete recomforte that was made to hym of Sadoyne.

1   Ye have all ynoughe understande here afore how Blanchardyn had the goode grace of the kynge of Prusse, of Sadoyne his sone, and the love of all the barons of the sayde royalme. And how he had reffused the kynges cosyne for to have her in maryage, but the grete love and fydelyté that he had toward his lady the proude pucelle in amours kept hym there fro. For rather he wold have deyed than to have falsed his feyth ayenst her for whome he had at herte so many a sorowful and hevy thought for to bere. For nother nyght nor daye he dyde non other thinge but thynke how and what manere he myght departe out of the contrey where he was inne for to go to gyve socoure unto the proude pucell [fol. 56v] in amours, his fayre love, that was his soverayn desyre and his right besy and contynually thoughte. Wherof it happed upon a daye amonge other, as Blanchardyn was entred in a gardyne wythin the kynges paleys alone, wythout eny feliship, for to complayne the better his hertes sorowes that in beholdyng upon the fayre flouris wherof nature had fayre appareylled the gardyne. And amonge other he sawe a rosier tree laden wyth many a fayr rose that had a smel ful swete, emonge whiche one was

ther that of flagraunt odoure and of beaulté passed all the other. Wherfore upon her he dyde arrest[1] his eyen and said in this maner, "Ha, noble rose, preelect[2] and chosen byfore all other flouris that ben about thee, howbeit they be right fayre. Thou puttest into my remembraunce, thurgh the fayrnes that I see in thee, the right parfyt and excellent beaulté of myn owne goode lady, the proude mayden in amours, whom God gyve all that whiche her noble herte wysheth and desyreth. I am so ferre from her that advyse it is to me,[3] and also I byleve the same, that I never shal see her nomore. I can not curse too moche myn unfortune that hath brought me, whiche was come to have the goode grace of the most parfyt creature that God and nature wythout comparison wold ever make, into the grete sorowes where I am now inne. Now most I be ferre from her; wolde God now that ye, myn owne swete lady, wyst that I am alive and how goode a wyll I have to socoure you yf it were to me possible." And in proferryng this wordes, the teeris fel grete from his eyen in grete haboundaunce without ceasse.

2   Sadoyne, that coude not dure[4] nor be without Blanchardyn, went him seking in al the place so longe that, at the last, he cam and sawe hym wythin the gardyne, and cam there as he was or ever Blanchardyn was aware of hym. He fonde him, the terres at the eyes of hym, makynge his full pituouse complayntes, the whiche Sadoyne had herde a part of [fol. 57r] hem. He cam and set hymself doun besyde Blanchardyn and prayed hym that he wolde telle him the cause of his sorowe and grete lamentacion, promyttyng to hym that it sholde never be told nor knowen by him. And saide unto him, "My right trusty felawe, ye do sobbe and make grete sorowe, wherfor I true[5] and thinke for veray trouth, that it is love that so ledes you." "Certes, Sadoyne," sayde Blanchardyn, "ye may byleve well for certayn that the god of love werreth ayenst me right sore to holde and kepe me here in this contrey. And to myn advyse, yf he wolde be content wyth reason, he sholde suffre that som worde were brought here to me to the comforte of one parte of my grete sorowe, from her for whos sake they be sore grounded wythin my penseful herte. I loke styl over the mountaynes and valeye als ferre as my sight can comprehende, but alas, I can not chuse nor see the toure wherynne she holdeth herself." "O my right trusty frende and dere felawe," sayde Sadoyne, "is it the toure of Babylonye where she doth holde her, or of Rome, of Spayne, or of Almanye?"[6] "Certes," sayde Blanchardyn, "it is not so ferre as ye wene, but syth that ye desyre so sore to knowe myn angwyshe and sorowe I shall telle you what is me befal. I am a servaunt reteyned wyth the lady of Tourmaday that is called of every man the proude mayden in amours. She is beseged wythin her cyté by Kynge Alymodes, a cruel tyraunt kynge of Cassydonye that hath had me as his prysoner here before, but by fortune of the see and the goode adventure, thanked be oure Lord I am escaped. He wold have, by strengthe and puyssaunce, to his spouse my sayd lady, but

---

[1]   rest *(pause)*

[2]   chosen before

[3]   advyse it is to me, *in my opinion (judgment)*

[4]   endure *(survive)*

[5]   believe

[6]   Germany

bycause that she wil not have him tyl her lord, he hath purposed to kepe his power[7] men of werre byfore her cyté of Tourmaday unto tyme that he have her at his wylle." After the wordes the teeres ranne doune from his eyen.

3   And whan Sadoyne sawe his true and feythfull felawe Blanchardyn make suche a sorowe, his herte bygan to quake wythin hymself [fol. 57v] for pyté that he had of Blanchardyn. And sayde thus unto hym, "Certaynly, dere felawe myne, yf ye wol do after me, we shal go wyth all pouer and myght to helpe and socoure your lady for whos love ye take suche a sorowe, and shal delyvere her from Kynge Alymodes handes." Blanchardyn, thenne beholdyng ful pyteously upon his felawe Sadoyne, sayde unto hym, "O the right grete recomforte of my sorowful lyf, wolde God it were so as ye saye, for the kyng Alymodes hath a doughter of his owne whiche is so fayr that God and nature can not amende her, nor in no lande can be choson no fayrer. Certaynly, yf we coude bringe this werke at an ende, she sholde be yours wythout faylle." "My frende dere," sayde Sadoyne, "it lieth in the wylle of the goddes. We have goode men of werre ynough for to furnysshe this enterpryse, whiche I sore do desyre for to gyve helpe to youre sorowes. I wyll go toward the kynge my fader for to have leve for you and for me." Whether Blanchardyn of this tydynge was glad, it is not to be asked.

---

[7] *strong*

The thirty fourth chapter conteyneth how Sadoyne toke leve of his fader the kyng and so dyde Blanchardyn and toke the see wyth a grete navé charged wyth men of were[1] for to go gyve socoure to the proude pucelle in amours, and of the provost of Tourmaday whiche they founde by the waye.

1   After many wordes proferred and sayde betwene the two yonge knyghtes, Sadoyne departed and cam tofore the kynge his fader. To whome, in the best wyse that he myght or coude, dyde shewe unto him his wyll, requiring of him that it myght be accomplisshed, shewyng unto him how that his royalme was in peas and tranquilité that tyme and that it was not lyke that werre shold happe there to befal. And bycause he was a yonge man, he wolde yet faine[2] excercyse himself in the noble crafte of armes, and that a lawfull and juste cause he had [fol. 58r] to do soo, for to gyve socoure and helpe the yonge knyght straunger, "that thourgh his prouesse[3] and grete worthynes hathe socoured you, and holpen[4] to putte out your mortall enmyes that were ferre come wythin this your royalme, and hath brought into your handes as prysonner your enmye, the kynge of Polonye, for to do your owne wylle upon hym, of the whiche good servyse he ought of rayson to be well rewarded." Whan the kynge of Prusse understode his son, he gaf to hymself grete marveylle and was wel abashed of that soudayne a wylle that was come to him. Nevertheles, whan he knewe and that he was advertysd by his son al alonge[5] of the cause and quarelle

---

[1] *war*
[2] *eagerly*
[3] *prowess (martial valor)*
[4] *helped*
[5] *fully*

of Blanchardyn, he was al ynough content and graunted hym his request. Wherof his son and eke[6] Blanchardyn cam and fel bothe doune humbly at the fote of hym and thanked him of that grete curtosye.

2   And for to see and furnysshe that this were doon, the kynge dyde make redy suche shippes as apparteyned[7] therunto and made them to be garnished well of vytaylles and of artyllery nedeful to suche an enterpryse. Upon whiche navye he sent wyth his son and wyth Blanchardyn the nombre of twelve thousand knyghtes of the most approved[8] and best chosen of al his royalme, and other men of werre in grete nombre. Al their arraye was made redy and the daye come that they sholde departe. The kynge, seenge the barkes and shippes of his sone to be furnysshed of men of werre and of vytaylles, of golde and sylver, and of alle thynge that were necessary to them, he was therof right glad. And syth dyde doo putte wyth the shippes foure ydoles his goddes that were all of fyne golde and garnyshed full richelly wyth grete perles and precyouse stones. And after this he entred hymself wythin the ship and toke his leve of his sone [fol. 58v] Sadoyne, prayng unto Blanchardyn that he shold have him for recomended, and toke his leve of them. Whan the kynge was come out of the ship where he had lefte his sone Sadoyne wyth Blanchardyn, he beganne to wepe. And after that he was gon from hem, they made to take up the ancres[9] and to hale[10] up their sayles wher in the wynde entred that had them soone ferre from the lande out of syght and toke the hyghe see as sone as they myght, sayllyng by the costes of many a strange regyon wythout fyndyng of eny adventure that is to be recounted.

3   And so longe they saylled bothe daye and nyght that they cam nyghe Tourmaday as two dayes journay, byfore whiche cyté was yet Kyng Alymodes at siege wyth his oost, wherof the fayr the proude pucell in amours was sore dispeysaunt.[11] And in especyall she was sore discomfited[12] at her herte for the love of her frende Blanchardyn that was the same tyme wyth his felawe Sadoyne sayllyng upon the see in grete gladnesse for the wynde and the see that were peasible. And saylled so longe that they perceyved a galeye from ferre that made fast waye ther as they went hemself, in whiche vessell was the provost of Tourmadaye and other servauntes to the proude pucelle in amours. And cam ayen from the oncle, the kyng of the Grete Norweghe, whiche they fonde but late ded[13] whan they cam there, where they retourned wythout expedicyon[14] of that wherfore they were goon thyder. Whan the provost and they of the galeye dyde perceyve the shippes of Blanchardyn, they were full sore affrayed bycause they knewe well anoon that they were all Sarrasyns.

---

[6] also

[7] pertained (were appropriate)

[8] tested (experienced)

[9] anchors

[10] haul

[11] displeased (unhappy)

[12] dejected

[13] but late ded, had recently died

[14] successful completion

4   And of that other parte, Blanchardyn and Sadoyne perceyved sone that they of the galleye were Crysten. They made anon after the sayd galleye for to enclose and take her, and whan they cam nyghe by her they called and asked of [fol. 59r] whens was the vessell, what they were and fro whens they came. And thenne the provost, wyth a grete drede and feer of his lyfe, lept forthe and sayde, "Lordes, we see wel that we can not escape you, but for drede of noo deth I shal not leve to tell unto you the trouth of all oure affayre. We all that be here come from the Grete Northweghe and were sent toward the kynge of the lande whiche was oncle to the proude mayden in love, whiche is oure lady and maystresse."

5   Blanchardyn right joyouse knewe ful sone the provost and thought that sone ynought[15] he sholde here of hym som goode tydynges of that thynge whiche he most desyred in this worlde. But the provost knewe not Blanchardyn the same tyme bycause he was made blak, disfygured, and sore chaunged of face by strengthe of the sonne, but trowed that he had ben a Sarrasyne as other were. Thenne cam Blanchardyn nyghe the bordours[16] of the galley and toke the provoste by the hand and made hym to come wythin his ship. Of dyverses thynges he questyoned hym, but the provost ansuered ferfully for he doubted them sore. So prayed he to Blanchardyn after he had exposed unto hym of whens he cam and what he was, that he wolde doo them no harme. Blanchardyn right humbly aysured hym and sayde, "Frende, take no feere at all, for nother damage nor evyl shal not be don to you nor to non of yours, for I shal myself conveye you yf nede be." The provost thanketh hym moche and was right glad. "Sir," sayde Blanchardyn to the provost, "ye have tolde me that ye be of the cité of Tourmaday. I praye you that ye wyl telle me in what regyon and what marche it is sette and who is lord there. I praye you telle me the trouth of it."

6   The provost thenne seeng that feabli[17] he myght speke without doubte or feer, he dyde reherce unto Blanchardyn al alonge how the royalme of Tourmaday was come to a doughter [fol. 59v] full fayre and goode that made herself to be called the proude pucelle in amours, that never wolde wedde kynge, duc, nor erle, how grete that he were, and that for the love of a gentyl[18] knyght that not longe agoo cam and socoured her in her werre that she had and yet hath ayenst the kynge Alymodes that wolde have her to his wyff. "But sire," sayde the provost, "by grete infortune, the worthy knyght wherof I do speke to you and the most valyaunt and most fayre that ever man myght or coude seke noowher in all the worlde, was taken of Kynge Alymodes folke byfore the cyté of Tourmaday. Whiche kynge hath sent hym into exile in ferre landes that none can not knowe where. But that men saye that of hym sholde be made a present to a kynge Sarrasyne whos brother the sayd knyght had slayen. Wherfor my sayd lady is in grete displaysure and ceaseth not nyght nor day to wysshe hym wyth her, prayng God for his retourne agayne. The sayd Kynge Alymodes is alwaye kepynge his siege byfore her cyté of Tourmaday and wasteth and distroyeth al the contrey about, for other harme can he not do to her. The towne and the castel are strong ynoghe and are vytayled alle ynough so that or ever he coude have

---

[15] enough
[16] sides (edges)
[17] in a whisper (weakly)
[18] courteous of high rank

them, my sayde lady sholde be for aaged."[19] Blanchardyn herde wel gladly the provost, and sayde to Sadoyne his felowe in his ere that of his lady in amours thees wordes were sayde. Sadoyne dyde here hem gladly and the devyses wyth Blanchardyn to the said provost of many thynges concernyng this matyre. And Blanchardyn coude understande noo thynge by the provost but that all was at his avantage, wherby he knewe that he was in his ladys grace as well as he was ever afore.

7   The provost thenne, seeng soo many fayre men of armes, he pryvely[20] demaunded of Blanchardyn yff [fol. 60r] they wolde be souldyours of the fayre the proude mayden in amours ayenst the kyng Alymodes and they shold be right well payed.[21] Thenne ansuered to hym Blanchardyn and sayde, "I byleve al ynough well that yf she wolde make of one of us a kyng, she myght of lyght[22] be served of us and of oure men." "Syre," sayde the provost, "it is no nede to speke more herof, for she shal never take, I am well sure, non other man tyl her lord but that self[23] knyght of whom I spake right now to you of, nor non shal have her royalme of her but only hymself."

8   "How thenne," sayd Blanchardyn, "thynke ye that her love be so stedfastly and so truly sette upon hym that Kynge Alimodes hath sent to be presented as ye saye? Is it your advyse that, yf of adventure he cam ayen to her, that she wolde sette ought by hym? For it is sayde of a custume[24] that the herte of a woman is mutable and inconstaunt and not in purpos stedfast." "Ha ha, sire," sayde the provoste, "pleysed God that he myght come to her ayen. Never happed so goode a daye to the contrey, nor to hym also, for he shold renewe manyfold the goode grace of her that so truli loveth hym." "Frende," sayde Blanchardyn, "I praye you telle me the name of the knyght of whom ye doo speke so moche." "Sir," sayde the provost, "the knyght of whom my sayde lady is so sore enamored upon hath to his name Blanchardyn. Ye may well be sure that she shal never forgete hym nor sette her herte from hym, though she were insured never to see hym, for she wol not here nother prayer nor requeste of no man in this world, al be he never so grete a kyng or prince. She dremeth often that her frende Blanchardyn cometh ayen and that they enbrace and kysse eche other in reconpence of the right evyl tyme in whiche they have be longe in grete displaisure one from another. And for to telle you the troughi[25] of it, it [fol. 60v] were not possyble to love more tenderly nor more truly than she doth hym. So oughte wel the said knyght to have her ryght dere yf he lyve yet." "Frende," sayd Blanchardyn "I doute not but he doth so, and advyse is to me that wyth al dilygence he shold himsilf come to socoure her at her nede after his power, yf he applye him is to do soo."

---

[19] *very aged*

[20] *privately*

[21] *pleased*

[22] of lyght, *quickly*

[23] *same*

[24] of a custome, *traditionally*

[25] *truth*

The thirty fifth chapter speketh of the grete devyses of the provost and of Blanchardyn and of the lettres that he sent to his lady the proude pucell in amours, and of the joye that she made whan she had red them.

1 Affter all the devyses above sayd, Blanchardyn drew hymsylf aside wythin his vessell and toke both ynke and paper and wrote a letter with his owne hande unto the fayer proude mayden in love, whiche lettres he toke[1] to the provost for to be presented unto his lady. The provoste toke them, promyttyng to do therwyth his devoyr.[2] And thenne Blanchardyn sayd unto the provoste, "Frende, all these shyppes and the armye that is herin are Sarasyns[3] and I am a paynem, and ful well I knowe Blanchardyn, wyche is enprysoned in paynems land where he suffreth grete evyls and grete sorowe. But so moche do I knowe of his doynge that he doth not care so moche for all that, as he doth of that he knoweth wel, that the proude pucell in amours is for his sake sore greved atte her hert." "Syr," sayd the provoste, "I praye to our Lorde that the knyght, for whos love my said lady taketh suche an hevynes atte herte more than I can tell you, maye retorne ayen wythin shorte tyme, for the pytyuoes complayntes that she daily maketh for her lover maketh us al to lyve in grete dyscomforte."

2 After dyverse talkynke don by Blanchardyn and the provost, they sepayred[4] hemsylf and toke leve of eche other. So went the provost and entred ayen into his galee holdyng [fol. 61r] goode fortune and a goode wynde, wherby wythin a whyle he was ferre a-fore the shyp where Blanchardyn was inne. And so sore exployted[5] wyth sayles and oores that at the ende of thre dayes he arryved wythin the haven of Tourmaday wyth his felyshyp, wythoute eny lette[6] were don to them. But a lytyl afore they had be ryght sore afrayed leste they shold be recountred by Kynge Alymodes folke, howbeyt that there was no ship that waye that coude have hurte theym. Notwythstandyng this, there were smal rennyng vesseles that oftymes dyspoyled and robbed theym that cam to the sayd haven of Tourmaday, as well by lande as upon the see.

3 Whan the provost was arryved, or ever he went in his owne hous nor noowhere, he and all his felyship went into our Ladyes chirche of Tourmaday for to yelde unto her thankes and praysynges of the goode adventure that was com to hym, they made theyr offrynges and syn departed. Ye may wele thynke that the provost was that tyme full well accompanyed of the barons, nobyl men, and bourgeys[7] of the sayd cyté for the grete love that they had unto hym and also that he was worthy therof. And thus accompanyed he cam into the paleys, where he fonde the proude pucell in amours that welcomed hym and made hym grete chere and was ryght glad of his commynge ayen.

4 And then the pucell asked hym tydynges of the kynge her uncle and how he had exployted and furnyshed her message. "Madame," sayd the provost, "I have ben in the

---

[1] *gave (entrusted)*

[2] *duty (best effort)*

[3] *Muslims*

[4] *separated*

[5] *hurried*

[6] *delay (hinderance)*

[7] *burgesses (town officials)*

Grete Norweyghe, wenyng to fynde ther the kynge your uncle, but thre dayes byfore my comyng thyder it pleased God that your uncle the kyng termyned[8] his lyff by deth that then toke hym. Wherby the barons of the realme ben in grete troubyl and have noo recomforte but in you, that are theyr lady by verey successyon as heyre[9] of the land most nexte parent.[10] Wherfore [fol. 61v] they sende worde to you by me that after the obsequyes[11] and fyneralles of your sayd uncle be doon, they shall approche puttyng theymself in ordynaunce for to helpe and socoure you as they ought for to do to their natural[12] lady and soverayn pryncès." Whan the nobyl mayden herde and understode the provost, she began to make grete sorowe, but the provost sayde unto her for to recomforte her, "Madame, ther nys so grete sorowe but that it may be forgoton at the laste, and afterwarde cometh som other message that is cause to rejoyse and brynge the creatures into consolacion. I saye this therfor, that after the pyteous tydynges that I have brought unto you of your uncles deth, I shall now telle you one thynge that of reason ought to please you well. Loke, here is a letter that a paynem knyght hath taken to me, whiche ful sore prayed me that I shulde dyrecte them unto you." The lady that wepte ryght sore toke the letter and red yt, wherof the tenore[13] was suche as foloweth.

5   "My ryght redoubted lady, the supportans[14] of my poure lyff, the gladnes of the hert of me and the thynge whiche in this worlde I most desyre, I me recomende ryght humbly unto your good grace. After the harde fortune that I had to be prysoner unto Kynge Alymodes, God my swete creatour, whom I yelde praysynges and lovynge, hath long preserved and kept me from deth and hath delyverd me from the peryles of the see, wherof I all alone am escaped. But myn enmyes that led me forth wyth them were all drowned and peryshed in the see, and not one that escaped alyve sauf myself alonely, to whom our Lord hath don thys grace, wherof I ought wel to joye myself in yevyng[15] unto hym thankes and praysynges evermore. After thys fortune I have ben syn, as force[16] compellyd me therto, servaunt unto a kynge Sarasyn as I had ben one of theym. Fro the whiche kyng, [fol. 62r] to myn worship and wyth grete love, I am departed, and hath taken me in my kepyng his sone and twelve thousand knyghtis right expert in armes, and other souldyours in grete nombre, for to come and socoure you and to take vengeaunce upon Kynge Alymodes the tyraunt. That was the thynge that most I dyde desyre in this world as of reason my dutye was. And to the surplus to the playsure of oure Lorde and hym playsed, ye shal understande by mouthe ferthere of myn astate.[17] And bycause ye shall gyve credence and feyth to this myn owne handewrytyng, I do now bringe to your remembrance that one onely kyssyng that I toke of yow not ferre wythout youre cyté of Tourmaday, afore that I was of

---

[8] ended

[9] heir

[10] apparent (in line of descent)

[11] funeral rites

[12] hereditary (by birth)

[13] contents

[14] support (spiritual help)

[15] giving

[16] necessity

[17] condition (estate)

you reteyned into youre noble servyse. My right redoubted lady, I praye to God to gyve you the complyshement of your noble desyres. Wryton upon the see by the hande of the knyght infortunate, thus signed Blanchardyn."

The thirty sixth chapter conteyneth and speketh of the joye that the proude pucelle in amours made for love of the commyng of her specyall frende Blanchardyn, and of the grete sorowe that she made anone after whan she see that fortune so lyghtly had hym and his navye ayen into the see ferre from the haven of Tourmaday.

1 Whan the proude mayden in amours had red the saide lettres al alonge and wel understand the tenoure[1] therof, the joye was not lytyl that she made for the reception of the same. She demaunded of the provost yf he knewe not hym that had taken the letters unto hym. He sayde, "nay," but unto her he recounted and tolde the manere and how as by a happe[2] he had fonde and met wyth a myghty navey, "upon whiche was a right grete excercyte[3] of folke of armes, but they were alle [fol. 62v] Sarrasyns and had theyre byleve upon their ydolles, and emonge them all was one knyght that coude speke to me." "Ha ha, provost," sayde the lady, "well ye have be deceyved whan ye dyde not knowe hym that somtyme ye have lodged in your house wyth you. It was, I ensure you, my moost dere frende Blanchardyn, that at my grete nede cometh to socoure and helpe me. How thenne have ye not knowe hym, a grete merveylle I have therof." "Madame," sayd the provost, "as to the body of hym, he may be lykened[4] well ynough to Blanchardyn, but the face of hym was dyed and blake as all other of his felyship were. Moche grete merveylle I gyve to myself that he dyde not dyscovere hymself unto me." The pucelle, heryng the provost speke, beganne to smyle and lawhe[5] strongly. Full sone was forgoton her onclis deth for cause of the right joyfull tydynges that she had herd of Blanchardyn, the whiche were full soone knowen though all the cyté, whiche thynge brought a newe joye to alle the enhabytantes there. But whosomever made joye therof, the proude pucell in amours rejoysshed herself above all other bycause that this nyghed her at herte. All ynough she red and overed[6] the sayd letters whiche she dyde kysse full ofte, soo sore was her thoughte upon Blanchardyn.

2 The nyght passed and the fayr day cam, and erly in the mornyng the pucelle rose from her bed. And whan she was clothed and opened the wyndowe and loked ferre upon the see, yf evere, by adventure, she myght see ne chuse the navye of Blanchardyn. She behelde so longe on every syde that she byganne to chuse and perceyve the saylles of the shippes of hym that so sore moche she had desyred. She was thenne recomforted of all thynges and remembred herself of non evyll that she had suffred byfore that. An hundred tymes she salued[7] and made obeyssaunce[8] to the shippes, prayng to God that they may

---

[1] *meaning*

[2] *chance (happenstance)*

[3] *company of warriors*

[4] *compared*

[5] *laugh*

[6] *read over (pondered)*

[7] *saluted*

[8] *homage (reverence)*

arryve sauf and sounde. [fol. 63r] Atte that hour her maystres was beside her, whiche was ful glad to see her thus mery and ful of joye, to whom the lady sayd that sone she shuld have socours of thirty thousand knyghtes and souldyors that ayenst King Alymodes shold helpe her.

3   As she was thus talkyng wyth her maystres and that the vessayls beganne to com nyghe and made redy all thynges to take lande, a south wynd rose up sodanly horryble and gret. The see byganne to ryse and swelle, and the wawes wexed so bygge and so grete that they semed to be mountayns. And was the tempeste so perelouse that they were constreyned to enter into the brode see agayne leste they sholde have smytten hemself agrounde,[9] and so wythdrew hemsylf fro lande. They were so sore tourmentyd that the cordes[10] and the saylles breke of all their shyppes or of the most partye, and were fayne to cutte off their mastes, habandounnynge[11] to the wynde and wawes of the see the conducte[12] of them alle. And were caste so ferre into the hyghe see that, in a shorte whyle, they knewe not in what marche[13] of the see they were. The proude pucell in amours, seeng thys grete infortune, wende[14] to have deyd anone for the grete dysplleasure that she toke of thys cursed adventure and reputed herself indygne[15] to have eny helpe nor socours. Whan she see her fortune thus torned ayenst her, she began to crye aloude sayng in thys wyse, "Alas my ryght trusty and feythful lover, I perceyve well that I shall never see you more. I am the cause of your inconvenyent,[16] ye were taken in my servyse." She made so grete mone and so pytefull complayntes as anybody in thys worlde myghte doo, always dyscomfortyng[17] her owne self wythouten mesure.

4   We shall leve to speke of the proude pucell in amours unto the tyme be comen that her sorowe be lefte [fol. 63v] and her joye recovered and renewed, and shal shewe you of Blanchardyn and of Sadoyne, his feythful felawe.

---

[9] smytten hemself agrounde, *have driven themselves aground*
[10] *ropes*
[11] *abandoning*
[12] *direction (guidance)*
[13] *region*
[14] *thought*
[15] *unworthy*
[16] *misfortune (injury)*
[17] *berating*

The thirty seventh chapiter conteyneth how Blanchardyn and Sadoyne arryved byfore the cyté of Cassydonye wher they founde Daryus that cam to speke wyth them.

1   Well ye have herde here above the ryght merveyllouse and horrybyl fortune that happed to Blanchardyn and to Sadoyne that daye they shold have taken lande atte the haven of Tourmadaye, whiche were all redy caste ferre from all costes and waited but the hour when they shold be drowned, wherof they were in a grete fere. Then sayd Blanchardyn to Sadoyne that he doubted ryght sore lest God were wroth upon theym bycause they had brought wyth theym theys cursed ydolles, and that hym semed yf he wold be baptysed and all his folk, and to byleve in our feith, that the tempeste shold breke.

He preched so longe Sadoyn and his folke, that they all of one assent and accorde promytted unto Blanchardyn that they sholde devoutly do baptyse hemself and shold byleve in the holy Crysten feyth, whan they shold come to lande or in place where hit myght be doon. The whyche thynge evyn so as they promysed it full devoutly, they ded accomplyshe hit afterward. They toke awaye the preciouse stones and the gold and sylver from theyre ydolles and maumetys[1] and syn cast them in the see wyth goode herte. Soo taryed not long after thys was doon that the tempeste ceassed and the see became swete and amyable, and became as a lytyll ryver.

2   After the ceasse of thys tempest, that had broughte theym so ferre oute of theyre knowleche that they wyste not where they were, fortune ledde theym in atte the havon of Cassydonye, where Daryus, the sone of Kyng Alymodes, was that daye [fol. 64r] and the fayre Beatryx his suster wyth hym, whiche was uttyrly fayre and replenysshed of all goode condicyons and maners that may be in a creature. Blanchardyn and Sadoyne, seeyng that they were comen tyl a sure havene and they and their folke all sauf, they were right glad. They thanked our Lord and had doune their saylles, cast their ancres and syth lepte a-lande, and their men of armes wyth them, whiche they renged[2] and dyde set hem in gode ordonaunce of battaylle al alonge the medowes that were there full fayre and grete, bycause that they knewe not in what marche they were arryved nor whether they of the contrey were frendes or enmyes. Sadoyne wende at fyrst that it had be Tourmaday, but they fonde a man and asked hym the name of the towne and who was lord of it. He ansuerd to them that it was the cyté of Cassydonye, wherof Alimodes is lord and kynge of this royalme, that for the tyme beyng was wyth a right grete puyssaunce of men of werre before Tourmaday kepyng there his siege, and that his sonn Daryus and the fayre Beatryx, his doughter, werre bothe togyder wythinne the towne of Cassydonye.

3   Blanchardyn was joyfull and glad to here these tydynges, and sayde all lawghyng to Sadoyne that they were well arryved upon their enmyes, and that every man sholde thynke to prove hymself well, for they must assaylle the towne bycause that the lady[3] that he dyde promytte to hym was within Cassydonye. "And morover," he sayde unto Sadoyne, "my right trusty felawe, we ben come to a goode haven. It is to us force that this cyté be wonne and conquested by oure strengthe and after that we shal go, to the playsure of God, for to socoure and helpe myn owne dere lady, the proude pucelle in amours." Sadoyne, heryng Blanchardyn that sayde [fol. 64v] to hym that the fayre Beatryx, whiche he had so sore desyred afore, was wythin the cyté of Cassydonye, was right glad that they were arryved there. He toke and gadred all newe corage wythin hymself and, mounted togyder on horsbacke, Blanchardyn and he and alle theyr folke dyde so and poynted[4] hemself for to fyght or for to gyve assawte to the towne. Evyn at that same houre that the sayde barouns were in the medowe renged one nyghe another and redy for to fyght, Daryus, Kynge Alymodes sone, was at a wyndowe of a grete toure wythin his paleys out of whiche he loked and behelde over and over the medowes and over the playne, whiche

---

[1] *images*

[2] *arranged in battle order*

[3] *Beatrix*

[4] *dressed (appointed)*

he see all coveryd with men of armes that were afore the towne, wherof he was right sore merveylled and wyst not yf they were frendes or foos.

4   He made hymself to be armed hastely and dyde publishe[5] though alle the towne and to them of his house that all sholde be armed on horsbacke and redy for to goo wyth hym wythout makynge eny delaye. For he sayde that he wold go to understande what folke they were that camen in armes so nyghe his towne. And after that Daryus commaunded was publyshed, ther were tenn thousand Cassydonyens soone redy, right well in harneys wel appoynted, that folowed hym and yssued out of the towne wyth Daryus, that was rydyng before hem all upon a right myghty courser. And Blanchardyn and Sadoyne, that sawe hym comen, made on her bataylles[6] and cam ayenst Daryus that sore hyghe bygann to calle and sayde, "Ye lordes that are here comen and have seased[7] my haven and taken lande, and that shewe tokens that your purpos is for to werre upon me, telle me yf ye be Sarrasyns."

5   Thenne Blanchardyn, his spere in [fol. 65r] hande and all armed fro top to too[8] byfore his bataylle, ansuered hym that they were not Sarrasyns. "But we ben," sayde he, "Crysten men that wyl go to gyve socoure and helpe unto that mayden the lady of Tourmaday, whereas the tyraunt Alymodes kepeth now his siege byfore the towne. But I wyl wel that thou know that in an evyl houre he cam ever there, for yf we may fynde hym we shall make hym to deye a shamefull dethe. And wyth this, yf it pleyseth unto Jhesu Cryst in whom we byleve, we shal this daye take by strengthe his cyté of Cassydonye. And see here by me Sadoyne, the sone of the kynge of Prusse, that shal mary his doughter thy suster the fayr Beatryx. So shall he rengne[9] in this lande, where he shal soone be obeyed, loved, and dred as a lord soverayne. And we shal not ceasse unto tyme that, to the playsure of Jhesu Cryst, we shall have all our wylle in this byhalve."

---

[5]   proclaim (announce)
[6]   made on her bataylles, *formed up their batallions*
[7]   seized
[8]   fro top to too, *from head to foot*
[9]   reign (rule)

The thirty eighth chapter conteyneth how the valyaunt Blanchardyn slewe Daryus and of the grete bataylle where the Cassydonyens were dyscomfyted and overthrawen and the cyté taken. And the fayr Beatryx was taken to mercy, and how Sadoyne and the fayre Beatryx made hemself to be baptyzed, and their folke wyth them.

1   Whan Daryus understode thees wordes, he knewe all ynough that it was Blanchardyn the worthy knight, wherof he gaff hymselff moche grete merveylle of the manere nor how he was escaped from thre score men to whom he had taken the charge to kepe hym and to have presented hym unto the kynge of Salamandrye. He wende to have tourned the brydell of his horsse, for he was right sore affrayed to see hym there byfore hym. [fol. 65v] But Blanchardyn perceyved it anone, and he, that well lerned was in all poyntes of werre, kept Darius therfro. He gaff his hors the spore and cam and kutte the waye betwene their

two bataylles,[1] for he was right wel horsed. He folowed Darius of so nyghe that he over reched hym with his swerde as he was fleyng at the right syde of hym, soo that his riche cote of maylle myght not warauntyze[2] hym. But he cutte bothe fleshe and bone and made in his body a grete wounde mortall, and syth recovered another stroke so that he smote hym doune ded to the grounde from his horse. Atte that oure were the Cassydonyens sore abasshed whan they sawe their lorde that laye upon the grounde sterk ded. They wyshed and complayned hym sore but neverthelesse, they avaunced themself full proudely and ranne upon their enmyes.

2 Thenne byganne the bataylle grete and cruell of bothe partes. Blanchardyn and Sadoyne made there merveylles of armes; they brake and cutte Cassydonyens on all sydes. No man was there so hardy that durste approche hem, where al as they came they made the presse to sprede abrode. Blanchardyn dyde espye[3] a knyght that bare the standarde of the Cassydonyens; he ranne upon hym and gaaff hym suche an horryble stroke upon his helme that he all to-brayned hym wyth his swerde. And thus he overthrewe doune bothe man and standarde so that the Cassydonyens had not syth the powere for to have dressyd it up ayen, but were slayne and all to-cutte and cloven that all the wayes were covered of bodyes ded and wounded men.

3 The same tyme was the fayre Beatryx at a wyndowe wythin the paleys lokyng upon the batayll, that sone perceyved and knewe that the losse was tourned upon her party. Wherfore she wyst [fol. 66r] well for certayne that impossyble was to her for to kepe the towne ayenst so grete a puyssaunce as she dyde see byfore her, consyderyng that the best defense and the moost worthy knyghtes of the lande were wyth her fader, the kynge Alymodes, at the siege byfore Tourmaday, and that suche as were issued out there were almost all overthrowen. Wel saw the fayre Beatryx that she muste yelde up herself. The same tyme passed Sadoyne byfore the wyndowe, that wyth bothe handes smote upon his enmyes. The fayre Beatryx called hym sayng in this manere, "Alas, right noble knyght, I gyve myself up unto you, prayeng that ye wol save bothe me and my cyté, and to take us into your mercy and pyté, havyng compassyon upon a yong mayden that yeldeth herself unto you." Sadoyne, lokyng toward the wyndowe, heved right soone his hande upward and sayde and promysed her that he sholde warauntyse her from all harme. He was right glad of these tydynges.

4 It was not longe after this that Blanchardyn and Sadoyne dyde mete togyder, havyng their swerdes in their fystes all dyed wyth the blode of their enmyes that they had al to-hewen[4] and cloven. And fynably[5] dyde so moche by their prouesse that, wythin a whyle, they made the Cassydonyens to fle, and discomfyted them and so nyghe they chassed them that they entred into the cyté wyth them. It was grete horrour to see the horryble occysion and slawghter that was made in the playne byfore the towne, where the bodyes lay by ded grete hepes here and there in many places. Whan Blanchardyn saw that they

---

[1] *armies (batallions)*

[2] *protect*

[3] *see (look steadily)*

[4] *cut to pieces*

[5] *finally (in the end)*

were com to their above⁶ of their enmyes, and that noo resystence at all was made ayenst hem, he made by a trompette to be proclamed that the slawhter sholde ceasse wythin the [fol. 66v] towne, syth that they were lordes and maysters of the same, the whiche thyng was don as yt was commaunded.

5   Sone after thys, Blanchardyn and Sadoyne cam to the paleys wythoute to fynd enybody that wold hem lete or gaynsey the entré therof. They went into the hall, where they founde the fayer Beatryx that cam ayenst them and yelded herself to them, prayng that they wold have pyté upon her. Blanchardyn toke the mayden by the hande sayng to her, "Fayer damesel, God forbede that evyl nor harme sholde be don to you." He cam toward Sadoyn and sayd unto hym, "My ryght trusty felawe, the promysse that byfore thys tyme I made unto you, I wol now quyte⁷ myself therof toward you. Take thys pucell; I geve her to you by suche a condycion that ye shal helpe me to socoure the proude pusell in amours." Sadoyne, ryght glad all laughyng, aunsuerd to Blanchardyn, "Frend myn, yt is wel reson that I do so and wyth ryght a good hert I shal goo to helpe you, for wel I am bounde therunto. Your promysse ye have ryght wele acquyted⁸ unto me, and an houndred thousand thankes I gyve you therfor." Sadoyne behelde the pucell Beatryx that so gentyl was and so odly⁹ fayr. He enbraced and kyssed her sayeng, "Fayr dameseyll, ye and I myself shal be babtysed, and after that I shall take you to myn own dere spouse and wyff; for I woll that thys false lawe and unabyl¹⁰ byleve and thys perverse sacryfyces that ben to this false idoles, ye leve and forsake." She aunswerd full mekely that she shulde so do wyth ryghte a goode wylle.

6   Wythin the same cyté of Cassydonye were the same tyme certeyne Crysten men that dwelled there under trybute,¹¹ that were ryghte glad whan they sawe that by the Crysten men the town was take. But by the comaundement of Blanchardyn, the preeste of the Crysten [fol. 67r] men that were dwellynge there assembled anone and made redy many tubbys and other vesselles full of fayre water whiche he blessed and halowed therynne. Sadoyne and Beatryx and all their people made hemself to be baptyzed, and namely all the people of that contrey were converted into our holy feythe. After these thynges thus happed and doon, Sadoyne wedded the fayre Beatryx, the doughter of Kynge Alymodes. The solemnytez¹² of the wedlok were made grete and notable, where the knyghtes and ladyes of the lande were. All of the noble clothyng wherof the pucelle was ornated¹³ wythall, it is no nede to telle you of it, but wel I dare saye that never in thoo dayes nor an hondred yere afore, men had not seen eny quene nor pryncesse more richely arayed. For so many a ryche jewell, so grete haboundance¹⁴ of precyouse stones and so grete a

---

⁶ *victory (success)*

⁷ *acquit (complete)*

⁸ *acquitted (carried out)*

⁹ *extraordinarily*

¹⁰ *useless (powerless)*

¹¹ *a tax paid for the privilege of legal residence in the city*

¹² *solemnities (ceremonies)*

¹³ *adorned (ornamented)*

¹⁴ *abundance*

tresoure was there wythin the paleys y-gadred[15] by the kyng Alymodes that it was a thyng infynyte, bycause that all the dayes of his lyff he had be a grete tyraunt. Soo had he taken and ravysshed and by stronge hande upon his neyghbours bothe ferre and nere, all that he fonde of grete value.

7   Thre dayes hool lasted the feste, and syth after Sadoyne byganne to enquyre of the governaunce and astate[16] of the lande, as to hym was nedefull to be doo. The evyll custumes he dyd brynge doune and sette up the goode, and syth putte goode provysyon for the justyse, and dyde stablysshe[17] provostes, ballyffes,[18] and rulers of the lande, and putte sure watche in all the townes and castelles. And by all the counseyll and goode advyse of Blanchardyn that was right wyse.

---

[15] *gathered*
[16] *condition*
[17] *establish*
[18] *bailiffs (administrative officials with judicial authority)*

The thirty ninth chapiter conteyneth how Blanchardyn fonde his fader the kynge of Fryse that was prysoner wythin [fol. 67v] **Cassydonye and of the pyteouse devyses that the fader and the sone had togydre.**

1   After these tydynges don and brought at an ende, it happed that one a day Blanchardyn, Sadoyne, and his wyff the fayer Beatryx were sittyng at the bord[1] takynge their recreacyon. The same tyme herde Blanchardyn a voyce of a man that full pyteuosly lamented hymself, wherof he toke grete merveylle, for he alredy had herde hym crye by whiles thre tymes. He demaunded of theym that were there byfore the table who myght be that wayled and cryed so pyteously.

2   Ther was a knyght that ansuered hym and sayde, "Syre it is not long agoo that Daryus made a coursse into Fryse wyth a grete nombre of shippes, insomoche that by tempeste of the see he was cast into an haven of the see of the sayde lande where he made grete wast, toke, and slewe many men, and many he dyde brynge wyth hym prysoners. Wherof emong other is one that called hymself lord of them alle, and the same is he that ye have herde crye so pyteously." Whan Blanchardyn herde speke of Fryse, he doubted hym well sone that it was som man of his lynage and sybbe,[2] and was sore dyspleased for the dystruction of his lande, and wel glad to be avenged wyth his owne hande upon the personne of Darius that the said distruction had commytted and don. Sadoyne thenne dyde sende incontynent toward the prysen and made to be brought out of it the noble kynge of Fryse. The tables were alredy taken up whan he was brought into the halle. Whan Blanchardyn sawe the noble kynge, his fader, he knewe hym anone, how well that he was ryght sore chaunged of face for grete sorowe and hardness of the pryson.

3   Blanchardyn coude not kepe hymself but that the grete [fol. 68r] teerys dropped fast out of his eyen for grete pyté that he had of his fader, and myght kepe his counteynaunce nor behave hymself. And whan he was come ayen to his manere, he demaunded

---

[1] *game table*
[2] *kin*

of his fader what lande he was of. The goode kynge ansuered hym and sayde, "I am a power[3] caytyf[4] kyng that somtyme regned in Fryselande, but thoughe fortune changeable my lande hath be wasted and lost by Darius, the sone of Kyng Alymodes. And after that he had uttirly dystroyed a grete part of my royalme, he brought me wyth hym to be here his prysoner lyvyng full pourly wythin a derke dongeon, and wold never putte me to noo raenson.[5] A fayr sone I had somtyme of myn owne spouse my wyff, whiche I helde and had full tenderly dere, but bycause I wolde not make hym a knyght, yongthe[6] movid hym and departed from me. And syth, as I have tolde you, myself, my royalme, and my folke have be thus dystroyed and wasted, what wol ye doo of me, I am but a man lost for ever more. I requyre[7] you that ye wyl slee me for to brynge my grete myserye at an ende, and nought to putte me ayen into the harde and tenebrouse[8] pryson where I and my knyghtes have be so longe, shortyng[9] oure dayes in suche poverté as ye may see." The goode kynge thenne, that thus reherced his angwysshe and displaysirs, bygane to wepe and sobbe right sore. Blanchardyn asked of the kynge yf he sawe his sone, whether he sholde knowe hym. "Alas," sayde the kyng, "wel am I sure that I shall never see hym."

4   Blanchardyn myght not conteyne hymself and sobbed full sore in his herte, and syth sayde unto the kynge his fader, "Syre, I spake wyth your sone not longe agoo whan he departed from us. We two felawes, this gentyllman and I, have ben alonge espace[10] wyth hym, and nothyng was partyd amonge us lyke as the one [fol. 68v] of us wold have yt that other was therof content. He loved me as he dyde hymself and I heeld[11] hym as dere as myself. We were long tyme togyder, insomoche that for grete love that he had to me, he gaff me this rynge of gold that ye now see on my fynger." The kyng loked upon the rynge and knew yt ryght well, but he knew not the fynger nor the hande that had yt on. "Certaynly," sayd the kyng, "I see and knowe right wel by the tokens that ye shewe unto me that ye have seen hym. Wherfor, sire, I requyre and praye you, for the recomforte of me that am a poure olde man and replenyshed wyth bytternes, that ye wol telle me where my sone Blanchardyn may be." Then Blanchardyn wyth grete payne spake wyth a lowe voyce aunswerde him and sayd, "Syr, ye muste knowe that he that ye askd for is ded." Whan the nobyl kyng understode hym, from a hyghe as he was he lete hymself falle donn to the erthe all in a swoun before all them that were there, for the grete dyspleasure that he toke atte his hert whan he herd that bytter and pytous tydynge that of new joyned unto his olde trybulacons. And then Blanchrdyn, seeng the sorow where the kyng his fader was ynne, toke repentaunce of that he had so longe hyd hymself, and wyth eyen all tempred[12] wyth teerys dyde put hymself upon his knees byfore the kynge his fader and ryght swetly

---

[3] *poor*

[4] *wretch (prisoner)*

[5] *ransom*

[6] *youth*

[7] *request (ask)*

[8] *dark (gloomy)*

[9] *spending (ending)*

[10] alonge espace, *a long time*

[11] *considered*

[12] *mixed*

cryed hym mercy sayeng in thys wyse, "My ryght doubted lord and fader, byfore you ye maye see your sone Blanchardyn that from you did departe wythoute your knowyng and lycense, wherof he asketh of you mercy and grace, and the offence that I dyde take and brynge wyth me your good courser, whiche ys wythoute pyere[13] amonge al other, wyth your good swerde, of whiche I have brought to deth Daryus your enmye."

5   Whan the kyng of Fryse, that alredy was come ayen to hymsylf, herde his son Blanchardyn speke, the [fol. 69r] whiche he knewe not atte that tyme well, for his sighte that was sore troubled of the derknes of the pryson in whiche he had suffred grete peyne and grete sorow. There nys no tounge of no creature mortall that unto you coude telle, wryte, or do[14] to be rehersed the grete joye that the same howre entred into the hert of that nobyl kyng prysoner, and of all the assystens[15] that were there the same daye, for theyr terys were parted among them. And in especyal Sadoyne and his wyff had of hit their parte, in suche a wyse that the teerys fell from their eyen al alonge their faces in so grete habondaunce that theyr ryche raymentes that they hadde on that daye were all wete wythall. The nobel kyng of Fryse was enbrased and kyssed of his sone Blanchardyn. The reverence and honoure that Sadoyne and his wyff made for love of Blanchardyn to his fader sholde be longe for to be recounted here. Wyth ryght grete joye and gladnes they had hym into the chamberes where was a bayne[16] redy made where they made hym to be wasshed clene, and syth toke hym clothyng accordyng to hys royal astate.[17] And in lykewyse they ded to all the knyghtes that had be prysoners wyth hym, every man after hys degree.

6   Blanchardyn, thenne seeng the adventure that was happed to hym, came toward the kyng hys fader and sayd unto hym, "My ryghte dere and honoured lorde and fader, I beseke you that ye woll telle me howe the quene my moder dyd byfore your harde infortune." "My ryght dere sone," said the kynge, "knowe now that never syth thy departyng thy sorowfull moder had no joye at her herte, and noon was there, myself nor noon other, that myghte recomforte her. Wherof thou mayst thynke wele that after that grevouse sorowe that she hath had of my takynge, and that she had never no worde from me [fol. 69v] syth that I was take and broughte here of the Sarasyns, wherby I knowe certeynli as I fere me that she ys rather ded than alyve." After thees wordes, the kynge byganne full sore to wepe and so ded Blanchardyn, so that Sadoyne nor Beatryx his wyff coude do no thynge to stynte[18] them.

---

[13] *equal (peer)*

[14] *cause*

[15] *squires (assistants)*

[16] *bath*

[17] *status (estate)*

[18] *stop*

The fortieth chapytur conteyneth how Blanchardyn and Sadoyne and the good kynge of Fryse toke the see wyth a grete excercyte of folke for to gyve socours unto the proude pucelle in amours.

1 After their teeris and pytuable reconyssaunce were past and chassed, they taryed the space of a moneth wythin the cyté of Cassydonye, abydyng that the kyng of Fryse fader unto Blanchardyn were hole and brought ayen into the astate of his owne strength, that was yet that tyme of resonabel age for to suffer[1] the excercise of armes. Blanchardyn, that all his hert and his thought had sette upon his ladye the proude pucell in amours, ryght sore desiryng to have her oute of thraldom[2] and power of Alymodes the kynge, and also seeng his fader broughte up ayen in good convalescence and helth, cam byfore Sadoyne and sayd, "My feythfull felawe and ryght trusty frende, God and fortune hath helped you so that ye be come to that thynge that ye moost dyd desire byfore this tyme, for the whiche thynge to be complete accordyng to my promyse I have holpen you the beste that I coude. So thanked be our Lord, ye are therof come to your above.[3] Wherfore I praye you that in lyke case ye woll do so to me, as in you ys my verey truste and parfyte confydence, whyche certaynly I knowe welle that ye woll doo. It ys soo that I beseke you now that ye woll helpe and socoure me now ayenste the kynge Alymodes, that by his grete crueltee and tyrannye kepeth shette[4] and [fol. 70r] closed that thynge that I oughte moste to be desirouse of in thys worlde, for to have her oute of servytude into franchyse.[5] It is my ryghte doubted ladye the proude pucell in amours." Whan Sadoyne understode the wordes of Blanchardyn, all smylyng he ansuerde unto hym and sayde, "My ryghte verey frende and goode felawe, your desyer and your wylle is myn own and nevere whyle I am man alyve nothynge shall be parted fer bytwene us. Your wylle and my wyll is but one wylle, so stedfasteli knytted that hit shall be lefte for an ensample to them that shal come herafter in perpetuall memorye. And your commaundementys and myn shal be wyth us two persones but one thynge. Late oure shyppes be made redy and appareyled. So shall we thenne goo for to gyve socoure and helpe unto her whos presence we so sore do desyre."

2 Thenne Blanchardyn, heryng the gracyous ansuer of Sadoyne his feythful felaw, he thanked hym right moche. And syn afterward, by ordenance of Sadoyne and Blanchardyn, the navey was apparelled and redy made, stored and garnyshed wyth good men of werre and wyth artylarye as was perteynyng to suche a thyng. And made hemself redy in fayr araye for to goo to socour and helpe her that passed all other of beauté that beseged was by Kyng Alymodes and his folke wythin her cyté of Tourmaday. After this that Blanchardyn and Sadoyne sawe their shyppes redy and well stored wyth vytaylles and of other thynges necessare to fynyshe their enterpryse to the socours and helpe of the proude pucel in amours. Sadoyne toke leve of his wyff, the fayre Beatryx, and so dyd Blanchardyn, whiche

---

[1] *bear (endure)*
[2] *subjection (unfree status)*
[3] *victory*
[4] *shut*
[5] *liberty (the status of a free person)*

they shall never see tyll that she and her husbonde Sadoyne have ben in grete peryll of their lyves, as hereafter ye shall mowe here.

3   Sadoyne, thorugh the counseyll of his felaw Blanchardyn, [fol. 70v] lefte wythin his cyté of Cassydonye foure thousand of goode knyghtes chosen for to defende and kepe it ayenst Kynge Alymodes yf by eny adventure he cam thider ayen, as he dyd afterwarde. After their leve thus taken of the fayr Beatryx, they departed and toke the see levynge behinde theym the fayr Beatryx that made so grete sorowe for her goode husbonde Sadoyne. Whan the barons were upon the see, the maryners made saylle. The wynde was ryght goode that broughte theym forth by suche a wyse[6] that, wythin a whyle, they were ferre fro the lande, and were togyder thirty grete shyppes and four score galeys subtyl.[7] Duryng the tyme that the goode kynge of Fryse, Blanchardyn, and Sadoyne and their folke shall be thus saylynge towarde Tourmaday, we shall retorne to speke of the tyraunte the kynge Alymodes and the proude pucell in amours.

---

[6] manner
[7] cleverly constructed

The forty first chapyter sheweth how Blanchardyn recounted to his fader and to Sadoyne the beaulté and the godnes of his lady the proude pucell in amours and of the provoste that cam ayenste hem.

1   We have herde heretofore howe Kynge Alymodes had beseged the nobel cyté of Tormaday where was the nobel lady the proude mayden in amours. Byfore whiche cyté he made gounes[1] and other engynes to be caste ayenste the walles bothe nyghte and daye for to brynge hem adoun, and wyth the same he made the toun sawted[2] ofte tymes ful sore, where he made grete losse of his folke. But yt is al ynough to be bylevyd for a trouth that it was not donn wythoute slaughter and damage to theym of the towne. The proude pucell in amours, seeng herself so sore expressyd,[3] her knyghtes and her men slayne, was ryght sory. And of that other partye, she had no hope of eny socours, but only of [fol. 71r] Blanchardyn in whom was al her trust. But by no manere she myght not knowe into what parte of the worlde he was dryven, and was in a grete feer lest he had ben drowned in the grete tempeste of wyndes that had reculed[4] them into the hyghe see from the costes of Tourmaday. Full often nyght and day she wyshed hym wyth her, and was so sory for hym that she wyst not what she sholde doo, and noo playsure she coude taken in no thynge but was evermore sorowyng at the herte of her. Insomoche that one daye, amonge other, erly in a mornyng, Kynge Alymodes made the towne to be assayled and was there made grete alarme and grete fray so that the noyse and the callynge that was made of bothe partyes cam unto the eerys[5] of the proude pucelle in amours, wherfor she rose out of her bed and bygan to wyshe sore after Blanchardyn.

---

[1] guns (cannons)
[2] attacked
[3] pressed hard in battle
[4] pulled back (withdrawn)
[5] ears

2   She cam toward a wyndowe whiche opened herself and as she dyde cast alwayes her syght toward the see. She trowed to have seen a grete nombre of shippes that were appyeryng upon the water and com sayllynge as her advyse was toward Tourmaday. She, seeng that thynge, for grete joye that she toke she wyst not what she sholde saye or thynke therof, whethr she was awakyng or aslepe, and for to be better in certaynté of the trouth she went up at a hyghe wyndowe and loked so longe tyl that she myght perceyve clerly that they were shyppes and vesselles of werre. "Ha, God," saide she, "myght som socours come to me of eny souldyours, for of noo man of my sybbe[6] I awayte for none syth that the kynge of the Grete Nourthweghe, myn oncle, is decessed that wold helpe me ayenst the tyraunt Kynge Alymodes." Atte the same houre Blanchardyn was upon the borde[7] of his ship and talked wyth the kynge of Fryse, his fader, [fol. 71v] and as they were thus in devyses, Blanchardyn loked on the see and byganne to espye[8] the toures of the paleys of Tourmaday and shewed them to his fader and to Sadoyne his felawe. He recounted to his fader the kynge of Fryse the beaulté, goodnes, and other goode vertues and maners that were in his lady, the proude pucelle in amours, and how he was in her goode grace and she lykewyse in his. And that yf God gaff hym that hap[9] that he myght come to bataylle ayenst her enmye, the kyng Alymodes, he sholde shewe to hym the benevolence that he ought[10] to his lady, and the grete malyvolence or evyll wylle that he had for her sake toward the tyraunt that by so grete wronge and wythout laufull cause made to her suche force and injurye. Thus talkyng of many thynges they exploytted[11] so by a goode wynde that they had, that they cam so nyghe the lande that they see playnly the tentes and the pavyllyons of Kynge Alymodes, the whiche Blanchardyn dyde shewe unto the kynge his fader and to his felawe Sadoyne.

3   The proude pucelle in amours, that at this houre was lenyng upon her wyndowe, sent hastely for the provost that he sholde come and speke wyth her, whiche cam anone to her. He entred into her chambre and right humbly salued the pucelle. She called hym nyghe her and shewed hym the right myghty navye that cam to arryve there. The provost, that was right wyse and subtyll, perceyved and knewe full sone that they were Crysten and sayde to his lady that he sholde go to them to wyte what folke they were, and yf he coude doo so moche by eny wyse that they wolde take her wages and serve her. He toke his leve and went oute of the chambre and cam streyght to the haven, where he toke a bote prest and garnyshed wyth eyght goode felawes, eche of them an ore in his [fol. 72r] hande, whiche wythin a short whyle brought the provost nyghe to the galleyes. And so wel they stered that they cam and borded the ship wherin Blanchardyn was that desyred sore to knowe what they were that so fast rowed toward his vessel. Thenne the provost, seeyng hymself arryved where he wolde be, right highly he salued theym that

---

[6]   kin
[7]   deck (side)
[8]   see at a distance
[9]   chance
[10]   owes
[11]   moved quickly

were wythin the ship. Blanchardyn, that lened upon the borde[12] of it, rendred to hym his salutacion. The provost thenne al on hyghe exposed and sayde the charge that he had of his maystres byhalve, the lady of Tourmaday. Blanchardyn, that wel knewe the provost, ansuered demaundyng of hym yf his lady was so sore oppressed by her enmyes as he sayde, and whether she might holde the towne longe ayenst them that had layde siege to it byfore her.

4   The provost ansuered to hym and sayde, "Ye right wel, but one thynge there is, that she may not have nother helthe nor joye but alweyes she most be chaunged[13] upon her bed where she can not have rest nor noo goode slepe by night nor by daye." "Frende," saide Blanchardyn, "wherof may come this dysease[14] unto her that so traveylleth and tourmenteth her? For myn advyse is this that at all endes she ought to force herself from her bed for to shewe herself, admonestyng her folke to do wel bycause they sholde take a better corage for the persone and sight of her." "Syre," sayde the provost, "be ye sure and knowe for a trouthe that, so moche I knowe by my lady, that she shal never have no parfytte joye at her herte for love of a knyght of whom she is enamored whiche she weneth to be peryshed and ded. But my hope is in God that he shall yet come ayen hyther, for men sayen comynly that he whome God wyll have kept may not be peryshed. Syre, I saye the same for the knyght that is the most parfyt in all beaulté and condicyons, that his lyke can not be founde. How be [fol. 72v] it that not long ago we herde tydynges of hym of a pylgryme that passed here byfore, that sayde to us for veray trouth that he and his felawe Sadoyne were arryved into the cyté of Cassydonye whiche they had taken and goten by force of armes, for the whiche tydynge my sayde lady hath be wel asswaged of her dysplaysure, trustyng in God that shortly she shal understande more playnly the certaynté therof."

5   Whan Blanchardyn understode the provost, he sayde unto hym that this whiche the pylgryme had sayd was true, and that Blanchardyn had sent hem there for to socoure and help his maistres. But som men wyl saye that he shal wedde the doughter of Kynge Alymodes, whiche is lady of the lande where he is, and that he shal maynteyne and kepe the contrey with her. "Ha, ha, sire, what is that that ye saye? What a grete synne and untrouth it were to Blanchardin to take nor have to his wyf another than the proude pucell in amours, that loveth him so truly and that so longe hath wayted and taryed after hym, and that for the grete love that she hath to him she hath reffused so many kynges and so hyghe prynces that dayly do requyre[15] her. Certes, whosomever brought her this sorowfull and pyteuose tydynge, I doubte not but that she shold slee herself for grete displaysir for suche. And so true I knowe her. Now God forbede that I be the brynger of thys tydynges, that so sore displaysaunt[16] shal be to me for to uttir and declare hem that I had almost as lief[17] to deye as to reherce them unto my said maystresse. But sire, syth it is therof as ye saye, and that ye come from Blanchardyn, I praye you to telle me yf he

---

[12] *side*

[13] *lying; (see note)*

[14] *discomfort (tribulation)*

[15] *ask for her (in marriage)*

[16] *displeasing (discomfiting)*

[17] *rather (prefer)*

wryteth or sendeth eny wordes to my sayde lady by you. For nothyng coude make me to byleve that this grete and lothely untrouthe sholde be in Blanchardyn, to leve and forsake her of whom he is so parfytly beloved for to take the doughter of [fol. 73r] a kynge, her enmye." "Frende," sayde Blanchardyn, "as for wrytyng or eny worde that he sholde sende, I knowe of none." "That rewyth me," sayde the provost, "so am I wel sore abashed how he can have a wylle to chose another lady than the proude pucelle in amours, whiche is the most fayr and the most noble and the most complet a lady and most plesaunt of all the remenaunt of the world. How thenne doeth not he remembre hymself of the courser and of the sleve of clothe of golde that she dyde send unto hym after the fyrst acqueyntaunce? Certaynly my herte can not judge to me that ever of suche a knyght as is Blanchardyn shold growe suche a wille to be do. Ha ha, madame," sayde the provost, "see here sore harde tydynges that shal be cause to brynge at an ende full myserably your laste dayes."

6   Whan Blanchardyn herde the provost speke thus, he bygan to smyle. Thenne the provost behylde hym ful ententyfly[18] and knewe hym, wherof he had so grete and so parfyt a joye that it can not be recounted. And after many wordes of reconyssaunce, the provoste tolde to hym of all how he was ever truly byloved and how his lady, the proude pucelle in amours, had borne and as yet bare suche a displeasure for and by the occasyon of hym, and that never syth that she receyved the letter that he dyde sende to her by hym, "she had no joye at her herte nor shal never have unto the tyme that she see you ayen." Blanchardyn sayde to hym, "Lat her take no care of nothing nor no doubte of my parte, for as to me I have alwayes be and evermore shall as longe I shall lyve her true and feythfull lover, and shall never fayle her of noo thyng that is or shal be in my power to doo for her. As to her that I more desire to complayse[19] than all the worlde, ye shal recomende me to her gode grace and from me ye shal presente unto her this rynge of golde. And as to the faytte [fol. 73v] of our men of werre that ben here, we have brought hem alle hyther only for to gyve unto her helpe and socoure. We shal kepe ourself wythin our vesselles bycause it is as now too late, and tomorne erly, whan we see houre and tyme goode and alle redy, we shal do sowne oure trompettes, hornes, and busynes. And ye that shal be wythin the cyté, see that ye be redy and appareylled for to yssue out at the same owre for to come ayenst oure enmyes, for from oure syde we shal assaylle them so quykly that they shal cursse the owre of oure commyng. And thus they shal be fought wythal of bothe sydes by suche a manere that wyth grete peyne they shal have leyser[20] to graunte unto us the victorye, yf God woll."

---

[18] attentively (intently)

[19] please (gratify)

[20] opportunity (leisure)

Here foloweth the forty second chapiter that conteyneth in hitself and speketh of the grete joye that the proude pucelle in love made whan she herde reherce by the provost the gracyouse tydynges of the commynge of here frende Blanchardyn.

1 The provost, herynge Blanchardyn speke so truly and benyngly,[1] he ansuered unto hym and sayde that, as to thier parte, suche a dyligence sal be made therupon that their enmyes shal knowe soone by grete strokes the grete corage of them of the towne. And thenne right joyouse he departed from Blanchardyn and toke leve of hym, sore desyryng of all his herte to fynde hymself byfore his sayde lady for to announce and telle to her this glad tydyng, and wend never to have come tyme[2] ynoughe there. He exployted so and made suche a dilygence that wyth grete joye and gladnesse he entred wythin the haven of Tourmaday without eny delaye nor lettyng by no maner, and cam to the towne where he fonde the noble mayden right nobly acompanyed of her knyghtes, ladyes, and gentyl women that were wyth her in grete nomber.

2 She, seeng the provost com a-land out of his bote makyng a mery [fol. 74r] contenance, was sore desired to know of hym som gode tydynges, for her hert judged her that he brought som. So taryed she not tyll that the provost were com toward her, but a grete pas[3] marched ayenst[4] hym. The provost made unto her the reverence, puttyng hymself upon his knee and sayd to her, "My ryght redubted lady, knowe ye for certayn that I have be wyth the ryght puyssaunt navye wyche is laden wyth men of armes that are come to helpe you. Of the whiche ben conducters[5] and chieff rulers the kynge of Fryse, the nobyl knyght Blanchardyn, his sone, and Sadoyne, his felaw. Madame, see here a rynge of gold that Blanchardyn sendeth to you by me wyth recommendacyons manyfold. Knowe, madame, that a grete joye ought to be encresed wythin you whan suche a socours is come to your grete comforte, for thes thre hyghe pryncys have brought wyth theym grete nomber of folkes, and they have a ryght perfyte desire to avenge your quarell upon Alymodes the tyraunt. And ye maye byleve for certeyn that the goode kynge of Fryse hath noon other desire than to avenge hymself, whan he shall com to the feelde, for the grete hurt, injurye, and damage that hath be doon unto hym by Daryus, the sone of Kyng Alymodes. Tomorowe by the mornyng shall the bataylle bygynne, wherfor Blanchardyn prayeth you by me that ye commaunde your captayns and men of armes that they be redy all to the ende that, whan the houre shall come that the trompettes and bussynes[6] of the oost of Blanchardyn shall begyn to soune, that your folke be redy for to take the feelde, and that quyckly they assaylle your enmyes of all sydes. And as to that parte of the prynces that come to your socours, they shal be redy att the same owre. And by all thus your enmyes shal fynde hemself oppressed both byfore and behynd, wherof Kyng Alymodes shal be in grete affray,[7] and ye shal be avenged upon hym to the [fol. 74v] playsure of

---

[1] *kindly (generously)*

[2] *soon*

[3] *distance*

[4] *toward*

[5] *leaders*

[6] *straight trumpets [OF buisine]*

[7] *alarm (assault)*

God. For he shal have a double displaysure, and in especyall whan the tydynges shal be recounted unto him of Daryus his sone, that hath be slayne and brought to his deth by the handes of Blanchardyn. And wyth this he shal fynde his cité of Cassydonye and all his grete royalme conquested and goten, and his doughter wedded, whiche by Blanchardyn hathe be yeven unto his felaw Sadoyne."

3   That tyme that the proude pucelle in amours had herd and understande the provost, never in her dayes had she so moche of displeasire but that these tydynges dyde redouble her joye over mesure, and thanked God of this goode adventure. So is there non that coude telle nor wryte the joye that the same tyme was in her and emonge all the people of the towne. She went ayen into her paleys replenysshed wyth joye and gladnesse and made to be cryed thurgh all the stretes and common places of the towne that all the stretes of the cyté sholde be hanged wyth clothes[8] the next day folowyng. And that, at the comyng in of Blanchardyn, every man sholde were his best clothyng, and that myrth and melody sholde be made thurgh al the cyté that same night, whereas were al maner of musical instrumentes. Whiche thing was don, for suche noyse and suche sowne was there made al that night, what of tambours,[9] trompettes, claryons, harp, lute, clavicordes,[10] and other diverse instrumentes, wyth the swete voyces of the ladyes and gentyl women that sange there, that it semed that God had descended among them from heven. And so grete was the joye wythin the cyté that the sowne therof was herde unto Kynge Alymodes oost. Merveylles it was to here the thankes, the lovenges and the praysynges, and the ryngyng of belles that were doon in all the chirches of the towne, yeldyng graces unto oure Lorde.

4   The kynge Alymodes, that was [fol. 75r] that same tyme wythin his tentes wyth his barons, gaff hymself grete merveylle of the joye and feste that he herde don wythin the cyté. He wyst not what he sholde thynke and doubted lest they had herde eny tydynges of som socours comyng unto them. For by no meanes he myght not see the socours that was come bycause that the paleys and the towne were bytwene hym and the see that he myght not loke ferre toward the seesyde. And also Blanchardyn and his navye, after that the provost was gon from hym, wythdrewe hem into the see, wherfor Alymodes nor his folke coude not see hem nor here them for the grete revyll and joye that was made by them of the cyté that made grete noyse. And at that self houre, Blanchardyn, wyth all his shippes and galeyes, cam and arryved wythin the haven and descended on lande wythout their enmyes were aware of hem, for the joye and noyse that wythin the towne was thus grete.

---

[8] *cloths (banners)*
[9] *small drums used on festive occasions*
[10] *small stringed keyboard instruments*

The forty third chapter folowed whiche conteyneth and speketh of the grete beaulté that was byfore Tourmaday ayenst the kynge Alymodes that was discomfyted, and of the takynge of Sadoyne wherof Blanchardyn was right sory as rayson was.

1 Well ye have herde heretofore the grete joye and gladnesse that was made wythin the cyté for the goode tydynges that the proude pusell in love had understand of Blanchardyn her lover, whiche that nyght made grete diligence for to accomplysshe that whiche Blanchardyn had sent her worde of. For she was herself that nyght in the towne house where she made to come al her captaynes tofore her, to whome by the provost she made to be tolde and related al alonge that was charged unto her by Blanchardyn. The captaynes and hedes of her werre were all glad of thees tydynges, right [fol. 75v] desyryng to putte it into execucyon. At the commaundement of ther lady they made hem all redy and putte hemself in araye for to sprynge out the next mornyng upon their enmyes, as by Blanchardyn was sent worde.

2 Of that other part, Kynge Alymodes, that was in grete affraye to knowe the cause and occasion wherfore they of the cyté were makynge suche a gladnesse, assembled his barons for to have advyse and counseyll upon this matiere. He commaunded that goode watche sholde be made al that nyght, and sette the scout watche wyth grete nombre of men that he sholde not be overtaken unbeware. And that same nyght, he sent for his shippes that were two mylle thens wythin an haven[1] for to have theym brought nerer his oost that he myght entre in them yf eny infortune happed to hym, and to wythdrawe his folke therinne yf nede were. Thus passed Kynge Alymodes the nyght over tyl the fayre daye came that the sonne byganne to ascende, castyng his bemes abrode upon the erthe. And as he was musyng upon the werke,[2] lokyng to and fro upon the see, he perceyved a right myghty navey wherof they that were come upon lande. He sawe hem in grete nombre alredy renged in a fayr ordeynaunce of batayll for to fyght nyghe by the see shoris a lytyl beyonde his ooste, wherof he was not awar afore that. And he was sore abashed and gretely merveylled how they were so soone landed wythout that he knewe therof. So fered he soone of this that was true, that it was Blanchardyn and his folke that were come there.

3 The worthy knyght Blanchardyn had ordeyned his folke in thre batayles wherof he led the formest,[3] the seconde he betoke to Sadoyne his felawe, and the thirde he gaf to be conducted to his fader, the kynge of Fryse. Whan Blanchardyn had al this thynges redy and all his ordeynaunces y-made, he made his trompettes, hornes, olyfauntes,[4] and busynes to be [fol. 76r] rongen and blowen so highe[5] that it was wonder to here them. They of the cyté thenne, that herde the sowne therof, yssued anone out of their towne by commaundement of their lady the proude mayden in amours, that sore admonested and prayed them to do wel to the ende that som goode tydynges might be reported by them.

---

[1] *cove (safe place)*

[2] *plan of action*

[3] *foremost*

[4] *battle trumpets made of ivory*

[5] *loudly*

Alimodes, seeng his enmyes com a-lande and in so fayre ordonaunce y-sette[6] of that one part, and of that other syde he sawe them of the cyté that cam wyth a grete puyssaunce upon hym and his folke, it is well ynough to be byleved that he was not wel assured. But nought therfore,[7] as a sharp and hardy knyght as he was, the best wyse that he myght or coude he ordeyned his bataylles, whiche he toke to be conducted and guyded to theym that semed hym worthy therof. The oostes beganne to approche eche other. The callyng and the crye arose so grete and hyghe betwyx them what by the sowne of trompettes, hornes, and bussynes as of the stour[8] dynnyng[9] and noyse that their horses made treddyng and wallopyng hyghe and harde upon the grounde, that it semed that all the foure elementes had fought there togyder. The duste bygganne to ryse so hyghe aboute them and so thykke that it toke away the bryghtnes of the sonne, so that they that were wythin the cyté sawe nother frendes nor enmyes.

4   They went to the chirche in grete devocyon, makyng their prayers to our Lord that he wolde helpe their frendes, and namely that noble lady, the proude pucelle in amours, alle barefote went from one chirche to another, prayng God that He wold graunte the victorie to her true lover Blanchardyn and to them that were with hym. And syth cam ayen to her paleys and mounted up to a highe toure for to see and beholde the batayl that was alredy bygonne. Right grete murdre and slaughter was ther made at settyng [fol. 76v] upon of bothe partyes. Many a knyght ded and brought to the grounde that never syn had power to releve[10] hemself, the horses of whom went rennyng upon the playn and into the medowes, the raynnes of their brydels[11] hangyng and drawyng upon the grounde.

5   Blanchardyn, at his comynge on that he made, recounted a duke cosyn germayn[12] to Kynge Alymodes, upon whom he sette the sharpe hed of his spere by so grete force that he perced his body thorugh and thorugh, so that the spere was seen from the breste to the backe of hym more than thre fote longe. And syn cam to the second, to the thyrd, and to the fourth, and never he rested nor ceassed hymself as long as the spere abode hole, whiche was sore bygge and oute of mesure grete, to slee and overthrawe his enmyes to the grounde. And or ever his spere was crased[13] or broken, he overthreu and slew seven of theym that deyd myserable ther amonge the horses fete. Then toke Blanchardyn his good swerde into his fyste wherof he brak salletes[14] and helmettes of fyn stele, and so braynd ther many one. He alto hewe his enmyes and made legges, armes, and fete to flee from the body of theym, that all the grounde aboute hym was dyed in red wyth blode of his adversaryes. He dyd so moche of armes that wythin a while his swerde was wele beknowen among his enmyes, insomoche that they made hym waye, fleeng.

---

[6] *situated (set up)*

[7] nought therfore, *nevertheless (in spite of)*

[8] *loud (strong)*

[9] *reverberation (din)*

[10] *recover (rise up)*

[11] raynenes of their brydels, *reins of their bridles*

[12] cosyn germayn, *close kin*

[13] *cracked (crushed)*

[14] *light, bowl-shaped helmets, usually without visors*

6   They dyd so moche by their ryght excellent proues[15] that they made to recule[16] theyr enmyes unto their tentes. And sore yll yt had ben wyth theym yf Kyng Alymodes had not socoured them, that cam of freshe wyth ten thousaund of his men. And to them he began to call and saye forth for the nobel barons, "Have thys daye rememberaunce of your wyves and chyldren that ye have lefte at home in care and myserye for dred that they have to lese you. Take ayen wythin yourself a good and vygoryus corage in [fol. 77r] shewynge of your force and vertue ayenste your enmyes." They began than to caste a crye amonge hem sore grete and wonderfull, tournynge their faces toward their enmyes.

7   Blanchardyn smote hymselfe wythynne theym fyrst of all, whom they knew full wele bycause that by hym and thorughe his cause they had receyved all the most losse that they had donn there, wherfore all their desire was for to close hym all aboute and slee hym yf they myghte have doon soo. And they, seenge that he had embated[17] hymself amonge them, dyde putte hemself togyder and enclosed hym rounde aboute, launchynge and castyng to hym speres and dartes insomoche that they wounded hym ful sore in many places of his body. And under him they slew his horse, but as a preu[18] knyght ryght valiante and hardy lepte lyghtli on his fete, enbrasyng[19] his sheelde, his swerde heved up in his fyste, wherwyth he smote and hewe bothe legges and armes from the bodyes of theym by suche a myghte and fyersnes and thorughe so grete strokes of hym, so that noon was so hardy of all his enmyes that durste abyde a full stroke of his handes.

8   Of that other partye was the kyng of Fryse and Sadoyne, that made the batayles of hys enmyes to trembel full fast and made roume[20] where grete preses were. Ryghte preu and valiant was the kyng of Fryse, for whomsoever he aryved upon he dyd shewe suche a puyssaunce that he had no power to escape but that he slew hym or wounded hym full ylle. Sadoyne, that was of grete corage and full of brennyng desire to acquyer to hymself the name of famouse proesse, chose Corboraunt, the brother of Kyng Alymodes, to whom he gaff suche a grete stroke wyth his swerde upon his helme that he overthrew hym from his horse doun to the grounde. And had kylde hym and broughte to his ende lightly[21] yf he had not ben ryghte sone socoured by King Alymodes, [fol. 77v] his brother, that cam upon Sadoyne acompanyed wyth six thousaund of his folke, wherof the battayl beganne of fresshe to be sore fyers and grete. Right grete was the effucyon[22] or shedyng of blode there of bothe partyes, but more of Alymodes parte that was assaylled and befought on eythre syde bothe behynde and before. Blanchardyn made there ryght a wondryng[23] of worthines and goode conducte. The kyng, his fader, folowed hym nyghe, and so dyde his felawe Sadoyne, for to confounde and overcome their enmyes, the whiche sawe hym

---

[15] *prowess (martial strength)*
[16] *retreat*
[17] *beat his way [OF s'embatre]*
[18] *brave (gallant)*
[19] *grabbing*
[20] *space (room)*
[21] *easily (quickly)*
[22] *spilling (flow)*
[23] a wondryng, *a wonder (marvel)*

fyghtyng and destroyeng and sleynge his enmyes in suche wyse that he raughte[24] noon upon the salate,[25] how stronge that he was, but that he claaf hym doun unto the tethe.

9 But his grete corage and grete prouesse had ben but lytell worthe to hym yf he had not be socoured anone of Sadoyne, his true felawe, that had herde the cry and the noyse that they made aboute Blanchardyn that trowed to have slayne hym. Sadoyne, seeng his true felawe Blanchardyn that faught on fote ayenst his enmyes, broched his hors wyth the spore, full of anger and of wrathe, his swerde in his hande dyed and all blody of the blode of his enmyes. Smot hymself into the presse where he dyde see it moost thyk, accompanyed wyth suche knyghtys as he well trustyd upon, callyng hygh after his baner. Wherby ten thousaund men of his felishyp folowed right soone the bak of hym, and namely the noble kynge of Fryse, that ful quykly cam to the rescue of his son Blanchardin. So smot they hemself all at one weyght[26] upon Kynge Alymodes folke and byganne to hewe and slee them, so that wythin a short tyme they brake the presse and made grete occycyon[27] upon their enmyes. To the rescue of Blanchardyn cam also the gode provost, and wyth him were they of the towne that ful wel dyde [fol. 78r] and bare hemself right wel, for so moche they deyde that, in a lytyl while, wolde their enmyes or not, that Sadoyne gat the place and brought a right myghty courser unto his felaw Blanchardyn, upon whiche he mounted up anone.

10 The kyng of Fryse, seeng his son Blanchardyn rescued and on horsbake ayen, brought his horse nere hym and demanded of hym how he dyde, and yf he felt hymself wounded or hurt in ony place where eny doubte were of his lyf. "Syre," sayde Blanchardyn, "no sore at all I fele wythin my body that can let[28] me to kylle and sle myn enmyes and yours." They thenne wythout eny moo wordes entred ayen bothe togyder into the bataylle toward them of the towne where Sadoyne was wyth them fyghtyng ayenst Alymodes and Corboraunt his brother. Blanchardyn, seeng them of the towne by the baner that they bare, in whiche was portrayed a fygure in lykenes of a mayde that represented the proude pucell in amours, he dyde shewe it unto his fader and to his felawe Sadoyne. He thenne toke corage and fyersnes more than ever he had don afore, admonestyng his fader and Sadoyne to do wel their parte. Soo putte themself into the thyckest of the batayll where they overthrewe and casted doune alle that founde hemself byfore them, wherby Kynge Alymodes folke reculed abak more than is the lengthe of an acre of lande. Alymodes, seeng his folke lese grounde and were smytten ded doun right by the hyghe prouesse and grete worthynes of Blanchardyn, desyred sore wythal his herte to joyne hymself wyth hym and so cam he at the one syde of Blanchardyn, his swerde in the hande for to slee hym yf he myght. But Blanchardyn, that ware[29] was and wel taught of all poyntes of werre, perceyved soone his manere of commyng ayenst hym and tourned brydel and went hymself upon Kynge Alymodes. And suche a stourdy stroke [fol. 78v] he gaf him upon the

---

[24] *struck (cut)*

[25] *light, bowl-shaped helmet, usually without a visor*

[26] *force (impetus)*

[27] *slaughter*

[28] *hinder*

[29] *vigilant (watchful)*

helmet that he brought him doune from his hors all astonyed, the whiche Blanchardin had taken right sone the hed from the body of hym, if socours and help had not come to hym of his folke that brought his hors to him ayen and remounted him on horsbak. Whan he see hymself on his hors, he cam ayen upon Blanchardyn, the swerde in his hande, requyryng to Blanchardyn that he wolde drawe out of the prese and that he had grete desyre to prove hymself upon hym. Whan Blanchardyn understode Kynge Alymodes, he was right glad and right lyberaly graunted to hym his requeste.

11   They two drewe themself out of the bataylle and byganne to bete and smyte one upon other so ofte and so thyk that the fyre came out of their armures that were of fyn stele, but Blanchardyn dyde serve hym wyth so peysaunt[30] and hevy strokes and so horryble, that Alymodes sholde never have departed from the place quyk[31] yf he had not be socoured of Corboraunt his brother. The batayll of thyem two dyde see playnly the proude pucell in amours, that was upon her highe toure where she praied God for the prosperyté of Blanchardyn. She called a yong knyght, a servaunt of hers, to whom she toke a sleve of whyt damaske and commaunded hym to presente hit hastely from her behalve unto Blanchardyn, prayng hym that for her sake and love to dye the whyt coloure into red wyth the blode of her enmyes. The gentylman, sore desyryng to accomplyshe his maystres commaundement, toke of his lady the sleve of whyt colour. He departed and made suche diligence that a present was therof made to Blanchardyn, rehersyng unto hym that that his lady, the proude pucelle in amours, had charged him to saye unto Blanchardyn. Whiche was right glad of the saide present, more than he sholde have be yf the messenger had brought to hym a mylyon[32] of fyn golde. And thanked moche [fol. 79r] his lady the proude pucelle in amours that behylde hym from her tour[33] as ferre as she myght chuse[34] hym, and enforced[35] his power for to parfurnysshe[36] her requeste. He smote upon his enmyes as it had be the thonder, and confoundyng and overthrawyng them ded to the grounde, for who that was that tyme y-raught of hym, his dayes were fynyshed.

12   Fynably,[37] the batayll lasted so longe that Kynge Alymodes and his Cassydonyens were rebuked, wold they or no, to their grete losse, hurt, and dommage. For of thre score thousand men that they were at the begynnyng, there abode of them that laye ded upon the playne more then thirty six thousaund. The remenaunt that myght be saved wythdrewe themself wyth Kynge Alymodes, that toke hastely the waye toward his shippes for to entre and save hymself therinne. But Sadoyne folowed hym of so nyghe at bak of hem that with grete peyne gaf them leyser[38] to save hemself. And so ferre he folowed and chassed them that he overtoke Kynge Alymodes brother, called Corboraunt, to whome he

---

[30] *forceful*
[31] *alive*
[32] *million (coins)*
[33] *tower*
[34] *see*
[35] *strengthened (reinforced)*
[36] *perform (carry out)*
[37] *In the end*
[38] *opportunity (time)*

gaff a reverse[39] wyth his swerde so grete that he made fle bothe the helme and the hed from the body of hym. Kynge Alymodes, seeng his brother slayne of a knyght alone, was full sory and an gred. He ascryed[40] to his folke that traytoure that had slayne his brother Corberaunt sholde be taken by them. "For he hath doon to us this daye so moche of evyl, bothe he and his felawes, that I shal never have joye at my herte tyl that I have hym ded or taken." They thenne from al sydes tourned upon Sadoyne and slewe his horsse and enclosed hym rounde aboute, so that his defendyng had nought proffyted to hym nor holpen, but that he shold have be there slayn, yf Kynge Alymodes had not ascryed and commaunded to his men that they sholde not sle hym but sholde take hym quyk,[41] [fol. 79v] whiche thynge was don of hem.

13   Grete crye, noyse, and houlyng made the Sarasyns at the takyng of Sadoyne, insomoche that Blanchardyn herde them, whiche cam rennyng there as the medlé[42] was wyth a grete nombre of folkys. But the kyng Alymodes, seeng hym comyng wyth puyssaunce, for fere that he had of hym, he departed and went hastely wyth suche as wold be saved wyth hym and entred hys shyppes, and brought wyth hym Sadoyne. For Blanchardyn coude never come tyme ynough to the rescue of hym, but or ever they were entred into theyr vessels they made grete losse of their men. But the sorow was ryght grete of Blanchardyn and of hys folke whan he wyste that the paynemys had wyth hem his trew felawe Sadoyne, wherof he was so dolaunt and so replenyshed wyth sorow and hevynes that nobody coude pease[43] hym by eny manere. He smote his hors wyth the spore alonge by the shores of the see, escryeng[44] as loude as he myght unto Kyng Alymodes that he wold take to hym ageyn his felaw Sadoyne, and that for his raensom he shulde geve hym thre score thousand pound of fyne gold wyth six thousand men of his folke that he had prysoners. Alymodes ansuerd that yf he wolde delyver the proude pucell in amours to hys wylle, that he shulde take hym ayen Sadoyne. Blanchardyn ansuerd that he was content and that whan he sholde have ayen Sadoyne and had delyverd the proude pucell in amours in his hande, he shold rather slee hymself than that she shold abyde wyth hym no while.

14   After these wordes, Alymodes, the kyng of Cassydonye, that was ryghte sore an gred, rose upon his fete and sayd to Blanchardyn that he loste[45] his wordes and that he sholde never see Sadoyne, but sholde have hym wyth hym into Cassydonye where he sholde make hym to be hanged byfore Beatryx, his [fol. 80r] doughter, sayeng that suche sholde be the rewarde of his folyshe love and that noon other raenson he sholde take for hym. And the sorowefull Sadoyne, that was that tyme upon the wale[46] of the ship sore harde y-bounde wyth yrons, bygan to calle and sayde wyth a hyghe voyce, "Farwel, my true felawe Blanchardyn. Ye shall never see me more, as I byleve." And thus they departed

---

[39] back-handed stroke (cut)
[40] called out (announced)
[41] alive
[42] combat [OF meleé]
[43] placate (appease)
[44] shouting
[45] wasted
[46] plank (side)

wythout eny more speche. The wynde was goode for them that sone brought them ferre from the coste of Tormaday and drewe towarde Cassydonye.

The forty fourth chapiter conteyneth in hitself how Blanchardin made hymself redy wyth his folke and navye for to socoure and helpe his felawe Sadoyne that Kynge Alymodes brought prysoner to Cassydonye.

1   Whan Blanchardyn dyde see that to hym was impossyble to have ayen by raenson his true felawe Sadoyne, he was right sory therfor, and none was there so grete frende wyth hym that coude recomforte hym. Sore pyteously he byganne to wyshe hym ayen sayng in this wyse, "Wo me, Sadoyne, my veray true felawe. For my sake ye have lefte your fader, your royalme, landes, lordshippes, and kynrede and your frendes, and have exposed the body of you and of your men to the socoure and help of me, and nowe, for myne owne cause, ye be prysoner. Ought not I wel to enforce myself that ye were delyvered from the evyll where ye be in at this tyme for the grete love that ye have unto me? Certes I ought to do it, and yf God be playsed, I shall acquyte myself therof."

2   The povere folke of Prusse, that is to wyte the barons and knyghtes that Sadoyne had brought wyth hym, were sore dyscomfyted[1] and full of sorowe for the absence of their maystre that they sawe was brought [fol. 80v] prysonner of the paynems, but Blanchardyn ryght humbly dyde recomforte hem the best wyse that he coude. After that the gayne[2] was parted emonge them that therof were worthy, Blanchardyn gaff commaundement that alle the shippes and other vesselles that were al aboute Tourmaday sholde be made redy and garnysshed wyth vytaylles suche as apparteyned,[3] and that his wylle was uttyrly sette for to goo to gyve socoure and helpe unto his felawe Sadoyne.

3   The fayr yong lady, the proude pucell in amours, was alredy come ayenst her true lover Blanchardyn, so may ye well ynough thynke and knowe for certayn that teerys were there shed and wepte of her parte in grete habondaunce. Whan the two mouthes met kyssyng eche other, the noble mayden was well recomforted of all her evylles past, but overmoche dysplaysed her to see her feythfull frende Blanchardyn that wolde goo ayen out of the lande. They cam wythin the cyté where they were receyved wyth grete feste and gladnesse, and syth after the owre of mydnyght was past, Blanchardin cam to the paleys where he fonde his love the proude pucelle in amours that sorowed right sore for the departyng of her frende Blanchardyn. But the best that to hym was possyble he dyde recomforte her, promyttyng to her that alssone[4] as he godely[5] myght, he sholde retourne ayen toward her.

4   Ther wythin was a knyght wyth her in whom she had a grete confydence, whiche had be noryshed in her paleys from the first tyme of his yonge age wyth the kynge of Tourmaday, her fader, that recomended hym at the owre of his deth unto his doughter. A full fayr knyght he was, but he was descended of a lowe kynrede, for his fader and his moder had be servauntes [fol. 81r] wythin the place, the whiche knyght, by his subtyl

---

[1] *dejected*

[2] *gain (spoils)*

[3] *pertained*

[4] *as soon*

[5] *possibly*

engyne⁶ and gode servyse that he made, came to be soo pryvé⁷ famylier wyth the kynge the proude pucelle in amours fader, that he added and gaffe more feyth and truste and more credence unto hym and his wordes than he dyde in eny other knyght or baron of his royalme, wherfore atte his decesse he had him moche recomended. But men saye in a comyn langage that never noo wodewoll⁸ dyde brede a sperhawke.⁹ I saye this for the knyght of whom I doo make here mencyon, whiche had to his name Subyon, for he was soo proude and so hawten¹⁰ that advyse was to hym,¹¹ for the grete auctoryté¹² that he was ynne, that non sholde have compared wyth hym. And therfore I saye that of churles¹³ bothe man and wyff can departe noo goode fruyte. And it is impossyble that yf eny grete lord, prynce, or baron gyve auctoryté or lene his eeres for to herken to a churles wordes, but that he shall be at the last deceyved by hym wythout more happe be. For men sayen that of a kerle¹⁴ may nought come but poyson and fylth that maketh the place to stynke where he haunteth¹⁵ ynne, as the same Subyon dyde.

5   Blanchardyn, seeng this knyght to be in grete auctoryté in the court of the proude pucelle in amours, and well honoured and gretely set by of all the offycers of the places, he dyde chuse the sayde knyght Subyon wythout eny counseyll of other for to playse the better the pucelle therby. And betoke unto hym the kepynge of the proude pucelle in amours noble personne wyth the charge and governaunce of an hondred knyghtes that sholde wayte upon hym, and made hym seneshall¹⁶ of all the royalme of Tourmaday and rewler of all the lande, wherof the noble mayden was right glad and knewe not what unto her sholde befall therby [fol. 81v] afterward, as herafter ye shall mowe understande playnly.

---

⁶ *ingenuity (wit)*

⁷ *intimately*

⁸ *green woodpecker; (see note)*

⁹ *sparrow hawk*

¹⁰ *arrogant (presumptuous)*

¹¹ advyse was to hym, *in his opinion (judgment)*

¹² *position of authority*

¹³ *persons of low rank or bad character*

¹⁴ *churl*

¹⁵ *frequents (lives)*

¹⁶ *chief administrator of a lord's lands and estates*

The forty fifth chapyter sheweth how Blanchardyn toke the see for to go socoure his felawe Sadoyne.

1   After that Blanchardyn had put provysion and kepyng for his lady and her lande, he toke his leve of her, whiche was wel sorowfull of eyther partyes, but the grete desyre that Blanchardyn had for to socoure and helpe his true felaw Sadoyne, to have hym out of the thraldom¹ into franchise,² retarded³ wythin his herte many sobbynges. The kyng of Fryse

---

¹ *bondage*

² *freedom (liberty)*

³ *stifled (impeded)*

came toward the proude pucell in amours and sayde to her in this maner of wyse, "Madame, it nede not to you to make eny sorowe, but be of goode chire and alle recomforted for, to the playsure of oure Lorde, we shal not have so soone acomplysshed oure enterpryse, but that I shal brynge to you ageyne my sone Blanchardyn." The proude pucelle in amours thenne ansuerde full mekely and sayde to the kynge fader unto Blanchardyn, "Sire, of that ye promytte to me I thanke you moche. I pray God that it may be soo and gyve you and hym grace to retourne wyth joye wythin short tyme, for the waytyng and taryng therof shal be sore noyouse[4] to me." The kynge of Fryse and the other barons thenne toke their leve of the pucelle and folowed Blanchardyn that had taken his shippyng alredy. Whan the proude pucelle in amours sawe her frende Blanchardyn departed, from her chambre where she lened upon a wyndowe that loked upon the see, makyng full pyteouse rewthes for her love that she sawe; nor never thens she wolde departe as longe as she myght see the shyppes that were sayllyng.

2   Whan Blanchardyn had taken the see wyth many shippes and galleyes, he had grete joye at his herte for the grete excercyte of folke that he conducted. And that wyth hym [fol. 82r] was the kynge his fader, of whom he was well recomforted, as of thre score thousand good men of warre that wyth hym were wele appoynted, what of Sadoynes folke as of hem of Tourmaday, whiche had all a goode wyll and grete desire to rescue their lord Sadoyne and to have hym oute of the handes of King Alymodes. The weder was fayr and clere and the see peasyble and styll. The ancres were drawen up and the sayles alofte, wherin the wynde smot and blew softe and good that sone brought them a goode waye fro the lande. Grete bruyt and revyl they made at their partyng, the see was covered wyth their sayles that sore brode were spred upon their vesselles. Many an horne, many an olyphaunt,[5] and many a claryon and trompettes were blowen there that made a joyefull noyse.

3   We shall here leve to telle of Blanchardyn and of his ryght puyssaunt excercyte,[6] that wyth force of saylles and oores goon saylyng on the see ful sore thretnyng Kyng Alymodes his enmye, and shall retourne to speke of Subyon and of his lady, the proude pucelle in amours, for to telle of their adventurys of the trayson of hym, and the grete comstaunce and feythfulnes of that other noble pucelle, in manere as here foloueth.

---

[4] *displeasing (annoying)*
[5] *battle trumpet made of ivory*
[6] *company of soldiers (army)*

The forty sixth chapter sheweth how Subyon to whom Blanchardyn atte his departyng had lefte the governaunce and kepynge of his lady the fayr proude pucell in amours and of all the royalme, made conspyracion ayenste her for to take her and have her to his wyff and of that whiche happed afterwarde.

1   Ye have well harde here afore whan Blanchardyn dyd departe from Tormaday, how he dyd ordeyne Subyon and made hym seneschall[1] and his leef tenaunt[2] generall of the

---

[1] *chief officer in a noble household and overseer of estates*
[2] *leef tenaunt, lieutenant, one to whom authority is delegated*

royalme of Tormaday, takynge to hym the rewle and the [fol. 82v] kepynge of the pucell unto tyme that he were comen ayen. Subyon, seeng hymself in suche an auctoryté and so haunsed[3] in worship, toke in his herte an unconstaunt pryde of the moevable[4] godes of fortune and wolde clymme[5] up yet into a more hyghe astate than he fortunably was comen unto, whiche myght wel have suffysed a better man than he was, for hym semed that the tyme was now come that he best myght brynge it aboute. He sawe that he was obeyed thurgh all the royalme, and that nothyng was don wythout his leve or commaundement whiche every man kept and obeyed. So dyde he so moche that wyth the most grete of the lande he made conspiracion,[6] insomoche that, by grete gyftes and promesses that he made to them, they promysed hym for to serve hym in accomplyssyng of all his wyll and to make him kynge of the lande. To this dyde consent many a traytour of the house of the pucell. Subyon sayde unto them all, "Lordes, ye knowe me al ynough and the grete auctoryté and power where I am now ynne. Wherby I may make yow all riche, yf ye wyl helpe truly to brynge my desyre at a gode ende. And that ye helpe me so moche that I may have to myn espouse the proude pucelle in amours and wedde her, of alle the godes and riches wherof she is endowed and wel garnysshed shal nothing therof be parted, but ye shal be perteners[7] to the hool as myself. And to me shal suffyse the name to be a kynge and to have the pucelle to myn owne wyf. And for the servyse that ye shal do to me in this byhalve,[8] ye shal have the reward suche as I have promysed unto you, and wyth this I shal kepe you ayenst al other that wold trouble or greve you by eny maner of wyse. For moche better it is to you to have a lord borne of this lande than to have a straunger. And ye may byleve certeynly that Blanchardyn shal never [fol. 83r] come ayen at thys syde. Kyng Alymodes is too myghty a lorde in his lande that shall sone overcome Blanchardyn. And yf so be that he wolde be so over proude to come hyder ayen, I shall make hym to be hanged wythoute eny respyte."[9] Then the false traytours and untrew men, to whiche Subyon made thys promyse, ansuerd to hym all wyth one voyce that they shulde helpe to bryng thys werke aboute that he shulde be kyng, and incontynent dide geve unto hym their feyth, makyng a grete and a solempne[10] ooth that they shulde be trew to hym of their promesses.

2   Alas, the good knyghte Blanchardyn was not aware that tyme of the grete treason that machyned[11] was ayenst hym. The ryght untrew Subyon was therof ryght glad, and sore desirouse to accomplysshe his dampnable enterpryse. At an ende, he and his complices in grete nombre went up to the paleys hall where he fonde the proude pucelle in love was, that but a lytyl afore was com fro the wyndowe where she had conveyed[12] wyth her eye

---

[3] *raised in status (enhanced)*

[4] *changeable (mutable)*

[5] *climb*

[6] *conspiracy*

[7] *partners*

[8] *matter (point)*

[9] *reprieve*

[10] *solemn*

[11] *plotted*

[12] *followed (escorted)*

her trewe lover Blanchardyn, and commended[13] hym and his fayer companye into the kepyng of our Lord, prayeng humbly that a goode retorne and a shorte he myght make. Thenne, whan she sawe that she myghte nomore see hem, she went awaye from the wyndowe as halfe in a swone sore tenderli wepynge.

3   And evyn at that tyme entred Subyon in her halle, and toke her by the hande and had her up fro the grounde and syn sayd, "Madame, dyscomforte you not thus for a stranger that fleeth from one lande to another, but gyve me wythoute mo wordes your love and goode wylle and ye shall doo as a wyse woman and well counseylled." Whan the noble mayden understode Subyon, ryght fyersli she bygan to loke upon hym, drawyng herselfe to the upperhande of hym, and sayde, "O thou ryght enfamouse[14] churle[15] and olde myschaunte,[16] how [fol. 83v] hast thou ben so hardy to speke thus of the sone of a kynge, the most preu[17] and the most valyant that ever gyrded eny swerde? How thenne arte thou now dronke or folyshe or from thy wyttes, that thou haste dare utter or profere suche wordes oute of thy mouthe?" Thenne Subyon al a hyghe ansuered and sayde, "Lady, speke nomore of hit, for ye shal never have non other man to youre husband and lorde but me, and tomorowe wythout lenger abydyng, wyl ye or not, I shal take and wedde you to my wyf and shal beslepe[18] your bed wyth you." And the traytours and felon conspiratours sayde unto their lady al togyder at ones,[19] "Madame, take and wedde Subyon. He is a man that shal kepe yow right wel and al your royalme, lordshipys, and landes." The good lady thenne hering the cursed and false traytours speke, saw wel that she was trahyshed[20] of all poyntes. But yf God of His grace purveyed not for her, she was lyke to be uttirly lost. To see that noble pucelle dyscomforted as she was, ther was noo man but ought to have compassion and pyté of her. She wyst of noo comforte to take unto her but to loke out at the wyndowe callyng after Blanchardyn that alredy had saylled ferre, and knewe nothynge of this adoo.[21] For yf he had knowlege therof the same tyme he sholde never have had joye at his herte tyl that she had be delyvered out of that grete hevynesse. The noble mayden made grete sorowe and tourmented herself ful piteously.

4   Thenne cam her maystresse sore discomforted that wyth grete peyne brought her into her chambre. The rewthe and doleaunce that this right parfit[22] and true lady made ought certeynly to styre and moeve all noble hertes to pyté and compassyon of her infortune, whan at the best tyme and most entier[23] of her age she had evermore sorowe, care, and grete displeysure. The night was to her sore long whiche she and her maystres passed, allwayes wepyng wythout onye ceasse. [fol. 84r] And the next day, Subyon, that to the

---

[13] entrusted
[14] vile (infamous)
[15] person of bad character (a term of contempt)
[16] villain (wretch)
[17] brave (gallant)
[18] sleep in
[19] once
[20] betrayed
[21] trouble (difficulty)
[22] perfect
[23] morally pefect (unblemished)

nobles of the lande had assigned an owre for to be at the paleys, cam wyth theym that helde part wyth hym into the halle, havyng their swerdes al naked under their mantelles. And whan the nobles of the lande were come there at his sendyng, Subyon dyde expose unto theym the cause wherfore he had called hem, and tolde them that he wolde be made kynge of Tourmaday, and that he wold wedde the proude pucelle in amours for many causes and raysons that were too long to be reherced.

Here foloweth the forty seventh that sheweth how the erle of Castelforde, the goode provost, and the knyght of the fery wyth their folke toke and bare awaye the proude pucelle wyth them into Castelforde magré[1] Subyon that besieged them wythin the sayde place, as ye shal here.

1   Whan the nobles of the lande that were there assembled understod Subyon, they had therof grete merveylle and loked upon eche other al abashed. Of that other part they marked[2] well that wyth Subyon were grete fuson of men al in harneys under their gownes, wherfore they see wel that force it was to them to consent his wyl at that owre and ansuered unto hym, syth that his playsure was so, they were content. But the olde erle of Castelforde, the goode provost, and the knyght of the fery sayde al thre togyder of one accorde that they sholde never be consentyng of that infydelyté and grete trayson, but cryed up alowde that men sholde taken Subyon for to be brought to pryson unto the tyme that Blanchardyn cam ayen. Subyon thenne called upon his folke and saide that they sholde avenge hym upon thees traytours. The gode erle, the provost, and the knyght of the fery called ayen in lyke wise upon their folke. So bygan the medlé[3] [fol. 84v] to be grete and fyers betuyx the two partyes, whiche were not equal, for overmoche were the traytours in grete multytude. So were constrayned the thre knyghtes and theyr men to wythdrawe themself togyder away.

2   Whan the proude pucell in amours sawe the erle departed, she ded call after hym ryght pyteousli, "Ha, ryghte nobel knyght, have pyté and compassyon upon thys pore chylde, whiche is now all alone amonge wolves famyshed be redy to devoure me." The goode erle then, the provost, and the knyght of the fery, their swerdes in their handes naked, toke and seysed her by force and broughte her donn the stayers of the paleys, where they founde their horses that bode there after hem, and lepte a-horsbak. And by the helpe of their frendes and kynnesmen, they sette the lady upon a myghty palfray magré Subyon and all his complyces. The provost guyded her horse by the reyn that was made faste to the brydell, and the good erle and the knyght of the fery cam behynde hem wyth their folke that had their swerdes al naked. And so moche they dyd by their highe proesse that, magré their enmyes, they conducted and broughte wyth them the pucell oute of her cyté of Tourmaday. That was not wythoute grete rewth and pyteouse clamors of the peple, for they were all in a grete dyspleasure for their noble and good lady that so pyteousli they sawe departe the town. The noble erle, the good provost, and the worthy knyght of the fery exployted so longe that wythoute eny let or combrauns[4] they and the

---

[1]   *in spite of [OF maugré]*

[2]   *observed (noted)*

[3]   *combat [OF meleé]*

[4]   *obstacle (hinderance)*

proude pucelle in amours arryved in saveté[5] wythin the fortres of Castelforde, where they were receyved of the countesse wyth hertly love and grete humylité. The proude pucell in amours thanked and rendred graces onto oure Lord that she was thus escaped oute of the handes of her enmye, wherof she thanked ryght moche the goode erle of Castelforde.

3   And [fol. 85r] Subyon, seeng that the pucell was thus caryed awaye, he was ryght wrooth and sory that she was scaped soo from hym. He made all hys folke to lepe on horsbak and foloued hem that had her awaye by the markes of their horses steppes. But at the entree of a forest that was there, they loste their trayne[6] and went oute of ther waye, wherby they myght not folowe nor overtake the pucell nor they that brought her wyth theim. And thus Subyon and his complyces inordynate purpos was tourned, chaunged, and fayled of their false and untrew enterprise. The ryght wycked and false Subyon had not refreyned[7] nor fulfylled his perverse and untreu corage, but sent hastyly to Tourmaday for folke and engynes,[8] ladders, and other habylymentes[9] of warre and made theim com afore Castelforde, where he dyd laye his siege and sware that he shulde never departe from afore the place unto the tyme that the castel were take and theym of wythin at his wyll. But it ys sayd often in a comyn langage that moche abydeth behynde that a fole thynketh, for the good erle, the provost, and the knyght of the fery wyth theyr folke ordeyned and provyded theymself soo that they fered but lytyl Subyon or noughte, and had more lette[10] and care to comforte the noble lady Eglantyne, otherwyse callyd the proude pucell in amours, than they had of Subyon. Castelforde was a stronge place and well appoynted to the were, soo that yt was inprenable[11] and fered not the shotte of the engynes, nor of bombardes.[12] It was purveyd ryghte well of vytaylles and of good men of werre.

4   Here we shall tarye[13] styll oure penne to wryte of theym that be byseged and of Subyon that kepte his seege byfore the fortresse of Castelforde, and shalle wryte of Alymodes, the untrew kynge, that ladde wyth hym the goode knyghte Sadoyne, felawe to Blanchardyn, [fol. 85v] toward the cyté of Cassydonye.

---

[5] *safety*

[6] *trail*

[7] *restrained*

[8] *siege machines or structures for assaulting walls*

[9] *munitions (apparatus)*

[10] *difficulty (impediment)*

[11] *impregnable*

[12] *cannons that shoot large stone balls*

[13] *pause (delay)*

Here foloweth the forty eighth chapter that conteyneth how Kyng Alymodes arryved before the cyté of Cassydonye, and how he spake to his doughter the fayr Beatryx and how for to doo to her a more grete despyte made a gybet to be dressed up for to have hanged there afore her eyen hyr goode husboode Sadoyne.

1   Ye have wele understonde here afore how Kyng Alymodes toke his shippyng hastely after the batayll that was afore Tormaday and brought Sadoyne prysoner wyth hym and saylled toward Cassydonye, where they arryved wythoute lettyng or perell. Whan they were comen into the haven, Alymodes made his ancres to be cast and toke lande there

wyth his folke, and syth made their horses to be had oute of the vesseles, wheropon they mounted and spred theymself upon the playn in a fayr ordenaunce of batayll. There beganne the trompettes, the hornes, the olyphauntes,[1] and the busynes to blowe, that suche a noyse made that the see and the erthe retentyssed[2] wythalle. The same tyme was the fayr Beatryx, the doughter of Kynge Alymodes, lenyng wyth bothe her armes upon a wyndowe wythin her paleys that loked toward the seesyde.

2   She sawe there in the playne a grete nombre of men of armes wherof she was right glad, wenyng to her that it had be Sadoyne, her true lover and wel beloved husbande, that had retourned ageyne wyth Blanchardyn. Hastely she made her stywarde to lepe a-horsbak and sent hym for to knowe what folke were arryved and landed in so grete nombre, whiche taryed not longe after that he was goon out of the towne that he sawe Alymodes and his folke that cam toward the towne a softe paas.[3] He asked hem what they were and yf they [fol. 86r] wyst not som goode tydynges of Sadoyne. Thenne cam Kyng Alymodes forthe and demaunded to the styward whiche his lady had lever[4] to see, other her fader or her lover Sadoyne. The styward ansuerd and sayde, "Syre, I knowe not your persone what ye be, nor to whom I speke, but wel I dare telle you that she careth not of her fader and that yf he cam ayen, he sholde not entre nor come ayen her nor come wythin the towne." And he tolde hym that they of the towne and of alle the lande of Cassydonye were becomen Cristen, and had crowned Sadoyne to their kynge and had made their homage unto hym and helde hym for their lorde soverayne.

3   Whan Alymodes understode the styward he was sore dolaunt and tryste of that. He sawe hymself thus unfortunable as to have lost his knyghtes and trowed to have come to reffut[5] in his lande that he fonde tourned to another lawe than his owne, the gates of the cyté and castell shet, and theym of wythin rebell ayenst hym, his right dere sone Daryus slayn and ded. Of that other part, he sawe his only doughter that denyed and defended[6] hym his comynge into his cyté of Cassydonye. He sayd full angerly to the styward that, "To an evyll owre hath your lady ben so madde as to mary herself to a ladde, a straunger, wythout my lycence and knowlege. She hath styred suche a thynge wherof she shal have yet at her herte grete sorowe and hevynes. For thou shalt nowe telle unto her that wyth me I doo brynge her yong ladde Sadoyne, whiche I shall tomorowe make to be hanged in despyte[7] of her byfore my cyté of Cassydonye."

4   Whan the goode styward understode hym that to hym spake, and knewe certaynly [fol. 86v] that it was Kynge Alymodes, wythout eny moo wordes departed from hym and cam hastely, brochyng his horsse wyth the spore, unto the cyté. He went into the paleys where he fonde his lady and recounted to her how it was Kyng Alymodes and his folke and what he had sayde, wherof she entred into a bytter displaysure and hertely sorowe.

---

[1] *ivory battle trumpets*

[2] *resounded (echoed)* [OF *retentir*]

[3] softe paas, *leisurely pace*

[4] *rather*

[5] *refuge (shelter)*

[6] *prevented*

[7] in despyte, *in order to spite*

5   Notwythstandyng this, as a vertuose lady made alle her folke to be redy in their harneys, whiche at that syde of the towne made to goo up upon the walles and towres for to deffende the towne, and charged them that they sholde not late her fader come wythin and non of them sholde speke wyth hym. Kynge Alymodes came rydyng toward the cyté wyth his bataylle[8] and aryved afore the castell where he sawe and knewe his doughter that loked out of a wyndowe. Wyth hym he brought Sadoyne to the ende that she myght see hym for to make to her a gretter dispite. Thenne called Kyng Alymodes alowde and sayde unto his doughter that anone hastely she sholde make to hym and his folke openyg of the gates of the castel and towne, sayng to her that over grete haste she had made to mary herself wythout his wyll, and that in an evyll oure she ever wedded Sadoyne, that for this cause for to doo to her a grete dyspite he shal tomorowe make hym to be hanged.

6   The fayre Beatryx, heryng her fader speke that he sone knewe, ansuered unto hym swetly and sayd by grete humylyté, full of sorowe and of compassyon and pyté for to refrene[9] and brynge to swetnes the harde corage and cruel wylle of Kynge Alymodes her fader, and namely for her goode husbande sake, trowyng[10] to eschewe[11] his deth therby. "Ha ha, my lorde, my dere fader, pardone your wrathe [fol. 87r] and evyll wylle to my lorde, my good husbonde, and to me, your only doughter, and be you sure my lorde, my dere fader, that whiche I have donn in this behalve I have donn it for the best. And yf ye woll byleve me, ye shall leve your folishe credence that ye geve upon your false goddes and shall byleve the Father, the Sone, and the Holy Goost, one onli God, that shalle make you to come to the blysse perdurable[12] that never shall fayll. And ye shall accorde wyth Blanchardyn and wyth Sadoyn of whom ye shall be served and dred of all your neyghbours, and shall lyve in grete worship and goode prosperyté alle your dayes. And I shall well doo wyth theym, that all that whiche I saye shall be made sure."

7   Whan thenne Kynge Alymodes herde thus speke his doughter, as a cruell man from his wyttes sayd unto her, "Ha, false and renyed[13] strompet, I were me lever ded than that I sholde byleve nor doo thi cursed counseyll, and that ever I sholde byleve in that same God of the Crystens that thou now preysest. I sholde me lever soffer to be drawen wyth horses.[14] And in despyte of hym and of thee, I shall doo to be executed in thy presence that that I have sayd, and after I shall make hym to be brent and to deye an evyl deth."

8   And whan she sawe that by no manere of meanes she myght not tourne ne chaunge the corage of her cruel fader, and that she herde hym saye blame of her God, her creatoure in whom she had sette her byleve and her herte, she by grete wrath sayd to hir fader, "O full ryght false and olde tyraunte, that worshypste false and desceyvable goddes and ydoles that canne not helpe thee nor theymselfe! What sekest thou here nor what moveth thee to come into this marche? Thou haste noughte to doo here, for thou shalt not sette

---

[8]   army (batallion)
[9]   restrain
[10] believing (thinking)
[11] avoid (escape)
[12] everlasting
[13] renegade (apostate)
[14] drawn and quartered (killed)

thy foote wythin my towne. Goo ayen [fol. 87v] to Tormaday to see the noble lande of that lady, she of whom thou arte amorouse soo moche that thou arte a fole become therfore. Olde unfamouse[15] myschaunt,[16] how arte thou soo folyshe and so overwenynge[17] as for to wene to have her? Thou haste that berde of thyne over-whyte therto, thy face is too mykel wonne,[18] and that olde skynne of thyn ys over mykel shronken togyder. Put thyselfe into some fayr hermytage and medel[19] thou no more wyth love. Leve this thoughte and make no more thyne accomptes for to entre wythin my cyté, for yf ye have taken and bounde my husbond that I see ther by thee, I shall have hym ayene, to the pleasure of our Lorde my creatour, some daye that shal be to your evyll adventure."

9   Whan Alymodes understode the reproches and the rygorouse wordes of his doughter, he wende to have lost his wyttes and to have deyd for anger and sorowe. Incontynent wythoute delaye he made his trompettes to be blowen and commaunded that the towne sholde be wele assaylled of all partyes. His men made hem redy after his commaundement and came and sawted[20] the towne full proudely. They that were wythin defended theym vygoryously as men of highe facion.[21] They kylled and slue and hurte sore many one, deffendynge hemselfe soo strongely ayenste their enmyes to theyr grete losse and damage and to wythdrawe themself ayen, wherfore Kynge Alymodes, sore angry and full of wrathe for the deth of many of his knyghtes that had be ther slayne, made his ryche pavylyons to be dressyd[22] and hanged byfore the towne and commaunded thorugh al his oost that they sholde rejoyse hemself and that they sholde make grete revell in sygne of joye, to the ende that the noyse therof shold come to the eeres of his doughter, for to gyve a more grete [fol. 88r] cause of dysplaysure and sorowe. Also he commaunded that Sadoyne sholde be beten.

10   And syth tomorowe in the mornyng as soone as the daye byganne to appiere, Kynge Alymodes commaunded expressely to the mareshall of his ooste that he shold doo make and to be sette up a galhouse[23] evyn byfore the castell, to the ende that his doughter myght better see hange at her ease her frende and lover Sadoyne. He ordeyned and comaunded that he shold be hanged. After this comaundement made by Kynge Alymodes, his mareshall dyde the kynges wyll to be accomplyssed and, accompanyed wyth fyve hondred men of armes, brought Sadoyne evyn at the place where the gybet[24] was made redy. Whan he cam there and sawe a payre of galhouse dressed up, where he trowed certaynly to have fynysshed hys dayes, the teerys habondantly fell doune from his eyen so byttyrly that they wette al his face. He byganne to make grete rewthe and pyteouse complayntes sayng in this wyse, "O my right true felawe and right dere frende Blanchardyn, this day

---

[15] *vile (infamous)*
[16] *villain (wretch)*
[17] *presumptuous (conceited)*
[18] *pale*
[19] *interfere (meddle)*
[20] *attacked*
[21] *ability (power)*
[22] *made ready*
[23] *gallows*
[24] *gibbet (stand for hanging)*

shall the seperacyon be made of the amyté[25] that is bytwene us bothe." And syth loked up toward the castel where he sawe his lady and wyf, the fayr Beatryce, and whan he dyde perceyve her face, he fyl doune in a swone alonge the erthe. The Sarrasyns that saw this lyfte hym up and gaf to hym grete and hevy strokes wyth staves. He byganne yet ayen to make rewthe and complayntes, wyshyng after Blanchardyn, and sayde how that he was come out of his contrey, whiche was ferre thens, for to helpe hym to socoure his lady, the proude pucelle in love, and syth that he shold never see hym, that he at the leste wyste yf he wolde avenge hym of this shamefull dethe or not that he most nowe suffre. And syth he saide ful sore sobbyng, "Alas, yf nedes I shal dey, I were of it all well [fol. 88v] content, soo that it were in the absence of her that maketh all my sorowes to encreace for her tendre love. Alas, myghte not fortune as well hurte or greve me by another manere of wyse than for to mak me deye shamefully byfore my owne true love, my goode wyffis presence? Alas, wo to me, unhappy man and more than myschaunte that I am. Ys ther non other remedye? Muste I nedes deye thus shamefully wythoute eny deffence makynge?" After thees wordes of complaynte that Sadoyne made, the cursed and felon paynems peyned hemselfe sore for to make redye suche thynges as served to make hym deye upon the galhouse that was sette up byfore the castell.

---

[25] *friendship*

The forty ninth chapter conteyneth how the fayer Beatryx sente her folke for to socoure her husbande Sadoyne, and was rescued from deth and brought wythin Cassydonye malgré[1] his enmyes.

1   Whan the fayr Beatryx, that at her wyndow was lenyng her hande over her brestes, and ful sore wepyng for love of her husband that she sawe in pereyl of his lyf, she lefte asyde her femenyn wyll, and toke wythin her the corage of a man vertuose in manere and faccion of a hardy byfyghtresse.[2] So ascryed[3] she highe[4] and sayd, "O my right good and trewe knyghtes, this daye I doo praye you and commaunde, that over all the best knyghtes that are now reynynge[5] in the wyde worlde, ye woll socoure the comforte of my joye, and that most is of all my lyffe that goeth to perdycyon, wythoute[6] yt be by youre benyngne grace. And upon all the gode socoures and servyces that ever ye woll doo to me, that at this tyme and owre, atte my requeste and prayer, ye woll enforce yourselfe to rescue oute of daunger of deth my lorde and youre, my gode husband Sadoyne, that I see yonder in grete parel of his lyf, but yf he be socoured right soone. And [fol. 89r] therfore yet ayen to you myn men, my true vasselles, I do full instantly pray that your naturell[7] lorde ye wyll help to have hym out of his harde enmyes handes, yf it be unto you possyble."

---

[1] *despite*

[2] *woman warrior [OF batailleresse (n. fem.), warrior]*

[3] *called out*

[4] *loudly*

[5] *present*

[6] *unless*

[7] *hereditary (by birth)*

2 The barons and knyghtes thenne of a right gode wyll, wythout answer nor replye makyng, in grete hast and wythout delaye, enflamed wyth yre and of cordyal[8] wrath for love of their lord that the Sarrasyns wolde doo deye thus pyteously so shameful a deth, and also for the love of their lady that they had full dere, went and armed hemself. And hastely in grete nombre of folke all a-fote lepte at a posterne out of the towne and cam al under covert from wythin the dyches[9] of the castel that were drye at that syde, wythout that they were a-spyed of no man except of Sadone, that soone perceyved theym comyng bycause he was alredy brought upon the ladder. Whan he had seen them, he that was as half ded a lityl afore toke ayen his strenthes and corage wythin hymself. He wrang[10] his fystes and brake the cordes al asonder that he was bounded wyth, and syth lept from the ladder whiche his legges enclosed togyder, lokyng upon a Sarrasyne that in his handes helde a grete guysarme[11] whiche is full goode and deffensable.[12] He toke hit from his fystes and gaf to hym suche a merveyllouse stroke wythall that he cloved hym unto the breste, and quykly gaf as moche to another, and syth to the thirde and to the fourthe, and scatered them abrode soo that none so hardy a paynym was there that durste come nyghe for to hurte hym.

3 Whan the mareshall of Kynge Alymodes oost sawe Sadoyne that al alone bare suche damage ayenst them alle, he wexed full of wrathe in his herte. He ascryed on his men and sayde that gretly and well they ought to hate hemself and to prayse hemself full lytyll, whan for one man alone they fled, and that it was a grete shame unto them that he had [fol. 89v] endured so long ayenst them all. He approched hymself toward Sadoyne, his swerde in his hand for to smyte hym, but Sadoyne, that was sore quyk and pert,[13] sawe him wel come and gaf hym wyth his guysarme suche an unmesurable stroke that he clove his hed unto the tethe and slewe him. Evyn at this owre the Cassydonyens that come were out of the cyté smotte hemself emonge the fyve hondred Sarrasyns byfore that they were aware of them. They beganne to slee doune right in every syde and stroke and smote upon the paynemys so that they delyvered lightly[14] the place of hem and none of them abode there but that he was ded or taken, excepte som that fled awaye that this tydynges brought to Alymodes that was full sory whan he understode this tydynge. Quykly he mounted a-horsbake and ranne as a mad man toward the gybette[15] where he fonde Sadoyne and his men that faught togydre. And whan Sadoyne saw hym come, he cam wyth a grete corage ayenst hym and leved[16] up his guysarme upon hym, where wythall he smote hym suche a stroke upon his shulders that he clove and overthrewe hym to the grownde, and sholde have take the lyf from him right soone yf he had not be socoured of his men.

---

[8] *heart-felt*

[9] *moats (ditches)*

[10] *wrung (twisted)*

[11] *battle axe*

[12] *able to give defense*

[13] *bold*

[14] delyvered lightly, *easily rid (emptied)*

[15] *stand for a noose*

[16] *raised*

But they came so fast by and by, and by so grete tourbes[17] and hepes, that force it was to Sadoyne to wythdrawe hymself and his men wythin the towne of Cassydonye, where he was receyved, as ye may thynke, right well wyth grete joye and gladnesse of my lady his wyf, the fayr Beatryce. And of that other part, the kynge Alymodes was so sore brought as to dispeyre himself bycause that he had thus lost his prysoner Sadoyne, and that he sawe his mareschall of his ost slayne, and sawe hymself bannyshed and chassed out of his towne and royalme, and also his doughter that was wedded to his mortayll enmye. Of that other part, [fol. 90r] he harde the revell and the joye that was made wythin the cyté that gaff a cause to renewe his sorowes and hevy fortune over many folde. The same tyme that Alymodes the kyng was in suche hevynes, Blanchardyn came sailynge upon the see, sore desiryng forto com in tyme that he myghte fynde his enmye the tyraunt Alymodes, whiche he fonde, as ye shall understond, by the historye whiche is folowyng.

---

[17] *multitudes (crowds)*

Here folowoth the fiftieth chapter whiche sheweth how Blanchardyn arryved in the haven of Cassydonye before whiche towne he fonde Alymodos the kynge.

1 Wel ye have herde here afore how Blanchardyn and the kynge of Fryse, his fader, departed from Tormaday wyth a gret excersite of men of armes for to come towarde Cassydonye for to rescue his felawe Sadoyne. They exployted soo long and made suche a dylygence, thorugh helpe of God and of goode wynde, that they arryved all hole and sounde wythin the sayd haven of Cassydonye.

2 Whan they were arryved, thay caste theyr ancres and had horses oute of the shippes. They descended on lande and mounted on horsbacke. Blanchardyn loked towarde the cyté, byfore the whiche he perceyved clerely the tentes and the pavyllyons of Kynge Alymodes ryght well sette there in gret nombre, wherof he toke in hymselfe a ryght parfit joye. He dyd shewe hem unto his fader and sayd, "Syre, ye maye espye and see byfore you oure enmyes, as I wene." In thes wordes talkyng togyder dyd arryve there foure of their men that were gon to clere the waye afore theym as ferre as Kynge Alymodes ooste, whiche, as they came ayen, recounted a paynem whiche they toke and broughte hym before Blanchardyn, that ryght dylygently exammyned hym, of whom he knewe for veraye trouth that it was Kynge Alymodes that lodged was byfore the cyté of Cassydonye wythin his tentes [fol. 90v] and pavyllyons, wherof he was ryght glade. He made hys folke hastely to putte theymselfe in ordenaunce of bataylle and syth beganne to marche fourth ayenst his sayd enmyes that alle redy were advertysed of his comynge, insomoche that bothe partyes came ayenste other, wherby Kyng Alymodes knew full sone that it was Blanchardyn, wherof he had no grete joye but became pencefull. Neverthelesse, as a knyght preu[1] and hardy as he was, toke corage in himselfe admonestynge his folke to do well. And of that other parte, Blanchardyn, the spere in the hande, came ridynge byfore the bataylle, settynge and kepyng his men in goode ordenaunce, praynge theym to enforce hemselfe to overcome their enmyes that they sawe before them. Ryghte gladde was Blanchardyn whan he wyste that his felawe Sadoyne was escaped oute of Kynge Alymodes handes al

---

[1] *brave (valiant)*

hole and sounde of all membres, thorugh the goode remedye and ryght grete prouesse that had moeved the herte of the fayr Batryce, his wyffe and treu love, wherof she canne not be praysed al ynough.

The fifty first chapter speketh of the grete batayll that was bytwyx Blanchardyn and Kyng Alymodes byfore Cassydonye, and how Alymodes was overcome, take and broughte prysoner into the cyté, and of the coronacyon of Sadoyn and of his wyff Beatryx.

1   Whan Sadoyne, that was the same tyme lokyng out at a wyndowe wythin his castell of Cassydonye and his wyf the fayr Beatryx by hym, sawe the two oostes that they wold joyne togyder to batayl, he gaf hymselfe gret mervayl, for he had seen them take lande, but he knewe hem not. So hadde he gret desire to know what they wer. He saw them com to eche other makynge grete cryes and callynges, so that emonge [fol. 91r] other he harde call Tourmaday. He dyde set al his entent for to know the baners and tokons of the lady of Tourmaday, so that incontynent after this he perceyved and knewe that it were they that by Blanchardyn, his felawe, were conducted and guyded. Hastely he made and comaunded to be publisshed[1] thorugh all the cyté that all men shold be in harneyse, whos commaundement they full dylygently acomplyshed. Sadoyne, armed of all his armes, mounted upon his courser and lept out of the towne wyth fifteen thousaund gode knyghtes valyaunt and hardy, that al at one poyse[2] smot hemself wythin Alymodes folke, wherof at their comyng on they slewe many one. Of that other part was Blanchardyn that made thynges wonderful unto men of sleeyng, hewyng, and gyvyng horryble strokes upon his enmyes. And who had seen hym at that tyme, he wold not have trowed that he had be a man mortal. He cravented[3] and overthrew al before him, clevyng them to the eerys and to the brestes of hem. He had be there longe whan his swerde was ryght well knowen in every of the ooste. He brake and departed the grete presses, so that his enmyes made waye byfore his swerde for grete drede that they had of hym, and they all fled that none durst abyde the peyse[4] of his hevy strokys. Sadoyne, his trewe felaw, cam that tyme and joyned his horse beside his.

2   Of their reconyssaunces and thankes that they made tyll eche other I make no mencyon at all, bycause at that tyme ther was nother of them bothe but that he had grete besynes in hande. Notwythstandyng what a-doo that they had, they embraced and colled[5] eche other and made grete knowleg,[6] gyvynge thankes to othre. And syn both togyder smote theymself amonge theyr enmyes al at ones, to whom they solde ful dere ther acqueyntance.[7] And wyth theym was the kynge of Fryse that of [fol. 91v] new had cast doune to the grounde that bare the chief standarde of Kyng Alymodes, wherof their enmeis made grete cries and grete noyse for their baner that laye upon the grounde. They

---

[1] *proclaimed (announced)*
[2] *instant*
[3] *vanquished [OF cravanter, overthrow]*
[4] *force*
[5] *hugged [OF col, neck]*
[6] *acknowledgement (recognition)*
[7] sold ful dere ther acqueyntance, *paid dearly for meeting them*

3   forced hemself as moche as they coude to have it up ayen, but the right grete prouesse of the forsaid thre princes kept them therfro. For they dyde so moche that wythin a whyle they bracke the presse and putte to flyght theyr enmyes.

3   The kynge Alymodes, seeng his folke that fled, his cheff standarde overthrawen and layng upon the grounde, his barons all to-bet adoune, and also sawe that impossyble it was to hym for to escape hymself quyk from the batoylle, wherfore, as sone as he myght or ever that a more grete myscheff sholde happe unto hym, cam and yelded hymself into the handes of Blanchardyn and of Sadoyne, prayng them right humbly for mercy and grace and that they wolde save his lyff. They toke hym as their prysoner, and after that the werke was ended and that all their enmyes were taken or slayn, they brought hym and entred wythin the cyté wyth grete tryumphe and glorye.

4   Yf the joye and the fayr welcome and honourable recepcion that of the fair Beatryx was made unto theym I wold reherce and telle, I sholde over longe tary myself. But the joye and the feste was there so grete that suche another was not seen byfore that tyme duryng this grete joye and feste. The barons and lordes of the lande that were there alle togyder of one accorde and one wylle crowned Sadoyne and receyved him to their kynge and to their lord. And the fayre Beatryx, his wyff, they also dyde crowne as heyre[8] of the lande. The feste beganne ayen to be right grete for joye of this coronacyon. [fol. 92r] The barons of the lande made their homage unto Sadoyne and toke and releved[9] their lord-shippes of hym and obeyed hym as their lordes naturell[10] as longe as they lyved and that Sadoyne and their ladye were togyder, wythout eny rebellyon.

5   Sadoyne helde and kept the lande all his tyme in goode unyon. They that were about hym rebell, he dompted[11] and subdewed them and brought them to his obeyssaunce.[12] Well and truly he loved and maynteyned justyce. The evyll customes he brought doune and areysed[13] and ordeyned other that were goode and most proffytable that he and his counseyll coude advyse. And by especyall all that was told hym ordeyned and advysed by Blanchardyn, he dyde and acomplysshed.

6   After that Sadoyne was crowned to be kynge and that he had achyeved and made alle his ordonaunces for to governe and holde his royalme in gode peas and unyon, Blanchardyn, his felawe, dysposed[14] himself for to retourne ayen toward Tormaday to the proude pucelle in amours, his lady that he desyred sore for to see. So made he to be appar-elled[15] his navye for to make his retourne, ayen levyng Sadoyne his felawe wyth the fayre Beatryx his wyff. He wyst not of nothyng that he sholde have enymore to do, for he knewe not of the venymouse malyce of the false traytoure Subyon, that wold have attempted a grete trayson ayenst hym and his lady, the proude pucelle in amours.

---

[8]   heir
[9]   restored
[10] hereditary (by birth)
[11] overthrew
[12] submission (obedience)
[13] established
[14] resolved (made ready)
[15] equipped

The fifty second chapter conteyneth how the proude mayden in love sent the provost toward Blanchardin whiche after thees tydynges exployted so sore that he arryved wyth alle his excercyte nyghe to the oost of Subyon.

1   Well ye have herde here afore that atte departyng that Blanchardin made fro Tormaday for to goo rescue [fol. 92v] hys felawe Sadoyne, he lefte his lady, the proude pucelle in amours, in the governaunce and kepyng of Subyon, the whiche, as ye have understonde afore, made conspyracion ayenst her for to have her to his wyff, and to make hymself kynge of Tourmaday to the ende that Blanchardyn were kepte therfro. But thorugh the prudence and worthynes of the noble erle of Castelforde, of the goode provost, and of the knyghte of the fery, a remedy was had ayenst his wycked malyce by suche a wyse that, wold Subyon or not and all his helpers, the noble lady proude of love was taken oute of his power and was brought by the forsayd two knyghtes and erle to the castel of Castelford, wherof Subyon was ryght sory. He cam and layde his seege trowyng for to have taken her, but the place was soo strong that it had no doubte of no seege, for it was garnyshed of good knyghtes fer to defende it, and wele furnyshed wyth all manere of vytaylles necessayré to suche a fortres. The lady that was shette¹ wythin was full sore and wroth for her frende Blanchardyn that he was soo ferre from her, and ryght moche desired his comyng ayen. She dyd calle to her the erle and the provost to whom full swetli she prayed that they wold sende toward Blanchardyn for to reherse and shewe unto hym the tydynges of the seege that byfore them was. "Madame," sayd the erle, "I am redy to do your pleasure, and me semeth it ought to be doon as ye saye. Ye most advyse and see by whom your message shal be made." The good provost then rose on his feet and sayd, "Madame, yf your wyll be, I shall gladli tak this vyage² in hand, and I shall never rest noowhere tyl that I have founde Blanchardyn." "Provost," sayd the pucell, "of this servyce that ye profer me I thanke you moche, for no better messenger I can not send, not that can better recounte and telle the danger where we ben now in."

2   The provost made a galley to [fol. 93r] be redy that was atte an haven there nyghe. He made her to be garnyshed wyth men and vytayllys, and syth, whan al thynge was redy, he toke his leve of the noble mayden his lady and of the eerle. And sone after the houre of mydnyghte, he departed pryvely oute of the castell and went and toke his shyppyng wythin his galley so stylle³ that of onybodye of the siege he was not aspyed.⁴ So moche exployted the provoste sailynge nyght and daye over the see, that by good wynde that he hadde, he arryved in a mornynge into the havon of Cassydonye, where he fonde many shyppes that made theymselfe redy by the ordonaunce of Blanchardyn. The provoste asked them after Blanchardyn; they tolde hym all that they knew of hym. The provoste descended a-lande and cam into the town and syth mounted to the paleys, where he fonde the barons that talkyd togyder. He salued Blanchardyn and Sadoyne that welcomde hym and made hym grete chere.

---

¹ *shut*
² *voyage*
³ *stealthily*
⁴ *seen*

3   Then spake Blanchardin to the provoste and asked hym of his tydynges. "Sire," sayd the provost, "ye shal knowe that tydynges I brynge, but they be not pleysaunte." He thenne rehersed and shewed unto him al alonge the grete untrouthe and false treyason that by Subyon hadde be made and machyned ayenste him and his lady the proude pucelle in amours. Blanchardin, heryng thees tydynges, was sore dolaunt. He called to his felawe Sadoyne and recounted to him alle that the provoste hadde reported and sayd, wherupon they ful sone, wythoute eny other inspecte,[5] concluded togyder that they sholde departe the nexte daye towarde Tormaday, and that they sholde never ceasse unto the tyme they had socoured the proude pucell in amours.

4   Their shyppes were redy and were garnyshed of folke and vytaylles. They toke their leve of the quene [fol. 93v] Beatryx, that was ryghte sory whan she sawe the departynge of her husbande Sadoyne. And entrynge into their vesseylles, saylled wyth so grete dilygence by the goode wynde that they had, so that they came wythout eny lette or adventure that ought to be tolde, and arryved wythin the haven of Tourmaday.

5   Whan they were come there, Blanchardyn sent the provost for to wyte of theym of the cyté yf they wolde gyfe up the cyté peasybly unto hym and he sholde receyve them to mercy. The provost descended a-lande and cam into the cyté, and exposed unto the burgeys and comynalté[6] the charge that he had of Blanchardyn. The cytezeyns and comon people of the towne, that understode the provost, were full glad of Blanchardyns comyng, and ansuered in this wyse al wyth one voyce, that his comyng was to theym right pleysaunt and agreable, and that whiche had be doon ayenst hym and their lady wythin the cyté was doon of force.

6   Whan the souldyours that Subyon had lefte there in garnyson[7] herde and understode the wylle of the people of the towne, they ansuered all that they sholde not suffre this, and that the cyté sholde be kepte for Subyon. Wherfore all the comynaltye of the towne went and armed them hastely and came upon the market place, where they bygynne to fyght ayenst the souldyours of the towne that wolde have kepte it for Subyon. Ryght grete slawghter was doon there, but the maystrye[8] and strengthe abode wyth the peple soo that they kyld or hurted sore alle them that were of Subyons folke, and syth toke the bodyes ded and caste hym over the walles of the towne into the dyches.

7   And after this they opened the gates of the towne, and in grete [fol. 94r] reverence and in token of humylyté cam the burgyes[9] and the people all barefote in maner of a processyon ayenst Blanchardyn and receyved to their lorde. And after that he and al his folke were entred wythin the cyté, he sent a spye unto the castel of Castelforde toward his lady, the proude pucell in amours, whiche spye dyde soo well that he entred into the sayd fortresse that he was not seen of theym that were atte the syege. He recounted and tolde unto the lady and to the erle how Blanchardyn and his felawe Sadoyne came for to socoure them, and that they were entred wythin Tormaday. Thise tidynges were to them moche

---

[5]   *examination (look into a matter)*
[6]   *common people*
[7]   *garrison*
[8]   *superior power (mastery)*
[9]   *town officials*

pleysaunt, for they were in a grete daunger of Subyon that domaged theym ryght sore and their place wyth their bombardes and other engynes of warre that he had do brynge there. And whan they of Castelforde understode by the sayd spye that Blanchardyn was comen wythin Tormaday, and that he came to gyve them socours and helpe ayenste Subyon, they beganne to make grete festes and grete joyes for his comynge and called and songe so highe that the noyse therof came unto Subyons eeres, that gaff hemself grete mervaylle why they ded soo.

8   On the morowe erly, Blanchardyn and Sadoyne departed from Tormaday and lefte there the good kyng of Fryse and foure thowsand goode men wyth hym for to kepe the towne. Whan Blanchardyn and his ooste were yssued oute of the cyté, he made two bataylles,[10] every one of ten thowsand men. The fyrst bataylle he betoke to be ledde by Sadoyne, his felawe, and that other bataylle he conducte himself and prayd and admonested his folke to doo welle, and syth toke their waye toward Castelforde, takyng a waye whiche was not moche haunted.[11] And alle at one peyse cam and spored their horses nyghe unto the [fol. 94v] ooste of Subyon or ever he was aware of hem. Nor he had not knowen nothynge of theyr commyng, but of a yoman of his owne that came from foragynge and sechyng[12] of heey[13] and ootes for his horses that advertysed hym, whiche came rennynge all his myght towarde Subyon and toolde hym on highe[14] that Blanchardyn came wyth a grete felyshyp for to fyghte wyth hym, and that yf he putte not his folke lyghtly[15] in ordonaunce for to receyve hym, he was in pereyll to lose hymselfe and all his ooste.

9   Whan Subyon understode that yoman, he chaunged coloure in face and was sore abashed. Wyth ryghte grete haste he made his folke to putte hemselfe in araye, and prayd them that they wold helpe hym at his nede, promyttynge theym for to make hem all ryche. They ansuerd that he sholde make therof no doute, and that they were stronge ynough for to resyste ayenste Blanchardyn, and promysed hym to yelde unto hym Blanchardin other quycke[16] or ded, or ever that the even sholde be come, and his felawe Sadoyne also. They were a thirty thowsand men ther that helde wyth Subyon that thus thretened Blanchardyn that they sholde smyte his hed off. But it ys sayd in comyn that whosoever rekeneth wythoute his hoste, he rekeneth twys for ones.[17] Thus hit happed wyth Subyones men as it foloweth.

---

[10]   battalions
[11]   frequented
[12]   searching
[13]   hay
[14]   on highe, *loudly*
[15]   quickly
[16]   alive
[17]   See Note.

The fifty third chapyter speketh how Blanchardyn and Sadoyne dyscomfyted Subyon and of the grete bataylle and manere how he was taken, and what folowed after.

1   Whan Blanchardin and Sadoyne sawe hem nyghe Subyons ooste, thay caste a ryght highe crye and smote hemselfe into their enmyes by suche a force and vertue [fol. 95r] that their comynge on they owerthrewe many of theym to grounde that never syth releved[1] hemself, but deyd myserable there bytwyx the horses feete. So grete and horyble byganne the batayll. The ayer was derke wyth shotte of arowes, quareylles,[2] and dartes that flowe bytwene bothe partyes. The duste and the brethe of men and of the horses was so thycke that wyth peyne they knew one from another. Then came they to fyghte wyth sperys, axes, guysarmes,[3] and swerdes, wherof they kylled and slew eche other. Blanchardyn and Sadoyne sette all their entent to slee their enmyes. Whan theyr speres were broken, they sette hande to their swerdes wherwyth they parted the grete presses. And wythin a while they had dyed themself in rede wyth the bloode of their enmyes that made unto them waye to passe by them.

2   And Blanchardyn, that ceassed not to renne here and there as a mad man, loked and sawe byfore hym a knyghte whiche was nyghe of sybbe unto Subyon that bare the cheff standarde. He tourned brydell to hym ward and wyth his goode swerde smote hym suche an horryble stroke that he clove him doune to the chynne and feell ded wyth the standarde to the erthe that was not after reysed up ayen, how be it that Subyon and his folke putte hem in peyne for to have hit brought up ayen, but Blanchardyn and Sadoyne kepte hem ther fro. Of that other parte, the good erle of Castelforde, the provost, and the knyght of the fery yssued out of the castell wyth a thousaund knyghtes that brake upon their enmyes, castyng a right hyghe crye, wherof Subyon and his men were sore affyerad. For he sawe his cheff banner overthrawen and hymself enclosed of al sydes, his men that fled and awayte non other but after the stroke of deth, wherunto he sawe hymself to be brought yf he fonde not som [fol. 95v] waye or meanes for to save hymself. He putte hymself to flyght, for hym thought the best manere for to flee was for to departe by tyme.[4]

3   Blanchardyn and Sadoyne, that always made watche over hym for to take and slee hym, sawe hym go out of the bataylle and set upon a myghty courser. They ranne anone after hym and chassed hym sore. He was well mounted upon a goode horse, wherfore they coude not overtake hym bycause the nyght byganne to comen and myght no lenger see hym. He toke and entred wythin a forest that was nyghe by. The remenaunt of his folke were al take by Blanchardynes men. Grete gayne they made there and a grete foyson of prysoners. They had grete joye and gladnesse they made of their victorye. But the erle of Castelforde and the barons merveylled them moche bycause they wyste not where their lordes Blanchardyn and Sadoyne were drawen. They soughte and serched them all aboute, but they fonde theym not.

---

[1] *recovered (rose up again)*

[2] *arrows with square heads*

[3] *battle axes*

[4] by tyme, *immediately*

4	And for to recounte of their adventure, they chased Subyon that was horsed at a vauntage better than they were. He walopped soo longe that he came into a valey where theves were, whiche were ten or twelve in nombre that were all grete murdrers, wherof the pryncypall and the mayster of them all was named Sylvayne, that knew well ynough Subyon, whiche came unto theym and sayd that he had grete nede of theym, and that two knyghtes chased hym for to slee him. And that yf it so happed that they myght catche and gete hem there wythin theyr caves, they sholde have of them so grete a butyne[5] and so grete goodes that they all shall evermore be ryche.

5	Whan the theves understode Subyon, they were sore desirouse to lodge theym wythin their streyngthe[6] prevely wythin a secrete chambre, whiche thyng they ded. But they had not so sone doon so that Blanchardyn and Sadoyne [fol. 96r] came there and asked the theves yf they wyste not to speke of a man that was mounted on horsbacke and armed as they were. They ansuerd that they wyste no tidynges of hym nor of none suche, but wel they said to Blanchardyn and to Sadoyne that yf they wolde be lodged there wythin for the nyghte that was comen, they sholde make theim gode chere of suche goodes as God had lent hem. Bycause they semed to be knyghtes, and that it was sore late to ryde eny ferther, and that noo housyng nor no retrayt[7] was nyghe by syx myles where they myght be lodged, the two barons, heryng the theves speke, consented for to lodge hemselfe for that nyght wyth theym.

6	They entred into their strengthe, and whan they were comen in and that they had seen the dysposicion[8] of the place, they judged in hemselfe that al thys meyné[9] were murderers and theves, wherefor they concluded within themselfe that they sholde lye al nyghte in their harneys and that they sholde not be dysgarnyshed of their swerdes. Whan Sylveyn the chief mayster of the theeves see that they had not putte off their harnes, he came toward them and said that they were in peax[10] and in a sure place, and that they myght wele putte of ther habilymentes of werre. Blanchardyn then ansuerd unto him and sayd that it was the costome of theire land not to putte off their armures for the fyrst nyght that they cam to a new lodgyng. The theves that sawe Blanchardyn and Sadoyne so fayr, so grete, and so wele armed durste not assaylle them, but Subyon, that was hidde wythin a chambre and that wele had herd theym, lept oute of it and gaaff them corage, and said that they were all wery of the batayl, and that a grete shame were to them, thirteen in nombre, yf they durste not sette upon two men.

7	Thenne came Sylvayn, his felawes wyth hym, and ascryed the two barons [fol. 96v] to dethe. Thenne saide Blanchardyn to Sadoyne, "We must defende oureself now, yf we thinke to scape quyk[11] out of this place and ever see oure ladyes paramours."[12] They lefte

---

[5] booty (plunder)
[6] stronghold
[7] shelter (secluded building)
[8] arrangement
[9] retinue (band of men)
[10] peace
[11] alive
[12] lovers

their wordes, drewe their swerdes, and set their sheildes afore theym. So bigan they to smyte amonge their felon enmyes. They all to-hewe and cleve them insomoche that eyght of theim fell doun ded to the erthe. The other foure trowed to have fled into saveté, but they were pursued so nyghe of Blanchardyn and of Sadoyne that they overtoke and slew thre of theim. The fourth, that was maister of hem all, fled wythin the place for to have saved hymself into the chambre where Subyon was. But of so nyghe he was folowed that Blanchardyn overtoke hym and smote hym suche a stroke wyth his swerde that he made his hede to flee fro the sholdres of hym, and fel ded evyn atte the dore of the chambre that he had opened all redy for to have saved him there wythinne, wher Subyon was in grete fere and drede. And not wythout a cause, for he well ynough byleved and knew that his dayes were come atte an ende, syth that he was fallen into Blanchardynes handes.

8   I shall here leve to speke of Blanchardyn, of Sadoyne, and of Subyon, that in grete fere was of his dethe, and shal retourne to speke of the proude pucelle in amours and of the barons that were wythin the castell of Castelforde.

The fifty fourth and last chapter conteyneth how Blanchardyn wedded his love the proude pucell in amours, and of the grete joye that was made there, and of the kynge of Fryse deth.

1   After that the batayll was fynysshed and that the folke of Subyon were all ded and taken, the proude pucell in amours cam doun from the toure where she and the countes of Castelforde were mounted for to see the batayll, and cam to the castel gate for to welcome Blanchrdyn and Sadoyn. Whan they were com there, they fonde the erle of Castelforde ...[1] and the other barons, who led with them a great plenty of prisoners, to force them into the courtyard. Then the proud pucelle in amours, seeing that her friend Blanchardyn was not come, she called the earl and asked him where Blanchardyn and Sadoyne were. "Madame," said the earl, "it is not long since that they were with us, so I don't know where they went nor do I know at what point they turned, for indeed we thought that they were coming to you."

2   When the noble damsel heard the earl and the provost who was there, who knew no tidings of the barons, from so high a place as she was she fell to the ground, calling out a very loud and piteous cry. Then those who had been taken there had great sorrow, for all thought that she was dead because in her they sensed no pulse nor breath. A pitiful thing it was to see the gentle countess and the other people who were there, but soon after the proud pucelle in amours came to herself, casting a deep sigh, then very piteously she began to complain, lamenting her true love Blanchardyn. There was no man or woman there who had such a hard heart that they did not have pity on her.

3   The good earl and the good countess comforted her as best they could, but it did no good; her sorrow began to strengthen more and more. They led her to a chamber, and when she was come there they led her to a couch to lie down. The countess and the ladies were milling about grieving and tearful because they could not at all console her, for she did not ever, for a moment, cease to make the most piteous and anguished complaints for

---

[1] See T-Note

her true love whom she thought to have lost. But hardly was there any delay before her plaints would be turned back joy, as you will hear later.

4 Blanchardyn and Sadoyne, who were in the dwelling of the thieves, where they found Subyon in a chamber where he was hiding, but little did it profit him, for when the two vassals saw him there, the joy which they were in was very great. They took and seized him and tied him hand and foot, then put him on a strong horse which they found there. Then they quickly bounded out of the place, and taking their destriers on which they mounted, set themselves on the way to Castelford, which was two leagues from there. Sadoyne went before and Subyon after, and Blanchardyn followed closely behind. The moon shone bright and clear, so the horses sped that in a little time they were before the gate of Castelford, which was closed. They began to call loudly, making themselves known.

5 When their coming was known, from all parts they came running to open up for them, and as soon as they entered there they dismounted at the stone pavement before the hall. Subyon was put in a very dark prison and was never otherwise since the hour that he had been taken; well he knew that he was sentenced to death. After the two barons entered there, their coming was announced to the proud pucelle in amours who had of it great joy as you could know well enough. Soon all her tears and regrets were changed to perfect joy and happiness. She raised herself in great haste, but no sooner was she up than Blanchardyn and Sadoyne came toward her, of which the joy was redoubled, for before all she kisses and embraces her love. They spoke together of many things. The joy, the recollections, and the great love which Blanchardyn made for the good earl of Castelford, to the provost, and to the knight of the ferry, with the sweet thanks, they would be too long if I wanted to recite them. But for the cause of brevity I will omit these. They passed the night.

6 Then when came the morning, they made themselves ready and mounted their horses, taking their way toward Tormaday where their coming was already known. The good king of Frise, father of Blanchardyn, and all those of the town went before together with all the confraternities of the city with crosses and standards to receive their lady and Blanchardyn who must be their lord. Very great joy and great celebration they made when they came together with them. The town was all hung and decked and strewn with fresh boughs; in the streets ladies and damsels of the town and maidens were at the windows singing and comporting themselves with joy. There were many and diverse instruments which sent forth melodious sounds. They rode on horseback to the palace where they all dismounted. Very great joy was manifest there.

7 After all were settled, by the council of the princes and so likewise by all those of the realm, Blanchardyn betrothed the beautiful proud pucelle in amours. Then, when the next morning came, the proud pucelle in amours was led to the cathedral accompanied by two kings, that is to say, of the king of Frise and of the king Sadoyne, and by the bishop of the city the two lovers were married and were crowned as king and queen of the kingdom of Tourmaday. Very grand and noble was the offering at the wedding mass.

8 After the mass was complete, they returned to the palace where the tables were set up. Water was poured, and then they sat down to eat. Of the elaborate dishes and courses accompanied by entertainments, I will not make a long account, for very richly were they

served of all that could satisfy the human body. Of the clothing and ornaments of which the bride and groom were adorned or dressed it is not possible to tell you. But indeed I dare say to you that never before or since this could one have or seen or known of more rich jewels or garments than on the two lovers were, for they were both so beautiful that God and nature could do nothing to improve them. Then after they had dined, tournament jousts, dances, and amusements began. Then afterwards, when it was the time and hour for supper, they seated themselves to eat. As they had been well served at dinner, so they were at supper.

9 When the supper was finished and it was time for them all to retire, the two lovers were led to a chamber where they went to bed together and conceived that night a son who in his time had the name Rambault the Frisian, the which made and achieved many and great deeds of prowess and died in the very piteous battle of Roncevaux, with Roland and Oliver, who if you would know more of them, look in his history which of them makes mention, and we will return to our subject. When the next day came, all within the palace got up and the festivities began again, which lasted one whole day.

10 After the solemnity of the celebrations and the wedding were passed, by the commandment of King Blanchardyn, Subyon and all his accomplices were put to death. Soon afterwards the barons of the kingdom of Frise arrived in Tourmaday to see the king their lord and the king Blanchardyn his son, of which the joy was strengthened. But when the good king knew and was well informed that the queen his wife was gone from this transitory world, then he greatly mourned for her, and so did the king Blanchardyn, who was very sad and grieved by this. But there is no sorrow so great that it should not finally come to an end. Notwithstanding this, the good king of Frise, for whatever comfort that one knew to offer him, he did not leave his sorrow; and so much so that of the great affliction that he had, he took to his sick-bed and died. The king Blanchardyn his son was in very keen unhappiness, and also the queen his wife who lamented greatly. He was buried, and his service and obsequies made, as fitting for a king.

11 After all the calamities and misfortunes of Blanchardyn and of his lady, as king and queen, replete and adorned of all good virtues, they lived the remainder of their life in peace and tranquility in the service of God, loved and respected by their neighbors, and had such grace of our Lord that before they departed the world they saw their son great in bearing arms and they made him to be crowned king of Frise. And they lived a very long time, in ruling them in this world, such that after their death they were greatly missed by their subjects, neighbors, and others who did not know them, so great was the renown of their life. In such a way they conducted themselves in this transitory world that they found peace in the kingdom of heaven. And Sadoyne, his loyal companion, returned to Cassydonye where he and the queen Beatrice lived in tranquility of soul and body.

12 This history does not mention anything further about the reign of the king Blanchardyn, nor of the queen his wife. So we will finish our history, praying to Father, Son, and Holy Spirit, that at the end of our days we might attain His grace. Amen.

Explicit expliciat. Quy plus vult scribere scribat.[2]

---

[2] *It is done, let it be done. Who would write more, let him write. [Lat.]*

Explanatory Notes to *Blanchardyn and Eglantine*

Dedication, Paragraph 1

late receyved in Frenshe from her good grace. See the General Introduction, pp. 2, 6–8 and Introduction to this romance, pp. 134–36, 146, for discussion of Margaret's patronage of Caxton.

reduce. To translate (*MED reducen* (v.), sense 4a).

auncyent hystoryes. Caxton may be referring to his own books such as *The Recuyell of Troy, Enydos, Jason, Le Morte D'Arthur*, and others of the Nine Worthies. His point, that it is as worthwhile for young gentlemen and ladies to read accounts of faithful lovers and military campaigns as it is for them to read devotional and didactic works, is a conventional justification for secular reading. The comment is relevant, for his patron was an early supporter of printing for the dissemination of devotional material.

stedfaste and constant. These comments may have had particular resonance for Margaret, who had earlier negotiated a much delayed marriage of her son, Henry VII, to Elizabeth, daughter of Edward IV. See the Introduction to this romance, p. 134.

Fryse. Frisia is a region on the North Sea, in what is now Holland and Germany. See Introduction to this romance, pp. 134–35, for the significance of this locale.

Dedication, Paragraph 2

rude and comyn Englyshe. Caxton employs a humility formula common in literary dedications. In his prologue to *Charles the Grete*, he asks pardon for the lack of gay terms and new eloquence in his translations (ed. Crotch, *Prologues and Epilogues*, p. 96). The prologues to *The Recuyell of Troy, Jason, Feats of Arms and Chivalry*, and *The Book of the Knight of the Tower* all contain similar phrases. See the General Introduction, pp. 13–14, for comments on Caxton's style.

arte of rethoryk. Rhetoric, along with grammar and logic, was part of the trivium that consituted the initial phase of formal education in the Middle Ages. The aureate prose fashionable in the fifteenth century made much use of rhetorical figures.

Table of Chapters, Paragraph 1

table. Tables of chapters were becoming common in manuscripts and books as chapter headings began to appear in long narratives. Tables accompanied many French texts of the period, and Caxton translated *Blanchardyn and Eglantine*'s from his source. When he created chapters in Malory's *Morte d'Arthur*, he included a table of contents in his volume. His prologue to the first edition of *The Game and Playe of the Chesse* (translated from French of Jean de Vignay) explains that the chapters of the book are written at its beginning so that "ye may see more playnly the mater wherof the book treteth" (ed. Crotch, *Prologues and Epilogues*, p. 12). All are examples of the striving for clarity and textual cohesion characteristic of curial prose style, discussed in the introduction to this volume.

Blanchardyn and Eglantine

Chapter 1, Paragraph 1

sore displesed. The author of the short prose *Blancandin* was the first to include the formulaic episode of the infertile royal couple whose prayer for a child is answered; the verse texts say only that their marriage was blessed by the birth of a son. The episode (*MIFL* D1925.3, T548.1) is a staple of romance plotting. Often, as in *Paris and Vienne*, the episode introduces the narrative by relating the birth of the protagonist. The meme also appears in the Middle English verse romances *Sir Tryamour*, *Northern Octavian*, and *Sir Gowther*.

Chapter 1, Paragraph 2

Blanchardyn. The name is derived from *blanche*, the French word for white. The color betokens purity and beauty.

brestis. That Blanchardyn is nursed by his own mother is a mark of distinction; it is also a detail that appears only in the long prose romances. Suckling one's own child was not the practice of the upper classes of late medieval Europe, whose infants were usually given to wet nurses as in *Paris and Vienne*. The noble lady who cares for the infant Blanchardyn does not perform this function. The fact that his mother does highlights the bond with her son, as well as the royal pedigree of the hero's nurture. A similar instance is found in the *Romance of Partenay*, where Melusine suckles her son Thierry, who grows twice as fast and large as other children. This romance has other features in common with *Blanchardyn and Eglantyne* (see note 9.2, below).

Chapter 1, Paragraph 3

sciences. Grammar, logic, and rhetoric (the trivium) constituted the basic curriculum of formal education, as appropriate to a prince. Blanchardyn's other accomplishments — hunting, chess, and polite conversation — were also necessary for a nobleman's education.

Explanatory Notes to Blanchardyn and Eglantine

Chapter 1, Paragraph 4

elder in age. BN does not mention age, saying rather that Blanchardyn excels those who are *les plus sagis* [more wise]. In both *The Story of the Grail* and *Lybeaus Desconus*, a noble youth is raised in ignorance of chivalry, though under very different circumstances. Both are raised alone in the forest by their mothers, who keep them from the practice of arms, fearing shame or loss. Blanchardyn's father's motives are unstated.

the goode byrde affeyteth hirself. "The good bird teaches herself." The proverbial expression refers to a hunting fowl whose natural abilities are such that it requires little training. The author employs the figure of speech as an instance of the romance trope "noble character will out"; see Whiting B305. Hunting birds being the prerogative of the aristocracy, the comparison of prince and noble fowl is apt.

Chapter 2, Paragraph 1

tapysserye. While tapestries depicting chivalric subjects were popular in the later Middle Ages, the Troy story was particularly important to the dukes of Burgundy since they traced their ancestry to the Trojan king, Priam. Philip the Good commissioned Raoul le Fèvre to render the story from Latin into French prose. Philip the Bold owned two tapestries depicting Hector; later Charles the Bold commissioned a series of tapestries illustrating episodes in the Trojan War (Forsyth, "Trojan War," p. 77; Farber, "Tapestry Collection of Philip the Bold," http://employees.oneonta.edu/farberas/arth/arth214_folder/tapestries_philip_bold.html). Only the prose *Blancandins*, composed for the court of Burgundy, mentions tapestries depicting the Trojan War; the verse texts refer generally to scenes of knights, horses, and arms.

Chapter 2, Paragraph 2

of Hector . . . and of Achilles. These figures are the canonical champions of the Trojan war. The first four were sons of King Priam of Troy. Hector and Troilus were killed by the Greek Achilles. In some versions of the Troy story, Paris and Deiphobus were responsible for Achilles's death.

Chapter 4, Paragraph 1

knyghtes and esquyers . . . yomen and grommes. The groups mentioned here — knights, esquires, yeomen, and grooms — comprise ranks within a noble household. Though the term squire still applied to young men of aristocracy or gentry who served as personal assistants to knights, the word also referred to men of the military and feudal landholding rank below that of knights. Yeomen were landholders and household officials below the rank of squire but above that of groom or page. Grooms were minor officials in any of the various departments of the household, here the stables. Besides appearing in the romance in order of precedence, individuals associate only with others of similar rank — knights and squires united by chivalry, yeomen and grooms by service in the royal establishment. Such catalogues of household members and attendants reflect the increased size of aristocratic households of the later

Middle Ages and the Burgundian program of ceremony and ostentation, a trend attested in England by the account books and ordinances of Edward IV and Henry VII.

Chapter 5, Paragraph 1

tenn of the clocke. The writer includes a contemporary detail, mentioning clock hours rather than canonical hours such as prime (see note 8.1, below). In fifteenth-century Germany and northern France, large public clocks were installed on churches and in town squares; their striking could be heard at a distance. The romance does not say that Blanchardyn heard a clock strike, only that he rode forth at that time.

Chapter 5, Paragraph 2

necstroke. The ritual of knighting included the candidate kneeling before his lord (or another superior designated to confer the rank) and receiving a slap on his shoulder with the flat of that person's sword. Blanchardyn's knighting is perfunctory and would not have been recognized in actual practice. The conferral of a knighthood usually included vows and, more formally, religious rituals of fasting and prayer.

Chapter 5, Paragraph 3

rest. Caxton provides a more precise picture of the mounted knight than his source which reads *au poing* [in the fist]. It was more common to brace the spere on a rest located on the breastplate, or against the body, not simply in the hand. Elsewhere, Caxton makes other substitutions that give more specific, or updated, details of military equipment (Despres, "Translation Techniques," p. 173).

Vassell. A vassal was one who owed military service to a lord. While the term could refer perjoratively to inferior status, it also had positive connotations of ideal vassalage and knightly prowess.

Chapter 7, Paragraph 1

berdles. This is an insult to Blanchardyn's masculinity imputing immaturity and inexperience.

Chapter 7, Paragraph 4

our herte . . . drawyng to the perfection. BN: *notre cuer qui est imparti* [our heart which is indivisible]. There is a metaphysical dimension to their love, for it completes the couple, making them a whole and thus perfect, according to the tenets of scholastic philosophy as applied to courtly love. When the lovers are separated by death, the survivor's heart is imperfect and powerless to keep the body alive, is drawn to the state of perfect love in union with its other part (*MED drauen* (v.), sense 2b, "to lead . . . spiritually; attract"; and sense 3b, "go toward . . . a state or condition").

Explanatory Notes to *Blanchardyn and Eglantine*

Chapter 8, Paragraph 1

pryme. One of the canonical hours of daily Christian prayer: matins (after midnight); lauds (dawn); prime (early morning); terce (third hour, mid-morning); sext (sixth hour, mid-day); nones (ninth hour, mid-afternoon); vespers (sunset); and compline (evening).

Chapter 8, Paragraph 2

fery. BN reads *gue* [ford]. The knight of the ferry is a real-world counterpart to otherworldly guides of romance who help knights across watery boundaries in their quest for chivalry.

Chapter 9, Rubric

Tormaday. The name may be related to the French *tour*, or tower, and Caxton frequently spells it "Tourmaday." The spelling also suggests "Tournai," the name of a town now in Belgium, which is mentioned in the *chansons des gestes* from which the author of the verse romance drew names and details (Stelboum, "William Caxton's Romance," p. 103).

Chapter 9, Paragraph 1

kingdom of Darye. This is the only time Eglantine's kingdom is named; it is not mentioned in the verse romance, and has not been associated with a particular location. Darye is the name of Darius the Great (d. 450 BCE) whose empire stretched from the Balkans to the Indus River.

Cassidonie. Perhaps Chalcedon (Kellner, p. cxix). This was a coastal town opposite Constantinople on the Bosporus and the the site of important battles in the Fourth Crusade (1198–1204).

Chapter 9, Paragraph 2

Eglantine. This is one of the two instances where the heroine's proper name appears in the romance (see 47.3). Caxton also names her in his Dedication and Table. In the French verse romances the character is referred to only as L'Orgueillese d'Amour; however, one of the provost's daughters has the name Aiglentine. The long French prose texts refer to the heroine as "Eglantine" a single time. The name, which is also a term for the briar rose, appears in several romances including *Le Bone Florence of Rome*, *Gerard de Nevres*, and the *Romance of Partenay*. In the latter, Eglantine is the daughter of the king of Bohemia who has been killed in combat with the pagan king of Cracow, which are contested regions in *Blanchardyn and Eglantine* as well. A better known Eglantine is Chaucer's Prioress, whose name is in keeping with other romance features of her portrait.

Chapter 9, Paragraph 3

arowes of love. This is a reference to the arrows shot by Cupid, Venus's son. Aimed at the heart, the arrows' wound brought fevers and burning love to the victim.

Chapter 9, Paragraph 4

brestys. The romance emphasizes Eglantine's bond to her mistress, a parallel to Blanchardyn's nurture (see 1.2).

Chapter 10, Paragraph 1

daungerouse. The word means both "hazardous, risky, dangerous," and "haughty, aloof . . . reluctant" (*MED daungerous* (adj.), senses 2a, 4); the latter has particular significance in the context of courtly love.

Chapter 12, Paragraph 3

folye or dishonoure. The ensuing dialogue between Eglantine and her mistress stresses the importance of circumspection and good reputation. Conduct books also emphasized these virtues.

Chapter 13, Paragraph 1

he dyde beholde. The idealized descriptions of the countryside around Tourmaday, and of the city itself, resemble scenes from lavish books of hours produced in northern European countries in the later Middle Ages. The long prose romance describes the countryside in more detail than other versions, and mentions Tourmaday's walls by the sea, as is appropriate to their Baltic location (ed. Greco, *Blancandin et l'Orgueilleuse*, pp. 45–46).

Chapter 14, Paragraph 2

mayntenaunce. Conduct, but also to affirm the dignity of one's rank by expenditures; spend money on a household, a court (*MED maintenen* (v.), sense 3a).

Chapter 14, Paragraph 3

bowe bakward. Saddles had high fronts and backs to keep the rider in place, and being bent backward over one's saddle was a common peril in combat and jousting.

Chapter 14, Paragraph 4

drewe his swerde . . . gaff it hym ageyn. Giving one's sword to one's vanquisher was an act symbolizing acceptance of defeat. Blanchardyn's returning it is a gesture of friendship and absolution.

Chapter 15, Paragraph 4

reverence. An act of respect, especially a bow (*MED reverence* (n.), sense 2). Attendance on the lord or lady was a matter of protocol in a noble household. The scene illustates polite behaviors as described in Caxton's *Boke of Curtasye*.

Chapter 15, Paragraph 5

holdeth. This threat is directed at the provost; Blanchardyn holds no lands [*tenementes*] from Eglantine.

Chapter 17, Paragraph 1

holdeth. Remains, continues; harbors an attitude (*MED holden* (v.) senses 13a, 10b).

Chapter 18, Paragraph 1

penoncelles. These various flags identified the nobles and their companies of soldiers. Though the terms are sometimes used interchangeably, the list is not redundant, as standards were borne by kings and battle leaders (the king of Poland and Subyon lose theirs); banners identified the companies led by knights bannerette, while penoncelles, or pennons, were borne by knights bachelors, the lowest rank of knighthood (*MED penoun* (n.), sense 1a).

Chapter 18, Paragraph 2

cognyssaunce. An emblem by which a knight's identity or allegiance to a sovereign is made known, here also in the sense of "a pennon with such a device" (*MED conissaunce* (n.), sense 2).

Trompettes, claryons, and other instrumentes. Various horns and other loud instruments were used to rally and direct troops in battle, and to announce the entrance of persons of high status.

Chapter 18, Paragraph 3

tambours. Large drums used to rally troops and intimidate foes (*MED tabour* (n.), sense 1c).

Chapter 18, Paragraph 4

gunnes. The term can refer to both siege engines that launch missiles, such as trebuchets and mangonels, and to cannons that fire them (*MED gonne* (n.), senses 1, 2).

bombardes. These large siege cannons were used defensively and offensively, especially in the fifteenth century, to batter down walls with large stone balls (*MED bombard* (n.), sense 1).

Chapter 19, Paragraph 4

sleves. Sleeves were detachable, being laced to the garment at each wearing, and were often embellished. The further bestowal of trappings for Blanchardyn's horse attests the donor's munificence. Eglantine gives him similar equipment (see 24.2).

Chapter 20, Paragraph 3

foure elementes. These are earth, air, fire, and water, the basic elements of all creation. In an ideal universe (as in a healthy body), they would be in harmony.

Chapter 20, Paragraph 4

lunge and lyvre. This alliterative formula, referring to internal organs in general, appears in other romances in similar battle contexts (*MED longe* (n.), sense 1c). Caxton has added this graphic detail, and the spear head emerging from the knight's back; his source is more general, and brief (Despres, "Translation Techniques," pp. 173–74).

swerde. This word seems to be a mistake, since Blanchardyn has been using a spear and takes up his sword a few lines later. The annotator has crossed out the word and written *speare* in the margin. See Textual Note.

he semed to be a man of the fayré. This is the first comparison of Blanchardyn to a fairy knight. The provost later repeats this observation to Eglantine (see 21.3). Blanchardyn's appearing to gallop in the air, as he kisses Eglantine and leaps past her company, is an echo of fairy mystique as well as a tribute to his horsemanship.

Chapter 20, Paragraph 9

Harpe, lute, sawtrye. These stringed instruments provided music to accompany indoor entertainments, and are frequently mentioned in romances in episodes of feasting and entertainment. In this scene women of various ranks are in attendance, the inclusion of the upper bourgeoise being noteworthy.

Chapter 20, Paragraph 11

thurste, honger, and shaketh for colde caused thrughe a hete intollerabyll. These are symptoms of lovesickness, the fever arising from the burning of love.

accident. Eglantine's wound of love may be a chance happening, but in the context, *accident* has religious significance as the outward physical manifestation of a sacramental mystery (the substance) (*MED accident* (n.), sense 2b).

Chapter 21, Paragraph 2

Sarasyn. The word is said to derive from Arabic *sharkeyn* meaning "eastern people" referring to Turks, Egyptians, and Persians, as distinguished from *maghribe* or "western people" (Stelboum, "William Caxton's Romance," p. 107). In Greek and Latin the word meant Arab, and appears in Old and Middle English referring to Turks, Arabs, or Muslims as well as to pagans in general (Calkin, *Saracens and the Making of English Identity*, p. 2). Christian writers used the term as an Islamophobic label associated with negative and racialized stereotypes of Muslims in order to denigrate enemies of European political and religious agendas (Heng, *Invention of Race*, pp. 111–12; Rajabzadeh, "Depoliticized").

Chapter 22, Paragraph 1

holde, the hand to. To stop or halt, as in the gesture of a raised, outward facing palm. The expression occurs in various forms such as "holden up hondes" and "holden hondes," which mean "to refrain from action," or to "restrain someone from acting." See Whiting H75; see also *MED hond(e* (n.), sense 6a; *holden* (v.1), sense 14a.

fayre shewes of their eyen whiche wauntonly. Caxton adds judgmental details to Eglantine's description of the daughters' behavior. BN says simply that they should refrain from the expressions and glances they made to the knight [*se departent de semblant et regars quelles font vers le chevalier*]. See the *Book of the Knight of the Tour-Landry* for Sir Geoffrey's instructions regarding control of the eyes and the gaze (*Knight of the Tour-Landry*, ed. Wright, p. 15).

Chapter 23, Paragraph 1

bere you in hande that. Affirm to you, an assertion that something is true (*MED beren* (v.1), sense 13g). The phrase often appears with the negative, as in "to be charged and born wrongly on hond," where "charged" suggests the raised hand gesture of swearing. See Whiting H65.

Chapter 23, Paragraph 2

behourdyng. Behorts [OF *behort*], combats fought with blunted weapons, were popular for the training of young knights, and tournaments often included such events. This word does not appear in BN.

Chapter 23, Paragraph 3

reverence. An act of respect, especially a bow (*MED reverence* (n.), sense 2). Attendance on the lord or lady was a matter of protocol in a noble household as described in Caxton's publication, *The Babees Boke* (ed. Furnivall, *Early English Meals and Manners*, pp. 250–58).

Chapter 23, Paragraph 4

yf rayson had not restrayned her. The vocabulary of formal argument predominates in this passage — *premysses, conclusyons, pryme face,* following the convention of debates between love and pride [*daunger*], emotion and reason. Later Eglantine tells Blanchardyn that she has debated the god of love (23.6).

Chapter 23, Paragraph 6

Wherof men may thynke . . . this caas acostumed. The narrator's comment draws attention to Blanchardyn's and Eglantine's facial expressions, the conventional blushing and pallor of courtly lovers.

Chapter 23, Paragraph 7

soubdayne fyre. The flame descending from heaven evokes the Pentecostal flame of the Holy Spirit that descended on Jesus's disciples following his crucifixion, anointing them to go forth and spread his message (Acts 2).

Chapter 24, Paragraph 1

can good skyle. To reason well, exercise sound judgement and discrimination; also to have the ability or skill to do something (*MED skil* (n.), senses 2b, 7b).

Chapter 24, Paragraph 2

clothe of golde crymosyn. Cloth of gold was a rich fabric woven with threads of gold and silk and often featuring red embroideries or patterns.

Chapter 24, Paragraph 4

kynge of geauntes, called Rubyon. Rubyon is introduced earlier (see 18.3) simply as a king accompanied by a king of giants who is fifteen feet tall and "foull and hydouse." The size of Blanchardyn's challenger intimidates other knights, but his appearance and stature are not mentioned again.

Chapter 24, Paragraph 7

above. The term means success, victory, and prosperity and often appears with such phrases as "ben at" and "comen to" (*MED above(n* (adv. as n.), sense 2a.).

Chapter 24, Paragraph 12

untrewe paynemys. This is an ironic condemnation. Romances often show Muslim kings berating their losing troops in an unchivalric display of fury.

Chapter 24, Paragraph 14

dromadaryes. Camels were exchanged as gifts and ransoms in the Middle Ages. In the Arab world, they were ridden in battle.

Chapter 25, Paragraph 2

Salmandry. This is Alexandria [*Alamandrie*] in Egypt; the verse texts of the romance give this name.

Chapter 25, Paragraph 3

for he whom God wolde preserve can not peryshe. See Whiting G276.

Chapter 26, Paragraph 1

Nourweye. The author of the French prose version felt a need to specify that Alymodes's city of Cassidoine is in Scandinavia (see note 9.1, above).

Chapter 26, Paragraph 5

Maryenbourgh. Literally "Mary's castle," now Malbork in western Poland, this site was part of Prussia until the fifteenth century. Marienburg was erected by the Order of Teutonic Knights in the thirteenth century; it was the site of many battles in the fourteenth and fifteenth centuries.

Pruce. This is Prussia, on the Baltic Sea in eastern Germany and western Poland.

Chapter 26, Paragraph 6

atte that tyme. The prose redactor must explain the Prussians' dark skin, a remnant of the Mediterranean setting of the original verse romance. French and English audiences of the fifteenth century would have known Prussians to be light-skinned, but Muslims, according to the stereotype, were dark-skinned, a color associated with evil and darkness.

hyghe Duche. High German language. This is Caxton's translation of *thioise*, meaning language of the Teutons [OF *tiois*] In the verse romances, Blancandin speaks Greek and other eastern languages.

Chapter 26, Paragraph 8

Grece. Greek parentage is part of Blanchardyn's incognito; it is more appropriate in the verse romance, which is set in the Mediterranean. In that version, Blancandin gives a more accurate account of his adventure.

Mocastre. This is the castle of Thomokastron on the Ionian Sea. Held by rebels to the Byzantine emperor, it surrendered to his forces in 1340. This detail appears only in the long prose version of the romance. The rebels were supported by Catherine of Valois, related to dukes of Burgundy (Nicol, *Reluctant Emperor*, pp. 41–43).

Mahon. From Muhammed, here used as the name of a deity. Blanchardyn is not averse to giving thanks to this god in order to pass among the Prussians, inserting the name in a formula where "God" would appear in a Christian context; later he says he will vanquish the Poles "though the helpe of the goddes" (28.3), but elsewhere, still incognito, he refers to the singular "God" and uses the Christian formula "oure Lorde" (32.4).

Chapter 27, Paragraph 2

Polonye. Wars between the Poles, the Prussians, and the Teutonic Knights were ongoing throughout the fifteenth century. See the Introduction to this romance, pp. 135–36.

Chapter 30, Paragraph 1

Well ye. The following episode, Darius's raid on Frisia and the capture of its spoils by the forces of Tourmaday, does not appear in the short prose *Blancandin* (Brussels, KRB, MS 3576/7).

Chapter 30, Paragraph 3

commodytees. The word refers to resources generally, but also has the more specific meaning of "crops or produce (of a manor)" (*MED commodite* (n.), senses 3a, 2a).

Chapter 30, Paragraph 5

y-blynded. Blindfolded. Later, when the king is rescued, his vision appears to be unimpaired, though initially dimmed by his confinement in darkness (39.5).

Chapter 32, Paragraph 1

in the mornyng or at evyn. To a void exposure to attack, the people of Tourmaday usually only went outside the city walls in early morning or at dusk.

Chapter 32, Paragraph 4

Grete Norweyghe. This is the Christian kingdom of Eglantine's uncle, always referred to as Grete Norweyghe to distinguish it from Alymodes's kingdom, Norweyghe. The designation may be the writer's attempt to differentiate areas of Norway, Sweden, and Denmark, whose boundaries were fluid and disputed in the fourteenth and fifteenth centuries (Stelboum, "William Caxton's Romance," p. 105).

Explanatory Notes to Blanchardyn and Eglantine

Chapter 33, Paragraph 1

preelect. A term applied to the Virgin Mary, meaning "divinely chosen beforehand" (*MED preelect* (adj.)). In thus describing the rose, a flower associated with the Virgin, Blanchardyn gives a religious cast to his meditation on his lady, whose name means "briar rose."

Chapter 34, Paragraph 5

sonne. The medieval European belief that dark pigmentation was caused by the heat of the sun accords with the conception of human geography and physiology found in the encyclopedias and natural histories of the time. The narrative seems to say that Blanchardyn's dark skin and disfigured face are caused by the sun, though earlier he has applied herbs to blacken his skin.

Chapter 36, Paragraph 1

dyed. Once again, the point is made that Blanchardyn appears to be dark skinned like the others in his party who are said to be "Sarrasyns." The provost's use of the word *dyed* suggests that he realizes the knight's color could be applied, since Eglantine has just revealed that he is Blanchardyn. His blackface is a disguise.

Chapter 37, Paragraph 1

tempeste shold breke. The motif of tempests abated by pious acts, whether jettisoning idols, prayer, or conversion, is common in romances, for example Marie de France's *Eliduc*, and *Florence of Rome* (*MIFL* C984.2, storm because of broken taboo; V52.6, mariners' prayer stops storm; D2141.1, storm magically stilled).

maumetys. Idols, pagan gods. The term, derived from the name Muhammed, reflects medieval Christian popular belief that his followers worshipped him as a god through images. This word is Caxton's addition. BN reads *decepuables et dampnables ydolles* [deceiving and damnable idols].

Chapter 37, Paragraph 5

all armed fro top to too. Proverbial (Whiting T421).

Chapter 38, Paragraph 6

trybute. This was a tax paid for security and protection (*MED tribut(e*, (n.)) The status of the Christian community in Cassydoyne resembles that of Jews in European cities.

Chapter 39, Paragraph 4

ded. This lie of Blanchardyn's is unnecessarily cruel and out of character for this loving son, though it is keeping with his trickster persona. The king's abject response is an opportunity for heightened pathos.

Chapter 41, Paragraph 4

chaunged. BN reads *couchid* [to lie down or recline]. Caxton uses *couchid* elsewhere, and in context *chaunged* is clearly a mistake, since Eglantine is lying on her bed.

he whome God wyll have kept may not be peryshed. Proverbial (Whiting G276).

Chapter 41, Paragraph 5

"Ha, ha, madame . . . your laste dayes." The provost, in an aside, addresses the absent Eglantine.

Chapter 42, Paragraph 3

thurgh all the stretes and common places of the towne that all the stretes of the cyté sholde be hanged wyth clothes. Decking streets with tapestries, cloths, or greenery was a common custom during celebrations. The festive music, ringing bells, and loud singing and praying are a fitting welcome for Blanchardyn and acts of thanksgiving, but they are also a strategy to unnerve Alymodes.

tambours. The context suggests small drums for festive occasions (*MED tabour* (n.), sense 1b). The catalogue of instruments which follows includes both loud and soft (trumpets and lutes), wind, brass, stringed, and keyboard instruments. The singing of the ladies in procession and the ringing of church bells completes the aural description of Blanchardyn's reception.

Chapter 43, Paragraph 4

alle barefote. To walk barefoot was a sign of humility, an act of penance, and a common practice on pilgrimage. See also 52.7, where townspeople welcome Blanchardyn in a barefoot procession.

Chapter 44, Paragraph 4

a knyght. The episode of Subyon features a stock character of romance: the treacherous steward who, given authority in his lord's absence, attempts to marry his wife to gain control of the realm. The Middle English romances *Sir Tryamour* and *Roswall and Lillian* also feature treacherous stewards.

never noo wodewoll dyde brede a sperhawke. Proverbial (see Whiting W566). Caxton's source reads *bruhier*, buzzard, a much less attractive bird than the *wodewoll*, or common woodpecker.

The French phrase makes a stronger contrast since buzzards feed on carrion while sparrow hawks take live prey and were considered noble birds. In this passage introducing Subyon, the narrator employs several proverbial expressions equating humble birth with filth and low morals to warn the reader of the danger in giving the low-born authority above their rank (see Whiting B305, C269, C270, C271). These proverbs appear only in the long prose romance.

Chapter 46, Paragraph 1

moevable godes of fortune. The word *moevable* is Caxton's addition; *goodes* refers to good things generally as well as to possessions, both subject to change.

Chapter 47, Paragraph 3

moche abydeth behynde that a fole thynketh. But much is lacking (left behind) in a fool's thoughts (see Whiting F448).

Eglantyne. Not in BN. Caxton added this second occurrence of the lady's name.

Chapter 48, Paragraph 6

your. In addressing her father with humility, Beatrix uses singular pronouns throughout this speech, hoping to mollify him with this form of polite address to a parent or superior.

Chapter 48, Paragraph 7

thi. Alymodes refers to Beatrix only by plural pronouns to express reproach and call attention to her subordinate status.

Chapter 48, Paragraph 8

thee. Beatrix responds to her father's angry dismissal by herself switching to plural pronouns to berate him.

Olde unfamouse myschaunt. Beatrix's angry and insulting rebuff to to her father is in keeping with the aggressive behavior of other Muslim princesses in romances and chansons. Her graphic characterization of his appearance is notable. See the Introduction to this romance, pp. 141–42, for further discussion of Beatrix.

Chapter 51, Paragraph 4

releved their lordshippes. Their feudal grants and titles were reaffirmed by Sadoyne (see *MED releven* (v.), sense 4c).

Chapter 52, Paragraph 9

whosoever rekeneth ... twys for ones. See Whiting H550. The proverb refers to paying a bill at a tavern or inn: he who neglects to consult his host when settling accounts (reckoning) ends up paying double. Subyon and his men will pay a high price for not taking Blanchardyn's prowess into account. *Rekeneth* also means "take heed," "pay attention" (*MED rekenen* (v.), sense 4e), and *host* may also be a pun on *host* in the sense of "army," which is appropriate in the proverb's context. The expression is used in similar circumstances in Lord Berners's translation of *Arthur of Little Britain,* as a warning when the emperor commands his men to assault Arthur's castle (trans. Bourcher, *Arthur of Little Britain,* p. 422).

Chapter 53, Paragraph 4

Sylvayne. The name means forest or woods, where outlaws often lived.

Chapter 54, Paragraph 6

confraternities. BN: *colleges.* These could be civic organizations, lay auxillaries to religious establishments, as well as faculties of schools.

Chapter 54, Paragraph 8

Water was poured. This is water for washing hands. This hygienic ritual begins the banquet, as stressed by books of manners. The description of the festivities appears only in the long prose version of the romance.

Chapter 54, Paragraph 9

Rambault the Frisian. In the *Chanson de Roland,* one Rembalt from Galacia is identified in a catalogue of Charlemagne's warriors as commanding a division of Flemings and barons from Frisia. These troops avenge the deaths of Charlemagne's nephew Roland, and Oliver, his brother in arms, slain by Muslims at the battle of Roncevaux. Rambault, king of Frisia, is the titular hero of a Burgundian romance contemporaneous with *Blanchardyn and Eglantine.*

Chapter 54, Paragraph 12

Explicit expliciat, Quy plus vult scribere scribat. A conventional colophon, based on the Latin *Explicit expliciat: scriptor ludere eat* [It is done, let it be done; the writer may go off to play].

Textual Notes to *Blanchardyn and Eglantine*

Title Page

At the bottom of the decorated title page inserted before the Dedication are two notes in nineteenth-century hands questioning the date 1485 in the title. Both refer to the typeface. One note is followed by the initial *W*; perhaps it was written by William Blades who was the first to systematically study Caxton's typefaces.

Dedication, Paragraph 1

Unto. So R. The first page of Caxton's print has an original woodcut border embellished by rubrication, including the title *Dedication* written at the top of the page in a professional Roman script with flourishes. See the Introduction to *Blanchardyn and Eglantine*, p. 147, for discussion of the book's ornamentation format.

Wyllyam Caxton. So R. In the right margin, a star has been written in black ink opposite the name.

prynce. So R. In the bottom margin below this line, *Wyllyam Caxton* is written in Roman letters. To the left of this, *The Printers Name* is written in script.

Dedication, Paragraph 3

Amen. So R. At the bottom of the page, a name, perhaps *Symon*, is written in brown ink followed by the numbers *1.6.6*; part of another inscription is visible at the lower edge. See the Introduction to *Blanchardyn and Eglantine*, pp. 147–48, for discussion of the book's evidence of early readers and owners.

Table of Chapters, Paragraph 1

Here. In R, *The Contents of the Chapters* is written in rubricated script at the top of the page. A finding aid appears in the right margin where the annotator has written *folio* in red ink. Beneath it, at the end of each chapter title, the corresponding folio is written in Arabic numerals. The list continues on leaves three and four, and it appears to be by the same hand as *The Contents of the Chapters*.

Table of Chapters, Paragraph 7

the of lady the. So R; emended to *the lady of* for sense.

Table of Chapters, Paragraph 13

and sorowe. So R. Not in BN.

Table of Chapters, Paragraph 14

departed fro hir. So R. Not in BN.

where as he dyd mervayllus armes. So R. Not in BN.

Table of Chapters, Paragraph 15

honorably. So R. Not in BN.

Table of Chapters, Paragraph 20

gladly. So R. Not in BN.

Table of Chapters, Paragraph 21

of Blanchardyn and other thynges. So R. Not in BN.

Table of Chapters, Paragraph 22

secretely. So R. Not in BN.

Table of Chapters, Paragraph 28

wyth a grete armye. So R. Not in BN.

Table of Chapters, Paragraph 37

and love. So R. Not in BN.

Table of Chapters, Paragraph 39

Capitulo xxxviii. So R. In the space between *Capitulo* and *xxxviii*, *chaptre* is hand-written in faint brown ink.

Table of Chapters, Paragraph 40

that thei had togyder. So R. Not in BN.

Table of Chapters, Paragraph 41

where they arryved . . . that they dyde. So R. Not in BN.

Table of Chapters, Paragraph 43

her frende and love. So R. Not in BN.

Table of Chapters, Paragraph 45

in grete distresse. So R. Not in BN.

Table of Chapters, Paragraphs 50–54

fol. 5r. The original page listing the remaining five chapters' titles is missing from R. However, a leaf has been inserted on which the titles are written in a professional gothic script and ornately rubricated. Their numbers and folios are listed in Arabic numerals in two columns on the right side of the page.

Blanchardyn and Eglantine

Chapter 1, Rubric

The first chapitre. The title of the chapter is set off by spacing and marked by an initial ¶; a blank line separates it from the text that follows.

Chapter 1, Paragraph 1

That. So R. The text begins with a capital letter *T* of floriated design, five lines tall. Caxton gave most of the chapter titles a similar, if scaled down, format.

Chapter 1, Paragraph 3

beyonde mesure ... of his age. So R. Not in BN.

Chapter 1, Paragraph 4

elder in age. So R. BN reads *les plus sagis* [more wise].

Notwythstandyng. In R, a ¶ sign marks this concluding sentence, emphasizing its proverbial statement.

Chapter 2, Rubric

and of theyre fayttes. So R. Not in BN. The title of the second chapter is set off by an initial ¶ and a partially blank line.

Chapter 2, Paragraph 1

It. So R. The initial capital letter is three lines tall and modestly embellished.

Chapter 2, Paragraph 2

and of Achilles. So R. Not in BN.

Chapter 2, Paragraph 3

and blasure. So R. Not in BN.

longe taryeng. So R. Not in BN.

Chapter 3, Rubric

The third chapitre. So R. The third chapter's title is marked with a ¶ and set off by blank lines before and after.

Chapter 3, Paragraph 1

Blanchardyn. So R. The initial letter is two lines tall. All of the following chapters begin with a similar large plain capital letter. These are not noted below.

where he was becomen. So R. Not in BN.

Chapter 4, Rubric

The fourth chapitre conteyneth . . . made for hym. So R. Not in BN. In R, the title of the fourth chapter is not separate from the text that precedes it, though it is marked by a ¶ sign.

Chapter 4, Paragraph 1

After. The initial *A*, located at the top of the folio, is two lines tall.

Chapter 5, Paragraph 2

alyght from his courser. So R. Not in BN.

and prayed hym. So R. Not in BN.

and that . . . lady unto hym. So R. Not in BN.

Chapter 5, Paragraph 3

and his good swerde y-girded. So R. BN: *sailly sur son destrier sans quelque avantage prendre* [leapt on his war horse without taking any (unfair) advantage].

Chapter 7, Paragraph 1

or haste. So R. Not in BN.

Chapter 7, Paragraph 4

our herte . . . drawyng to the perfection. So R. BN: *notre cuer qui est imparti* [our heart which is indivisible].

Chapter 7, Paragraph 5

or wythout ceasse. So R. Not in BN.

Chapter 8, Paragraph 1

that are wonte to growe in wodes. So R. Not in BN.

Chapter 8, Paragraph 2

fery. So R. BN reads *gue* [ford].

Chapter 8, Paragraph 3

and goodely manere. So R. Not in BN.

Chapter 9, Rubric

Tormaday. So R. In the space between the title and the text that follows, a seventeenth-century hand has written in black ink... *and the counsell he gave him touching the proude pucelle in amours or proud lady in love.* Eglantine is introduced in this chapter, and the writer wanted to note this important fact in the title.

Chapter 9, Paragraph 1

After. So R. A faint bracket in the left margin marks this paragraph.

knight... R lacks a leaf here. The missing passage is supplied in the translation from BN that follows. Kellner includes the passage (pp. 35–36).

Chapter 9, Paragraph 3

me semeth not. So R. In the right margin, a faint bracket marks the line where the knight of the ferry replies to Blanchardyn.

How be it. So R. A faint bracket here continues into the right margin, and the letter *H* in *How* has been lightly circled. The sentence it begins relates Blanchardyn's first stirrings of love for the proud lady.

good. So R. Not in BN.

Chapter 9, Paragraph 4

and welthe. So R. Not in BN.

or cusse. So R. Not in BN.

Chapter 10, Rubric

as foloweth. So R. Not in BN.

Chapter 11, Paragraphs 2–3

Blanchardyn, seeyng the oure and the poynt... alone wythout eny companye. So R. These paragraphs are marked by faint brackets in the right margin to indicate the pivotal episode of the kiss.

Chapter 12, Rubric

as herafter foloweth. So R. Not in BN.

Chapter 12, Paragraph 3

nor knowen. So R. Not in BN.

but that I sholde complayne me. So R. Not in BN.

and shal deye. So R. Not in BN.

saynge strongly ayenst hit. So R. Not in BN.

and uttre. So R. Not in BN.

that is now happed to you of one man. So R. Not in BN.

Chapter 13, Rubric

havyng styl his thought fast upon here beaulté. So R. Not in BN.

as herafter foloweth. So R. Not in BN.

Chapter 13, Paragraph 1

upon her whyte palfray amblyng. So R. Not in BN.

hanged. So R. Not in BN. Caxton's Eglantine is more brutal than her French counterpart, who only wants to *prendre* [seize, apprehend] the offending knight.

Chapter 13, Paragraphs 2–3

wherof he was glad ... provostis place of Tourmaday. So R. Not in BN.

Chapter 13, Paragraph 3

Who that wol lodge ... entre this inne. So BN. R: prose. Edited following modern conventions of verse format for ease of reading. Caxton prints the ballade as prose, offset with a paraph mark and a capital letter similar to those at the beginnings of chapters.

Chapter 14, Paragraph 4

in this maner. So R. Not in BN.

to your plesure and behouffe. So R. Not in BN.

wherof the provost thanked hym gretly. This is the last line on the folio. Beneath it an early owner has described his family's coat of arms:

> *John Dewe of Chesterton ownethe me Anno domini 1500*
> *md, that I found wrytten in an old booke, that (Rich?)ard*
> *Dewe my predecessor of the halle of Chesterton, in the*
> *reigne of Richard the second, gott in the feild in Ireland*
> *am (arms) aunciente red with three barres yellowe therein*
> *a yellowe castell in a blewe feild hee(?) was then and ...*

The note is written in brown ink. The remainder has been trimmed off, perhaps when the pages were rebound. A John Dew received his B.A. from Cambridge in 1484–1485 and was a fellow of Gonville Hall there from 1488 to 1500. Chesterton is a neighborhood in modern Cambridge. See the Introduction to this romance, pp. 147–48, for discussion of the book's owners.

Chapter 15, Paragraph 1

his evyll wylle. So R. Not in BN.

behavoure and. So R. Not in BN.

Chapter 15, Paragraph 3

and goode wylle. So R. Not in BN.

Chapter 16, Paragraph 1

In suche. So R. Remains of an annotation in brown ink appear in the gutter of the left margin.

Chapter 16, Paragraph 2

that so fyers was ayenst the god of love. So R. Not in BN.

Chapter 17, Paragraph 1

soverayne desyre and. So R. Not in BN.

Chapter 18, Rubric

wyth a myghty power of folke. So R. Not in BN.

Chapter 19, Rubric

all of whyte sylke. So R. Not in BN.

Chapter 20, Paragraph 3

affrayed. So R. Remains of an annotation appear in the gutter of the left margin.

Chapter 20, Paragraph 4

appiered. So R. Not in BN.

swerde. R: ~~swerde~~ *speare.* The word *swerde* has been crossed out and the annotator has written *speare* in brown ink in the right margin. The name *John New* is written below in a similar hand. See Explanatory Note.

of proesse. So R. Not in BN.

Chapter 20, Paragraph 7

in her herte. So R. Not in BN.

Yf ye wolde. R reads *Yf yf.* An annotator corrected the second *yf* by writing an *e* over the *f*. A smudged cross has been written in brown ink on the right margin. It appears beside the important passage in which Eglantine determines to take Blanchardyn as her lover.

noo man infydele. So R. Caxton omitted a detail from his source: that Eglantine will wed no infidel having *ydoles dyaboliques* [diabolical idols].

Chapter 20, Paragraph 9

or wythdrawe his men. So R. Not in BN.

Chapter 20, Paragraph 10

lenyng upon. So R. A black ink cross is written in the right margin.

specyall. So R. This word is underlined and the annotator's hand has written *frend* in the margin, in brown ink.

nor how to mayntene herself. So R. Not in BN.

ne take no maner of reste. So R. Not in BN.

Chapter 21, Rubric

as it foloweth. So R. Not in BN.

Chapter 21, Paragraph 2

hoste. So R. The word is underlined, and the annotator has written *guest* by it in the margin, in brown ink. This is not a correction, but a definition. *MED* defines *host* as an invited guest or a paying guest (*host* (n.2), senses 2a, b).

Chapter 21, Paragraph 3

feyré. So R. The letter *y* is written in brown ink at the end of this word.

Chapter 22, Rubric

the yonge knyght, as it folowed here. So R. Not in BN.

Chapter 22, Paragraph 1

fayre shewes of their eyen whiche wauntonly. So R. BN: *semblant et regars quelles font* [expressions and glances that they made].

Chapter 22, Paragraph 2

and in all manere norreture right parfyt. So R. Not in BN.

Chapter 23, Rubric

twenty third. R: *xxiiii.* The last *i* is crossed out and the annotator has written *chap~.23d* in the margin, in brown ink.

Chapter 23, Paragraphs 1–2

After the humble leve . . . "I thanke you," sayde Blanchardyn. So R. Faint brackets set off these paragraphs an important passage in which Blanchardyn rejects the Provost's suggestion that Eglantine is in love with him.

Chapter 23, Paragraph 1

hyghe. So R. A partial signature in brown ink, perhaps *Rich . . . Furm . . .*, is visible at the edge of the right margin.

Chapter 23, Paragraph 2

and behourdyng. So R. Not in BN.

Chapter 23, Paragraph 4

and taken. So R. Not in BN.

as longeth tyl a knyght to doo. So R. Not in BN. A partial signature, *Mary L.*, is written in dark brown ink along the lower edge of the page; the bottoms of the letters have been trimmed off.

promette. So R. An annotator emended the spelling, writing in *ss* in brown ink.

Chapter 23, Paragraph 6

god of love. R: *of god love.* Emended to *god of love* for sense.

Chapter 24, Rubric

twenty fourth. R: *xxiiii.* The last *i* is crossed out and the annotator has written *chap~ 24th* in the left margin, in brown ink.

Chapter 24, Paragraphs 2–3

After the gracyouse leve of the lady . . . proceded to hym of veraye noblenes. So R. Faint brackets in the side margin mark the beginning and end of this important passage, which narrate the lover's exchange of gifts and Eglantine's first public acknowledgment of her favor, followed by the appointment of Blanchardyn as seneschal.

Chapter 24, Paragraph 7

speciall. So R. This word is underlined, and the annotator has written *frend* in the margin in brown ink.

Chapter 24, Paragraph 9

and cursed man. So R. Not in BN.

Chapter 24, Paragraph 10

harde. So R. Not in BN.

Chapter 25, Paragraph 1

Thus after . . . lost his lyff. So R. The first two paragraphs of this chapter are set off by faint marginal brackets. The passage narrates Beatrice's plea to Alymodes and his sparing of Blanchardyn's life.

Chapter 25, Paragraph 2

for whom ye have caused your humble supplycacion. So R. Not in BN.

So. So R. This word is preceded by a space and a paraph mark, creating a visual break on the page. Here a reader has inserted a marginal bracket before the conclusion of Alymodes's address to Beatrice.

Chapter 25, Paragraph 3

for he whom God wolde preserve can not peryshe. So R. Not in BN.

Chapter 26, Paragraph 1

for to have wrake upon hym. So R. Not in BN.

Chapter 26, Paragraph 3

wyshyng full often . . . above all other. So R. Not in BN.

Chapter 27, Paragraph 2

The kynge . . . provysion were had. So R. Not in BN.

Chapter 28, Rubric

How. So R. The annotator has written *Chap~ 28th* in the left margin by this unnumbered title.

Chapter 28, Paragraph 3

Vassall. So R. Not in BN.

and sette. So R. Not in BN.

Chapter 29, Paragraph 1

hylles and dales here and there. So R. BN: *les champs dont les maistres gisoyent mors entre les pies sur les champs* [the fields where their masters lie dead between their feet on the ground]. Caxton omits the detail about the horses' riders, though the formula appears in several other battle scenes.

Chapter 29, Paragraph 2

twenty four. So R. BN: *dix* [ten].

Chapter 29, Paragraph 4

bycause that they sholde be more sure of hym. So R. Not in BN.

Chapter 29, Paragraph 5

under thy swerde. So R. Not in BN.

royalme. So R. BN: *de mon people deffendeur. De veufes et orphenins secure garde et droiture* [defender of my people. Of old people and orphans, safe keeping and justice].

to be understande. So R. Not in BN.

descended of. So R. BN: *sans nulle doubte et as bien averi fie tes paroles* [without any doubt and as your speech well attests].

Chapter 30, Paragraph 4

Daryus, that of his beynge ther was soone advertysed. So R. BN: *Daire et toute sa navire y vint arriver et prendre port par ung bien matin. Il fist jette les ancres puis saillirent hors tous ensamble moult joyeux de ce que hors de la tourmente de la mer estoient eschappez. Mais pas bien ne scavoient en quel pays ils estoient arrivez.* [Darius and all his navy arrived there and made port in a fair morning. He made the anchors to be dropped then they rushed out all together very joyous that they were escaped from tempest of the sea. But they did not know in what country they had arrived.]

Chapter 30, Paragraph 6

for the love . . . myserably has loste. So R. Not in BN.

Chapter 31, Rubric

for love of . . . them there. So R. Not in BN.

Chapter 31, Paragraph 2

The maronners bygan . . . wyth grete joye. So R. Not in BN.

Chapter 32, Paragraph 4

had. So R. The sense seems to be *had* **not** *som.* K emends.

Chapter 32, Paragraph 5

for or ever . . . oute of syght. So R. Not in BN.

And the provost . . . costes of Nourtheweghe. So R. Not in BN.

where he arryved . . . it is sayd. So R. Not in BN.

the goode yonge knyght. So R. Not in BN.

wyth Sadoyne. So R. Not in BN.

Chapter 33, Rubric

wythin a gardyne. So R. Not in BN.

Sadoyne. So R. BN includes the phrase *en promettant que de tout son povoir lui aideroit* [promising that he will help him with all his power].

Chapter 33, Paragraph 1

without ceasse. So R. Not in BN.

Chapter 33, Paragraph 2

from her . . . my penseful herte. So R. Not in BN.

Chapter 36, Paragraph 1

that at my grete nede . . . I have therof. So R. Not in BN.

Chapter 36, Paragraph 3

maystres and that the. So R. Faintly written in the right margin, a large arrow points to the end of this line. In the adjacent passage, Eglantine sees Blanchardyn's navy overtaken by a storm and swept from Tourmaday.

Chapter 36, Paragraph 4

his feythful felawe. So R. Not in BN.

Chapter 37, Paragraph 1

maumetys. So R. BN : *decepuables et dampnables ydolles* [deceiving and damnable idols].

Chapter 37, Paragraph 5

and all armed fro top to too. So R. Not in BN.

Chapter 38, Rubric

And the fayr Beatryx was taken to mercy. So R. Not in BN.

Chapter 39, Paragraph 3

and myght kepe his counteynaunce nor behave hymself. So R. Not in BN.

harde and. So R. Not in BN.

shortyng oure dayes . . . ye may see. So R. Not in BN.

Chapter 39, Paragraph 5

or do to be rehersed. So R. Not in BN.

prysoner. So R. Not in BN.

Chapter 39, Paragraph 6

no. In R, a bracket in brown ink marks the end of this line. In the passage that follows, the king of Frisia relates the death of Blanchardyn's mother.

Chapter 40, Paragraph 2

and his folke within her cyté of Tourmaday. So R. BN: *le quel par sa cruaulte est cause que le royaulme de Frize avoit este degaste par Daire son filz, dont le bon roy pere de Blanchandin avoit grant desir de sen vengier, tres convoitant de soy trouver en lieu ou il lui peust porter dommage car il estoit encorres de bon eaige pour porter et excerciser les armes* [which by his cruelty is the cause that the realm of Frise had been laid waste by Darius his son, on which the good king father of Blanchardin had great desire to take revenge, longed to find himself in a place where he could cause him harm, for he was still of a good age to bear and use arms].

Chapter 41, Paragraph 4

chaunged. So R. BN: *couchid.* See Explanatory Note.

Chapter 41, Paragraph 6

yf God woll. So R. Not in BN.

Chapter 42, Rubric

Here foloweth . . . in hitself and. So R. Not in BN.

Chapter 42, Paragraph 1

so truly and benyngly. So R. Not in BN.

their enmyes shal knowe . . . of the towne. So R. Not in BN. Caxton considerably embellishes the ferocity of the Provost's reply. BN reads only *que de nul tort nen seront reprins* [will not recover from the harm (done to them)].

Chapter 42, Paragraph 4

that wythin the towne was thus grete. So R. Not in BN.

Chapter 43, Paragraph 2

for to have theym . . . entre in them. So R. BN: *pour ce que la endroit ou il estoit logie ny avoit quelque perilage de la mer si la fist venir aupres de lui ancre pour ce que le temps estoit douls et la mer quoyt il le fist affin que . . .* [because the place where he was quartered had no peril of the sea, he made them come there near to him to anchor because the weather was calm and the sea quiet, he made it so that . . .].

Chapter 43, Paragraphs 2–3

Thus passed Kynge Alymodes the nyght . . . nother frendes nor enmyes. So R. Marks between the lines of text set off this passage beginning the extended account of the final battle between Blanchardyn's army and the forces of Alymodes; similar marks appear again at the end of the following paragraph.

Chapter 43, Paragraph 5

a duke. So R. Not in BN.

Chapter 43, Paragraph 6

They dyd . . . excellent proues. So R. In BN, this passage relating the retreat of Alymodes's forces and ensuing battle follows the account of the king of Frisia and Sadoyne's combat with Corburant which appears in paragraph 8.

They began . . . toward their enmyes. So R. Not in BN.

Chapter 43, Paragraph 10

his felawe. So R. Not in BN.

had taken . . . body of hym. So R. BN: *eust occis* [had killed].

Chapter 43, Paragraph 11

They two drewe themself out. So R. Brackets in the outside margins mark this paragraph which recounts the single combat, on horseback, of Blanchardyn and Alymodes.

their armures that were of fyn stele. So R. BN: *lachier qui en leurs heaulmes estoit* [laces which were on their helmets].

yf the messenger . . . of fyn golde. So R. Not in BN.

Chapter 44, Paragraph 3

in grete habondaunce. So R. Not in BN.

Chapter 44, Paragraph 4

I saye this. In R, this sentence and the three following it are preceded by ¶s. Caxton thus gives visual emphasis to the lesson. See the Explanatory Note for additional commentary.

Chapter 45, Paragraph 2

wyth hym. So R. An early hand has written *Blanchardyn* at the bottom left corner of the page, in brown ink.

Chapter 46, Paragraph 1

and so haunsed in worship. So R. Not in BN.

whiche myght wel ... than he was. So R. Not in BN.

that shall sone overcome Blanchardyn. So R. Not in BN.

Chapter 47, Rubric

as ye shal here. So R. Not in BN.

Chapter 47, Paragraph 3

Eglantyne, otherwyse callyd the proude pucell in amours. So R. Not in BN.

Chapter 47, Paragraph 4

tarye styll oure penne to wryte. So R. BN: *vous lairons a parler de ceulx* [we leave you to speak of those ...].

wryte. So R. BN: *parlerons* [we will speak].

Chapter 48, Paragraph 1

wyth bothe her armes. So R. Not in BN.

Chapter 48, Paragraphs 6–9

The fayre Beatryx, heryng her fader speke . . . that Sadoyne sholde be beten. So R. Faint brackets in the side margin mark the beginning and end of this passage recounting the heated exchange between Alymodes and Beatrix as she pleads with him to spare Sadoyne and accept Christianity.

Chapter 48, Paragraph 6

that ye geve upon your false goddes. So R. Not in BN.

one onli God. So R. Not in BN.

Chapter 48, Paragraph 8

goddes and. So R. Not in BN.

Chapter 48, Paragraph 9

for the deth . . . be ther slayne. So R. Not in BN.

Chapter 48, Paragraph 10

bytterly. So R. Not in BN.

in this wyse. So R. Not in BN

that he most nowe suffre. So R. Not in BN.

Chapter 49, Paragraph 2

whiche is full goode and deffensable. So R. Not in BN.

Chapter 49, Paragraph 3

my lady. So R. BN reads *sa dame* [his lady].

Chapter 50, Paragraph 2

parfit. R: *parft.* I follow Kellner's emendation.

Chapter 51, Paragraph 2

and thankes. So R. Not in BN.

tyll eche other. So R. Not in BN.

and colled. So R. Not in BN.

Chapter 51, Paragraph 3

from the bataylle. So R. Not in BN.

Chapter 51, Paragraph 5

and subdewed. So R. Not in BN.

Chapter 51, Paragraph 6

and unyon. So R. Not in BN.

venymouse malyce of the false traytoure. So R. Not in BN.

a grete trayson. So R. BN: que par Subien avoit este procedee alencontre de sa dame [he knew not that Subyon had been advancing against his lady].

the proude pucelle in amours. So R. Not in BN.

Chapter 52, Paragraph 1

for to goo rescue hys felawe Sadoyne. So R. Not in BN.

and telle. So R. Not in BN.

Chapter 52, Paragraph 3

and shewed. So R. Not in BN.

Chapter 52, Paragraph 7

of theym. So R. Not in BN.

and tolde. So R. Not in BN.

Chapter 52, Paragraph 8

and ootes for his horses. So R. Not in BN.

Chapter 53, Rubric

and what folowed after. So R. Not in BN.

Chapter 53, Paragraph 1

fol. 95r. Brown stains on this folio suggest that the pages missing from the end of R were damaged and discarded in rebinding. Similar stains on fol. 4, the last original page of the Table of Chapters, may explain why the leaf was added there when the volume was restored.

of theym. So R. Not in BN.

to passe by them. So R. Not in BN.

Chapter 53, Paragraph 2

Subyon. R: *Sadoyne,* emended; in the context, a mistake.

Chapter 53, Paragraph 3

He was well mounted. So R. A faint bracket in the right margin marks the passage recounting the flight of Subyon into the forest following the defeat of his troops.

Chapter 53, Paragraph 4

there wythin theyr caves. So R. Not in BN.

Chapter 53, Paragraph 5

by syx myles. So R. Not in BN.

Chapter 53, Paragraph 7

Subyon was. So R. BN: *ne la neust este trouve se par adventure neust este Silvain leur maistre qui leans se cuidoit bouter* [there (Subyon) would not have been found, if, by chance, Silvain their master had not thought to hide himself in that place].

that he had opened . . . there wythinne. So R. Not in BN.

Chapter 53, Paragraph 8

and of the barons ... castell of Castelforde. So R. Not in BN.

Chapter 54, Paragraph 1

Castelforde ... R is incomplete for the last leaves are lacking. I have supplied the missing part of the narrative with my translation of BN. Kellner includes the passage from that manuscript (pp. 206–19).

Appendix: *Paris and Vienne*, Cépède's Prologue

This prologue appears in all manuscripts of the long version but in none of the manuscripts or prints of the short version, including Caxton's. The following translation is based on Paris, Bibliothèque Nationale de France, MS fr. 1480.[1]

Alanus, who was most wise,[2] has written in the book of his doctrines an axiom which says in Latin, "*Hoc crede quod tibi verum esse videtur*,"[3] and would furthermore say that this maxim, is translated out of Latin into French: "*Tu croyras les chouses qui te resembleront estre veritables*." I undertake this theme in the present case because I have all my life taken pleasure in the reading romances and chronicles of the ancient histories, as of the life of Lancelot, of Tristan, of Florimond, of Guy of Warwick, who performed many brave acts in their life according to what I have found written. And many things I have found there which are very impossible to believe. And many other books I have seen, but among them I have chosen a book, written in the Provençal language, which was drawn from another book written in the Catalan language. This book contains the life of a baron who was called Godfrey d'Alencon, who was dauphin of Vienne, who had a daughter who was called Vienne, who was a paragon of beauty. And how a knight who was called Paris, son of a baron who was named messire Jacques, was enamored of the said Vienne so that for love of her he did in his life many great deeds, as you will hear later. And because the matter is reasonable and credible enough, and also because the story is quite pleasing — for it is a good thing to hear recounted the great deeds of the ancients in times past — I undertake to translate the history for you from Provençal into French. I would request and beg all those who read the said book, that if they find written there anything which is not well done, that they will pardon my defects and amend them according to their good judgment, for my ability is not sufficient to that which is needed to well treat it [the material], and also for I am not French by birth but was born and raised in the city of Marseilles. And if it pleases you to know that from Saint Pierre I take my name, of the Cypède for surname, and commenced to write this book in the year of our lord 1432, the third day of the month of September.

---

[1] Leach, *Paris*, pp. xiv–xv.
[2] Alain de Lille (1128–1203) was the author of *De Planctu Natura* and other influential theological and philosophical treatises. Blending mysticism with rationalism, his writings demonstrated that the natural world as well as religious truths could be apprehended by human reason without the aid of revelation.
[3] The aphorism translates as "Believe that which appears to you to be true (credible)."

Bibliography

Manuscripts and Early Prints

Brussels, KBR, MS 3576/7. [*Blanchardyn and Eglantine*, short prose]

Brussels, KRB, MS BR 9632/3, fols. 1r–137v. [*Paris et Vienne*, long Burgundian prose]

Carpentras, Bibliothèque Municipale (Inguimbertine), MS 1792, fols. 285–288.

Carpentras, Bibliothèque Municipale (Inguimbertine), papiers de Peiresc, nº 23, t. 2, fol. 286. [*Paris and Vienne*, long version]

Caxton, William. *Blanchardyn and Eglantine*. Westminster: William Caxton, 1489. USTC: 500150; ISTC: ib00690400; ESTC: S108419. Manchester, John Rylands Library, Incunable 15027. Online at: https://luna.manchester.ac.uk/luna/servlet/detail/Manchester~20~20~17~190274: Bookreader-15027?qvq=q:Bookreader%2B15027&mi=0&trs=1. [Base text]

Columbia, University of Missouri, Elmer Ellis Library, Special Collections, Fragmenta Manuscripta 157, 1 fol. [*Paris and Vienne*]

Paris, Bibliothèque de France, Arsenal, MS 3000. [*Paris and Vienne*, long version]

Paris, Bibliothèque Nationale de France, MS fr. 375, fols. 254v–267r. [*Blanchardyn and Eglantine*, verse version]

Paris, Bibliothèque Nationale de France, MS fr. 1464. Online at https://gallica.bnf.fr/ark:/12148/btv1b525052213/f9.item. [*Paris and Vienne*, long version]

Paris, Bibliothèque Nationale de France, MS fr. 1479. [*Paris and Vienne*, long version]

Paris, Bibliothèque Nationale de France, MS fr. 1480. [*Paris et Vienne*, long version]

Paris, Bibliothèque Nationale de France, MS fr. 19152, fols. 174v–192v. Online at https://gallica.bnf.fr/ark:/12148/btv1b52513419n?rk=42918;4. [*Blanchardyn and Eglantine*, verse]

Paris, Bibliothèque Nationale de France, MS fr. 20044. Online at https://gallica.bnf.fr/ark:/12148/btv1b10721305x. [*Paris et Vienne*, short version]

Paris, Bibliothèque Nationale de France, MS fr. 24371. Online at https://gallica.bnf.fr/ark:/12148/btv1b90580821/. [*Blancandin et l'Orgueilleuse d'Amour*, long prose]

Paris, Bibliothèque Nationale de France, MS nouvelles acquisitions françaises 10169. [*Paris and Vienne*, long version]

Paris et Vienne. Antwerp: Gherard Leeu, 1487. USTC: 70658; ISTC: ip00112800. Paris: Bibliothèque Nationale de France, Département Réserve des livres rares, RES-Y2-159. Online at https://gallica.bnf.fr/ark:/12148/btv1b8600062n. [*Paris et Vienne*, short prose]

Philadelphia, University of Pennsylvania, Kislak Center for Special Collections, Rare Books and Manuscripts, Lawrence J. Schoenberg Collection, MS Codex 862 (formerly MS French 22). [*Blanchardyn and Eglantine*, verse]

Stories dei nobilissimi amanti Paris e Viena. Treviso: Michael Manzolus, 1481. USTC: 999397; ISTC: ip00115500. London, British Library, IA.28369. [*Paris and Vienne*, short version]

Thystorye of the noble ryght valyaunt and worthy knyght Parys, and of the fayr Vyenne de daulphyns doughter. Westminster: William Caxton, 1485. USTC: 500113; ISTC: ip00113500. London, British Library, C.10.b.10. Online at http://access.bl.uk/item/viewer/ark:/81055/vdc_100102251449.0x000001#?c=0&m=0&s=0&cv=76&xywh=-982%2C-345%2C11693%2C6873. [Base text]

Turin, Biblioteca nazionale universitaria, MS L V 44, fols. 136r–188r. [*Blanchardyn and Eglantine*, verse]

Vienna, Österreichische Nationalbibliothek, Cod. 3432. [*Paris and Vienne*, long version]

Vienna, Österreichische Nationalbibliothek, Cod. 3438. [*Blanchardyn and Eglantine*, long prose version]

Primary Sources

The Babees Book. In Furnivall, ed. *Early English Meals and Manners*. Pp. 250–58.

Babbi, Anna Maria, ed. *Paris et Vienne: romanzo cavalleresco del xv secolo, Parigi, Bibliothèque Nationale, ms. fr. 20044*. Scienza sella letteratura e del linguaggio 10. Milan: Francoangeli, 1992. [short version]

Boethius. *The Consolation of Philosophy*. Trans. Victor Watts. London: Penguin, 1999.

The Boke of Curtasye. In Furnivall, ed. *Early English Meals and Manners*. Pp. 177–205.

Bourcher, John, Lord Berners, trans. *The History of the Valiant Knight Arthur of Little Britain*. Ed. Edward Vernon Utterson. London: White, Cochrand, and Co., 1814.

Caxton, William. *The History of Jason: Translated from the French of Raoul le Fèvre by William Caxton*. Ed. John Munro. EETS e.s. 111. London: Kegan Paul, Trench, Trübner and Co., 1913.

———. *Godeffroy of Bologne, or The Siege and Conqueste of Jeruslaem*. Ed. Mary Noyes Colvin. EETS e.s. 64. London: Oxford University Press, 1893. Reprint Bungay: Richard Clay and Sons, 1926.

———. *Paris and Vienne*. Ed. MacEdward Leach. EETS e.s. 234. London: Oxford University Press, 1957.

———. *Caxton's Blanchardyn and Eglantine c. 1489: from Lord Spencer's Unique Imperfect Copy, Completed by the Original French and the Second English Version of 1595*. Ed. Leon Kellner. EETS e.s. 58. London: Oxford University Press, 1890. Reprint, Bungay: Richard Clay and Co., 1962. [Manchester: Rylands Library 15027]

———. *Caxton's Eneydos, 1490*. Ed. W. T. Culley and F. J. Furnivall. EETS e.s. 57 London: Oxford University Press, 1890. Reprint, 1962.

———. *The Book of the Knight of la Tour Landry*. Ed. Thomas Wright. London: EETS, 1906. Reprint, New York: Greenwood Press, 1969.

———. *Le Morte D'Arthur*. Ed. Janet Cowen. 2 vols. London: Penguin, 1969.

———. *The Book of the Ordre of Chyvalry*. Ed. Alfred T. P. Byles. EETS o.s.168. London: Oxford University Press, 1926. Reprint, New York: Oxford University Press, 1971.

———. *Aesop's Fables*. Ed. Bamber Gascoigne and Christina Gascoigne. London: Hamish Hamilton, 1984.

———. *The Game and Playe of the Chesse*. Ed. Jenny Adams. METS. Kalamazoo, MI: Medieval Institute Publications, 2009.

———. *Caxton's Golden Legend*. Ed. Mayumi Taguchi, John Scahill, and Satoko Tokunaga. 2 vols. EETS 355, 357. Oxford: Oxford University Press, 2020, 2021.

Cépède, Pierre de la. *Paris et Vienne*. Ed. Rosalind Brown-Grant and Marie-Claude de Crécy. Textes Littéraires du Moyen Age 38. Paris: Classiques Garnier, 2015.

Chaucer, Geoffrey. *The Riverside Chaucer*. Ed. Larry D. Benson et al. 3rd ed. Boston: Houghton Mifflin, 1987.

Chrétien de Troyes. *The Story of the Grail*. Trans. David Staines. In *The Complete Romances of Chrétien de Troyes*. Bloomington: Indiana University Press, 1990.

Christine de Pisan. *The Book of Deeds of Arms and of Chivalry*. Trans. Sumner Willard. Ed. Charity Canon Willard. University Park: University of Pennsylvania Press, 1999.

Crotch, W. J. B., ed. *The Prologues and Epilogues of William Caxton*. EETS o.s. 176. London: Oxford University Press, 1928. Reprint, New York: Burt Franklin, 1971.

"Der altfranzosische Roman *Paris et Vienne*." Ed. Robert Kaltenbacher. *Romanische Forschungen* 15, no. 2 (1904), 321–688a, 688a–i; 688k–z. [BNF MS fr. 1480. Cépède's original version]

Edward of Norwich. *The Master of Game*. Ed. William A. Baillie-Grohman and Florence N. Baillie-Grohman. Philadelphia: University of Pennsylvania Press, 2005.

Froissart, Jean. *Chronicles*. Ed. Geoffrey Brereton. Baltimore: Penguin, 1968.

Furnivall, Frederick J., ed. *Early English Meals and Manners: John Russell's Boke of Nurture, Wynkyn de Worde's Boke of Kervynge, The Boke of Curtasye, R. Weste's Booke of Demeanor, Seager's Schoole of Vertue, The Babees Book, Aristotle's A B C, Urbanitatis, Stans Puer ad Mensam, The Lytylle Childrenes Lytil Boke, For to serve a Lord, Old Symon, The Birched School-Boy, etc*. EETS o.s. 32. Oxford: Oxford University Press, 1868. Reprint, Oxford: Oxford University Press, 1931.

Gerbert de Montreuil. *Gerard de Nevers: Prose Version of the Roman de la Violette*. Ed. Lawrence F. H. Lowe. Elliott Monographs in the Romance Languages and Literatures 22. Princeton: Princeton University Press, 1928.

Gower, John. *Confessio Amantis*. Ed. Russell Peck. 2nd ed. Vol. 1. METS. Kalamazoo, MI: Medieval Institute Publications, 2006.

Greco, Rosa Anna, ed. *Blancandin et l'Orgueilleuse d'Amours: versioni in prosa del xv secolo*. Alessandria: Edizioni dell'Orso, 2002. [Brussels, KBR, MS 3576/7, short prose; and Vienna, Österreichische Nationalbibliothek, Cod. 3438, long prose]

Heffernan, Carol Falvo, ed. *Le Bone Florence of Rome*. Manchester: Manchester University Press, 1976.

Hudson, Harriet, ed. *Four Middle English Romances*. METS. Kalamazoo, MI: Medieval Institute Publications, 1995, 2006.

———. "Octavian." In *Four Middle English Romances*. Pp. 39–95.

———. "Sir Tryamour." In *Four Middle English Romances*. Pp. 145–193.

Kohanski, Tamarah, and C. David Benson, eds. *The Book of John Mandeville*. METS. Kalamazoo, MI: Medieval Institute Publications, 2007.

Laskaya, Anne, and Eve Salisbury, eds. *The Middle English Breton Lays*. METS. Kalamazoo, MI: Medieval Institute Publications, 1995.

———. "Sir Launfal." In Laskaya and Salisbury, *The Middle English Breton Lays*. Pp. 201–62.

———. "Sir Gowther." In Laskaya and Salisbury, *The Middle English Breton Lays*. Pp. 263–307.

Marie de France. "Eliduc." In *The Lais of Marie de France*. Trans. Glyn Burgess and Keith Busby. London: Penguin, 1999.

Purdie, Rhiannon, ed. "Roswall and Lillian." In *Shorter Scottish Medieval Romances*. Scottish Text Society 5. Suffolk, UK: Scottish Text Society, 2013.

Russell, John. "The Boke of Nurture." In Furnivall, ed. *Early English Meals and Manners*. Pp. 1–112.

Salisbury, Eve and James Weldon, eds. *Lybeaus Desconus*. METS. Kalamazoo, MI: Medieval Institute Publications, 2013.

Sargent, Barbara Nelson, ed. *Le Livre de Roy Rambaux de Frise*. Chapel Hill: University of North Carolina Press, 1967.

Skeat, Walter, ed. *The Romans of Partenay, or of Lusignen: Otherwise Known as The Tale of Melusine*. EETS o.s. 22. London: Trübner and Co., 1866.

The Song of Roland. Trans. D. D. R. Owen. Woodbridge: Boydell, 1990.

Sweetser, Franklin P., ed. *Blancandin et l'Orgueilleuse d'Amour: roman d'aventure du XIIIe siècle*. Genève: Librairie Droz, 1964. Philadelphia: University of Pennsylvania Press. [MS Codex 862, French verse version.]

Twiti, William. *The Middle English Text of "The Art of Hunting."* Ed. David Scott-MacNab. Heidelberg: Winter, 2009.

Wynkyn de Worde, *The Boke of Kervynge*. In Furnivall, ed. *Early English Meals and Manners*. Pp 147–174.

Secondary Sources

Adams, Tracy. "Printing and the Transformation of the Middle English Romance." *Neophilologus* 82, no. 2 (1998), 291–310.

———. "'Noble, wyse and grete lords, gentilmen and marchauntes': Caxton's Prologues as Conduct Books for Merchants." *Parergon* 22, no. 2 (2005), 53–76.

Akbari, Suzanne Conklin. *Idols in the East: European Representations of Islam and the Orient 1100–1450*. Ithaca, NY: Cornell University Press, 2009.

Alberghini, Jennifer. "'A kysse onely': The Problem of Female Socialization in William Caxton's *Blanchardyn and Eglantine*." *Studies in the Age of Chaucer* 44 (2022), 347–57.

Archibald, Elizabeth, Megan G. Leitch, and Corinne Saunders, eds. *Romance Rewritten: The Evolution of Middle English Romance: A Tribute to Helen Cooper*. Cambridge: D. S. Brewer, 2018.

Barron, Caroline. "Chivalry, Pageantry and Merchant Culture in Medieval London." In *Heraldry, Pageantry and Social Display in Medieval England*. Ed. Peter Coss and Maurice Keen. Woodbridge: Boydell, 2002. Pp. 219–41.

Bartlett, Anne Clark. "Translation, Self-Representation, and Statecraft: Lady Margaret Beaufort and Caxton's *Blanchardyn and Eglantyne* (1489)." *Essays in Medieval Studies* 22 (2005), 53–66.

Blades, William. *The Biography and Typography of William Caxton, England's First Printer*. London: Trübner, 1877.

Blake, N. F. *Caxton and His World*. London: André Deutsch, 1969.

———, ed. *Caxton's Own Prose*. London: André Deutsch, 1973.

———. *William Caxton and English Literary Culture*. London: Hambledon Press, 1991.

Bornstein, Diane. *Mirrors of Courtesy*. Hamden, CT: Archon, 1975.

———. "William Caxton's Chivalric Romances and the Burgundian Renaissance in England." *English Studies* 57, no. 1 (1976), 1–10.

———. *The Lady in the Tower: Medieval Courtesy Literature for Women*. Hamden, CT: Archon, 1983.

Brown-Grant, Rosalind. *French Romance of the Later Middle Ages: Gender, Morality, and Desire*. Oxford: Oxford University Press, 2008.

———. "Adolescence, Anxiety and Amusement in Versions of *Paris et Vienne*." *Cahiers de recherches médiévales et humanistes* 20 (2010), 59–70.

———. "Narrative Style in Burgundian Prose Romances of the Later Middle Ages." *Romania* 130 (2012), 355–406.

Burke-Severs, J., ed. *MWME*. Vol. 1. Ed. J. Burke-Severs. New Haven: Connecticut Academy of Arts and Sciences, 1967.

Burnley, J. D. "Curial Prose in England." *Speculum* 61, no. 3 (1986), 593–614.

Calkin, Siobhain Bly. *Saracens and the Making of English Identity: The Auchinleck Manuscript*. New York: Routledge, 2005.

Cartlidge, Neil. "Medieval Romance Mischief." In Archibald, Leitch, and Saunders, *Romance Rewritten*. Pp. 27–47.

Cohen, Jeffrey Jerome. "On Saracen Enjoyment: Some Fantasies of Race in Late Medieval England and France." *Journal of Medieval and Early Modern Studies* 31, no. 1 (2001), 113–46.

Cooper, Helen. *The English Romance in Time: Transforming Motifs from Geoffrey of Monmouth to the Death of Shakespeare*. Oxford: Oxford University Press, 2004.

———. "Prose Romances." In *A Companion to Middle English Prose*. Ed. A. S. G. Edwards. Cambridge: D. S. Brewer, 2004. Pp. 215–29.

———. "Going Native: The Caxton and Mainwaring versions of *Paris and Vienne*." Yearbook of English Studies 41, no. 11 (2011), 21–34.

Cope, Christopher. *The Lost Kingdom of Burgundy: A Phoenix Frustrated*. New York: Dodd, Mead & Company, 1987.

Cotton, William T. "Fidelity, Suffering, and Humor in *Paris and Vienne*." In *Chivalric Literature: Essays on Relations between Literature and Life in the Later Middle Ages*. Ed. Larry D. Benson and John Leyerle. Studies in Medieval Culture 14. Kalamazoo, MI: Medieval Institute Publications, 1980. Pp. 91–100.

De Weever, Jacqueline. *Sheba's Daughters: Whitening and Demonizing the Saracen Woman in Medieval French Epic*. New York: Garland, 1998. Reprint, London: Routledge, 2015.

Deacon, Richard. *A Biography of William Caxton: The First English Editor, Printer, Merchant, and Translator*. London: Frederick Muller, 1976.

Derrien, Eve. "*Blancandin* ou l'apprentissage de la royauté." In *La Figure du roi: actes du colloque du Centre d'études médiévales et dialectes de Lille 3, 24–26 Septembre 1998*. Ed. Marie-Madeline Castellani. Vol. 1. Bien dire et bien aprandre 17. Lille: Université Charles de Gaulle, 1999. Pp. 91–101.

Despres, Joanne M. "Translation Techniques in the Romances of William Caxton." Ph.D. Dissertation: University of Pennsylvania, 1991.

"Dew, John." In *A Cambridge Alumni Database*. Compilers John Venn and A. B. Emden. University of Cambridge. Online at https://venn.lib.cam.ac.uk/cgi-bin/search-2018.pl?sur=Dew&suro=c&fir=John&firo=w&cit=&cito=c&c=all&z=all&tex=&sye=1483&eye=1500&col=GonH&maxcount=50.

Dictionnaire du Moyen Français, 17th edition. Ed. Robert Martin, et al. Nancy: Centre National de la Recherche Scientifique, Université de Lorraine, 2020–. Online at http://zeus.atilf.fr/dmf/.

Dockray, Keith. "Why did Fifteenth-Century English Gentry Marry?: The Pastons, Plumptons and Stonors Reconsidered." In *Gentry and Lesser Nobility in Late Medieval Europe*. Ed. Michael Jones. New York: St. Martins, 1986. Pp. 61–80.

Dunn, Charles. "Romances Derived from English Legends." In Burke-Severs, *MWME*, pp. 17–37.

Edlich-Muth, Miriam. "From Magic to Miracle: Reframing *Chevalere Assigne*." In Archibald, Leitch, and Saunders, *Romance Rewritten*. Pp. 173–88.

Edwards, A. S. G., and Carol M. Meale. "The Marketing of Printed Books in Late Medieval England." *The Library* 15 (1993), 95–124.

Farber, Allen. "Tapestry Collection of Philip the Bold." *SUNY - Oneonta Art History Home Page*. Online at http://employees.oneonta.edu/farberas/arth/arth214_folder/tapestries_philip_bold.html.

Finlayson, John. "The Source of Caxton's *Paris and Vienne*." *Philological Quarterly* 46, no. 1 (1967), 130–35.

Forsyth, William H. "The Trojan War in Medieval Tapestries." *The Metropolitan Museum of Art Bulletin* n.s. 14, no. 3 (Nov. 1955), 76–84. Online at https://doi.org/10.2307/3257653.

Goodman, Jennifer R. *Malory and William Caxton's Prose Romances of 1485*. Ph.D. Dissertation: Harvard University, 1981. Reprint, New York: Garland, 1987.

———. "'That wommen holde in ful greet reverence': Mothers and Daughters Reading Chivalric Romances." In Smith and Taylor, *Women, the Book and the Worldly*. Pp. 25–30.

———. "Caxton's Continent." In *Caxton's Trace: Studies in the History of English Printing*. Ed. William Kuskin. Notre Dame, IN: Notre Dame University Press, 2006. Pp. 101–23.

Hellinga, Lotte. "The Malory Manuscript and Caxton." In *Aspects of Malory*. Ed. Toshiyuki Takamiya and Derek Brewer. Cambridge: D. S. Brewer, 1981. Pp. 127–41.

Heng, Geraldine. "Jews, Saracens, 'Black Men', Tartars: England in a World of Racial Difference." In *A Companion to Medieval English Literature and Culture c. 1350–1500*. Ed. Peter Brown. Malden, MA: Blackwell, 2007. Pp. 247–69.

———. *The Invention of Race in the European Middle Ages*. Cambridge: Cambridge University Press, 2018.

The Holy Bible: Douay-Rheims Bible. Rockford, IL: Tan Books and Publishers, 1899. Online at www.drbo.org.

Hornstein, Lillian Hurlands. "Miscellaneous Romances." In Burke-Severs, *MWME*, pp.144–72.

Houlbrooke, Ralph. "The Making of Marriage in mid-Tudor England: Evidence from the Records of Matrimonial Contract Litigation." *Journal of Family History* 10, no. 4 (1985), 339–52.

Hudson, Harriet. "Construction of Class, Family, and Gender in Some Middle English Popular Romances." In *Class and Gender in Early English Literature: Intersections*. Ed. Britton J. Harwood and Gillian R. Overing. Bloomington: Indiana University Press, 1994. Pp. 76–94.

———. "Rebellious Daughters and Rotten Chickens: Gender and Genre in Caxton's *Paris and Vienne*." *Medievalia et Humanistica* 29 (2003), 81–102.

Hull, Suzanne W. *Chaste, Silent, and Obedient: English Books for Women 1475–1640*. San Marino, CA: Huntington Library, 1982.

Jewers, Caroline A. *Chivalric Fiction and the History of the Novel*. Gainesville: University Press of Florida, 2000.

Karras, Ruth Mazo. *From Boys to Men: Formations of Masculinity in Late Medieval Europe*. Philadelphia: University of Pennsylvania Press, 2003.

Kennedy, Kathleen. "Moors and Moorishness in Late Medieval England." *Studies in the Age of Chaucer* 42 (2020), 213–51.

Krug, Rebecca. "Margaret Beaufort's Literate Practice: Service and Self-Inscription." In *Reading Families: Women's Literate Practice in Late Medieval England*. Ithaca, NY: Cornell University Press, 2002. Pp. 65–113.

Kuskin, William. "Caxton's Worthies Series: The Production of Literary Culture." *English Literary History* 66, no. 3 (1999), 511–51.

———. *Symbolic Caxton: Literary Culture and Print Capitalism*. Notre Dame, IN: University of Notre Dame Press, 2008.

Leitch, Megan. "Thinking Twice about Treason in Caxton's Prose Romances: Proper Chivalric Conduct and the English Printing Press." *Medium Aevum* 81, no. 2 (2012), 41–69.

Lester, G. A., ed. *Sir John Paston's 'Grete Boke': A Descriptive Catalogue, With an Introduction, of British Library MS Landsdowne 285*. Cambridge: D. S. Brewer, 1984.

Lewis, Katherine J. *Kingship and Masculinity in Late Medieval England*. New York: Routledge, 2013.

Marchal, Matthieu. "De l'existence d'un manuscrit de la prose de *Blancandin et l'Orgueilleuse d'Amours* produit dans l'atelier du Maître de Wavrin." In *L'Art du récit a la cour de Bourgogne: l'activité de Jean de Wavrin et de son atelier. Acts du colloque international organisé les 24 et 25 octobre 2013 à l'Université du Littoral — Côte d'Opale (Dunkerque)*. Ed. Jean Devaux and Matthieu Marchal. Paris: Honoré Champion, 2018. Pp. 265–85.

Matheson, Lister M. "Printer and Scribe: Caxton, the *Polychronicon*, and the *Brut*." *Speculum* 60, no. 3 (July 1985), 593–614. Online at https://doi.org/10.2307/2848177.

McSheffery, Shannon. *Love and Marriage in Late Medieval London*. Kalamazoo, MI: Medieval Institute Publications, 1995.

Meale, Carol M. "Wynkyn de Worde's Setting-Copy for *Ipomydon*." *Studies in Bibliography* 35 (1982), 156–171.

———. "Caxton, de Worde, and the Publication of Romance in Late Medieval England." *The Library* 14, no. 4 (1992), 283–98.

Middle English Dictionary. Ed. Frances McSparran, et. al. Ann Arbor: University Library, 2000—. Online at https://quod.lib.umich.edu/m/middle-english-dictionary/dictionary.

Morse, Ruth. "Historical Fiction in Fifteenth-Century Burgundy." *Modern Language Review* 75, no. 1 (1980), 48–64.

Naber, Antoinette. "Les goûts littéraires d'un bibliophile de la cour de Bourgogne." In *Courtly Literature: Culture and Context, Selected Papers from the 5th Triennial Congress of the International Courtly Literature Society, Dalfsen, The Netherlands, 9–16 August, 1986*. Ed. Keith Busby and Erik Kooper. Amsterdam: John Benjamins, 1990. Pp. 459–64.

Nall, Catherine. "Margaret Beaufort's Books: a New Discovery." *Journal of the Early Book Society for the Study of Manuscripts and Printing History* 16 (2013), 213–20.

Nicholls, Jonathan. *The Matter of Courtesy: Medieval Courtesy Books and the Gawain-Poet*. Woodbridge: D. S. Brewer, 1985.

Nicol, Donald M. *The Reluctant Emperor: A Biography of John Cantacuzene, Byzantine Emperor and Monk, c. 1295–1383*. Cambridge: Cambridge University Press, 1996.

Olson, Rebecca. "Margaret Beaufort, Royal Tapestries, and Confinement at the Tudor Court." *Textile History* 48, no. 2 (2017), 233–47.

———. "The Continuing Adventures of *Blanchardyn and Eglantine*: Responsible Speculation about Early Modern Fan Fiction." *PMLA* 134, no. 2 (2019), 298–314.

Painter, George D. *William Caxton: A Quincentenary Biography of England's First Printer*. London: Chatto and Windus, 1976.

Pearsall, Derek. "The English Romance in the Fifteenth Century." *Essays and Studies* 29 (1976), 56–83.

Pender, Patricia. "'A Veray Patronesse': Margaret Beaufort and the Early English Printers." In *Gender, Authorship, and Early Modern Women's Collaboration*. Ed. Patricia Pender. Cham: Palgrave-MacMillan, 2017. Pp. 219–43.

Rajbzadeh, Shokoofeh. "The Depoliticized Saracen and Muslim Erasure." *Literature Compass* 16 (2019), 1–8.

Ramsey, Lee C. *Chivalric Romances: Popular Literature in Medieval England*. Bloomington: Indiana University Press, 1983.

Rawcliffe, Carole. "The Politics of Marriage in Later Medieval England: William, Lord Botreaux, and the Hungerfords." *Huntington Library Quarterly* 51, no. 3 (1988), 168–75.

Schlauch, Margaret. *Antecedents of the English Novel 1400–1600 (from Chaucer to Deloney)*. London: Oxford University Press, 1963.

Schutte, Valerie. "Lady Margaret Beaufort and the Wives of Henry VIII." In *Mary I and the Art of Book Dedications: Royal Women, Power, and Persuasion*. New York: Palgrave-MacMillan, 2015. Pp. 7–32.

Smith, Lesley, and Jane H. M. Taylor, eds. *Women, the Book and the Worldly: Selected Proceedings of the St. Hilda's Conference, 1993*. Vol. 2. Cambridge: D. S. Brewer, 1995.

Stelboum, Judith P. "William Caxton's Romance of *Blanchardyn and Eglantine*." Ph.D. Dissertation: New York University, 1968. Online at https://www.proquest.com/docview/302432621.

Stuip, René. "*Blanchandin*, Jean de Créquy et Marienburg." *Etudes médievales* 1 (1999), 347–56.

Summit, Jennifer. "William Caxton, Margaret Beaufort and the Romance of Female Patronage." In Smith and Taylor, *Women, the Book and the Worldly*. Pp. 151–65.

Thompson, Stith. *Motif-Index of Folk-Literature: A Classification of Narrative Elements in Folktales, Ballads, Myths, Fables, Mediaeval Romances, Exempla, Fabliaux, Jest-Books, and Local Legends*. Rev. and enl. ed. 6 vols. Bloomington: Indiana University Press, 1955–1958.

Van der Schaaf, Baukje Finet. "Les incunables français, néerlandais, allemand et anglais de *L'Histoire du très vaillant chevalier Paris et de la belle Vienne*, fille du dauphin et leur rapport à la tradition manuscrite du récit." In *L'épopée romane: actes du XVe Congrès International Rencesvals 2000*. Poitiers: University of Poitiers, 2002. Pp. 825–36.

Veenstra, Jan R. "'Le prince qui se veult faire de nouvel roy': The Literature and Ideology of Burgundian Self-Determination." In *The Ideology of Burgundy: The Promotion of National Consciousness 1364–1565*. Ed. D'Arcy Jonathan Dacre Boulton and Jan R. Veenstra. Leiden: Brill, 2006. Pp. 195–221.

Vines, Amy N. *Women's Power in Late Medieval Romance*. Cambridge: D. S. Brewer, 2011.

Wang, Yu-Chiao. "Caxton's Romances and Their Early Tudor Readers." *Huntington Library Quarterly* 67, no. 2 (2004), 173–88.

Whiting, Bartlett Jere, and Helen Wescott Whiting. *Proverbs, Sentences, and Proverbial Phrases from English Writings mainly before 1500*. Cambridge, MA: Belknap Press of Harvard University Press, 1968.

Willard, Charity Cannon. "Patrons at the Burgundian Court: Jean V de Créquy and His Wife, Louise de la Tour." In *The Search for a Patron in the Middle Ages and the Renaissance*. Ed. David G. Wilkins and Rebecca L. Wilkins. Medieval and Renaissance Studies 12. Lewiston, ME: Mellen, 1996. Pp. 55–62.

Williams, Elizabeth. "England, Ireland, and Iberia in *Olyuer of Castylle*: The View from Burgundy." In *Boundaries in Medieval Romance*. Ed. Neil Cartlidge. Cambridge: D. S. Brewer, 2008. Pp. 93–102.

 # Glossary

ABBREVIATIONS: **adj.**: adjective; **adv.**: adverb; **conj.**: conjunction; **contr.**: contraction; **Lat.**: Latin; **n.**: noun; **OF**: Old French; **pron.**: pronoun; **pa.**: past; **p.**: participle; **pr.**: present; **prep.**: preposition; **v.**: verb.

This glossary includes only glossed words that occur more than three times in the texts.

abashed, abasshe (v.) *confounded, surprise*
abridge (v.) *shorten, abridge*
abyde, abye (v.) *stay, remain, abide*
admonest (v.) *exhort, counsel*
adventure (n.) *chance, fortune, fate; event, exploit; knightly feats of arms*
advertyse (v.) *notice, inform, observe*
advyse (n.) *opinion, judgment;* **advyses**, *deliberations*
advyse (v.) *notice, consider*
affray (n.) *alarm, attack, commotion*
affrayed (pa. p.) *frightened, afraid*
afore (adv.) *before*
alonge (adj.) *alone*
alonge (adv.) *fully, at length*
alonge (prep.) *along*
alwey (adv.) *always*
alyght (v.) *dismount*
amended (v.) *added to, improved*
amyté (n.) *friendship*
ancred (v.) *anchored*
ancres (n.) *anchors*
angwysshe (n.) *anguish, sorrow*
anone (adv.) *immediately*
apparaylle (n.) *preparation, equipment*
appareylled (v.) *equipped, prepared*
apparteyne (v.) *pertain, be appropriate*
ar (prep.) *before, ere*
araye (n.) *order; apparel, equipment, adornment*
araye (v.) *dress; make a show of armed force*
areyse (v.) *raise, arise, awaken*
ascrye (v.) *exclaim, call out, call to battle*

astate (n.) *condition, social status, estate*
astonyed (p.) *stunned, unconscious*

---

bataylle (n.) *battalion; battle*
beaulté, beawté (n.) *beauty*
behalve, byhalve (n.) *sake, account*
behavoure (n.) *deportment, demeanor, manners*
beholden (v.) *indebted, obligated*
behove, byhove, behouffe (n.) *advantage, benefit*
behoveth, behoven (v.) *is requisite, necessary*
bethynke (v.) *consider, reflect*
bordour, bord (n.) *edge, side*
breke, brake (v.) *disclose; break, shatter in pieces*
brente, brennyng (v.) *burnt, burning*
broched (v.) *spurred;* see **brochynge**
brochynge (pr. p.) *spurring, piercing*
bruyt (n.) *din, clamor; renown, reputation; report*

---

caas (n.) *circumstance, event*
capitulo (n.) *chapter*
Cassydoyne (n.) *Chalcedon, in Turkey*
charge (v.) *dash forth; fill; order*
chose, choys, chuse (v.) *see, discern by sight; select, designate*
claryons (n.) *slender, shrill-sounding trumpets*
clove, cloven (v.) *cleave, split in parts*
companye (n.) *entourage, company of knights*
comyn (adj.) *ordinary, of the common people*

333

comyns (n.) *people without rank or title*
conveye (v.) *bring, escort, convey*
corage (n.) *courage, spirit, heart*
couched, cowched (v.) *recline, rest; position a spear for attack*
counseyl (n.) *advice; council of advisors*
counseyl (v.) *advise*
countenaunce (n.) *expression, face*
cours (n.) *a charge in battle or tournament*
courser (n.) *war horse, swift horse*
cusse (n.) *kiss*

---

damoysel (n.) *young unmarried woman of rank; female attendant*
demaund (v.) *ask, request, demand*
despyte (n.) *contempt, disdain; an act designed to insult, humiliate, or harm*
destrayned (pa. p.) *preturbed, distressed*
destrier (n.) *war horse, charger*
detrenched (v.) *cut in pieces, sliced*
devoyer (n.) *duty, task, one's best effort*
devyse (v.) *recount, consult*
devyses (n.) *reports, plans, consultations*
do, doo (v.) *perform or complete an activity; to cause or make something happen*
dolaunt (adj.) *sad, grieving*
dommage (n.) *damage; misfortune*
doubte (v.) *fear, question*
doubted (pa. p.) *respected; feared; see* **doubte** (v.)
dyde (v.) *did*
dyscomfyte (v.) *defeat, overcome*
dyscomfyted (pa. p.) *defeated; discomforted, dejected; see* **dyscomfyte** (v.)
dyspose (v.) *resolve*
dysposycyon (n.) *arrangement, condition*

---

eerys (n.) *ears*
eke (adv.) *also, in like manner*
enbrased (v.) *embraced, seized*
ende (n.) *purpose, result*

enforce (v.) *strengthen, reinforce; rape*
engine (n.) *plan, machination; machine, particularly one used in warfare*
entendement (n.) *intention, will; understanding*
enterpryse (n.) *undertaking, deed of arms*
espye (v.) *see, look stealthily, spy*
estate (n.) *condition, state of being; social status*
evyl (adj.) *wretched, harmful*
evyl (adv.) *very badly*
excercyte (Lat. *exercitus*) (n.) *company of warriors, army*
exployted (v.) *exerted, hurried, made an effort*
extraction, extraccion (n.) *lineage, descent*

---

fast (adj.) *secure*
fast (adv.) *firmly*
fayne (adv.) *gladly, eagerly*
fayte, feat (n.) *occurrence, act, especially of armed combat*
felawe (n.) *companion, comrade, fellow*
felawship, felauship (n.) *fellowship, companionship, company of people especially warriors*
felon (adj.) *wicked, treasonous, criminal*
ferre (adv.) *far*
fery (n.) *river passage, crossing*
fest (n.) *festivity, feast*
fest (v.) *entertain hospitably, celebrate*
foison, foyson (n.) *abundance, plenty*
force (n.) *power, necessity; aggression;* **it is ~**, *it is necessary*
free (adj.) *noble, generous, gracious*
Fryse (n.) *Frisia*
furnysshe (v.) *supply, satisfy, carry out*
fyers (adj.) *fierce, powerful, high spirited*

---

gaaff (v.) *gave*
galleye (n.) *large seagoing vessel with sails and oars, ship*

Glossary

garnysshe (v.) *adorn, decorate; supply; prepare for defense, fortify*
gayne (n.) *gain, profit*
gaynsaye (v.) *to speak or act against, forbid, gainsay*
gentyll (adj.) *of aristocratic status; noble, courteous, refined*
goddes (n.) *gods; goddess*
godes (n.) *goods, possessions*
greve (v.) *grieve, lament; trouble, injure*
grevous (adj.) *injurious, extreme*

---

haboundance (n.) *abundance, large number*
hardy (adj.) *bold, courageous, daring*
harneys (n.) *military equipment, armor*
haven (n.) *harbor, port*
hem (pron.) *him, them*
hemself (pron.) *themselves*
her (pron.) *her, their*
here (v.) *hear*
hevy (adj.) *heavy; having great force; sad*
hevyness (n.) *sadness, depression*
highe (adj.) *loud; elevated; exhalted*
hold (v.) *keep, affirm; obligate*
holden (pa. p.) *beholden, obligated, indebted; see* **hold** (v.)
holpen (v.) *aided, helped*
host (n.) *army*
hyely (adv.) *loudly; greatly*
hym (pron.) *him*

---

incontinent (adv.) *immediately, at once*
indygnacion (n.) *anger, wrathful disposition; scorn*
infortune (n.) *misfortune*

---

jape (n.) *jest, trick*
jape (v.) *trick, deceive; to behave foolishly*
jovencel (n.) *(OF) youth, young knight*

---

kepe (v.) *keep, protect, restrain*

---

lette (v.) *delay, hinder, prevent*
lette, letting (n.) *delay, obstruction; trouble*
leve (n.) *permission; formal departure*
leve (v.) *leave; cease*
leve, lever (adv.) *rather, prefer*
lightly (adv.) *quickly, easily*
lyght (v.) *mount, alight*
lynage (n.) *ancestry, lineage*

---

maner (n.) *behavior, conduct; method, procedure; kind, variety*
marche (n.) *territory, region, boundary lands*
Maryenborough (n.) *Marienburg in Poland*
maynten (v.) *behave, maintain composure, conduct oneself; support, uphold, especially a challenge in a tournament*
mayntenaunce (n.) *conduct, behavior; support, maintenance*
mayster, maister (n.) *tutor; leader, captain*
maystres (n.) *governess; lady*
melancolye (n.) *sadness, one of the four humors*
membre (n.) *limb, body part*
merveylle (n.) *marvel, wonder*
merveylle (v.) *wonder, admire, be astonished*
mete (adj.) *fitting, appropriate*
mete (n.) *meat, food, a meal*
mete (v.) *encounter, meet*
mo, moo, mowe, more (adj.) *to a greater extent or amount*
mo, moo, mowe, more (adv.) *again, additionally*
mo, moo, mowe, more (n.) *more, additional things, persons, etc.*
moyen (n.) *means, course of action*

---

ne (conj.) *nor*
nevewe (n.) *nephew*
nyghe (prep.) *near*
nys (contr. of **ne is**) *is no*

---

occysion (n.) *slaughter, carnage*
oost (n.) *army, host*
or (prep.) *before*
ordynaunce (n.) *order, arrangement; military equipment*
ought (pn.) *anything*
ought (v.) *owe; should*
owre (n.) *hour*

---

paas (n.) *pace, gait; pass, pathway, road*
palays (n.) *palace*
palfray (n.) *horse for riding, not combat*
parelle (n.) *peril*
parfytte, parfit (adj.) *excellent, perfect*
paynem (n.) *pagan, non-Christian*
pensefull (adj.) *thoughtful, melancholy*
peryshe (v.) *die; shipwreck*
peyne, payne (n.) *pain; diligence, care; threat*
playn (adj.) *clear, obvious*
playne (adv.) *clearly*
playne (n.) *plain, level open area*
Polonye (n.) *Poland*
postern (n.) *back entry, secret passageway*
pourveye, purvey (v.) *provide, supply*
power (adj.) *poor, wretched*
power (n.) *strength, ability, resources; military unit, men at arms*
poynt (n.) *particular, detail; feat of arms; moment*
poynt (v.) *appoint, establish*
praty (adj.) *pretty, attractive*
presse (n.) *crowd, thick of a fight*
prest (adj.) *ready for action, prepared*
prevely (adv.) *secretly, privately*
proffer (v.) *offer, give*
promesse (n.) *promise, vow*
promise, promytte (v.) *promise*
promyttyng (pr. p.) *promising*; see **promise, promytte** (v.)
prouese, proes, prowesse (n.) *strength, skill in combat; courage*
provost (n.) *chief magistrate, military officer*
prys (n.) *prize; honor, esteem*
pucelle (n.) *maiden*
putte (v.) *place, move*
puyssaunce (n.) *strength; military might*
puyssaunt (adj.) *strong, powerful*
pyté (n.) *pity*
pytoyable (adj.) *pitiful, lamentable*

---

raenson (n.) *ransom, payment*
raughte, rought (v.) *attack, strike with a sword; achieve*
rayson (n.) *reason*
recommend (v.) *commend, extol; entrust*
recountre (v.) *come together, collide*
recule (v.) *retreat, draw back*
redoubted (pa. p.) *revered, honored*
reherce (v.) *tell, recount*
renged (pa. p.) *arranged, drawn up in battle order*
renne (v.) *run, charge*
renommee (n.) *renown, fame*
replenysshe (v.) *fill*
requyre (v.) *ask, request; require*
reteyne (v.) *engage in service, employ*
reverence (n.) *gesture of respect and obeisance, curtsey, bow*
rewthe (n.) *regret, sorrow*
royalme (n.) *realm, kingdom*

---

sage (adj.) *learned, wise*
Salmandry (n.) *Alexandria, Egypt*
salue, salewe (v.) *greet with respect, salute*
sauf (adj.) *safe, unharmed*
sauf (prep.) *except*
seche (v.) *seek, search for*

self (adj.) *same*
shewe (v.) *show, express*
shewynges (n.) *expressions, demonstrations*
socoure (n.) *aid, assistance*
socoure (v.) *save, help, succor*
softe (adj.) *gentle, soft*
softly (adv.) *quietly, gently*
sone (adv.) *soon*
sone (n.) *son*
sore (adv.) *greatly, severely, forcefully*
souldan (n.) *sultan*
souldyour (n.) *soldier*
sowne (n.) *sound*
sowne (v.) *make noise; play an instrument*
specyall (n.) *beloved, friend*
spory, spore (n.) *spur*
stourdy (adj.) *fierce, brave*
styl, stylle (adv.) *continually; without movement*
subtyl (adj.) *clever, keen*
subtylly (adv.) *perceptively, skillfully*
suffre (v.) *allow; endure pain*
surely (adv.) *safely*
syn, synce (prep.) *afterwards, since*
syth (adv.) *afterward, subsequently*
syth (conj.) *because, seeing that*

---

tarye (v.) *pause, linger, delay*
tofore (adv.) *before, previously*
tofore (prep.) *in front of*
Tormaday, Tourmaday (n.) (OF *tour*) *Eglantine's city*
trow (v.) *think, believe*
tryste (adj.) *sad*
trystesse (n.) *sorrow*

---

unnethe (adv.) *with difficulty, hardly*

---

vaunce (v.) *advance, move forward*
veray (adj.) *true, actual*
vysage (n.) *face, expression*
vytaylle (n.) *food, provisions*

---

walloped (v.) *galloped*
warauntyse (v.) *guarantee, protect*
wene, wende (v.) *think, suppose, believe*
werke (n.) *action, deed; skill; edifice, fortification*
wete, wite, wyte (v.) *think, know*
wexe (v.) *become, grow, increase*
wont (v.) *tend, accustomed*
worship (n.) *honor, respect, renown*
wroth (adj.) *angry, stirred to wrath*
wyse (adj.) *wise, intelligent*
wyse (n.) *manner, way*
wyte, wote, wyst (v.) *know, knew;* **that is to ~,** *that is to say, namely*
wythall (adv.) *completely, entirely*
wythin (prep.) *inside*
wythout (conj.) *unless*
wythout (prep.) *outside; in the absence of*
wytte (n.) *mind, intellect; wisdom, knowledge*

---

y- *prefix forming past participle*
yate (n.) *gate*
yeven, yoven (v.) *given*
yssue (n.) *conclusion; children, progeny*
yssue (v.) *go out, leave*

Middle English Texts Series

The Floure and the Leafe, The Assembly of Ladies, The Isle of Ladies, edited by Derek Pearsall (1990)

Three Middle English Charlemagne Romances, edited by Alan Lupack (1990)

Six Ecclesiastical Satires, edited by James M. Dean (1991)

Heroic Women from the Old Testament in Middle English Verse, edited by Russell A. Peck (1991)

The Canterbury Tales: Fifteenth-Century Continuations and Additions, edited by John M. Bowers (1992)

Gavin Douglas, *The Palis of Honoure*, edited by David Parkinson (1992)

Wynnere and Wastoure and The Parlement of the Thre Ages, edited by Warren Ginsberg (1992)

The Shewings of Julian of Norwich, edited by Georgia Ronan Crampton (1994)

King Arthur's Death: The Middle English Stanzaic Morte Arthur and Alliterative Morte Arthure, edited by Larry D. Benson, revised by Edward E. Foster (1994)

Lancelot of the Laik and Sir Tristrem, edited by Alan Lupack (1994)

Sir Gawain: Eleven Romances and Tales, edited by Thomas Hahn (1995)

The Middle English Breton Lays, edited by Anne Laskaya and Eve Salisbury (1995)

Sir Perceval of Galles and Ywain and Gawain, edited by Mary Flowers Braswell (1995)

Four Middle English Romances: Sir Isumbras, Octavian, Sir Eglamour of Artois, Sir Tryamour, edited by Harriet Hudson (1996; second edition 2006)

The Poems of Laurence Minot, 1333–1352, edited by Richard H. Osberg (1996)

Medieval English Political Writings, edited by James M. Dean (1996)

The Book of Margery Kempe, edited by Lynn Staley (1996)

Amis and Amiloun, Robert of Cisyle, and Sir Amadace, edited by Edward E. Foster (1997; second edition 2007)

The Cloud of Unknowing, edited by Patrick J. Gallacher (1997)

Robin Hood and Other Outlaw Tales, edited by Stephen Knight and Thomas Ohlgren (1997; second edition 2000)

The Poems of Robert Henryson, edited by Robert L. Kindrick with the assistance of Kristie A. Bixby (1997)

Moral Love Songs and Laments, edited by Susanna Greer Fein (1998)

John Lydgate, *Troy Book Selections*, edited by Robert R. Edwards (1998)

Thomas Usk, *The Testament of Love*, edited by R. Allen Shoaf (1998)

Prose Merlin, edited by John Conlee (1998)

Middle English Marian Lyrics, edited by Karen Saupe (1998)

John Metham, *Amoryus and Cleopes*, edited by Stephen F. Page (1999)

Four Romances of England: King Horn, Havelok the Dane, Bevis of Hampton, Athelston, edited by Ronald B. Herzman, Graham Drake, and Eve Salisbury (1999)

The Assembly of Gods: Le Assemble de Dyeus, or Banquet of Gods and Goddesses, with the Discourse of Reason and Sensuality, edited by Jane Chance (1999)

Thomas Hoccleve, *The Regiment of Princes*, edited by Charles R. Blyth (1999)

John Capgrave, *The Life of Saint Katherine*, edited by Karen A. Winstead (1999)

John Gower, *Confessio Amantis*, Vol. 1, edited by Russell A. Peck; with Latin translations by Andrew Galloway (2000; second edition 2006); Vol. 2 (2003); Vol. 3 (2004)

Richard the Redeless and Mum and the Sothsegger, edited by James M. Dean (2000)

Ancrene Wisse, edited by Robert Hasenfratz (2000)

Walter Hilton, *The Scale of Perfection*, edited by Thomas H. Bestul (2000)

John Lydgate, *The Siege of Thebes*, edited by Robert R. Edwards (2001)

Pearl, edited by Sarah Stanbury (2001)

The Trials and Joys of Marriage, edited by Eve Salisbury (2002)

Middle English Legends of Women Saints, edited by Sherry L. Reames, with the assistance of Martha G. Blalock and Wendy R. Larson (2003)

The Wallace: Selections, edited by Anne McKim (2003)

Richard Maidstone, *Concordia (The Reconciliation of Richard II with London)*, edited by David R. Carlson, with a verse translation by A. G. Rigg (2003)

Three Purgatory Poems: The Gast of Gy, Sir Owain, The Vision of Tundale, edited by Edward E. Foster (2004)

William Dunbar, *The Complete Works*, edited by John Conlee (2004)

Chaucerian Dream Visions and Complaints, edited by Dana M. Symons (2004)

Stanzaic Guy of Warwick, edited by Alison Wiggins (2004)

Saints' Lives in Middle English Collections, edited by E. Gordon Whatley, with Anne B. Thompson and Robert K. Upchurch (2004)

Siege of Jerusalem, edited by Michael Livingston (2004)

The Kingis Quair and Other Prison Poems, edited by Linne R. Mooney and Mary-Jo Arn (2005)

The Chaucerian Apocrypha: A Selection, edited by Kathleen Forni (2005)

John Gower, *The Minor Latin Works*, edited and translated by R. F. Yeager, with *In Praise of Peace*, edited by Michael Livingston (2005)

Sentimental and Humorous Romances: Floris and Blancheflour, Sir Degrevant, The Squire of Low Degree, The Tournament of Tottenham, and The Feast of Tottenham, edited by Erik Kooper (2006)

The Dicts and Sayings of the Philosophers, edited by John William Sutton (2006)

"Everyman" and Its Dutch Original, "Elckerlijc," edited by Clifford Davidson, Martin W. Walsh, and Ton J. Broos (2007)

The N-Town Plays, edited by Douglas Sugano, with assistance by Victor I. Scherb (2007)

The Book of John Mandeville, edited by Tamarah Kohanski and C. David Benson (2007)

John Lydgate, *The Temple of Glas*, edited by J. Allan Mitchell (2007)

The Northern Homily Cycle, edited by Anne B. Thompson (2008)

Codex Ashmole 61: A Compilation of Popular Middle English Verse, edited by George Shuffelton (2008)

Chaucer and the Poems of "Ch," edited by James I. Wimsatt (revised edition 2009)

William Caxton, *The Game and Playe of the Chesse*, edited by Jenny Adams (2009)

John the Blind Audelay, *Poems and Carols*, edited by Susanna Fein (2009)

Two Moral Interludes: The Pride of Life and Wisdom, edited by David Klausner (2009)

John Lydgate, *Mummings and Entertainments*, edited by Claire Sponsler (2010)

Mankind, edited by Kathleen M. Ashley and Gerard NeCastro (2010)

The Castle of Perseverance, edited by David N. Klausner (2010)

Robert Henryson, *The Complete Works*, edited by David J. Parkinson (2010)

John Gower, *The French Balades*, edited and translated by R. F. Yeager (2011)

The Middle English Metrical Paraphrase of the Old Testament, edited by Michael Livingston (2011) The *York Corpus Christi Plays*, edited by Clifford Davidson (2011)

Prik of Conscience, edited by James H. Morey (2012)

The Dialogue of Solomon and Marcolf: A Dual-Language Edition from Latin and Middle English Printed Editions, edited by Nancy Mason Bradbury and Scott Bradbury (2012)

Croxton Play of the Sacrament, edited by John T. Sebastian (2012)

Ten Bourdes, edited by Melissa M. Furrow (2013)

Lybeaus Desconus, edited by Eve Salisbury and James Weldon (2013)

The Complete Harley 2253 Manuscript, Vol. 2, edited and translated by Susanna Fein with David Raybin and Jan Ziolkowski (2014); Vol. 3 (2015); Vol. 1 (2015)

Oton de Granson, Poems, edited and translated by Peter Nicholson and Joan Grenier-Winther (2015) *The King of Tars,* edited by John H. Chandler (2015)

John Hardyng Chronicle, edited by James Simpson and Sarah Peverley (2015)

Richard Coer de Lyon, edited by Peter Larkin (2015)

Guillaume de Machaut, The Complete Poetry and Music, Volume 1: The Debate Poems, edited and translated by R. Barton Palmer (2016)

Lydgate's Fabula Duorum Mercatorum and Guy of Warwyk, edited by Pamela Farvolden (2016)

The Katherine Group (MS Bodley 34), edited by Emily Rebekah Huber and Elizabeth Robertson (2016)

Sir Torrent of Portingale, edited by James Wade (2017)

The Towneley Plays, edited by Garrett P. J. Epp (2018)

The Digby Mary Magdalene Play, edited by Theresa Coletti (2018)

Guillaume de Machaut, The Complete Poetry and Music, Volume 9: The Motets, edited by Jacques Boogart (2018)

Six Scottish Courtly and Chivalric Poems, Including Lyndsay's Squyer Meldrum, edited by Rhiannon Purdie and Emily Wingfield (2018)

Gavin Douglas, "The Palyce of Honour," edited by David John Parkinson (2018)

Guillaume de Machaut, The Complete Poetry and Music, Volume 2: The Boethian Poems, Le Remede de Fortune and Le Confort d'Ami, edited by R. Barton Palmer (2019)

John Lydgate's "Dance of Death" and Related Works, edited by Megan L. Cook and Elizaveta Strakhov (2019)

The Roland and Otuel Romances and the Anglo-French Otinel, edited by Elizabeth Melick, Susanna Fein, and David Raybin (2020)

Christine de Pizan's Advice for Prices in Middle English Translation: Stephen Scrope's "The Epistle of Othea" and the Anonymous "Lytle Bibell of Knighthod," edited by Misty Schieberle (2020)

Of Knyghthode and Bataile, edited by Trevor Russell Smith and Michael Livingston (2021)

The Destruction of Jerusalem, or Titus and Vespasian, edited by Kara L. McShane and Mark J. B. Wright (2021)

"The Owl and the Nightingale" and the English Poems of Oxford, Jesus College, MS 29 (II), edited by Susanna Fein (2022)

🕮 Commentary Series

Haimo of Auxerre, *Commentary on the Book of Jonah,* translated with an introduction and notes by Deborah Everhart (1993)

Medieval Exegesis in Translation: Commentaries on the Book of Ruth, translated with an introduction and notes by Lesley Smith (1996)

Nicholas of Lyra's Apocalypse Commentary, translated with an introduction and notes by Philip D. W. Krey (1997)

Rabbi Ezra Ben Solomon of Gerona, *Commentary on the Song of Songs and Other Kabbalistic Commentaries,* selected, translated, and annotated by Seth Brody (1999)

John Wyclif, *On the Truth of Holy Scripture,* translated with an introduction and notes by Ian Christopher Levy (2001)

Second Thessalonians: Two Early Medieval Apocalyptic Commentaries, introduced and translated by Steven R. Cartwright and Kevin L. Hughes (2001)

The "Glossa Ordinaria" on the Song of Songs, translated with an introduction and notes by Mary Dove (2004)

The Seven Seals of the Apocalypse: Medieval Texts in Translation, translated with an introduction and notes by Francis X. Gumerlock (2009)

The "Glossa Ordinaria" on Romans, translated with an introduction and notes by Michael Scott Woodward (2011)

Nicholas of Lyra, Literal Commentary on Galatians, translated with an introduction and notes by Edward Arthur Naumann (2015)

Early Latin Commentaries on the Apocalypse, edited by Francis X. Gumerlock (2016)

Rabbi Eliezer of Beaugency: Commentaries on Amos and Jonah (with selections from Isaiah and Ezekiel), by Robert A. Harris (2018)

Carolingian Commentaries on the Apocalypse by Theodulf and Smaragdus, edited and translated by Francis X. Gumerlock (2019)

Honorius Augustodunensis, "Exposition of Selected Psalms," edited by David Welch, translated by Catena Scholarium, with Introduction by Ann W. Astell (2023)

Secular Commentary Series

Accessus ad auctores: Medieval Introduction to the Authors, edited and translated by Stephen M. Wheeler (2015)

The Vulgate Commentary on Ovid's Metamorphoses, Book 1, edited and translated by Frank Coulson (2015)

Brunetto Latini, "La rettorica," edited and translated by Stefania D'Agata D'Ottavi (2016)

John of Garland, "Integumenta Ovidii": Texts, Translation, and Commentary, edited and translated by Kyle Gervais (2022)

Documents of Practice Series

Love and Marriage in Late Medieval London, selected, translated, and introduced by Shannon McSheffrey (1995)

Sources for the History of Medicine in Late Medieval England, selected, introduced, and translated by Carole Rawcliffe (1995)

A Slice of Life: Selected Documents of Medieval English Peasant Experience, edited, translated, and with an introduction by Edwin Brezette DeWindt (1996)

Regular Life: Monastic, Canonical, and Mendicant "Rules," selected and introduced by Douglas J. McMillan and Kathryn Smith Fladenmuller (1997); second edition, selected and introduced by Daniel Marcel La Corte and Douglas J. McMillan (2004)

Women and Monasticism in Medieval Europe: Sisters and Patrons of the Cistercian Reform, selected, translated, and with an introduction by Constance H. Berman (2002)

Medieval Notaries and Their Acts: The 1327–1328 Register of Jean Holanie, introduced, edited, and translated by Kathryn L. Reyerson and Debra A. Salata (2004)

John Stone's Chronicle: Christ Church Priory, Canterbury, 1417–1472, selected, translated, and introduced by Meriel Connor (2010)

Medieval Latin Liturgy in English Translation, edited by by Matthew Cheung Salisbury (2017)

Henry VII's London in the Great Chronicle, edited by Julia Boffey (2019)

Jewish Daily Life in Medieval Northern Europe, 1080–1350, edited by Tzafrir Barzilay, Eyal Levinson, and Elisheva Baumgarten (2022)

Wills and Testaments in Medieval England from the Thirteenth to the Sixteenth Century, edited by Robert A. Wood (2023)

Medieval German Texts in Bilingual Editions Series

Sovereignty and Salvation in the Vernacular, 1050–1150, introduction, translations, and notes by James A. Schultz (2000)

Ava's New Testament Narratives: "When the Old Law Passed Away," introduction, translation, and notes by James A. Rushing, Jr. (2003)

History as Literature: German World Chronicles of the Thirteenth Century in Verse, introduction, translation, and notes by R. Graeme Dunphy (2003)

Thomasin von Zirclaria, "Der Welsche Gast (The Italian Guest)," translated by Marion Gibbs and Winder McConnell (2009)

Ladies, Whores, and Holy Women: A Sourcebook in Courtly, Religious, and Urban Cultures of Late Medieval Germany, introductions, translations, and notes by Ann Marie Rasmussen and Sarah Westphal-Wihl (2010)

Neidhart: Selected Songs from the Riedegg Manuscript, introduction, translation, and commentary by Kathryn Starkey and Edith Wenzel (2016)

Varia

The Study of Chivalry: Resources and Approaches, edited by Howell Chickering and Thomas H. Seiler (1988)

Studies in the Harley Manuscript: The Scribes, Contents, and Social Contexts of British Library MS Harley 2253, edited by Susanna Fein (2000)

The Liturgy of the Medieval Church, edited by Thomas J. Heffernan and E. Ann Matter (2001; second edition 2005)

Johannes de Grocheio, "Ars musice," edited and translated by Constant J. Mews, John N. Crossley, Catherine Jeffreys, Leigh McKinnon, and Carol J. Williams (2011)

Aribo, "De musica" and "Sententiae," edited and translated by T. J. H. McCarthy (2015)

Guy of Saint-Denis, "Tractatus de tonis," edited and translated by Constant J. Mews, Carol J. Williams, John N. Crossley, and Catherine Jeffreys (2017)

Anthony Munday, The Honourable, Pleasant, and Rare Conceited Historie of Palmendos: A Critical Edition, edited by Leticia Álvarez-Recio (2022)

"Blandin de Cornoalha," A Commic Occitan Romance: A New Critical Edition and Translation, edited by Wendy Pfeffer, translated by Margaret Burrell and Wendy Pfeffer (2022)

"The Miracle of Theophilus," by Gautier de Coinci, edited and translated by Jerry Root (2022)